D1602085

VOLUME 62

SCREEN WORLD™

The Films of 2010

BARRY MONUSH

An Imprint of Hal Leonard Corporation

Published in 2011 by Applause Theatre & Cinema Books
An Imprint of Hal Leonard Corporation
7777 West Bluemound Road
Milwaukee, WI 53213

Trade Book Division Editorial Offices
33 Plymouth Street, Montclair, NJ 07042

Printed in the United States of America
Book design by Tony Meisel

ISBN 978-1-55783-787-5
ISSN 1545–9020

www.applausebooks.com

In memory of
John Willis

whose mission to chronicle the history of motion pictures and theater made these worlds accessible for countless fans and admirers, and who was instrumental in changing my life for the better; with much gratitude.

CONTENTS

The Kids are On-Line but the Movies are Still Alright

Looking on the bright side, I suppose there's something positive to be said about a movie year in which Hollywood can create something as outstanding and relevant to our times as *The Social Network* and still have it *not* win the Academy Award for Best Picture. (This movie was so brilliantly written by Aaron Sorkin that even the supposed 'throw away' lines are great. My favorite, Andrew Garfield quipping "And he *does* own a watch," about Justin Timberlake's arrogant tardiness). Turns out there was formidable enough competition around to make voters look elsewhere to bestow the top prize, as they did with one of the most literate crowd-pleasers in many an age, *The King's Speech*. As for me, I'm thrilled that these movies were made at all, and one winning the industry's highest honor does not cancel out the other's value. Good work is good work. Maybe the real excitement should be over the fact that both of them did very nicely at the box office. True, if you scan down the list of the highest grossing 2010 releases, *The Social Network* still falls a few notches below *Yogi Bear*, so maybe there's not cause for celebration yet. But take heart; there was also great ticket-buying interest not only in these intelligent offerings but in a movie about ballet (*Black Swan*) and a traditional western (the remake of *True Grit*, which, well done as it was, still doesn't quite eclipse the original, for my money). That's another hopeful sign that the industry can't gauge what is a 'sure thing' and what is not; which will keep movie-going pleasurable, despite Hollywood's better efforts to make it predictable.

The Social Network was not the only outstanding movie to reflect the current public mania for the internet, the need to live as much of life on-line as possible, as a one-of-a-kind documentary, *Catfish*, proved just as fascinating as director David Fincher's dramatization of the founding of Facebook, in telling the unbelievable but true tale of how modern technology has changed our ways of connecting, and questions our definitions of reality in the process.

There was also a superior Americanization of a foreign chiller, *Let Me In*; one of director-writer Mike Leigh's all-time best, *Another Year*, an unsettling and incisive examination of how some unlucky folks are denied the good fortune to find love and happiness; a masterful exercise in paranoia, *The Ghost Writer*, which presented 76-year-old Roman Polanski at one of his career peaks; *Secretariat*, a nicely done dramatization of one of the seminal events in racing history; *Daybreakers*, a stylishly gruesome and atmospheric vampire parable; *Diary of a Wimpy Kid*, a subversively cheeky look at the ever-ridiculous rituals of school life; *You Will Meet a Tall Dark Stranger*, yet another perceptive and bitterly funny take on the human condition by Woody Allen; *The Other Guys*, a Will Ferrell comedy that actually produced some good laughs for a change; *Get Him to the Greek*, which found an ideal role to bring out the better side of the manic Russell Brand; *Unstoppable*, a crackerjack race-against-time thriller; *Please Give*, a comedy so smartly done that it remains a mystery why its creator, Nicole Holofcener, has not risen from under-the-wire cult director to the front rank of modern filmmakers; *City Island*, a surprisingly lovable comedy about a dysfunctional family; a strange and visually stunning revision of *Alice in Wonderland*, just as one would expect from Tim Burton; *Flipped*, a sweet bit of romantic teen nostalgia that, alas, barely got any bookings in theaters; *The Town*, a gritty crime drama that second-time director Ben Affleck pulled off like a seasoned pro; *It's Kind of a Funny Story*, a life-affirming peek into a psychiatric ward, of all places; *Nowhere Boy*, another worthy bit of biographical speculation about the ever-fascinating Beatles; *The Extra Man*, which depicted the world of Manhattan's lunatic fringe with great insight and humor; *The Kids are All Right*, which happily made families headed by same sex couples look like a very feasible and natural part of today's world; *Machete*, a rude, crude and often hilarious update on grind-house trash of yore; the disturbingly downbeat *Buried*, which managed to stay inside a coffin for its entire running time and yet grip you; the similarly claustrophobic but more hopeful *127 Hours*, which also held your interest with a minimal change of scenery; the classy and easy-to-take *How Do You Know*, which somehow managed to be rejected by critics *and* audiences, despite being tailor-made for maximum popular consumption; some amusing comedies that allowed Steve Carell to shine, *Date Night* and *Dinner for Schmucks*; both *Shutter Island* and *Inception*, which beyond their techno and visual pleasures, provided fine acting showcases for the ever-impressive Leonardo DiCaprio; and the so-accurate-it-hurts depiction of today's undependable job market in one of too many sadly unsung movies released in 2010, *The Company Men*.

For top-notch acting you had your pick among the stellar cast of *The King's Speech*, which not only included Oscar-winner Colin Firth but the marvelous Geoffrey Rush at his very best; two Edward Nortons for the price of one in the enjoyably nutty *Leaves of Grass*; one of the finest performances of Michael Douglas's career in *Solitary Man*, certainly the most glaring omission among the year's Oscar nominees; absolutely *everybody* in *The Social Network*, from one of the most exciting rising actors, Andrew Garfield, to the always watchable Jesse Eisenberg, who also did fine work in *Holy Rollers* and the aforementioned *Solitary Man*; Emma Stone, cleverly sending up high school conformity in *Easy A*; Casey Affleck for finally nailing a role that suited him all too well, in *The Killer Inside Me*; a prime showcase for the wonderful Robert Duvall in *Get Low*; not only Oscar winners Melissa Leo and Christian Bale, but the less-heralded, subtler performances of Amy Adams and Mark Wahlberg in *The Fighter*; Paul Giamatti for finding the humanity in the self-centered, severely screwed up title character in *Barney's Version*; Natalie Portman, giving her all and then some to *Black Swan*, which made her such a right choice to take home the Best Actress Oscar; Tommy Lee Jones capturing the inner torment of that rare bird, a corporate executive with a conscience, in *The Company Men*; and Jim Carrey who deserved a round of applause for not giving a damn about pleasing his usual fan-base, with his no-holds-barred depiction of a gay con artist in *I Love You Phillip Morris*, a movie which, of course, had to spend years shopping around for a distributor.

There were sequels galore on the market; the usual dependency on the overly-familiar; too many tickets sold to movies *without* live actors in them; and more worthwhile pictures slipping under the radar than can be listed here. It's a crowded market out there and when you consider all the multi-tasking that's distracting much of the world it's a wonder certain titles get seen at all, ever, no matter what the format. According to some reports, cinemas are starting to lose a lot of the customarily dependable youth market, no doubt because they'd prefer to view things in the microscopic world of iPods and other such do-dads. Perhaps this will result in a greater shift towards movie production aimed at those who savor words over noise, humanity over hardware, thoughtful insight over rapidly consumed and quickly forgotten fluff. Furthermore, let's hope the increasing competition from whatever this week's newest form of media consumption is will keep movie makers on their toes, enticing them to keep creating better and better product, regardless of who it is aimed at, in hopes of drawing away attention from the tiny little piece of machinery in your hand.

– Barry Monush

ACKNOWLEDGMENTS

Abramorama, Anchor Bay, Anthology Film Archives, Apparition, Balcony Releasing CBS Films, The Cinema Guild, Cinema Libre, Columbia Pictures, Scott Denny, DreamWorks, Brian Durnin, E1 Entertainment, Film Forum, First Independent Pictures, First Look, First Run Features, Focus Features, Fox Searchlight, Freestyle Releasing, Ben Hodges, IFC Films, International Film Circuit, Tim Johnson, Marybeth Keating, Kino International, Koch Lorber Films, Lionsgate, Tom Lynch, MGM, Magnolia Films, Anthony Meisel, Miramax Films, Music Box Films, New Line Cinema, New Yorker Films, Oscilloscope, Overture Films, Paladin, Paramount Pictures, Paramount Vantage, Regent/here!, Roadside Attractions, Rogue Pictures, Greg Rossi, Screen Gems, Screen Media, Seventh Art Releasing, Samuel Goldwyn Films, James Sheridan, Sony Pictures Classics, Strand Releasing, Summit Entertainment, TLA Releasing, TriStar, Truly Indie, Twentieth Century Fox, United Artists, Universal Pictures, Variance Films, Walt Disney Pictures, Warner Bros., The Weinstein Company

DOMESTIC FILMS A

2010 Releases / January 1–December 31

YOUTH IN REVOLT

(DIMENSION) Producer, David Permut; Executive Producers, Bob Weinstein, Harvey Weinstein, Nan Morales; Co-Producers, Steve Longi, Miranda Freiberg; Director, Miguel Arteta; Screenplay, Gustin Nash; Based on the novel *Youth in Revolt: The Journals of Nick Twisp* by C.D. Payne; Photography, Chuy Chávez; Designer, Tony Fanning; Costumes, Nancy Steiner; Music, John Swihart; Editors, Pamela Martin, Andy Keir; Animation Director, Peter Sluszka; Casting, Joanna Colbert, Richard Mento, Meredith Tucker; a David Permut/Shangri-La Entertainment production; Dolby; Color; Rated R; 90 minutes; Release date: January 8, 2010.

CAST

Nick Twisp/Francois Dillinger	**Michael Cera**
Sheeni Saunders	**Portia Doubleday**
Estelle Twisp	**Jean Smart**
George Twisp	**Steve Buscemi**
Jerry	**Zach Galifianakis**
Lance Wescott	**Ray Liotta**
Bernice Lynch	**Jade Fusco**
Lacey	**Ari Graynor**
Vijay Joshi	**Adhir Kalyan**
Lefty	**Erik Knudsen**
Paul Saunders	**Justin Long**
Taggarty	**Rooney Mara**
Mrs. Saunders	**Mary Kay Place**
Mr. Saunders	**M. Emmet Walsh**
Mr. Ferguson	**Fred Willard**
Trent	**Jonathan Bradford Wright**

Lise Lacasse (Matron), Michael Collins (Old Man), Gregory F. Anderson, Connell Brown (Sailors), Randall Godwin, Tony Fanning (Officers), Francine Roussel (Headmistress), Oscar the Dog (Albert), Chuy Chávez, Miguel Arteta (Illegal Immigrants), Bruce Lawson (Officer A. Fanning), Sudhi Rajagopal (Officer T. Cahill), Roz Music (Store Clerk), Christa B. Allen (Teenage Girl), Trevor Duke (Chad), Arnaud Crowther, Danielle Nicole Czirmer (French Students)

A frustrated, virginal teen's obsession with a girl he has met in a trailer park leads him to create an alternate persona who encourages him to bring forth his untapped rebellious side in order to win the woman of his dreams.

Michael Cera, Michael Cera

Michael Cera, Adhir Kalyan

Michael Cera © Dimension Films

Michael Cera, Portia Doubleday

Amy Adams, John Lithgow © Universal Studios

Amy Adams, Matthew Goode

LEAP YEAR

(UNIVERSAL) Producers, Gary Barber, Roger Birnbaum, Jonathan Glickman, Chris Bender, Jake Weiner; Executive Producers, J.C. Spink, Su Armstrong; Director, Anand Tucker; Screenplay, Deborah Kaplan, Harry Elfont; Photography, Newton Thomas Sigel; Designer, Mark Geraghty; Costumes, Eimer Ní Mhaoldomhnaigh; Music, Randy Edelman; Editor, Nick Moore; a Spyglass Entertainment presentation of a Barber/Brinbaum, Benderspink production; American-Irish; Dolby; Panavision; Color; Rated PG; 105 minutes; Release date: January 8, 2010

CAST
Anna	**Amy Adams**
Declan	**Matthew Goode**
Jeremy	**Adam Scott**
Jack	**John Lithgow**
Seamus	**Noel O'Donovan**

Tony Rohr (Frank), Pat Laffan (Donald), Alan Devlin (Joe), Ian McElhinney (Priest), Dominique McElligott (Bride), Mark O'Regan (Captain), Maggie McCarthy (Eileen), Peter O'Meara (Ron), Macdara Ó Fathara (Father Malone), Kaitlin Olson (Libby), Liza Ross (Edith), Marcia Warren (Adele), Michael J. Reynolds (Jerome), Ben Caplan (Realtor), Catherine Walker (Kaleigh), Michael FitzGerald (Fergus), Brian Milligan (Bobbo), Flaminia Cinque (Carla), Vincenzo Nicoli (Stefano), Mali Harries, Sarah Hadland (Gaelic Air Reps), David Herlihy (Landlord), David Fynn (Agent), Breffni McKenna (Tommo), Gabriella Gabitas (Wife), Robert Bannon (Waiter), Roman Stefanski (Husband), Martin T. Sherman (Guy), Liam Kelly (Doorman), Pat Deery, John Burke (Sozzled Regulars), Ruth McGill (Woman in Village), Declan Mills (Tailor)

Hoping to benefit from the Irish tradition of permitting women to propose to their suitors on Leap Day, Anna flies to Dublin only to end up in a small village where she hopes to engage someone to drive her to her destination.

WONDERFUL WORLD

(MAGNOLIA) Producers, Glenn Williamson, Miranda Bailey, Matthew Leutwyler; Executive Producer, Lampton Enochs; Co-Producer, Julie Sandor; Associate Producers, Amanda Marshall, Joanna Colbert; Director/Screenplay, Josh Goldin; Photography, Daniel Shulman; Designer, Kristin Bicksler; Costumes, Liz Staub; Music, Craig Richey; Original Songs, Dan Zanes; Editor, Jeff Canavan; Casting, Richard Mento; a Cold Iron Pictures & K5 International presentation of an Ambush Entertainment and Back Lot Pictures production; Dolby; Color; Rated R; 89 minutes; Release date: January 8, 2010

CAST
Ben Singer	**Matthew Broderick**
Khadi	**Sanaa Lathan**
Ibou	**Michael Kenneth Williams**
The Man	**Philip Baker Hall**
Cyril	**Jesse Tyler Ferguson**
Sandra	**Jodelle Ferland**

Patrick Carney (Evan), Christy Reese (Cassie), Zacharias E. Foppe (Leon), Cristen Barnes (Suzie), Mia Alicia Ford (Cyril's Daughter), Paul T. Taylor (Doug), James Burton (McRory), Dan Zanes (Sweeny), John Hambrick (Judge Bissel), Drew Waters (City Lawyer #1), Odessa Sykes (Laugh Zone MC), Carey Bowers (Standup Comic), Linda Leonard (Doctor), David George (Male Nurse), Williams Ragsdale (Bufford), David Jenson (Tow Truck Driver), Michael Showers (Lawyer on TV), Thomas Ike Awagu (African Man)

A failed children's folk singer's pessimistic outlook is turned around by the arrival of the sister of his Senegalese roommate.

Matthew Broderick, Dan Zanes, James Burton

Jodelle Ferland, Sanaa Lathan © Magnolia

Denzel Washington

Evan Jones, Denzel Washington

Jennifer Beals, Gary Oldman

THE BOOK OF ELI

(WARNER BROS.) Producers, Joel Silver, Denzel Washington, Broderick Johnson, Andrew A. Kosvoe, David Valdes; Executive Producers, Steve Richards, Susan Downey, Erik Olsen; Co-Producers, Steven P. Wegner, Yolanda T. Cochran, John David Washington; Directors, The Hughes Brothers (Allen Hughes, Albert Hughes); Screenplay, Gary Whitta; Photography, Don Burgess; Designer, Gae Buckley; Costumes, Sharen Davis; Music, Atticus Ross; Music Supervisor, Deva Anderson; Editor, Cindy Mollo; Visual Effects Supervisor, Jon Farhat; an Alcon Entertainment presentation of a Silver Pictures production; Dolby; HD Widescreen; Color; Rated R; 118 minutes; Release date: January 15, 2010

CAST

Eli	**Denzel Washington**
Carnegie	**Gary Oldman**
Solara	**Mila Kunis**
Redridge	**Ray Stevenson**
Claudia	**Jennifer Beals**
Martz	**Evan Jones**
Hoyt	**Joe Pingue**
Martha	**Frances de la Tour**
George	**Michael Gambon**
Engineer	**Tom Waits**

Chris Browning (Hijack Leader), Richard Cetrone, Lateef Crwoder, Keith Davis, Don Theerathada, Thom Williams, Lora Martinez-Cunningham (Hijackers), Scott Wilder (Middle-Aged Man), Heidi Pascoe (Middle-Aged Woman), Jennifer Caputo, Eddie Perez, Spencer Sano, Karin Silvestri (Bikers), Mike Gunther, John Koyama, Mike McCarty (Snipers), Scott Michael Morgan (Construction Thug Leader), Sala Saker (Construction Thug), Arron Shiver (Bartender), Justin Tade (Town Doctor), Mike Seal (Door Guard), Richard Smith (Orpheum Patron), Paul Crawford, Edward Duran, David Wald, Jermaine Washington (Town Thugs), Kofi Elam, Clay Fontenot, Al Goto, Brad Martin, Tim Rigby (Convoy Thugs), Luis Bordonada, Robert Powell (Carnegie Gunmen), Angelique Midthunder (Gatling Gun Gunner), Todd Schneider (Caddy Driver), Darrin Prescott (Suburban Driver), Laurence Chavez (Ice Cream Truck Driver), Brian Lucero (Alcatraz Guard), David Midthunder (Alcatraz Soldier), Malcolm McDowell (Lombardi)

While wandering the devastated landscape, decades after most of the world has been annihilated, Eli encounters a despotic ruler who swears to gain possession by whatever means possible of the Bible Eli carries.

Mila Kunis ©Warner Bros.

THE SPY NEXT DOOR

(LIONSGATE) Producer, Robert Simonds; Executive Producers, Ryan Kavanaugh, Tucker Tooley, Ira Shuman Solon So; Co-Producer, Kenneth Halsband; Director, Brian Levant; Screenplay, Jonathan Bernstein, James Greer, Gregory Poirier; Photography, Dean Cundey; Designer, Stephen Lineweaver; Costumes, Lisa Jensen; Music, David Newman; Music Supervisors, Happy Walters, Season Kent; Editor, Lawrence Jordan; Senior Visual Effects Supervisor, Ed Jones; Stunts, Bob Brown; Casting, Jeanne McCarthy, Nicole Abellera; a Relativity Media and Robert Simonds Company production; Dolby; Technicolor; Rated PG; 92 minutes; Release date: January 15, 2010

CAST
Bob Ho	**Jackie Chan**
Gillian	**Amber Valletta**
Farren	**Madeline Carroll**
Ian	**Will Shadley**
Nora	**Alina Foley**
Poldark	**Magnus Scheving**
Creel	**Katherine Boecher**
Larry	**Lucas Till**

Billy Ray Cyrus (Colton James), George Lopez (Glaze), Mia Stallard (Cute Girl), Maverick McWilliams (Chad), Quinn Mason (Carl), Margaret Murphy (Mom), Esodie Geiger (Principal), Arron Shiver (Scientist), Richard Christie (Judge), Kayleigh Burgess (Cute Gymnast), Stacey Johnson (Princess' Mom), Frank Bond (Waiter), Stephen Eiland (Taxi Driver), Tim Connolly, Troy Brenna, Jeff Chase, Mark Kubr, David Mattey, Scott Workman (Russian Thugs)

In an effort to ingratiate himself with his neighbor, undercover CIA agent Bob Ho agrees to babysit her three kids while she is away, little aware that one of the children has accidentally downloaded valuable information that makes him the target of Russian spies.

Will Shadley, Jackie Chan, Madeline Carroll © Lionsgate

Dwayne Johnson, Stephen Merchant, Julie Andrews © 20th Century Fox

TOOTH FAIRY

(20TH CENTURY FOX) Producers, Jason Blum, Mark Ciardi, Gordon Gray; Executive Producer/Story, Jim Piddock; Co-Producer, Kevin Halloran; Director, Michael Lembeck; Screenplay, Lowell Ganz, Babaloo Mandel, Joshua Sternin, Jeffrey Ventimilia, Randi Mayem Singer; Photography, David Tattersall; Designer, Marcia Hinds; Costumes, Angus Strathie; Music, George S. Clinton; Music Supervisors, Frankie Pine; Editor, David Finfer; Visual Effects, Prime Focus, CIS Vancouver; Special Effects Supervisor, Alex Burdett; Stunts, Guy Bews; Casting, Mindy Marin (U.S.), Coreen Mayrs, Heike Brandstatter (Canada); a Mayhem Pictures/Blumhouse production, presented with Walden Media; Dolby; Deluxe color; Rated PG; 101 minutes; Release date: January 22, 2010

CAST
Derek Thompson	**Dwayne Johnson**
Carly	**Ashley Judd**
Tracy	**Stephen Merchant**
Mick Donnelly	**Ryan Sheckler**
Ziggy	**Seth MacFarlane**
Lily	**Julie Andrews**

Chase Ellison (Randy), Destiny Grace Whitlock (Tess), Brandon T. Jackson (Duke), Billy Crystal (Jerry), Dan Joffre (Tooth Fairy #1), Ellie Harvie (Permit Woman), Barclay Hope (Coach), Michael Daingerfield (Announcer), Josh Emerson (Kyle), Dale Wolfe (Color Commentator), Steve Bewley (Brad), Brendan Penny (Josh), Lee Tichon (Andreas), Darien Provost (Gabe), David Quinlan (Gabe's Dad), Ron Toffolo (Sports Reporter), Jill Morrison (Shelter Cove Mom), Stephen Holmes (Shelter Cove Dad), Alex Ferris (Shelter Cove Kid), Steve Levy (Himself), Simon King (Dave), Juno Ruddell (Sally), Rukiya Bernard (Amnesia Woman), O.L. Bramble (Amnesia Man), Maya Washington (Amnesia Daughter), Candus Churchill (Amnesia Grandma), Rudy Richards (Amnesia Grandpa), Maya Mack (Amnesia Granddaughter), B.J. Harrison (Amnesia Aunt), Alvin Sanders (Amnesia Uncle), Tanessa Holomon (Amnesia Kid), Storma Sire (Amnesia Daughter-in-Law), Joanna Reid (Amnesia Distant Cousin), Christina Schild (Poltergeist Woman), Nicholas Carella (Poltergeist Man), Nicole Muñoz (Kelly), Brendan Meyer (Ben), Kevin Atwell (Kevin), Daniel Bacon (Fan), Derek Gilroy (Crazed Fan), Brendan Beiser (Teddy's Dad), Dee Jay Jackson (Cop), Peter Kelamis (Talent Show Teacher), John Kirincich (Ref for Game #3), John Tench (Inmate), Fiona Hogan (Scared Woman)

As his punishment for quashing the dreams of children, an arrogant hockey player is sentenced to serve two weeks as a tooth fairy.

LEGION

(SCREEN GEMS) Producers, David Lancaster, Michel Litvak; Executive Producers, Gary Michael Walters, Scott Stewart, Jonathan Rothbart; Co-Producers, Steve Beswick, Marc Sadeghi; Director, Scott Stewart; Screenplay, Peter Schink, Scott Stewart; Photography, John Lindley; Designer, Jeff Higinbotham; Costumes, Wendy Partridge; Music, John Frizzell; Music Supervisor, Chris Douridas; Editor, Steven Kemper; Stunts, John Medlen; Casting, Rick Montgomery; a Bold Films production; Dolby; Super 35 Widescreen; Deluxe color; Rated R; 104 minutes; Release date: January 22, 2010

CAST

Michael	**Paul Bettany**
Jeep Hanson	**Lucas Black**
Kyle Williams	**Tyrese Gibson**
Charlie	**Adrianne Palicki**
Percy Walker	**Charles S. Dutton**
Howard Anderson	**Jon Tenney**
Gabriel	**Kevin Durand**
Audrey Anderson	**Willa Holland**
Sandra Anderson	**Kate Walsh**
Bob Hanson	**Dennis Quaid**
Gladys Foster	**Jeanette Miller**
Minivan Boy	**Cameron Harlow**

Doug Jones (Ice Cream Man), Josh Stamberg (Burton), Yancey Arias (Estevez), Danielle Lozeau (Teenage Girl), Luce Rains (Raggedy Man), Bryan Chapman (Football Player), Denny Pierce (Minivan Dad), Kaye Wade (Elderly Woman), Chuck Hicks (Elderly Man), Stephen Oyoung (Warehouse Guard), Tyra Danielle (Woman with Presents), Django Marsh (Voice of Minivan Boy)

A stranger arrives at a diner in the Mojave Desert to help a small band of citizens do battle against warrior angels bent on bringing on the apocalypse.

Charles S. Dutton, Lucas Black, Adrianne Palicki, Dennis Quaid, Tyrese Gibson
© Screen Gems

Kevin Durand

Paul Bettany

Willa Holland, Kate Walsh

Brendan Fraser, Courtney B. Vance, Ayanna Berkshire © CBS Films

Harrison Ford, Brendan Fraser

Jared Harris, Brendan Fraser

EXTRAORDINARY MEASURES

(CBS FILMS)   Producers, Michael Shamberg, Stacey Sher, Carla Santos Shamberg; Executive Producers, Harrison Ford, Nan Morales; Director, Tom Vaughan; Screenplay, Robert Nelson Jacobs; Based on the book *The Cure* by Geeta Anand; Photography, Andrew Dunn; Designer, Derek R. Hill; Costumes, Deena Appel; Music, Andrea Guerra; Editor, Anne V. Coates; Casting, Margery Simkin; a Double Feature Films production; Dolby; Panavision; Deluxe color; Rated PG; 106 minutes; Release date: January 22, 2010

CAST

John Crowley	**Brendan Fraser**
Dr. Robert Stonehill	**Harrison Ford**
Aileen Crowley	**Keri Russell**
Megan Crowley	**Meredith Droeger**
Patrick Crowley	**Diego Velazquez**
John Crowley Jr.	**Sam M. Hall**
Dr. Kent Webber	**Jared Harris**
Erich Loring	**Patrick Bauchau**
Pete Sutphen	**Alan Ruck**
Dr. Renzler	**David Clennon**
Sal	**Dee Wallace**
Marcus Temple	**Courtney B. Vance**
Wendy Temple	**Ayanna Berkshire**

P.J. Byrne (Dr. Preston), Andrea White (Dr. Allegria), G.J. Echternkamp (Niles), Vu Pham (Vinh Tran), Derek Webster (Cal Dunning), Jana Lee Hamblin (Renzler Scientist #1), Shelly Lipkin (Senior Scientist), Chris Harder (Researcehr), Eric Derovanessian (Security Officer), Patrick Ferguson (Reception Nurse), Jeanette McMahon (Jane, Day Nurse), Brennan Claire (Julia), Tra'Renee Chambers (Marcy, Night Nurse), Quigley Provost-Landrum (Maria), Kimberly Howard, Melanie Sanders (ICU Nurses), Lily Mariye (Dr. Waldman), Sherilyn Lawson (Kate, Day Nurse), Eric Martin Reid (ICU Doctor), Sharonlee McLean (Stonehill's Secretary), Bryce Flint-Sommerville (Van Driver), Jeanine Jackson (Nell Madden), Gavin Bristol (Webber's Assistant), Robert Blanche (Armed Guard), Olga Sanchez (Pediatric Nurse), Chrisse Roccaro (Mega Store Cashier), Michael Shamberg, John Crowley (Renzler Venture Capitalists), Christopher Desmond Williams (Security Officer #2)

Desperate to find a cure for his two children who are suffering from Pompe disease, pharmaceuticals executive John Crowley enlists the aid of a brilliant doctor in hopes of providing him with the needed funds to put his theory of how to cure the disease to work.

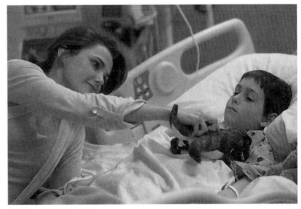

Keri Russell, Diego Velazquez

Danny Huston, Mel Gibson

Mel Gibson, Bojana Novakovic

Mel Gibson, Shawn Roberts

Ray Winstone © Warner Bros.

EDGE OF DARKNESS

(WARNER BROS.) Producers, Graham King, Tim Headington, Michael Wearing; Executive Producers, Dan Rissner, David M. Thompson, Suzanne Warren, Gail Lyon, E. Bennett Walsh; Director, Martin Campbell; Screenplay, William Monahan, Andrew Bovell; Based on the television series written by Troy Kennedy Martin; Photography, Phil Meheux; Designer, Tom Sanders; Costumes, Lindy Hemming; Music, Howard Shore; Editor, Stuart Baird; Second Unit Director, John Mahaffie; Casting, Pam Dixon; a GK Films (U.S.)/BBC Films (U.K.)/Icon Prods. (U.S.) production, presented in association with GK Films; American-British; Dolby; Panavision: Technicolor; Rated R; 117 minutes; Release date: January 29, 2010

CAST

Thomas Craven	**Mel Gibson**
Darius Jedburgh	**Ray Winstone**
Jack Bennett	**Danny Huston**
Emma Craven	**Bojana Novakovic**
Burnham	**Shawn Roberts**
Millroy	**David Aaron Baker**
Whitehouse	**Jay O. Sanders**
Moore	**Denis O'Hare**
Senator Jim Pine	**Damian Young**
Melissa	**Caterina Scorsone**
Agent One	**Frank Grillo**

Wayne Duvall (Chief of Police), Gbenga Akinnagbe (Det. Darcy Jones), Gabrielle Popa (Young Emma), Paul Sparks (Northampton Police Detective), Christy Scott Cashman (Det. Vicki Hurd), Dossy Peabody (Annie, Bennett's Assist.), Gordon Peterson (Interviewer), Peter Epstein (Agent Two), Tom Kemp (Paul Honeywell), Tim Sawyer (Doctor), Molly Schreiber (Reporter #1), Amelia Broome (Tina), Celeste Oliva (Janet), Scott Winters (Northmoor Doctor), Joe Stapleton, Nico Evers-Swindell (State Troopers), Solveig Romero (Hospital Nurse), Ali Reza Farahnakian (Northampton Doctor), Rick Avery (Robinson Jr.), Peter Hermann (Sanderman), Bill Thorpe (Watch Sergeant), Charles Harrington (Craven's Neighbor), Lisa Hughes, Paula Ebben, Kathy Curran (News Reporters), Frank Ridley (Automatic Weapons Cop), David Curtis (Security Officer Northmoor), Tom Duffy (Boston Police Detective)

Swearing to track down the men who cold-bloodedly killed his daughter in front of him, Boston cop Thomas Craven discovers that the crime is tied to the government-connected corporation for which she worked.

Jon Heder, Dax Shepard, Will Arnett, Danny DeVito

Kristen Bell, Alexis Dziena, Peggy Lipton © Walt Disney Pictures

WHEN IN ROME

(TOUCHSTONE) Producers, Gary Foster, Mark Steven Johnson, Andrew Panay; Executive Producers, Mindy Farrell, Steven Roffer, Ezra Swerdlow; Co-Producers, Rikki Lea Bestall, Kim Winther; Director, Mark Steven Johnson; Screenplay, David Diamond, David Weissman; Photography, John Bailey; Designer, Kirk M. Petruccelli; Costumes, Sarah Edwards; Music, Christopher Young; Music Supervisor, Dave Jordan; Editors, Andrew Marcus, Ryan Folsey; Casting, Kathleen Chopin; a Walt Disney Studios Motion Pictures release of a Touchstone presentation of a Gary Foster production; Dolby; Panavision; Technicolor; Rated PG-13; 91 minutes; Release date: January 29, 2010

Kristen Bell, Anjelica Huston

CAST

Beth	**Kristen Bell**
Nick	**Josh Duhamel**
Celeste	**Anjelica Huston**
Al	**Danny DeVito**
Antonio	**Will Arnett**
Lance	**Jon Heder**
Gale	**Dax Shepard**
Joan	**Alexis Dziena**
Stacy	**Kate Micucci**
Priscilla	**Peggy Lipton**
Umberto	**Luca Calvani**

Keir O'Donnell (Father Dino), Bobby Moynihan (Puck), Kristen Schaal (Ilona), Judith Malina (Umberto's Grandma), Lee Pace (Brady Sacks), Natalie Joy Johnson (Secretary), Charlie Sanders, Eugene Cordero (Poker Players), Eric Zuckerman (Hansom Cab Driver), Pasquale Esposito (Police #1), Valentina Roma (Nick's Date), Francesco De Vito (Cabbie), Carlo Giuliano, Tommaso Matelli (Wedding Guests), Bob Dwyer (Cop), Ebony Jo-Ann (Customer), Erin Miller (Patron), Quisha Saunders (Kim), Alexa Havins (Lacy), Carlo D'Amore (Italian Translator), Geoffrey Cantor (Dr. Moskowitz), Abe Goldfarb, J.T. Arbogast (Executives), Lawrence Taylor, Shaquille O'Neal, David Lee, Brian Kenny, Sebastian Saraceno (Themselves), Gloria Colonnello (Guest #3), John Mainieri (Man in Elevator), George Deihl Jr. (News Reporter), Brook Whitmore (Guggenheim Party Bartender), Bing Putney (Guggenheim Party Waiter), Elizabeth Olin (Guggenheim Party Girl #1), Ghostface Killah (Guggenheim DJ), Nico Toffoli (Wedding Guest), Don Johnson (Beth's Dad)

After falling in love with a sportswriter while attending her sister's wedding in Rome, Beth scoops up some coins from a fountain adorned with a statue of Venus and suddenly finds herself desired by a whole slew of suitors.

Kristen Bell, Josh Duhamel

DEAR JOHN

(SCREEN GEMS) Producers, Marty Bowen, Wyck Godfrey, Ryan Kavanaugh; Executive Producers, Jeremiah Samuels, Toby Emmerich, Michele Weiss, Tucker Tooley; Associate Producer, Michael Disco; Co-Producers, Kenneth Halsband, Jamie Linden; Director, Lasse Halström; Screenplay, Jamie Linden; Based on the novel by Nicholas Sparks; Photography, Terry Stacey; Designer, Kara Lindstrom; Costumes, Dana Campbell; Music, Deborah Lurie; Music Supervisors, Happy Walters, Season Kent; Editor, Kristina Boden; Casting, Joanna Colbert, Richard Mento; a Temple Hill and Relativity Media production; Dolby; Panavision; Technicolor; Rated PG-13; 107 minutes; Release date: February 5, 2010

Braeden Reed, Henry Thomas © Screen Gems

CAST

John Tyree	**Channing Tatum**
Savannah Curtis	**Amanda Seyfried**
Mr. Tyree	**Richard Jenkins**
Tim Wheddon	**Henry Thomas**
Noodles	**D.J. Cotrona**
Rooster (Dan Rooney)	**Cullen Moss**
Starks	**Gavin McCulley**
Berry	**Jose Lucena Jr.**
Captain Stone	**Keith Robinson**
Randy	**Scott Porter**
Susan	**Leslea Fisher**
Daniels	**William Howard**
Mr. Curtis	**David Andrews**
Mrs. Curtis	**Mary Rachel Dudley**

Bryce Hayes (Yellow Shirt), Braeden Reed (Alan, 6 years old), Luke Benward (Alan, 14 years old), Tom Stearns, Michael Harding (Coin Dealers), Brett Rice (Pastor), David Dwyer (Steve the Owner), Anthony Osment (Other Surfer), Jim Wenthe (Professor), Matt Blue (Doctor), Lauree Bradway, Glenn M. Tatum, Martin Coleman Bowen (Party Guests), Maxx Hennard (Berg), Jay Phillips (Young Beret), Steven O'Connor (Col. Kittrick), Jessica A. Lucas (Nurse), Teresa Smith (Tim's Nurse), Bryce Hogarth Aremendariz (John, 7 years old), Shelley Reid (Airport Security Guard), Cenk Otay (Screaming Man), Russell A. Turner (Adams), Lisa Burrascano (Woman in Park), Mary Fischer (Helpful Nurse)

Channing Tatum, Amanda Seyfried

Special Forces soldier John Tyree and Savannah Curtis fall in love during her spring break from school only to be separated when he is obliged to return to active duty overseas.

Amanda Seyfried, Richard Jenkins

Channing Tatum

Benicio Del Toro, Emily Blunt, Anthony Hopkins

THE WOLFMAN

(UNIVERSAL) Producers, Scott Stuber, Benicio Del Toro, Rick Yorn, Sean Daniel; Executive Producers, Bill Carraro, Ryan Kavanaugh; Director, Joe Johnston; Screenplay, Andrew Kevin Walker, David Self; Based on the motion picture screenplay by Curt Siodmak; Photography, Shelly Johnson; Designer, Rick Heinrichs; Costumes, Milena Canonero; Music, Danny Elfman; Editors, Dennis Virkler, Walter Murch; Visual Effects Supervisor, Steve Begg; Visual Effects, The Moving Picture Co., Double Negative, Peerless Camera Co.; Special Effects Supervisor, Paul Corbould; Special Makeup Effects Designer, Rick Baker; Stunts, Steve Dent, Wendy Armstrong; Casting, Priscilla John; a Stuber Pictures production, presented in association with Relativity Media; Dolby; Color; Rated R; 102 minutes; Release date: February 12, 2010

CAST

Lawrence Talbot	**Benicio Del Toro**
Sir John Talbot	**Anthony Hopkins**
Gwen Conliffe	**Emily Blunt**
Abberline	**Hugo Weaving**
Maleva	**Geraldine Chaplin**
Singh	**Art Malik**
Dr. Hoenegger	**Antony Sher**
Constable Nye	**David Schofield**
Ben Talbot	**Simon Merrells**
Gwen's Maid	**Gemma Whelan**
Young Lawrence	**Mario Marin-Borquez**
Young Ben	**Asa Butterfield**
Solana Talbot	**Cristina Contes**

Malcolm Scates (Butcher), Nicholas Day (Col. Montford), Michael Cronin (Dr. Lloyd), David Sterne (Kirk), Roger Frost (Rev. Fisk), Rob Dixon (Squire Strickland), Clive Russell (MacQueen), Oliver Adams (Gypsy Boy), Emil Hostina (Bear Handler), Rick Baker (First Gypsy Killed), Emily Cohen (Little Gypsy Girl), Jessica Manley (Gypsy Mother), Dave Fisher (Gypsy Man, Stones), Olga Fedori (Maleva's Daughter), Lorraine Hilton (Mrs. Kirk), John Owens, Richard James (Asylum Doctors), Barry McCormick (Asylum Orderly), Jordan Coulson (Wolf Boy), Ian Peck (Creepy Guard), David Keyes (Custodian), Shaun Smith (Carter), Jack Nightingale, C.C. Smiff (Police Officers), Anthony Debaeck (Driver), Branko Tomovic (Gypsy Man)

Following the death of his brother, Lawrence Talbot returns to his home in the English countryside where a bite from a wolf turns him into a rampaging beast at the sight of every full moon. Remake of the 1941 Universal film that starred Lon Chaney Jr. and Claude Rains.

2010 Academy Award winner for Best Makeup.

Benicio Del Toro © Universal Studios

Hugo Weaving

Benicio Del Toro

VALENTINE'S DAY

(NEW LINE CINEMA) Producers, Mike Karz, Wayne Rice; Executive Producers, Toby Emmerich, Samuel J. Brown, Michael Disco, Diana Pokorny; Director, Garry Marshall; Screenplay, Katherine Fugate; Story, Katherine Fugate, Abby Kohn, Marc Silverstein; Photography, Charles Minsky; Designer, Albert Brenner; Costumes, Gary Jones; Music, John Debney; Music Supervisor, Julianne Jordan; Editor, Bruce Green; Casting, Deborah Aquila, Tricia Wood; a Wayne Rice/Karz Entertainment production; Distributed by Warner Bros.; Dolby; Color; Rated PG-13; 124 minutes; Release date: February 12, 2010

CAST

Morley Clarkson	**Jessica Alba**
Susan	**Kathy Bates**
Kara Monahan	**Jessica Biel**
Holden	**Bradley Cooper**
Sean Jackson	**Eric Dane**
Dr. Harrison Copeland	**Patrick Dempsey**
Edgar	**Hector Elizondo**
Kelvin Moore	**Jamie Foxx**
Julia Fitzpatrick	**Jennifer Garner**
Jason	**Topher Grace**
Liz	**Anne Hathaway**
Alex	**Carter Jenkins**
Reed Bennett	**Ashton Kutcher**
Paula Thomas	**Queen Latifah**
Willy	**Taylor Lautner**
Alphonso	**George Lopez**
Estelle	**Shirley MacLaine**
Grace	**Emma Roberts**
Capt. Kate Hazeltine	**Julia Roberts**
Edison	**Bryce Robinson**
Felicia	**Taylor Swift**

Queen Latifah © New Line Cinema

Jessica Biel, Jamie Foxx

Larry Miller (Oversized Baggage Agent), Beth Kennedy (Mrs. Claudia Smart), Katherine LaNasa (Pamela Copeland), Kristen Schaal (Ms. Gilroy), Erin Matthews (Flight Attendant), Christine Lakin (Heather), Lauren Reeder (Hotel Clerk Michelle), Joey Sorge (Amos), Julia Springer (Olivia Copeland), Alec Nemser (Charlie), Kathleen Marshall (Siena Bouquet Nikki), Rick Batalla (Michael), Anna Kulinova (Bulgarian Girl), Cassie Rowell (Coffee Barista), Faline England, Jim McCann (Flower Shop Customers), Shea Curry (Indian Restaurant Friend Elise), Alexis Peters (Friend Dana), Wedil David (Rani's Mom Rehka), Natalie Timmermans (Indian Bride), Jennifer Leigh Warren (Party Singer), Scott Crumly (Indian Restaurant Valet), Jonathan Morgan Heit (Soccer Tough Franklin), Megan Suri (Rani), Brooklynn Proulx (Madison), Karolinah Villarreal (Gwen), Angelo Salvatore Restaino (Alex's Friend Gideon), Scott Marshall (Mr. Schwabbe), Kelly Flynn (Referee), Sam Marshall (Soccer Son), Mandy Medlin (Teacher), Larrs Jackson (Airport Chauffer Redmond), Cleo King (TSA Supervisor Daisy Bell), Corena Chase (TSA Security Officer), Justin Michael Duval (TSA Security Guard), Heidi Brucker (Southwest Gate Agent), Lily Marshall-Fricker (Lily), Kamilla Bjorlin (Sherry Donaldson), Anna Aimee White (Weather Girl), Stefanie Sherk (Stage Manager), Marty Nadler, Scott Sener (Cameramen), Colin Owens (Anchor), Calvin Jung (Flower Mart Simon), Serena Poon (Chinese Vendor), Kazumi Nakamura (Japanese Vendor), Gwenda Perez (Spanish Vendor), Kiko Kiko (Dodger Grandmother), Joseph Leo Bwarie (Mailroom, Danny), Robert Belushi (Mailroom, Ted), Jaclyn Miller (ACM Receptionist), Joe Smith (ACM Restaurant Waiter), Katie Joy Horwitch (ACM Outdoor Café Waitress), Lisa Roberts Gillian (Young Nurse), Barbara Marshall (Head Nurse), Stephanie Fabian (Candy Striper), Sandra Taylor (Beach Girl Candy), Sarah Lilly (Lady with Dog), Tony Scruggs (Beverly Wilshire Waiter), Roberta Valderrama (Angry Girlfriend), Cyrus Alexander (Cisco the Cheater), Peter Allen Vogt (Cupid), Paul Vogt (Shouting Sheldon), Bonnie Aarons (Strange Lady), Adreama Gonzalez (Cemetery Ticket Vendor), Matt Merchant (Loud Guy), Lisa Valenzuela (Loud Lady), Howard Storm (Louder Guy), Jennifer Amy, Kristin Mellian (Bistro Gardens Waitresses), Rance Howard (Bistro Gardens Diner), Travina Springer (Sign Language Interpreter), Tracy Reiner (French Photographer), Hannah Storm (Herself), Mike Greenberg, Mike Golic (ESPN Radio Announcer Voices), Paul Williams (Voice of Romeo Midnight), Garry Marshall (Musician), Joe Mantegna (Angry Driver)

A look at various romantic hookups and heartbreaks in the Los Angeles area on Valentine's Day.

Taylor Swift

Jessica Alba

Carter Jenkins, Emma Roberts

Bradley Cooper, Julia Roberts

Topher Grace, Anne Hathaway

Patrick Dempsey, Jennifer Garner

Brandon T. Jackson, Alexandra Daddario, Logan Lerman

Alexandra Daddario, Logan Lerman, Brandon T. Jackson

Logan Lerman

Logan Lerman © 20th Century Fox

Logan Lerman

Pierce Brosnan, Brandon T. Jackson

Rosario Dawson, Steve Coogan

Melina Kanakaredes, Sean Bean, Kevin McKidd

PERCY JACKSON & THE OLYMPIANS: THE LIGHTNING THIEF

(20TH CENTURY FOX) Producers, Karen Rosenfelt, Chris Columbus, Michael Barnathan, Mark Radcliffe; Executive Producers, Thomas M. Hammel, Greg Mooradian, Guy Oseary, Mark Morgan; Director, Chris Columbus; Screenplay, Craig Titley; Based on the novel by Rick Riordan; Photography, Stephen Goldblatt; Designer, Howard Cummings; Costumes, Renee April; Music, Christophe Beck; Editor, Peter Honess; Visual Effects Supervisor, Kevin Mack; Makeup Effects Designer, Bill Terezakis; Stunts, Bob Brown; Casting, Janet Hirshenson, Jane Jenkins, Coreen Mayrs, Keike Brandstatter; a Fox 2000 Pictures presentation of a 1492 Pictures/Sunswept Entertainment production; Dolby; Super 35 Widescreen; Deluxe color; Rated PG; 119 minutes; Release date: February 12, 2010

CAST
Percy Jackson	**Logan Lerman**
Grover	**Brandon T. Jackson**
Annabeth	**Alexandra Daddario**
Luke	**Jake Abel**
Zeus	**Sean Bean**
Mr. Brunner/Chiron	**Pierce Brosnan**
Hades	**Steve Coogan**
Persephone	**Rosario Dawson**
Athena	**Melina Kanakaredes**
Sally Jackson	**Catherine Keener**
Poseidon	**Kevin McKidd**
Gabe Ugliano	**Joe Pantoliano**
Medusa	**Uma Thurman**
Mrs. Dodds/Fury	**Maria Olsen**
Ferryman	**Julian Richings**

Bonita Friedericy (Hysterical Woman), Annie Ilonzeh, Marie Avgeropoulos, Luisa D'Oliveira, Christie Laing, Marielle Jaffe, Elisa King, Tania Saulnier, Crystal Tisiga, Alexis Knapp (Aphrodite Girls), Charlie Gallant (Lotus Land Bellhop), Chelan Simmons, Andrea Brooks, Jocelyn Ott (Lotus Land Waitresses), Max Van Ville (Seventies Kid – Casino), Dimitri Lekkos (Apollo), Ona Grauer (Artemis), Stefanie von Pfetten (Demeter), Conrad Coates (Hephaestus), Erica Cerra (Hera), Dylan Neal (Hermes), Luke Camilleri (Dionysus), Holly Hougham, Ina Geraldine Guy, Raquel Riskin, Yusleidis Oquendo, Janine Edwards (Grover Girls), Valerie Tian (Cute Girl), Violet Irene Columbus (Nymph Warrior), Sarah Smyth, Merritt Patterson (Pretty Girls), Julie Luck (WGHP News Anchor), Andrea Day (Field News Reporter), John Stewart, Dee Jay Jackson, Matthew Garlick (Poker Buddies), Stan Carp (Old Fisherman), Suzanne Ristic (Maid at Motel), Richard Harmon (Smart Ass Kid), Robin LeMon (Museum Tour Guide), Doyle Devereux (Museum Employee), Tom Pickett (Parthenon Janitors), V.J. Delos-Reyes, Tim Aas, Keith Blackman Dallas, Spencer Atkinson (Parthenon Janitors), Maya Washington, Victor Ayala (Percy's Classmates), Zane Holtz (50's Tough), Eli Zaougdakis, Matt Reimer, Rob Hayter, Loyd Bateman, Shawn Beaton (Sons of Ares), Jarod Joseph, Reilly Dolman, Paul Cummings (College Buddies), Julie Brar (Cute Girlfriend), Dejan Loyola (Boyfriend), Mario Casoria (Cook), Dorla Bell (Waitress), Caroline Matthews (Waitress with Cleaver), Jade Pawluk (Screaming Diner), Patrick Currie (Stuffy Croupier), Darian Arman , Mariela Zapata (Warriors), David L. Smith (Poet)

Accused of stealing Zeus' master lightning bolt, Percy Jackson, a teenager who realizes he is the half-human love child of Poseidon, sets out to find the real culprit.

Uma Thurman, Logan Lerman

SHUTTER ISLAND

(PARAMOUNT) Producers, Mike Medavoy, Arnold W. Messer, Bradley J. Fischer, Martin Scorsese; Executive Producers, Chris Brigham, Laeta Kalogridis, Dennis Lehane, Gianni Nunnari, Louis Phillips; Co-Producers, Joseph Reidy, Emma Tillinger, Amy Herman; Director, Martin Scorsese; Screenplay, Laeta Kalogridis; Based on the novel by Dennis Lehane; Photography, Robert Richardson; Designer, Dante Ferretti; Costumes, Sandy Powell; Music Supervisor, Robbie Robertson; Editor, Thelma Schoonmaker; Visual Effects Supervisor, Rob Legato; Visual Effects, The Basement, the Syndicate, New Deal Studios; Special Visual Makeup, Legacy Effects; Stunts, George Aguilar; Casting, Ellen Lewis, Meghan Rafferty; a Phoenix Pictures production in association with Sikella Productions and Appian Way; Dolby; Panavision; Deluxe color; Rated R; 138 minutes; Release date: February 19, 2010

Ben Kingsley

CAST

Teddy Daniels	**Leonardo DiCaprio**
Chuck Aule	**Mark Ruffalo**
Dr. Crawley	**Ben Kingsley**
Dr. Naehring	**Max von Sydow**
Dolores	**Michelle Williams**
Rachel 1	**Emily Mortimer**
Rachel 2	**Patricia Clarkson**
George Noyce	**Jackie Earle Haley**
Warden	**Ted Levine**
Deputy Warden McPherson	**John Carroll Lynch**
Laeddis	**Elias Koteas**
Bridget Kearns	**Robin Bartlett**
Peter Breene	**Christopher Denham**

Nelli Sciutto (Nurse Marino), Joseph Sikora (Glen Miga), Curtiss I'Cook (Trey Washington), Raymond Anthony Thomas (Orderly Ganton), Joseph McKenna (Inmate Billings), Ruby Jerins (Little Girl), Tom Kemp, Bates Wilder (Ward C Guards), Lars Gerhard (Dying Commandant), Matthew Cowles (Ferry Captain), Jill Larson (Manacled Woman), Ziad Aki (Tattoo'd Man), Dennis Lynch (Red-Headed Man), John Porell (Wild-Eyed Man), Drew Beasley (Younger Boy), Joseph Reidy (Operator), Bree Elrod, Michael E. Chapman (Patients), Thomas B. Duffy (Guard), Ken Cheeseman, Steve Witting (Doctors), Keith Fluker, Darryl Wooten (Orderlies), Michael Byron (McPherson's Driver), Gary Galone (Gate Guard), Gabriel Hansen (Young Guard)

Federal Marshals Teddy Daniels and Chuck Aule arrive on Shutter Island to investigate the mysterious disappearance of an inmate from the island's asylum.

Leonardo DiCaprio

Leonardo DiCaprio, Mark Ruffalo

Mark Ruffalo, Leonardo DiCaprio, Max von Sydow, Ben Kingsley

Mark Ruffalo, Leonardo DiCaprio © Paramount Pictures

Michelle Williams

Ben Kingsley, Mark Ruffalo, Leonardo DiCaprio

Leonardo DiCaprio, Michelle Williams

Ted Levine, Mark Ruffalo, Leonardo DiCaprio

COP OUT

(WARNER BROS.) Producers, Marc Platt, Polly Johnsen, Michael Tadross; Executive Producers, Adam Siegel, Robb Cullen, Mark Cullen; Director/Editor, Kevin Smith; Screenplay, Robb Cullen, Mark Cullen; Photography, David Klein; Designer, Michael Shaw; Costumes, Juliet Polcsa; Music, Harold Faltermeyer; Special Effects Coordinator, Jeff Brink; Stunts, Jery Hewitt; Casting, Jennifer Euston; a Marc Platt production; Dolby; Super 35 Widescreen; Color; Rated R; 113 minutes; Release date: February 26, 2010

Bruce Willis, Michelle Trachtenberg

CAST

Jimmy Monroe	**Bruce Willis**
Paul Hodges	**Tracy Morgan**
Barry Mangold	**Adam Brody**
Hunsaker	**Kevin Pollak**
Gabriela	**Ana de la Reguera**
Poh Boy	**Guillermo Diaz**
Ava	**Michelle Trachtenberg**
Dave	**Seann William Scott**
Roy	**Jason Lee**
Capt. Romans	**Sean Cullen**

Juan Carlos Hernández (Raul), Cory Fernandez (Juan), Ana de la Reguera (Gabriela), Jason Hurt, Jeff Lima (Youths), Albert Bonilla (Julio), Robinson Aponte, Jeremy Dash (Bangers), Mando Alvarado (Mexican Man), Francie Swift (Pam), Rashida Jones (Debbie), Keith Joe Dick (Big Al), Ernest O'Donnell (Masked Man#1), Jim Norton (George), Harry L. Seddon (NYC Police E.S.U. – SWAT), Susie Essman (Laura), John D'Leo (Kevin), Adrian Martinez (Tino), Marcus Morton (Tommy), Fred Armisen (Russian Lawyer), Hannah Ware (Russian Lawyer's Wife), Ephraim López (Busboy), Mark Consuelos (Manuel), Jayce Bartok (Eddie), Larissa Drekonja (Hourly Housekeeper), Jacinto Taras Riddick (Darnell), Jeff Chena (Cop), Jordan Carlos (Eric), Robb Cullen (Coroner), Raymond Quinlan (Priest), Michael A. Pitt (The Neighbor), Ryan Quinlan (Groom), Elliot Santiago (Lonzo), Joye Giambattista (Pito), Stracy Diaz (Bruja), Chazz Menendez (Jose)

An attempt by cop Jimmy Monroe to retrieve a valuable stolen baseball card brings him and his partner Paul into contact with a dangerous drug smuggler.

Guillermo Diaz © Warner Bros.

Tracy Morgan

Kevin Pollak, Adam Brody

Brett Rickaby, Timothy Olyphant, Radha Mitchell

Danielle Panabaker

Timothy Olyphant, Joe Anderson © Overture Films

THE CRAZIES

(OVERTURE) Producers, Michael Aguilar, Dean Georgaris, Rob Cowan; Executive Producers, George A. Romero, Jeff Skoll, Jonathan King; Director, Breck Eisner; Screenplay, Scott Kosar, Ray Wright; Photography, Maxime Alexandre; Designer, Andrew Menzies; Costumes, George L. Little; Music, Mark Isham; Editor, Billy Fox; Visual Effects Supervisor, Ron Thornton; Prostethic Makeup Effects, Robert Hall; Stunts, E.J. Foerster; Casting, John Papsidera; an Aguilar/Georgaris production, presented with Participation Media in association with Imagenation Abu Dhabi; Dolby; Super 35 Widescreen; Color; Rated R; 101 minutes; Release date: February 26, 2010

CAST

Sheriff David Dutton	**Timothy Olyphant**
Dr. Judy Dutton	**Radha Mitchell**
Russell Clank	**Joe Anderson**
Becca Darling	**Danielle Panabaker**
Deardra Farnum	**Christie Lynn Smith**
Bill Farnum	**Brett Rickaby**
Nicholas	**Preston Bailey**
Mayor Hobbs	**John Aylward**
Pvt. Billy Babcock	**Joe Reegan**
Intelligence Officer	**Glenn Morshower**

Larry Cedar (Ben Sandborn), Gregory Sporleder (Travis Quinn), Mike Hickman (Rory Hamill), Lisa K. Wyatt (Peggy Hamill), Justin Welborn (Curt Hamill), Chet Grissom (Kevin Miller), Tahmus Rounds (Nathan), Brett Wagner (Jesse), Alex Van (Red), Anthony Winters (Town Pastro), Frank Hoyt Taylor (Mortician Charles Finley), Justin Miles (Scotty McGregor), Marian Green (Mrs. McGregor), E. Roger Mitchell (Fire Chief Tom), Michael Cole (Site Coordinator), Mark Oliver (Rescue Worker), Lynn Lowrty (Woman on Bike), Chris Carnel, Jimmy Waitman, Jay Pearson (Car Wash Lunatics), Kathryn Kim, Lori Beth Edgeman (Distraught Moms), Al Greffenius, Gene L. Hamilton, Steve Pilchen (Diner Crazies), Lexie Behr (Lizzie), Adam Dingeman (Snickering Boy), Megan Hensley (Babbling Teen), Ann Roth, Mary Lynn Owen (Distraught Women), Michael "Mickey" Cole (Distraught Boy), Billie McNabb (Waitress), Elizabeth Barrett (Lone Woman), Rachel Storey (Molly Hutchins), Bruce Aune (Newscaster), Jacqueline Sherrard (Local Girl), Pierce Gagnon, Matthew Lintz (Distraught Sons), Wilbur T. Fitzgerald (Distraught Husband)

When select citizens of a small Iowa town begin behaving irrationally, the military arrives to quarantine the area, leading Sheriff David Dutton to believe that a sinister coverup is taking place. Remake of the 1973 film that starred Lane Carroll.

Joe Anderson, Timothy Olyphant

ALICE IN WONDERLAND

(WALT DISNEY PICTURES) Producers, Richard D. Zanuck, Joe Roth, Suzanne Todd, Jennifer Todd; Executive Producer/Editor, Chris Lebenzon; Co-Producer, Katterli Frauenfelder; Director, Tim Burton; Screenplay, Linda Woolverton; Based on the books *Alice's Adventures in Wonderland* and *Through the Looking Glass* by Lewis Carroll; Photography, Dariusz Wolski; Designer, Robert Stromberg; Costumes, Colleen Atwood; Music, Danny Elfman; Senior Visual Effects Supervisor, Ken Ralston; Visual Effects Supervisors, Sean Phillips, Carey Villegas; Visual Effects & Animation, Sony Imageworks Inc.; Animation Supervisor, David Schaub; Makeup Designer, Valli O'Reilly; Stunts, Garrett Warren; Casting, Susie Figgis; a Roth Films/Zanuck Co. production; Dolby; Deluxe color; 3D; Rated PG; 108 minutes; Release date: March 5, 2010

Anne Hathaway, Bloodhound

CAST

Mad Hatter	**Johnny Depp**
Alice Kingsleigh	**Mia Wasikowska**
Red Queen	**Helena Bonham Carter**
White Queen	**Anne Hathaway**
Stayne, Knave of Hearts	**Crispin Glover**
Tweedleedum/Tweedledee	**Matt Lucas**
Helen Kingsleigh	**Lindsay Duncan**
Lady Ascot	**Geraldine James**
Lord Ascot	**Tim Pigott-Smith**
Charles Kingsleigh	**Martin Csokas**
Hamish	**Leo Bill**
Aunt Imogene	**Frances de la Tour**
Margaret Kingsleigh	**Jemma Powell**
Lowell	**John Hopkins**

VOICE CAST

Absolem, the Blue Caterpillar	**Alan Rickman**
Cheshire Cat	**Stephen Fry**
White Rabbit	**Michael Sheen**
Bayard	**Timothy Spall**
Dormouse	**Barbara Windsor**
Jabberwocky	**Christopher Lee**
Dodo Bird	**Michael Gough**
Executioner	**Jim Carter**
Tall Tower Faces	**Imelda Staunton**
March Hare	**Paul Whitehouse**

Cheshire Cat

John Surman, Peter Mattinson (Colleagues), John Hopkins (Lowell), Eleanor Gecks (Faith Chattaway), Eleanor Tomlinson (Fiona Chattaway), Rebecca Crookshank (Strange Woman Kisser), Mairi Ella Challen (6-Year-Old Alice), Holly Hawkins (Woman with Large Nose), Lucy Davenport (Woman with Big Ears), Joel Swetow (Man with Large Belly), Jessica Oyelowo (Woman with Large Poitrine), Ethan Cohn (Man with Large Chin), Richard Alonzo (Man with Big Forehead), Harry Taylor (Ship Captain), Chris Grabher (High Top Hat Juggler), Caroline Royce, Bonnie Parker, Simone Sault, Leigh Daniels, Carl Walker, Matt Dempsey, Chris Grierson, Dale Mercer (Party Dancers), David Lale, John Bass, Nicholas Levy, Patrick Roberts, Phillip Granell, Stephen Giles (Party Musicians), Hilary Morris (Maypole Dancer), Jacqueline Delamora (White Queen Loyalist)

A grown-up Alice Kingsleigh returns to the dreamland she once knew as Wonderland, where a prophecy states that she must fight the dreaded Jabberwocky and save the place from the wicked rule of the Red Queen.

2010 Academy Award winner for Best Costume Design and Best Art Direction. This film received an additional Oscar nomination for visual effects.

Helena Bonham Carter

Johnny Depp

Anne Hathaway © Walt Disney Pictures

Matt Lucas, Matt Lucas

Mia Wasikowska

The Blue Caterpillar

Dodo, Helena Bonham Carter

Ellen Barkin, Don Cheadle

Ethan Hawke

BROOKLYN'S FINEST

(OVERTURE) Producers, Basil Iwanyk, John Langley, John Thompson, Elie Cohn; Executive Producers, Mary Viola, Jesse Kennedy, Robert Greenhut, Antoine Fuqua, Avi Lerner, Danny Dimbort, Trevor Short, Boaz Davidson, Marco Weber; Co-Producer, Kat Samick; Director, Antoine Fuqua; Screenplay, Michael C. Martin; Photography, Patrick Murguia; Designer, Therese Deprez; Costumes, Juliet Polcsa; Music, Marcelo Zarvos; Music Supervisor, John Houlihan; Editor, Barbra Tulliver; Casting, Mary Vernieu, Suzanna Smith Crowley; a Millennium Films presentation of a Thunder Road Film Productions and Nu Image Production in association with Langley Films, Inc; Dolby; Super 35 Widescreen; Color; Rated R; 132 minutes; Release date: March 5, 2010

CAST

Eddie	**Richard Gere**
Tango	**Don Cheadle**
Sal	**Ethan Hawke**
Caz	**Wesley Snipes**
Carlo	**Vincent D'Onofrio**
Ronny Rosario	**Brían F. O'Byrne**
Lt. Bill Hobarts	**Will Patton**
Angela	**Lili Taylor**
Agent Smith	**Ellen Barkin**
E. Quinlan	**Jesse Williams**
Chantel	**Shannon Kane**
Det. Patrick Leary	**Wass Stevens**

Armando Riesco (Det. George Montress), Wade Allain-Marcus (C-Rayz), Logan Marshall-Green (Melvin Panton), Michael Kenneth Williams (Red), Hassan Iniko Johnson (Beamer), Jas Anderson (K. Rock), John D'Leo (Vinny), George DeNoto (Vito), Alison Cordaro (Vicky), Frencesca Carchia (Lynette), Raquel Castro (Katherine), Stella Maeve (Cynthia), Reilly Stith (Myeisha), Josh Thompson (JoJo), Bruce MacVittie (Father Scarpitta), Robert John Burke (State Trooper #1), Jerry Speziale (Capt. Geraci), Sarah Thompson (Sarie), Rodney "Bear" Jackson (Suspicious Man #1), Cle "Bone" Sloan ("The Dragon"), Michael Pemberton (Capt. Jenkins), Ziare Paige (Man Man), Gregory Young (Wiz), Randy Eastman (J-Mill), Thomas Jefferson Byrd (Uncle Jeb), Alain Lauture (Kid with Braids), Joe Adams (Doctor), Alok Tewari (Pakistani Man), Matlok (Student), Zachary Fuqua (Z-Man), Lela Rochon, Ed Moran, Isiah Whitlock (Investigators), Leonid Citer (Union Rep), Nicoye Banks (Slim), Tobias Truvillion (Gutta), Tawny Cypress (Allisa), Jeanine Ramirez (Reporter), Rosalyn Coleman (Crying Mother), Paul Diomede (Arguing Man), Diana Bologna (Arguing Woman)

Three different stories of three increasingly disillusioned Brooklyn police officers: a soon-to-retire veteran; an undercover cop who finds himself in the uncomfortable position of turning on a friend; and one so desperate to make financial ends meet he considers stealing some money from a drug raid.

Jesse Williams, Richard Gere © Overture Films

GREEN ZONE

(UNIVERSAL) Producers, Tim Bevan, Eric Fellner, Lloyd Levin, Paul Greengrass; Executive Producers, Debra Hayward, Liza Chasin; Co-Producer, Mairi Bett; Director, Paul Greengrass; Screenplay, Brian Helgeland; Inspired by the book *Imperial Life in the Emerald City* by Rajiv Chandrasekaran; Photography, Barry Ackroyd; Designer, Dominic Watkins; Costumes, Sammy Sheldon; Music, John Powell; Editor, Christopher Rouse; Visual Effects Supervisor, Peter Chiang; Digital Visual Effects, Double Negative; Stunts, Markos Rounthwaite, Gary Connery; Casting, Amanda Mackey, Cathy Sandrich Gelfond, Dan Hubbard, John Hubbard; a Working Title production, presented in association with Studio Canal and Relativity Media; Dolby; Super 35 Widescreen; Color; Rated R; 114 minutes; Release date: March 12, 2010

Amy Ryan, Matt Damon

CAST

Roy Miller	**Matt Damon**
Clark Poundstone	**Greg Kinnear**
Martin Brown	**Brendan Gleeson**
Lawrie Dayne	**Amy Ryan**
Freddy	**Khalid Abdalla**
Briggs	**Jason Isaacs**

Igal Naor (Gen. Al Rawi), Raad Rawi (Ahmed Zubaidi), Said Faraj (Seyyed Hamza), Michael O'Neill (Col. Bethel), Faical Attougui (Al Rawi Bodyguard), Aymen Hadouchi (Ayad Hamza), Nicoye Banks (Perry), Jerry Della Sallas (Wilkins), Sean Huze (Conway), Michael Dwyer, Edouard H.R. Gluck, Brian Siefkes, Adam Wendling, Abdul Henderson, Paul Karsko, Robert Miller, Eugene Cherry, Alexander Drum, Brian Van Riper, Matthew Knott, Nathan Lewis (MET D's), John Roberson (Infantry Sgt). James Brown (Soldier at WMD Site), Bijan Daneshmand (Zubaidi's Aide), Bryan Reents (Poundstone Aide), Michael Judge (JMOC Tech), Patrick St. Espirit (Military Intel 2 Star), Allen Vaught (Col. Jonathan Vaught), Paul Rieckhoff (Gonzales), Martin McDougall (Brown's Aide), Antoni Corone (Col. Lyons), Timothy Ahern (General at VTC), Ben Sliney (Bureaucrat at VTC), Whitley Bruner (Senior CIA Man at VTC), Intishal Al Timimi (Hawkish Iraqi), Driss Roukhe (Tahir al-Malik), Muayad Ali (Qasim), Jamal Selmaoui (Hawkish Aide), Mohamed Kafi (Iraqi Officer), Kadhum Sabur (Mystery Man), Boubker Hilal (Qasim Aide), Soumaya Akaaboune (Sanaa), Thamou El Metouani (Seyyed's Housekeeper), Salah Eddine Elamari, Naji El Jouhary, Aroun Benchkaroun (Seyyed's Sons), Hajar Machroune (Seyyed's Daughter), Scott Berendes, Abdelkrim Assad, Michael Diaz, Tyler Christen, Adam Mackey, Ben Holland, Jeffrey Carisalez,k Jonathan Stone, James Hodges, Larry Lewis (TF221's), William Oakes (Camp Cropper Tech), Ziad Adwan (Translator), Ian Bendel, Venie Joshua, Miguel Berroa, Peter Shayhorn (Camp Cropper Guards), Miguel Palaugalarza, Christopher Lilly (Camp Cropper Wardens), Sabir Ed-Dayab (Iraqi Prisoner), Omar Berdouni (Righteous Ali), Alex Moore, Alistair Bailey, Eric Loren (CIA Techs), Paul Cloutier (Special Forces Tech), Wallace Bagwell (Alpha Leader 1), William Meredith (CPA Presser), Tommy Campbell (Chopper Comms Commander), James Wills (Chopper Coms Tech), Jered Bezemek (Convoy Commander), Johnny Nilson (Republican Palace Reporter), Salman Hassan, Ammar Khdir, Youssif Falah-Jassem, Latif Al Anzi (Zubaidi Conference Speakers)

Greg Kinnear, Matt Damon

Chief Warrant Officer Roy Miller's failure to find alleged weapons of mass destruction in Iraq causes him to question the real motives behind the U.S. invasion.

Jason Isaacs, Matt Damon © Universal Studios

REMEMBER ME

(SUMMIT) Producers, Nicholas Osborne, Trevor Engelson; Executive Producers, Carol Cuddy, Robert Pattinson; Director, Allen Coulter; Screenplay, Will Fetters; Photography, Jonathan Freeman; Designer, Scott P. Murphy; Costumes, Susan Lyall; Music, Marcelo Zarvos; Music Supervisor, Alexandra Patsavas; Editor, Andrew Mondshein; Casting, Joanna Colbert, Richard Mento; an Underground Films production; Dolby; Deluxe color; Rated PG-13; 113 minutes; Release date: March 12, 2010

CAST
Tyler Hawkins	**Robert Pattinson**
Ally Craig	**Emilie de Ravin**
Sgt. Neil Craig	**Chris Cooper**
Diane Hirsch	**Lena Olin**
Aidan Hall	**Tate Ellington**
Caroline Hawkins	**Ruby Jerins**
Charles Hawkins	**Pierce Brosnan**
Janine	**Kate Burton**
Les Hirsch	**Gregory Jbara**

Caitlyn Paige Rund (Allyssa Craig, 11 years), Martha Plimpton (Allysa's Mom), Moisés Acevedo, Noel Rodriguez (Muggers), Kevin McCarthy (Police Chief), Athena Currey (Tootbrush Girl), Angela Pietropinto (Diner Waitress), David Deblinger (NYU Professor), Lee Brock (Uptight Mommy), Meghan Markle (Megan), Emily Wickersham (Miami Blonde), Kelli Barrett (Miami Brunette), Jon Trosky, Drew Leary (Musicians), Bob Colletti, Scott Burik, William Cote Kruschwitz, Douglas Crosby (Queens Guy), Chris McKinney (Leo), Scott Nicholson (Escorting Officer), Tricia Paoluccio (Receptionist), Peyton Roi List, Morgan Turner (Taunting Classmates), Olga Merediz (Aidan's Professor), Ebrahim Abe Jaffer (Indian Restaurant Waiter), David Anzuelo (Carny Game Attendant), Sándor Técsy (Cab Driver), Justin Grace (Rookie Cop), Michael Hobbs (Oak Room Waiter), Jane Harnick (Birthday Girl's Mom), Emily Godshall (Birthday Girl), Andera Navedo (Caroline's Teacher), Bill Burns (Bailiff), Christopher Clawson (Michael Hawkins)

A confused teen still devastated by his brother's suicide plots a revenge of sorts on the cop who arrested him by making a play for the man's daughter, who is also suffering from a personal loss.

Robert Pattinson, Pierce Brosnan © Summit

Robert Pattinson, Emilie de Ravin

Tate Ellington, Robert Pattinson

Robert Pattinson, Emilie de Ravin

Jay Baruchel, Alice Eve

Jay Baruchel, T.J. Miller, Nate Torrence, Mike Vogel

Adam LeFevre, Debra Jo Rupp © DreamWorks

SHE'S OUT OF MY LEAGUE

(DREAMWORKS/PARAMOUNT) Producers, Jimmy Miller, David Householter; Executive Producer, George Gatins; Director, Jim Field Smith; Screenplay, Sean Anders, John Morris; Photography, Jim Denault; Designer, Clayton Hartley; Costumes, Molly Maginnis; Music, Michael Andrews; Music Supervisor, Deva Anderson; Editor, Dan Schalk; Casting, Allison Jones; a Mosaic Media Group production; Dolby; Super 35 Widescreen; Deluxe color; Rated R; 106 minutes; Release date: March 12, 2010

CAST
Kirk Kettner	**Jay Baruchel**
Molly McCleish	**Alice Eve**
Stainer	**T.J. Miller**
Jack	**Mike Vogel**
Devon	**Nate Torrence**
Marnie	**Lindsay Sloane**
Dylan	**Kyle Bornheimer**
Debbie	**Jessica St. Clair**
Patty	**Krysten Ritter**
Mrs. Kettner	**Debra Jo Rupp**
Mr. Kettner	**Adam LeFevre**
Katie	**Kim Shaw**
Wendy	**Jasika Nicole**

Geoff Stults (Cam), Hayes MacArthur (Ron), Andrew Daly (Mr. Fuller), Sharon Maughan (Mrs. McCleish), Trevor Eve (Mr. McCleish), Adam Tomei (Randy), Robin Shorr (Tina Jordan), Patrick Jordan (Bowler), Tom Stoviak (Museum Director), Rick Applegate ("Plane Doctor"), Heather Morgan Leigh (Flight Attendant), Chuck Aber (Pilot), Jason McCune (Restaurant Patron), Yan Xi (Karen), Alex Cole (Scotty Reese), Joseph F. Eberle (Hockey Bartender), Phil Spano (Hockey Coordinator), Jeff Adams, Mila Cermak, Mike Gaffney, Todd Gally, Jim Gricar, Rob Hofmann, Jason Lewis, Ed Nusser, Jory Rand, Matthew Richert, Tom Rieck, Joe Sager (Hockey Players)

Hapless airline security worker Kirk Kettner is stunned when a chance encounter with a breathtakingly beautiful woman leads to a relationship.

Lindsay Sloane, Jay Baruchel

America Ferrera, Lance Gross © Fox Searchlight

Forest Whitaker, Carlos Mencia

OUR FAMILY WEDDING

(FOX SEARCHLIGHT) Producers, Edward Saxon, Steven J. Wolfe; Co-Producer, Scott G. Hyman; Director, Rick Famuyiwa; Screenplay, Wayne Conley, Malcolm Spellman, Rick Famuyiwa; Story, Wayne Conley; Photography, Julio Macat; Designer, Linda Burton; Costumes, Hope Hanafin; Music, Transcenders; Music Supervisor, Barry Cole; Editor, Dirk Westervelt; Casting, Kim Taylor-Coleman; a Sneak Preview Entertainment/Edward Saxon production; Dolby; Super 35 Widescreen; Deluxe color; Rated PG-13; 101 minutes; Release date: March 12, 2010

CAST

Brad Boyd	**Forest Whitaker**
Lucia Ramirez	**America Ferrera**
Miguel Ramirez	**Carlos Mencia**
Angela	**Regina King**
Marcus Boyd	**Lance Gross**
Sonia Ramirez	**Diana Maria Riva**

Lupe Ontiveros (Momma Cecilia), Anjelah Johnson (Isabella Ramirez), Charlie Murphy (T.J.), Shannyn Sossamon (Ashley McPhee), Tonita Castro (Aunt Rosita), Anna Maria Horsford (Diane Boyd), Warren Sapp (Wendell Boyd), Shondrella Avery (Keisha Boyd), Sterling Ardrey (Ardom Boyd), Skylan Brooks (Buddy Boyd), Castulo Guerra (Father Paez), Joseph Mencia (Manny Ramirez), Vivek Shah (Maitre d'), Matt Sauter (Waiter), Paul Costa (Mixologist), Joaquin Pastor (DJ Spine-Sane), James Lesure (Officer Turman), Alejandro Patino (Goat Truck Driver), Jacqueline Mazarella (Dress Shop Owner), Joseph Vassallo (Tux Shop Owner), Ella Joyce (Earlene), Sy Richardson (Sonny), Noel G. (Raymond Mata), Charles Grisham (Westside Player), Caroline Aaron (Elaine), Mimi Michaels, Carlee Avers (Tipsies), Hayley Marie Norman (Sienna), Gordon E. James (Frat Boy #2), Gina Rodriguez (Bridesmaid), Gabriel G. Alvarez (Cousin James)

Racial tensions erupt between Hispanic truck driver Miguel Ramirez and black talk show host Brad Boyd when their offspring announce their upcoming marriage.

THE BOUNTY HUNTER

(COLUMBIA) Producer, Neal H. Moritz; Executive Producers, Wink Mordaunt, Ori Marmur, Robyn Meisinger, Donald J. Lee Jr., Ryan Kavanaugh; Director, Andy Tennant; Screenplay, Sarah Thorp; Photography, Oliver Bokelberg; Designer, Jane Musky; Costumes, Sophie de Rakoff; Music, George Fenton; Editor, Troy Takaki; Stunts, Peter Bucossi; Casting, Kathleen Chopin; an Original Film production, presented in association with Relativity Media; Dolby; Arri Widescreen; Deluxe color; Rated PG-13; 110 minutes; Release date: March 19, 2010

CAST

Nicole Hurley	**Jennifer Aniston**
Milo Boyd	**Gerard Butler**
Stewart	**Jason Sudeikis**
Sid	**Jeff Garlin**
Irene	**Cathy Moriarty**

Peter Greene (Mahler), Joel Marsh Garland (Dwight), Dorian Missick (Bobby Singer), Siobhan Fallon Hogan (Teresa), Carol Kane (Dawn), Adam Rose (Jimmy), Christine Baranski (Kitty Hurley), Gio Perez (Uncle Sam), Jason Kolotouros (Gelman), Matt Malloy (Gary), David Costabile (Arthur), Lynda Gravatt (Judge), Jayne Houdyshell (Landlady), Ritchie Coster (Ray), Mark Budd (Stickman), Mary Testa (Maid at the Taj), Harry Zittel (Pedicab Driver), Charles Techman (Track Vet), Tracy Thorne (Membership Director), Christian Borle (Caddy), Amanda Dutton (Darla), Eddie J. Mitchell (Jonathan), Adam LeFevre (Edmund), Charlie Hewson (Rich Guy), Lou Sumrall (Bone), Brooke Allison Stroebele (Strip Club Waitress), Eric Zuckerman (Kenny), Wally Dunn (Depository Clerk), Mike Sheehan (Desk Sergeant), Shaun Hasas (Dealer), Patrick Mitchell (Jeremy)

When investigative reporter Nicole Hurley skips bail, her vengeful ex-husband Milo Boyd is assigned to take her into custody.

Gerard Butler, Jennifer Aniston © Columbia Pictures

Jennifer Aniston

THE RUNAWAYS

(APPARITION) Producers, John Linson, Art Linson, Bill Pohlad; Executive Producers, Joan Jett, Kenny Laguna, Brian Young; Co-Producers, Frank Hildebrand, David Grace; Director/Screenplay, Floria Sigismondi; Based on the book *Neon Angel* by Cherie Currie; Photography, Benoit Debie; Designer, Eugenio Caballero; Music, Lillian Berlin; Music Supervisor, George Drakoulias; Editor, Richard Chew; Casting, Wendy O'Brien; a River Road Entertainment and a Linson Entertainment production; Dolby; Super 35 Widescreen; Color; Super 16-to-35mm; Rated R; 102 minutes; Release date: March 19, 2010

Dakota Fanning, Kristen Stewart

CAST

Joan Jett	**Kristen Stewart**
Cherie Currie	**Dakota Fanning**
Kim Fowley	**Michael Shannon**
Sandy West	**Stella Maeve**
Lita Ford	**Scout Taylor-Compton**
Robin	**Alia Shawkat**
Marie Currie	**Riley Keough**
Scottie	**Johnny Lewis**
Cherie's Mom	**Tatum O'Neal**
Cherie's Dad	**Brett Cullen**
Tammy	**Hannah Marks**
Aunt Evie	**Jill Andre**

Ray Porter (Band Member), Kiaya Snow (Cashier), Allie Grant (Club Girl), Brendan Sexton III (Derek), Shammy Dee (DJ), Aaron Mouser (Fat Employee), Peggy Stewart (Grandma Oni), Robert Romanus (Guitar Teacher), Jay Thames (Headliner's Roadie), Masami Kosaka (Japanese Journalist), Masayuki Yonezawa (Japanese Photographer), Hiroshi Sakata (Japanese Promoter), P.D. Mani (Cake Shop Manager), Mickey Petralia (Record Executive), Antonella Sigismondi (Rockabilly Saleslady), Nick Eversman (Rocker Boy), Keir O'Donnell (Rodney Bingenheimer), Lisa Long (Sandy's Mom), J.R. Nutt (Skinny Employee), Alejandro Patino (Grocery Store Manager), John Konesky (Studio Engineer), Tim Winters (Wolfgang), Adam Silver (Boy in Audience), Koji Wada (Announcer)

The true story of how eccentric producer/songwriter Kim Fowley brought together a group of teens to become one of the first all-girl hard-rock bands, the Runaways.

Alia Shawkat, Scout Taylor-Compton, Stella Maeve, Kristen Stewart, Dakota Fanning

Michael Shannon

Dakota Fanning, Michael Shannon © Apparition

Zachary Gordon, Karin Konoval

Kaye Capron, Robert Capron

Rachael Harris, Zachary Gordon

Karan Brar, Zachary Gordon, Robert Capron

Robert Capron, Zachary Gordon, Chloë Grace Moretz

Zachary Gordon, Robert Capron, Grayson Russell

Grayson Russell, Zachary Gordon, Robert Capron © 20th Century Fox

Robert Capron (center), Zachary Gordon

DIARY OF A WIMPY KID

(20TH CENTURY FOX) Producers, Nina Jacobson, Brad Simpson; Executive Producer, Jeff Kinney; Co-Producer, Ethan Smith; Director, Thor Freudenthal; Screenplay, Jackie Filgo, Jeff Filgo, Gabe Sachs, Jeff Judah; Based on the book by Jeff Kinney; Photography, Jack Green; Designer, Brent Thomas; Costumes, Monique Prudhomme; Music, Theodore Shapiro; Music Supervisor, Julia Michels; Editor, Wendy Greene Bricmont; Visual Effects Supervisor, Mark Dornfeld; Animation, Custom Film Effects; Stunts, Dave Hospes; Casting, Heike Brandstatter, Ronna Kress, Coreen Mayrs; a Fox 2000 Pictures presentation of a Color Force production in association with Dune Entertainment and DayDay Films; Dolby; Deluxe color; Rated PG; 92 minutes; Release date: March 19, 2010

CAST

Greg Heffley	**Zachary Gordon**
Rowley Jefferson	**Robert Capron**
Susan Heffley	**Rachael Harris**
Frank Heffley	**Steve Zahn**
Rodrick Heffley	**Devon Bostick**
Angie Steadman	**Chloë Grace Moretz**
Fregley	**Grayson Russell**
Patty Farrell	**Laine MacNeil**
Chirag Gupta	**Karan Brar**
Manny Heffley	**Connor Fielding, Owen Fielding**
Collin	**Alexis Ferris**
Coach Malone	**Andrew McNee**
Mrs. Norton	**Belita Moreno**
Mr. Winsky	**Rob LaBelle**
Pete Hosey	**Nicholas Carey**
Carter	**Samuel Patrick Chu**
Wade	**Donnie MacNeil**
Shelly	**Samantha Page**
Marley	**Ava Hughes**
Darren Walsh	**Harrison Houde**
Dieter Muller	**Severin Korfer**
Mrs. Flint	**Jennifer Clement**
Mrs. Irvine	**Karin Konoval**
Vice Principal Roy	**Raugi Yu**
Rowley's Mom	**Kaye Capron**
Archie Kelly	**Jake D. Smith**
Arthur	**Talon Dunbar**
Bryce Anderson	**Owen Best**

Naomi Dane (Cheese Girl), Willem Jacobson (Cheese Boy), Sean Bygrave (Coach Brewer), Maxine Miller (Elderly Woman), Taya Clyne (Granddaughter), Nathaniel Marten (Grown-Up Greg), Rylee Stiles (Preston), Nikki Frazer, Greta Gisbon (Lunch Kids), Peter New (Grown-Up Quentin), Nathan Smith (Kindergarten Boy), Kina Mori McWatt (Kindergarten Girl), Dylan Bell (Kindergarten Greg), Madison Bell (Kindergarten Patty), Adom Osei (Marty Porter), Alfred E. Humphreys (Mr. Jefferson), Brent Chapman (Mr. Parnell), Cainan Wiebe (Quentin), Ryan Grantham (Rodney James), Cole Heppell (Quentin's Sidekick), Ethan Shankaruk (Snot Kid), Jesse Wheeler (Unpopular '80's Boy), Paul Hubbard (Brock Brannigan), Brett Dier (80's Breakdancer), Brandon Barton (80's Jock Boy), Cindy Busby (80's Popular Girl), Alicia Takase Lui, Jay Sidhu, Tori Christianson, Emerald Schreier, Benjamin D. Mitchell, Haris Cash, Mariah Crudo (Audition Kids), Alistair Abell, Tara McGuire (Voices of Reporters), Aidan Gebert, Cameron Krpan, Paolo Tolfo (Löded Diper)

11-year-old middle-schooler Greg Heffley makes it his goal to rise in popularity among his peers, all the while wondering if he can get his best friend Rowley to abandon his nerdy ways.

CITY ISLAND

(ANCHOR BAY) Producers, Andy Garcia, Raymond de Felitta, Zachary Matz, Lauren Versel,; Executive Producers, Maria Teresa Arida, Lucia Seabra, Milutin G. Gatsby, Michael Roban, Grzegorz Hajdarowicz,; Co-Executive Producers, Luis de Val, Antonio Gijon, Rene Garcia; Director/Screenplay, Raymond de Felitta; Photography, Vanja Cernjul; Designer, Franckie Diago; Costumes, Tere Duncan; Music, Jan A.P. Kaczmarek; Editor, David Leonard; Casting, Sheila Jaffe, Meredith Tucker; a CineSon Productions & Medici Entertainment presentation in association with Lucky Monkey Pictures, Gremi Film Production and Filmsmith; Dolby; Color; Rated PG-13; 103 minutes; Release date: March 19, 2010

CAST

Vince Rizzo	**Andy Garcia**
Joyce Rizzo	**Julianna Margulies**
Tony Nardella	**Steven Strait**
Vivian Rizzo	**Dominik Garcia-Lorido**
Vince Rizzo Jr.	**Ezra Miller**
Molly	**Emily Mortimer**
Michael Malakov	**Alan Arkin**
Denise	**Carrie Baker Reynolds**
Cheryl Plinoff	**Hope Glendon-Ross**
Bruno	**Louis Mustilo**
Casting Assistant	**Jee Young Han**
Tanya	**Sharon Angela**
Matt Cruniff	**Curtiss Cook**
Security Man	**Paul Romero**
Working Class Guy	**Paul Diomede**
Bouncer	**Vernon W. Campbell**

Lora Chio, Yeyveniy Dekhtyar, Steven J. Klaszky, Jennifer Larkin, Benjamin Mathes (Actors), Marshall Efron (Man with Dog Monologue)

A prison security guard with secret aspirations to be an actor further disrupts his already dysfunctional family by bringing home a parolee who happens to be his illegitimate son.

Emily Mortimer, Andy Garcia

Steven Strait, Dominik Garcia-Lorido, Andy Garcia, Julianna Margulies, Ezra Miller

Dominik Garcia-Lorido, Julianna Margulies, Andy Garcia

Ezra Miller, Julianna Margulies, Dominik Garcia-Lorido, Andy Garcia

Andy Garcia, Steven Strait

Julianna Margulies, Andy Garcia

Hope Glendon-Ross, Carrie Baker Reynolds, Ezra Miller © Anchor Bay

Julianna Margulies, Steven Strait, Dominik Garcia-Lorido, Carrie Baker Reynolds, Ezra Miller, Hope Glendon-Ross, Andy Garcia

Ben Stiller

Brie Larson, Ben Stiller, Juno Temple

Greta Gerwig, Rhys Ifans, Ben Stiller © Focus Features

GREENBERG

(FOCUS FEATURES) Producers, Scott Rudin, Jennifer Jason Leigh; Executive Producer, Lila Yacoub; Director/Screenplay, Noah Baumbach; Story, Jennifer Jason Leigh, Noah Baumbach; Photography, Harris Savides; Designer, Ford Wheeler; Costumes, Mark Bridges; Music, James Murphy; Music Supervisor, George Drakoulias; Editor, Tim Streeto; Casting, Francine Maisler; a Scott Rudin production; Dolby; Panavision; Deluxe color; Rated R; 107 minutes; Release date: March 19, 2010

CAST

Roger Greenberg	**Ben Stiller**
Florence Marr	**Greta Gerwig**
Ivan Schrank	**Rhys Ifans**
Beth	**Jennifer Jason Leigh**
Sara	**Brie Larson**
Muriel	**Juno Temple**
Phillip Greenberg	**Chris Messina**
Carol Greenberg	**Susan Traylor**
Eric Beller	**Mark Duplass**
Gina	**Merritt Wever**
Peggy	**Mina Badie**
Megan	**Blair Tefkin**
Johno	**Jake Paltrow**

Koby Rouviere (Greenberg Boy), Sydney Rouviere (Greenberg Girl), Emily Lacy, Aaron Wrinkle, Heather Lockie (Gallery Band Members), Chris Coy (Guy at Gallery), Zach Chassler (Marlon), Charlotte Vida Silverman (Beller's Daughter), Nicole Luizzi (Vet Receptionist), Nora Isela Monterroso, Robert E. Wolfe M.D. (Vets), Luke Clements (Guitarist), Alfredo Marin (Bus Boy), Jeremy Barber, Anna Culp, Erica Huggins, Dale JE Hebert II, Sophie Savides (Musso and Frank's Patron), Trace Webb (Victor), Jessica Mills (Second Vet Receptionist), Maria Snow (Receptionist), Layla Delridge (Girl with Beer), Dave Franco (Rich), Max Hoffman (Jerry), Ramona Gonzalez (Anita), Alessandra Balazs (Olivia), Nick Nordella (Jordan), Trent Gill (Kid at Stereo), Emily Kuntz, Zosia Mamet, Zoe Di Stefano, Cole M. Grief-Neil (Guests), Micah Schaffer (Guy with Joint)

Following a nervous breakdown Roger Greenberg moves into his brother's L.A. home where he finds himself attracted to his sibling's caretaker.

Jennifer Jason Leigh

HOT TUB TIME MACHINE

(MGM) Producers, John Cusack, Grace Loh, Matt Moore; Executive Producer, Michael Nelson; Director, Steve Pink; Screenplay, Josh Heald, Sean Anders, John Morris; Story, Josh Heald; Photography, Jack Green; Designer, Bob Ziembicki; Costumes, Dayna Pink; Music, Christophe Beck; Music Supervisors, Dana Sano, Steve Pink; Casting, Susie Farris; a Metro-Goldwyn-Mayer Pictures and United Artists presentation of a New Crime production; Dolby; Color; Rated R; 99 minutes; Release date: March 26, 2010

CAST

Adam	**John Cusack**
Lou	**Rod Corddry**
Nick Webber	**Craig Robinson**
Jacob	**Clark Duke**
Phil	**Crispin Glover**
April	**Lizzy Caplan**
Blaine	**Sebastian Stan**
Jennie	**Lyndsy Fonseca**
Kelly	**Collette Wolfe**
Repair Man	**Chevy Chase**

Charlie McDermott (Chaz), Aliu Oyofo (Nick at 17), Jake Rose (Adam at 17), Brook Bennett (Lou at 17), Crystal Lowe (Zoe), Jessica Paré (Tara), Kellee Stewart (Courtney), Julia Maxwell (Lucy), Geoff Gustafson (Dr. Jeff), Adam Sabla, Austin Warren, Jocelyn C. Waugh, Curtis Santiago, Ryan Guldemond, Jeremy Page, Anthony Dallas (Nick's Band), Rob LaBelle (Stewart), Odessa Rojen (Young Courtney), Viv Leacock (Courtney's Dad), Brendan Fletcher (Sleazy Guy), Jamie Switch (Massive Cell Phone Guy), Jacob Blair (Gunnar), Chad Garner, Donald McDonald, Chad MacDonald, Anthony Pagni ("Poison" Band Member), Blaine Anderson (MC), Emmanuella Bezjak (Lucy's Friend), Lynda Boyd (Adam's Secretary), Michael Roberds (Manager), Daren Herbert (Receptionist), Megan Holmes ("Where's the Bee" Girl), Curtis Dekker (Soft Seven Guy), Ecstasia Sanders (Girl at Club), Eddie Ruttle, Heathcliffe Scaddan (Beer Luge Guys), Peter Wilson (Beer Luge Guys), Rhys Williams, Brent Lister, Lars Anderson, Paul Dzenkiw (Cronies), Amy Esterle, Dawn Natalia (Hot Tub Girls), Ava Leemet (Candy Girl), Willy Lavendel, Crystal Tisiga (Fancy Ski Guys), Marie West (Winterfest Bartender), William Zabka (Rick Steelman)

Returning to the ski resort where they spent some of the wildest times of their youth, three disillusioned men and the nephew of one of them are transported back to the mid-1980s, by way of a magical hot tub.

Chevy Chase

Collette Wolfe, Rob Corddry © MGM

Craig Robinson, Rob Corddry, John Cusack, Clark Duke

Crispin Glover

HOW TO TRAIN YOUR DRAGON

(DREAMWORKS/PARAMOUNT) Producer, Bonnie Arnold; Executive Producers, Kristine Belson, Tim Johnson; Co-Producers, Karen Foster, Doug Davison, Roy Lee, Michael Connolly; Director, Chris Sanders, Dean DeBlois; Screenplay, Will Davies, Chris Sanders, Dean DeBlois; Based on the book by Cressida Cowell; Designer, Kathy Altieri; Music, John Powell; Editors, Darren Holmes, Maryann Brandon; Head of Character Animation, Simon Otto; Head of Story, Alessandro Carloni; Head of Layout, Gil Zimmerman; Character Design, Nico Martlet; Visual Consultant, Roger Deakins; Casting, Leslee Feldman; a DreamWorks Animation presentation; Distributed by Paramount Pictures; Dolby; Widescreen; Deluxe/Technicolor; 3D; Rated PG; 98 minutes; Release date: March 26, 2010

VOICE CAST

Hiccup	**Jay Baruchel**
Stoick the Vast	**Gerard Butler**
Gobber	**Craig Ferguson**
Astrid	**America Ferrera**
Snotlout	**Jonah Hill**
Fishlegs	**Christopher Mintz-Plasse**
Tuffnut	**T.J. Miller**
Ruffnut	**Kristen Wiig**
Ack	**Robin Atkin Downes**
Starkard	**Philip McGrade**
Hoark the Haggard	**Kieron Elliott**
Phlegma the Fierce	**Ashley Jensen**

A scrawny member of a Viking tribe defies the warring principles of his village by befriending an injured dragon.

This film received Oscar nominations for animated feature and original score.

Gobber, Snotlout, Ruffnut, Astrid, Tuffnut, Fishlegs

Fishlegs

Astrid, Hiccup, Toothless © DreamWorks

Gobber, Stoick the Vast

Monstrous Nightmare, Stoick the Vast

Hiccup, Toothless

Ruffnut, Snotlout, Astrid, Fishlegs, Tuffnut

Ruffnut, Tuffnut

Toothless, Hiccup

Toothless, Hiccup

THE LAST SONG

(TOUCHSTONE) Producers, Adam Shankman, Jennifer Gibgot; Executive Producer, Tish Cyrus; Co-Producer, Dara Weintraub; Director, Julie Anne Robinson; Screenplay, Nicholas Sparks, Jeff Van Wie; Based on the novel by Nicholas Sparks; Photography, John Lindley; Designer, Nelson Coates; Costumes, Louise Frogley; Music, Aaron Zigman; Music Supervisor, Buck Damon; Editor, Nancy Richardson; Casting, Amanda Mackey, Cathy Sandrich Gelfond; Distributed by Walt Disney Studios Motion Pictures; a Touchstone Pictures presentation of an Offspring Entertainment production; Dolby; Panavision; Deluxe color; Rated PG; 108 minutes; Release date: March 31, 2010

CAST

Ronnie Miller	**Miley Cyrus**
Steve Miller	**Greg Kinnear**
Jonah Miller	**Bobby Coleman**
Will Blakelee	**Liam Hemsworth**
Scott	**Hallock Beals**
Kim	**Kelly Preston**
Marcus	**Nick Lashaway**
Blaze	**Carly Chaikin**
Susan Blakelee	**Kate Vernon**
Ashley	**Melissa Ordway**
Tom Blakelee	**Nick Searcy**
Lance	**Michael Jamorski**
Cassie	**Carrie Malabre**

Lance E. Nichols (Pastor Harris), Stephanie Leigh (Megan Blakelee), Phil Parham (Megan's Husband), Bonnie Johnson (Neighbor), Rhoda Griffis (Doctor), Anthony Paderewski (Security Guard). April Moore, Todd Smith (Firemen at Church)

Forced to spend the summer at the Georgia shore with her divorced dad, Ronnie Miller finds herself falling in love with a local teen.

Greg Kinnear, Bobby Coleman © Touchstone Pictures

Liam Hemsworth, Miley Cyrus

Liam Hemsworth

Pierce Brosnan, Susan Sarandon © Paladin

THE GREATEST

(PALADIN) Producers, Lynette Howell, Beau St. Clair; Executive Producers, Pierce Brosnan, Aaron Kaufman, Doug Dey, Ron Hartenbaum, Douglas Kuber, Myles Nestel, Anthony Callie; Co-Producers, Katie Mustard, Amanda J. Scarano; Associate Producers, Nissa Ren Cannon, Chris Charalambous; Director/Screenplay, Shana Feste; Photography, John Bailey; Designer, Judy Rhee; Costumes, Luca Mosca; Music, Christophe Beck; Editor, Cara Silverman; Casting, Laura Rosenthal, Ali Farrell; a Barbarian Film Group in association with Oceana Media Finance presentation of a Silverwood Films/Irish Dreamtime production; Dolby; Panavision; Color; Rated R; 99 minutes; Release date: April 2, 2010

CAST
Allen Brewer	**Pierce Brosnan**
Grace Brewer	**Susan Sarandon**
Rose	**Carey Mulligan**
Ryan Brewer	**Johnny Simmons**
Bennett Brewer	**Aaron Johnson**
Ashley	**Zoë Kravitz**
Jordan Walker	**Michael Shannon**
Joan	**Jennifer Ehle**

Amy Morton (Lydia), Deirdre O'Connell (Joyce), Maryann Urbano (Cheryl), Kevin Hagan (Priest), Miles Robbins (Sean Brewer), Cara Seymour (Janis), Ramsey Faragallah (Dr. Shambus), Colby Minifie (Latral), Portia (Toni), Dante E. Clark (Dante), Ron Scott (Police Officer), Miguel Cervantes, Maya Ri Sanchez (EMT's), Lindsay Beamish (Shea), Eric Santiago (Partygoer), John Boyd (Wyatt), Cynthia Boorujy (Rose's Doctor), Hannah Hodson (Amy), Miriam Cruz (Gloria), Joel de la Fuente (Allen's Doctor), James Biberi (Prison Security Guard), Wai Ching Ho (Piano Teacher), Louis D'Agostino (Friend #1), Alexander Flores (Geeky Student)

After the tragic death of their son, the grieving Brewer family reluctantly takes in the pregnant girlfriend he left behind.

Tyler Perry's

WHY DID I GET MARRIED TOO?

(LIONSGATE) Producers, Tyler Perry, Reuben Cannon; Executive Producer, Michael Paseornek; Co-Producers, Roger M. Bobb, Joseph P. Genier; Director/Screenplay, Tyler Perry; Photography, Toyomichi Kurita; Designers, Ina Mayhew, Maybe Berke; Costumes, Keith G. Lewis; Music, Aaron Zigman; Music Supervisor, Joel C. High; Editor, Maysie Hoy; Casting, Kim Williams, Alpha Tyler; a Reuben Cannon/Lionsgate production, presented with TPS; Dolby; Color; Rated PG-13; 121 minutes; Release date: April 2, 2010

CAST
Patricia	**Janet Jackson**
Sheila	**Jill Scott**
Dianne	**Sharon Leal**
Gavin	**Malik Yoba**
Mike	**Richard T. Jones**
Angela	**Tasha Smith**
Troy	**Lamman Rucker**

Michael Jai White (Marcus), Tyler Perry (Terry), Louis Gossett Jr. (Porter), Cicely Tyson (Ola), Nia Iman Muhammad (Kenya Bobb), Tyson Gilmore (T.J.), Valarie Pettiford (Harriet), Marc Farley (Stage Manager), K Callan (Ms. Tannenbaum), Zoë Grace Hargrove (Daughter), Frank Roberts (Doctor), Richard Whiten (Philip), Yaniv Moyal (Alex), Steve Warren (Man), Seth Powell (Marcus Jr.), Rodney Peete (Walter), Brian Daye (Technical Director), Chris Moses (Ross), Carra Patterson (Kelly), Victor Webster (Ray), Laveranues Coles Jr., Roger Lodge (Sportscasters), Sheri Mann Stewart (College Professor), Jonté Moaning (Cake Dancer). Dwayne Johnson (Patricia's Co-Worker)

Four couples vacation together in the Bahamas, where the various problems inherent in each of their relationships come to the surface.

Janet Jackson, Malik Yoba © Lionsgate

Medusa

Liam Neeson

Polly Walker, Ralph Fiennes

Sam Worthington

Gemma Arterton, Sam Worthington

Alexa Davalos, Mads Mikkelsen

Liam Cunningham, Mads Mikkelsen, Gemma Arterton

Ian Whyte © Warner Bros.

CLASH OF THE TITANS

(WARNER BROS.) Producers, Basil Iwanyk, Kevin De La Noy; Executive Producers, Richard D. Zanuck, Thomas Tull, Jon Jashni, William Fay; Director, Louis Leterrier; Screenplay, Travis Beacham, Phil Hay, Matt Manfredi; Based on the motion picture directed by Desmond Davis and written by Beverley Cross; Photography, Peter Menzies Jr.; Designer, Martin Laing; Costumes, Lindy Hemming; Music, Ramin Djawadi; Editors, Martin Walsh, Vincent Tabaillon; Visual Effects Supervisor, Nick Davis; Prosthetics Supervisor, Conor O'Sullivan; Special Effects and Animatronics Supervisor, Neil Corbould; Stunts, Paul Jennings; Casting, Lucinda Syson, Elaine Grainger; a Thunder Road Film/Zanuck Co. production, presented in association with Legendary Pictures; Dolby; Panavision; 3D; Techincolor; Rated PG-13; 106 minutes; Release date: April 2, 2010

CAST

Perseus	**Sam Worthington**
Zeus	**Liam Neeson**
Hades	**Ralph Fiennes**
Calibos/King Acrisius	**Jason Flemyng**
Io	**Gemma Arterton**
Andromea	**Alexa Davalos**
Danae	**Tine Stapelfeldt**
Draco	**Mads Mikkelsen**
Apollo	**Luke Evans**
Athena	**Izabella Miko**
Solon	**Liam Cunningham**
Ixas	**Hans Matheson**
Ozal	**Ashraf Barhom**
Kucuk	**Mouloud Achour**
Sheikh Sulieman	**Ian Whyte**
Eusebios	**Nicholas Hoult**
Kepheus	**Vincent Regan**
Cassiopeia	**Polly Walker**
Aged Cassiopeia	**Katherine Koeppky**
Prokopion	**Luke Treadaway**
Spyros	**Pete Postlethwaite**
Marmara	**Elizabeth McGovern**
Tekla	**Sinead Michael**
Pemphredo	**Ross Mullan**
Enyo	**Robin Berry**
Deino	**Graham Hughes**
Phaedrus	**Martin McCann**
Belo	**Rory McCann**

Adrian Bouchet (Soldier, Zeus Statue), Kaya Scodelario (Peshet), Alexander Siddig (Hermes), Tamer Hassan (Ares), Danny Huston (Poseidon), William Houston (Ammon), Jamie Sives (Captain), Phil McKee (Harbormaster), Geoffrrey Beevers (Noble, Basilica), Michael Grady-Hall, Laura Kachergus (Citizens, Argos), David Kennedy (Kepheus' General), Nina Young (Hera), Jane March (Hestia), Nathalie Cox (Artemis), Agyness Deyn (Aphrodite), Paul Kynman (Hephaestus), Natalia Vodianova (Medusa), Charlotte Comer (Demeter)

In order to save Andromeda from being sacrificed to the dreaded Krakken, Perseus, the illegitimate son of Zeus, journeys to the underworld in hopes of obtaining the head of Medusa. Remake of the 1981 MGM film of the same name that starred Harry Hamlin, Laurence Olivier, and Judi Bowker.

DATE NIGHT

(20TH CENTURY FOX) Producer/Director, Shawn Levy; Executive Producers, Joe Caracciolo Jr., Josh McLaglen, Tom McNulty; Screenplay, Josh Klausner; Photography, Dean Semler; Designer, David Gropman; Costumes, Marlene Stewart; Music, Christophe Beck; Editor, Dean Zimmerman; Stunts, Jack Gill, Andy Gill; Casting, Donna Isaacson; a 21 Laps production; Dolby; HD Widescreen; Deluxe color; Rated PG-13; 88 minutes; Release date: April 9, 2010

Leighton Meester

CAST

Phil Foster	**Steve Carell**
Claire Foster	**Tina Fey**
Det. Arroyo	**Taraji P. Henson**
Armstrong	**Jimmi Simpson**
Collins	**Common**
D.A. Frank Crenshaw	**William Fichtner**
Holbrooke	**Mark Wahlberg**
Katy	**Leighton Meester**
Haley Sullivan	**Kristen Wiig**
Brad Sullivan	**Mark Ruffalo**
Taste	**James Franco**
Whippit	**Mila Kunis**
Miletto	**Ray Liotta**
Det. Walsh	**Bill Burr**
Oliver Foster	**Jonathan Morgan Heit**
Charlotte Foster	**Savannah Argenti**
Claw Maitre D'	**Nick Kroll**
Claw Hostess	**Olivia Munn**
Natanya	**Gal Gadot**
Wendy	**Lauren Weedman**
Teaneck Waiter	**Darren Le Gallo**
Peppermint Hippo Doorman	**J. Razor**
House-Hunting Woman	**Gillian Vigman**
House-Hunting Man	**Chayim Frenkel**
Young Man	**Jon Bernthal**
Young Woman	**Ari Graynor**
Himself	**Will.i.am**
VIP Thug	**Sho Brown**
Exotic Dancers	**Jahnel Curfman, Stella Angelova**
Miletto Thugs	**Joe Starr, John Cenatiempo**
Claw Hotties	**Katie Gill, Michelle Galdenzi**
Book Club Members	**Stacey Scowley, Lourdes Regala**
VIP Room Bodyguard	**Hal Devi**

Dani Playel, Kat Howland, Alandrea Martin (VIP Room Dancers), Sterling Cooper (Tweak), J.B. Smoove (Cabbie)

During an evening in Manhattan, Jersey couple Phil and Claire Foster's decision to accept a dinner reservation that doesn't belong to them results in a night of mayhem when they are mistaken for blackmailers who possess a valuable flash drive.

Common, Jimmi Simpson

Tina Fey, Steve Carell

Tina Fey, Steve Carell, Mark Wahlberg

Steve Carell

Steve Carell, Tina Fey

Steve Carell, J.B. Smoove © 20th Century Fox

Mila Kunis, James Franco

Karen Young, Jamey Sheridan

Steve Buscemi © Paladin

HANDSOME HARRY

(PALADIN) Producers, Jamin O'Brien, Marilyn Haft; Executive Producers, Fred Berner, Elizabeth Kling; Director, Bette Gordon; Screenplay, Nicholas T. Proferes; Photography, Nigel Bluck; Designer, Rene Sekula; Costumes, Michael Anzalone; Music, Anton Sanko; Editor, Keiko Deguchi; Casting, Todd M. Thaler; a Worldview Entertainment production; Color; HD; Widescreen; Not rated; 94 minutes; Release date: April 16, 2010

CAST
Harry Sweeney	Jamey Sheridan
Thomas Kelly	Steve Buscemi
Judy Rheems	Mariann Mayberry
Professor Porter	Aidan Quinn
Peter Rheems	John Savage
David Kagan	Campbell Scott

Titus Welliver (Gebhardt), Karen Young (Muriel), Jayne Atkinson (Kelly's Wife), Bill Sage (Pauley), Emily Donahue (Kelly's Daughter), Asher Grodman (Bobby Sweeney), Andrew Dolan (Sam), Rutanya Alda (Mrs. Schroeder), Kevin Reed (Young Kagan), Blake Lowell (Young Kelly), Tom Degnan (Young Harry), Elizabeth Hess (Kagan's Mother), Danny Lane (Young Rheems), Reathel Bean (Kagan's Fatehr), Nicholas Carriere (Bartender), Anita Hollander (Sarah), June Stein (Neighborhood Woman), Carmen López (Kagan's Maid), Blake Hammond (Hank), Sidney Williams, Brian Russell (Customers), Philip Willcox, Doug Goodenough, Jordan Cooper, Brian Lindvall (Quartet Members), John Ferrier (Priest), Jon Bates (Bandleader)

On his deathbed, Thomas Kelley asks a friend from their days in the navy to convey his apologies to another former sailor whom the two men had wronged.

THE CITY OF YOUR FINAL DESTINATION

(SCREEN MEDIA) Producers, Paul Bradley, Pierre Proner; Co-Producer, Richard Hawley; Director, James Ivory; Screenplay, Ruth Prawer Jhabvala; Based on the novel by Peter Cameron; Photography, Javier Aguirresarobe; Art Director, Andrew Sanders; Costumes, Carol Ramsey; Music, Jorge Drexler; Editor, John David Allen; a Hyde Park Intl. presentation of a Merchant Ivory Prods. production, in association with Goldcrest Features, Falkhan Entertainment Group; Dolby; Color; Rated PG-13; 114 minutes; Release date: April 16, 2010

CAST
Adam	Anthony Hopkins
Omar Razaghi	Omar Metwally
Caroline	Laura Linney
Arden Langdon	Charlotte Gainsbourg
Pete	Hiroyuki Sanada
Mrs. Van Euwen	Norma Aleandro
Deirdre	Alexandria Maria Lara
Alma	Norma Argentina
Deirdre's Escort	Eliot Mathews

César Bordón, Diego Velazquez (Helpful People at the Bus Depot), Ambar Mallman (Portia Gund), Arturo Goetz, Marcos Montes, Sophie Tirouflet (Mrs. Van Euwen's Guests), Luciano Suardi (Dr. Pereira), Carlos Torres (Barbar), Pietro Gian (Taxi Driver), Julia Perez (Nurse), Agustín Pereyra Lucena (Guitarist), Pablo Druker (Conductor), Eliot Mathews (Deirdre's Escort), Andrew Sanders (Caroline's Escort), Nicholas Blandullo (Young Adam), James Martin (Postman), Sofia Viruboff (Adam's Mother), Julieta Vallina (Schoolbus Lady)

Having been refused permission to write a book on the late writer Jules Gund, a young Iranian-American academic journies to the author's Uruguayan estate where he encounters the man's many quarreling heirs.

Anthony Hopkins © Screen Media

Aaron Johnson, Christopher Mintz-Plasse

Christopher Mintz-Plasse, Mark Strong © Lionsgate

KICK-ASS

(LIONSGATE) Producers, Matthew Vaughn, Brad Pitt, Kris Thykier, Adam Bohling, Tarquin Peck, David Reid; Executive Producers, Pierre Lagrange, Stephen Marks, Mark Millar, John S. Romita Jr., Jeremy Kleiner; Co-Producer, Jane Goldman; Director, Matthew Vaughn; Screenplay, Jane Goldman, Matthew Vaughn; Based on the comic book by Mark Millar, John S. Romita Jr.; Photography, Ben Davis; Designer, Russell De Rozario; Costumes, Sammy Sheldon; Music, John Murphy; Music Supervisor, Ian Neil; Visual Effects Supervisor, Mattias Lindahl; Casting, Lucinda Syson, Sarah Halley-Finn; a MARV Films/Plan B production; Dolby; Panavision; Technicolor; Rated R; 117 minutes; Release date: April 16, 2010

CAST
Dave Lizewski (Kick-Ass)	**Aaron Johnson**
Chris D'Amico (Red Mist)	**Christopher Mintz-Plasse**
Frank D'Amico	**Mark Strong**
Mindy Macready (Hit Girl)	**Chloë Grace Moretz**
Marty	**Clark Duke**
Katie Deauxma	**Lyndsy Fonseca**
Todd	**Evan Peters**
Damon Macready (Big Daddy)	**Nicolas Cage**
Big Joe	**Michael Rispoli**
Sgt. Marcus Williams	**Omari Hardwick**
Det. Gigante	**Xander Berkeley**

Jason Flemyng (Lobby Goon), Garrett M. Brown (Mr. Lizewski), Deborah Twiss (Mrs. Zane), Sophie Wu (Erika Cho), Elizabeth McGovern (Mrs. Lizewski), Stu "Large" Riley (Huge Goon), Johnny Hopkins, Ohene Cornelius (Gang Kids), Corey Johnson (Sporty Goon), Kenneth Simmons (Scary Goon), Anthony Desio (Baby Goon), Carlos Besse Peres (Buttons), Randall Batinkoff (Tre Fernandez), Dexter Fletcher (Cody), Russell Bentley (Medic), Tamer Hassan (Matthew), Yancy Butler (Angie D'Amico), Adrian Martinez (Ginger Goon), Tim Plester (Danil), Joe Bacino (Posh Goon), Hubert Boorder (Oscar Juarez), Chris McGuire, Max White, Dean Copkov (Diner Fight Guys), Jacob Cartwright (Running Teenager), Maurice DuBois, Dana Tyler (News Anchors), Craig Ferguson (Himself), Omar Soriano (Leroy), Katrena Rochell (Junkie), Kofi Natei (Rasul), Dan Duran (Reporter), Louis Young (Breaking News Reporter), Val Jobara (Nervous Goon), Quinn Smith (Big Mean Boy)

A mild-mannered teen turns into a makeshift superhero named Kick-Ass and soon becomes both an internet sensation and the target of an angry mob boss.

Aaron Johnson, Chloë Grace Moretz, Nicolas Cage

Evan Peters, Aaron Johnson, Clark Duke

DEATH AT A FUNERAL

(SCREEN GEMS) Producers, Sidney Kimmel, William Horberg, Chris Rock, Share Stallings, Laurence Malkin; Executive Producers, Jim Tauber, Bruce Toll, Dean Craig, Glenn S. Gainor; Director, Neil LaBute; Screenplay, Dean Craig; Photography, Rogier Stoffers; Designer, Jon Gary Steele; Costumes, Maya Lieberman; Music, Christophe Beck; Editor, Tracey Wadmore-Smith; Casting, Victoria Thomas; a Sidney Kimmel Entertainment/Wonderful Films/Parabolic Pictures/Stable Way Entertainment production; Dolby; Panavision; Deluxe color; Rated R; 92 minutes; Release date: April 16, 2010

Chris Rock, Regina Hall, Martin Lawrence

CAST

Reverend Davis	**Keith David**
Cynthia	**Loretta Devine**
Frank	**Peter Dinklage**
Duncan	**Ron Glass**
Uncle Russell	**Danny Glover**
Michelle	**Regina Hall**
Brian	**Kevin Hart**
Ryan	**Martin Lawrence**
Oscar	**James Marsden**
Norman	**Tracy Morgan**
Aaron	**Chris Rock**
Elaine	**Zoe Saldana**
Jeff	**Columbus Short**
Derek	**Luke Wilson**

Regine Nehy (Martina), Bob Minor (Edward), Alexander Folk (Middle Aged Man), Leslie Rivers (Older Lady), Bronwyn Hardy, Willi Willis, Betty K. Bynum (Mourners), Jamison Young (Asian Man)

Family battles erupt and complications ensue at a funeral starting when the wrong corpse is delivered to the viewing. Remake of the 2007 film of the same name, with Peter Dinklage repeating his role from that version.

Columbus Short, James Marsden, Ron Glass, Loretta Devine © Screen Gems

Peter Dinklage

Tracy Morgan, Danny Glover

Amber Heard

THE JONESES

(ROADSIDE ATTRACTIONS) Producers, Doug Mankoff, Andrew Spaulding, Derrick Borte, Kristi Zea; Executive Producers, Sheetal Talwar, Tom Luse, Paul Young, Peter Principato; Co-Producers, Scott Lochmus, Jessica Stamen; Director/Screenplay, Derrick Borte; Photography, Yaron Orbach; Designer, Kristi Zea; Costumes, Renee Kalfus; Music, Nick Urta; Music Supervisor, Susan Jacobs; Casting, Pam Dixon; a Vistaar Religare presentation in association with WSG Pictures and FilmNation Entertainment of an Echo Lake presentation; Dolby; Super 35 Widescreen; Color; Rated R; 93 minutes; Release date: April 16, 2010

CAST

Steve Jones	**David Duchovny**
Kate Jones	**Demi Moore**
Jenn Jones	**Amber Heard**
Mick Jones	**Ben Hollingsworth**
Larry	**Gary Cole**
Summer	**Glenne Headly**
KC	**Lauren Hutton**
Sylvia	**Catherine Dyer**
Billy	**Chris Williams**
Naomi	**Christine Evangelista**
Mary Beth	**Ashley LeConte Campbell**

Robert Pralgo (Alex "The Hammer" Baynor), Justin Price (Skateboarder), Kim Wall (Bethany), Tiffany Morgan (Melanie Baynor), Ric Reitz (Bob), Mark Oliver (Man#1), Andrew DiPalma (Will), Jenson Goins (Ami), Steve Barnes, Jason MacDonald (Guys), Wilbur Fitzgerald, Charles Van Eman (Golfers), Hayes Mercure (Tim), Ron Clinton Smith (Policeman), Jennifer Van Horn (Loretta), Ava Lauren Borte, Ella Archer Borte (Girls at Country Club), Roy McCrerey (Rich Guy), Christoph Vogt (Mover), Jayson Warner Smith (Maitre D'), Sonya Thompson (Restaurant Patron), James Belyeu (Waiter #1), Jacob G. Akins (Furniture Mover), John Atwood (Ken), Danielle Barnum (Sommelier), Jason Horgan (Mr. Stallings), Gregory Wright (Steve's Friend on Lawnmower), Kip Watson (Makeup Artist), Sandra Kahlert Borte (Mother at Country Club), Joel Chivington (Kid taking Golf Lesson)

Four people posing as the perfect upscale suburban family are sent to infiltrate a wealthy community with the express intention of encouraging their all-too-willing neighbors to purchase expensive products.

Ben Hollingsworth, Amber Heard, Demi Moore, David Duchovny
© Roadside Attractions

David Duchovny, Demi Moore

Jennifer Lopez, Alex O'Loughlin

Jennifer Lopez, Linda Lavin, Tom Bosley

Jennifer Lopez, Alex O'Loughlin © CBS Films

THE BACK-UP PLAN

(CBS FILMS) Producers, Todd Black, Jason Blumenthal, Steve Tisch; Executive Producers, Rodney Liber, David Bloomfield; Director, Alan Poul; Screenplay, Kate Angelo; Photography, Xavier Pérez Grobet; Designer, Alec Hammond; Costumes, Karen Patch; Music, Stephen Trask; Music Supervisor, Linda Cohen; Editor, Priscilla Nedd Friendly; Casting, David Rubin, Richard Hicks; an Escape Artists production; Dolby; Super 35 Widescreen; Deluxe color; Rated PG-13; 104 minutes; Release date: April 23, 2010

CAST

Zoe	**Jennifer Lopez**
Stan	**Alex O'Loughlin**
Mona	**Michaela Watkins**
Clive	**Eric Christian Olsen**
Playground Dad	**Anthony Anderson**
Daphne	**Noureen DeWulf**
Carol	**Melissa McCarthy**
Arthur	**Tom Bosley**
Lori	**Maribeth Monroe**
Olivia	**Danneel Harris**
Dr. Scott Harris	**Robert Klein**
Nana	**Linda Lavin**

Carlease Burke (Tabitha), Amy Block (Sara), Jennifer Elise Cox (Baby Store Sales Clerk), Adam Rose (Louie), Cesar Milan (Himself), Peggy Miley (Shirley), Sadie May Beebe (Dakota), Logan Lauriston (Mack), Barbara Perry (Wedding Singer), Chalo González (Band Leader), Art Frankel ("Not Me" Man), Anselm King (Cab Driver), Elisabeth Abbott, Lili Mirojnick (Pregnant Women), Donna Ponterotto (Woman in Gym), Mario Gavras (Mario), Riley B. Smith, Samantha Hall, Jared Gilmore, Rowan Blanchard (Mona's Kids), Wes Whitehead (Cheese Customer), John Ronald Dennis, Bunny Gibson, Stan Mazin, Beverly Polcyn, Bobbie Bates, Birl Jonns, Anushka Jones, Skip Cunningham, Jack Mattis, Felix Chavez (Conga Line Dancers), Olivia Jones, Riley Jones, Isabelle Jones, Skylar Weber, Zachary Weber (Infants), Nubbins, Nip, Tuck (Nuts)

Having just gotten pregnant through artificial insemination, Zoe then finds herself in an awkward situation when she soon afterwards meets and falls in love with Stan.

Michaela Watkins, Jennifer Lopez

THE LOSERS

(WARNER BROS.) Producers, Joel Silver, Akiva Goldsman, Kerry Foster; Executive Producers, Andrew Rona, Steve Richards, Sarah Aubrey, Stuart Besser; Co-Producer, Richard Mirisch; Director, Sylvain White; Screenplay, Peter Berg, James Vanderbilt; Based on the comic book series by Andy Diggle, Jock, published by DC Comics/Vertigo; Photography, Scott Kevan; Designer, Aaron Osborne; Costumes, Magali Guidasci; Music, John Ottman; Editor, David Checel; Visual Effects Supervisors, Jesper Kjolsrud, Simon Hughes; Visual Effects, Image Engine; Casting, Mary Vernieu, Venus Kanani; a Weed Road Pictures production, presented in association with Dark Castle Entertainment; Dolby; Super 35 Widescreen; Color; Rated PG-13; 98 minutes; Release date: April 23, 2010

Chris Evans © Warner Bros.

CAST

Clay	**Jeffrey Dean Morgan**
Aisha	**Zoe Saldana**
Jensen	**Chris Evans**
Roque	**Idris Elba**
Pooch	**Columbus Short**
Cougar	**Óscar Jaenada**
Max	**Jason Patric**
Wade	**Holt McCallany**

Peter Macdissi (Vkram), Peter Francis James (Fadhil), Tanee McCall (Jolene), Mark Ginther, Daniel Kalal, Colin Follenweider, Garrett Warren (Goliath Guards), Rey Hernandez (Armored Car Guard), Ernesto Morales (Nabil), Evan Mirand (Lead Chryon Guard), Noel Estrella (Indian Thug Leader), Gunner Wright (Jet Pilot), Robert Slavonia (Mr. Anderson), Debbie Ann Rivera (Mr. Anderson's Secretary), Kirk Sullivan (Transport Helicopter Pilot), Marcos Davila (Thug on Bus), Alanis M. Salinas (Little Girl at Compound), Maneul O. Velazquez (Boy with Teddy Bear), Thomas R. Nunan III (Pentagon Official), John Galindez (MIG Pilot), Lindsey Sutton, Alan J. Trudeau (EMTs), Rafael Lopez Diaz (Short Indian Scientist), Norman Grant (Delivery Room Doctor), Krissy Korn (Referee)

A group of unorthodox Special Forces operatives are enlisted to eliminate their onetime boss who had betrayed them during a disastrous mission in the Bolivian jungles.

Holt McCallany, Jason Patric

Zoe Saldana

Jeffrey Dean Morgan, Idris Elba

Amanda Peet

Ann Guilbert, Sarah Steele

Catherine Keener, Oliver Platt

Oliver Platt, Rebecca Hall, Ann Guilbert, Amanda Peet, Catherine Keener

Oliver Platt

Rebecca Hall, Amanda Peet

Rebecca Hall, Thomas Ian Nicholas © Sony Classics

Sarah Steele

PLEASE GIVE

(SONY CLASSICS) Producer, Anthony Bregman; Associate Producer, Stefanie Azpiazu; Executive Producer, Caroline Jaczko; Director/Screenplay, Nicole Holofcener; Photography, Yaron Orbach; Designer, Mark White; Costumes, Ane Crabtree; Music, Marcelo Zarvos; Editor, Robert Frazen; Casting, Jeanne McCarthy; a Likely Story production; Dolby; Color; Rated R; 90 minutes; Release date: April 30, 2010

CAST

Kate	**Catherine Keener**
Mary	**Amanda Peet**
Alex	**Oliver Platt**
Rebecca	**Rebecca Hall**
Andra	**Ann Guilbert**
Abby	**Sarah Steele**
Eugene	**Thomas Ian Nicholas**
Cathy	**Elizabeth Keener**
Marissa	**Elise Ivy**
Adam	**Josh Pais**
Mrs. Portman	**Lois Smith**
Erin	**Amy Wright**
Dr. Lerner	**Scott Cohen**
Blind Date	**Paul Sparks**
Transvestite Homeless Person	**Harmonica Sunbeam**
Man Waiting for a Table	**Arthur French**
Leaf Man	**Neal Lerner**
Salesgirls	**Mandy Olsen, Emma Myles**
Tommy	**John Srednicki**
Kevin	**Timothy Doyle**
Big Back	**Rebecca Budig**
Carrie-Ann	**Romy Rosemont**
Anita	**Kathleen Doyle**
Don	**Kevin Corrigan**
Elyse	**Elizabeth Berridge**
Homeless Man	**Charles Techman**
Mr. Melnick	**Portia**
Jason	**Jason Kingsley**

Griffin Frazen, Reggie Austin, Maddie Corman, Alice Spivak, Sarah Vowell, Jason Mantzoukas, Erica Berg, Michael Panes (Shoppers), Regina Marie Healy (Abby #2), Creighton James (Ambulance Guy), Maria Barrientos (Elena), Jamie Tirelli (Dario), David Weininger (Funeral Director)

Kate feels the guilt of living well while coping with the poverty and sadness that surrounds her as a resident of New York.

Sarah Steele, Catherine Keener

Jackie Earle Haley

Jackie Earle Haley

Rooney Mara © New Line Cinema

A NIGHTMARE ON ELM STREET

(NEW LINE CINEMA) Producers, Michael Bay, Andrew Form, Brad Fuller; Executive Producers, Mike Drake, Robert Shaye, Michael Lynne, Richard Brener, Walter Hamada, Dave Neustadter; Co-Producer, John Rickard; Director, Samuel Bayer; Screenplay, Wesley Strick, Eric Heisserer; Story, Wesley Strick; Based on characters created by Wes Craven; Photography, Jeff Cutter; Designer, Patrick Lumb; Costumes, Mari-An Ceo; Music, Steve Jablonsky; Editor, Glen Scantlebury; Special Prosthetics Effects Designer, Andrew Clement; Special Effects Coordinator, John D. Milinac; Casting, Lisa Fields; a Platinum Dunes production; Distributed by Warner Bros.; Dolby; Panavision; Color; Rated R; 95 minutes; Release date: April 30, 2010

CAST

Freddy Kruger	**Jackie Earle Haley**
Quentin Smith	**Kyle Gallner**
Nancy Holbrook	**Rooney Mara**
Kris Fowles	**Katie Cassidy**
Jesse Braun	**Thomas Dekker**
Dean Russell	**Kellan Lutz**
Alan Smith	**Clancy Brown**
Dr. Gwen Holbrook	**Connie Britton**
Nora Fowles	**Lia Mortensen**
Little Kris	**Julianna Damm**
Jesse's Father	**Christian Stolte**

Katie Schooping Knight, Hailey Schooping Knight, Leah Uteg (Creepy Girls), Don Robert Cass (History Teacher), Kurt Naebig (Dean's Father), Kyra Krumins (Little Nancy), Brayden Coyer (Little Jesse), Max Holt (Little Dean), Andrew Fiscella (Inmate), Bob Kizer (Swim Coach), Pete Kelly (Officer), Jason Brandstetter (County Jail Cop), Rob Riley (Minister), Scott Lindvall (Paramedic), Dominick Coviello (Pharmacist), Parker Bagley (Paxton, Friend in Diner), Jennifer Robers (Dean's Mom), Tania Randall (Nurse), Logan Stalzer (Little Logan), Christopher Woods (Little Christopher), Aaron Yoo (Marcus Yeon)

A group of teenagers have the same dream in which they are tormented by a disfigured man with knives for fingers who threatens to kill each of them before they wake up. Remake of the 1984 film that starred Robert Englund.

Katie Cassidy, Thomas Dekker, Rooney Mara

Annette Bening, Jimmy Smits

Cherry Jones, Annette Bening © Sony Classics

MOTHER AND CHILD

(SONY CLASSICS) Producers, Lisa Maria Falcone, Julie Lynn; Executive Producers, Alejandro González Iñárritu; Co-Producer, Jonathan McCoy; Associate Producers, Tom Heller, Karen Graci; Director/Screenplay, Rodrigo García; Photography, Xavier Pérez Grobet; Designer, Christopher Tandon; Costumes, Susie DeSanto; Music, Edward Shearmur; Music Supervisor, Barklie Griggs; Editor, Steve Weisberg; Casting, Heidi Levitt; a Mockingbird Pictures production, presented in association with Everest Entertainment; Dolby; HD Widescreen; Color; Rated R; 126 minutes; Release date: May 7, 2010

Samuel L. Jackson, Naomi Watts

CAST

Elizabeth	**Naomi Watts**
Karen	**Annette Bening**
Lucy	**Kerry Washington**
Paul	**Samuel L. Jackson**
Paco	**Jimmy Smits**
Ada	**S. Epatha Merkerson**
Sister Joanne	**Cherry Jones**
Joseph	**David Ramsey**
Nora	**Eileen Ryan**
Sofia	**Elpidia Carrillo**
Cristi	**Simone Lopez**
Steven	**Marc Blucas**
Tracy	**Carla Gallo**
Ray	**Shareeka Epps**
Letitia	**Lisagay Hamilton**
Tom	**David Morse**

Shareeka Epps, Kerry Washington

Alexandria Salling (Karen, age 14), Connor Kramme (Tom, age 14), Kay D'Arcy (Karen's Hydrotherapy Patient), Bradford Alex (Physical Therapist), Michael Warren (Winston), Latanya Richardson (Carol), Amy Brenneman (Dr. Eleanor Stone), Tatanya Ali (Maria), Sean Scarborough (Maria's Husband), Ahmed Best (Julian), Brendan Ball (Paul's Niece), Veronica Welch (Paul's Sister), Dawn Deibert (Judge), Gloria Garayua (Melissa), Elizabeth Peña (Amanda), Lawrence Pressman (Dr. Morgan), Britt Robertson (Violet), Gabrielle Abitol (Adoption Agency Worker), Karen Graci (Ray's Nurse), Eugene Collier (Hospital Security Guard), Evette Cord (Adoption Agency Lawyer), Juliette Amara (Ella, age 2), Susan Nimoy (Rebecca)

Three intersecting stories about women who have been affected by adoption: a physical therapist is unnerved by the tenuous relationship she has with her ailing mother; a no-nonsense lawyer has an affair with her boss, looking strictly for phyisicality with no emotional attachment; disappointed because they can't conceive, a couple seek to adopt.

IRON MAN 2

(PARAMOUNT) Producer, Kevin Feige; Executive Producers, Alan Fine, Stan Lee, David Maisel, Denis L. Stewart, Louis D'Esposito, Jon Favreau, Susan Downey; Co-Producers, Jeremy Latcham, Victoria Alonso; Director, Jon Favreau; Screenplay, Justin Theroux; Based on characters from the Marvel comic book created by Stan Lee, Don Heck, Larry Lieber, Jack Kirby; Photography, Matthew Libatique; Designer, J. Michael Riva; Costumes, Mary Zophres; Music, John Debney; Music Supervisor, Dave Jordan; Editors, Richard Pearson, Dan Lebental; Casting, Sarah Finn, Randi Hiller; a Marvel Entertainment presentation; Dolby; Super 35 Widescreen; Color; Rated PG-13; 124 minutes; Release date: May 7, 2010

CAST

Tony Stark (Iron Man)	**Robert Downey Jr.**
Pepper Potts	**Gwyneth Paltrow**
Lt. Col. James "Rhodey" Rhodes (War Machine)	**Don Cheadle**
Natalie Rushman (Black Widow)	**Scarlett Johansson**
Justin Hammer	**Sam Rockwell**
Ivan Vanko (Whiplash)	**Mickey Rourke**
Nick Fury	**Samuel L. Jackson**
Agent Coulson	**Clark Gregg**
Howard Stark	**John Slattery**
Happy Hogan	**Jon Favreau**
Voice of Jarvis	**Paul Bettany**
U.S. Marshal	**Kate Mara**
Christine Everhart	**Leslie Bibb**
Senator Stern	**Garry Shandling**

Christiane Amanpour, Larry Ellison, Adam "DJ AM" Goldstein, Stan Lee, Elon Musk (Themselves), Philippe Bergeron (Det. Lemieux), James Bethea, Michael Bruno (Security Force), Katie Clark (Expo Fan), Luminita Docan (Russian Newscaster), François Duhamel (French Photographer), Tim Guinee (Maj. Allen), Eric L. Haney (Gen. Meade), Yevgeni Lazarev (Anton Vanko), Isaiah Guyman Martin IV (AV Operator), Helena Mattsson (Rebecca), Keith Middlebrook (Expo Cop), Anya Monzikova (Rebeka), Margy Moore (Bambi Arbogast), Olivia Munn (Chess Roberts), Alejandro Patino (Strawberry Vendor), Davin Ransom (Young Tony Stark), Karim Saleh (Guard), Brian Schaeffer (Hammer Expo Tech), Phillipe Simon (French Waiter), Jack White (Jack)

Ivan Vanko uses his technical expertise to assume the alter ego of Whiplash and destroy Iron Man. Sequel to the 2008 film with Downey and Paltrow repeating their roles; Don Cheadle replaces Terrance Howard.

Gwyneth Paltrow, Robert Downey Jr., Sam Rockwell, Leslie Bibb
© Paramount Pictures

Robert Downey, Jr.

Scarlett Johansson

Mickey Rourke

Christopher Egan

Gael García Bernal, Amanda Seyfried

Milena Vukotic, Lydia Biondi, Amanda Seyfried, Marina Massironi, Luisa Ranieri

LETTERS TO JULIET

(SUMMIT) Producers, Caroline Kaplan, Ellen Barkin, Mark Canton; Line Producer, Marco Valerio Pugini; Executive Producer, Ron Schmidt; Director, Gary Winick; Screenplay, Jose Rivera, Tim Sullivan; Photography, Marco Pontecorvo; Designer, Stuart Wurtzel; Costumes, Nicoletta Ercole; Music, Andrea Guerra; Music Supervisor, John Houlihan; Editor, Bill Pankow; Casting, Cindy Tolan, Ellen Lewis, Beatrice Kruger; an Applehead Pictures production, a Mark Canton production; Dolby; Super 35 Widescreen; Color; Rated PG; 105 minutes; Release date: May 14, 2010

CAST

Sophie	**Amanda Seyfried**
Charlie	**Christopher Egan**
Victor	**Gael García Bernal**
Claire	**Vanessa Redgrave**
Lorenzo	**Franco Nero**
Lorraine	**Marcia DeBonis**
Isabella	**Luisa Ranieri**
Francesca	**Marina Massironi**
Donatella	**Lydia Biondi**
Maria	**Milena Vukotic**
Angelina	**Luisa de Santis**
Patrica	**Ashley Lilley**
Viticoltore	**Giordano Formenti**
Signor Ricci, Olive Farmer	**Paolo Arvedi**
Cheese Supplier	**Dario Conti**
Lorenzo Jr.	**Daniel Baldock**

Ivana Lotito (Young Girl), Remo Remotti (Farm House Lorenzo), Angelo Infanti (Chess Playing Lorenzo), Giacomo Piperno (Lorenzo on Lake), Fabio Testi (Count Lorenzo), Sara Armentano (Folks Home Nurse), Benito Deotto (Folks Home Lorenzo), Marcello Catania (Take Him Loreno), Silvana Bosi (Take Him Lorenzo's Wife), Elio Veller (Grocer Lorenzo), Sandro Dori (Priest Lorenzo), Adriano Guerri (Waiter Lorenzo), Oliver Platt (*New Yorker* Editor)

While visiting Verona, Italy, Sophie discovers a letter written to Shakespeare's Juliet from many years before and becomes determined to find the woman responsible and reunite her with the man she once loved.

Vanessa Redgrave, Franco Nero © Summit

ROBIN HOOD

(UNIVERSAL) Producers, Brian Grazer, Ridley Scott, Russell Crowe; Executive Producers, Charles J.D. Schlissel, Michael Costigan, Jim Whitaker, Ryan Kavanaugh; Director, Ridley Scott; Screenplay, Brian Helgeland; Story, Brian Helgeland, Ethan Reiff, Cyrus Voris; Photography, John Mathieson; Designer, Arthur Max; Costumes, Janty Yates; Music, Marc Streitenfeld; Editor, Pietro Scalia; Casting, Jina Jay; Stunts, Steve Dent; Special Effects Coordinator, Nigel Nixon; a Brian Grazer production in association wth Scott Free Prods., presented with Imagine Imagine Entertainment in association with Relativity Media; American-British; Dolby; Panavision; Color; Rated PG-13; 140 minutes; Release date: May 14, 2010

Mark Strong

CAST

Robin Longstride	**Russell Crowe**
Marion Loxley	**Cate Blanchett**
Sir Walter Loxley	**Max von Sydow**
William Marshall	**William Hurt**
Godrey	**Mark Strong**
Prince John	**Oscar Isaac**
King Richard the Lionheart	**Danny Huston**
Eleanor of Aquitaine	**Eileen Atkins**
Friar Tuck	**Mark Addy**
Sheriff of Nottingham	**Matthew Macfadyen**
Little John	**Kevin Durand**
Will Scarlet	**Scott Grimes**
Allan A'Dayle	**Alan Doyle**
Sir Robert Loxley	**Douglas Hodge**
Isabelle of Angoulême	**Léa Seydoux**
Baron Baldwin	**Robert Pugh**
Baron Fitrobert	**Gerald McSorley**
Belvedere	**Velibor Topic**
Loop	**Ciaran Flynn**
Father Tancred	**Simon McBurney**

William Hurt, Eileen Atkins

Denise Gough (Village Mother), John Nicholas (Farmer Paul), Thomas Arnold (Captain of the Royal Barge), Pip Carter (Royal Equery), Mark Lewis Jones (Stone Mason Longstride), Bronson Webb (Jimoen), Denis Menochet (Adhemar), Jamie Beamish (Church Deacon), John Atterbury (Exchequer), Luke Evans (Sheriff's Thug), Roy Holder (Gaffer Tom), Mark David (Baron Baldwin's Grandson), Ruby Bentall (Margaret Walter's Maid), Ned Dennehy (Sentinel), Nicolas Simon (Slovenly French Cook), Lisa Millett (Walter's Cook), Stuart Martin (Messenger), Jessica Raine (Princess Isabel of Glouchester), Steve Evets (Ragged Messenger), Eric Rulliat (Ruffian), Abraham Belaga (King Philip's Aide), Jack Downham (Young Robin), Richard Riddell (Sentry), David Bertrand (French Captain), Arthur Darvill (Groom), Giannina Facio (Lady-in-Waiting), Hannah Barrie (Woman at Bog), Lee Battle (Soldier Boy), Nicky Bell (Soldier Two), Andrea Ware (Little John's Wench), John O'Toole (Tom the Pig Man), Ralph Ineson (Northerner), Zuriel De Peslouan (French Informant), Jack Curran (Distinctive Man), Samuel Dupuy (French Flagship Captain), Nick Lucas (Justiciar), Alan Charlesworth (Cardinal Roger), Lothaire Gerard (French Boy), Mat Laroche (Laughing French Soldier), Chris Jared (Equerry), Joseph Hamilton, James Hamilton, James Burrows, Danny Clarke, Tom Blyth (Feral Children)

Following the Crusades, Robin Longstride returns to England where he finds the newly crowned King John making life miserable for the population, allowing the monarch's scheming advisor to use this opportunity to unleash an invasion of the country by France.

Léa Seydoux, Oscar Isaac

Russell Crowe, Cate Blanchett

Russell Crowe

Russell Crowe, Mark Addy

Matthew Macfadyen

Russell Crowe, Max von Sydow

Danny Huston © Universal Studios

Common, Queen Latifah

Paula Patton, Queen Latifah, Pam Grier

JUST WRIGHT

(FOX SEARCHLIGHT) Producers, Debra Martin Chase, Queen Latifah, Shakim Compere; Co-Producers, M. Blair Breard, Gaylyn Fraiche, Jarrod Moses; Director, Sanaa Hamri; Screenplay, Michael Elliot; Photography, Terry Stacey; Designer, Nicholas Lundy; Costumes, David Robinson; Music, Wendy Melvoin, Lisa Coleman; Music Supervisor, Julia Michels; Editor, Melissa Kent; Basketball Stunt Coordinator, Mark Ellis; Casting, Avy Kaufman; a Flavor Unit/Debra Martin Chase production; Dolby; Deluxe color; Rated PG; 111 minutes; Release date: May 14, 2010

CAST

Leslie Wright	**Queen Latifah**
Scott McKnight	**Common**
Morgan Alexander	**Paula Patton**
Lloyd Wright	**James Pickens Jr.**
Ella McKnight	**Phylicia Rashad**
Janice Wright	**Pam Grier**
Mark Matthews	**Laz Alonso**
Angeo Bembrey	**Mehcad Brooks**
Nelson Kaspian	**Michael Landes**
Morgan's Friend	**Lindsay Michelle Nader**
Dr. Taylor	**Peter Hermann**
Kim Strother	**Bella Goldsmith**
Paul	**Leo Allen**

Dwight Howard, Dwyane Wade, Rashard Lewis, Bobby Simmons Jr., Jalen Rose, Rajon Rondo, Marv Albert, Michael R. Fratello, Kenny Smith, Stuart Scott, Elton Brand, Terence Blanchard, Tim Walsh, Rod Thorn, Leo Ehrline, J.J. Thorn (Themselves), Richard D'Alessandro (Chauffeur), Fabian Almazan, Ben Street, Kendrick Scott (Jazz Band), Brely Evans (Sabrina), Rupak Ginn (Raj), Paolo Montalban (Sommelier), Allen Iaccarino, Joe Felix, Marty Krzywonos (Hecklers), Lauren Dellolio (Waitress), Deborah S. Craig (Maitre d'), Neville Page (Jellyfish Documentary Narrator), Otis Best Jr., Divine Compere, Larkey Cummings, Gustavo Conha, Kedric Dines Jr., Corey Elvin, Andrew Lewis, Carter Lewis, Michael Murry, Deandre Pierre, Lance Rivera Jr., Iman Watson, Elijah Wright (Rucker Park Kids)

Physical therapist Leslie Wright lands her dream job working for injured NBA star Scott McKnight and falls in love with him, only to see her hopes for romance dashed when her friend Morgan captures Scott's attention.

Common

TiMER

(PRESENT PICTURES) Producers, Rikki Jarrett, Jac Schaeffer, Jennifer Glynn; Director/Screenplay, Jac Schaeffer; Photography, Harris Charalambous; Designer, Maya Sigel; Music, Andrew Kaiser; Editor, Peter Samet; a Truckbeef LLC production; Dolby; Color; HDCAM; Rated R; 99 minutes; Release date: May 14, 2010

CAST

Oona O'Leary	**Emma Caulfield**
Steph	**Michelle Borth**
Mikey	**John Patrick Amedori**
Dan the Man	**Desmond Harrington**
Marion	**JoBeth Williams**
Matchmaker Patty	**Patty Kali Rocha**
Rick	**Muse Watson**
Dutch	**John Ingle**
Jesse	**Hayden McFarland**
Paul DePaul	**Tom Irwin**
Dr. Serious	**Mark Harelik**
Brian	**Scott Holroyd**
Manager Larry	**Eric Jungmann**

Bianca Brockl (Soledad), Cristina Cimellaro (Host), Sean C. Francis (CEO), Christine Joaquin (Cindy), Celene Lee (Tammi), Nicki Norris (Delphine), Alan Rice (Dude), Ho-Kwan Tse (Scientist), Katherine Von Till (Local News Anchor), Devin Williamson (Brother), Christopher T. Wood (News Anchor), Kelvin Yu (Nelson)

In an alternate version of present day Los Angeles when people can wear a "TiMer" device allowing them to know the exact number of days and minutes until you meet your soul mate, Oona O'Leary faces an uncertain future.

Emma Caulfield, John Patrick Amedori © Present Pictures

Frey Ranaldo, Sage Ranaldo © IFC Films

Ronald Bronstein, Frey Ranaldo

DADDY LONGLEGS

(IFC FILMS) a.k.a. *Go Get Some Rosemary*; Producers, Casey Neistat, Tom Scott; Co-Producers, Sam Lisenco, Josh Safdie, Benny Safdie, Brett Jutkiewicz, Zach Treitz, Michael Zana, Sophie Dulac; Executive Producer, Andy Spade; Associate Producers, Eléonore Hendricks, Matt Walker, Charles Merzbacher; Directors/Screenplay, Josh Safdie, Benny Safdie; Photography, Brett Jutkiewicz, Josh Safdie; Designer, Sam Lisenco; Editors, Josh Safdie, Benny Safdie, Brett Jutkiewicz, Ronald Bronstein; a NASA Entertainment presentation of a Sophie Dulac productions co-production of a Red Bucket Films production; Color; Not rated; 98 minutes; Release date: May 14, 2010

CAST

Lenny	**Ronald Bronstein**
Sage Sokol	**Sage Ranaldo**
Frey Sokol	**Frey Ranaldo**
Leni	**Eléonore Hendricks**
Principal Puccio	**Victor Puccio**

Sean Price Williams (Dale), Dakota Goldhor (Roberta), Aren Topdjian (Aren, Boyfriend), Abel Ferrara (Robber), Leah Singer (Paige, Mother), Salvatore Sansone (Salvie), Jake Braff (Jake), Ted Barron (Jeff), Larry Chamberlain (Batman), Wayne Chin (Rick), Alex Greenblatt (Friend), Lee Ranaldo (Stepfather)

An irresponsible, 34-year-old divorced dad must face the decision of whether he wants to be a more important and prominent part of his young sons' lives, beyond his annual, two-week visit.

HOLY ROLLERS

(FIRST INDEPENDENT PICTURES) Producers, Danny A. Abeckaser, Tory Tunnell, Per Melita, Jen Gatien; Executive Producers, Kevin Asch, Isaac Gindi, Marat Rosenberg, Dave Berlin; Co-Producers, Robert Profusek, Ryan Silbert; Director, Kevin Asch; Screenplay, Antonio Macia; Photography, Ben Kutchins; Designer, Tommaso Ortino; Costumes, Jacki Roach; Music, MJ Mynarski; Music Supervisors, Kevin Wyatt, Scott Vener; Editor, Suzanne Spangler; Casting, Sig De Miguel, Stephen Vincent; a Deerjen Films/Lookbook Films/Safehouse Pictures and Gulfstream Films production, presented in association with Shaman Productions, Inc.; Color; Rated R; 89 minutes; Release date: May 21, 2010

Justin Bartha, Jesse Eisenberg © First Independent Pictures

CAST
Sam Gold	**Jesse Eisenberg**
Yosef Zimmerman	**Justin Bartha**
Rachel Apfel	**Ari Graynor**
Jackie Solomon	**Danny A. Abeckaser**
Mendel Gold	**Mark Ivanir**
Ephraim	**Q-Tip**
Elka Gold	**Elizabeth Marvel**
Leon Zimmerman	**Jason Fuchs**
Ruth Gold	**Hallie Kate Eisenberg**
Rebbe Horowitz	**Bern Cohen**
Andrew	**Charlie Hewson**
David	**Andrew Levitas**
Josh	**Marc Rose**

Omer Barnea (Elijah), Stella Keitel (Zeldny Lazar), David Vadim (Mr. Maxim), Eli Gelb (Ezra, Young Hasid Mule), Penny Bittone (Ivan), Evan Mathew Weinstein (Young Hasidic Father), Court Young, Caroline Stefanie Clay (Customs Agents), Karina Arroyave (Gloria), Lou Cantres (Carlos the Mailman), Keith Davis (Security Guard), Sruli Federman (Sruli Lazar), Alizée Guinochet (Tabitha), Rachel Heller (Girl), Sruli Leider (Sam's Friend), Joseph R. McConnell (Thug), Leslie C. Nemet (Young Hasidic Mother), Robert Oppel (Tattooed Inmate), Roderick Pannell (Thug #1), Ori Pfeffer (Beni), Zoe Portanova (Party Girl), Tim Schuebel (U.S. Customs Agent), Sammuel Soifer (Shmuely Lazar), Anita Storr (Passenger going through Customs)

Sam Gold, a young Hasidic Jew from an Orthodox Brooklyn community, is recruited by his neighbor to serve as a drug mule.

Jesse Eisenberg, Justin Bartha

Danny A. Abeckaser, Ari Graynor

Jesse Eisenberg, Justin Bartha, Jason Fuchs

Fiona, Shrek

Shrek, Donkey © DreamWorks

Shrek, Rumplestiltskin

SHREK FOREVER AFTER

(DREAMWORKS) Producers, Teresa Cheng, Gina Shawy; Executive Producers, Aron Warner, Andrew Adamson, John H. Williams; Director, Mike Mitchell; Screenplay, Josh Klausner, Darren Lemke; Photography, Yong Duk Jhun; Art Directors, Max Boas, Michael Hernandez; Music, Harry Gregson-Williams; Editor, David Teller; Animation Supervisor, Marek Kochout; Character Technical Director, Lucia Modesto; Character Effects Animator, Noah Peterson; Distributed by Paramount Pictures; Dolby; Color; 3D; Rated PG; 93 minutes; Release date: May 21, 2010

VOICE CAST

Shrek	**Mike Myers**
Donkey	**Eddie Murphy**
Princess Fiona	**Cameron Diaz**
Puss in Boots	**Antonio Banderas**
Queen	**Julie Andrews**
Brogan	**Jon Hamm**
King Harold	**John Cleese**
Cookie	**Craig Robinson**
Rumplestiltskin/Priest/Krekraw Ogre	**Walt Dohrn**
Gretched	**Jane Lynch**
Patrol Witch/Wagon Witch #2	**Lake Bell**
Dancing Witch/Wagon Witch #1	**Kathy Griffin**
Guard Witch	**Mary Kay Place**

Kristen Schaal (Pumpkin Witch/Palace Witch), Meredith Vieira (Broomsy Witch), Ryan Seacrest (Father of Butter Pants), Cody Cameron (Pinocchio/Three Pigs), Larry King (Doris), Regis Philbin (Mabel), Christopher Knights (Blind Mice), Conrad Vernon (Gingerbread Man), Aron Warner (Wolf), Jasper Johannes Andrews, Ollie Mitchell (Ogre Babies), Miles Christopher Bakshi (Ogre Baby/Villager Kid), Nina Zoe Bakshi (Ogre Baby/Tourist Girl/Villager Girl)

Bored with his life of domesticity, Shrek makes a deal with Rumpelstiltskin to return to his life as an ogre only to be sent to a nightmare version of Far Far Away, where he and his beloved Fiona have never even met. Third in the DreamWorks series following *Shrek* (2001), *Shrek 2* (2004), and *Shrek the Third* (2007).

Puss in Boots

SOLITARY MAN

(ANCHOR BAY) Producers, Paul Schiff, Steven Soderbergh, Heidi Jo Markel, Dana Golomb; Executive Producers, Avi Lerner, Danny Dimbort, Boaz Davidson, Trevor Short; Co-Producer, Jared Goldman; Directors, Brian Koppelman, David Levien; Screenplay, Brian Koppelman; Photography, Alvin Kuchler; Designer, Robert Pearson; Costumes, Jenny Gering; Music, Michael Penn; Editor, Tricia Cooke; Casting, Avy Kaufman; a Nu Image production, a Paul Schiff production, presented in association with Millennium Films; Dolby; Color; Rated R; 90 minutes; Release date; May 21, 2010

CAST

Ben Kalmen	**Michael Douglas**
Nancy Kalmen	**Susan Sarandon**
Jimmy Merino	**Danny DeVito**
Jordan Karsch	**Mary-Louise Parker**
Susan Porter	**Jenna Fischer**
Allyson Karsch	**Imogen Poots**
Daniel Cheston	**Jesse Eisenberg**
Steve Heller	**Richard Schiff**
Scotty Porter	**Jake Siciliano**
Gary Porter	**David Costabile**
Peter Hartofilias	**Ben Shenkman**
Carol Solomonde	**Anastasia Griffith**
Ted Loof	**Alex Kaluzhsky**
Nurse	**Simona Levin Williams**
Sgt. John Haverford	**James Colby**
Nascarella	**Arthur Nascarella**
Dr. Steinberg	**Bruce Altman**
Bill Rayle	**Nick M. Toomey**
Irate Student	**Adam Pally**
Todd the Building Manager	**Lenny Venito**
Maitre D'	**Greg McFadden**
Waiter	**Ricky Garcia**
Dean Edward Gitelson	**Doug McGrath**
Tall Girl	**Gillian Jacobs**
Allyson's Attractive Friend	**Katherine Owens**
Kelly	**Arizona Muse**
Shadow	**Sean Patrick Reilly**
Maureen	**Olivia Thirlby**

Six and a half years after receiving a discouraging medical report, once-successful car dealer Ben Kalmen continues to lead a hedonistic existence, much to the dismay of his friends and family.

Imogen Poots, Michael Douglas, Jesse Eisenberg

Jake Siciliano, Jenna Fischer, Michael Douglas

Danny DeVito

Michael Douglas, Susan Sarandon

Imogen Poots

Mary-Louise Parker

Susan Sarandon

Michael Douglas, Jesse Eisenberg © Anchor Bay

Jesse Eisenberg, Olivia Thirlby

SEX AND THE CITY 2

(NEW LINE CINEMA) Producers, Michael Patrick King, Sarah Jessica Parker, Darren Starr, John Melfi; Executive Producers, Toby Emmerich, Richard Brener, Marcus Viscidi; Director/Screenplay, Michael Patrick King; Based on the TV series created by Darren Starr, based on characters from the book by Candace Bushnell; Photography, John Thomas; Designer, Jeremy Conway; Costumes, Patricia Field; Music, Aaron Zigman; Music Supervisor, Julia Michels; Editor, Michael Berenbaum; Casting, Bernard Telsey; a Darren Starr production, presented in association with Home Box Office, in association with Village Roadshow Pictures; Dolby; Panavision; Deluxe color; Rated R; 146 minutes; Release date: May 27, 2010

CAST

Carrie Preston	**Sarah Jessica Parker**
Samantha Jones	**Kim Cattrall**
Charlotte Goldenblatt	**Kristin Davis**
Miranda Hobbes	**Cynthia Nixon**
Aidan Shaw	**John Corbett**
Mr. Big	**Chris Noth**
Steve Brady	**David Eigenberg**
Harry Goldenblatt	**Evan Handler**
Jerry "Smith" Jerrod	**Jason Lewis**
Stanford Blatch	**Willie Garson**
Anthony Marantino	**Mario Cantone**
Herself	**Liza Minnelli**

Lynn Cohen (Magda), Alice Eve (Erin), Noah Mills (Nicky), Max Ryan (Rikard Spiriti), Omid Djalili (Mr. Safir), Billy Stritch (Band Leader), Art Malik (Shiekh Khalid), Raza Jaffrey (Butler Guarau), David Alan Basche (David), Viola Harris (Gloria Blatch), Gerry Vichi (Leo Blatch), Kamilah Marshall, Shayna Steele, Jordan Ballard (Bewitched Singers), Norm Lewis (Reginald), Manuel Herrera (Sergio), Alexandra Carl (Waitress at Inn), Lilian Pizzuto, Sabrina Pizzuto, Savanna Mae Dezio, Sienna Cheryl Dezio (Rose Goldenblatt), Joseph Pupo (Brady Hobbes), Neal Bledsoe (Kevin), Ron White (Tom), Selenis Leyva (Teacher), Condola Rashad (Meghan), Jennifer Ferrin (Patience), Kevin Brown (Usher), Miley Cyrus, Tim Gunn, Tuesday Knight (Themselves), Dhaffer L'Abidine (Mahmud), Penélope Cruz (Carmen Garcia Carrion), Fatima Nouali, Meryem Zaimi (Security Women), Walton Nuñez (Butler Adbul), Akhmiss Abdelmalek (Butler Adman), Abdesselam Bouhasni (Butler Resir), Najat Kheir Allah (Real Housewife of Abu Dhabi), Azzdeine Riyad (Shifty Man), Mohamd Belfikh (Show Salesman), Daoud Heidami (Abed), Alexander Wraith (Nightclub Waiter), Adesola A. Osakalumi, Nnamudi Amobi (Nightclub DJs), Tory Ross, Loretta Ables-Sayre, Ronica V. Reddick (Singers), Mohammed Moutawakil (Outraged Man), Zohra Sadiki (Outraged Woman), Jamal Selmaoui, Mostafa Hnini (Security Guards), Antony Bunsee (Beydoun), Waleed Zuaiter (Shahib), Piter Marek (Khalil), Tarek Moussa (Omar), Abderrahim Daris (Angry Old Man), Mohamed Kafi, Adil Louchgui, Belmjahed Abdelhak, Mustafa Alyassri, Sultan Alyassri (Angry Men), Raya Meddine (Annesha), Goldy Notay (Basimah), Anoush Nevart (Jihan), Deepa Purohit, Nicoel Shalhoub, Chriselle Almeida, Marjan Neshat (Stewardesses), Jimmy Palumbo (William the Doorman), Jack O'Brien (New Firm Law Partner), Megan Boone (Allie), Nick Adams, Paul Canaan, Joshua Cruz, Van Hughes, Robert Lenzi, Jay Armstrong Johnson, Michael Mahany, Kyle Dean Massey, Jeffrey Omura, Andrew Rannells, Matthew Risch, Nicholas Rodriguez, Ryan Silverman, Will Taylor, Max Von Essen, Dashaun Young (Wedding Chorus), John Antorino (Golfer), Minglie Chen (Bergdorf Salesgirl), Zack Clark (Bartender #1), Peter Conboy (Tourist), Alexandra Fong, Parker Fong (Lily York Goldenblatt), Nadine Isenegger, Natalie Lomonte (Liza Dancers), Kelli O'Hara (Ellen), Michael T. Weiss (Handsome Man at Wedding)

Believing that her marriage to Mr. Big has already grown stale, Carrie Preston, along with friends Miranda and Charlotte, accepts an offer from their pal Samantha Jones to join her on an all-expense-paid trip to Abu Dhabi where she hopes to sort out her problems. Sequel to the 2008 film *Sex and the City* (New Line Cinema).

Evan Handler, David Eigenberg, Chris Noth

Sarah Jessica Parker © New Line Cinema

Kristin Davis, Sarah Jessica Parker, Kim Cattrall, Cynthia Nixon

Ben Kingsley, Jake Gyllenhaal, Richard Coyle

PRINCE OF PERSIA: THE SANDS OF TIME

(WALT DISNEY PICTURES) Producer, Jerry Bruckheimer; Executive Producers, Mike Stenson, Chad Oman, John August, Jordan Mechner, Patrick McCormick, Eric McLeod; Director, Mike Newell; Screenplay, Boaz Yakin, Doug Miro, Carlo Bernard; Screen Story, Jordan Mechner, based on his video game series *Prince of Persia*; Photography, John Seale; Designer, Wolf Kroeger; Costumes, Penny Rose; Music, Harry Gregson-Williams; Editors, Michael Kahn, Martin Walsh, Mick Audsley; a Jerry Bruckheimer Films presentation; Dolby; Super 35 Widescreen; Deluxe Color; Rated PG-13; 116 minutes; Release date: May 28, 2010

CAST

Dastan	**Jake Gyllenhaal**
Nizam	**Ben Kingsley**
Tamina	**Gemma Arterton**
Sheik Amar	**Alfred Molina**
Seso	**Steve Toussaint**
Garsiv	**Toby Kebbell**
Tus	**Richard Coyle**
King Sharam	**Ronald Pickup**
Bis	**Reece Ritchie**

Gísli Örn Garðarsson (Hassansin Leader), Claudio Pacifico (Hassansin Porcupine), Dave Pope (Hassansin Giant Scimitar), Domonkos Pardanyi (Hassansin Double-Bladed Halberd), Massimilano Ubladi (Hassansin Long Razor), Furdik Vladimir (Hassansin Grenade Man), Christopher Greet (Regent of Alamut), William Foster (Young Dastan), Elliot James Neale (Young Bis), Selva Raslingham (Persian Captain), Daud Shah (Asoka), Daisy Doidge-Hill (Young Guardian Girl), Charlie Banks (King Sharam as a Boy), Jesse Mathews (Nizam as a Boy), Rohan Siva (Bloodied Alamut Soldier), Dimitri Andreas (Head Servant), Stephen Pope (Roham), Trampas Thompson (Mounted Herald), Joseph Bedlem (Garsiv's Lieutenant), Rachid Abbad (Rafa), Farzana Dua Elahe (Tamina's Maid Servant), Aziz El Kibachi (Mughal Sulan), Simon De Selva (General), Felix Augusto Quadros (Spy), Amin Mohammad Fouladi, Masoud Abbasi, Mehrdad Azmin, Zartosht Safari, Ali Nourbakhsh, Parham Bahadroan, Ehsan Parvizian, Shohreh Shojaeifard, Babake Babakinejad (Musicians)

Having come into possession of a magical dagger that can turn back time, Dastan finds himself framed for the murder of his adopted father, the King, causing him to flee the kingdom and try to find a means of proving his innocence.

Jake Gyllenhaal © Walt Disney Pictures

Jake Gyllenhaal, Gemma Arterton

Colm Meaney, Russell Brand © Universal Studios

Jonah Hill, Elisabeth Moss

Jonah Hill, Sean Combs

Russell Brand

GET HIM TO THE GREEK

(UNIVERSAL) Producers, Judd Apatow, Nicholas Stoller, David Bushell, Rodney Rothman; Executive Producer, Richard Vane; Co-Producer, Jason Segel; Director/Screenplay, Nicholas Stoller; Based on characters created by Jason Segel; Photography, Robert Yeoman; Designer, Jan Roelfs; Costumes, Leesa Evans; Music, Lyle Workman; Music Supervisor, Jonathan Karp; Editors, William Kerr, Mike Sale; an Apatow production, presented in association with Relativity Media and Spyglass Entertainment; Dolby; Color; Rated R; 109 minutes; Release date: June 4, 2010

CAST

Aaron Green	**Jonah Hill**
Aldous Snow	**Russell Brand**
Daphne Binks	**Elisabeth Moss**
Jackie Q	**Rose Byrne**
Jonathan Snow	**Colm Meaney**
Sergio Roma	**Sean Combs**
Lena Snow	**Dinah Stabb**

Zoe Salmon, Lars Ulrich, Mario López, Pink, Billy Bush, Kurt F. Loder, Christina Aguilera, Tom Felton, Rick Schroder, Pharrell, Meredith Vieira, Paul Krugman (Themselves), Tyler McKinney (African Child in Video), Chad Cleven, Jonathan Chris Lopez, Vero Felice Monti, Danny O'Leary (Paparazzi in Los Angeles), Aziz Ansari (Matty), Kali Hawk (Kali), Nick Kroll (Kevin), Brandon Andrew Johnson, Ivan Shaw, Ellie Kemper (Pinnacle Executives), Jake Johnson (Jazz Man), Da'Vone McDonald (Sergio's Security Guard), Derek Resallat (Dr. Coltrane), Karl Theobald (Duffy Servant Dude), Gee Sekweyama, Jamie Sives (Aldous' Mates in London), Zoe Richard, Jessica Ellerby (Club Girls in London), Tony Van Silva (Old Man on Bike), Meddy Ford, Rebecca Kinder (Party Girls in Limo), Jim Piddock (Limousine Driver in London), Kristen Bell (Sarah Marshall),Ryan Shiraki (Rianna the Hairdresser), José Ramón Rosario (Limousine Driver in New York), Sean Manniion (*Today Show* Sound Guy), David Auerbach (*Today Show* Stage Manager), Howard F. Strawbridge (*Today Show* Lighting Director), Stephen G. Lucas (*Today Show* Director), Lenny Widegren, Roger Manning Jr., Sean Hurley, Victor Indrizzo (Infant Sorrow), Ato Essandoh (Smiling African Drummer), Bashiri Johnson, Kimati Dinizulu, Gary Fritz, Jelanie Johnson, Daoud Woods, Sheldon Goode, Mauwena Kodjovi (African Percussionists), Richard Child, Caroline Limata, John J. Schneider (*Today Show* Audience Members), Aurora Nonas-Barnes (Oak Room Girl), Jennifer Perry (Flirtatious Party Girl), Lindsey Broad (Pocket Dial Girl), Nicole Sciacca (Dancer at Nightclub in New York), Thomas Nowell (S&M Guy Who Looks like Moby), Duane Sequira (Drug Dealer in New York), Ronald J. Garner (TSA Agent at JFK), Joyful Drake (Sergio's Baby Mama), Francesca DelBanco (Admiral Club Attendant), T.J. Miller (Brian the Concierge), Neal Brennan (Guy at Brian's House), Stephanie Faracy (Wendy), Brian Duprey (Frank Look-Alike), Kyle Diamond (Sammy Look-Alike), Thomas R. Wallek (Joey Look-Alike), Drew Anthony Carrano (Dean Look-Alike), Kelly Ann Buckman (Waitress), Giusy Castiglione, Christine T. Nguyen, Diana Terranova (Lap Dancers in Vegas), Ava Vassileva (Topless Party Girl), Carla Gallo (Destiny), Carlos Jacott (Navigator Driver in Vegas), Rino Romano (Voice), Joe Benson (DJ Voice), Sarah Haskins (Girl in Crowd at Standard Hotel), Andrew Burlinson (Hipster in the Crowd), Tom Chadwick (Tom the Assistant), Mike Viola, Dan Rothchild (Furry Walls), Dayton Knoll, Chris J. Evans, Hannah Cowley, Hannah Schick, Megan Presley (VH1 Storyteller Audience)

Hapless record company employee Aaron Green is given the unenviable task of escorting self-destructive rock star Aldous Snow from London to his sold-out return engagement at Los Angeles' Greek Theater.

KILLERS

(LIONSGATE) Producers, Scott Aversano, Ashton Kutcher, Jason Goldberg, Mike Karz; Executive Producers, William S. Beasley, Josie Rosen, Peter Morgan, Michael Paseornek, John Sacchi, Christopher Pratt, Chad Marting; Co-Producer, Karyn Spencer Murphy; Director, Robert Luketic; Screenplay, Bob DeRosa, T.M. Griffin; Story, Bob DeRosa; Photography, Russell Carpenter; Designer, Missy Stewart; Costumes, Ellen Mirojnick, Johanna Argan; Music, Rolfe Kent; Music Supervisor, Tracy McKnight; Editors, Richard Francis-Bruce, Mary Jo Markey; Casting, Deborah Aquila, Tricia Wood, Jennifer Smith; an Aversano Films and Katalyst Films production, a Lionsgate production; Dolby; Color; Rated PG-13; 93 minutes; Release date: June 4, 2010

CAST

Spencer Aimes	**Ashton Kutcher**
Jen Kornfeldt	**Katherine Heigl**
Mr. Kornfeldt	**Tom Selleck**
Mrs. Kornfeldt	**Catherine O'Hara**
Vivian	**Katheryn Winnick**
Mac Bailey	**Kevin Sussman**
Olivia Brooks	**Lisa Ann Walter**

Casey Wilson (Kristen), Rob Riggle (Henry), Martin Mull (Holbrook), Alex Borstein (Lily Baily), Usher Raymond IV (Kevin the Manager), Letoya Luckett (Amanda), Michael Daniel Cassady (Milo), Larry Joe Campbell (Pete Denham), Mary Birdsong (Jackie Vallero), Ric Reitz (Dougie Vallero), John Atwood (Don Nootbar), Bruce Taylor (Mr. Stafford), Sharan C. Mansfield (Mildred), Adeline Gorgos (Gorgeous Blodne), Ariel Winter (Sadie), Jean-Charles Fonti (Jean Paul), Nazareth Agopian (Jasper Leveneux), Christophe Carotenuto (Leveneux's Adjutant), Blandine Bury (Leveneux's Mistress), Ghislain Caroslo (Courier), Michel Bellier (Maitre D'), David Marchal (Waiter), Pascal T'Hooft (Guard), David Mitnik (Gagged Man), Winston Story (Eurocreep), Lauren Glazier (Stewardess), George Duskin (Trap Shooter)

Spencer Aimes is glad to leave behind his life as a professional assassin in order to wed Jen Kornfeldt, only to discover, three years into their marriage, that they are themselves the target of assassins.

Ashton Kutcher, Tom Selleck © Lionsgate

Marmaduke, Lee Pace ©20th Century Fox

MARMADUKE

(20TH CENTURY FOX) Producer, John Davis; Executive Producers, Arnon Milchan, Tariq Jalil, Jeffrey Stott, Derek Dauchy; Director, Tom Dey; Screenplay, Tim Rasmussen, Vince Di Meglio; Based upon the comic created by Brad Anderson and Phil Leeming; Photography, Greg Gardiner; Costumes, Karen Matthews; Music, Christopher Lennertz; Music Supervisors, Dave Jordan, Jojo Villanueva; Editor, Don Zimmerman; a Davis Entertainment Company production, presented by Regency Enterprises; Dolby; Color; Rated PG; 87 minutes; Release date: June 4, 2010

CAST

Voice of Marmaduke	**Owen Wilson**
Phil Winslow	**Lee Pace**
Debbie Winslow	**Judy Greer**
Don Twombly	**William H. Macy**
Barbara Winslow	**Caroline Sunshine**
Brian Winslow	**Finley Jacobsen**
Sarah Winslow	**Mandy Haines, Milana Haines**

VOICE CAST: Emma Stone (Maizie), George Lopez (Carlos), Christopher Mintz-Plasse (Giuseppe), Steve Coogan (Raisin), Stacy Ferguson (Jezebel), Kiefer Sutherland (Bosco), Marlon Wayans (Lightning), Damon Wayans Jr. (Thunder), Sam Elliott (Chupadogra), Randall Montgomery (Sweater Dog), Hope Levy, Anjelah N. Johnson (Afghans), Devon Werkheiser (Drama Dog #1/Shroom Dog #2/Golden Dog/Cocker Spaniel), Chris Colfer (Drama Dog #2/Shroom Dog #1/Beach Dog #1), David Z. Price (Party Dog #2/Beagle), Hudson Thames (Delinquent Dog), Francisco Ramos, Bernardo de Paula, Eddie "Piolin" Sotelo (Purse Dogs), Todd Glass (Doberman/Shasta), Ryan Devlin, Jeffrey Garcia (Beach Dogs), King "AB" Kedar (Surfing Award Dog/Beach Dog #4), Liza Lapira (Party Dog #1), Jack McGee (Dalmatian), Josh Gad (Bandana Dog)
ADDITIONAL CAST: David Walliams (Anton Harrison), Raugi Yu (Drama Trainer), Glenn McCuen (Bodie), Frank Topol (Bosco's Owner), Graylen Cameron (Giant Teenage Boy), Alex Rockhill (Dog Catcher), Cameron Cowles, John Daily, Tyler Abiew (Skater Boys), Heather Doerksen (Jessica), Ashley Liu (Executive), Madison Desjarlais (Brunette), Erin Kerr (Redhead), Nicole Muñoz (3rd OC Girl), Christopher Attadia (Jock), Jason Bryden (Man on Bench), Izaak Smith (Basketball Captain), Keith Blackman Dallas (Emergency Road Worker), Peter-John Prinsloo (Lead Fireman), Colin Decker, Charles Jarman, Garvin Cross, Chris Bradford (Firemen), Graham MacDonald (Orange County Policeman), David Stanfield (Announcer)

Phil Winslow and his family move to a new neighborhood where their enormous Great Dane, Marmaduke, proceeds to wreck havoc in his customary manner.

THE A-TEAM

(20TH CENTURY FOX) Producers, Stephen J. Cannell, Spike Seldin, Tony Scott, Jules Daly, Alex Young, Iain Smith; Executive Producers, Ridley Scott, Marc Silvestri, Ross Fanger; Director, Joe Carnahan; Screenplay, Joe Carnahan, Brian Bloom, Skip Woods; Based on the Television series created by Frank Lupo, Stephen J. Cannell; Photography, Mauro Fiore; Designer, Charles Wood; Costumes, Betsy Heimann; Music, Alan Silvestri; Editors, Roger Barton, Jim May; a Stephen J. Cannell/Top Cow/Scott Free production; Dolby; Panavision; Deluxe color; Rated PG-13; 117 minutes; Release date: June 11, 2010

Bradley Cooper, Sharlto Copley, Liam Neeson, Quinton "Rampage" Jackson

CAST

Col. John "Hannibal" Smith	**Liam Neeson**
Lt. Templeton "Faceman" Peck	**Bradley Cooper**
Clarisa Sosa	**Jessica Biel**
Cpl. Bosco "B.A." Baracus	**Quinton "Rampage" Jackson**
Murdock	**Sharlto Copley**
Lynch	**Patrick Wilson**
General Morrison	**Gerald McRaney**
Director McCready	**Henry Czerny**
General Javier Tuco	**Yul Vazquez**
Pike	**Brian Bloom**
Gammons	**Maury Sterling**
Ravech	**Terry Chen**
Chopshop Jay	**Omari Hardwick**
Oskar Shunt	**David Hugghins**

Jacob Blair (Agent Blair), Rad Daly (Agent Daly), Kyle Riefsnyder (Agent Kyle), Andrew Coghlan (Army Hospital Attendant), James O'Sullivan (Army Hospital Courier), C. Ernst Harth (Crematorium Attendant), Stefan Arngrim (Crazy Howard Little), Christian Tessier (Tahoe Prison Deputy), William Stewart, Marc-Anthony Massiah (Tahoe Inmates), Kwesi Ameyaw, Robert Conway (Dutch Customs Agents), Gardiner Millar (Prison Warden), Anita Brown (Attractive Prison Guard), Alex Madison (General Tuco's Wife), Benny Hernandez, Jimmy Ortega (Mexican Captor), Bo Anzo (Mike "The Operator"), Neil Schell (Army Meddac Hospital XO), Leah Carnahan (Army Meddac Nurse), Michael St. John Smith (Cemetery Chaplain), Shaw Madson (Station Polizei), Katie Boskovich (FOB French Reporter), Sam Radjinia (Morrison's Arab Goon #2), Billy Wickman (Flight Control Tech), Brendan Penny (C130J Pilot #1), Jeanne-Melanie Haasbroek (Army Hospital Therapist Elke), Tom Butler, John Callahan (Judge Advocates), Dirk Benedict (Pensacola Prisoner Milt), Dwight Schultz , Don Kodel (German Doctors), Natalie L. James (Lynch Secretary), Vince Murdocco, Fraser Aitcheson (Pike Goons), Jason Schombing (Flight Control Commander), Stephane Fromont (Gate Guard), Frank Maier (German Fisherman), Anne Maier (German Wife), Hitesh Jogia, Marwan Al-Shami, Ali Bordbar (Iraqi Liaisons), Jennifer Cheon (Lynch Woman), Peter Fletcher (Police Captain), Alfred Jajjo (Mint Worker), Jon Johnson (Honor Guard), Craig Loblaw (Police Detective), Patrick Merle (Frankfurt Police Officer), Julian Paul (Prison MP), Rafael Pellerin (Soccer Kid), Ralph Shaw (Ukulele Performer), Darin Wong (Killer Operatiive), Corey Burton (Narrator), Jon Hamm (Other Lynch)

Bradley Cooper

Hoping to clear themselves of false charges, a quartet of soldiers accepts a deal from a CIA operative to recover the stolen printing plates that led to their court-martials. Based on the 1983-87 NBC series that starred George Peppard, Dwight Schultz, Mr. T, and Dirk Benedict. Schultz and Benedict make appearances here.

Jessica Biel © 20th Century Fox

Han Wen Wen, Jaden Smith © Columbia Pictures

Jaden Smith, Jackie Chan

THE KARATE KID

(COLUMBIA) Producers, Jerry Weintraub, Will Smith, Jada Pinkett Smith, James Lassiter, Ken Stovitz; Executive Producers, Dany Wolf, Susan Ekins, Han San Ping; Director, Harald Zwart; Screenplay, Christopher Murphey; Story, Robert Mark Kamen; Photography, Roger Pratt; Designer, François Ségun; Costumes, Han Feng; Music, James Horner; Music Supervisor, Pilar McCurry; Editor, Joel Negron; Co-Producer, Solon So; an Overbrook Entertainment/Jerry Weintraub production in association with China Film Group Corporation; American-Chinese; Dolby; Super 35 Widescreen; Color; Rated PG; 140 minutes; Release date: June 11, 2010

CAST

Dre Parker	**Jaden Smith**
Mr. Han	**Jackie Chan**
Sherry Parker	**Taraji P. Henson**
Mei Ying	**Han Wen Wen**
Master Li	**Rongguang Yu**
Meiying's Dad	**Zhensu Wu**
Meiying's Mom	**Zhiheng Wang**
Cheng	**Zhenwei Wang**
Dre's Detroit Friend	**Jared Minns**
Liang	**Shijia Lü**
Zhuang	**Yi Zhao**
Song	**Bo Zhang**
Harry	**Luke Carberry**

Cameron Hillman (Mark), Ghye Samuel Brown (Oz), Rocky Shi (Ur Dang), Ji Wang (Mrs. Po), Harry Van Gorkum (Music Instructor), Tess Liu (History Teacher), Xinhua Guo (Tournament Doctor), Jijun Zhai (Mat 4 Referee), Shun Li (Mat 5 Referee), Yanyan Wu (Mrs. Xie), Tao Ji (Announcer), Chen Jing (Man on Planet Speaking Chinese), Wentai Liu (Dude from Detroit), Geliang Liang (Ping Pong Man), Xu Ming (Bao), Hannah Joy (Diane), Michelle Yeoh (Cobra Trainer)

Forced to move to China with his mom, young Dre Parker is taught kung fu by a maintenance man in order to take on the school bully. Remake of the 1984 Columbia film of the same name that starred Ralph Macchio and Pat Morita.

Taraji P. Henson

Jaden Smith, Jackie Chan

WINTER'S BONE

(ROADSIDE ATTRACTIONS) Producers, Anne Rosellini, Alix Madigan-Yorkin; Executive Producers, Jonathan Scheuer, Shawn Simon; Co-Producer, Kate Dean; Director, Debra Granik; Screenplay, Debra Granik, Anne Rosellini; Based on the novel by Daniel Woodrell; Photography, Michael McDonough; Designer, Mark White; Costumes, Rebecca Hofherr; Music, Dickon Hinchliffe; Editor, Affonso Gonçalves; Casting, Kerry Barden, Paul Schnee; an Anonymous Content and Winter's Bone production; Dolby; Color; HD; Rated R; 99 minutes; Release date: June 11, 2010

CAST

Ree Dolly	**Jennifer Lawrence**
Teardrop	**John Hawkes**
Little Arthur	**Kevin Breznahan**
Merab	**Dale Dickey**
Sheriff Baskin	**Garret Dillahunt**
Sonya	**Shelley Waggener**
April	**Sheryl Lee**
Gail	**Lauren Sweetser**
Ashlee	**Ashlee Thompson**
Mike Satterfield	**Tate Taylor**
Blond Milton	**William White**
Megan	**Casey MacLaren**
Sonny	**Isaiah Stone**
Connie	**Valerie Richards**
Alice	**Beth Domann**
Floyd	**Cody Brown**
Thump Milton	**Ronnie Hall**
Victoria	**Cinnamon Schultz**
Recruiter	**Russell Schalk**
Spider Milton	**Brandon Gray**
Baby Ned	**Andrew Burnley, Phillip Burnley**
Tilly	**Charlote Jeane Lucas**
Pickin' Session Vocalist	**Marideth Sisco**
Buster Leroy	**Raymond Vaughan Jr.**

Informed that her delinquent, ex-con dad has signed away their house and land as collateral, Ree becomes determined to track him down when she learns the house will be seized unless he shows up for a scheduled court appearance.

This film received Oscar nominations for picture, actress (Jennifer Lawrence), supporting actor (John Hawkes), and adapted screenplay.

Ashlee Thompson, Jennifer Lawrence, Isaiah Stone

Ashlee Thompson, Jennifer Lawrence, Isaiah Stone

Jennifer Lawrence

Jennifer Lawrence

Jennifer Lawrence © Roadside Attractions

Dale Dickey

Lauren Sweetser

John Hawkes

Joan Rivers

Joan Rivers © IFC Films

JOAN RIVERS: A PIECE OF WORK

(IFC FILMS) Producers, Ricki Stern, Annie Sundberg, Seth Keal; Executive Producer/ Screenplay, Ricki Stern; Directors, Ricki Stern, Annie Sundberg; Photography, Charles Miller; Music, Paul Brill; Editor, Penelope Falk; a Breakthru Films production; Dolby; Color; Rated R; 84 minutes; Release date: June 11, 2010.

WITH
Joan Rivers, Melissa Rivers, Don Rickles, Kathy Griffin, Florian Klein, Emily Kosloski, Mark Phillips, Larry A. Thompson, Patrick Alparone, Edgar Cooper Endicott, Flo Fox, Florian Klein, Jocelyn Pickett

Documentary that follows a year in the life of comedian Joan Rivers.

STONEWALL UPRISING

(FIRST RUN FEATURES) Producers/Directors, Kate Davis, David Heilbroner; Screenplay, David Heilbroner; Based on the book *Stonewall: The Riots That Sparked the Gay Revolution* by David Carter; Photography, Buddy Squires; Music, Gary Lionelli; Editor, Kate Davis; a Q-Ball Productions Film for American Experience; Stereo; Color/Black and white; HDCAM; Not rated; 82 minutes; Release date: June 16, 2010.

WITH
Virginia Appuzo, Martin Boyce, Raymond Castro, Prof. William Eskridge, Jerry Hoose, Tommy Lanigan-Schmidt, Dick Leitsch, Eric Marcus, John O'Brien, Seymour Pine, Fred Sergeant, Lucian Truscott, Doric Wilson
AND Paul Bosche, John DiGiacomo, Dana Gaiser, Noah Goldman, J. Michael Grey, David Huggins, Louis Mandelbaum, Leroy S. Mobley, Samual Morkofsky, Alfredo del Rio (Reenactment Actors)

Documentary depicting the events that led to the gay uprising at New York's Stonewall Inn in June of 1969, launching a turning point in gay rights.

© First Run Features

CYRUS

(FOX SEARCHLIGHT) Producer, Michael Costigan; Executive Producers, Ridley Scott, Tony Scott; Directors/Screenplay, Jay Duplass, Mark Duplass; Photography, Jas Shelton; Designer, Annie Spitz; Costumes, Roemehl Hawkins; Music, Michael Andrews; Editor, Jay Deuby; Co-Producer, Chrisann Verges; a Scott Free production; Dolby; DTS; Deluxe; Rated R; 92 minutes; Release date: June 18, 2010

CAST
John	John C. Reilly
Cyrus	Jonah Hill
Molly	Marisa Tomei
Jamie	Catherine Keener
Tim	Matt Walsh
Thermostat Girl	Diane Mizota
Ashley	Kathy Ann Wittes
Pretty Girl	Kathryn Aselton
Pastor	Jamie Donnelly
Roger	Tim Guinee
Stranger at Reception	Charlie Brewer
Rusty	Steve Zissis

Seven years after the collapse of his marriage, John believes he has finally found happiness when he begins dating Molly, only to find their relationship hindered by her 21-year-old oddball son Cyrus.

John C. Reilly

Jonah Hill, Marisa Tomei, John C. Reilly

Marisa Tomei, Jonah Hill, John C. Reilly, Catherine Keener

John C. Reilly, Jonah Hill © Fox Searchlight

JONAH HEX

(WARNER BROS.) Producers, Akiva Goldsman, Andrew Lazar; Executive Producers, Ravi Mehta, Thomas Tull, Jon Jashni, William Fay, Matt LeBlanc, John Goldstone; Co-Producers, Richard Middleton, Miri Yoon, Margot Lulick; Director, Jimmy Hayward; Screenplay, Neveldine & Taylor; Story, William Farmer, Neveldine & Taylor; Based on comic books written by John Albano, illustrated by Tony DeZuniga, published by DC Comics; Photography, Mitchell Amundsen; Designer, Tom Meyer; Costumes, Michael Wilkinson; Music, Marco Beltrami, Mastodon; Editors, Fernando Villena, Tom Lewis; Visual Effects Supervisor, Ariel Velasco Shaw; Visual Effects, Hydraulx, Soho VFX, Pixel Magic; Casting, Bernard Telsey; a Mad Chance/Weed Road production, presented in association with Legendary Pictures; Dolby; Panavision; Technicolor; Rated PG-13; 81 minutes; Release date: June 18, 2010

CAST
Jonah Hex	**Josh Brolin**
Quentin Turnbull	**John Malkovich**
Lilah	**Megan Fox**
Burke	**Michael Fassbender**
Lt. Grass	**Will Arnett**
Lt. Evan	**John Gallagher Jr.**

Aidan Quinn (President Ulysses Grant), Tom Wopat (Col. Slocum), Michael Shannon (Don Cross Williams), Wes Bentley (Adelman Lusk), Julia Jones (Cassie), Luke James Fleischmann (Travis), Rio Hackford (Grayden Nash), David Jensen (Turnbull's Henchman), Billy Blair (Billy, Turnbull's Gang), Sean Boyd (Preacher, Turnbull's Gang), John McConnell (Stunk Crick Sheriff), Jackson Townsend (Stunk Crick Mayor), T.J. Toups, Ned Coleman, Jack Wirt (Stunk Crick Deputies), Ty Holland (Dumbass Outlaw), J.D. Evermore (Union Officer on Train), Scott Staggers (Union Letter Writer), Jimmy Hayward (Train Wood Tender), Michael Arnona (Train Engineer), Noel Murano (Surviving Soldier), Preston Acuff (Union Officer at Fed Reserve), Jonathan Watts Bell, Vincent Riverside (Roughnecks at Tent), Stephen S. Chen (Old Chinese Guy), Joe Billingiere, L.W. Gray Hawk Perkins (Medicine Men), Bill Martin Williams (Union Commanding Officer), Milos Milicevic (Burly Turnbull Guard), Eric Woods (Turnbull's Lookout), Maureen Brennan (Mother on Train), John Kennon Kepper (Boy on Train), Seth Gabel (Advisor), Bruce Sunpie Barnes (Singer), Andy Ryan (Barber), Darin Heames (Bartender), Mitchell Amundsen (Customer), Matt Lasky (Dead Turnbull Guard), Rance Howard (Telegrapher), Antal Kalik (Huge Bar Patron), Michael Papajohn (Saber Guard), Tait Fletcher (Nasty Gunner), Paul Zies (Henchman #1), Brian Eldering (Lookout), Lance Reddick (Smith), Jake Radaker (Boy), Jeffrey Dean Morgan (Jeb Turnbull)

In the years following the Civil War, Jonah Hex, an embittered bounty hunter swearing vengeance on Quentin Turnbull for killing his family, is enlisted by the government to help stop Turnbull from destroying the Union with a deadly secret weapon.

John Malkovich, Wes Bentley © Warner Bros

Kate Hudson, Casey Affleck © IFC Films

THE KILLER INSIDE ME

(IFC FILMS) Producers, Chris Hanley, Bradford L. Schlei, Andrew Eaton; Executive Producers, Jordan Gertner, Lilly Bright, Chad Burris, Alan Liebert, Randy Mendelsohn, Fernando Sulichin; Co-Producers, Susan Kirr, Bob Film & Film I Vast with Anna Croneman, Tomas Eskilsson; Director, Michael Winterbottom; Screenplay, John Curran; Based on the novel by Jim Thompson; Photography, Marcel Zyskind; Designers, Rob Simons, Mark Tildesley; Costumes, Lynette Meyer; Music, Melissa Parmenter, Joel Cadbury; Editor, Mags Arnold; Casting, Mary Vernieu, J.C. Cantu; a Hero Entertainment presentation of a Muse, Stone Canyon, Revolution production in association with Curiously Bright Entertainment and Indion Entertainment Group; Dolby; Panavision; Technicolor; Rated R; 108 minutes; Release date: June 18, 2010

CAST
Lou Ford	**Casey Affleck**
Amy Stanton	**Kate Hudson**
Joyce Lakeland	**Jessica Alba**
Chester Conway	**Ned Beatty**
Joe Rothman	**Elias Koteas**
Sheriff Bob Maples	**Tom Bower**
Howard Hendricks	**Simon Baker**
Billy Boy Walker	**Bill Pullman**
Johnnie Pappas	**Liam Aiken**
Bum	**Brent Briscoe**
Deputy Jeff Plummer	**Matthew Maher**

Jay R. Ferguson (Elmer Conway), Blake Brigham (6-year-old Lou), Noah Crawford (Young Mike), Michael Gibbons (Turnkey), Zach Josse (13-year-old Lou), Blake Lindsley (Max's Diner Waitress), Rosa Pasquarella (Nurse), Caitlin Turner (Helen), Arletta Knight Fink (Courthouse Secretary), Jed Fox, Russell Stewart (Dispatchers), Donna E. Jones (Courthouse Diner Waitress)

Ordered to evict a prostitute from her residence because of her involvement with the son of one of the town's preeminent businessman, psychopathic Deputy Sheriff Lou Ford instead becomes the woman's lover.

Cameron Diaz, Tom Cruise

Cameron Diaz, Tom Cruise

Cameron Diaz, Tom Cruise

KNIGHT AND DAY

(20TH CENTURY FOX) Producers, Cathy Konrad, Steve Pink, Todd Garner; Executive Producers, Joe Roth, Arnon Milchan, E. Bennett Walsh; Director, James Mangold; Screenplay, Patrick O'Neill; Photography, Phedon Papamichael; Designer, Andrew Menzies; Costumes, Arianne Phillips; Music, John Powell; Editor, Michael McCusker; a Regency Enterprises presentation of a Pink Machine/ Todd Garner/Tree Line Film production; Dolby; Super 35 Widescreen; Deluxe color; Rated PG-13; 111 minutes; Release date: June 23, 2010

CAST

Roy Miller	**Tom Cruise**
June Havens	**Cameron Diaz**
Fitzgerald	**Peter Sarsgaard**
Antonio	**Jordi Mollà**
Director George	**Viola Davis**
Simon Fleck	**Paul Dano**
Bernhard	**Falk Hentschel**
Rodney	**Marc Blucas**
Braces	**Lennie Loftin**
April Havens	**Maggie Grace**
Danny	**Rich Craig**
Frank Jenkins	**Dale Dye**
Molly	**Celia Weston**

Gal Gadot (Naomi), Jack A. O'Connell (Wilmer), Trevor Loomis (Eduardo), Nilaja Sun (Allison), Tommy Nohilly (Randy Mechanic), Taylor Treadwell (Gate Agent), Christian Finnegan (Ticket Agent), Nicholas Reese Art (Kid at Airport), Brian Dykstra (TSA Officer), Brian Tarantina (Scrap Yard Man), Natasha Paczkowski (Petra the Tailor), Jerrell Lee (Fireman Paul), Matthew Lawler (Passerby Agent), Ronn Surels (Flight Attendant), Eric Robert Bradshaw Bennett (18 Wheeler Driver), Scott Wahle, Sara Underwood (Newscasters), Helen L. Welsh (Neighbor), King Orba (Smuggler), Adam Gregor (Train Cook), Mitch E. Bowan (Medivac EMT), Gerald T. Carbajal (Doctor in Hallway)

June Havens finds herself involved in a global pursuit when secret agent Roy Miller enlists her aid in trying to stay one jump ahead of FBI agents who are intent of getting hold of a special device Roy is trying to keep out of their hands.

Cameron Diaz, Tom Cruise © 20th Century Fox

David Spade, Adam Sandler, Chris Rock, Rob Schneider, Kevin James

Maya Rudolph, Chris Rock © Columbia Pictures

Rob Schneider, Joyce Van Patten

GROWN UPS

(COLUMBIA) Producers, Adam Sandler, Jack Giarraputo; Executive Producers, Barry Bernardi, Tim Herlihy, Allen Covert, Steve Koren; Director, Dennis Dugan; Screenplay, Adam Sandler, Fred Wolf; Photography, Theo Van de Sande; Designer, Perry Andelin Blake; Costumes, Ellen Lutter; Music, Rupert Gregson-Williams; Music Supervisors, Michael Dilbeck, Brooks Arthur, Kevin Grady; Editor, Tom Costain; Casting, Roger Mussenden, Jeremy Rich; a Happy Madison production, presented in association with Relativity Media; Dolby; Technicolor; Rated PG-13; 102 minutes; Release date: June 25, 2010

CAST

Lenny Feder	**Adam Sandler**
Eric Lamonsoff	**Kevin James**
Kurt McKenzie	**Chris Rock**
Marcus Higgins	**David Spade**
Rob Hilliard	**Rob Schneider**
Roxanne Chase-Feder	**Salma Hayek Pinault**
Sally Lamonsoff	**Maria Bello**
Deanne McKenzie	**Maya Rudolph**
Gloria	**Joyce Van Patten**

Ebony Jo-Ann (Mama Ronzoni), Di Quon (Rita), Steve Buscemi (Wiley), Colin Quinn (Dickie Bailey), Tim Meadows (Malcolm), Madison Riley (Jasmine Hilliard), Jamie Chung (Amber Hilliard), Ashley Loren (Bridget Hilliard), Jake Goldberg (Greg Feder), Cameron Boyce (Keithie Feder), Alexys Nycole Sanchez (Becky Feder), Ada-Nicole Sanger (Donna Lamonsoff), Frank Gingerich (Bean Lamonosoff), Nadji Jeter (Andre McKenzie), China Anne McClain (Charlotte McKenzie), Dan Patrick (Norby the Ride Guy), Tim Herlihy (Pastor), Blake Clark (Bobby "Buzzer" Ferdinando), Norm MacDonald (Geezer), Jonathan Loughran (Robideaux), Kevin Grady (Muzby), Richie Minervini (Tardio), Jackie Sandler (Tardio's Wife), Sadie Sandler, Sunny Sandler (Tardio's Daughters), Dennis Dugan (Referee), Lisa M. Francis (Bailey's Wife), Berkeley Holman (Bailey's Son), Michael Cavaleri (Young Lenny Feder), Andrew Bayard (Young Eric Lamonsoff), Jameel McGill (Young Kurt McKenzie), Kyle Brooks (Young Marcus Higgins), Joshua Matz (Young Rob Hilliard), J.D. Donaurma (Higgins' Father), Billy Concha (Scoreboard Guy), Alec Musser (Water Park Stud), Henriette Mantel (Waitress), Hunter Silva (Young Bailey), Christopher Borger (Young Malcolm), Connor Panzer (Young Robideaux), Jeremy Weaver (Young Muzby), Daniel Cohen (Young Tardio), Jonathan Crowley (Milk Kid)

Following the death of their high school basketball coach, five friends gather for a vacation during which they begin to question the choices they have made in life.

Salma Hayek Pinault, Adam Sandler

RESTREPO

(NATIONAL GEOGRAPHIC) Producers/Directors/Photography, Sebastian Junger, Tim Hetherington; Executive Producers, John Battsek, Nick Quested; Music Supervisor, Ruy Garcia; Editor, Michael Levine; an Outpost Films production; Dolby; Color; Rated R; 94 minutes; Release date: June 25, 2010.

WITH

Dan Kearney, Lamont Caldwell, Kevin Rice, Misha Pemble-Belkin, Kyle Steiner

Documentary following the Second Platoon, Battle Company, 173rd Airborne Brigade as they engage in combat with the Taliban in Afghanistan's Korengal Valley.

This film received an Oscar nomination for documentary feature.

Kyle Steiner

Misha Pemble-Belkin, Ross Murphy

Joe Pesci, Helen Mirren © E1 Entertainment

LOVE RANCH

(E1 ENTERTAINMENT) Producers, Taylor Hackford, Lou DiBella, Marty Katz; Executive Producers, Mark Jacobson, Marcus Schöffer; Co-Producers, Jeff Waxman, Lisa Ann Dennis; Director, Taylor Hackford; Screenplay, Mark Jacobson; Photography, Kieran McGuigan; Designer, Bruno Rubeo; Costumes, Melissa Bruning; Music, Chris Bacon; Editor, Paul Hirsch; Casting, Nancy Klopper; an Aramid Entertainment Fun presentation of a VIP Medienfonds 3 co-production in association with Rising Star of an Anvil Films/DiBella Entertainment production; American-German; Dolby; Color; HD-to-35mm; Rated R; 118 minutes; Release date: June 30, 2010

CAST

Grace Bontempo	**Helen Mirren**
Charlie Bontempo	**Joe Pesci**
Armando Bruza	**Sergio Peris-Mencheta**
Irene	**Gina Gershon**
Mallory	**Taryn Manning**
Christina	**Scout Taylor-Compton**
Samantha	**Bai Ling**

Elise Neal (Alan), Bryan Cranston (James Pettis), Rick Gomez (Tom Macy), M.C. Gainey (Warren Stamp), Gil Birmingham (Johnny Cortez), Emily Rios (Muneca), Melora Walters (Janelle), Raoul Trujillo (Hernan Prado), Bo Brown (Leroy Colter), Wendell Pierce (Naasih Mohammed), Harve Presnell (Dr. Smathers), Leslie Jordan (Martin Hainsworth), Niki J. Crawford (Tawny), Esodie Geiger (Reba), Dylan Kenin (McMurphy), Suzanne Michaels (Stella Sands), Roseanne Vau (Mary French), Kevin Wiggins (Husband), Beth Bailey (Wife), Mia Stallard (Chrissy), Stephen Eiland (Fat Customer), Mark Sivertsen (Horny Fan), Chad Brummett (Drunken Fan), Steven Quezada, Dale O'Malley (Drunks), Ryil Adamson (Bellner), Maulik Pancholy (Dr. Singh), Vic Brwoder (Orderly), Rocky Burke (Fight Referee), Daniel Caplin (Ring Doctor), Guadalupe Contreras (Ring Announcer), William E. Marshall (Colter's Manager), Robert Padilla (Bruza's Cut Man), Dominic Orlandi (Sports Reporter), Rio Hackford (Ranch Bartender), Bob Harvey (New Year's Eve John), Philip R. Keay (John #1), Jerry Gardner, John Hardman, Luce Rains, Christopher Hagen, Allan Pacheo (Ranch Johns), Neil Summers (Drunken John)

Finding no satisfaction in her marriage, brothel madam Grace Bontempo has a fling with the Argentinian prizefighter her husband has decided to manage.

ECLIPSE

(SUMMIT) Producers, Wyck Godfrey, Karen Rosenfelt; Executive Producers, Marty Bowen, Greg Mooradian, Mark Morgan, Guy Oseary; Co-Producer, Bill Bannerman; Director, David Slade; Screenplay, Melissa Rosenberg; Based on the novel by Stephenie Meyer; Photography, Javier Aguirresarobe; Designer, Paul Denham Austerberry; Costumes, Tish Monaghan; Music, Howard Shore; Music Supervisor, Alexandra Patsavas; Editors, Art Jones, Nancy Richardson; Special Effects Supervisor, Alex Burdett; Casting, Stuart Aikins, Sean Cossey, Rene Haynes; a Temple Hill production in association with Maverick/Imprint and Sunswept Entertainment; Dolby; Super 35 Widescreen; Color; Rated PG-13; 124 minutes; Release date: June 30, 2010

Ashley Greene, Jackson Rathbone

CAST

Bella Swan	**Kristen Stewart**
Edward Cullen	**Robert Pattinson**
Jacob Black	**Taylor Lautner**
Victoria	**Bryce Dallas Howard**
Charlie Swan	**Billy Burke**
Jane	**Dakota Fanning**
Dr. Carlisle Cullen	**Peter Facinelli**
Esme Cullen	**Elizabeth Reaser**
Jasper	**Jackson Rathbone**
Emmett Cullen	**Kellan Lutz**
Alice Cullen	**Ashley Greene**
Rosalie	**Nikki Reed**
Jessica	**Anna Kendrick**
Mike	**Michael Welch**
Eric	**Justin Chon**
Angela	**Christian Serratos**
Riley	**Xavier Samuel**
Reese	**Sarah Clarke**
Billy Black	**Gil Birmingham**
Bree	**Jodelle Ferland**
Mr. Biers	**Paul Jarrett**
Mrs. Biers	**Iris Quinn**
Embry Call	**Kiowa Gordon**
Quil Ateara	**Tyson Houseman**
Jared	**Bronson Pelletier**
Paul	**Alex Meraz**
Leah Clearwater	**Julia Jones**
Emily	**Tinsel Korey**
Sam Uley	**Chaske Spencer**
Sue Clearwater	**Alex Rice**
Seth Clearwater	**BooBoo Stewart**
The Cold One	**Peter Murphy**
Alec	**Cameron Bright**
Demetri	**Charlie Bewley**

William Belleau, Justin Rain (Quileute Warriors), Monique Ganderton (Beautiful Vampiress), Byron Chief-Moon (Taha Aki), Mariel Belanger (Third Wife), Dawn Chubai (Reporter), Jack Huston (Royce King), Ben Geldreich (John), Daniel Cudmore (Felix), Leah Gibson (Nettie), Kirsten Prout (Lucy), Cainan Wiebe (Newborn Boy), Catalina Sandino Moreno (Maria)

Bella Swan is torn between her love for vampire Edward Cullen and her devotion to werewolf Jacob Black, as a destructive group of rampaging vampires heads for Seattle with the intention of eliminating Bella. Third in the series, following *Twilight* (2008) and *New Moon* (2009).

Nikki Reed, Kellan Lutz

Taylor Lautner, Kristen Stewart

Bryce Dallas Howard © Summit

Danielle Cudmore, Dakota Fanning, Cameron Bright, Charlie Bewley

Robert Pattinson, Kristen Stewart

Tinsel Korey, Chaske Spencer, Tyson Houseman, Bronson Pelletier, Kiowa Gordon, Alex Meraz

Xavier Samuel (center)

THE LAST AIRBENDER

(PARAMOUNT) Producers, M. Night Shyamalan; Sam Mercer, Frank Marshall; Executive Producers, Kathleen Kennedy, Scott Aversano, Michael Dante DiMartino, Bryan Konietzko; Director/Screenplay, M. Night Shyamalan; Based on the series *Avatar: The Last Airbender* created by Michael Dante DiMartino, Bryan Konietzko; Photography, Andrew Lesnie; Designer, Philip Messina; Costumes, Judianna Makovsky; Music, James Newton Howard; Editor, Conrad Buff; Co-Producer, Jose L. Rodriguez; Visual Effects & Animation, Industrial Light & Magic; a Nickelodeon Movies presentation of a Blinding Edge Picture, Kennedy/Marshall Company production; Dolby; Super 35 Widescreen; 3D; Deluxe color; Rated PG; 103 minutes; Release date: July 1, 2010

Aasif Mandvi

CAST

Aang	**Noah Ringer**
Prince Zuko	**Dev Patel**
Katara	**Nicola Peltz**
Sokka	**Jackson Rathbone**
Uncle Iroh	**Shaun Toub**
Commander Zhao	**Aasif Mandvi**
Fire Lord Ozai	**Cliff Curtis**
Princess Yue	**Seychelle Gabriel**
Katara's Grandma	**Katharine Houghton**
Master Pakku	**Francis Guinan**
Monk Gyatso	**Damon Gupton**
Azula	**Summer Bishil**

Jackson Rathbone, Nicola Peltz

Randall Duk Kim (Old Man in Temple), John D'Alonzo (Zhao's Assistant), Keong Sim (Earthbending Father), Isaac Jin Solstein (Earthbending Boy), Edmund Ikeda (Old Man of Kyoshi Town), John Noble (The Dragon Spirit), Morgan Spector, Ritesh Rajan (Fire Nation Soldiers), Manu Narayan, Karim Sioud (Fire Nation Prison Guards), Kevin Yamada (Earth Kingdom Prisoner), Ted Oyama (Kyoshi Villager), Georgie DeNoto (Teahouse Child), Manuel Kanian (Nervous Prison Guard), Chris Brewster (Kicking Firebender), Ryan Shams (Lead Archer), Jeffrey Zubernis, Brian Johnson (Water Tribe Soldiers), J.W. Cortes (Fire Lord Attendant)

As the Fire Nation continues its quest for world domination, a pair of water benders rescues a young boy who turns out to be an Avatar and the last of the air bending nation, thereby making him the key factor in bringing peace to the four kingdoms. Based on the animated series *Avatar, The Last Airbender*.

Dev Patel © Paramount Pictures

Noah Ringer

Agnes, Edith, Gru's Mom, Margo © Universal Studios

DESPICABLE ME

(UNIVERSAL) Producers, Chris Meledandri, Janet Healy, John Cohen; Executive Producers, Nina Rowan, Sergio Pablos; Directors, Chris Renaud, Pierre Coffin; Screenplay, Cinco Paul, Ken Daurio; Story, Sergio Pablos; Lighting and Compositing, Kim White; Music, Pharrell Williams, Heitor Pereira; Music Supervisor, Kathy Nelson; Editors, Pamela Ziegenhagen-Shefland, Gregory Perler; Designer, Yarrow Cheney; Art Director, Eric Guillon; Story Supervisor, Dave Rosenbaum; Supervising Technical Director, Etienne Pecheux; a Chris Meledandri, Illumination Entertainment production; Dolby; Color; HD; 3D; Rated PG; 95 minutes; Release date: July 9, 2010

VOICE CAST

Gru	**Steve Carell**
Vector	**Jason Segel**
Dr. Nefario	**Russell Brand**
Gru's Mom	**Julie Andrews**
Mr. Perkins	**Will Arnett**
Miss Hattie	**Kristen Wiig**
Margo	**Miranda Cosgrove**
Edith	**Dana Gaier**
Agnes	**Elsie Fisher**
Jerry the Minion	**Jemaine Clement**
Carnival Barker/Tourist Dad	**Jack McBrayer**
Fred McDade	**Danny McBride**
Tourist Mom	**Mindy Kaling**

Pierre Coffin (Tim the Minion/Bob the Minion/Mark the Minion/Phil the Minion/Stuart the Minion), Chris Renaud (Dave the Minion), Rob Huebel (Anchorman), Ken Daurio (Egyptian Guard), Ken Jeong (Talk Show Host), Charles Bright, Katie Leigh, Ranjani Brow, Scott Menville, Holly Dorff, Edie Mirman, Jackie Gonneau, Al Rodrigo, Wendy Hoffman, Jakob Roston, James Kyson-Lee, Hans Tester, Tony Lee, Debi Mae West (Additional Voices)

When a rival villain makes off with the Great Pyramid of Giza, would-be villain Gru decides he must pull off something even more heinous and therefore plots to shrink the Moon and steal it

Gru, Dr. Nefario

Minions, Gru

Vector

THE KIDS ARE ALL RIGHT

(FOCUS) Producers, Gary Gilbert, Jeffrey Levy-Hinte, Celine Rattray, Jordan Horowitz, Daniela Palin Lundberg, Philippe Hellmann; Director, Lisa Cholodenko; Screenplay, Lisa Cholodenko, Stuart Blumberg; Photography, Igor Jadue-Lillo; Designer, Julie Berghoff; Costumes, Mary Claire Hannan; Music, Carter Burwell; Music Supervisor, Liza Richardson; Editor, Jeffrey M. Werner; Casting, Laura Rosenthal; a Focus Features and Gilbert Films presentation of an Antidote Films, Mandalay Vision and Gilbert Films production; Dolby; Technicolor; Rated R; 104 minutes; Release date: July 9, 2010

CAST

Nic	**Annette Bening**
Jules	**Julianne Moore**
Paul	**Mark Ruffalo**
Joni	**Mia Wasikowska**
Laser	**Josh Hutcherson**
Tanya	**Yaya DaCosta**
Jai	**Kunal Sharma**
Clay	**Eddie Hassell**
Sasha	**Zosia Mamet**
Luis	**Joaquin Garrido**
Brooke	**Rebecca Lawrence**
Stella	**Lisa Eisner**
Joel	**Eric Eisner**
Waily Girl	**Sasha Spielberg**
Clay's Dad	**James MacDonald**
Bartender	**Margo Victor**

A lesbian couple is surprised to learn that their teenage children have secretly tracked down the sperm donor who is their biological father.

This film received Oscar nominations for picture, actress (Annette Bening), supporting actor (Mark Ruffalo) and original screenplay.

Annette Bening, Julianne Moore, Josh Hutcherson, Mia Wasikowska, Mark Ruffalo

Annette Bening, Julianne Moore

Annette Bening, Josh Hutcherson, Julianne Moore, Mia Wasikowska

Annette Bening, Julianne Moore

Annette Bening, Julianne Moore

Yaya DaCosta, Mark Ruffalo

Mia Wasikowska, Josh Hutcherson © Focus Features

Mark Ruffalo, Josh Hutcherson

Josh Hutcherson, Mia Wasikowska, Mark Ruffalo

Adrien Brody, Laurence Fisburne

Alice Braga, Walter Goggins, Adrien Brody © 20th Century Fox

Topher Grace, Alice Braga

PREDATORS

(20TH CENTURY FOX) Producers, Robert Rodriguez, John Davis, Elizabeth Avellan; Executive Producer, Alex Young; Co-Producer, Bill Scott; Director, Nimród Antal; Screenplay, Alex Litvak, Michael Finch; Based on characters created by Jim Thomas, John Thomas; Photography, Gyula Pados; Designers, Steve Joyner, Caylah Eddleblute; Costumes, Nina Proctor; Music, John Debney; Editor, Dan Zimmerman; Special Makeup and Creature Effects, Greg Nicotero, Howard Berger; Visual Effects Supervisor, Robert Rodriguez; Casting, Mary Vernieu, J.C. Cantu; a Troublemaker Studios/Davis Entertainment Co. production in association with Dune Entertainment; Dolby; Panavision; Color; Rated R; 107 minutes; Release date: July 9, 2010

CAST

Royce	**Adrien Brody**
Edwin	**Topher Grace**
Isabelle	**Alice Braga**
Stans	**Walter Goggins**
Nikolai	**Oleg Taktarov**
Noland	**Laurence Fishburne**
Cuchillo	**Danny Trejo**
Hanzo	**Louis Ozawa Changchien**
Mombasa	**Mahershalalhashbaz Ali**

Carey Jones (Tracker Predator/Falconer Predator), Brian Steele (Berzerker Predator), Derek Mears (Classic Predator)

A motley crew of commandos is individually dispatched to a distant planet where they are forced to use their wiles to survive against a deadly alien force. Previous films in the 20th Century-Fox sci-fi series are *Predator* (1987), *Predator 2* (1990), and *Alien vs. Predator* (2004).

Topher Grace

THE SORCERER'S APPRENTICE

(WALT DISNEY PICTURES) Producer, Jerry Bruckheimer; Executive Producers, Todd Garner, Nicolas Cage, Mike Stenson, Chad Oman, Norman Golightly, Barry Waldman; Director, Jon Turteltaub; Screenplay, Matt Lopez, Doug Miro, Carlo Bernard; Screen Story, Lawrence Konner, Mark Rosenthal, Matt Lopez; Photography, Bojan Bazelli; Designer, Naomi Shohan; Costumes, Michael Kaplan; Music, Trevor Rabin; Editor, William Goldenberg; Special Effects Supervisor, John Nelson; Visual Effects, Asylum, Double Negative, One of Us, Ghost VFX, Rising Sun Pictures, Method; Stunts, George Marshall Ruge; Casting, Ronna Kress; a Jerry Bruckheimer Films presentation of a Saturn Films/Broken Road production; Dolby; Deluxe color; Super 35 Widescreen; Rated PG; 108 minutes; Release date: July 14, 2010

Alfred Molina, Toby Kebbell

CAST

Balthazar Blake	**Nicolas Cage**
Dave Stutler	**Jay Baruchel**
Horvath	**Alfred Molina**
Becky	**Teresa Palmer**
Drake Stone	**Toby Kebbell**
Bennet	**Omar Benson Miller**
Veronica	**Monica Bellucci**
Morgana	**Alice Krige**
Young Dave	**Jake Cherry**
Merlin	**James A. Stephens**
Sun-Lok	**Gregory Woo**

Wai Ching Ho (Chinese Woman), Jason Moore (Subway Mugger), Robert B. Capron (Young Dave's Pal), Peyton Roi List (Young Becky), Sándor Técsy (Russian Man), Marika Daciuk (Russian Woman), Nicole Ehringer (Abigail Williams), Adriane Lenox (Ms. Algar), Ethan Peck (Andre), Manish Patel (NYU Clerk), Oscar A. Colon (Fry Cook), Joe Lisi (Police Captain), William Devlin (Police Officer), Victor Cruz (Auto Impound Clerk), Melissa Gallagher (Woman on the Street), Parisa Fitz-Henley (Bennet's Girlfriend), Brandon Gill (Student in Bathroom), Henry Yuk (Chinese Dragon Carrier), Jordan Johnston (Mean Kid), Izuchukwu Mozie (African Boy), Amit Soni (Indian Boy), Maha Chehlaoui (Hot Girl), Adria Barratta, Rosie Moss (Students), Ian Alda (Physics Student), Ian McShane (Narrator)

Jay Baruchel © Walt Disney Pictures

Arthurian wizard Balthazar enlists the aide of a modern day physics student to help him stop the evil Morgana from regaining her power and destroying the world.

Nicolas Cage, Jay Baruchel

Nicolas Cage, Jake Cherry

Michael Caine, Leonardo DiCaprio

Joseph Gordon-Levitt

Ken Watanabe, Lukas Haas

Leonardo DiCaprio, Ellen Page

Tom Hardy

Ken Watanabe, Marion Cotillard

Leonardo DiCaprio, Marion Cotillard

Leonardo DiCaprio, Ken Watanabe, Joseph Gordon-Levitt, Tom Hardy, Cillian Murphy, Tom Berenger, Ellen Page

Cillian Murphy, Leonardo DiCaprio, Tom Hardy

Leonardo DiCaprio, Ellen Page © Warner Bros.

INCEPTION

(WARNER BROS.) Producers, Emma Thomas, Christopher Nolan; Executive Producers, Chris Brigham, Thomas Tull; Director/Screenplay, Christopher Nolan; Photography, Wally Pfister; Designer, Guy Hendrix Dyas; Costumes, Jeffrey Kurland; Music, Hans Zimmer; Editor, Lee Smith; Visual Effects Superivsor, Paul Franklin; Visual Effects, Double Negative, New Deal Studios; Special Effects Supervisor, Chris Courbould; Stunts, Tom Struthers, Sy Hollands, Brent Woolsey; Casting, John Papsidera; a Syncopy production, in association with Legendary Pictures; Dolby; Panavision; Technicolor; Rated PG-13; 148 minutes; Release date: July 16, 2010

CAST

Dom Cobb	**Leonardo DiCaprio**
Saito	**Ken Watanabe**
Arthur	**Joseph Gordon-Levitt**
Mal	**Marion Cotillard**
Ariadne	**Ellen Page**
Eames	**Tom Hardy**
Robert Fischer Jr.	**Cillian Murphy**
Browning	**Tom Berenger**
Miles	**Michael Caine**
Yusuf	**Dileep Rao**
Maurice Fischer	**Pete Postlethwaite**
Nash	**Lukas Haas**
Tadashi	**Tai-Li Lee**
Phillipa (3 years)	**Claire Geare**
James (20 months)	**Mangus Nolan**
Phillipa (5 years)	**Taylor Geare**
James (3 years)	**Johnathan Geare**
Japanese Security Guard	**Tohoru Masamune**
Saito's Attendant	**Yuji Okumoto**
Elderly Bald Man	**Earl Cameron**
Lawyer	**Ryan Hayward**
Flight Attendant	**Miranda Nolan**
Cab Driver	**Russ Fega**
Thin Man	**Tim Kelleher**
Blonde	**Talulah Riley**

Nicolas Clerc, Coralie Deykere, Silvie Laguna, Virgile Bramly, Jean-Michel Dagory (Bridge Sub Cons), Helena Cullinan, Mark Fleischmann, Shelley Lang (Penrose Sub Cons), Adam Cole, Jack Murray, Kriag Thornber, Angela Nathenson, Natasha Beaumont (Bar Son Cons), Marc Raducci, Carl Gilliard, Jill Maddrell, Alex Lombard, Nicole Pulliam (Lobby Sub Cons), Peter Basham (Fischer's Jet Captain), Michael Gaston (Immigration Officer), Felix Scott, Andrew Pleavin (Businessmen), Lisa Reynolds (Private Nurse), Jason Tendell (Fischer's Driver), Jack Gilroy (Old Cobb), Shannon Welles (Old Mal)

Wealthy Saito hires "extractor" Dom Cobb, who is able to invade other people dreams, to enter the dreams of a rival businessman.

2010 Academy Award winner for Best Cinematography, Best Visual Effects, Best Sound Mixing, and Best Sound Editing.

This film received additional Oscar nominations for picture, original screenplay, art direction, and original score.

SALT

(COLUMBIA) Producers, Lorenzo di Bonaventura, Sunil Perkash; Executive Producer, Ric Kidney, Mark Vahradian, Ryan Kavanagh; Director, Phillip Noyce; Screenplay, Kurt Wimmer; Photography, Robert Elswit; Designer, Scott Chambliss; Costumes, Sarah Edwards; Music, James Newton Howard; Editors, Stuart Baird, John Gilroy; Visual Effects Supervisor, Robert Grasmere; Stunts, Wade Eastwood; Casting, Avy Kaufman; a di Bonaventura Pictures production, presented in association with Relativity Media; Dolby; Panavision; Deluxe color; Rated PG-13; 100 minutes; Release date: July 23, 2010

Angelina Jolie

CAST

Evelyn Salt	**Angelina Jolie**
Ted Winter	**Liev Schreiber**
Peabody	**Chiwetel Ejiofor**
Orlov	**Daniel Olbrychski**
Mike Krause	**August Diehl**
Secretary of Defense	**Andre Brugher**
Russian President Matveyev	**Olek Krupa**

Corey Stoll (Shnaider), Hunt Block (U.S. President Lewis), Gaius Charles (CIA Officer), Daniel Pearce (Young Orlov), Cassidy Hinkle (12-Year-Old Chenkov), Vladislav Koulikov (Chenkov's Father), Olya Zueva (Chenkov's Mother), Kevin O'Donnell (Young CIA Officer), Zach Shaffer (CIA Security Officer), Albert Jones (CIA Technician), Zoe Lister Jones (CIA Security Hub Tech), Paul Juhn (North Korean Torturer), Tika Sumpter (Front Deskwoman), David Bishins (Security Supervisor), Yara Shahidi (Salt's Young Neighbor), Gary Wilmes (Advisor to U.S. President), Jordan Lage (National Security Advisor), Jeremy Davidson (President's Secret Service Agent), Michelle Ray Smith (Lead Bunker Officer), Marion McCorry (CIA Director Medford), Vladimir Tevlovski (KA Executioner), Steve Cirbus (FBI Agent), Roslyn Ruff (Neural Tech), Jeb Brown (Bunker Technician), Lara Apponyi (BBC Newscaster), Vitali Baganov (New Russian President), Peter Weireter (Security Officer), Ryan Shams (Interrogation Tech), Colleen Wrthmann (Secret Service Tactical Officer), Liam Joynt (White House Gate Officer), Victoria Cartagena (Portico Checkpoint Agent), Armand Schultz (Martin Crenshaw), Ivo Velon (Basayev), Kamar De Los Reyes (Secret Service Agent), Victor Slezak (One-Star General), Dionne Audain (Communications Agent), Jalil Jay Lynch (DC Taxi Driver), Mike Colter (CIA Tactical Leader), Beverly Kirk (White House Reporter), Barbara Harrison (DC Reporter), Lynn C. Sanders (Bishop), Theresa Caggiano (Subway Cop), Nick Poltoranin, Vladimir Troitsky, Hristo Hristov (Russian KA Agents), James Nuciforo (Military Aide), Jose L. Rodriguez (North Korean Border MP), Avis Boone (Rink Petroleum Security), Scott Dillin, Alex Jones, Angelo Lopez (Presidential Bunker Techs), Stephen Breach (Police Captain), Mike Conneenn (Washington Reporter), Gregory R. Kelly (News Anchor), Elizabeth Kaldein (NY1 Reporter), Angel David (Burly Agent), Frank Harts (2nd Floor Secret Service Agent)

Angelina Jolie

CIA Agent Evelyn Salt finds herself on the run after a defector accuses her of being a Russian spy whose next mission is to assassinate the Russian president.

This film received an Oscar nomination for sound mixing.

Angelina Jolie © Columbia Pictures

Chiwetel Ejiofor, Liev Schreiber

Paul Reubens, Shirley Henderson © IFC Films

Ciarán Hinds

Michael Lerner

LIFE DURING WARTIME

(IFC FILMS) Producers, Christine Kunewa Walker, Derrick Tseng; Executive Producers, Elizabeth Redleaf, Mike S. Ryan; Director/ Screenplay, Todd Solondz; Photography, Ed Lachman; Designer, Roshelle Berliner; Costumes, Catherine George; Music Supervisor, Doug Bernheim; Editor, Kevin Messman; Casting, Gayle Keller; a Werc Werk Works production; Dolby; Technicolor; HD; Not rated; 98 minutes; Release date: July 23, 2010

CAST

Joy Jordan	**Shirley Henderson**
Bill Maplewood	**Ciarán Hinds**
Trish Maplewood	**Allison Janney**
Harvey Weiner	**Michael Lerner**
Billy Maplewood	**Chris Marquette**
Mark Weiner	**Rich Pecci**
Jacqueline	**Charlotte Rampling**
Andy	**Paul Reubens**
Helen Jordan	**Ally Sheedy**
Timmy Maplewood	**Dylan Riley Snyder**
Mona Jordan	**Renee Taylor**
Allen	**Michael Kenneth Williams**
Wanda	**Gaby Hoffman**

Roslyn Ruff (Waitress), Rebecca Chiles (Hostess), Emma Hinz (Chloe), Carmen Marie Colon Mejia (Sarah), Fernando Samalot (Eddie), Meng Ai (Jesse)

The three Jordan sisters attempt to cope with the various miscommunications and unhappiness in their lives.

Dylan Riley Snyder, Allison Janney

Selena Gomez, Joey King © 20th Century Fox

RAMONA AND BEEZUS

(20TH CENTURY FOX) Producers, Denise Di Novi, Alison Greenspan; Co-Producer, Brad Van Arragon; Director, Elizabeth Allen; Screenplay, Laurie Craig, Nick Pustay; Based on the novels by Beverly Cleary; Photography, John Bailey; Designer, Brent Thomas; Music, Mark Mothersbaugh; Music Supervisor, Julia Michels; Editor, Jane Moran; Casting, Christian Kaplan (U.S.), Coreen Mayrs, Heike Brandstatter (Canada); a Fox 2000 Pictures and Walden Media presentation of a Di Novi Pictures production; Dolby; Panavision; Deluxe color; Rated G; 103 minutes; Release date: July 23, 2010

CAST
Ramona Quimby	**Joey King**
Beatrice "Beezus" Quimby	**Selena Gomez**
Robert Quimby	**John Corbett**
Dorothy Quimby	**Bridget Moynahan**
Aunt Bea	**Ginnifer Goodwin**
Hobart	**Josh Duhamel**
Howie Kemp	**Jason Spevack**
Susan	**Sierra McCormick**
Mrs. Meacham	**Sandra Oh**

Kathryn Zenna (Mrs. Kushner), Janet Wright (Grandma Kemp), Ruby Curtis (Willa Jean), Hutch Dano (Henry Huggins), Patti Allan (Mrs. Pitt), Garnet Harding (D. Garnet Harding), Daniel A. Vasquez (Little Kid), Andrew McNee (Mr. Clay), Tom Pickett (Mr. Cardoza), Lynda Boyd (Mother of Triplets), Dace Norman (Triplet Boy), George C. Wolfe (Casting Director), Nancy Robertson (Casting Associate), Calista Bashuk (TV Commercial Girl), Eileen Barrett (Minister), Donnelly Rhodes (Crusty Photographer), Ian Bruce Thompson (Bus Driver), Brandi Alexander (Casting Wrangler), Aila McCubbing, Zanti McCubbing (Roberta Quimby), Miller (Picky Picky)

Teenage Beatrice endures the rambunctious behavior of her 9-year-old sister Ramona, while their family faces an unexpected financial crisis.

SPOKEN WORD

(VARIANCE) Producers, Karen Koch, William T. Conway; Director, Victor Nunez; Screenplay, William T. Conway, Joe Ray Sandoval; Photography, Virgil Mirano; Designer, Bryce Perrin; Costumes, Lahly Poore; Music, Michael Brook; Music Supervisors, Guilherme Campellon, Emily Kaye; Editors, Victor Nunez, Justin Geoffrey; a New Mexico Media Partners presentation of a Luminaria production; Color; Super 16; Not rated; 116 minutes; Release date: July 23, 2010

CAST
Cruz	**Kuno Becker**
Emilio	**Miguel Sandoval**
Cruz, Sr.	**Rubén Blades**
Shea	**Persia White**
Ramon	**Antonio Elias**
Gabrielle	**Monique Curnen**

Beth Bailey (Reporter), Jernard Burks (Renegade), Monique Candelaria (Cruz Montoya's Mother), Deborah Chavez (Candace), Maurice Compte (George), Courtney Cunningham (Robyn), Stephen Elland (Big Mike), Eddie L. Fauria (Old Head Ted), Joe Manuel Gallegos Jr. (Deputy Sheriff Aragon), Castulo Guerra (Dr. Lopez), Johnnie Hector (Luis), Andre Kinney (Roberto), Jonathan Lund (Gangster), Rashaan Nall (Cloudy), Rick A. Ortega Jr. (Sheriff Carlos Sandoval), Chris Ranney (Bartender)

A successful San Francisco spoken word artist reluctantly returns to his home In New Mexico to see his dying father and finds himself mired in the violent and dysfunctional world he gladly left behind.

Kuno Becker, Persia White

Rubén Blades © Variance

GET LOW

(SONY CLASSICS) Producers, Dean Zanuck, David Gundlach; Co-Producer, Richard Luke Rothschild; Executive Producers, Dariusz Gasiorowski, Harrison Zanuck, Joseph Rappa, Oliver Simon, Daniel Baur, Robert Duvall, David Ginsberg, C. Gaby Mitchell, Alain Midzic; Director/Editor, Aaron Schneider; Screenplay, Chris Provenzano, C. Gaby Mitchell; Story, Chris Provenazno, Scott Seeke; Photography, David Boyd; Designer, Geoffrey Kirkland; Costumes, Julie Weiss; Music, Jan A. P. Kaczmarek; Music Supervisor, Evelyn Klean; Casting, Lisa Mae, Craig Fincannon; a K5 International presentation of a Zanuck Independent production in co-production with David Gundlach Productions, Lara Enterprises TVN in association with Butcher's Run Films; Dolby; Panavision; Deluxe Color; Rated PG-13; 100 minutes; Release date: July 30, 2010

CAST

Felix Bush	**Robert Duvall**
Mattie Darrow	**Sissy Spacek**
Frank Quinn	**Bill Murray**
Buddy Robinson	**Lucas Black**
Rev. Gus Horton	**Gerald McRaney**
Rev. Charlie Jackson	**Bill Cobbs**
Carl	**Scott Cooper**
Kathryn Robinson	**Lori Beth Edgeman**
WKNG Announcer	**Linds Edwards**
Bonnie	**Andrea Powell**
Tom	**Chandler Riggs**
Grier	**Danny Vinson**
Gary	**Blerim Destani**
Orville	**Tomasz Karolak**
Photographer	**Andy Stahl**
Mr. Feldman	**Marc Gowan**
Mary Lee Stroup	**Arin Logan**

A cantankerous old Tennessee hermit decides to throw his own funeral while he is still alive, claiming he wants the community to speak up about the stories they've heard about him.

Lucas Black, Lori Beth Edgeman

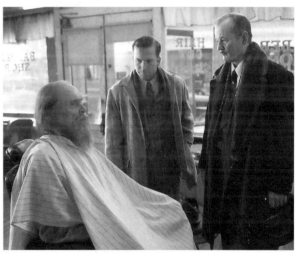

Robert Duvall, Lucas Black, Bill Murray

Robert Duvall, Lucas Black, Bill Cobb

Sissy Spacek © Sony Classics

Amanda Crew

Charlie Tahan, Zac Efron

CHARLIE ST. CLOUD

(UNIVERSAL) Producer, Marc Platt; Executive Producers, Michael Fottrell, Ryan Kavanaugh, Ben Sherwood; Director, Burr Steers; Screenplay, Craig Pearce, Lewis Colick; Based on the novel *The Death and Life of Charlie St. Cloud* by Ben Sherwood; Photography, Enrique Chediak; Designer, Ida Random; Costumes, Denise Wingate; Music, Rolfe Kent; Editor, Padraic McKinley; Casting, Heike Bradnstatter, Allison Jones, Coreen Mayrs; a Marc Platt production, presented in association with Relativity Media; Dolby; Hawk Scope Widescreen; Deluxe Color; Rated PG-13; 99 minutes; Release date: July 30, 2010

CAST

Charlie St. Cloud	**Zac Efron**
Sam St. Cloud	**Charlie Tahan**
Tess Carroll	**Amanda Crew**
Alistair Wooley	**Augustus Prew**
Tink Weatherbee	**Donal Logue**
Claire St. Cloud	**Kim Basinger**
Florio Ferrente	**Ray Liotta**
Sully	**Dave Franco**
Connors	**Matt Ward**
Latham	**Miles Chalmers**
Green	**Jesse Wheeler**
Carla Ferrente	**Desiree Zurowski**
Ben Carroll	**Adrian Hough**
Grace Carroll	**Jill Teed**

Valerie Tian, Grace Sherman, Brenna O'Brien (Girls in Toy Store), Tegan Moss (Cindy), Julia Maxwell (Rachel), Paul Chevray (Hoddy Snow), Paul Duchart (Reverend Polk), Renu Bakshi (Reporter), Darren Dolynski (Ambulance Driver), Sophie Stukas (Mary Rogers), Marci T. House (Photographer), Ted Whittall (Principal), Natasha Denis (Julie), D. Neil Mark (EMT)

Five years after his little brother has been killed in a car accident, a grieving and guilt-stricken Charlie St. Cloud continues his relationship with his sibling, believing he can communicate with him in the afterlife.

Charlie Tahan, Zac Efron

Zac Efron, Augustus Prew © Universal Studios

Katie Holmes, Paul Dano

Kevin Kline © Magnolia

Marian Seldes, Paul Dano

John C. Reilly

THE EXTRA MAN

(MAGNOLIA) Producers, Anthony Bregman, Stephanie Davis; Executive Producers, Agnes Mentre, Vincent Maraval, Stefanie Azpiazu, Jonathan Ames, Shari Springer Berman, Robert Pulcini; Co-Producer, Rebecca Rivo; Directors, Shari Springer Berman, Robert Pulcini; Screenplay, Robert Pulcini, Jonathan Ames, Shari Springer Berman; Based on the novel by Jonathan Ames; Photography, Terry Stacey; Designer, Judy Becker; Costumes, Suttirat Anne Larlarb; Music, Klaus Badelt; Music Supervisor, Linda Cohen; Editor, Robert Pulcini; Casting, Ann Goulder; a Wild Bunch presentation of a Likely Story/3 Arts production; Dolby; Super 35 Widescreen; Deluxe color; Rated R; 108 minutes; Release date: July 30, 2010

CAST

Henry Harrison	**Kevin Kline**
Louis Ives	**Paul Dano**
Gershon Gruen	**John C. Reilly**
Mary Powell	**Katie Holmes**
George	**John Pankow**
Meredith Lagerfeld	**Celia Weston**
Katherine Hart	**Patti D'Arbanville**
Lois Huber	**Lynn Cohen**
Vivian Cudlip	**Marian Seldes**
Aresh	**Dan Hedaya**
Otto Bellman	**Jason Butler Harner**

Alicia Goranson (Sandra), Marisa Ryan (Tanya), Barbara Christie (Margaret Chase Cudlip), Alex Burns (Brad), Jackie Hoffman (Pushy Woman), Justis Bolding (Wine Pourer), Beth Fowler (Ms. Marsh), Rafael Sardina (Chicken Man), Jean Brassard (Waiter), David Boston (Neighbor), Graeme Malcolm (Narrator), Kevin Sculin (Drag Club Patron), Lisa Brescia (Teacher), Victoria Barabas (Daisy), Peter Kybart (Maitre D), Gisele Alicea (Miss Pepper), John Leighton (Valet), Lewis Payton (Usher), Elizabeth Blancke-Biggs (Diva), Betty Hudson (Maid), Jonathan Ames (Gentleman), Alicia Goranson (Sandra), Philip Carlson (Preacher)

Hoping to make a place in New York society, Louis Ives leaves his Princeton prep school job and heads for the city where he links up with Henry Harrison, a penniless but wiley older fellow who makes his living squiring around wealthy Manhattan widows.

DINNER FOR SCHMUCKS

(PARAMOUNT/DREAMWORKS) Producers, Walter F. Parkes, Laurie MacDonald, Jay Roach; Executive Producers, Francis Veber, Sacha Baron Cohen, Amy Sayres, Jon Poll, Roger Birnbaum, Gary Barber; Director, Jay Roach; Screenplay, David Guion, Michael Handelman; Inspired by the film *Le diner de cons* by Francis Veber; Photography, Jim Denault; Designer, Michael Corenblith; Costumes, Mary Vogt; Music, Theodore Shapiro; Editor, Alan Baumgarten, Jon Poll; Casting, Jeanne McCarthy, Nicole Abelloera; a Spyglass Entertainment presentation of a Parkes + MacDonald production, an Everyman Pictures production; Dolby; Super 35 Widescreen; Color; Rated PG-13; 114 minutes; Release date: July 30, 2010

CAST

Barry Speck	**Steve Carell**
Tim Conrad	**Paul Rudd**
Therman	**Zach Galifianakis**
Kieran	**Jemaine Clement**
Julie	**Stephanie Szostak**
Darla	**Lucy Punch**
Lance Fender	**Bruce Greenwood**
Müeller	**David Walliams**
Caldwell	**Ron Livingston**
Susana	**Kristen Schaal**
Davenport	**P.J. Byrne**
Robin	**Andrea Savage**
Josh	**Nick Kroll**
Henderson	**Randall Park**
Birgit	**Lucy Davenport**
Marco, the Blind Swordsman	**Christopher O'Dowd**
Lewis the Ventriloquist	**Jeff Dunham**
Madame Nora, Pet Psychic	**Octavia Spencer**
Vincenzo, Vulture Lover	**Patrick Fischler**
Chuck, Beard Champion	**Rick Overton**
Patrick	**Eric Winzenried**
Christina, Bird Girl	**Nicole LaLiberte**
Monique, Bird Girl	**Maria Zyrianova**
Maitre D'	**Scott Weintraub**

Informed by his boss that he must bring the most idiotic person possible to a business dinner in order to compete with others of the same ilk, Tim believes he has found the perfect specimen in the guiless, socially inept Barry Speck. Based on the 1998 French film *The Dinner Game.*

Christopher O'Dowd, Zach Galifianakis

Lucy Davenport, David Walliams

Ron Livingston, David Walliams, Bruce Greenwood, Larry Wilmore

Lucy Punch, Paul Rudd, Stephanie Szostak

Octavia Spencer, Patrick Fischler, Paul Rudd, Steve Carell, Rick Overton, Jeff Dunham

Steve Carell, Jemaine Clement

Steve Carell

Steve Carell, Paul Rudd

Steve Carell, Paul Rudd © Paramount/DreamWorks

THE OTHER GUYS

(COLUMBIA) Producers, Will Ferrell, Adam McKay, Jimmy Miller, Patrick Crowley; Executive Producers, David Householter, Chris Henchy, Kevin Messick; Director, Adam McKay; Screenplay, Adam McKay, Chris Hency; Photography, Oliver Wood; Designer, Clayton Hartley; Costumes, Carol Ramsey; Music, Jon Brion; Editor, Brent White; Special Effects Supervisors, Mark Hawker, Danny Cangemi; Casting, Allison Jones; a Gary Sanchez/Mosaic production; Dolby; Panavision; Deluxe color; Rated PG-13; 107 minutes; Release date: August 6, 2010

CAST

Allen Gamble	**Will Ferrell**
Terry Hoitz	**Mark Wahlberg**
Dr. Sheila Gamble	**Eva Mendes**
Capt. Gene Mauch	**Michael Keaton**
David Ershon	**Steve Coogan**
Roger Wesley	**Ray Stevenson**
P.K. Highsmith	**Samuel L. Jackson**
Christopher Danson	**Dwayne Johnson**
Martin	**Rob Riggle**
Fosse	**Damon Wayans Jr.**
Jimmy	**Bobby Cannavale**

Derek Jeter, Brooke Shields, Rosie Perez, Tracy Morgan (Themselves), Larnell Stovall, Jalil Jay Lynch, Roy T. Anderson (Rastas), Andrew Secunda, Sara Chase (Press Conference Reporters), David Gideon (Mayor), Josh Church (Hot Dog Guy), Michael Delaney (Bob Littleford), Alison Becker (Financial News Anchor), Warren Kelley (NYSE Official), Zoe Lister-Jones (Therapist), Sean Heilig, Matthew J. McCarthy, Adam Phillips (Therapy Cops), Tess Kartel (Brazilian Woman), Rob Mars, C.C. Taylor (Wesley's Guards), Zach Woods (Douglas), Jake Quinn, Patrick Ferrell (Precinct Detectives), Andy Buckley (Don Beaman), Elizabeth Kaledin (NY1 Reporter), Will Lyman (Frontline Narration App), Rob Huebel (Officer Watts), Peter R. Thewes (Hazmat Officer), Robin Ng (Waiter), Natalie Zea (Christinith), Brett Gelman (Hal), Malachy McCourt (Old Man in Irish Bar), Barry Carl, Benjamin Magnuson, Thomas McDonnell III, Jimmy O'Donnell, Kevin Osborne, Pierce Turner, James Archie Worley (Irish Singers), Lindsay Sloane (Francine), Shakiem Evans (Dancer), Danielle Cell (Brenda), Brianne Moncrief (Ershon's Assistant), Adam McKay (Dirty Mike), Oliver Wood (Captain Salty), James Mazzola, Patrick Crowley (Homeless Dudes), Ben Schwartz (Beaman's Assistant), Tara Copeland (Police Dispatcher), Eamon Speer (Ice Cream Man), Patrick Reale (Beaman Tow Cop), Zak Orth (Accountant), Pete Antico (Chechen Rebel), Viola Harris (Mama Ramos), Jamie Dugal (Schoolgirl), Chris Gethard (Clerk), Michael Fawcett (Minister), Pilar Angelique (Stunning Woman), Anne Heche (Pamela Boardman), Tracy Morgan (Himself), Josef Sommer (D.A. Radford), Ice-T (Narrator)

Terry Hoitz and Allen Gamble grab their chance to get away from their lowly positions on the police force when the precinct's two star cops are put out of commission.

Eva Mendes, Will Ferrell

Michael Keaton © Columbia Pictures

Samuel L. Jackson, Dwayne Johnson

Will Ferrell, Steve Coogan, Mark Wahlberg

Terry Crews, Luke Wilson

Luke Wilson, James Caan © Paramount Vantage

MIDDLE MEN

(PARAMOUNT VANTAGE) Producers, Christopher Mallick, William Sherak, Jason Shuman, Michael J. Weiss; Director, George Gallo; Screenplay, George Gallo, Andy Weiss; Photography, Lukas Ettlin; Designer, Bob Ziembicki; Costumes, Sharen Davis; Music, Brian Tyler; Music Supervisor, Tricia Holloway; Editor, Malcolm Campbell; a Mallick Media presentation of a Oxymoron Entertainment production in association with Blue Star Entertainment; Dolby; Panavision; Deluxe color; Rated R; 99 minutes; Release date: August 6, 2010

CAST

Jack Harris	**Luke Wilson**
Wayne Beering	**Giovanni Ribisi**
Buck Dolby	**Gabriel Macht**
Jerry Haggerty	**James Caan**
Diana Harris	**Jacinda Barrett**
Curt Allmans	**Kevin Pollak**
Audrey Dawns	**Laura Ramsey**
James	**Terry Crews**
Nikita Sokoloff	**Rade Sherbedgia**
Frank Griffin	**Kelsey Grammer**

Graham McTavish (Ivan), Jason Antoon (Denny Z), Robert Forster (Louie La La), John Ashton (Morgan), Martin Kove (U.S. Senator), Diane Sorrentino (Raven Swallows), Stacey Alysson (Alexandra Raines), Richard Wilk (Hard Rock Hotel Host), Robert Della Cerra (Bil Romero), Leon "Bubba" Ganter (Reggie), Dexter Jasper (Peanut), Melissa Bustamante (Laura), Claudia Jordan (Cynthia), Jack Barnes (Adam, 5 months), Christian Michael Clark (Michael, age 9), Hunter Gomez (Young Jack,a ge 15), Shannon Whirry (Screaming Mother), Price Mitchum (Goth Kid), Suzanne Kent (Woman in Vet's Office), John Edmund Parcher (Supervisor), Ky-Moni Abraham (Bartender), Tami Donaldson (Receptionist), Aighleann McKiernan (Waitress), Ginger Williams (Secretary), Nick Sowell (Josh Posner), Ron Cadwell (Towncar Driver), Sanel Bdulimic (Russian Thug #1), Argam Pogosjan (Cousin Yuri), Brady Stanley (Teenage Michael), Shane Shields (Dean Loomis), Tom Nogan (Farmer), Jesse Jane (Herself), Jim Devoti, Krista Braun (News Reporters), Raj Suri (Pakistani Terrorist), Frank Pesce (Bar Patron), Tisa McCay (AVN Bartender), Malorie Charak (AVN Guest), Gregory Nicholas Vrotsos (Arresting Officer), Julie Lott (Jessie "River Dancer"), Lauren Gallagher (Scared Hooker), Brittany Blasier (Cocktail Waitress)

The true story of how Texas businessman Jack Harris paid an instrumental part in bringing pornography to the Internet.

Luke Wilson, Laura Ramsey

Gabriel Macht, Rade Sherbedgia, Giovanni Ribisi

Aidan Quinn, Penelope Ann Miller © Warner Bros.

Israel Broussard, Callan McAuliffe

Madeline Carroll, Callan McAuliffe

FLIPPED

(WARNER BROS.) Producers, Rob Reiner, Alan Greisman; Executive Producers, Martin Shafer, Liz Glotzer, David Siegel; Co-Producer, Frank Capra III; Director, Rob Reiner; Screenplay, Rob Reiner, Andrew Scheinman; Based on the novel by Wendelin Van Draanen; Photography, Thomas del Ruth; Designer, Bill Brzeski; Costumes, Durinda Wood; Music, Marc Shaiman; Editor, Robert Leighton; Casting, Janet Hirshenson, Jane Jenkins; a Castle Rock Entertainment presentation of a Rob Reiner/Alan Greisman production; Dolby; Color; Rated PG; 90 minutes; Release date: August 6, 2010

CAST

Juli Baker	**Madeline Carroll**
Bryce Loski	**Callan McAuliffe**
Patsy Loski	**Rebecca De Mornay**
Steven Loski	**Anthony Edwards**
Chet Duncan	**John Mahoney**
Richard Baker	**Aidan Quinn**
Trina Baker	**Penelope Ann Miller**
Daniel Baker	**Kevin Weisman**
Young Juli	**Morgan Lily**
Young Bryce	**Ryan Ketzner**

Gillian Pfaff (Young Lynetta), Michael Boza, Beau Lerner (Teasing Boys), Jacquelyn Evola, Taylor Goothuis, Elly Bryant (Playground Girls), Ashley Taylor (Sherry Stalls), Israel Broussard (Garrett), Cody Horn (Lynetta), Frankie Potochick (Neighborhood Kid), Quintin Hicks, Wallace Bridges (Tree Workers), Inga Wilson (Mrs. Kimble), Jake Reiner (Skyler), Michael Christopher Bolten (Mark Baker), Shane Harper (Matt Baker), Lidna Auwers (Mrs. Meisner), Ruth Crawford (Mrs. Steuby), Stefanie Scott (Dana Tessler), Joseph Varsanik Tyler Moylan, Tristan DeRoches (Boys in Hallway), Pat Lentz (Mrs. McClure), Spencer Rohatynski, Chase Gall (Basket Boys), Matthew Gold (Eddie Trulock), Alora Catherine Smith (Melanie), Kelley Donnelly (Liz), Sophina Saggau (Macy), Michele Messmer (Pello's Mom)

In early 1960's Michigan, teenagers Bryce Loski and Juli Baker experience their first romance.

John Mahoney, Callan McAuliffe

TWELVE

(HANNOVER HOUSE) Producers, Sidonie Dumas, Ted Field, Charlie Corwin, Jordan Melamed, Bob Salerno: Executive Producer, J. Andrew Greenblatt; Co-Producer, Michael Bederman; Director, Joel Schumacher; Screenplay, Jordan Melamed; Based on the novel by Nick McDonell; Photography, Seven Fierberg; Designer, Ethan Tobman; Music, Harry Gregson-Williams; Editor, Paul Zucker; Casting, Lauren Bass, Jessica Kelly, Suzanne Smith; a Gaumont presentation of a Radar Pictures/Original Media production in association with Artina Films; Dolby; Color; Rated R; 94 minutes; Release date: August 6, 2010

CAST
White Mike	**Chace Crawford**
Chris	**Rory Culkin**
Hunter	**Philip Ettinger**
Sara Ludlow	**Esti Ginzburg**
Lionel	**Curtis Jackson**
Gabby	**Zoë Kravitz**
Claude	**Billy Magnussen**

Emily Meade (Jessica Brayson), Emma Roberts (Molly), Ellen Barkin (Jessica's Mother), Kiefer Sutherland (Narrator), Ako (Mrs. Fong), Dionne Audain (Nana's Mother), Gregg Bello (Det. Keminski), Maxx Brawer (Andrew), Jermaine Crawford (NaNa), Chanel Farrell (Shelly), Alexander Flores (Arturo), Alice Barrett Mitchell (White Mike's Mom), Alexandra Neil (Mimi Kenton), Ethan Peck (Sean), Charles Austin Saxton (Mark Rothko), Erik Per Sullivan (Timmy), Nico Tortorella (Tobias), Jeremy Allen White (Charlie), Isiah Whitlock (Det. Dumont).

Feeling lost after the death of his mother, White Mike decides to make a living selling drugs to the rich and spoiled teenagers of Manhattan.

Rory Culkin, Esti Ginzburg © Hannover House

Chace Crawford

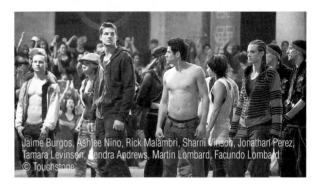
Jaime Burgos, Ashlee Nino, Rick Malambri, Sharni Vinson, Jonathan Perez, Tamara Levinson, Kendra Andrews, Martin Lombard, Facundo Lombard © Touchstone

STEP UP 3D

(TOUCHSTONE/SUMMIT) Producers, Patrick Wachsberger, Erik Feig, Adam Shankman, Jennifer Gibgot; Executive Producers, Bob Hayward, David Nicksay, Meredith Milton; Director, Jon M. Chu; Screenplay, Amy Andelson, Emily Meyer; Based on characters created by Duane Adler; Photography, Ken Seng; Designer, Devorah Herbert; Costumes, Kurt & Bart; Music, Bear McCreary; Music Supervisor, Buck Damon; Editor, Andrew Marcus; Choreographers, Jamal Sims, Nadine "Hi Hat" Ruffin, Dave Scott, Richmond Talauega, Anthony Talauega; Casting, Joanna Colbert, Richard Mento; a Walt Disney Studios Motion Pictures release of a Touchstone Pictures and Summit Entertainment presentation of a Summit Entertainment production in association with Offspring Entertainment; Dolby; Color; 3D; Rated PG-13; 106 minutes; Release date: August 6, 2010

CAST
Luke	**Rick Malambri**
Moose	**Adam G. Sevani**
Natalie	**Sharni Vinson**
Camille	**Alyson Stoner**

Keith Stallworth (Jacob), Kendra Andrews (Anala), Stephen "tWitch" Boss (Jason), Martin Lombard, Facundo Lombard (The Santiago Twins), Oren "Flearock" Michaeli (Carlos), Joe Slaughter (Julien), Daniel "Cloud" Campos (Kid Darkness), Aja George, Straphanio "Shonnie" Solomon, Terence Dickson (The Ticks), Chadd "Madd Chadd" Smith (Vladd), Britney "B" Thomas (B.), Terrance Harrison (Radius), Jonathan "Legacy" Perez (Legz), Jaime "Venum" Burgos (Mohawk), Ivan "Flipz" Velez (Spinz), Ashlee Nino (Stix), Tamara Levinson (Bend), Ricardo "Boogie Frantick" Rodriguez Jr. (Wave), Mari Koda (Jenny Kido), Harry Shum Jr. (Cable), Christopher Scott (Hair), Luis Rosado (Monster), LaJon "Lil Duda" Dantzler (Smiles), Janelle Cambridge (Fly), Jalen R. "JStyles" Testerman (Arcade Rats), Joshua Allen, Jeffrey "Machine" McCann, Beau "Casper" Smart, Philip "Spee-D" Albuquerque, Ricard Steelo Vasquez, Moises "Moy" Rivas, Ivan Koumaev, Sharya Howell, Caryl A. Land, Nick Wilson, Nick DeMoura (House of Samuari), Bailey Hanks (NYU Tour Guide), Robin Lord Taylor (Punk Kid), Alex Zelenty (Emo Skater), Jimmy Smagula (Balloon Vendor), Christopher Place (Police Officer), Mark Blum (NYU Professor), Alex Charak (Nerd Student), Carolina Ravassa (Kristin), Ally Maki (Jenny), Jamal Sims (Red Hook Announcer), Kevin Chew (Gwai Announcer), Ken Marks (Walter), Mark Tallman (Door Person), Jennifer Van Dyck (Natalie's Mom), Kylie Liya Goldstein (Ice Cream Girl), David Brown (Ice Cream Man), Rhapsody James (Woman watering Plants), Dylan Hartigan (Scooter Boy), Sal Mistretta (Diner Customer), Sonnie Brown (Mrs. Kido), Akira Takayama (Mr. Kido), Grandmaster Caz (World Jam Announcer), Nadine "Hi Hat" Ruffin, Raymond Del Barrio, Marley Marl (World Jam Judges), Dan Ziskie (NYU Dean)

A group of New York street dancers compete against some of the top hip hop dancers in a high-stakes showdown. Previous entries in the Disney series: *Step Up* (2006) and *Step Up 2 the Streets* (2008).

James Franco

Julia Roberts

Javier Bardem, Julia Roberts

Julia Roberts

Julia Roberts, Hadi Subiyanto © Columbia Pictures

Julia Roberts, Billy Crudup

Lucia Guzzardi, Julia Roberts

Richard Jenkins, Julia Roberts

EAT PRAY LOVE

(COLUMBIA) Producers, Dede Gardner; Executive Producers, Brad Pitt, Stan Wlodkowski, Jeremy Kleiner; Director, Ryan Murphy; Screenplay, Ryan Murphy, Jennifer Salt; Based on the book by Elizabeth Gilbert; Photography, Robert Richardson; Designer, Bill Groom; Costumes, Michael Dennison; Music, Dario Marianelli; Music Supervisor, PJ Bloom; Editor, Bradley Buecker; Casting, Francine Maisler; a Plan B Entertainment production; Dolby; Deluxe color; Rated PG-13; 140 minutes; Release date: August 13, 2010

CAST

Liz Gilbert	**Julia Roberts**
David Piccolo	**James Franco**
Richard from Texas	**Richard Jenkins**
Delia Shiraz	**Viola Davis**
Stephen	**Billy Crudup**
Felipe	**Javier Bardem**
Ketut Liyer	**Hadi Subiyanto**
Andy Shiraz	**Mike O'Malley**
Sofi	**Tuva Novotny**
Giovanni	**Luca Argentero**
Luca Spaghetti	**Giuseppe Gandini**
Giulio	**Andrea Di Stefano**
Swami Shivananda	**Michael Cumpsty**
Corella	**Sophie Thompson**
Tulsi	**Rushita Singh**
Wayan Nuriasih	**Christine Hakim**
Armenia	**Arlene Tur**
Ian	**David Lyons**
Leon	**TJ Power**
Nyomo	**I. Gusti Ayu Puspawati**
Andre	**A. Jay Radcliff**
Bookstore Girl	**Ashlie Atkinson**
Woman in Play	**Lisa Roberts Gillan**
Play Walk-Out	**Ryan O'Nan**
The Guru	**Gita Reddy**
NYU Student Boyfriend	**Dwayne Clark**
NYU Student Girlfriend	**Jennifer Kwok**
Laundromat Gal	**Mary Testa**
Andrea Sherwood	**Welker White**

Elijah Tucker, Karen Trindle, Zach Dunham, Clair Oaks, Ned Leavitt, Lynn Margileth (Chant Leaders), Jose Ramon Rosario (Storage Building Guy), Lucia Guzzardi (Landlady), Roberto Di Palma (Large Man at Trattoria), Silvano Rossi (Paolo the Barber), Ludovica Virga, Marco Lastrucci (Arguing Fruit Customer), Elena Arvigo (Maria), Andrea Di Stefano Giulio), Remo Remotti (Older Soccer Fan), Vanessa Marini (Clothing Store Salesgirl), Lydia Biondi (Ruffina), Emma Brunetti (Paola), Chiara Brunetti (Claudia), Ajay Bhandari (Liz's Bag Holder), Ritvik Tyagi (Madhu), Sd Pandey (Man in Temple), Anand Yeshwant Bapat (Indian Shop Salesman), Micky Dhameejani (Rijul), Peter Davis (Disc Jockey), Shona Benson (Sharon in Seva Office), Dean Allan Tolhurst (Balinese Realtor), Richard V. Vogt (Man in Restaurant)

Following a painful divorce, New York writer Liz Gilbert decides to spend a year abroad hoping to find both culinary and spiritual pleasures, while also searching for romance.

Viola Davis, Julia Roberts

Eric Roberts, Steve Austin

Jet Li, Dolph Lundgren, Sylvester Stallone

Jason Statham

THE EXPENDABLES

(LIONSGATE) Producers, Avi Lerner, John Thompson, Kevin King Templeton; Executive Producers, Danny Dimbort, Boaz Davidson, Trevor Short, Les Weldon, Jon Feltheimer, Jason Constantine, Ed Kowan, Basil Iwanyk, Guymon Casady; Co-Producers, Robert Earl, Matt O'Toole; Director, Sylvester Stallone; Screenplay, David Callaham, Sylvester Stallone; Story, David Callaham; Photography, Jeffrey Kimball; Designer, Franco-Giacomo Carbone; Music, Brian Tyler; Editors, Ken Blackwell, Paul harb; Visual Effects Supervisor, Wes C. Caefer; Visual Effects, Worldwide FX; Stunts, Chad Stahelski; Casting, Deborah Aquila, Tricia Wood; a Nulmage production, presented with Millennium Films; Dolby; Super 35 Widescreen; Color; Rated R; 103 minutes; Release date: August 13, 2010

CAST

Barney Ross	**Sylvester Stallone**
Lee Christmas	**Jason Statham**
Yin Yang	**Jet Li**
Gunner Jensen	**Dolph Lundgren**
James Munroe	**Eric Roberts**
Toll Road	**Randy Couture**
Paine	**Steve Austin**
General Garza	**David Zayas**
Sandra	**Giselle Itié**
Lacy	**Charisma Carpenter**
The Brit	**Gary Daniels**
Hale Caesar	**Terry Crews**
Tool	**Mickey Rourke**
Paul	**Hank Amos**
Trench	**Arnold Schwarzenegger**
Mr. Church	**Bruce Willis**

Amin Joseph (Pirate Leader), Senyo Amoaku (Tall Pirate), Antonio Rodrigo Nogueira, Antonio Rogerio Nogueira (Garza's Bodyguards), Sassa Nascimento (Vilena Customes Agent), R.A. Rondell (Gunner's Goon), Tze Yep (Gagged Hostage), Preshas Jenkins (Gunner's Pirate), Ronn Surels (American Operative), Lauren Jones (Cheyenne), Pirazeres Barbosa (Old Woman Bartender), Jose Vasquez, Daniel Arrias (Cell Guards), Antonio Gullo (Farmer), Javier Lambert (Squad Leader), Tastu Carvalho (Palace Guard), Marcio Rosario (Royal Guard Leader), Paulo Bastos (Vilenan Soldier)

A team of mercenaries is assembled to infiltrate a South American island and dispose of despotic General Garza and the cocaine dealer with whom he is in league.

Sylvester Stallone, Giselle Itié © Lionsgate

Michael Cera, Mary Elizabeth Winstead, Johnny Simmons, Ellen Wong,
Alison Pill, Mark Webber © Universal Studios

Mae Whitman

SCOTT PILGRIM VS. THE WORLD

(UNIVERSAL) Producers, Marc Platt, Eric Gitter, Nira Park, Edgar Wright; Executive Producers, Ronaldo Vasconcellos, J. Miles Dale; Co-Producers, Joe Nozemack, Lisa Gitter, Steve V. Scavelli; Director, Edgar Wright; Screenplay, Michael Bacall, Edgar Wright; Based on the Oni Press graphic novels by Bryan Lee O'Malley; Photography, Bill Pope; Designer, Marcus Rowland; Costumes, Laura Jean Shannon; Music, Nigel Godrich; Music Supervisor, Kathy Nelson; Editors, Jonathan Amos, Paul Machliss; Special Effects Supervisor, Arthur Langevin; Visual Effects Supervisor, Frazer Churchill; Visual Effects, Double Negative, Mr. X; Stunts, Brad Allan; Fight Coordinator, Peng Zhang; a Marc Platt/Big Talk Films production; Dolby; Super 35 Widescreen; Deluxe Color; Rated PG-13; 112 minutes; Release date: August 13, 2010

Michael Cera, Jason Schwartzman

CAST

Scott Pilgrim	**Michael Cera**
Ramona Flowers	**Mary Elizabeth Winstead**
Wallace Wells	**Kieran Culkin**
Lucas Lee	**Chris Evans**
Stacey Pilgrim	**Anna Hendrick**
Kim Pine	**Alison Pill**
Todd Ingram	**Brandon Routh**
Gideon Gordon Graves	**Jason Schwartzman**
Envy Adams	**Brie Larson**
Julie Powers	**Aubrey Plaza**
Young Neil	**Johnny Simmons**
Stephen Stills	**Mark Webber**
Knives Chau	**Ellen Wong**

Kieran Culkin

Ben Lewis (Other Scott), Nelson Franklin (Comeau), Kristina Pesic (Sandra), Ingrid Haas (Monique), Marlee Otto, Will Bowes, Celin Lepage, Mark LeRoy (Partygoers), Kjartan Hewitt (Jimmy), Chantelle (Tamara Chen), Matt Watts (Promoter), Erik Knudsen (Crash), Maurie W. Kaufmann (Joel), Abigail Chu (Trasha), Satya Bhabha (Matthew Patel), Christine Watson (Demon Hipster Chick), Don McKellar (Director), Emily Kassie (Winifred Hailey), Jung-Yul Kim (Goon), Mae Whitman (Roxy Richter), Tennessee Thomas (Lynette Guycott), Keita Saitou (Kyle Katayanagi), Shota Saito (Ken Katayanagi), Michael Lazarovitch (Some Guy), John Patrick Amedori (Lollipop Hipster), Joe Dinicol, Cragi Strickland (Elevator Hipsters), Thomas Jane, Clifton Collins Jr. (Vegan Police)

Before he can win the girl of his dreams, Scott Pilgrim must do battle with all seven of her previous lovers.

VAMPIRES SUCK

(20TH CENTURY FOX) Producers, Peter Safran, Jason Friedberg, Aaron Seltzer; Executive Producer, Arnon Milchan; Co-Producers, Jerry P. Jacobs, Hal Olofsson; Directors/ Screenplay, Jason Friedberg, Aaron Seltzer; Photography, Shawn Maurer; Designer, William Elliott; Costumes, Alix Hester; Music, Christopher Lennertz; Music Supervisors, Dave Jordan, Jojo Villanueva; Editor, Peck Prior; Visual Effects Supervisors, Ray McIntyre Jr., Jamison Goei; Casting, Nancy Foy; a Regency Enterprises presentation of a New Regency/3 in the Box production; Dolby; Deluxe color; Rated PG-13; 82 minutes; Release date: August 18, 2010

CAST

Becca Crane	**Jenn Proske**
Edward Sullen	**Matt Lanter**
Frank Crane	**Diedrich Bader**
Jacob White	**Christopher N. Riggi**
Daro	**Ken Leong**
Jennifer	**Anneliese Van Der Pol**

David DeLuise (Old Man Scully), Kelsey Ford (Iris), Dave Foley (Principal Smith), Jeff Witzke (Dr. Carlton), Arielle Kebbel (Rachel), B.J. Britt (Antoine), Charlie Weber (Jack), Emily Brobst (June), Bradley Dodds (Salvatore), Ken Jeong (Daro), Mike Mayhall (Nicholas), Rett Terrell (Max), Stephanie Fischer (Rosalyn), Nick Eversman (Jeremiah), Zane Holtz (Alex), Crista Flanagan (Eden), Jun Hee Lee (Derric), Michael Hanson (Rick), Parker Dash (Drunken Festival Goer), Leo Fabian (Biker Dude), Randal Reeder (Gross Bearded Biker), Krystal Mayo (Buffy the Vampire Slayer), Ike Barinholtz (Bobby White), Amanda Jacobs (Team Edward Girl), Ryan Glorioso (Science Teacher), Bryan Philip Cruz (Chinese Food Delivery Guy), Aida Garrett (Mean Girl), Marissa Cavazos, Sarah Colbert (Team Jacob Girls), Marcelle Baer (Hot Girl), Alyssa Overbeck (Trendy Girl), Nedal "Ned" Yousef, Rodrigo Lloreda, John Franklin, Nick Gomez (Jacob's Pack), Celeste Roberts (Matronly Faculty Member), Greg Washington (Photographer), John Bemecker (Vampire), Helena Barrett (Alice), Sara Blanche (Pretty Girl), Matthew Warzel (John), Michelle Lang (Innocent Woman), Valerie Morgan (Woman in Line)

In the Pacific Northwest teenager Becca Crane hooks up with vampire Edward Sullen in this spoof of the *Twilight* films.

Arielle Kebbel, B.J. Britt, Charlie Weber © 20th Century Fox

Jason Bateman, Jennifer Aniston © Miramax

THE SWITCH

(MIRAMAX) Producers, Albert Berger, Ron Yerxa; Executive Producers, Nathan Kahane, Jennifer Aniston, Kristin Hahn; Co-Producers, Allan Loeb, Brian Bell, Kelly Konop, Mary Lee, Steven Pearl; Directors, Josh Gordon, Will Speck; Screenplay, Allan Loeb; Based on the short story *Baster* by Jeffrey Eugenides; Photography, Jess Hall; Designer, Adam Stockhausen; Costumes, Kasia Walicka Maimone; Music, Alex Wurman; Music Supervisor, Steven Baker; Editor, John Axelrad; Casting, Douglas Aibel; a Mandate Pictures presentation of a Bona Fide/ Echo Films production; Dolby; Super 35 Widescreen; Color; Rated PG-13; 101 minutes; Release date: August 20, 2010

CAST

Kassie Larson	**Jennifer Aniston**
Wally Marrs	**Jason Bateman**
Roland	**Patrick Wilson**
Leonard	**Jeff Goldblum**
Debbie	**Juliette Lewis**
Sebastian Larson	**Thomas Robinson**

Kelli Barrett (Jessica), Jason Jones (Climbing Wall Guide), Scott Elrod (Declan), Todd Louiso (Artie), Bryce Robinson (Older Sebastian), Victor Pagan (Knit Hat Guy), Rebecca Naomi Jones, Jeremy J. Mohler (Party Guests), Will Swenson (Stage Actor), Edward James Hyland (Man in Theater), Caroline Dhavernas (Pauline), Brian Podnos (Waiter), Carmen M. Herlihy (Woman on Bus), Lily Pilblad (Girl at Pizzeria)

Having accidentally disposed of the sperm that is intended for his friend Kassie's artificial insemination, Wally decides to replace it with his own. Seven years later he encounters Kassie's grown son, whom he realizes is actually his own biological offspring.

LOTTERY TICKET

(WARNER BROS.) Producers, Mark Burg, Oren Koules, Andrew A. Kosove, Broderick Johnson, Matt Alvarez; Executive Producers, Ice Cube, Timothy M. Bourne, Steven P. Wegner; Co-Producers, Brad Kaplan, Andrew Wilson, Yolanda T. Cochran; Director, Erik White; Screenplay, Aboul Williams; Story, Erik White, Aboul Williams; Photography, Patrick Cady; Designer, Roshelle Hernandez; Costumes, Sandra Hernandez; Music, Teddy Castellucci; Editor, Harvey Rosenstock; Casting, Kim Taylor-Coleman; an Alcon Entertainment presentation of a Burg-Koules production, a Cube Vision production; Dolby; Technicolor; Rated PG-13; 95 minutes; Release date: August 20, 2010

CAST

Kevin Carson	**Bow Wow**
Benny	**Brandon T. Jackson**
Stacie	**Naturi Naughton**
Sweet Tee	**Keith David**
David Semaj	**Charlie Murphy**
Lorenzo	**Gbenga Akinnagbe**
Jimmy the Driver	**Terry Crews**
Grandma	**Loretta Devine**

Ice Cube (Mr. Washington), Bill Bellamy (Giovanni), Mike Epps (Rev. Taylor), Faheem Najm (Junior), Teairra Mari (Nikki Swayze), Chris Williams (Doug), Vince Green (Malik), Leslie Jones (Tasha), Malieek Straughter (Deangelo), Jason Weaver (Ray-Ray), Stacie Davis (Reporter), Andre Mayron (Officer Ross), D.J. "Bishop" Rogers (Customer), Britanny Eady (Attractive Lady), Timfreit D'Rane (Angry Man), Mike Pniewski (Carl), Sky Cameron (Little Girl), Eric J. Little, Taneka Johnson, Tonea Stewart, IronE Singleton, Darryl D. Moore (Random Neighbors), Daniella Lewis, Shantis Thompson (Voices), Maria Duarte (Bonnie Berry), Mike DeFoor (Janitor), Bobby L. Graham Sr. (Brother Conner), L. Stephanie Ray (Rev. Taylor's Ex-Wife), Lance Toland (Helicopter Pilot), Patricia L. Bostick, Marlon Gandy, Bobby Lee Graham Jr., Nanella O. Graham, Daniel Theodore Harris, Gloria O. Henderson, Nanella Henderson-Lynch, Edward R. Lynch, Valerie D. McBride, Gloria Graham Potter, Jean Vincent Ricks, Dorothy Geer Sims, Barry Taylor, Synthia M. Willis (Singers)

When Kevin Carson unexpectedly wins a $370 million lottery prize, he must wait three days to collect his money, thereby having to face every possible sycophantic friend and neighbor hoping to get in on the prize.

Brandon T. Jackson, Ice Cube, Bow Wow, Naturi Naughton © Warner Bros.

Jerry O'Connell © Dimension

PIRANHA

(DIMENSION) Producers, Mark Canton, Marc Toberoff, Alexandre Aja, Gregory Levasseur; Executive Producers, Bob Weinstein, Harvey Weinstein, Alix Taylor, Louis G. Friedman, J. Todd Harris, Chako van Leeuwen; Director, Alexandre Aja; Screenplay, Peter Goldfinger, Josh Stolberg; Photography, John R. Leonetti; Designer, Clark Hunter; Costumes, Sanja Milkovic; Music, Michael Wandmacher; Editor, Baxter; Special Makeup Effects, Gregory Nicotero, Howard Berger; Visual Effects Supervisors, David Wentworth, Kevin O'Neill; Casting, Alyssa Weisberg; a Mark Canton/IPW production in associatgion with Aja/Levasseur Prods.; Dolby; Panavision; Color; 3-D; Rated R; 88 minutes; Release date: August 20, 2010

CAST

Sheriff Julie Forester	**Elisabeth Shue**
Novak	**Adam Scott**
Derrick Jones	**Jerry O'Connell**
Deputy Fallon	**Ving Rhames**
Kelly	**Jessica Szohr**
Jake Forester	**Steven R. McQueen**
Mr. Goodman	**Christopher Lloyd**
Matt Boyd	**Richard Dreyfuss**

Kelly Brook (Danni), Riley Steele (Crystal), Paul Scheer (Andrew), Brooklynn Proulx (Laura Forester), Sage Ryan (Zane Forester), Eli Roth (Wet T-Shirt Host), Ricardo Chavira (Sam), Dina Meyer (Paula), Cody Longo (Todd Dupree), Brian Kubach (Brett), Ashlynn Brooke (Cheerleader), Cavin Gray-Schneider (Frat Boy Driver), Bo Jacober (Geeky Party Guy), Franck Khalfoun (Deputy Green), Genevieve Alexandra (Propeller Girl), Devra Korwin (Mrs. Goodman), Nick Magee (Boy in Parasail Boat), Gianna Michaels (Parasailing Girl), Bonnie Morgan (Sorotiy Girl, Inner-Tube), Gregory Nicotero (Boat Captain), Tim Bishop (Drunk Kid, Cannonball), Carmen Prisco (Drunk Dumb Jock), Maarsen Roney (Drunk Laughing Jock), Jason Spisak (Deputy Taylor), Kym Stus, Nicole Randall (Trampoline Girls), Christopher Vejnoska (Party-Goer, Floating Stage), Nancy Walers (Girl Cut in Half), Tyrone Williams (DJ), Matt Bercia (Fat Frat Boy)

An earthquake unleashes a swarm of deadly piranha on the Lake Victoria resort.

Pat Tillman © Weinstein Co.

Pat Tillman, Kevin Tillman

THE TILLMAN STORY

(WEINSTEIN CO.) Producer, John Battsek; Executive Producers, Molly Thompson, Robert DeBitteto, Robert Sharenow, Andrew Ruhemann, Michael Davies; Co-Producer, Caitrin Rogers; Director, Amir Bar-Lev; Screenplay, Amir Bar-Lev, Joe Bini, Mark Monroe; Photography, Sean Kirby, Igor Martinovic; Music, Philip Sheppard; Music Supervisor, Liz Gallacher; Editors, Joshua Altman, Joe Bini, Gabriel Rhodes; Narrator, Josh Brolin; an A&E IndieFilms presentation of a Passion Pictures/Axis Films production in association with Diamond Docs and Embassy Row; Color; Super 16-to-HD; Rated R; 94 minutes; Release date: August 20, 2010.

Documentary on how pro-football star-turned-soldier Pat Tillman's death in Afghanistan was covered up by the Bush administration.

THE LAST EXORCISM

(LIONSGATE) Producers, Eric Newman, Eli Roth, Marc Abraham, Thomas A. Bliss; Executive Producers, Huck Botko, Andrew Gurland, Phil Altmann, Ron Halpern; Co-Producers, Patty Long, Gabrielle Neimand; Director, Daniel Stamm; Screenplay, Huck Botko, Andrew Gurland; Photography, Zoltan Honti; Designer, Andrew Bofinger; Music, Nathan Barr; Editor, Shilpa Khanna; Casting, Lauren Bass; a Spike Entertainment and StudioCanal presentation of an Arcade Pictures production; Dolby; Color; Rated PG-13; 87 minutes; Release date: August 27, 2010

CAST
Cotton Marcus	**Patrick Fabian**
Nell Sweetzer	**Ashley Bell**
Iris Reisen	**Iris Bahr**
Louis Sweetzer	**Louise Herthum**
Caleb Sweetzer	**Caleb Landry Jones**
Pastor Manley	**Tony Bentley**
John Marcus	**John Wright Jr.**
Shanna Marcus	**Shanna Forrestall**
Justin Marcus	**Justin Shafer**

Carol Sutton (Shopkeeper), Victoria Patenaude (Motorist), John Wilmot (Spindly Man), Becky Fly (Becky Davis), Denise Lee (Nurse), Logan Craig Reid (Logan Winters), Sofia Hujabre (Café Manager), Adam Grimes (Daniel Moskowitz)

A preacher who has done his share of bogus exorcisms allows a camera crew to follow him to New Orleans to confront what appears to be another false alarm, only to find a young woman who does indeed appear to be possessed.

Patrick Fabian, Ashley Bell

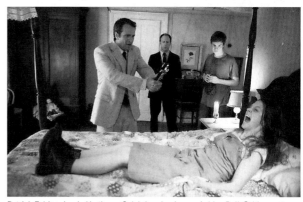

Patrick Fabian, Louis Herthum, Caleb Landry Jones, Ashley Bell © Lionsgate

Matt Dillon, Jay Hernandez © Screen Gems

Michael Ealy, Chris Brown, Idris Elba, Hayden Christensen, Paul Walker

TAKERS

(SCREEN GEMS) Producers, Will Packer, Tip "T.I." Harris, Jason Geter; Executive Producers, Glenn S. Gainor, Gabriel Casseus, Chris Brown, Morris Chestnut; Director, John Lussenhop; Screenplay, Peter Allen, Gabriel Casseus, John Luessenhop, Avery Duff; Photography, Michael Barrett; Designer, Jon Gary Steele; Costumes, Maya Lieberman; Music, Paul Haslinger; Editor, Armen Minasian; Visual Effects Supervisor, Rocco Passionino; Casting, Lindsey Hayes Kroeger, David H. Rapaport; a Rainforest Films production in association with Grand Hustle Films; Dolby; Deluxe Color; Rated PG-13; 107 minutes; Release date: August 27, 2010

CAST

Jack Welles	**Matt Dillon**
John Rahway	**Paul Walker**
Gordon Jennings	**Idris Elba**
Eddie Hatcher	**Jay Hernandez**
Jake Attica	**Michael Ealy**
Ghost	**Tip "T.I." Harris**
Jesse Attica	**Chris Brown**
A.J.	**Hayden Christensen**

Steve Harris (Lt. Carver), Johnathon Schaech (Scott), Marianne Jean-Baptiste (Naomi), Zoe Saldana (Rachel Jansen), Gaius Charles (Max), Gideon Emery (Sergei), Zulay Henao (Monica), Glynn Turman (Chief Detective Duncan), Nicholas Turturro (Franco Dalia), Isa Briones (Sunday), Andrei Runtso (Constantine), Vladiir Tevloski (Ethan), Tim Sitarz, Gokor Chivichyan, Roman Mitichyan, Vladimir Orlov, Mike Smith (Russians), Harrison Miller (Eddie Jr.), Karl Knuth (Scott's Bodyguard), Conrade Gamble (Haitian Thug), Jermaine Holt (Dealer #2), Martin Shuler (Prison Guard), Kelvin Brown (Security Guard #1), Danny Epper, Bobby McLaughlin (Bank Guards), Nancy Wetzel (Chopper News 14 Reporter), Andrew Fiscella (Security Chief), Juna Kim (Asian Girls), Natasha Ellie (African American Girl), Will McFadden (Haitian's Lawyer), Daniel Stevens (Slick), Troy Brenna (Sweatpants), Gino Anthony Pesi (Paulie Jr.), Mike Wood (Police Tech), Terrell Lee (Parole Officer), Noelle Smith (Officer of the Day), Lanny Joon (Vice Cop), Roger Stoneburner (Wasted Junkie), Erik Stabenau, Jim Lewis (Armed Drivers), Matt Taylor, Marcus Young (Armed Guards), Jimmy Roberts, Dustin Meier (Guards), James Martinez (Officer in Charge), Laura Shay Griffin (Receptionist), Ashleigh Falls (Frumpy Bank Teller), JoAnna Rhambo (Woman in Underwear at Gordon's), Bryan Ross (Officer #4), Nathan Bell (Cop in a Hole), Joe DiGiandomenico, Craig Susser (TV News Reporters), Ben Skorstad (2nd News Helicopter Pilot), Brad Jensen (News 14 Chopper Pilot), Michael Duisenberg (News Reporter Channel 8), Christopher "Critter" Antonucci (News 14 Camera Crew), John Meier, Scott Wilder (Police Officers in Chase), Patrick Stickland (Doorman), Paul Stephen Hubbard (Internal Affairs Officer)

Zoe Saldana, Michael Ealy

L.A. Dective Welles sets out to nab a team of highly professional thieves who are hoping to pull off a daring armored car robbery.

THE AMERICAN

(FOCUS) Producers, Anne Carey, Jill Green, Ann Wingate, Grant Heslov, George Clooney; Executive Producer, Enzo Sisti; Director, Anton Corbijn; Screenplay, Rowan Joffe; Based on the novel *A Very Private Gentleman* by Martin Booth; Photography, Martin Ruhe; Designer, Mark Digby; Costumes, Suttirat Anne Larlarb; Music, Herbert Gronemeyer; Editor, Andrew Hulme; Special Effects Coordinator, Renato Agostini; Stunts, Franco Salamon; Casting, Beatrice Kruger; American-British; a This is That/Greenlit/Smokehouse production; Dolby; Super 35 Widescreen; Technicolor; Rated R; 105 minutes; Release date: September 1, 2010

Violante Placido, George Clooney

CAST

Jack/Edward	**George Clooney**
Clara	**Violante Placido**
Mathilde	**Thekla Reuten**
Father Benedetto	**Paolo Bonacelil**
Pavel	**Johan Leysen**
Ingrid	**Irina Björklund**
Fabio	**Filippo Timi**
Anna	**Anna Foglietta**
Hunters	**Lars Hjelm, Björn Granath**
Man on Vespa	**Giorgio Gobbi**
Old Cheese Vendor	**Silvana Bosi**
Waiter at Market	**Guido Palliggiano**
Postmaster	**Antonio Rampino**

Ilaria Cramerotti, Angelica Novak, Isabelle Adriani (Hookers), Raffaele Serao (Barman in Town Square Bar), Sandro Dori (Waiter at Locanda Grapelli)

A hit man for hire goes into hiding when he realizes someone has targeted him for death.

Thekla Reuten, George Clooney

George Clooney

Irina Björklund, George Clooney © Focus Features

J.R. Ackerley, Tulip

Tulip, J.R. Ackerley © New Yorker Films

MY DOG TULIP

(NEW YORKER) Producers, Norman Twain, Howard Kaminsky, Frank Pellegrino; Directors, Paul Fierlinger, Sandra Fierlinger; Screenplay/Animator, Paul Fierlinger; Based on the novel by J.R. Ackerley; Music, John Avarese; a My Dog Tulip Co. production; Color; Not rated; 81 minutes; Release date: September 1, 2010

VOICE CAST

J.R. Ackerley	**Christopher Plummer**
Nancy/Greengrocer's Wife	**Lynn Redgrave**
Ms. Canvenini	**Isabella Rossellini**
Mr. Plum/Pugilist	**Peter Gerety**
Captain Pugh/Mr. Blandish	**Brian Murray**
Army Veterinarian	**Paul Hecht**
Bicyclist/Rude Veterinarian	**Euan Morton**

A middle-aged bachelor becomes the owner of an Alsatian dog who becomes a pivotal part of his life during her 14 year life span.

GOING THE DISTANCE

(NEW LINE CINEMA/WB) Producers, Adam Shankman, Jennifer Gibgot, Garrett Grant; Executive Producers, Dave Neustadter, Richard Brener, Michael Disco; Director, Nanette Burstein; Screenplay, Geoff LaTulippe; Photography, Eric Steelberg; Designer, Kevin Kavanaugh; Costumes, Catherine Marie Thomas; Music, Mychael Danna; Music Supervisor, Dana Sano; Editor, Peter Teschner; Casting, Juel Bestrop, Kathleen Chopin, Seth Yanklewitz; an Offspring Entertainment production; Dolby; Super 35 Widescreen; Color; Rated R; 103 minutes; Release date: September 3, 2010

CAST

Erin	**Drew Barrymore**
Garrett	**Justin Long**
Dan	**Charlie Day**
Box	**Jason Sudeikis**
Corinne	**Christina Applegate**
Will	**Ron Livingston**

Oliver Jackson-Cohen (Damon), Jim Gaffigan (Phil), Natalie Morales (Brandy), Kelli Garner (Brianna), June Diane Raphael (Karen), Rob Riggle (Ron), Sarah Burns (Harper), Terry Beaver (Professor), Matt Servitto (Hugh), Leighton Meester (Amy), Tuffy Questell (Airport ISA Agent), Charlie Hewson (Douchebag), Taylor Schwencke (Maya), Mike Birbiglia (Toby the Waiter), Meredith Hagner (Tanning Salon Employee), Benita Robledo (Diner Waitress), Stink Fisher (Muscle Guy), Kristen Schaal (Bartender), Graham Davie (Zach), Zach Page (Zander), Mick Hazen (Zeff), Sean Gustavus Tarjyoto (Awkward Nerd), Cass Buggé, Sandie Rosa (Girlfriends), Adam Harrison, Piers Hewitt, Todd Howe, Nathan Nicholson (The Boxer Rebellion), Samantha Futerman, Natalie Knepp (Very Young Intern), Happy Anderson (Terry), Sondra James (Elderly Woman), Maya Morris, Jennifer Bronstein (Not it Girl), Maria Conte Di Angelis (Receptionist), Ethan F. Hamburg (Newsroom Co-Worker), Anna Gorecky, Josephine-Dana April Micari (Diesel Records Secretary), Loretta Fox (Sandy), Carole Raphaelle Davis (Carmen), Ron Bottitta (Creepy Guy)

Erin and Garrett begin a relationship in Manhattan, only to wonder if they can sustain it when she is obliged to move back west to San Francisco.

Justin Long, Drew Barrymore © New Line Cinema

Danny Trejo

Jeff Fahey, Robert De Niro © 20th Century Fox

MACHETE

(20TH CENTURY FOX) Producers, Robert Rodriguez, Elizabeth Avellan, Rick Schwartz; Executive Producers, Ashok Amritraj, Edward Borgerding, Alan Bernon, Myles Nestel; Co-Executive Producers, Peter Fruchtman, Jerry Fruchtman, Jacky Gilardi Jr., Darby Parker, Alastair Burlingham, Steve Robbins, Anthony Gudas; Directors, Robert Rodriguez, Ethan Maniquis; Screenplay, Robert Rodriguez, Alvaro Rodriguez; Photography, Jimmy Lindsey; Dcsgincr, Chris Stull; Costumes, Nina Proctor; Music, Chingon; Editors, Robert Rodriguez, Rebecca Rodriguez; Visual Effects Supervisor, Robert Rodriguez; Stunts, Russell Towery; Casting, Mary Vernieu, JC Cantu; an Overnight production in association with Troublemaker Studios; Dolby; Deluxe color; Rated R; 105 minutes; Release date: September 3, 2010.

CAST

Machete	**Danny Trejo**
Senator John McLaughlin	**Robert De Niro**
Sartana	**Jessica Alba**
Torrez	**Steven Seagal**
Luz	**Michelle Rodriguez**
Booth	**Jeff Fahey**
Padre	**Cheech Marin**
Von	**Don Johnson**
Sniper	**Shea Whigham**
April	**Lindsay Lohan**
Osiris Ampanour	**Tom Savini**
Julio	**Daryl Sabara**
Jorge	**Gilberto Trejo**
Von's Henchman	**Billy Blair**

Jessica Alba

Cheryl Chin (Torrez Henchwoman), Ara Celi (Reporter), Felix Sabates (Doc Felix), Electra Avellan (Nurse Mona), Elise Avellan (Nurse Lisa), Marci Madison (Nurse Fine), Vic Trevino (Federale Officer), Mayra Leal (Chica, Naked Girl), Alejandro Antonio (Chief), Juan Pareja (Rico), Alicia Marke (June), Mitchell lance Adams, Jason Douglas (Patrolmen), Brent Smiga (Sniper's Henchman), Chris Warner (Hospital Security Guard), Jim Henry (Guard), Tina Rodriguez (Tristana), Roland Ruiz (Luis), Greg Ingram (Cristos), Tito Larriva (Culebra Cruzado), Hugo Perez (Van Driver), Nina Leon (Machete's Wife), Doran Ingram (Von's Minute Man), James Brownlee (Henchman), Nimród Antal (Booth's Bodyguard), Dimitrius Puldio, Scott Jefferies (Bodyguards).

Machete, an illegal alien working as a day laborer in Texas, is hired to assassinate a political candidate, only to realize he has been set up to take the fall for the crime, causing him to seek revenge. The character of Machete first appeared in a mock trailer in the 2007 film *Grindhouse*.

Danny Trejo, Steven Seagal

PRINCE OF BROADWAY

(ELEPHANT EYE FILMS) Producer, Darren Dean; Director/Photography/Editor, Sean Baker; Screenplay, Sean Baker, Darren Dean; Designer, Stephonik Youth Baker; Associate Producers, Blake Ashman, Victoria Tate; a Cre Films presentation; Color; HD; Not rated; 102 minutes; Release date: September 3, 2010

CAST

Lucky	**Prince Adu**
Levon	**Karren Karaguillian**
Prince	**Aiden Noesi**
Karina	**Keyali Mayaga**
Linda	**Kat Sanchez**
Nadia	**Victoria Tate**

Chris Bergoch (Snowbound Victim), Brea Cola (Serena), Roger Harkavy (Defense Attorney), Adesuwa Addy Iyare (Herself), Kurt Leitner (Davenport), Cindy Lopez (Duana), Mark Newell (Undercover Cop), Edwin Morteye (Ralphie), Michael Adrienne O'Hagan (Snowbound Victim's Girlfriend), Justen Oriolo (Size 13), Edward Pagan (Hector), Tony Roach (DNA Doctor), Allison Carter Thomas (Midwestern Tourist), Mala Wright (Customer)

Shop vendor Lucky's carefree existence is disrupted when an ex-girlfriend orders him to take care of their infant son.

Prince Adu © Elephant Eye Films

Joaquin Phoenix

Joaquin Phoenix © Magnolia

I'M STILL HERE

(MAGNOLIA) Producers, Joaquin Phoenix, Casey Affleck, Amanda White; Director, Casey Affleck; Screenplay, Casey Affleck, Joaquin Phoenix; Photography, Casey Affleck, Magdalena Gorka; Music, Joaquin Phoenix; Editors, Casey Affleck, Dody Dorn; a They Are Going to Kill Us Prods. presentation; Dolby; Color; HD; Rated R; 107 minutes; Release date: September 10, 2010.

WITH

Joaquin Phoenix, Casey Affleck, Nicole Acacio, Tim Affleck, Norm Block, Sean Combs, Billy Crystal, Mos Def, Amanda Demme, Danny DeVito, Jamie Foxx, Eliot Ganyon, Danny Glover, David Grutman, Anthony Langdon, David Letterman, Matt Maher, Larry McHale, Jack Nicholson, Edward James Olmos, Sue Patricola, Carey Perloff, Natalie Portman, Jamison Reeves, Eddie Rouse, Mike Snedegar, Christine Spines, Ben Stiller, Patrick Whitesell, Bruce Willis, Robin Wright

Mock documentary in which actor Casey Affleck films his brother-in-law, Joaquin Phoenix, as he makes the decision to quit acting and become a hip hop artist.

GASLAND

(ABRAMORAMA) Producers, Trish Adlesic, Josh Fox, Molly Gandour; Executive Producers, Debra Wigner, Hunter Gray; Director/Screenplay, Josh Fox; Photography, Josh Fox, Matthew Sanchez; Editor, Matthew Sanchez; an Intl. Wow Company production; Color; Digital Video; Not rated; 105 minutes; Release date: September 15, 2010.

WITH
Josh Fox, Weston Willis, Amee Ellsworth, Jess Ellsworth, John Fenton, John Hanger, Maurice Henchey, Mike Markham, Lewis Meeks, Marsha Mendenhall, Wilma Subra, Calvin Tillman

Documentary on the dangers of natural gas drill..

This film received an Oscar nomination as documentary, feature.

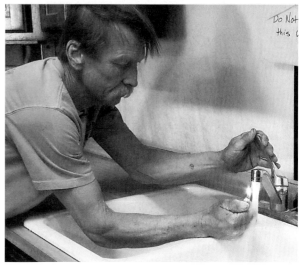

Gasland © Abramorama

Paddy, Marcel ©Lionsgate

ALPHA AND OMEGA

(LIONSGATE) Producers, Richard Rich, Ken Katsumoto, Steve Moore; Executive Producers, Noah Fogelson, Max Madhavana, Michael Paseornek; Directors, Anthony Bell, Ben Gluck; Screenplay, Christopher Denk, Steve Moore; Story, Steve Moore; Art Director, Donald A. Towns; Animation Supervisor, Satish Thokade; Music, Chris Bacon; Music Supervisors, Jay Faires, Tracy McKnight; Editor, Joseph L. Campana; Casting, Bernie Van De Yacht; Presented with Crest Animation; Dolby; Color; 3D; Rated PG; 88 minutes; Release date: September 17, 2010

VOICE CAST

Humphrey	**Justin Long**
Kate	**Hayden Panettiere**
Tony	**Dennis Hopper**
Winston	**Danny Glover**
Marcel	**Larry Miller**
Paddy	**Eric Price**
Eve	**Vicki Lewis**
Lilly	**Christina Ricci**
Garth	**Chris Carmack**
Shakey	**Kevin Sussman**
Salty	**Brian Donovan**
Sweets	**Bitsie Tulloch**

Two wolves from rival packs find themselves unexpectedly tranquilized and transported by rangers from Canada to Idaho, from which they hope to escape and return to their warring tribes.

Kate, Humphrey

John Ortiz, Daphne Rubin-Vega

Amy Ryan, Tom McCarthy, Daphne Rubin-Vega

Philip Seymour Hoffman, Amy Ryan © Overture Films

JACK GOES BOATING

(OVERTURE) Producers, Marc Turtletaub, Peter Saraf, Beth O'Neil, Emily Ziff; Executive Producers, Philip Seymour Hoffman, John Ortiz; Co-Producer, George Paaswell; Director, Philip Seymour Hoffman; Screenplay, Rob Glaudini, based on his play; Photography, Mott Hupfel; Designer, Thérèse DePrez; Costumes, Mimi O'Donnell; Music, Grizzly Bear; Additional Score, Evan Lurie; Editor, Brian A. Kates; Casting, Avy Kaufman; Casting, Avy Kaufman; a Big Beach and Cooper's Town production in association with Labyrinth Theater Company and Olfactory Productions; Dolby; Color; Rated R; 91 minutes; Release date: September 17, 2010

CAST

Jack	**Philip Seymour Hoffman**
Connie	**Amy Ryan**
Clyde	**John Ortiz**
Lucy	**Daphne Rubin-Vega**
Dr. Bob	**Tom McCarthy**
Uncle Frank	**Richard Petrocelli**
Italian Woman	**Lola Glaudini**
Ungainly Swimmer	**Ralph Osorio**
MTA Worker	**Stephen Adly Guirgis**
Drunk Man on Subway	**Mason Petit**
Waldorf Doorman	**Trevor Long**
Happy Husband	**Stephen Mailer**
Happy Wife	**Elizabeth Rainer**

Theodore Mailer (Young Son), Count Stovall (Men's Room Attendant), Salvatore Inzerillo (Cannoli), Elizabeth Rodriguez (Waldorf Event Assistant), Beth Cole (Teacher), Oliver Foot-E' (Swimming Teacher), Byron West (Swimming Student), Shawna Bermender (Becky), Cordell Stahl (MTA Orientation Leader)

Lucy and Clyde set their shy friend Jack up with Connie, hoping that the relationship will blossom into something solid, just as their own marriage begins to unravel.

Philip Seymour Hoffman

THE TOWN

(WARNER BROS.) Producers, Graham King, Basil Iwanyk; Executive Producers, Thomas Tull, Jon Jashni, William Fay, David Crockett; Director, Ben Affleck; Screenplay, Peter Craig, Ben Affleck, Aaron Stockard; Based on the novel *Prince of Thieves* by Chuck Hogan; Photography, Robert Elswit; Designer, Sharon Seymour; Costumes, Susan Matheson; Music, Harry Gregson-Williams, David Buckley; Editor, Dylan Tichenor; Casting, Lora Kennedy; a GK Films production, a Thunder Road Film production, presented in association with Legendary Pictures; Dolby; Panavision; Technicolor; Rated R; 124 minutes; Release date: September 17, 2010

Chris Cooper © Warner Bros.

CAST

Doug MacRay	**Ben Affleck**
Claire Keesey	**Rebecca Hall**
FBI Agent Adam Frawley	**Jon Hamm**
James "Jem" Coughlin	**Jeremy Renner**
Krista Coughlin	**Blake Lively**
Dino Ciampa	**Titus Welliver**
Fergie Colm	**Pete Postlethwaite**
Stephen MacRay	**Chris Cooper**
Albert "Gloansy" Magloan	**Slaine**
Desmond Elden	**Owen Burke**
Rusty	**Dennis McLaughlin**
Agent Quinlan	**Corena Chase**
Henry	**Brian Scannell**
Henry's Girl	**Kerri Dunbar**
Vericom Crew Chief	**Tony V.**
Alex Colazzo	**Isaac Bordoy**
Beacon G.I. Joe Driver	**Michael Yebba**
Inside Man at Fenway	**Jimmy Joe Maher**
Young Security Guard	**Mark Berglund**
BPD Sergeant at Krista's Accident	**Daniel Woods**
Cashcom Guards	**Ralph Boutwell, Michael Romig**
Atlantic Truck Courier	**Michael Malvesti**
Arnold Washton	**Jack Neary**
Morton Previt	**Edward O'Keefe**
Task Force Agent Conlan	**Joe Lawler**
FBI SWAT Team Leader	**Ben Hanson**
FBI SWATs	**Brian A. White, Richard Caines**
Police Captain	**Frank Garvin**
Cop Giving Statement	**Danny Ring**

Blake Lively, Ben Affleck

Gary Galone (Internal Affairs Officer at Fenway), David Catanzaro (Fenway Detective), Jeremiah Kissel (Claire's Lawyer), Malik McMullen (Plain Clothed FBI Agent), Charles C. Winchester III, Adam J. Husband (Gate D Police Officers), Danny DeMiller (Eskimo Story Speaker), Sarah Rawlinson, Sean Locke, Peter Looney (NA Speakers), Lennin Pena (Colazzo's Friend), James McKittrick (Cop Who Looks Away), Ted Arcidi (Cedar Junction C.O.), Bryan Connolly (Cedar Junction C.O. Visitors Area), Quan Liang Chen (Monument Laundry Owner), Alex Winston (Police Photographer), Michael F. Murphy (Michael Houlihan), Michele Cressinger (Margie), Kimberly Mahoney (Warren Tavern Waitress), Bobby Curcuro (Man in Harvard Square), Ginaya Green, Nicole Page (Krista's Friends), Georgia Lyman (Neptune's Waitress), Robert Boyden (Vericom Employee), Jamie Ghazarian (Dancer at Foxy Lady)

A Boston bank robber finds himself falling in love with the woman he and his cohorts took as a getaway hostage during their last heist.

This film received an Oscar nomination for supporting actor (Jeremy Renner).

Jeremy Renner, Slaine, Owen Burke, Ben Affleck

Rebecca Hall, Ben Affleck

Ben Affleck, Jeremy Renner

Pete Postlethwaite

Jon Hamm, Titus Welliver

Jon Hamm

Jeremy Renner

Dan Byrd, Emma Stone

Stanley Tucci, Emma Stone, Bryce Clyde Jenkins, Patricia Clarkson
© Screen Gems

Emma Stone, Aly Michalka

Penn Badgley, Emma Stone

EASY A

(SCREEN GEMS) Producers, Zanne Devine, Will Gluck; Co-Producer, Mark B. Johnson; Director, Will Gluck; Screenplay, Bert V. Royal; Photography, Michel Grady; Designer, Marcia Hinds; Costumes, Mynka Draper; Music Supervisor, Wende Crowley; Editor, Susan Littenberg; Casting, Lisa Miller Katz; an Olive Bridge Entertainment production; Dolby; Deluxe color; Rated PG-13; 93 minutes; Release date: September 17, 2010

CAST

Olive Penderghast	**Emma Stone**
Woodchuck Todd	**Penn Badgley**
Marianne	**Amanda Bynes**
Brandon	**Dan Byrd**
Mr. Griffith	**Thomas Haden Church**
Rosemary Penderghast	**Patricia Clarkson**
Micah	**Cam Gigandet**
Mrs. Griffith	**Lisa Kudrow**
Principal Gibbons	**Malcolm McDowell**
Rhiannon	**Aly Michalka**
Dill Penderghast	**Stanley Tucci**

Fred Armisen (Pastor), Juliette Goglia (Eighth Grade Olive), Jake Sandvig (Anson), Morgan Rusler (Mr. Abernathy), Nicki Tyler-Flynn (Mrs. Abernathy), Braeden Lemasters (Eighth Grade Kid), Mahaley Hessam (Nina), Jameson Moss (Evan), Blake Hood (Kennedy Peters-Booth), Bryce Clyde Jenkins (Chip Penderghast), Neil Soni (Zia), Stacey Travis (Marianne's Mom), Bonnie Burroughs (Micah's Mom), Eddie Applegate (Micah's Grandfather), Norma Michaels (Micah's Grandmother), Yolanda Snowball (Receptionist), Andrew Fleming (Doctor), Johanna Braddy (Melody Bostic), David Gore (Pre-Teen Ki), Lalaine (Gossipy Girl), D'Anthony Wayne Palms (Josh Wisniewski), Ryan Parker (Kurt), Rawson Thurber (Quiznos Guy), Chris De Lorenzo (Spectator in the Gym), Jillian Johnston (Server), Nancy Karr, Clay Black, Brad Etheridge, Veerta Motiani, Michael Strauss (Singing Servers), Lance Kerfuffle (Clerk), Drew Koles (Boy), Max Crumm (Pontius), Jeremiah Hu (Judas), Jessica Jann (Jezebel), Danni Katz (Harlot)

Unable to convince her friend that she has *not* yet lost her virginity, Olive Penderghast decides to lie about her sex life and soon gets a reputation as the most promiscuous girl in high school.

CATFISH

(UNIVERSAL/ROGUE) Producers, Andrew Jarecki, Marc Smerling, Ariel Schulman, Henry Joost; Co-Producer, Zac Stuart Pontier; Directors, Ariel Schulman, Henry Joost; Photography, Henry Joost, Ariel Schulman, Yaniv Schulman; Music Supervisor, Susan Jacobs; Editor, Zac Stuart-Pontier; a Relativity Media presentation of a Supermarche/Hit the Ground Running production; Color; DV; Rated PG-13; 86 minutes; Release date: September 17, 2010.

WITH
Yaniv "Nev" Schulman, **Ariel Schulman**, **Henry Joost**, **Angela Wesselman**, **Vince Pierce**, **Abby Pierce**

Documentary in which Ariel Schulman and Henry Joost set out to record the daily life of the former's brother, Yaniv, who ends up making an unexpected connection on the internet with a Michigan family who may not be what they seem to be.

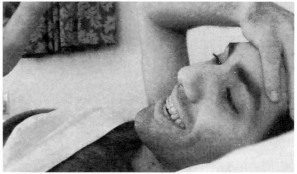
Nev Schulman

Airel Schulman, Henry Joost, Nev Schulman

Nev Schulman

Nev Schulman

Nev Schulman © Rogue Pictures

LEAVES OF GRASS

(FIRST LOOK FEATURES) Producers, Tim Blake Nelson, Edward Norton, Bill Migliore, John Langley, Elie Cohn, Kristina Dubin; Executive Producers, Avi Lerner, Danny Dimbort, Trevor Short, Boaz Davidson, David Koplan, Stuart Blumberg, Eric Gitter; Director/Screenplay, Tim Blake Nelson; Photography, Roberto Schaefer; Designer, Max Biscoe; Costumes, Caroline Eselin; Music, Jeff Danna; Music Supervisor, Randall Poster; Editor, Michelle Botticelli; Casting, Avy Kaufman; a Millennium Films and Langley Films presentation of a Class 5 Films production; Dolby; Color; Rated R; 104 minutes; Release date: September 17, 2010

Edward Norton, Edward Norton

CAST

Bill Kincaid/Brady Kincaid	**Edward Norton**
Janet	**Keri Russell**
Pug Rothbaum	**Richard Dreyfuss**
Daisy Kincaid	**Susan Sarandon**
Ken Feinman	**Josh Pais**
Colleen	**Melanie Lynskey**
Rabbi Zimmerman	**Maggie Siff**
Professor Nathan Levy	**Lee Wilkof**
Buddy Fuller	**Steve Earle**
Suzie Feinman	**Lisa Benavides-Nelson**
Miss Greenstein	**Lucy DeVito**
Professor Sorenson	**Ty Burrell**
Shaver	**Randall Reeder**
Bolger	**Tim Blake Nelson**

Kent Jude Bernard (Philosophy Student), Amelia Campbell (Maggie Harmon), Leo Fabian (Wadell), Tina Parker (Sharon), Jenna Podell (Staci Feinman), Henry Max Nelson (Gabe Feinman), Alyssia Dujmovich (Jilly), Ken Cheeseman (Jimmy Fuler), Naima Imani Lett (Sally), Tim Ware (Minister Davies), Robin McGee (Salesman), Chris Friehofer (Doctor)

Keri Russell, Edward Norton © First Look Features

Believing his twin brother has died, philosophy professor Bill Kincaid returns home to the rural Oklahoma roots he gladly left behind, only to discover that his sibling is very much alive and wanting Bill to pose as him to settle some shady business negotiations.

Richard Dreyfuss

Susan Sarandon, Edward Norton

Bojana Novakovic, Jenny O'Hara, Bokeem Woodbine, Logan Marshall-Green, Geoffrey Arend

Jacob Vargas, Chris Messina, Matt Craven © Universal Studios

Logan Marshall-Green

Bokeem Woodbine, Bojana Novakovic

DEVIL

(UNIVERSAL) Producers, M. Night Shyamalan, Sam Mercer; Executive Producers, Drew Dowdle, Trish Hofmann; Co-Producers, Ashwin Rajan, John Rusk; Director, John Erick Dowdle; Screenplay, Brian Nelson; Story, M. Night Shyamalan; Photography, Tak Fujimoto; Designer, Martin Whist; Costumes, Erin Benach; Music, Fernando Velazquez; Editor, Elliot Greenberg; Visual Effects Supervisors, Rocco Passionino, Mark Dornfeld; Casting, Debra Zane; a Media Rights Capital presentation of a The Night Chronicles production; Dolby; Super 35 Widescreen; Color; Rated PG-13; 80 minutes; Release date: September 17, 2010

CAST

Det. Bowden	**Chris Messina**
Mechanic, Tony	**Logan Marshall-Green**
Salesman, Vince	**Geoffrey Arend**
Young Woman, Sarah	**Bojana Novakovic**
Old Woman	**Jenny O'Hara**
Guard, Ben	**Bokeem Woodbine**
Lustig	**Matt Craven**
Ramirez	**Jacob Vargas**
Det. Markowitz	**Joshua Peace**
Elsa Nahai	**Caroline Dhavernas**
Dwight	**Joe Cobden**
Cheryl	**Zoie Palmer**
Henry	**Vincent Laresca**

Rudy Webb (Old Janitor), Craig Eldridge (Donnelly), Robert Lee (Chinese Man), Genadijis Dolganovs (Janitor), Joe Pingue (Business Bureau Clerk), Killian Gray (Uni), Michael Rhoades (Fire Captain), Kelly Jones (Firefighter Kurtzy), Lee Oliveira, Jay Hunter (Firefighters), Jonathan Potts (Wayne Kazan), Alice Poon (Officer Choi), Stacy Chbosky (Car Crash Woman), Gage Munroe (Jesse Bowden)

Five people find themselves trapped in a high-rise elevator where a seemingly supernatural force is unleashed upon them.

Francisco and His Mother

Geoffrey Canada (right) © Paramount Vantage

WAITING FOR 'SUPERMAN'

(PARAMOUNT VANTAGE) Producer, Lesley Chilcott; Executive Producers, Jeff Skoll, Diane Weyermann; Co-Producer, Eliza Hindmarch; Director, Davis Guggenheim; Screenplay, Davis Guggenheim, Billy Kimball; Photography, Erich Roland, Bob Richman; Music, Christophe Beck; Editors, Greg Finton, Jay Cassidy, Kim Roberts; a Patricipant Media presentation in association with Walden Media of an Electric Kinney Films production; Dolby; Color; Rated PG; 102 minutes; Release date: September 24, 2010.

WITH
Geoffrey Canada, Michelle Rhee, Bill Strickland, Randi Weingarten, The Black Family, The Esparza Family, The Hill Family

Documentary about America's failing school system.

STRAPPED

(TLA RELEASING) Producers, Joseph Graham, Bill Parker; Executive Producers, Raymond Murray, Derek Curl, Claire Kohler, Eric Moore; Co-Producer, Robert Merck; Director/Screenplay, Joseph Graham; Photography, Matthew Boyd; Designer, William King; Music, Count; Editor, Sharon Franklin; an AltarBoy production; Color; HD; Not rated; 92 minutes; Release date: September 24, 2010

CAST

Hustler	**Ben Bonenfant**
John	**Artem Mishin**
Gypsy Troubadour	**Michael Carlisi**
Sam	**Paul Gerrior**
Leon	**Carlo D'Amore**
Susan	**Katherine Celio**
David	**Michael Klinger**
Jacob	**Raphael Barker**

Following a sexual transaction, a hustler tries to find his way out of an apartment building only to be talked into further encounters by the other interested tenants.

Artem Mishin, Ben Bonenfant

Ben Bonenfant © TLA Releasing

Betty White, Jamie Lee Curtis, Sigourney Weaver, Odette Yustman, Kristen Bell

Kristen Chenoweth

Billy Unger, Jimmy Wolk, Victor Garber, Jamie Lee Curtis

Kyle Bornheimer © Touchstone

YOU AGAIN

(TOUCHSTONE) Producers, John J. Strauss, Eric Tannenbaum, Andy Fickman; Executive Producer, Mario Iscovich; Director, Andy Fickman; Screenplay, Moe Jelline; Photography, David Hennings; Designer, Craig Stearns; Costumes, Genevieve Tyrrell; Music, Nathan Wang; Editors, David Rennie, Keith Brachmann; Casting, Gail Goldberg; a Frontier Pictures production; Dolby; Technicolor; Rated PG; 105 minutes; Release date: September 24, 2010

CAST
Marni	**Kristen Bell**
Gail	**Jamie Lee Curtis**
Ramona	**Sigourney Weaver**
Joanna	**Odette Yustman**
Georgia King	**Kristen Chenoweth**
Mark	**Victor Garber**
Grandma Bunny	**Betty White**
Will	**Jimmy Wolk**
Charlie	**Sean Wing**
Tim	**Kyle Bornheimer**
Ben	**Billy Unger**
Taylor	**Christine Lakin**
Kendall	**Meagan Holder**
Richie	**Patrick Duffy**

Anna White (LouAnne), Brytni Sarpy (Marcia), Gelsey Weiss (Gail), Tammy To (Jennifer), Mimi Karsh (Lori), Amye Karsh (Lori), Amye Wilmes (Lucian), Henry G. Sanders (Chaplain), Shanola Hampton (Tammy), Jenna Leigh Green (Heather), Christopher Khai (Murata), Ashley Fink (Sunday), Paul Nygro (Strauss), Reginald VelJohnson (Mason Dunlevy), Daryl Hall, Joan Oates (Themselves), T-Bone Wolk, Mike Braun, Charlie Dechant, Zev Katz, Eliot Lewis (The Band), Lisa Valenzuela (Moe), L.J. Benet (Eric), Amy Reiss (Mary Ann), Chambers Stevens (Iscovich), Coby McLaughlin (Sean), Brittany Wilkinson (Teenage Gail), Anne Winfree (Teenage Ramona), Catherine Bach (Daisy), Staci Keanan (Dana), Chopper (Coco Puff), Dwayne Johnson (Airplane Security), Cloris Leachman (Helen)

Marni is horrified to learn that her brother is about to marry the very same girl who made Marni's high school years a living hell.

WALL STREET: MONEY NEVER SLEEPS

(20TH CENTURY FOX) Producers, Edward R. Pressman, Eric Kopeloff; Executive Producers, Celia Costas, Alex Young, Alessandro Camon; Director, Oliver Stone; Screenplay, Allan Loeb, Stephen Schiff; Based on characters created by Stanley Weiser and Oliver Stone; Photography, Rodrigo Prieto; Designer, Kristi Zea; Costumes, Ellen Mirojnick; Music, Craig Armstrong; Executive Music Producer, Budd Carr; Editors, Julie Monroe, David Brenner; Casting, Sarah Halley Finn, Kathleen Chopin; an Edward R. Pressman production; Dolby; Super 35 Widescreen; Deluxe color; Rated PG-13; 130 minutes; Release date: September 24, 2010

Josh Brolin, Eli Wallach

CAST

Gordon Gekko	**Michael Douglas**
Jake Moore	**Shia LaBeouf**
Bretton James	**Josh Brolin**
Winnie Gekko	**Carey Mulligan**
Julie Steinhardt	**Eli Wallach**
Jake's Mother	**Susan Sarandon**
Louis Zabel	**Frank Langella**
Dr. Masters	**Austin Pendleton**
Realtor	**Sylvia Miles**
Treasury Secretary	**John Bedford Lloyd**
Audrey	**Vanessa Ferlito**
Robby	**John Buffalo Mailer**
New York Fed Chief	**Jason Clarke**

Christian Baha (Hedge Fund Chief), Maria Bartiromo (News Host), Waltrudis Buck (Zabel's Secretary), Alice Burla (13 Year Old Pianist), Anthony Cochrane (Shoe Salesman, London), Frank Ciornei (Gekko's Landlord), Michael Genet (James' Butler), Richard Green (Boxer), Limor Hakim (Rumor Spreading Executive at Window), Edward Henzel (Rumor Spreading Executive), Sondra James (Lady at Book Signing), Harry Kerrigan (Prison Guard), Nan Lu (Chinese Executive), Edmund Lyndeck (Patient), Tom Mardirosian (District Attorney), Manu Narayan (Quant Analyst), Annika Pergament (Reporter), Annie McEnroe Pressman (Woman at Birthday), Eric Purcell (Jeweler), Eliyas Qureshi (Cabbie), Dieter Riesle (Swiss Bank Official), Mouriel Roubini (Economist on TV), Oliver Stone (Investor), Richard Stratton (Prison Cage Guard), Faye Wattleton (Professor at Fordham), Catherine Wolf (Zabel's Wife), Thomas Belesis, Darin Guerrasio, Greg Hildreth (Zabel Traders), George Steven Blumenthal, Emmett Fitzsimmons, Madison Mason (Bank Presidents), Michael Cumpsty, Jean Pigozzi (Churchill Schwartz Partners), Natalie Morales, Olaf Rogge (Churchill Schwartz Traders), Carrie Lee, Rhonda Schaffler (Reuters Reporters), Eloise DeJoria, Coralie C. Paul (Women at Party), Sean Stone, James P. Anderson, Mark Russell Gray (Hedge Fund Traders), Richard Crawford, Paul Grunert (Barbers, London), Vincent Farrell Jr., Ron Insana, Andrew Serwer (TV Analysts), Anthony Scaramucci, Melissa Francis, Warren Buffett, Graydon Carter, James Chanos, Sunil Hirani, Thomas M. Joyce, Joe Keenan, Steven Liesman (Themselves), Ali Velshi (Panelist on TV), Jim Cramer, David Faber, Sue Herera, Larry Kudlow, Melissa Lee, Becky Quick, Carl Quintanilla (Newscasters), Ed Bergtold, Mike DiGiacinto, Kevin Keeels, Ben Nisman, Tim Wilson (Traders at Urinals), Laura Dawn, Amber Dixon Brenner (Winnie's Office Co-Workers), Curzon Dobell, Leonard Logsdail (London Tailors), Charlie Sheen (Bud Fox)

Michael Douglas, Shia LaBeouf © 20th Century Fox

After serving time in prison for corporate malfeasance, one-time Wall Street hot shot Gordon Gekko seizes his chance to become a "player" again and to connect with the daughter he never knew when he takes young investment trader Jake Moore under his wing. Sequel to the 1987 film *Wall Street* (20th) with Michael Douglas, Charlie Sheen, and Sylvia Miles repeating their roles.

Shia LaBeouf, Josh Brolin, Michael Douglas

Aaron Tveit, James Franco

Andrew Rogers, Jon Hamm © Oscilloscope

HOWL

(OSCILLOSCOPE) Producers, Elizabeth Redleaf, Christine Kunewa Walker, Rob Epstein, Jeffrey Freidman; Executive Producers, Gus Van Sant, Jawal Nga; Co-Producers, Brian Benson, Andrew Peterson, Mark Steele; Directors/Screenplay, Rob Epstein, Jeffrey Friedman; Photography, Edward Lachman; Designer, Therese DePrez; Costumes, Kurt and Bart; Music, Carter Burwell; Editor, Jake Pushinsky; Animation Designer, Eric Drooker; Casting, Benie Telsey; a Werc Werk Works production in association with Telling Pictures and Rabbit Bandini Prods.; Dolby; Technicolor/Black and white; Not rated; 84 minutes; Release date: September 24, 2010

CAST

Allen Ginsberg	**James Franco**
Ralph McIntosh	**David Strathairn**
Jake Ehrlich	**Jon Hamm**
Judge Clayton Horn	**Bob Balaban**
Professor David Kirk	**Jeff Daniels**
Gail Potter	**Mary-Louise Parker**
Mark Schorer	**Treat Williams**
Luther Nichols	**Alessandro Nivola**

Todd Rotondi (Jack Kerouac), Jon Prescott (Neal Casady), Aaron Tveit (Peter Orlovsky), Sean Patrick Reilly, Alex Emanuel, Allyson Reilly (Six Gallery), Andrew Rogers (Lawrence Ferlinghetti), Cecilia Foss (Beatnik Poet), Kaydence Frank, Heather Klar (Poet Girls), Joe Toronto (Sailor), Johary Ramos (Hustler)

The true story of the uproar that erupted over Alan Gisnberg's 1955 poem "Howl," and the subsequent efforts to stop the work from being published.

LEGEND OF THE GUARDIANS: THE OWLS OF GA'HOOLE

(WARNER BROS.) Producer, Zareh Nalbandian; Executive Producers, Donald De Line, Deborah Snyder, Lionel Wigram, Chris DeFaria, Kathryn Lasky, Bruce Berman; Director, Zack Snyder; Screenplay, John Orloff, Emil Stern; Based on the novels entitled *Guardians of Ga'Hoole* by Kathryn Lasky; Designers, Simon Whiteley, Grant Freckelton; Music, David Hirschfelder; Editor, David Burrows; a Village Roadshow Pictures production, an Animal Logic production; American-Australian; Dolby; 3D; Color; Rated PG; 90 minutes; Release date: September 24, 2010

VOICE CAST

Soren	**Jim Sturgess**
Gylfie	**Emily Barclay**
Kludd	**Ryan Kwanten**
Twilight	**Anthony LaPaglia**
Grimble	**Hugo Weaving**
Nyra	**Helen Mirren**
Allomere	**Sam Neill**
Ezylryb	**Geoffrey Rush**

Abbie Cornish (Otulissa), Miriam Margolyes (Mrs. Plithiver), David Wenham (Digger), Adrienne DeFaria (Eglantine), Joel Edgerton (Metal Beak), Essie Davis (Marella), Deborra-Lee Furness (Barran), Sacha Horler (Strix Struma), Bill Hunter (Bubo), Barry Otto (Echidna), Richard Roxburgh (Boron), Angus Sampson (Jutt), Leigh Whannell (Jatt), Gareth Young (Pete), Amanda Bishop, Anthony Cogin, Trent Dalzell, James Evans, Lelda Kapsis, Andrew McDonnell, John Xintavelonis (Additional Voices)

Soren, a young barn owl raised by the wicked owls of St. Aggie's, escapes to the island of Ga'Hoole to help its inhabits combat their enemy.

Digger, Gylfie, Twilight, Mrs. Plithiver © Warner Bros.

Soren

THE SOCIAL NETWORK

(COLUMBIA) Producers, Scott Rudin, Dana Brunetti, Michael De Luca, Ceán Chaffin; Executive Producer, Kevin Spacey; Director, David Fincher; Screenplay, Aaron Sorkin; Based upon the book *The Accidental Billionaires* by Ben Mezrich; Photography, Jeff Cronenweth; Designer, Donald Graham Burt; Costumes, Jacqueline West; Music, Trent Reznor, Atticus Ross; Editors, Angus Wall, Kirk Baxter; Casting, Laray Mayfield; a Scott Rudin/Michael De Luca/Trigger Street production, presented in association with Relativity Media; Dolby; Widescreen; Deluxe color; Rated PG-13; 121 minutes; Release date: October 1, 2010

CAST

Mark Zuckerberg	**Jesse Eisenberg**
Eduardo Saverin	**Andrew Garfield**
Sean Parker	**Justin Timberlake**
Cameron and Tyler Winklevoss	**Armie Hammer**
Divya Narendra	**Max Minghella**
Tyler Winklevoss (Body)	**Josh Pence**
Christy	**Brenda Song**
Marylin Delpy	**Rashida Jones**
Sy	**John Getz**
Gage	**David Selby**
Gretchen	**Denise Grayson**
Larry Summers	**Douglas Urbanski**
Erica Albright	**Rooney Mara**
Dustin Moskovitz	**Joseph Mazzello**
Chris Hughes	**Patrick Mapel**
Alice	**Malese Jow**
Amelia Ritter	**Dakota Johnson**
Mr. Cox	**Barry Livingston**
Billy Olsen	**Bryan Barter**
Henry	**Henry Roosevelt**
KC	**Shelby Young**
Stuart Singer	**Victor Z. Isaac**
Vikram	**Abhi Sinha**
Bob	**Mark Saul**
Reggie	**Cedric Sanders**
Anne	**Inger Tudor**
Tori	**Mariah Bonner**
Intern Eric	**Kyle Fain**
Intern Ian	**Christopher Khai**
Sharon	**Emma Fitzpatrick**
Andrew	**Jeffrey Thomas Border**
Howard Winklevoss	**John Hayden**
Peter Thiel	**Wallace Langham**
Prince Albert	**James Shanklin**

Dustin Fitzsimmons (Phoenix Club President), Toby Meuli (Phoenix Member Playing Facemash), Alecia Svensen (Girl at Phoenix Club), Jami Owen, James Dastoli, Robert Dastoli, Scotty Crowe, Jayk Gallagher (Students Playing Facemash), Marcella Lentz-Pope (Erica's Roommate), Trevor Wright (B.U. Guy in Bra), Marybeth Massett (Mrs. Cox), Randy Evans (Student in Communications Officer), Carrie Armstrong (Court Reporter), Pamela Roylance (Ad Board Chairwoman), Brian Palermo (CS Lab Professor), Brett Leigh (Phoenix Club Hazer), Chris Gouchoe (Phoenix Club Pledge), Nicholas Tubbs, Kevin Chui, Richard Ferris, Anh Nguyen, Dane Nightingale, Stephen Fuller, John He (A Capella Group), Nick Smoke, Cali Fredrichs (KC's Friends), Steve Sires (Speaker, Bill Gates), Nancy Linari (Larry Summers' Secretary), Aaron Sorkin (Ad Executive), Courtney Arndt (Victoria's Secret Model), Felisha Terrell (Beautiful Woman), Zoe De Toledo (Harvard Rowers' Coxman), Simon Barr, Alex Leigh, Phil Turnham, Richie Steele, Chris Friend, Tom Harvey (Harvard Rowers), Ray Poulter, Bob Hewitt, Dave Lambourn, James Padmore, Sebastian Kouba, Charles Herbert, Robin Dowell, Nathan Hillyer (Hollandia Rowers), Alex Reznik (Prince Albert's

Aide), Oliver Muirhead (Mr. Kenwright), Sarah Shane Adler, Amy Ferguson (Stoned Girls), Monique Edwards (Bank Teller), Cayman Grant (Peter Thiel's Assistant), Scott Lawrence (Maurice), Peter Holden, Darin Cooper (Facebook Lawyers), Jared Hillman (Mackey), Caitlin Gerard (Ashleigh), Lacey Beeman, Cherilyn Rae Wilson (Sorority Girls), Caleb Jones (Fraternity Guy), Franco Vega, Andrew Thacher (Policemen), Alex Olijnyk (Hollandia Rower's Coxman)

The story behind how Harvard student Mark Zuckerberg's claim that he invented Facebook prompted law suits from others who insisted that they were being denied their credit for involvement in the creation of the website as well as the substantial money made from it.

2010 Academy Award winner for Best Adatped Screenplay, Best Film Editing, and Best Original Score.

This film received additional Oscar nominations for picture, actor (Jesse Eisenberg), director, cinematography, and sound mixing.

Andrew Garfield, Joseph Mazzello, Jesse Eisenberg, Patrick Mapel

Jesse Eisenberg, John Getz

Rooney Mara, Jesse Eisenberg

Jesse Eisenberg, Brenda Song, Andrew Garfield

Justin Timberlake, Jesse Eisenberg

Jesse Eisenberg © Columbia Pictures

Max Minghella, Armie Hammer

Armie Hammer, Max Minghella

Chloë Grace Moretz, Kodi Smit-McPhee

Chloë Grace Moretz, Kodi Smit-McPhee

Chloë Grace Moretz

Kodi Smit-McPhee, Chloë Grace Moretz © Overture Films

Kodi Smit-McPhee

Kodi Smit-McPhee

Elias Koteas

Jimmy "Jax" Pinchak, Nicolai Dorian, Dylan Minnette, Brett DelBuono

Richard Jenkins

LET ME IN

(OVERTURE) Producers, Simon Oakes, Alex Brunner, Guy East, Tobin Armbrust, Donna Gigliotti, John Nordling, Carl Molinder; Executive Producers, Nigel Sinclair, John Ptak, Philip Elway, Fredrik Malmberg; Co-Producer, Vicki Dee Rock; Co-Executive Producers, Andy Mayson, Marc Schipper; Director/Screenplay, Matt Reeves; Based on the screenplay and the novel *Lat den rätte kommma in* (*Let the Right One In*) by John Ajvide Lindqvist; Photography, Greig Fraser; Designer, Ford Wheeler; Costumes, Melissa Bruning; Music, Michael Giacchino; Music Supervisor, Liz Gallacher; Editor, Stan Salfas; Special Effects Coordinator, Werner Hahnlein; Visual Effects Supervisors, Brad Parker, Sean Faden, Charlie Itirriaga, Marko Forker, Noel Hooper, Mike Uguccioni; Casting, Avy Kaufman; a Hammer Films production in association with EFTI, presented with Exclusive Media Group; Dolby; Panavision; Technicolor; Rated R; 115 minutes; Release date: October 1, 2010

CAST

Owen	**Kodi Smit-McPhee**
Abby	**Chloë Grace Moretz**
The Father	**Richard Jenkins**
Owen's Mother	**Cara Buono**
The Policeman	**Elias Koteas**
Virginia	**Sasha Barrese**
Larry	**Dylan Kenin**
Jack	**Chris Browning**
Mr. Zoric	**Ritchie Coster**
Kenny	**Dylan Minnette**
Mark	**Jimmy "Jax" Pinchak**
Donald	**Nicolai Dorian**
Nurse	**Rebekah Wiggins**
Seth	**Seth Adkins**
Lanky Kid	**Ashton Moio**
Kenny's Brother	**Brett DelBuono**
Girl in Pool	**Gwendolyn Apple**
Video Arcade Counterman	**Colin Moretz**
Scottie Tate	**Rowbie Orsatti**
Principal	**Brenda Wehle**
Football Players	**Galen Hutchison**, **Dean Satriano**
Admitting Nurse	**Rachel Hroncich**
Day Nurse	**Deborah Mazor**
Train Conductor	**Frank Bond**
Newscaster	**Kayla Anderson**

Tobin Espeset, Ben Bode, Juliet Lopez, Jon Kristian Moore (Paramedics)

A bullied boy befriends a new girl in his neighborhood; little realizing that she is in fact a vampire. Remake of the 2008 Swedish film *Let the Right One In*.

Richard Jenkins, Chloë Grace Moretz

Zoë Kravitz

IT'S KIND OF A FUNNY STORY

(FOCUS) Producers, Kevin Misher, Ben Browning; Executive Producers, Jeremy Kipp Walker, Michael Maher, Peter Rawlinson, Patrick Baker; Directors/Screenplay, Ryan Fleck, Anna Boden; Based on the novel by Ned Vizzini; Photography, Andrij Parkeh; Designer, Beth Mickle; Costumes, Kurt and Bart; Music, Broken Social Scene; Music Supervisor, Andrea von Foerster; Editor, Anna Boden; Casting, Cindy Tolan; a Misher Films production, a Wayfare Entertainment production, presented in association with Wayfare Entertainment; Dolby; Color; Rated PG-13; 100 minutes; Release date: October 8, 2010

CAST

Craig Gilner	**Keir Gilchrist**
Noelle	**Emma Roberts**
Dr. Eden Minerva	**Viola Davis**
Lynn Gilner	**Lauren Graham**
George Gilner	**Jim Gaffigan**
Nia	**Zoë Kravitz**
Bobby	**Zach Galifianakis**
Smitty	**Jeremy Davies**
Humble	**Matthew Maher**
Dr. Mahmoud	**Aasif Mandvi**
Muqtada	**Bernard White**
Solomon	**Daniel London**
The Professor	**Novella Nelson**

MacIntyre Dixon (Roger), Adrian Martinez (Johnny), Lou Myers (Jimmy), Thomas Mann (Aaron), Mary Birdsong (Bobby's Ex), Dana De Vestern (Alissa Gilner), Karen Chilton (Nurse Harper), Jared Goldstein (Ronny), Alan Aisenberg (Scuggs), Rosalyn Coleman (Monica, "Under Pressure" Nurse #1), Molly Hager (Becca), Ato Blankson-Wood (Jennifer), Caitlin Kinnunen (Science Geek), Stephen Scarpulla (HS Director), Jee Young Han (HS Do-Gooder), Leo Allen (Mr. Reynolds), Morgan Murphy (Joanie), Billy McFadden (Little Craig), Susan Blommaert (HS Teacher), Ethan Herschenfeld (Acid Head), Ben Folstein (Neil), Kenya Brome, Delia Reed ("Under Pressure" Nurses), Stewart Steinberg (Charlie, Custodian), Valentina de Angelis (Jenna)

Feeling severly stressed and depressed, a teenager signs himself into a psychiatric hospital, where circumstances force him to reside with the adult patients.

Jeremy Davies, Keir Gilchrist, Emma Roberts © Focus Features

Zach Galifianakis, Keir Gilchrist

STONE

(OVERTURE) Producers, Holly Wiersma, Jordan Schur, David Mimran; Executive Producers, Avi Lerner, Danny Dimbort, Trevor Short, Rene Besson; Co-Producer, Ed Cathell III; Director, John Curran; Screenplay, Angus MacLachlan; Photography, Maryse Alberti; Designer, Tim Grimes; Costumes, Vicki Farrell; Music, Jon Brion; Music Supervisor, Selena Arizanovic; Editor, Alexandre De Franceschi; Casting, Laura Rosenthal; a Mimran Schur Pictures/Holly Wiersma production; Dolby; Super 35 Widescreen; Color; Rated R; 105 minutes; Release date: October 8, 2010

CAST

Jack Mabry	**Robert De Niro**
Gerald Creeson ("Stone")	**Edward Norton**
Lucetta	**Milla Jovovich**
Madylyn Mabry	**Frances Conroy**
Young Jack	**Enver Gjokaj**
Young Madylyn	**Pepper Binkley**
Miss Dickerson	**Sandra Love Aldridge**
Guard Peters	**Greg Trzaskoma**
Candace	**Rachel Loiselle**
Warden	**Peter Lewis**
Janice	**Sarab Kamoo**

Dave Hendricks (Pastor), Wayne David Parker (Frank), Madeline Loiselle (Katie), Kylie Tarnopol, Bailey Tarnopol, Madison Tarnopol (Young Candace), Richard Murphy, Richard Goteri, Ron Lyons (Guards), Linda Boston (Lead Teacher), Jan Cartwright, Jane Burkey, Connie Cowper, Bonnie Clevering (Madelyn's Friends), Wallace Bridges (Police Captain), James Oscar Lee, Marcus Sailor (Sincere Inmates), Brian Peter (Teach, Inmate), David Strohschein, Jason Waugh, Lamont Bell, John Bostic (Inmates), Jordyn Thomas (Child), Rory Mallon (Walters), Trudy Mason (Bobby's Widow), Sammy Publes (Liquor Store Owner), Tevis R. Marcum, Jonathan Stanley, Rod McIntosh (Lucetta's Men), John Lewis (Black Inmate), Chris Molte, Tobiasz Daszkiewicz (White Power Inmates), Troy Coulon (Ex-Con), Mike Shreeman (Larry), Thomas Mahard (Some Guy), Kitty Joy Schur (Girl), Tom Lowell (Infirmary Guard), Bonzai Vitale (ND Driver)

Jack Mabry, a wearied parole officer on the brink of retirement, finds himself taking on a difficult case in a prisoner who will do anything to get out of jail, going so far as to encourage his girlfriend to persuade Jack in her own manner.

Milla Jovovich, Robert De Niro © Overture Films

Robert De Niro

Edward Norton

Robert De Niro, Frances Conroy

SECRETARIAT

(WALT DISNEY PICTURES) Producers, Gordon Gray, Mark Ciardi; Executive Producers, Bill Johnson, Mike Rich; Co-Producer, Kim Winther; Director, Randall Wallace; Screenplay, Mike Rich; Suggested by the book *Secretariat: The Making of a Champion* by William Nack; Photography, Dean Semler; Designer, Tom Sanders; Costumes, Michael T. Boyd; Diane Lane's Costumes, Julie Weiss; Music, Nick Glennie-Smith; Editor, John Wright; Special Effects Coordinator, John Milinac; Casting, Sheila Jaffe; a Mayhem Pictures production; Dolby; Panavision; Deluxe color; Rated PG; 123 minutes; Release date: October 8, 2010

Fred Dalton Thompson, Diane Lane © Walt Disney Pictures

CAST

Penny Chenery	**Diane Lane**
Lucien Laurin	**John Malkovich**
Jack Tweedy	**Dylan Walsh**
Hollis Chenery	**Dylan Baker**
Miss Ham	**Margo Martindale**
Eddie Sweat	**Nelsan Ellis**
Ronnie Turcotte	**Otto Thorwarth**
Bull Hancock	**Fred Dalton Thompson**
Ogden Phipps	**James Cromwell**
Chris Chenery	**Scott Glenn**
E.V. Benjamin	**Mike Harding**
Robert Kleburg	**Richard Fullerton**
John Galbreath	**Tim Ware**
Pancho Martin	**Nestor Serrano**
Laffit Pincay	**Keith Austin**
Bill Nack	**Kevin Connolly**
Andy Beyer	**Eric Lange**
Seth Hancock	**Drew Roy**
Sarah Tweedy	**Carissa Capobianco**
Kate Tweedy	**AJ Michalka**
Chris Tweedy	**Sean Cunningham**
John Tweedy	**Jacob Rhodes**
Earl Jansen	**Graham McTavish**
Jimmy Gaffney	**Tom Foley**
Paul Feliciano	**Grant Whitacre**
Obnoxious Owner	**Forry Smith**
CBS Anchor	**Tom Clark**
Dr. Manuel Gilman	**Ken Strunk**

Dylan Walsh, Dylan Baker, Diane Lane

Jazz Undy, Michael Guthrie (Fans), Cullen Wallace (Che Wannabe), Mike Battaglia (Derby Official), Wynn Reichert (Pastor), Tony Renaud, Tim Layden, Bill Nack (Reporters), Jennifer Trier (Receptionist), Pamela Pryor (Waitress), Kate Ward (Belmont Guest), Andrew Wallace (Belmont Singer), Rusty Hendrickson (Burger Joint Cook), Michael Boyd, Michael Mills (Golfers), Albert Duhon (Berated Stable Hand0, Audrey Scott (6-Year-Old Penny), Slaid Parker (New York Taxi Driver), Joe Chrest (Sports Broadcaster), Jason Schwartz (Spectator), Reid Cherner, Hank Goldberg, Dick Jerardi, John McClain, Jay Privman (Hack Pack), Penny Chenery (Preakness Spectator)

The true story of how Penny Chenery's prize colt Sectretariat broke all records to become the 1973 Triple Crown Winner and one of the greatest race horses of all time.

Drew Roy, Diane Lane

AJ Michalka, Sean Cunningham, Dylan Walsh, Jacob Rhodes,
Carissa Capobianco

Kevin Connolly, Eric Lange

John Malkovich, Diane Lane

Otto Thorwarth, Nelsan Ellis

Sean Cunningham, Margo Martindale, Jacob Rhodes, Diane Lane

Otto Thorwarth

LIFE AS WE KNOW IT

(WARNER BROS.) Producers, Barry Josephson, Paul Brooks; Executive Producers, Denise Di Novi, Scott Niemeyer, Norm Waitt, Katherine Heigl, Nancy Heigl, Bruce Berman; Director, Greg Berlanti; Screenplay, Ian Deitchman, Kristin Rusk Robinson; Photography, Andrew Dunn; Designer, Maher Ahmad; Costumes, Debra McGuire; Music, Blake Neely; Editor, Jim Page; Casting, John Papsidera; a Gold Circle Films/Josephson Entertainment production, presented in association with Village Roadshow Pictures; Dolby; Technicolor; Rated PG-13; 113 minutes; Release date: October 8, 2010

Hayes MacArthur, Christina Hendricks

CAST
Holly Berenson	Katherine Heigl
Eric Messer	Josh Duhamel
Sam	Josh Lucas
Sophie	Alexis Clagett, Brynn Clagett, Brooke Clagett
Alison Novak	Christina Hendricks
Peter Novak	Hayes MacArthur
Janine Groff	Sarah Burns
Beth	Jessica St. Clair
Older Sophie	Brooke Liddell, Kiley Liddell
Amy	Britt Flatmo
Ted	Rob Huebel
DeeDee	Melissa McCarthy
Lonnie	DeRay Davis
Simon	Kumail Nanjiani

Andrew Daly (Scott), Bill Brochtrup (Gary), Will Sasso (Josh), Majandra Delfino (Jenna), Jason MacDonald (Cousin), Tara Ochs (Cousin's Wife), Wilbur Fitzgerald (Peter's Dad), Melissa Ponzio (Victoria, Stripper Cousin), Reggie Lee (Alan Burke), Markus Flanagan (Chef Phillipe), Brook Josephson (Liz), Chanta Rivers (CPS Worker), Eric Phillips (Stoned Teenager), Andy Buckley (George Dunn), L. Warren Young (Officer Young), Johanna Jowett (Jill), Jody Thompsno (Worker), Horace Toney (Court Clerk), Millie Fairchild (Older Woman), Rob Nagle (Neighbor Dad), Katie Kneeland (Patron), Patricia French (Judge Gorling), Ron Clinton Smith (Contractor), Antwan Mills (Airport Security), Steve Nash (Himself), Shayne Kohout (Pregnant Woman with DeeDee), Danielle L. Grant (Ticket Counter Lady), Eddie Frierson (Voice of Sports Announcer)

Josh Duhamel, Clagett Baby © Warner Bros.

When their friends are killed in a car accident, Holly Berenson and Eric Messer, who have never been able to stand one another, are given custody of the baby who has been left behind, forcing them to share a home together while they try to raise the child.

Katherine Heigl, Josh Lucas

Josh Duhamel, Clagett Baby, Katherine Heigl

Mark Hogancamp

© The Cinema Guild

MARWENCOL

(THE CINEMA GUILD) Producers, Jeff Malmberg, Tom Putnam, Matt Radecki, Chris Shellen, Kevin Walsh; Director/Editor, Jeff Malmberg; Photography, Jeff Malmberg, Tom Putnam, Matt Radecki, Kevin Walsh; Music, Ash Black Buffalo; an Open Face production in association with Different by Design; Color; DV; Super 8; Not rated; 83 minutes; Release date: October 8, 2010.

WITH
Mark Hogancamp, Tod Lippy, David Naugle, Emmanuel Nneji, Colleen Vargo

Documentary on how Mark Hogancamp created an alternate universe with his own backyard playset after an attack left him brain-damaged.

JACKASS 3D

(PARAMOUNT) Producers, Jeff Tremaine, Spike Jonze, Johnny Knoxville; Executive Producers, Van Toffler, Derek Fred, Trip Taylor; Co-Producers, Sean Cliver, Dimitry Elyashkevich, Bam Margera; Director, Jeff Tremaine; Screenplay, Preston Lacy; Photography, Dimitry Elyashkevich; Designer, JxPx Blackmon; Music Supervisor, Ben Hochstein; Editors, Seth Casriel, Matthew Probst, Matthew Kosinski; Special Effects Supervisor, Elia P. Popov; Stunts, Charles Grisham, Roy Farfel, Jason Rodiguez, Durk Tyndall; a Dickhouse production, presented with MTV Films; Dolby; Color; 3D; Rated R; 93 minutes; Release date: October 15, 2010

WITH
Johnny Knoxville, Bam Margera, Ryan Dunn, Steve-O, Jason "Wee Man" Acuña, Preston Lacy, Christ Pontius, "Danger Ehren" McGhehey, Dave England, April Margera, Phil Margera, Spike Jonze, Seann William Scott, Jeff Tremaine, Will Oldham, Loomis Fall, Tony Hawk, Eric Koston, Trip Taylor, Rick Kosick, Dimitry Elyashkevich, Greg Iguchi, Brandon Novak, Manny Puig, Judd Leffew, Lance Bangs, Gregory J. Wolf, Josh Brown, Mat Hoffman, Rakeyohn, Omar Von Muller, Wendy de Coito, Madison Clapp, Jack Polick, Sean Cliver, Mike Kassak, Seamus Frawley, Jukka Hilden, Jarno Leppälä, Hannu-Pekka Parviainen, Jarno Laasala, Erik Ainge, Jared Allen, Will Bakey, Andy Bell, Mark Zupan, Tommy Passemante, Parks Bonifay, Jess Margera, Gary Leffew, Brett Leffew, David Weathers, Rip Taylor, John Taylor, Jesse Merlin, Edward Barbanell, David A. Kipper, Kerry Getz, Priya Swaminathan, Scott Shriner, Brian Bell, Rivers Cuomo, Terra Jole, Stevie Lee, Dana Michael Woods, Chris "Little Kato," Tony Elliott, Mark Povinelli, Kevin Thompson, Anne Bellamy, Angie Simms

A group of men subject themselves to a series of deliberately outrageous and often painful stunts, in 3D. Previous entries in the Paramount series: *Jackass* (2002) and *Jackass Number Two* (2006).

Chris Pontius © Paramount Pictures

Bruce Willis, John Malkovich, Helen Mirren

Ernest Borgnine, Karl Urban

Mary-Louise Parker © Summit

RED

(SUMMIT) Producers, Lorenzo di Bonaventura, Mark Vahradian; Executive Producers, Gregory Noveck, Jake Myers; Director, Robert Schwentke; Screenplay, Jon Hoeber, Erich Hoeber; Based on the graphic novel by Warren Ellis, Cully Hamner; Photography, Florian Ballaus; Designer, Alec Hammond; Costumes, Susan Lyall; Music, Christophe Beck; Music Supervisor, Julianne Jordan; Editor, Thom Noble; Special Effects Coordinator, Laird McMurray; Visual Effects Supervisor, James Madigan; Casting, Deborah Aquila, Tricia Wood; a di Bonaventura Pictures production; Dolby; Super 35 Widescreen; Color; Rated PG-13; 110 minutes; Release date: October 15, 2010

CAST

Frank Moses	**Bruce Willis**
Sarah Ross	**Mary-Louise Parker**
Marvin Boggs	**John Malkovich**
Victoria	**Helen Mirren**
William Cooper	**Karl Urban**
Joe Matheson	**Morgan Freeman**
Ivan Simanov	**Brian Cox**
Robert Stanton	**Julian McMahon**
Cynthia Wilkes	**Rebecca Pidgeon**
Henry, the Records Keeper	**Ernest Borgnine**
Gabriel Singer	**James Remar**
Alexander Dunning	**Richard Dreyfuss**

Chris Owens (Hanged Man), Jacqueline Fleming (Marna), Randy Wade Kelley (Paramedic), Jason Giuliano (Endercott), Alec Rayme (Cop at Intersection), Lawrence Turner (Retirement Home Assassin), Emily Kuroda (Mrs. Chan), Joe Chrest (Retirement Home Detective), Justine Wachsberger (Nurse), Tara Yelland (Wilkes' Secretary), Jefferson Brown (Fred), Audrey Wasilewski (Businesswoman), Dimitry Chepovetsky, Matthew Olver (Surveillance Tech), Jason Weinberg (Lead CIA Tactical Officer), Tony De Santis (Security Chief), Greg Bryk (Firefighter), Heidi von Palleske (Neighbor), Neil Whitely (FBI Commander), Robert Morse (Interrogator), Joshua Peace (Interrogation Surveillance Tech), Michelle Nolden (Michelle Cooper), Jake Goodman (Cooper's Son), Tess Goodman (Cooper's Daughter), Desiree Beausoleil (Security Woman), Laura DeCarteret (Fundraiser Greeter), Jonathan Lloyd Walker (Agent Burbacher), Murray McRae (Intro Speaker), Cindy Dukoff (Banquet Guest), Thomas Mitchell (Lone Agent), Bernadette Couture, Chavis Brown, Aaron Khon (Agents)

Retired CIA agent Frank Moses rounds up some former fellow agents in order to help him find out who has ordered him dead, and what is the larger conspiracy behind this plan.

Richard Dreyfuss (back to camera), John Malkovich, Morgan Freeman, Bruce Willis

CONVICTION

(FOX SEARCHLIGHT) Producers, Andrew Sugerman, Andrew S. Karsch, Tony Goldwyn; Executive Producers, Hilary Swank, Markus Barmettler; Director, Tony Goldwyn; Screenplay, Pamela Gray; Photography, Adriano Goldman; Designer, Mark Ricker; Costumes, Wendy Chuck; Music, Paul Cantelon; Muisc Supervisor, Liz Gallacher; Editor, Jay Cassidy; Casting, Kerry Barden, Paul Schnee; a Longfellow Pictures production, an Andrew Sugerman production in association with Oceana Media Finance and Prescience, presented in association with Omega Entertainment; Dolby; Color; Rated R; 107 minutes; Release date: October 15, 2010

CAST

Betty Anne Waters	**Hilary Swank**
Kenny Waters	**Sam Rockwell**
Abra Rice	**Minnie Driver**
Nancy Taylor	**Melissa Leo**
Barry Scheck	**Peter Gallagher**
Mandy Marsh	**Ari Graynor**
Rick	**Loren Dean**
Richard	**Conor Donovan**
Ben	**Owen Campbell**
Roseanna Perry	**Juliette Lewis**
Elizabeth Waters	**Karen Young**
Brenda Marsh	**Clea DuVall**

Thomas Mahard, Laurie Brown (Law Professors), John Pyper-Ferguson (Aidan), Ele Bardha (Don), Rusty Mewha (Desk Sergeant), Marc Macaulay (Officer Boisseau), Bailee Madison (Young Betty Anne), Tobias Campbell (Young Kenny), Frank Zieger (Boyfriend), J. David Moeller (Grandpa), Scott Philyaw (Cop), Tobiasz Daszkiewicz (Guy in Bar), Iris Ingram (Guy's Girlfriend), John Lepard (Minister), Jake Andolina (State Trooper), Talia Balsam (Prosecuting Attorney), Wallace Bridges (Global Van Lines Witness), Marty Bufalini (Defense Attorney), Doug Hamilton (Medical Examiner), Sarab Kamoo (Kathleen Higgins), Hugh McGuire (Trial Judge), Michele Messmer (Mrs. Brow), Annabel Armour (Social Service Woman), Toya Brazell (Court Clerk), Heather Kozlakowski (Jury Foreman), Matt Hollerbach, Zack Fealk (Law Students), Linda Hurd (Bar Exam Woman), Michael Liu (Huy Dao), Paul Burt (Prison Guard "Stash"), York Griffith (Desk Sergeant #2), Gordon Michaels (Lt. Daniels), Alana Jo Beckman (Neighborhood Girl), Ethan Cutkosky (Neighborhood Boy), Eddie Huchro (Courthouse Clerk), Jane Alderman (Mrs. Halloran), Janet Ulrich Brooks (Dr. McGilvray), Gary Davis, Rick Le Fevour (Prison Guards), Jennifer Roberts (Martha Coakley), Linda Boston (Release Judge), Kam Carman, Julia Ho, Peter Carey (Reporters), Melissa Bickerton (Admissions Counselor)

The true story of how Betty Anne Waters earned a law degree in order to prove that her brother was wrongly imprisoned for a murder he didn't commit.

Hilary Swank, Sam Rockwell

Hilary Swank © Fox Searchlight

Minnie Driver, Hilary Swank

Sam Rockwell, Melissa Leo

HEREAFTER

(WARNER BROS.) Producers, Clint Eastwood, Kathleen Kennedy, Robert Lorenz; Executive Producers, Steve Spielberg, Frank Marshall, Tim Moore, Peter Morgan; Director/Music, Clint Eastwood; Screenplay, Peter Morgan; Photography, Tom Stern; Designer, James J. Murakami; Costumes, Deborah Hopper; Editors, Joel Cox, Gary D. Roach; Visual Effects Supervisor, Michael Owens; Casting, Fiona Weir; a Kennedy/ Marshall production, a Malpaso production; Dolby; Panavision; Technicolor; Rated PG-13; 129 minutes; Release date: October 15, 2010

CAST

George Lonegan	**Matt Damon**
Marie LeLay	**Cécile De France**
Billy	**Jay Mohr**
Melanie	**Bryce Dallas Howard**
Marcus/Jason	**George McLaren,**
	Frankie McLaren
Didier	**Thierry Neuvic**
Dr. Rousseau	**Marthe Keller**
Jackie	**Lyndsey Marshal**
Christos	**Richard Kind**

Steven R. Schirripa (Carlo, Cooking Teacher), Jenifer Lewis (Candace), Cyndi Mayo Davis (Island Hotel Clerk), Lisa Griffiths (Stall Owner), Jessica Griffiths (Island Girl), Ferguson Reid, Derek Sakakura (Rescuers), Charlie Creed-Miles (Photographer), Rebekah Staton, Declan Conlon (Social Workers), Marcus Boyea, Franz Drameh, Tex Jacks, Taylor Doherty (Teenagers), Mylène Jampanoï (Reporter Jasmine), Stéphane Freiss (Guillaume Belcher), Laurent Bateau (TV Producer), Calum Grant (Factory Worker), Joe Bellan (Tony), Tom Beard (Priest), Andy Gathergood, Helen Elizabeth (Jackie's Friends), Jean-Yves Berteloot (Publishing Executive Michael), Niamh Cusack, George Costigan (Foster Parents), Claire Price (Marcus' Teacher), Surinder Duhra (Islamic Teacher), Sean Buckley (Dr. Meredith), Audrey Brisson (Hospice Receptionist), Jess Murphy (Dying Woman), Michael Cuckson (Hospice Husband), Jennifer Thorne (Hospice Mother), Barry Martin (Hospice Father), Charlie Holliday (Union Rep), John Nielsen (Factory Supervisor), Anthony Allgood (Visitor), Mathew Baynton (College Receptionist), Pearce Quigley (Channeler), Paul Antony-Barber (Nigel), Meg Wynn Owen (Mirror Lady), Selina Cadell (Mrs. Joyce), Tom Price (Man), Céline Sallette (Secretary), Celia Shuman (Neighbor), Joanna Croll (Tour Guide), Jack Bence (Ricky), Derek Jacobi (Himself), Tim Fitzhigham (Bearded Author), Chloe Bale (Hotel Receptionist)

A construction worker who has tried to resist his psychic gift is drawn into the lives of a French woman who has had visions of the afterlife and a British boy who has lost his twin.

This film received an Oscar nomination for visual effects.

Marthe Keller, Cécile De France © Warner Bros.

Bryce Dallas Howard

Cécile De France, Matt Damon

Frankie McLaren, George McLaren

James Gandolfini, Kristen Stewart

WELCOME TO THE RILEYS

(SAMUEL GOLDWYN FILMS) Producers, Michael Costigan, Giovanni Agnelli, Scott Bloom; Executive Producers, Ken Hixon, Manny Mashouf, Ridley Scott, Tony Scott, Steve Zaillian; Line Producer, Bergen Swanson; Director, Jake Scott; Screenplay, Ken Hixon; Photography, Christopher Soos; Designer, Happy Massee; Costumes, Kim Bowen; Music, Marc Streitenfeld; Music Supervisor, Randall Poster; Editor, Nicolas Gaster; Casting, Elizabeth Coulon; a Destination Films presentation of a Scott Free and Argonaut Pictures production; Dolby; Technicolor; Rated R; 110 minutes; Release date: October 29, 2010

CAST
Doug Riley	**James Gandolfini**
Mallory	**Kristen Stewart**
Lois Riley	**Melissa Leo**
Jerry	**Joe Chrest**
Harriet	**Ally Sheedy**
Tara	**Tiffany Coty**
Vivian	**Eisa Davis**

Lance E. Nichols (Hamilton "Ham" Watkins), Peggy Walton Walker (Brenda), Sharon Landry (Sharon), Kathy Lamkin (Charlene), Kerry Cahill (Waitress), Ken Hixon (Danny), Elliott Grey (Randy), David Jensen (Ed), Greg DiLeo (Ernie), Denee Tyler (Parking Officer), Lara Grice (Sales Clerk), Jack Moore (Roger), George Eaton (Desk Clerk), James Holbrook (Driver), Crhris Kuttruff (Jay-Jay), Kim Collins (Bondsman), Mark Adam (Day Manager), Russell Steinberg (Conventioneer)

A man who has never fully recovered from the loss of his teenage daughter, meets a young runaway girl with whom he forms a platonic bond.

Melissa Leo, James Gandolfini © Samuel Goldwyn Films

CLIENT 9:
THE RISE AND FALL OF ELIOT SPITZER

(MAGNOLIA) Producers, Alex Gibney, Jedd Wider, Todd Wider. Maiken Baird; Co-Producer, Peter Elkind; Executive Producers, Mason Speed Sexton, Molly Thompson, Robert DeBitetto, Robert Sharenow; Director/Screenplay, Alex Gibney; Photography, Maryse Alberti; Music, Pete Nashel; Editor, Plummy Tucker; an A&E IndieFilms in association with Wider Film Projects and Jigsaw Productions presentation; Dolby; Color; Rated R; 117 minutes; Release date: November 5, 2010.

WITH
Eliot Spitzer; **Wrenn Schmidt** (Angelina), **Kim Allen** (Times Square Lip-Sync Singer), **Laura Somma** (Woman on the Train)

Documentary on how New York Governor Eliot Spitzer fell from his prominent position because of a scandal involving prostitution.

Silda Wall Spitzer, Eliot Spitzer © Magnolia

Juliette Lewis, Zach Galifianakis

Robert Downey Jr., Jamie Foxx

Robert Downey Jr., Zach Galifianakis

Michelle Monaghan © Warner Bros.

DUE DATE

(WARNER BROS.) Producers, Todd Phillips, Dan Goldberg; Executive Producers, Thomas Tull, Susan Downey, Scott Budnick; Director, Todd Phillips; Screenplay, Alan R. Cohen, Alan Freedland, Adam Sztykiel, Todd Phillips; Story, Alan R. Cohen, Alan Freedland; Photography, Lawrence Sher; Designer, Bill Brzeski; Costumes, Louise Mingenbach; Music, Christophe Beck; Music Supervisors, Randall Poster, George Drakoulias; Editor, Debra Neil-Fisher; Casting, Juel Bestrop; a Green Hat Films production, presented in association with Legendary Pictures; Dolby; Super 35 Widescreen; Technicolor; Rated R; 95 minutes; Release date: November 5, 2010

CAST

Peter Highman	**Robert Downey Jr.**
Ethan Tremblay	**Zach Galifianakis**
Sarah Highman	**Michelle Monaghan**
Darryl	**Jamie Foxx**
Heidi	**Juliette Lewis**
Lonnie	**Danny McBride**
Airport Screener	**RZA**
TSA Agent	**Matt Walsh**
Limo Driver	**Brody Stevens**
Patrick	**Jakob Ulrich**
Alex	**Naiia Ulrich**
Barry	**Todd Phillips**
Carl	**Bobby Tisdale**

Sharon Morris (Airport X-Ray), Nathalie Fay, Emily Wagner (Flight Attendants), Steven M. Gagnon (Air Marshal), Paul Renteria (Border Guard), Marco Rodriguez (Federali Agent), Mimi Kennedy (Sarah's Mom), Tymberlee Hill (New Mother), Keegan-Michael Key (New Father), Aaron Lustig (Dr. Greene), Jon Cryer (Alan Harper), Charlie Sheen (Charlie Harper).

Tossed off an airplane because of a misunderstanding, Peter Highman is forced to travel cross country with the same lunatic who got him in trouble, in order to get to his wife before she gives birth.

Tim Griffin, Bruce McGill © Summit

Naomi Watts, Sean Penn

FAIR GAME

(SUMMIT) Producers, Bill Pohlad, Janet Zucker, Jerry Zucker, Akiva Goldsman, Jez Butterworth, Doug Liman; Executive Producers, Jeff Skoll, David Bartis, Mari Jo Winkler-Ioffreda, Kerry Foster, Mohammed Khalaf; Co-Producers, Kim Winther, Avram Ludwig, David Sigal; Director/Photography, Doug Liman; Screenplay, Jez Butterworth, John-Henry Butterworth; Based on the books *The Politics of Truth* by Joseph Wilson and *Fair Game* by Valerie Plame Wilson; Designer, Jess Gonchor; Costumes, Cindy Evans; Music, John Powell; Music Supervisor, Julianne Jordan; Editor, Christopher Tellefsen; Casting, Joseph Middleton; a River Road Entertainment and Participant Media presentation in association with Imagenation Abu Dhabi of a River Road/Zucker Productions/Weed Road Pictures/Hypnotic production; Dolby; Color; Rated PG-13; 106 minutes; Release date: November 5, 2010

CAST

Valerie Plame	**Naomi Watts**
Joe Wilson	**Sean Penn**
Sam Plame	**Sam Shepard**
Fred	**Ty Burrell**
Scooter Libby	**David Andrews**
Diana	**Brooke Smith**
Bill ▇	**Noah Emmerich**
Jim Pavitt	**Bruce McGill**
Jack ▇	**Michael Kelly**

Sonya Davison (Chanel Suit), Vanessa Chong, Stephanie Chali (Tabir Secretaries), Anand Tiwari (Hafiz ▇), Jessica Hecht (Sue), Norbert Leo Butz (Steve), Rebecca Rigg (Lisa), Tom McCarthy (Jeff), Ashley Gerasimovich (Samantha Wilson), Quinn Broggy (Trevor Wilson), Nicholas Sadler (CIA Tour Leader), Iris Bahr (CPD Agent), Ghazil (Minister of Mines – Niger), Kristoffer Winters (Joe Turner), Louis Ozara Changchien, Remy Auberjonois (Nervous Analysts), Sean Mahon (CIA Analyst #1), Mohamed Hanaa Abdel Fattah (Professor Badawi), Rashmi Rao (Kim), David Denman (Nervous Dave), Liraz Charhi (Dr. Zahraa ▇), Tim Griffin (Paul ▇), Sunil Malhotra (Ali ▇), Kevin Makely (Jordan Officer #1), Mousa Al Stari (Mukhabarat Officer), Khaled Nabawy (Hammad ▇), Rafat Basel (Hammad's Son), Maysa Abdel Sattar (Hammad's Wife), Judith Resnik (B.U. Professor), Ben Mac Brown, Satya Bhabha (B.U. Students), Nabil Koni, Mohammad Al Sawalqa (Iraqi Scientists), Jenny Maguire (Beth ▇), David Warshofsky (Pete ▇), Geoffrey Cantor (Ariel Fleischer), David Iklu, Deidre Goodwin, Donna Placido (Journalists), Adam LeFevre (Karl Rove), Brian McCormack (Steven Hadley), James Rutledge (Andrew Card), Tricia Munford (Cathie Martin), Michael Goodwin (David Addington), Nasser (Mr. Tabir ▇), Chet Grissom (Dir. of CIA Operations), James Joseph O'Neil (Internal Security Officer), Danni Lang, Jane Lee (Supporters), James Moye, Judy Naier (Field Reporters), Polly Holliday (Diane Plame), Kola Ogundrian, Byron Utley (Businessmen), Anastasia Barzee (Right Wing Reporter), Sanousi Sesay (DC Cab Driver)

Adam LeFevre, David Andrews

When the Bush administration ignores diplomat Joe Wilson's report on the absence of weapons of mass destruction in Iraq, he makes his findings public, prompting them to retaliate by exposing his wife's position as a CIA agent.

Sam Shepard, Naomi Watts

127 HOURS

(FOX SEARCHLIGHT) Producers, Christian Colson, Danny Boyle, John Smithson; Executive Producers, Bernard Bellew, John J. Kelly, François Ivernel, Cameron McCracken, Lisa Marie Falcone, Tessa Ross; Director, Danny Boyle; Screenplay, Danny Boyle, Simon Beaufoy; Based on the book *Between a Rock and a Hard Place* by Aron Ralston; Photography, Anthony Dod Mantle, Enrique Chediak; Designer/Costumes, Suttirat Larlarb; Music, A.R. Rahman; Song: "If I Rise" music by A.R. Rahman, lyrics by Dido and Rollo Armstrong; Editor, Jon Harris; Casting, Donna Isaacson; a Pathé presentation in association with Everest Entertainment of a Cloud Eight/Decibel Films/Darlow Smithson production; Dolby; Super 35 Widescreen; Technicolor; Rated R; 94 minutes; Release date: November 5, 2010

James Franco, Clémence Poésy

CAST

Aron Ralston	**James Franco**
Kristi	**Kate Mara**
Megan	**Amber Tamblyn**
Aron's Friend	**Sean A. Bott**
Aron, age 5	**Koleman Stinger**
Aron's Dad	**Treat Williams**
Brian	**John Lawrence**
Aron's Mom	**Kate Burton**
Sonja, age 10	**Bailee Michelle Johnson**
Aron, age 15	**Parker Hadley**
Rana	**Clémence Poésy**
Blue John	**Fenton G. Quinn**
Sonja	**Lizzy Caplan**
Boy on Sofa	**P.J. Hull**
Eric Meijer	**Pieter Jan Brugge**
Monique Meijer	**Rebecca Olson**
Andy Meijer	**Jeffrey Wood**
Dan	**Norman Lehnert**
Helicopter Co-Pilot	**Xmas Lutu**
Helicopter Pilot	**Terry S. Mercer**
Zach	**Darin Southam**

The true story of how Aron Ralston spent 127 hours trapped in an isolated slot canyon before resorting to drastic means to free himself and save his life.

This film received Oscar nominations for picture, actor (James Franco), adapted screenplay, film editing, original score, and original song ("If I Rise").

James Franco, Kate Mara, Amber Tamblyn

James Franco

James Franco

James Franco

James Franco

James Franco

James Franco © Fox Searchlight

MEGAMIND

(DREAMWORKS) Producers, Lara Breay, Denise Nolan Cascino; Executive Producers, Stuart Cornfeld, Ben Stiller; Director, Tom McGrath; Screenplay, Alan Schoolcraft, Brent Simons; Designer, David James; Art Director, Timothy J. Lamb; Music, Hans Zimmer, Lorne Balfe; Editor, Michael Andrews; Head of Story, Catherine Yuh Rader; Head of Character Animation, Jason Schleifer; Visual Effects Supervisor, Philippe Denis; Head of Layout, Nol Le Meyer; Stereoscopic Supervisor, Phil Captain 3D McNally; a DreamWorks Animation SKG Presentation of a PDI/DreamWorks production; Distributed by Paramount; Dolby; Color; 3D; Rated PG; 95 minutes; Release date: November 5, 2010

Metroman

VOICE CAST

Megamind	**Will Ferrell**
Roxanne Ritchie	**Tina Fey**
Titan	**Jonah Hill**
Minion	**David Cross**
Metro Man	**Brad Pitt**
Megamind's Father	**Justin Theroux**
Bernard	**Ben Stiller**
Megamind's Mother	**Jessica Schulte**
Lord Scott/Prison Guard	**Tom McGrath**
Lady Scott	**Emily Nordwind**
Warden	**J.K. Simmons**

Ella Olivia Stiller, Quinn Dempsey Stiller (Schoolchildren), Brian Hopkins (Prisoner), Christopher Knights (Prison Guard), Mike Mitchell (Father in Crowd), Jasper Johannes Andrews (Crying Baby), Jack Blessing (Newscaster), Stephen Kearin (Mayor)

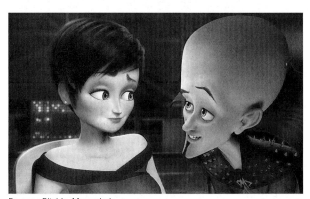
Roxanne Ritchie, Megamind

When brilliant but unsuccessful super-villain Megamind finally manages to defeat his nemesis, Metro Man, he takes over Metro City only to realize that he must face a new villain.

Roxanne Ritchie, Minion

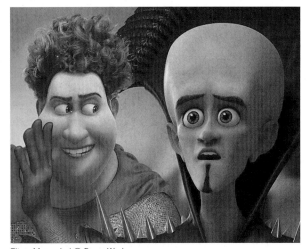
Titan, Megamind © DreamWorks

Janet Jackson, Omari Hardwick

Kimberly Elise, Michael Ealy © Lionsgate

FOR COLORED GIRLS

(LIONSGATE) Producers, Tyler Perry, Paul Hall, Roger M. Bobb; Director/Screenplay, Tyler Perry; Based upon the stage play entitled *For Colored Girls Who Have Considered Suicide When the Rainbow is Enuf* by Ntozake Shange; Executive Producers, Ozzie Areu, Joseph P. Genier, Nzingha Stewart, Michael Paseornek; Photography, Alexander Gruszynski; Designer, Ina Mayhew; Costumes, Johnetta Boone; Music, Aaron Zigman; Music Supervisor, Joel C. High; Editor, Maysie Hoy; Co-Producer, Charisse Nesbit; Casting, Robi Reed; a 34th Street Films presentation; Dolby; Deluxe color; Rated R; 134 minutes; Release date: November 5, 2010

CAST
Crystal/Brown	**Kimberly Elise**
Jo/Red	**Janet Jackson**
Juanita/Green	**Loretta Devine**
Tangie/Orange	**Thandie Newton**
Yasmine/Yellow	**Anika Noni Rose**
Kelly/Blue	**Kerry Washington**
Nyla/Purple	**Tessa Thompson**
Gilda	**Phylicia Rashad**
Alice/White	**Whoopi Goldberg**
Rose	**Macy Gray**
Beau Willie	**Michael Ealy**
Carl	**Omari Hardwick**
Frank	**Richard Lawson**
Donald	**Hill Harper**
Bill	**Khalil Kain**
Renee	**Rayna Tharani**
Kenya	**Jaycee Williams**
Kwame	**Thomas "Deuce" Jessup**
Katina	**May Zayan**
Dr. Davis	**John Crow**
Driver	**Joe Amato**
Girl #1	**Ambrya Underwood**
Nurses	**Jackie Prucha, Roevely Rancell**
Waitress	**Holly Crawshaw**
Security Guard	**David Feigenbaum**

Michael Cory Davis, Jason Graham, Ayo Sorrells, Kendrick Cross (Men), Karen Slack, Andrea Jones-Sojola, Jeanette Illidge (Sopranos), Jazmia Battle, Morgan Caldwell, Sakinah Davis, Ashlee Gillum, Chantia Robinson, Sarah Soto, Alexis Whitehead, Brionna Williams (Dancers)

A look into the lives of nine different women as their stories of turmoil and damaged relationships intersect.

Anika Noni Rose, Kerry Washington, Janet Jackson, Kimberly Elise, Phylicia Rashad, Loretta Devine, Tessa Thompson, Thandie Newton

Whoopi Goldberg, Tessa Thompson

Diane Keaton

Rachel McAdams, Diane Keaton, Harrison Ford

Rachel McAdams © Paramount Pictures

MORNING GLORY

(PARAMOUNT) Producers, J.J. Abrams, Bryan Burk; Executive Producers, Sherryl Clark, Guy Riedel; Director, Roger Michell; Screenplay, Aline Brosh McKenna; Photography, Alwin Küchler; Designer, Mark Friedberg; Costumes, Frank Fleming; Music, David Arnold; Editors, Dan Farrell, Nick Moore, Steven Weisberg; Associate Producer, Lindsey Weber; Casting, Ellen Lewis, Marcia DeBonis; a Bad Robot production, in association with Goldcrest Pictures Limited; Dolby; Panavision; Deluxe color; Rated PG-13; 102 minutes; Release date: November 10, 2010

CAST
Becky Fuller	**Rachel McAdams**
Mike Pomeroy	**Harrison Ford**
Colleen Peck	**Diane Keaton**
Adam Bennett	**Patrick Wilson**
Jerry Barnes	**Jeff Goldblum**
Lenny Bergman	**John Pankow**
Ernie Appleby	**Matt Molloy**
Becky's Mom	**Patti D'Arbanville**
Paul McVee	**Ty Burrell**

Noah Bean (First Date), Jack Davidson (Dog-Walking Neighbor), Vanessa Aspillaga (Anna), Jeff Hiller (Sam – Channel 9 Producer), Linda Powell (Louanne), Mike Hydeck (Ralph), Joseph J. Vargas (Channel 9 Director), Mario Frieson (Channel 9 Technical Director), Kevin Herbst (Channel 9 Associate Director), Jerome Weinstein (Fred), Stephen Park (Channel 9 Weatherperson), David Fonteno (Oscar), Adrian Martinez (IBS Lobby Guard), J. Elanie Marcos (Lisa Bartlett), Rizwan Manji, Jay Russell, Finnerty Steeves, Rick Younger, Arden Myrin, Caroline Clay, Katharine Hyde, Allen Warnock, Welker White, Maddie Corman, Jeremy Beiler (*Daybreak* Producers), Jonathan Forte (First Intern), Kevin Pariseau (Horse Teeth Reporter), Chris Sieber (Groundhog Reporter), Liz Keifer (Jerry's Wife), Lauren Cohn (Crafts Expert), Jayne Houdyshell (Stage Manager), Miguel A. Hernandez Jr. (Editor), Alice Callahan (Girl at Schiller's), Miles O'Brien (IBS Anchorperson), Elaine Kaufman, Bob Schieffer, Morley Safer, Chris Matthews, Curtis "50Cent" Jackson, Tony Yayo, DJ Whoo Kid, Lloyd Banks (Themselves), Don Roy King (Merv, *Daybreak* Director), Robert Caminiti (*Daybreak* Associate Director), Stefani I. Cohen (*Daybreak* Timing Production Assistant), Gray Winslow (*Daybreak* Technical Director), Kristine Nielsen (Fan), Paul Uricoli (IBS Evening News Producer), Rosalynd Darling (*Daybreak* Fan on Plaza), Gio Perez (Second Intern), Pepper Brinkley (Jerry's Assistant), Steve McAuliff (Animal Expert), Vincent J. Robinson (Bagpiper), Don Hewitt, Sr. (Joe the Cameraperson), Reed Birney (Governor Willis), Carmen M. Herlihy (Becky's Assistant), Bruce Altman, Kathleen McNenny, Jason Kravits (Television Executives), John Bundy (Magician)

After Becky Fuller is put in charge of a struggling morning news show, she attempts to bring fresh life to the program by hiring Mike Pomeroy to co-anchor the show, against his better judgment.

Rachel McAdams, Harrison Ford

SKYLINE

(UNIVERSAL) Producers, The Brothers Strause, Kristian James Andresen, Liam O'Donnell; Executive Producers, Ryan Kavanaugh, Brett Ratner, Tucker Tooley, Brian Tyler, Brian Kavanaugh-Jones; Co-Producer, Paul Barry; Line Producer, Tracey Landon; Directors/Visual Effects Supervisors, The Brothers Strause (Colin Strause, Greg Strause); Screenplay, Joshua Cordes, Liam O'Donnell; Photography, Michael Watson; Designer, Drew Dalton; Costumes, Bobbie Mannix; Music, Matthew Margeson; Editor, Nicholas Wayman Harris; Creature Designers, Alec Gillis, Tom Woodruff Jr.; Casting, Liz Dean; a Rogue presentation of a Hydraulix Entertainment production , a Transmission production, a Relativity Media production in association with Rat Entertainment; Dolby; Color; Rated PG-13; 94 minutes; Release date: November 12, 2010

CAST
Jarrod	**Eric Balfour**
Elaine	**Scottie Thompson**
Candice	**Brittany Daniel**
Denise	**Crystal Reed**
Ray	**Neil Hopkins**
Oliver	**David Zayas**
Terry	**Donald Faison**

Robin Gammell (Walt), Tanya Newbould (Jen), J. Paul Boehmer (Colin), Phet Mahathongdy O'Donnell (Airplane Mom/Bartender), Byron McIntyre (Limo Driver), Jackie Marin (Girl in Pool), Tony Black (Derek), Eliza Till (Girl at Party), James Huang, Erik Rondell (Soldiers), Johnny De Beer (Rocket Soldier), Lauren Marin (Abducted Girl), Matt Frels (Abducted Guy), Pam Levin (Pregnant Abductee)

Extra-terrestrials descend upon Earth with the intent of consuming the population, prompting a group of terrified Los Angelenos to take refuge in an apartment building where they hope to battle the aliens and stay alive.

Eric Balfour, Scottie Thompson

© Universal Studios

Lena Dunham, David Call

Lena Dunham, Jemima Kirke © IFC Films

TINY FURNITURE

(IFC FILMS) Producers, Kyle Martin, Alicia Van Couvering; Co-Producer, Alice Wang; Director/Screenplay, Lena Dunham; Photography, Jody Lee Lipes; Art Directors, Chris Trujillo, Jade Healy; Music, Teddy Blanks; Editor, Lance Edmands; a Tiny Ponies production; Dolby; Color; Not rated; 98 minutes; Release date: November 12, 2010

CAST
Aura	**Lena Dunham**
Siri	**Laurie Simmons**
Nadine	**Grace Dunham**
Candice	**Rachel Howe**
Frankie	**Merritt Wever**
Charlotte	**Jemima Kirke**

Alex Karpovsky (Jed), David Call (Keith), Amy Seimetz (Ashlynn), Graland Hunter (Noelle), Isen Ritchie (Jacob), Mike S. Ryan (Homeless Man)

Aura, a recent college graduate, returns to her family's TriBeCa loft in order to come to terms with her past life and what the future holds for her.

UNSTOPPABLE

(20TH CENTURY FOX) Producers, Julie Yorn, Tony Scott, Mimi Rogers, Eric McLeod, Alex Young; Executive Producers, Chris Ciaffa, Rick Yorn, Jeff Kwatinetz; Director, Tony Scott; Screenplay, Mark Bomback; Photography, Ben Seresin; Designer, Chris Seagers; Costumes, Penny Rose; Music, Harry Gregson-Williams; Editors, Chris Lebenzon, Robert Duffy; Co-Producer, Lee Trink; Casting, Denise Chamian; Stunts, Gary Powell; a Prospect Park/Scott Free production; Dolby; Super 35 Widescreen; Deluxe Color; Rated PG-13; 98 minutes; Release date: November 12, 2010

CAST

Frank Barnes	**Denzel Washington**
Will Colson	**Chris Pine**
Yardmaster Connie Hooper	**Rosario Dawson**
Dewey	**Ethan Suplee**
Galvin	**Kevin Dunn**
Inspector Werner	**Kevin Corrigan**
Bunny	**Kevin Chapman**
Ned	**Lew Temple**
Gilleece	**T.J. Miller**
Darcy	**Jessy Schram**
Judd Stewart	**David Warshofsky**
Janeway	**Andy Umberger**
Nicole	**Elizabeth Mathis**
Maya	**Meagan Tandy**
Michael Colson	**Dylan L. Bruce**
Clark	**Jeff Hochendoner**
Ryan Scott	**Ryan Ahern**
Baker	**Christopher Lee Philips**
Hoffman	**Kevin McClatchy**
Galvin's Assistant	**Toni Saldana**
Captain Allen	**Patrick F. McDade**
Red Truck Driver	**Bill Laing**
Brewster Dispatcher	**Scott A. Martin**
Devereaux	**Richard Pelzman**
Diner Waitress	**Lissa Brennan**
Findlay Police Officer	**Barry Ben Sr.**
Findlay Reporter	**Heather Leigh**
Horse Trailer Owner	**Carla Bianco**
Hazmat Worker	**Keith Michael Gregory**
RA Official	**L. Derek Leonidoff**
Marie, Checkout Girl	**Gretchen Bluemle**
Mrs. Hermann, Old Lady	**Diane Jonardi**

Aisha Hinds (Railway Safety Campaign Coordinator), Khalio Walker, Gilda Estelle Chestney, Kam Bott, Kevin Bott, Max Schuler (Hero Kids), Corey Parker Robinson (Lead Officer #1), Christopher Stadulis (Police Officer #2), Alicia Murton (Teacher), David Flick (Train Engineer), Jeff Wincott (Jesse – Will's Brother), Nathan Hollabaugh (Young Cop), Rebecca Harris (Pauline), Rick Chambers, Mike Clark, Tom Stoviak, Ellen Gamble, Shelby Camptella, Adrienne Wehr (News Reporters), Wililam Ward III, Jennifer Boresz (Reporters), Victor Gojcaj (Groundman), Maxx Hennard (Tower Operator), Joe Coyle, Dihlon McManne, Charoles Van Eman (GEO Golfers), Joshua Elijah Reese (Young Engineer), John D. Leonard, Thomas Riley (Brewster Men), Jeremiah Fragale (Cop), Jason McCune (Radar Gun Cop), Adam Kroloff (Railroad Spokesperson), Jake Andolina (Evacuation Police Officer), Jarrod DiGiorgi, Tami Dixon, Sean Derry (Control Room Staff), Amy Arce (TV Reporter), Matt Cates (State Trooper), Chase Ellison (Teenage Witness), Juan M. Fernandez (White Shirt Reporter), Steven Gonzales (Another News Reporter), Rick Rader (Train Employee Witness), Carly Steel (Reporter in Helicopter), Warren Sweeney (Press Representative), Stephen Monroe Taylor (Truck Driver), Stephen Nelson (Reporter at Keating Summit), Christie Stawicki (Onlooker)

A veteran engineer and a young conductor race against time to catch up with and stop an unmanned 39-car train carrying a powerful cargo of combustible liquids.

This film received an Oscar nomination for sound editing.

Chris Pine, Denzel Washington © 20th Century Fox

Chris Pine

Chris Pine

Chris Pine

Denzel Washington, Chris Pine

Rosario Dawson

Denzel Washington

Denzel Washington

Alan Rickman

Bill Nighy, Emma Watson, Rupert Grint, Daniel Radcliffe

Ralph Fiennes, Jason Isaacs

Daniel Radcliffe (in front of) Mark Williams, David Thewlis, Robbie Coltrane

HARRY POTTER AND THE DEATHLY HALLOWS PART 1

(WARNER BROS.) Producers, David Heyman, David Barron, J.K. Rowling; Executive Producer, Lionel Wigram; Co-Producers, John Trehy, Tim Lewis; Director, David Yates; Screenplay, Steve Kloves; Based on the novel by J.K. Rowling; Photography, Eduardo Serra; Designer, Stuart Craig; Costumes, Jany Temime; Music, Alexandre Desplat; Editor, Mark Day; Visual Effects Supervisor, Tim Burke; Special Makeup Effects, Nick Dudman; Casting, Fiona Weir; a Heyday Films production; Dolby; Panavision; Color; Rated PG-13; 146 minutes; Release date: November 19, 2010

CAST

Harry Potter	**Daniel Radcliffe**
Ron Weasley	**Rupert Grint**
Hermione Granger	**Emma Watson**
Bellatrix Lestrange	**Helena Bonham Carter**
Rubeus Hagrid	**Robbie Coltrane**
Lord Voldemort	**Ralph Fiennes**
Alastor "Mad-Eye" Moody	**Brendan Gleeson**
Xenophilius Lovegood	**Rhys Ifans**
Lucius Malfoy	**Jason Isaacs**
Rufus Scrimgeour	**Bill Nighy**
Professor Severus Snape	**Alan Rickman**
Dolores Umbridge	**Imelda Staunton**
Molly Weasley	**Julie Walters**
Arthur Weasley	**Mark Williams**
Draco Malfoy	**Tom Felton**
Dobby	**Toby Jones**
Ginny Weasley	**Bonnie Wright**
Fred Weasley	**James Phelps**
George Weasley	**Oliver Phelps**
Luna Lovegood	**Evanna Lynch**
Vernon Dursley	**Richard Griffiths**
Dudley Dursley	**Harry Melling**
Hermione's Dad	**Ian Kelly**
Hermione's Mum	**Michelle Fairley**
Petunia Dursley	**Fiona Shaw**
Charity Burbage	**Carolyn Pickles**
Narcissa Malfoy	**Helen McCrory**
Wormtail	**Timothy Spall**
Yaxley	**Peter Mullan**
Pius Thicknesse	**Guy Henry**
Antonin Dolohov	**Arben Bajraktaraj**
Professor Albus Dumbledore	**Michael Gambon**
Fleur Delacour	**Clémence Poésy**
Ollivander	**John Hurt**
Remus Lupin	**David Thewlis**
Kreacher	**Simon McBurney**

Graham Duff, Adrian Annis, Emil Hostina, Paul Khanna, Richard Strange, Anthony John Crocker, Peter G. Reed, Granville Saxton, Judith Sharp, Ashley McGuire, Penelope McGhie, Bob Yves Van Hellenberg Hubar, Tony Kirwood, Jon Campling, Simon Grover (Death Eaters), Rod Hunt (Thorfinn Rowle), Suzanne Toase (Alecto Carrow), Ralph Ineson (Amycus Carrow), David Ryall (Elphias Doge), George Harris (Kingsley Shacklebolt), Andy Linden (Mundungus Fletcher), Domhnall Gleeson (Bill Weasley), Natalia Tena (Nymphadora Tonks), Frances de La Tour (Madame Maxime), Matyelok Gibbs (Auntie Muriel), Eva Alexander (Waitress), Matthew Lewis (Neville Longbottom), Devon Murray (Seamus Finnigan), William Melling (Nigel), Freddie Stroma (Cormac McLaggen), Amber Evans, Ruby Evans (Twins), Katie Leung (Cho Chang), David O'Hara (Albert Runcorn), Steffan Rhodri (Reg Cattermole), Nick Moran (Scabior), Sophie Thompson (Mafalda Hopkirk), Daniel Tuite (Skinny Ministry Wizard), Daisy Haggard (Ministry Lift Voice),

George Potts (Balding Wizard), Rose Keegan (Red Haired Witch), Ned Dennehy (Scared Man), Kate Fleetwood (Mary Cattermole), Rade Serbedzija (Gregorovitch), Jamie Campbell Bower (Young Grindelwald), Hazel Douglas (Bathilda Bagshot), Adrian Rawlins (James Potter), Geraldine Sommerville (Lily Potter), Miranda Richardson (Rita Skeeter), Michael Byrne (Gellert Grindelwald), David Legeno (Fenrir Greyback), Samuel Roukin (Snatcher), Warwick Davis (Griphook)

As Voldemort's Death Eaters seize control of the Ministry of Magic, Harry Potter and his friends Ron and Hermione attempt to track down and destroy the Horcruxes that will allow them to vanquish Voldemort. The seventh film in the Warner Bros. series following *Harry Potter and the Sorcerer's Stone* (2001), *Harry Potter and the Chamber of Secrets* (2002), *Harry Potter and the Prisoner of Azkaban* (2004), *Harry Potter and the Goblet of Fire* (2005), *Harry Potter and the Order of the Phoenix* (2007), and *Harry Potter and the Half-Blood Prince* (2009). The second half of this installment, and the series finale, was released on July 15, 2011.

This film received Oscar nominations for art direction and visual effects.

Daniel Radcliffe, Clémence Poésy, Robbie Coltrane, Dohmnall Gleeson, Mark Williams

Daniel Radcliffe, Emma Watson, Rupert Grint

Sophie Thompson, Daniel Radcliffe, Kate Fleetwood, Steffan Rhodri

Rhys Ifans

Robbie Coltrane, Daniel Radcliffe © Warner Bros.

THE NEXT THREE DAYS

(LIONSGATE) Producers, Olivier Delbosc, Marc Missonnier, Michael Nozik, Paul Haggis; Executive Producers, Agnes Mentre, Anthony Katagas; Director/Screenplay, Paul Haggis; Based on the film *Pour Elle*, by Fred Cavayé, with a screenplay by Fred Cavayé and Guillaume Lemans; Photography, Stéphane Fontaine; Designer, Laurence Bennett; Costumes, Abigail Murray; Music, Danny Elfman; Editor, Jo Francis; Co-Producer, Eugenie Grandval; Casting, Randi Hiller; a Highway 61 Films production; Dolby; Deluxe color; Rated PG-13; 133 minutes; Release date: November 19, 2010

CAST

John Brennan	**Russell Crowe**
Lara Brennan	**Elizabeth Banks**
George Brennan	**Brian Dennehy**
Lieutenant Nabulsi	**Lennie James**
Nicole	**Olivia Wilde**
Luke	**Ty Simpkins**
Grace Brennan	**Helen Carey**
Damon Pennington	**Liam Neeson**
Detective Quinn	**Jason Beghe**
Meyer Fisk	**Daniel Stern**
David	**Jonathan Tucker**
Mouss	**RZA**
Alex	**Kevin Corrigan**

Michael Buie (Mick Brennan), Moran Atias (Erit), Remy Nozik (Jenna), Toby Green, Tyler Green (Three Year Old Luke), Aisha Hinds (Det. Collero), Veronica Brown, Lisa Ann Goldsmith (Guards), Leslie Merrill (Elizabeth Gesas), Alissa Haggis (Junkie), James Donis (Prison Major), Rachel Deacon (Duty Nurse), Glenn Taranto (Hospital Security Guard), Derek Cecil (Dr. Becsey), Kaitlyn Wylde (Julie), Zachary Sondrini (Photoshop Kid), Lauren Haggis (Lyla), Tyrone Giordano (Mike), James Ransone (Harv), Etta Cox (Notary), Barry Bradford (Jail Guard, Entry Hall), Rick Warner (County Jail Captain), James Francis Kelly III (Lab Van Driver), Denise Dal Vera (Eugenie), Nazanin Boniadi (Elaine), Jeff Hochendoner (Alex's Thug Buddy), Allan Steele (Sgt. Harris), Quantia Mali (Phone Operator), Trudie Styler (Dr. Byrdie Lifson), David Flick (Male Nurse), Fabio Polanco (Phone Repairman), Sean Huze, Jonathan Berry (Prison Guards), Tamara Gorski (Hospital Nurse), Patrick Brennan (Hospital Guard), Brenna McDonough (Brenda), Kathy Fitzgerald (Neighbor), Tom Quinn (Elderly Man), Melissa Jackson (Air Canada Clerk), Patrick F. McDade (Airport Security Chief)

After his wife is arrested and incarcerated for a crime she didn't commit, and their final appeal is rejected, John Brennan decides that the only solution is to break her out of prison.

Liam Neeson, Russell Crowe

Ty Simpkins, Elizabeth Banks

Olivia Wilde, Russell Crowe

Russell Crowe, Daniel Stern © Lionsgate

Anne Hathaway, Jake Gyllenhaal

Anne Hathaway, Jake Gyllenhaal © 20th Century Fox

Jake Gyllenhaal, Oliver Platt

Josh Gad, Jake Gyllenhaal

LOVE AND OTHER DRUGS

(20TH CENTURY FOX) Producers, Scott Stuber, Edward Zwick, Marshall Herskovitz, Charles Randolph, Pieter Jan Brugge; Executive Producers, Arnon Milchan, Margaret Riley; Director, Edward Zwick; Screenplay, Charles Randolph, Edward Zwick, Marshall Herskovitz; Based on the book *Hard Sell: The Evolution of a Viagra Salesman* by Jamie Reidy; Photography, Steven Fierberg; Designer, Patti Podesta; Costumes, Deborah L. Scott; Music, James Newton Howard; Music Supervisor, Randall Poster; Editor, Seven Rosenblum; Casting, Victoria Thomas; a Fox 2000 Pictures and Regency Enterprises presentation of a New Regency/Stuber Pictures/Bedford Falls production; Dolby; Super 35 Widescreen; Deluxe Color; Rated R; 112 minutes; Release date: November 24, 2010

CAST
Jamie Randall	**Jake Gyllenhaal**
Maggie Murdock	**Anne Hathaway**
Bruce Winston	**Oliver Platt**
Dr. Stan Knight	**Hank Azaria**
Josh Randall	**Josh Gad**
Trey Hannigan	**Gabriel Macht**
Cindy	**Judy Greer**
Dr. James Randall	**George Segal**
Nancy Randall	**Jill Clayburgh**

Kate Jennings Grant (Gina), Katheryn Winnick ("Lisa"), Kimberly Scott (Gail), Peter Friedman (California Man), Nikki Deloach (Christy), Natalie Gold (Dr. Helen Randall), Megan Ferguson (Farrah), Michael Benjamin Washington (Richard), Bingo O'Malley (Sam), Dorothy Silver (Sophie), Lucy Roucis (Un-Convention Parkinson's Speaker), Joan Augustin (Joan), Michael Chernus (Jerry), Kate Easton (Amber), Michael Buffer (Pfizer Convention MC), Maite Schwartz (Texas), Max Osinski (Ned), Ian Harding, Josh Breslow, Ian Novick, Tess Soltau, Constance Brenneman, Nicole Thomas, Jasper Soffer (Pfizer Trainees), Kwame Rakes (Doctor in Parking Lot), Scott Cohen (Ted Golstein), Sharon Wilkins (La Boheme Receptionist), Brian Hutchison (Homeless Man), Dana Dancho (Smiling Receptionist), Lisa Ann Goldsmith (Nurse Janice), Rick Applegate (Viagra Doctor), Ray Godshall (Friendly Senior), Jean Zarzour (Viagra Sample Nurse), Harry O'Toole (Man with Walker), Jennifer Delaeo (Viagra Receptionist), Deidre Goodwin, Geneva Carr, Vanessa Asprillaga (Viagra Nurses), Patricia Cray (Kindly-Looking Woman), Frank Catanzazo, Brian E. Jay, Frank Ferraro, Judy Pergl, Kim Cagni, K (Themselves), Kristin Spatafore, Larissa S. Emanuele (Convention Girls), Loretta Higgins (PET Scan Doctor), Kimberyl M. Rizzo (Front Desk Receptionist), Jason Bernard (Quack Doctor), Nicole Perrone (Determined Receptionist), Jo Newman (Bree), Christina Fandino (Khae), Teri Clark Linden (ER Receptionist), Keivn McClatchy (Justin)

A fast-talking, womanizing pharmaceutical salesman meets his challenge when he falls in love with an independent young woman afflicted with early onset Parkinson's disease.

Alan Cumming

Cam Gigandet

Christina Aguilera, Eric Dane © Screen Gems

Cher

Christina Aguilera, Cher

Julianne Hough, Kristen Bell

Peter Gallagher

Stanley Tucci, Cher

Christina Aguilera

BURLESQUE

(SCREEN GEMS) Producer, Donald De Line; Executive Producers, Stacy Kolker Cramer, Risa Shapiro; Director/Screenplay, Steven Antin; Photography, Bojan Bazelli; Designer, Jon Gary Steele; Costumes, Michael Kaplan; Music, Christophe Beck; Music Supervisor, Buck Damon; Executive Music Producer, Christina Aguilera; Executive Music Consultant, C. "Tricky" Stewart; Choreographers, Denise Faye, Joey Pizzi; Editor, Virginia Katz; Casting, John Papsidera; a De Line Pictures production; Dolby; Super 35 Widescreen; Deluxe color; Rated PG-13; 119 minutes; Release date: November 24, 2010

CAST

Tess	**Cher**
Ali	**Christina Aguilera**
Marcus	**Eric Dane**
Jack	**Cam Gigandet**
Georgia	**Julianne Hough**
Alexis	**Alan Cumming**
Vince	**Peter Gallagher**
Nikki	**Kristen Bell**
Sean	**Stanley Tucci**
Natalie	**Dianna Agron**
Harold Saint	**Glynn Turman**
Mark the DJ	**David Walton**
Dave	**Terrence Jenkins**
Coco	**Chelsea Traille**
Scarlett	**Tanee McCall**
Jesse	**Tyne Stecklein**
Anna	**Paula Van Oppen**
Loretta	**Isabella Hoffman**
Mr. Anderson	**James Brolin**
Dwight	**Stephen Lee**
Preacher	**Denise Faye**
Ali's Hotel Manager	**Baldeep Singh**
Greg	**Michael Landes**
Marla	**Wendy Benson**
Loft Assistant	**Tisha French**
Brittany	**Katerina Mikailenko**
Pary Guest at Marcus' House	**Jay Luchs**
Ditsy Waitress	**Katelynn Tilley**

Gwen Van Dam (Curler Woman at Grundy Bus Stop), Catherine Natale (Curler Woman's Friend), Jonathon Trent (Damon, Bumper Band Member), Blair Redford (James, Bumper Band Member), Taylor Graves, Adam Driggs, Alvino Lewis, Jimmy R.O. Smith, Leah Katz (Bumper Band Members), Melanie Lewis, Sarah Mitchell, Tara Nicole Hughes, Aisha Francis, Deanna Walters, Loriel Hennington (Main Dancers), Robert Kirkland, Black Thomas, Sean Van der Wilt, Corey Anderson, Timor Seffens, Jaquel Knight (Bartenders), Samantha Abrantes, Samantha Faye Lee, Michelle Brooke, Jamie Lee Ruiz (Can Can Dancers), Viktoria Shvartsman, Shannon Beach (Contortionists), Jeskilz, Jenny Robinson, Talia-Lynn Prairie, Meredith Ostrowsky, Katrina Norman, Micki Duran, Ashley Ashida Dixon, Rachele Brooke Smith, Tiana Brown, Jersey Maniscalco, Allison Kyler, Audra Griffis, Jacquelyn Dowsett (Dancers)

Ali arrives in Los Angeles hoping to break into show business and ends up the star attraction at a burlesque club in grave financial danger.

TANGLED

(WALT DISNEY PICTURES) formerly *Rapunzel*; Producer, Roy Conli; Executive Producers, John Lasseter, Glen Keane; Directors, Nathan Greno, Byron Howard; Screenplay, Dan Fogelman; Music, Alan Menken; Original Songs, Alan Menken (music) and Glenn Slater (lyrics); Associate Producer, Aimee Scribner; Editor, Tim Mertens; Visual Effects Supervisor, Steve Goldberg; Art Director, David Goetz; Desginer, Douglas Rogers; Character CG Supervisor, Jesus Canal; Head of Story, Mark Kennedy; Layout Supervisor, Scott Beattie; Animation Supervisors, Glen Keane, John Kahrs; Character TD/Technical Animation Supervisor, Frank Hanner; Dolby; 3D; DeLuxe color; Rated PG; 100 minutes; Release date: November 24, 2010

Flynn Ryder, Pascal

VOICE CAST

Rapunzel	**Mandy Moore**
Flynn Ryder (Eugene FitzHerbert)	**Zachary Levi**
Mother Gothel	**Donna Murphy**
Stabbington Brother	**Ron Perlman**
Captain of the Guard	**M.C. Gainey**
Big Nose Thug	**Jeffrey Tambor**
Hook Hand Thug	**Brad Garrett**
Short Thug	**Paul F. Tompkins**
Vlad	**Richard Kiel**
Young Rapunzel/Little Girl	**Delaney Rose Stein**
Guard #1/Thug #1	**Nathan Greno**
Guard #2/Thug #2	**Byron Howard**
Guard #3	**Tim Mertens**

Michael Bell, Bob Bergen, Susanne Blakeslee, June Christopher, Roy Conli, David Cowgill, Terri Douglas, Chad Einbinder, Pat Fraley, Eddie Frierson, Jackie Gonneau, Nicholas Guest, Bridget Hoffman, Daniel Kaz, Anne Lockhart, Mona Marshall, Scott Menville, Laraine Newman, Paul Pape, Lynwood Robinson, Fred Tatasciore, Hynden Walch, Kari Wahlgren (Additional Voices)

Flynn Ryder, Rapunzel, Pascal

When bandit Flynn Ryder ends up in a tower in which Rapunzel has been imprisoned since childhood by the wicked Mother Grothel, she bargains with him to free her and take her to see the world she's missed out on.

This film received an Oscar nomination for original song ("I See the Light").

Rapunzel

Mime Thug, Flynn Ryder

Hook Hand, Flynn Ryder, Vlad, and Thugs

Maximus, Rapunzel

Rapunzel, Flynn Ryder

Mother Gothel, Rapunzel © Walt Disney Pictures

Flynn Ryder

Mother Gothel (center), the Stabbington Brothers

Billy Bob Thornton, Carla Gugino

Billy Bob Thornton, Moon Bloodgood

Dwayne Johnson © CBS Films

FASTER

(CBS FILMS) Producers, Martin Shafer, Liz Glotzer, Tony Gayton, Robert Teitel; Executive Producers, Joe Gayton, Dara Weintraub; Director, George Tillman Jr.; Screenplay, Tony Gayton, Joe Gayton; Photography, Michael Grady; Designer, David Lazan; Costumes, Salvador Perez; Music, Clint Mansell; Editor, Dirk Westervelt; Casting, Sarah Halley Finn; a TriStar Pictures presentation of a Castle Rock Entertainment/State Street Pictures production; Dolby; Super 35 Widescreen; Color; Rated R; 98 minutes; Release date: November 24, 2010

CAST

Driver	**Dwayne Johnson**
Cop	**Billy Bob Thornton**
Killer	**Oliver Jackson-Cohen**
Cicero	**Carla Gugino**
Lily	**Maggie Grace**
Marina	**Moon Bloodgood**
The Evangelist	**Adewale Akinnouye-Agbaje**
Warden	**Tom Berenger**
Roy Grone	**Mike Epps**
Sergeant Mallory	**Xander Berkeley**

Mauricio Lopez (Prison Guard), James Gaines (Inmate), Jan Hoag (Receptionist), Courtney Gains (Telemarketer), Michael Irby (Vaquero), Josh Clark (Uniform), Michael Blain-Rozgay (TV Anchor), Sid S. Liufau (Kenny), Aaron Behr, Jeffrey Daniel Phiilips (Cohorts), Matt Gerald (Driver's Brother), John Cirigiliano (Old Guy), Jonna Walsh (Teen Girl), Kiyomi Calloway (Little Girl), Aedin Mincks (Tommy), Michole Briana White (TV Anchor #2), Clint Palmer (Ranch House Husband), Jennifer Carpenter (Woman), Stephanie Nash (TV Reporter), Geraldine Kearns (Preacher's Wife), Buzz Belmondo (Preacher), Lester Speight (Baphomet), Ski Cutty Carr (Bouncer), Steven Charles (Cowboy), Julia Pace Mitchell (Cashier), Jack Wallace (Bathroom Attendant), Julius Tennon, Seth Burben (Doctors), Sara Arrington, Stacey Ashmont (Nurses), Annie Corley (Mother), Jeffri Kent Norat (Detective), Nadja Minyon (Evangelist's Wife),

An ex-con sets out to kill those who double-crossed him during a heist and caused the death of his brother.

Maggie Grace, Oliver Jackson–Cohen

I LOVE YOU PHILLIP MORRIS

(ROADSIDE ENTERTAINMENT) Producers, Andrew Lazar, Far Shariat; Executive Producer, Luc Besson; Line Producer, Richard Middleton; Co-Producer, Miri Yoon; Associate Producers, Jeffrey Harlacker, Linda Fields Hill; Directors/ Screenplay, John Requa, Glenn Ficarra; Based on the book by Steven McVicker; Photography, Xavier Grobert; Designer, Hugo Luczyc-Wyhowski; Costumes, David C. Robinson; Music, Nick Urata; Music Supervisor, Gary Calamar; Editor, Thomas J. Nordberg; Casting, Bernie Telsey; a EuroCorp presentation of a Mad Chance production; American-French; Dolby; Color; Rated R; 98 minutes; Release date: December 3, 2010

CAST

Steven Russell	**Jim Carrey**
Phillip Morris	**Ewan McGregor**
Debbie	**Leslie Mann**
Jimmy	**Rodrigo Santoro**
Lindholm	**Antoni Corone**
Birkheim	**Brennan Brown**
Cleavon	**Michael Mandel**

Annie Golden (Eudora), Marylouise Burke (Barbara Bascombe), David Jensen (Judge), Dameon Clarke (Houston Lawyer), Clay Chamberlin (Cellmate, Arnie), Louis Herthum (Doctor), Morgana Shaw (Steven's Mom), Joe Chrest (Steven's Dad), Griff Furst (Mark), Aunjanue Ellis (Reba), Devere Jehl (Samuel), Michael Showers (Gary), Beth Burvant (Sara), Deyne Ladson (Neil), John Kennon Kepper (9-year-old Steven), Alyssa Tate (Child Stephanie), Andrew Sensenig (Screecher), David Stanford (Paramedic), Bill Dykes (Latino Man), Tony Bentley (Racist Client), Kathrin Middleton (Saleswoman), Donovan Guidry (Moustached Man), Nicholas Alexander (Steven's 11-year-old Brother), Michael Beasley (Release Officer), Sean Boyd (Policeman), Maureen Brennan (Vera), Marcus Lyle Brown (Young Doctor), Trey Burvant (Blake), Ken Clement (County Corrections Officer), Miriam Cruz (Helen), David Dahlgren (Physician), Tommy Davis (Todd), Michael Ducote (SWAT Commander), Ashley Duggan-Smith (Secretary #3), Lela Edgar (Blond Wife), J.D. Evermore (Bossy Guard), Jon Eyez (2nd Prisoner), Evan Fitzpatrick (Red-Haired Boy), Shane Fitzpatrick (Little Girl), Shane Fuller (Male Nurse), Jeff Galpin (Lead Officer), Lawrence Gamell Jr. (Driving Cop), James Garrity (Night Guard), Lone Gisclair (Little Boy), Geraldine Glenn (Mandi), Douglas M. Griffin (Steven's Attorney), Jessica Heap (Secreary), Tim Hickey (Blond Inmate), Keith Hudson (Produce Manager), Jeremy Aaron Johnson, Aron Ten Eyck (Policemen), Jacqueline King (Lawyer), Alexa Kuve (Cherubic Secretary), Frederick Lewis (Yoakum), Sharon London (Clerk), Audrey Lynn (Married Woman), Marc Macaulay (Houston Cop), Reginald Mack (Jail Guard), Danny Marlin (Infirmary Orderly), Sammi Jack Martincak (12-year-old Stephanie), Anne McKenzie (Facelift Wife), Thelma Medina (Huge Nurse), Wendy Michaels (Housewife), John Mourain (Taxi Driver), Randall Newsome (Cop), Lance Nichols (Houston Judge), Antonio Paone (Cab Driver), Liann Pattison (Mrs. Lindholm), Sherrie Peterson (D.A.), Clyde Raymond (Houston Doctor), Dane Rhodes (Bald Prisoner), Johnny Rock (New Cellmate), Archie Sampier (Yard Guard), Andy Sims (Corrections Officer), Thomas Thomason (Lawrence), Deneen D. Tyler (Caretaker), Chris Wecklein (Baylor), Scotty Whitehurst (Orderly), Bill Martin Williams (Duty Officer), Jaymon Yates (First Prisoner), Don Yesso (Guard)

The true story of how con man Steven Russell concocted one outrageous scheme after another in order to keep up the high level of living he desired for himself and his lover, Phillip Morris, whom he'd met while in prison.

Jim Carrey, Ewan McGregor

Jim Carrey (center)

Rodrigo Santoro, Jim Carrey © Roadside Attractions

Natalie Portman, Vincent Cassel

Natalie Portman, Winona Ryder

Mila Kunis

Natalie Portman

Natalie Portman, Mila Kunis © Fox Searchlight

Natalie Portman

Vincent Cassel, Natalie Portman

BLACK SWAN

(FOX SEARCHLIGHT) Producers, Mike Medavoy, Arnold W. Messer, Brian Oliver, Scott Franklin; Director, Darren Aronofsky; Screenplay, Mark Heyman, Andrés Heinz, John McLaughlin; Story, Andrés Heinz; Photography, Matthew Libatique; Designer, Thérèse DePrez; Music, Clint Mansell; Music Supervisors, Jim Black, Gabe Hilfer; Choreographer, Benjamin Millepied; Editor, Andrew Weisblum; Casting, Mary Vernieu; a Prøtøzøa and Phoenix Pictures production presented in association with Cross Creek Pictures; Dolby; Technicolor; Rated R; 108 minutes; Release date: December 3, 2010

CAST

Nina Sayers (The Swan Queen)	**Natalie Portman**
Lily (The Black Swan)	**Mila Kunis**
Thomas Leroy (The Gentleman)	**Vincent Cassel**
Erica Sayers (The Queen)	**Barbara Hershey**
Beth Macintyre (The Dying Swan)	**Winona Ryder**
David (The Prince)	**Benjamin Millepied**
Veronica (Little Swan)	**Ksenia Solo**
Galina (Little Swan)	**Kristina Anapau**
Madeline (Little Swan)	**Janet Montgomery**
Andrew (Suitor)	**Sebastian Stan**
Tom (Suitor)	**Toby Hemingway**
Sergio (Rothbart)	**Sergio Torrado**
Mr. Fithian (Patron)	**Mark Margolis**
Mrs. Fithian (Patron)	**Tina Sloan**
Mr. Stein (Patron)	**Abraham Aronofsky**
Costumer Georgina	**Marcia Jean Kurtz**
Stage Manager Sebastian	**Shaun O'Hagan**
Sexy Waiter Scott	**Christopher Gartin**
Administrator Susie	**Deborah Offner**
Uncle Hank	**Stanley B. Herman**
Physical Therapist	**Michelle Rodriguez Nouel**
Understudy for Siegfried	**Kurt Froman**
Conductor	**Marty Krzywonos**
Nurse	**Leslie Lyles**
Jaded Piano Player	**John Epperson**
Piano Player	**Arkadiy Figlin**
Violin Player	**Timothy Fain**
Lady in the Lane	**Sarah Lane**
Man in Stall	**Liam Flaherty**
Rich Gent	**Patrick Heusinger**

Marina Stavitskaya, Olga Kostritzky, Christine Redpath, Alexandra Damiani (Ballet Mistresses), Rebecca Azenberg, Laura Bowman, Holly L. Fusco, Abigail Mentzer, Barette Vance, Lillian di Piazza, Megan Dickinson, Jessy Hendrickson, Geneviève Lebean, Gina Artese, Rachel Jambois, Ryoko Sadoshima, Kaia A. Tack, Lauren Fadeley, Sarah Hay, Adrianna de Svastich, Jamie Wolf, Carrie Lee Riggins (Corps de Ballet)

Given the chance to take the lead in a production of *Swan Lake*, Nina Sayers finds herself embroiled in a bizarre competitive relationship with fellow ballerina Lily, which begins to take its toll on her sanity.

2010 Academy Award winner for Best Actress (Natalie Portman).

This film received additional Oscar nominations for picture, director, cinematography and film editing.

Barbara Hershey, Natalie Portman

ALL GOOD THINGS

(MAGNOLIA) Producers, Marc Smerling, Andrew Jarecki, Bruna Papandrea, Michael London; Executive Producers, Janice Williams, Barbara A. Hall, Bob Weinstein, Harvey Weinstein, Michelle Krumm; Director, Andrew Jarecki; Screenplay, Marcus Hinchey, Marc Smerling; Photography, Michael Seresin; Designer, Wynn Thomas; Costumes, Michael Clancy; Music, Rob Simonsen; Music Supervisor, Susan Jacobs; Editors, David Rosenbloom, Shelby Siegel; Co-Producers, David Rosenbloom, Marcus Hinchey; Casting, Douglas Aibel; a Groundswell Productions, Hit the Ground Running Films presentation; Dolby; Color; Rated R; 101 minutes; Release date: December 3, 2010

CAST
David Marks	**Ryan Gosling**
Katie Marks	**Kirsten Dunst**
Sanford Marks	**Frank Langella**
Deborah Lehrman	**Lily Rabe**
Malvern Bump	**Philip Baker Hall**
Daniel Marks	**Michael Esper**

Diane Venora (Janice Rizzo), Nick Offerman (Jim McCarthy), Kristen Wiig (Lauren Fleck), Stephen Kunken (Todd Fleck), John Cullum (Richard Panatierre), Maggie Kiley (Mary McCarthy), Liz Stauber (Sharon McCarthy), Marion McCorry (Ann McCarthy), Mia Dillon (Katie's Aunt), Tom Kemp (Katie's Uncle), Trini Alvarado (Sarah Davis), Tom Riis Farrell (Barry Davis), Bruce Norris (Brian Callender), Francie Swift (Kelly Callender), David Margulies (Mayor), Glenn Fleshler (Sidney Greenhaus), Stephe Singer (Solly Sachs), Francis Guinan (Daniel Patrick Moynihan), Ellen Sexton (Moynihan's Wife), William Jackson Harper (Moynihan's Assistant), Ashlie Atkinson (Bonnie Felder), Donna Bullock (Divorce Attorney), Pamala Tyson (Lula Baxter), Julie Moran (Herself), Diane Kagan (Scream Therapist), Socorro Santiago (Nurse), Barbara Ann Davison (Woman at Baby Shower), Zabryna Guevara (Waitress), Lanny Flaherty (Rooming House Landlord), Robert Clohessy (Building Superintendent), Lazaro Perez (Building Elevator Operator), Michelle Hurst (Newscaster), Craig Walker (Assistant District Attorney), Lola Pashalinski (Woman at Luxor), Jerry Grayson (Man at Luxor), Anthony Torn (Theater Manager), Zoe Lister-Jones (Press Conference Reporter), Tristan Comeau (Young David), Amelia Martin (David's Mother), Matthew Floyd Miller (Young Sanford), Peter Becerra (Officer at Search),Mary A. Kelly (Vermont Realtor), Jeong Kim (Waiter at Disco), Andy Tsay (Waiter), Ruel Jusi (Butler), Arwen, Jordie (Ivan the Dog)

The marriage between the son of a wealthy real estate developer and a young woman leads to tragedy when the young man's fragile mental state begins to unravel.

Ryan Gosling, Kirsten Dunst © Magnolia

Anthony Mackie, Kerry Washington

NIGHT CATCHES US

(MAGNOLIA) Producers, Ron Simons, Sean Costello, Jason Orans; Co-Producers, Katie Mustard, Adam Spielberg, Tanya Hamilton; Director/Screenplay, Tanya Hamilton; Photography, David Tumblety; Designer, Beth Mickle; Costumes, Maren Reese; Music, The Roots; Music Supervisor, Dave Golden; Editors, Affonso Gonçalves, John Chimples; Casting, Lois Drabkin; a SimonSays Entertainment production in association with Gigantic Pictures; Dolby; Color; Rated R; 88 minutes; Release date: December 3, 2010

CAST
Patricia Wilson	**Kerry Washington**
Marcus Washington	**Anthony Mackie**
Dwayne "DoRight" Miller	**Jamie Hector**
Detective David Gordon	**Wendell Pierce**
Jimmy Dixon	**Amari Cheatom**
Iris Wilson	**Jamara Griffin**
Colin Dixon	**Sadiq Afif**

Tariq Trotter (Bostic Washington), Novella Nelson (Eloise Johnson), Ron Simons (Carey Ford), Damali Mason (Auntie Lorraine), Jann Ellis (Auntie Cecile), Thomas Roy (Old Man Harrison), Bill Zielinski (Frank Cherry), Christopher Kadish (Partner), Nakia Dillard (T.T.), Matt Russell (Young Detective), Kevin C. Walls (Art Lyle (Police Officers), Whitney Wilcox (Child in Kitchen), Tariq Rasheed (Neil Wilson), Steve Kaufmann (Cop #2)

A former member of Philadelphia's Black Power movement returns to his old neighborhood after a mysterious absence and soon finds himself at odds with the group that had once been such an instrumental part of his life.

Jamara Griffin, Anthony Mackie
© Magnolia

Angelina Jolie, Johnny Depp

Rufus Sewell, Angelina Jolie

Angelina Jolie © Columbia Pictures

THE TOURIST

(COLUMBIA) Producers, Graham King, Tim Headington, Roger Birnbaum, Gary Barber, Jonathan Glickman; Executive Producers, Lloyd Phillips, Bahman Naraghi, Olivier Courson, Ron Halpern; Director, Florian Henckel von Donnersmarck; Screenplay, Florian Henckel von Donnersmarck, Chistopher McQuarrie, Julian Fellowes; Photography, John Seale; Designer, Jon Hutman; Costumes, Colleen Atwood; Music, James Newton Howard; Editors, Joe Hutshing, Patricia Rommel; Casting, Susie Figgis a GK Films presentation in association with Spyglass Entertainment of a GK Films and Birnbaum/Barber production in association with StudioCanal; Dolby; Color; Rated PG-13; 103 minutes; Release date: December 10, 2010

CAST

Frank Tupelo	**Johnny Depp**
Elise Clifton-Ward	**Angelina Jolie**
Inspector John Acheson	**Paul Bettany**
Chief Inspector Jones	**Timothy Dalton**
Reginald Shaw	**Steve Berkoff**
The Englishman	**Rufus Sewell**
Colonello Lombardi	**Christian De Sica**
Sergente Cerato	**Alessio Boni**
Tenente Narduzzi	**Daniele Pecci**
Tenente Tommassini	**Giovanni Guidelli**

Raoul Bova (Conte Filippo Gaggia), Bruno Wolkovitch (Capitaine Courson), Marc Ruchmann (Brigadier Kasier), Julien Baumgartner (Brigadier Ricuort), François VIncentelli (Brigadier Marion), Clément Sibony (Brigadier Rousseau), Jean-Claude Adelin (Brigadier Cavillan), Jean-Marie Lamour (Café Waiter, Jean Michel), Nicolas Guillot (Café Head Waiter, Jérôme), Mhamed Arezki (Courier Achmed Techabli), Igor Jijikine (VIrginsky), Vladimir Tevlovski (Liputin), Alec Utgoff (Fedka), Mark Zak (Shigalyov), Meri Marcoré (Hotel Concierege Alessio), Gabriele Gallinari (Hotel Bell Boy Luca), Riccardo De Torrebrung (Hotel Waiter Guido), Maurizio Casagrande (Waiter Antonio), Nino Frassica (Brigadiere Mele), Gwilym Lee (Senior Technician Mountain), Steven Robertson (Junior Technician Pinnock), Iddo Goldberg (Jones' Assistant Whitfield), Renato Scarpa (Arturo the Tailor), Giancarlo Previati (Gala Coordinator Dalla Pietà), Giovanni Esposito (Interpreter Coppa), Marino Narduzzi (Elise's Driver Stefano), Tino Giada (Elise's Driver Mauro), Bruno Biolotta (Sniper Chief Giordani), Ralf Moeller (Jail Bird Lunt)

Hoping to throw the CIA off the trail of her lover, agent Elise Clifton-Ward hooks up with an innocent American tourist, so that she can use him as a decoy.

Paul Bettany, Timothy Dalton

Chris Cooper, Alan Cumming

Russell Brand, Alfred Molina

Helen Mirren, Felicity Jones, Djimon Hounsou

THE TEMPEST

(TOUCHSTONE/MIRAMAX) Producers, Julie Taymor, Robert Chartoff, Lynn Hendee, Julia Taylor-Stanley, Jason K. Lau; Executive Producers, Ron Bozman, Tino Puri, Rohit Khattar, Stewart Till, Anthony Buckner, Greg Strasburg; Director/ Screenplay, Julie Taymor; Based on the play by William Shakespeare; Photography, Stuart Dryburgh; Designer, Mark Friedberg; Costumes, Sandy Powell; Music, Elliot Goldenthal; Editor, Françoise Bonnot; a Chartoff/Hendee, TalkStory, Artemis Films production in association with Mumbai Mantra Media Limited; Dolby; Color; Rated PG-13; 110 minutes; Release date: December 10, 2010

CAST
Propsera	**Helen Mirren**
Trinculo	**Russell Brand**
Prince Ferdinand	**Reeve Carney**
Gonzalo	**Tom Conti**
Antonio	**Chris Cooper**
Sebastian	**Alan Cumming**
Caliban	**Djimon Hounsou**
Miranda	**Felicity Jones**
Stephano	**Alfred Molina**
King Alonso	**David Strathairn**
Ariel	**Ben Whishaw**
Boatswain	**Jude Akuwudike**

A shipwreck engineered by the wizard Prospera brings a diverse boatload of passengers to the island where she keeps her daughter under her watchful eye.

This film received an Oscar nomination for costume design.

Ben Whishaw © Touchstone

THE CHRONICLES OF NARNIA: THE VOYAGE OF THE DAWN TREADER

(20TH CENTURY FOX) Producers, Mark Johnson, Andrew Adamson, Philip Steuer; Executive Producer, Douglas Gresham, Perry Moore; Director, Michael Apted; Screenplay, Christopher Markus, Stephen McFeely, Michael Petroni; Photography, Dante Spinotti; Designer, Barry Robison; Costumes, Isis Mussenden; Music, David Arnold; Editor, Rick Shaine; Visual Effects Supervisor, Angus Bickerton; Casting, Nina Gold, Christine King; a Fox 2000 Pictures and Walden Media presentation; Dolby; Color; 3D; Rated PG; 113 minutes; Release date: December 10, 2010

Skandar Keynes © 20th Century Fox

CAST

Lucy Pevensie	**Georgie Henley**
Edmund Pevensie	**Skandar Keynes**
Caspian	**Ben Barnes**
Eustace Scrubb	**Will Poulter**
Drinian	**Gary Sweet**
Lord Bern	**Terry Norris**
Lord Rhoop	**Bruce Spence**
Coriakin	**Bille Brown**
Lillandil	**Laura Brent**
Voice of Aslan	**Liam Neeson**
Voice of Reepicheep	**Simon Pegg**
The White Witch	**Tilda Swinton**

Colin Moody (Auctioneer), Anna Popplewell (Susan Pevensie), William Moseley (Peter Pevensie), Shane Rangi (Tavros), Arthur Angel (Rhince), Arabella Morton (Gael), Rachel Blakely (Gael's Mum), Steven Rooke (Faun), Tony Nixon (1st Mate), David Vallon (Slave Trader), Jared Robinson (Intake Officer), Roy Billing (Chief Dufflepud), Neil G. Young, Greg Poppleton, Nicholas Nelid (Dufflepuds), Nathaniel Parker (Caspian's Father), Daniel Poole (Young Man), Mirko Grillini (Telmarine Sailor), Ron Kelly (Steward), Laurence Coy (Photographer), Douglas Gresham, Michael Maguire (Slavers), Catarina Hebbard (Gael's Aunt), Tamati Rangi (Minotaur), Lucas Ross (Handsome Soldier), Megan Hill (Pretty Young Nurse), David Suchet (Trader), Ross Price (First Mate)

Aslan, Georgie Henley, Skandar Keynes, Ben Barnes

Lucy and Edmund Pevensie return to the fantastical other-world of Narnia, where they join Caspian and the crew of the Dawn Treader on a series of adventures on which rests the fate of Narnia itself. Third in *The Chronicles of Narnia* series following *The Lion, the Witch and the Wardrobe* (Disney, 2005) and *Prince Caspian* (Disney, 2008).

Georgie Henley

Reepicheep, Will Poulter

THE FIGHTER

(PARAMOUNT) Producer, David Hoberman, Todd Lieberman, Ryan Kavanaugh, Mark Wahlberg, Dorothy Aufiero, Paul Tamasy; Executive Producers, Tucker Tooley, Darren Aronofsky, Leslie Varrelman, Keith Dorrington, Eric Johnson; Co-Producers, Jeff Waxman, Kenneth Halsband; Director, David O. Russell; Screenplay, Scott Silver, Paul Tamasy, Eric Johnson; Story, Keith Dorrington, Paul Tamasy, Eric Johnson; Photography, Hoyte Van Hoytema; Designer, Judy Becker; Costumes, Mark Bridges; Music, Michael Brook; Music Supervisors, Happy Walters, Season Kent; Casting, Sheila Jaffe; a Relativity Media presentation in association with the Weinstein Company of a Relativity Media, Mandeville Films, Closest to the Hole production; Dolby; Super 35 Widescreen; Technicolor; Rated R; 115 minutes; Release date: December 10, 2010

CAST

Mickey Ward	**Mark Wahlberg**
Dicky Eklund	**Christian Bale**
Charlene Fleming	**Amy Adams**
Alice Ward	**Melissa Leo**
Himself	**Mickey O'Keefe**
George Ward	**Jack McGee**
'Little Alice' Eklund	**Melissa McMeekin**
Cathy 'Pork' Eklund	**Bianca Hunter**
Cindy 'Tar' Eklund	**Erica McDermott**
Donnna Eklund Jaynes	**Jill Quigg**
Gail 'Red Dog' Eklund	**Dendrie Taylor**
Phyllis 'Beaver' Eklund	**Kate O'Brien**
Sherri Ward	**Jenna Lamia**
Sal Lanano	**Frank Renzulli**
Gary 'Boo Boo' Giuffrida	**Paul Campbell**
Kassie Ward	**Catilin Dwyer**
Karen	**Chanty Sok**
Lou Gold	**Ted Arcidi**
Mike Toma	**Ross Bickell**
Wolfie	**Sean Malone**
Gilberto Brown, aka Jose	**José Antonio Rivera**
HBO Cameramen	**Richard Farrell, Matthew Muzio**
HBO Producer	**Steven Barkhimer**
Themselves	**Art Ramalho, Sugar Ray Leonard**

Jackson Nicoll (Little Dicky), Allison Folland (Laurie Carroll), Sean Doherty (Jimmy, Laurie's Husband), Sue Costello (Becky), Thomas Benton (Businessman), Ray Greenhalge (Ray Ramalho), Tino Kimly (Pran), Epifanio Melendez (Carlos Garcia), Jeremiah Kissel (Bald Businessman), Sean Eklund (Man in Diner), Rouen Chea (Chan), Brian A. Nguyen (Brian), Rikki Kleiman (Court Clerk), Michael Dell'Orto (WBU Commissioner), Paul Locke, Kim Carrell (Reporters), Colin Hamell (John Hyland), Dale Place (Referee Micky Vann), Eddie Lee Anderson (Referee Joe Cortez), Bonnie Aarons (Crackhead Bonnie), Joe Lupino (Referee Mitch Halpern), Walter Driscoll (Court Officer), Matt Russell (Photo Guy on Street), A. Joseph Denucci, Richard A. Eklund, George Michael Ward, Richard Eklund Jr., Jack Greenhalge, Kevin Paige (Men on Street), David A. Ramalho Sr. (Trainer), Ziad Akl (Inmate), Simon Hamlin (Movie Patron), Gerald Greenhalge (Uncle Jerry), Matthew Russell, Tommy Eklund (Running Kids), Rita Mercier, Deborah Bolanger, Kerry Moore (Women on Street), Philip D. Herbert (Micky's Cutman), Raul Vera (Sanchez Trainer), Jack Lally (Neary Trainer), Carlos L. Smith (Sugar Ray Leonard Bodyguard), Jerrell Lee, Hugh K. Long (Fight Spectators), Catherine Lynn Stone (Fan), Eric Weinstein (Micky's Friend), Bo Cleary (Cop), Anthony Molinari (Neary), Peter Cunningham (Mike 'Machine Gun' Mungin), Miguel Espino (Alfonso Sanchez), Anthony 'Ace' Thomas (Castillo), Brian Christensen (Drunk Guy), Jen Weissenberg (Drunk Girl), Michael Buffer, Larry Merchant, Jim Lampley, Emanuel Steward, Roy Jones Jr., George Foreman, Don Dunphy (Fight Announcer)

Micky Ward hopes to compete for the world light welterweight title despite the burden of having to train under his undependable half-brother, Dicky, a former boxer who is now battling a crack addiction.

2010 Academy Award winner for Best Supporting Actor (Christian Bale) and Best Supporting Actress (Melissa Leo).

This film received additional Oscar nominations for picture, supporting actress (Amy Adams), director, original screenplay, and film editing.

Christian Bale, Mark Wahlberg

Christian Bale, Art Ramalho, Melissa Leo, Mark Wahlberg

Mickey O'Keefe, Mark Wahlberg, Melissa McKeekin, Steven Barkhimer, Art Ramalho, Melissa Leo, Jenna Lamia, Richard Farrell, Dendrie Taylor

Mark Wahlberg, Amy Adams

Mickey O'Keefe, Mark Wahlberg, Christian Bale

Mark Wahlberg, Jack McGee, Melissa Leo, Christian Bale, Jackson Nicoll

Mark Wahlberg, Christian Bale

Mark Wahlberg, Amy Adams © Paramount Pictures

Mark Wahlberg

THE COMPANY MEN

(WEINSTEIN CO.) Producers, Claire Rudnick Polstein, Paula Weinstein, John Wells; Executive Producer, Barbara A. Hall; Director/Screenplay, John Wells; Photography, Roger Deakins; Designer, David J. Bomba; Costumes, Lyn Paolo; Music, Aaron Zigman; Editor, Robert Frazen; Casting, Laura Rosenthal; a Battle Mountain Films production in association with Spring Creek Productions; Dolby; DeLuxe color; Rated R; 109 minutes; Release date: December 10, 2010

Kevin Costner, Ben Affleck

CAST

Bobby Walker	**Ben Affleck**
Phil Woodward	**Chris Cooper**
Jack Dolan	**Kevin Costner**
Gene McClary	**Tommy Lee Jones**
Sally Wilcox	**Maria Bello**
Maggie Walker	**Rosemarie DeWitt**
James Salinger	**Craig T. Nelson**
Mifflin	**Thomas R. Kee**
Connors	**Craig Mathers**
Karlson	**Gary Galone**

Suzanne Rico (Gail), Adrianne Krstansky (Carol), Lewis D. Wheeler (Ken), Celeste Oliva (Jane), Tom Kemp (Conal), Nancy Villone (Diane), Chris Everett (Barbara), Lance Greene (Landry), Kathy Harum (Karen), Allyn Burrows (Stevens), Anthony Estrella (Haspel), David Catanzaro (Archer), Anthony O'Leary (Drew), Angela Rezza (Carson), Sasha Spielberg (Sarah), Maryann Plunkett (Lorna), Patricia Kalember (Cynthia), Dana Eskelson (Dierdre Dolan), James Colby (Davey), John Doman (Dysert), Richard Snee (Speaker), Ellen Colton (MK&T Receptionist), Eamonn Walker (Danny), Cady Huffman (Joanna), Gene Amoroso (Balding Man), Annette Miller (Nan), Tonye Patano (Joyce Robertson), David De Beck (Hansen), Kent Shocknek (Herb Rittenour), William Hill (Kevin Walker), Carolyn Pickman (Fran Walker), Jeff Barry (Dale), David Wilson Barnes (Troy Thayer), Brian White (Mike), Denece Ryland (FMR Receptionist), Rena Maliszweski (Robin), Cindy Lentol (Dana), Scott Winters (Ed), Sanjit De Silva (Tom), Austin Lysy (Liam), Elizabeth Dann (Norvell Receptionist), Dossy Peabody (Jane Nefeld)

Chris Cooper

Three employees of Boston's GTX Corporation face uncertain futures when they are among those whose jobs are eliminated.

Tommy Lee Jones, Ben Affleck

Ben Affleck, Rosemarie DeWitt © Weinstein Co.

Beau Garrett

Michael Sheen, Garrett Hedlund

Jeff Bridges

Garrett Hedlund © Walt Disney Pictures

TRON: LEGACY

(WALT DISNEY PICTURES) Producers, Sean Bailey, Jeffrey Silver, Steven Lisberger; Executive Producer, Donald Kushner; Director, Joseph Kosinski; Screenplay, Edward Kitsis, Adam Horowitz; Story, Edward Kitsis, Adam Horowitz, Brian Klugman, Lee Sternthal; Based on characters created by Steven Lisberger, Bonnie MacBird; Photography, Claudio Miranda; Designer, Darren Gilford; Costumes, Michael Wilkinson; Music, Daft Punk; Music Supervisor, Jason Bentley; Editor, James Haygood; Special Effects Supervisor, Alex Burdett; Dolby; 3D; Color; Rated PG; 127 minutes; Release date: December 17, 2010

CAST

Kevin Flynn/Clu	**Jeff Bridges**
Sam Flynn	**Garrett Hedlund**
Quorra	**Olivia Wilde**
Alan Bradley/Tron	**Bruce Boxleitner**
Jarvis	**James Frain**
Gem	**Beau Garrett**
Castor/Zuse	**Michael Sheen**
Rinzler	**Anis Cheurfa**

Serinda Swan, Yaya DaCosta, Elizabeth Mathis (Sirens), Yurij Kis (Half Faced Man), Conrad Coates (Bartik), Daft Punk (Masked DJ's), Ron Selmour (Chattering Homeless Man), Dan Joffre (Key Security Guard #1 – Ernie), Darren Dolynski (Young Man on Recognizer), Kofi Yiadom (Disc Opponent #2), Steven Lisberger (Shaddix), Donnelly Rhodes (Grandpa Flynn), Belinda Montgomery (Grandma Flynn), Owen Best (7 Year Old Sam Flynn), Matt Ward (Iso Boy), Zoe Fryklund (Iso Girl), Dean Redman (Light Jet Sentry), Mi-Jung Lee (Debra Chung), Christopher Logan (Nervous Program), Sheldon Yamkovy (Destitute Program), Dale Wolfe (Irv Culpepper), Joanne Wilson, Catherine Lough Haggquist, Shaw Madson (Reporters), Thomas Bradshaw (Security Guard #2), Shafin Karim (East Indian Taxi Driver), Rob Daly (Lead Sentry), Mike Ching (Blue Gaming Program), Michael Teigen (Green Gaming Program), Brent Stait (Purple Gaming Program), Amy Esterle (Young Mrs. Flynn), Cody Laudan (End of the Line Club Bouncer), Jeffrey Nordling (Richard Mackey), Christine Adams (Claire Atkinson), Kate Gajdosik (News Anchor), Jack McGee (Police Photographer), Dawn Mander (Crying Program), John Reardon (Young Kevin Flynn), Cillian Murphy (Edward Dillinger)

Investigating the unexplained disappearance of his father, young Sam Flynn finds himself caught in the same cyber universe where his dad has been living for 20 years. Sequel to the 1982 Disney film *TRON* with Jeff Bridges and Bruce Boxleitner repeating their roles.

This film received an Oscar nomination for sound editing.

Miles Teller, Nicole Kidman

Nicole Kidman, Tammy Blanchard © Lionsgate

Sandra Oh, Aaron Eckhart

Dianne Wiest

RABBIT HOLE

(LIONSGATE) Producers, Leslie Urdang, Dean Vanech, Nicole Kidman, Per Saari, Gigi Pritzker; Executive Producers, Dan Revers, William Lischak, Linda McDonough, Brian O'Shea; Co-Producers, Caroline Jaczko, Geoff Linville; Director, John Cameron Mitchell; Screenplay, David Lindsay-Abaire, based on his play; Photography, Frank G. DeMarco; Designer, Kalina Ivanov; Costumes, Ann Roth; Music, Anton Sanko; Music Supervisor, Robin Urdang; Editor, Joe Klotz; Casting, Sig de Miguel, Stephen Vincent; an Olympus Pictures/Blossom Films/Oddlot Entertainment production; Dolby; Color; Rated PG-13; 92 minutes; Release date: December 17, 2010

CAST

Becca Corbett	**Nicole Kidman**
Howie Corbett	**Aaron Eckhart**
Nat	**Dianne Wiest**
Jason	**Miles Teller**
Izzy	**Tammy Blanchard**
Gabby	**Sandra Oh**
Auggie	**Giancarlo Esposito**
Rick	**Jon Tenney**
Kevin	**Stephen Mailer**
Craig	**Mike Doyle**
Rhonda	**Roberta Wallach**
Peg	**Patricia Kalember**
Donna	**Ali Marsh**
Ana	**Yetta Gottesman**

Colin Mitchell (Sam), Deidre Goodwin (Reema), Julie Lauren (Debbie), Rob Campbell (Bob), Jennifer Roszell (Sotheby's Receptionist), Marylouise Burke (Librarian), Jay Wilkison (Gary), Ben Hudson (Sammy), Salli Saffioti (Lori), Ursula Clare Parker (Lilly), Phoenix List (Danny), Sandi Carroll (Abby), Teresa Kelsey (Mary), Sara Jane Blazo (Jason's Mother), Brady Parisella (Caden)

Becca and Howie Corbett try to go about their normal lives after suffering the tragic loss of their 4-year-old son.

This film received an Oscar nomination for actress (Nicole Kidman).

Tom Cavanaugh, Boo Boo, Yogi

Andrew Daly © Warner Bros.

YOGI BEAR

(WARNER BROS.) Producer, Donald De Line, Karen Rosenfelt; Executive Producers, Andrew Haas, James Dyer, Lee Berger; Director, Eric Brevig; Screenplay, Jeffrey Ventimilia, Joshua Sternin, Brad Copeland; Based on characters created by Hanna-Barbera Productions; Photography, Peter James; Designer, David R. Sandefur; Costumes, Liz McGregor; Music, John Debney; Music Supervisor, Julianne Jordan; Editor, Kent Beyda; Stunts, Augie Davis; Special Effects Supervisor, Ken Durey; Visual Effects & Animation, Rhythm & Hues Studio; a Sunswept Entertainment/De Line Pictures production, in association with Rhythm & Hues; Dolby; Technicolor; 3D; Rated PG; 80 minutes; Release date: December 17, 2010

Tom Cavanaugh, Anna Faris

CAST

Voice of Yogi Bear	**Dan Aykroyd**
Voice of Boo Boo	**Justin Timberlake**
Rachel	**Anna Faris**
Ranger Smith	**Tom Cavanaugh**
Ranger Jones	**T.J. Miller**
Chief of Staff	**Nate Corddry**
Mayor Brown	**Andrew Daly**
Narrator	**Josh Robert Thompson**
Mayor's Tailor	**David Stott**
Dirty Shopper	**Greg Johnson**
Stylist	**Christy Quillam**
Elderly Purse Lady	**Patricia Aldersley**
Purse Snatcher	**Tim McLachlan**

Hayden Vernon, Dean Knowsley, Barry Duffield, Michael Morris, Will Wallace (Security Guards), Suzana Srpek (Picnic Table Mom)

Troublesome picnic scavenger Yogi Bear joins forces with his nemesis Ranger Smith to stop Jellystone Park from being sold to developers.

Yogi

HOW DO YOU KNOW

(COLUMBIA) Producers, James L. Brooks, Paula Weinstein, Laurence Mark, Julie Ansell; Executive Producers, John D. Schofield, Richard Sakai; Director/Screenplay, James L. Brooks; Photography, Janusz Kaminski; Designer, Jeannine Oppewall; Costumes, Shay Cunliffe; Music, Hans Zimmer; Music Supervisor, Nick Angel; Editor, Richard Marks, Tracey Wadmore-Smith; Co-Producer, Aldric La'Auli Porter; Casting, Francine Maisler; a Gracie Films production; Dolby; DeLuxe Color; Rated PG-13; 121 minutes; Release date: December 17, 2010

Paul Rudd, Jack Nicholson © Columbia Pictures

CAST

Lisa Smalls	**Reese Witherspoon**
George Madison	**Paul Rudd**
Matty	**Owen Wilson**
Charles Madison	**Jack Nicholson**
Annie	**Kathryn Hahn**
Ron	**Mark Linn-Baker**
Al	**Lenny Venito**
Coach Sally	**Molly Price**
George's Lawyer	**Ron McLarty**
Terry	**Shelly Conn**
Bullpen Pitcher	**Domenick Lombardozzi**
Doorman	**John Tormey**
Riva	**Teyonah Parris**
Psychiatrist	**Tony Shalhoub**
Softball Coach	**Dean Norris**

Donna Dundon (Annie's Mom), Cyrus Newitt (Annie's Dad), Will Blagrove, Andrew Wilson, David Gregory (Matty's Teammates), Yuki Matsuzaki (Tori), Bill McKinley (Maitre d'), Jim Bouton (Bullpen Coach), Tara Subkoff (Subpoena Woman), Mary Gallagher (Coach), Aileen Zoccola, Sachi Jonas, Amanda Moshay (Players' Wives), Lyssa Lee Roberts (Groped Girl), Seth Sanders (Cocky Agent), Elyse Braner, Ryann Hendricks, Jessi Moore, Amanda Freed, Jaime Wohlbach, Anjelica Selden, Lovieanne Jung, Suze Kilner, Brian Distance, Michael Toolan-Roche, Caitlin Hanrahan, Deanna Vecchio, Samantha Yodowitz, Crystl Bustos, Andrea Duran, Jackie Dempsey, Tara Henry, Carri Martin (U.S. National Team)

Reese Witherspoon, Owen Wilson

Lisa drifts into a relationship with a major league pitcher after being cut from her softball team, only to find herself attracted to a businessman who is being accused of a financial crime.

John Tormey, Reese Witherspoon

Reese Witherspoon, Paul Rudd

Dustin Hoffman, Barbra Streisand © Universal Studios

Laura Dern

Ben Stiller, Barbra Streisand

Robert De Niro, Owen Wilson, Ben Stiller, Harvey Keitel

LITTLE FOCKERS

(UNIVERSAL/PARAMOUNT) Producers, Jane Rosenthal, Robert De Niro, Jay Roach, John Hamburg; Executive Producers, Nancy Tenenbaum, Daniel Lupi, Meghan Lyvers, Andrew Miano, Ryan Kavanaugh; Director, Paul Weitz; Screenplay, John Hamburg, Larry Stuckey; Based on characters created by Greg Glienna and Mary Ruth Clarke; Photography, Remi Adefarasan; Designer, William Arnold; Costumes, Mary Maginnis; Music, Stephen Trask; Editors, Greg Hayden, Leslie Jones, Myron Kerstein; Casting, Joseph Middleton; a Tribeca/Everyman Pictures production presented in association with Relativity Media; Dolby; Color; Rated PG-13; 98 minutes; Release date: December 22, 2010

CAST

Jack Byrnes	**Robert De Niro**
Greg Focker	**Ben Stiller**
Kevin Rawley	**Owen Wilson**
Dina Byrnes	**Blythe Danner**
Pam Focker	**Teri Polo**
Andi Garcia	**Jessica Alba**
Prudence	**Laura Dern**
Bernie Focker	**Dustin Hoffman**
Roz Focker	**Barbra Streisand**
Randy Weir	**Harvey Keitel**

Erika Jensen, Robert Miano, Katharine Kramer, Roy Jones Jr., Derek Resallat (Party Parents), Keivn Hart (Nurse Louis), Daisy Tahan (Samantha Focker), Colin Baiocchi (Henry Focker), Tom McCarthy (Dr. Bob), Yul Vazquez (Junior), Jack Axelrod (Chappy), Clent Bowers (Mr. Androvsky), Olga Fonda (Svetlana), Laksh Singh (Dr. Patel), Trula Marcus (Stage Producer), Jake Keiffer (Rufus), Rob Huebel (Sleazy Doctor), John Di Maggio, Jordan Peele, Kello Kirkland Powers (EMTs), Deepak Chopra (Himself), Robbie Tucker (EHS Tough Kid), Nick Kroll (Young Doctor), Sergio Calderón (Gustavo), Aaron Zachary Philips (Confused Child), David Pressman, Hugh Dane (Doctors), Richard Cotovsky (Newspaper Vendor), Amy Stiller (Kristen), Trinity Warren, Cade Rogers, Ava Rose Williams, Frankie M. Torres (Climbing Kids), Kyla Warren, Eric Haisan, Ryder Bucaro, Callder West Griffith, Lei'lah Star, David Williams (Party Kids), Randy Chuang, Joe Thamawt (Monks), Harry Bali (Sadu), Paul Herman (Caricature Artist), Leslie Garavito (Fire Pit Child), Cort Rogers, Troy Brown (Bounce House Kids), Vladimir Kubr (Ballpit Kid), Semere-Ab Etmet Yohannes (Fire Walker), Nicole Pano (Art Teacher), Michael Naughton (Anatomy Professor), Celina Zambón (Carmencita), Shih Chou (Party Monk), Stan Egi (Man on Subway), Antonio Bolivar, Michelle Castillo, Theodore M. Crisell, Neisha Folkes, Jilana Laufer, Molly Rogers (Flamenco Dancers)

Feeling the passing of time, Jack Byrnes decides it is time to anoint his son-in-law, Greg Focker, the patriarch of the Focker-Byrnes families. Third in the series following *Meet the Parents* (Universal, 2000) and *Meet the Fockers* (Universal, 2004).

Hailee Steinfeld, Barry Pepper

Hailee Steinfeld, Jeff Bridges

Jeff Bridges © Paramount Pictures

Hailee Steinfeld

Hailee Steinfeld, Matt Damon

Matt Damon

Hailee Steinfeld, Matt Damon, Jeff Bridges

Josh Brolin, Hailee Steinfeld

TRUE GRIT

(PARAMOUNT) Producers, Scott Rudin, Ethan Coen, Joel Coen; Executive Producers, Steven Spielberg, Robert Graf, David Ellison, Paul Schwake, Megan Ellison; Directors/Screenplay, Joel Coen, Ethan Coen; Based on the novel by Charles Portis; Photography, Roger Deakins; Designer, Jess Gonchor; Costumes, Mary Zophres; Music, Carter Burwell; Editor, Roderick Jaynes; Casting, Ellen Chenoweth; a Skydance Productions presentation of a Scott Rudin/Mike Zoss production; Dolby; Super 35 Widescreen; Color; Rated PG-13; 110 minutes; Release date: December 22, 2010

CAST

Marshal Rooster Cogburn	**Jeff Bridges**
Mattie Ross	**Hailee Steinfeld**
LaBeouf	**Matt Damon**
Tom Chaney	**Josh Brolin**
Lucky Ned Pepper	**Barry Pepper**
Col. Stonehill	**Dakin Matthews**
Undertaker	**Jarlath Conroy**
Emmett Quincy	**Paul Rae**
Moon (The Kid)	**Domhnall Gleeson**
40-Year-Old Mattie	**Elizabeth Marvel**
Yarnell	**Roy Lee Jones**
Bear Man	**Ed Lee Corbin**
Sheriff	**Leon Russom**
Harold Parmalee	**Bruce Green**
Boarding House Landlady	**Candyce Hinkle**
Mr. Lee	**Peter Leung**
Cole Younger	**Don Pirl**
Cross-Examining Lawyer	**Joe Stevens**
First Lawyer	**David Lipman**
Judge Parker	**Jake Walker**
Stableboy	**Orlando Smart**
Ferryman	**Ty Mitchell**
Repentant Condemned Man	**Nicholas Sadler**
Unrepentant Condemned Man	**Scott Sowers**
Condemned Indian	**Jonathan Joss**
Woman at Hanging	**Maggie A. Goodman**
Indian Youths at Bagby's	**Brandon Sanderson**
	Ruben Nakai Campana

14-year-old Mattie Ross hires ornery, one-eyed Marshal "Rooster" Cogburn to capture the man responsible for the murder of her father.

Remake of the 1969 Paramount film that starred John Wayne, Kim Darby, and Glen Campbell.

This film received Oscar nominations for picture, actor (Jeff Bridges), supporting actress (Hailee Steinfeld), directors, adapted screenplay, cinematography, art direction, costume design, sound mixing, and sound editing.

Jeff Bridges

SOMEWHERE

(FOCUS) Producers, G. Mac Brown, Roman Coppola, Sofia Coppola; Executive Producers, Francis Ford Coppola, Paul Rassam, Fred Roos; Director/Screenplay, Sofia Coppola; Photography, Harry Savides; Designer, Anne Ross; Costumes, Stacey Battat; Music, Phoenix; Editor, Sarah Flack; Casting, Courtney Bright, Nicole Daniels; an American Zoetrope production, presented in association with Pathé Distribution, Medusa Film, Tohokushinsha; Dolby; Technicolor; Rated R; 98 minutes; Release date: December 22, 2010

Chris Pontius, Elle Fanning

CAST

Johnny Marco	**Stephen Dorff**
Cleo	**Elle Fanning**
Sammy	**Chris Pontius**
Rebecca	**Michelle Monaghan**

Erin Wasson, Alexandra Williams, Nathalie Fay (Party Girls), Kristina Shannon (Bambi), Karissa Shannon (Cindy), John Prudhont (Chateau Patio Waiter), Ruby Corley (Patio Girl), Angela Lindvall (Blonde in Mercedes), Maryna Linchuk, Meghan Collison, Jessica Miller (Vampire Models), Lala Sloatman (Layla), Renee Roca (Ice Skating Instructor), Aurelien Wiik (French Guy), Lauren Hastings (Pretty Girl), Amanda Anka (Marge), Ellie Kemper (Claire), Brian Gattas (Studio PR Man), Randa Walker (Eager PR Woman), Sylvia Desrochers (Rebecca's Publicist), Christopher James Taylor (Press Photographer), Silvia Bizio (Italian Journalist), Noel De Souza (Indian Journalist), Lisa Lu (Chinese Journalist), Alexander Nevsky (Russian Journalist), Aida Talka-O'Reilly (Egyptian Journalist), Emanuel Levy (Israeli Journalist), H.J. Park (Korean Journalist), Jordu Schell, Joey Rocket, Jack Firman Jr. (SPFX Make-up Artists), Io Bottoms (Receptionist), Paul Greene (Ron the Masseur), Eliza Coupe (Hotel Room Neighbor), Nicole Trunfio (Brunette Bikini Beauty), Tim Starks (LAX VIP Services), Mary McNeal (Airline Rep), Ferruccio Calamari (Milan VIP Handler), Antonio Bracciani (Milan Airport Policeman), Davide Borella (Hotel Manager – Milan), Munzio Alfredo "Pupi" D'Angieri (Pupi), Jo Champa (Pupi's Wife), Greta Zamparini (Pupi's PR), Stefano Fiorentino (Young Rich Man), Laura Chiatti (Sylvia), Giorgia Surina (Italian TV Reporter), Simona Ventura, Nino Frassica (Telegatto Hosts), Maurizio Nichetti (Telegatto Award Recipient), Valeria Marini (Telegatto Special Guest), Paola Turani, Marica Pellegrinelli (Telegatto Girls), Martina Chiriaco, Jennifer Iacono, Angela Lanotte, Simona Lucla Tauro (Telegatto Dances), Marco Gandolfi Vannini (Italian Limo Driver), Philip Pavel (Hotel Manager), Romulo Laki (Romulo), Damian Delgado (Victor), Laura Ramsey (Naked Blonde with Sailor Cap), Nathalie Love (Young Wasted Girl), Caitlin Keats (Chateau Lobby Guest), David Jean Thomas (Casino Croupier), Peter McKernan (Helicopter Pilot), Patrick McKernan (Helicopter Ground Safety), C.C. Sehffield (Woman Getting Haircut), Ray Garcia (Parking Valet), Benicio Del Toro (Himself).

Stephen Dorff

Feeling listless and alienated by the pressures of movie stardom, Johnny Marco finds some meaning to his life when his daughter Cleo comes to stay with him for an extended period of time.

Stephen Dorff, Elle Fanning

Stephen Dorff, Elle Fanning © Focus Features

Gwyneth Paltrow, Tim McGraw

COUNTRY STRONG

(SCREEN GEMS) Producers, Jenno Topping, Tobey Maguire; Executive Producer, Meredith Zamsky; Director/Screenplay, Shana Feste; Photography, John Bailey; Designer, David J. Bomba; Costumes, Stacey Battat; Music, Michael Brook; Music Supervisor, Randall Poster; Song: "Coming Home" by Bob DiPiero, Tom Douglas, Hillary Lindsey and Troy Verges/performed by Leighton Meester; Editors, Carol Littleton, Conor O'Neill; Casting, Laura Rosenthal, Liz Dean; a Material Pictures production; Dolby; DeLuxe color; Rated PG-13; minutes; Release date: December 22, 2010

CAST

Kelly Canter	**Gwyneth Paltrow**
James Canter	**Tim McGraw**
Beau Hutton	**Garrett Hedlund**
Chiles Stanton	**Leighton Meester**
Winnie	**Marshall Chapman**
Hair Stylist	**Lari White**
JJ	**Jeremy Childs**
Joe	**JD Parker**
Travis' Mom	**Lisa Stewart Seals**

Jackie Welch (Teacher), Cinda McCain (Misty), Gabe Sipos (Travis), Sandra Harris (Orderly), Megan Henderson (Herself), Dan Beene (Bob), Reegus Flenory (Security Guard), Terri Minton (James's Assistant), Ed Bruce (Clint), Darrin Dickerson (Tex), Alana Grace (Ginny), Katie Groshong (Richard's Assistant), Candace Michelle Coffee (Denise), Katie Cook (Gossip Show Host), Adam Skaggs, Travis Nicholson (PA's), Denita Odigie (PR Girl in Classroom), Jeffrey Buckner Ford (Richard), Jeri Sager (Stylist), Kirt Lahew (Biker), Ranjit Bhullar (Doctor), Tina White (Interviewee), Brett Warren (Jesse Clark), Olivia Haley, Jim Melton (Fans), Holly Watson, Brad Schmitt, Andy Cordan (Interviewers), Cory Younts, Skylar Wilson, Josh Graham, Chris Scruggs, Loney Hutchins, Ian Fitchuk (Beau's Bandmates), Bucky Baxter, John Bohlinger, Neal Casal, Chris Clark, Jim Lauderdale, Doug Frasure, Amanda Shires, John Deaderick (Kelly's Bandmates), Johnny Gates, Jamie Jarbeau, Matt Scanlon, Michael Ollin Lotten, Smith Curry (Chiles' Bandmates), Kristen Wilkinson, David Angeli, Gregory Martin, Sara Reist (String Quartet Members), James Hamlet, Steve Hinson (Honky Tonk Band Members), Fred Eltringham, Gary Nicholson, Beau Stapleton, Danny Flowers (Stuiod Band Members), Nancy Amons, Jim Taylor, Jonathan Martin, Katrina Hagger Smith, Nick Beres, Kelly Sutton, Shane Tallant, Katrina Smith, Christine Maddela, Stephanie Langston (Reporters)

A rising singer-songwriter hooks up with fallen country star Kelly Canter in an effort to get her career back on track.

This film received an Oscar nomination for original song ("Coming Home").

GULLIVER'S TRAVELS

(20TH CENTURY FOX) Producers, John Davis, Gregory Goodman; Executive Producers, Jack Black, Benjamin Cooley; Director, Rob Letterman; Screenplay, Joe Stillman, Nicholas Stoller; Photography, David Tattersall; Designer, Gavin Bocquet; Costumes, Sammy Sheldon; Music, Henry Jackman; Music Supervisor, Dave Jordan; Editors, Dean Zimmerman, Alan Edward Bell; Visual Effects, Weta Digital Ltd.; Visual Effects Supervisor, Guy Williams; Casting, Priscilla John (UK); Jeanne McCarthy (US); Stunts, Franklin Henson; a Davis Entertainment Company production; Dolby; DeLuxe color; 3D; Rated PG-13; 85 minutes; Release date: December 25, 2010

CAST

Lemuel Gulliver	**Jack Black**
Horatio	**Jason Segel**
Princess Mary	**Emily Blunt**
Darcy Silverman	**Amanda Peet**
King Theodore	**Billy Connolly**
General Edward	**Chris O'Dowd**
Dan	**T.J. Miller**
Jinks	**James Corden**
Queen Isabelle	**Catherine Tate**
King Leopold	**Emmanuel Quatra**
Prince August	**Olly Alexander**
Nigel, Travel Writer	**Richard Laing**
Foreman	**David Sterne**

Stweart Scudamore (Blefuscian Captain), Jonathan Aris (Lilliputian Scientist), Jake Nightingale, Okezie Morro, Christopher Middleton (Blefuscian Sentries), Danni Benattar (Giant Princess), Bradley Ford, Noah St. Bean, Zachary Harris (Boys), Charlize Hyams, Nieve Stenton, Rafiella Brooks (Girls), Robert Gilbert (Mark), Harry Peacock (Lilliputian Royal Guard), Gemma Whelan (Lilliputian Rose), Ian Porter (Business Desk Editor), Stink Fisher (Construction Worker), Bentley Kalu (New York Tribune Staffer), Meredith Vieira (Lilliputian), Joe Lo Truglio (Butt-crack Man), Christopher Lee Shefstad (Vendor)

Sent on assignment to write about the Bermuda Triangle, Lemuel Gulliver wakes up in Lilliput where his enormous size puts him in awe of the tiny residents in this update on the classic Jonathan Swift story.

Jack Black © 20th Century Fox

BLUE VALENTINE

(WEINSTEIN CO.) Producers, Jamie Patricof, Lynette Howell, Alex Orlovsky; Executive Producers, Doug Dey, Jack Lechner, Scott Osman, Ryan Gosling, Michelle Williams; Co-Producer, Carrie Fix; Director, Derek Cianfrance; Screenplay, Derek Cianfrance, Joey Curtis, Cami Delavigne; Photography, Andrij Parekh; Designer, Inbal Weinberg; Costumes, Erin Benach; Music, Grizzly Bear; Music Supervisor, Joe Rudge; Casting, Cindy Tolan; an Incentive Filmed Entertainment presentation of a Silverwood Films/Hunting Lane Films production in association with Chrysler/Shade Pictures/Motel Movies/Cottage Industries; Dolby; Color; Rated R; 120 minutes; Release date: December 29, 2010

CAST

Dean	**Ryan Gosling**
Cindy	**Michelle Williams**
Frankie	**Faith Wladkya**
Jerry	**John Doman**
Bobby	**Mike Vogel**
Marshall	**Marshall Johnson**
Gramma	**Jen Jones**
Glenda	**Maryann Plunkett**
Jamie	**James Benatti**
Jo	**Barbara Troy**
Charley	**Carey Westbrook**
Dr. Feinberg	**Ben Shenkman**
Mimi	**Eileen Rosen**
Professor	**Enid Graham**

Ashley Gurnari (Checker), Jack Parshutich (Billy), Samii Ryan (Amanda), Mark Benginia (Concierge), Timothy Liveright (Doctor), Tamara Torres (Maria), Robert Russell (Justice of the Peace), Michelle Nagy (Music Teacher), Felicia Reid (Nurse), Melvin Jurdem (Old Man), Alan Malkin (Cab Driver), Derik Belanger (Tony), Isabella Frogoletto, Madison Ledergerber (Children), Jaimie Jensen (Pregnant Woman)

A non-linear look into the married lives of Dean and Cindy and their ups and downs over the years.

This film received an Oscar nomination for actress (Michelle Williams).

Ryan Gosling, Michelle Williams © Weinstein Co.

Ryan Gosling

Michelle Williams

DOMESTIC FILMS B

2010 Releases / January 1–December 31

GARBAGE DREAMS (Iskander Films) Producer/Director/Photography, Mai Iskander; Executive Producer, Tiffany Schauer; Music, Raz Mesinai; Editor, Kate Hirson; a co-production with Movieart in association with Chicken & Egg Pictures; Color; HD; Not rated; 79 minutes; Release date: January 6, 2010. Documentary on how three Egyptian teens find their job of collecting and recycling garbage under threat by international sanitation companies

Garbage Dreams © Iskander Films

SWEETGRASS (Cinema Guild) Producer, Ilisa Barbash; Director/Photography, Lucien Castaing-Taylor, Ilisa Barbash; a Peabody Museum, Cambridge production; Dolby; Color; DV-to-35mm; Not rated; 101 minutes; Release date: January 6, 2010. Documentary follows a group of modern-day cowboys as their lead their flocks of sheep up into the Absaroka-Beartooth Mountains of Montana. **WITH** John Ahern, Elaine Allestad, Lawrence Allestad, Pat Connolly

Sweetgrass © Cinema Guild

FLOODING WITH LOVE FOR THE KID (Independent) Director/Screenplay/Photography/Editor/Designer, Zachary Oberzan; Based on the novel *First Blood* by David Morrell; Color; Not rated; 107 minutes; Release date: January 8, 2010. **CAST**: Zachary Oberzan

WAITING FOR ARMAGEDDON (First Run Features) Producers, David Heilbroner, Franco Sacchi; Directors, Kate Davis, Franco Sacchi, David Heilbroner; Photography, Franco Sacchi, Kate Davies; Music, Gary Lionelli; Editor, Mike Nuget; Eureka Film Productions and Q-Ball Productions; Color; HDCAM; Not rated; 74 minutes; Release date: January 8, 2010. Documentary on America's Evangelical community and their beliefs in Biblical prophecies regarding the Rapture and Armageddon. **WITH** James Bagg, Laura Bagg, Tony Edwards, Devonna Edwards, Dr. H. Wayne House

Waiting for Armageddon © First Run Features

CRAZY ON THE OUTSIDE (Freestyle) Producers, Brian Reilly, Brett Gregory, Anastasia Stanecki; Executive Producers, Justin Moritt, Richard Baker; Director, Tim Allen; Screenplay, Judd Pillot, John Peaslee; Photography, Robbie Greenberg; Designer, Rob Pearson; Costumes, Valerie Laven-Cooper; Music, David Newman; Music Supervisors, Manish Raval, Tom Wolfe; Editor, Scott Conrad; Casting, Anne McCarthy, Jay Scully, Freddy Luis; a Boxing Cat Films presentation; Dolby; Color; Rated PG-13; 96 minutes; Release date: January 8, 2010. **CAST**: Tim Allen (Tommy), Sigourney Weaver (Vicki), Ray Liotta (Gray), Jeanne Tripplehorn (Angela), J.K. Simmons (Ed), Julie Bowen (Christy), Kelsey Grammer (Frank), Jon Gries (Edgar), Darla Delgado (Gray's Girlfriend), Daniel Booko (Cooper Luboja), Robert Baker (Lance), Karle Warren (Alex Luboja), Malcolm Goodwin (Rick), Vanessa Ross (Christy's Friend), Casey Sander (Prison Guard), Kate Clarke (Tommy's Mother), Kenton Duty (Ethan Papadopolous), Hector Atreyu Ruiz (Prisoner), Meeghan Holaway (Tina), Tahmus Rounds (Pee Man), Helen Slayton-Hughes (Grandma), John Hayden (Judge Pierce), Brian Graham (Convict), Evelyn Iocolano (Denise), Wayne Morse (Holding Cell Cop), Jeff Kueppers (Steve), Tommy Gerrits (Dentist Patient), Ricky Marciano (Parent), Scarlett Chorvat (Cindy)

Tim Allen, Ray Liotta in *Crazy on the Outside* © Freestyle Releasing

BITCH SLAP (Freestyle) Producers/Screenplay, Eric Gruendemann, Rick Jacobson; Director, Rick Jacobson; Photography, Stuart Asbjomsen; Designer Vali Tirsoaga; Costumes, Rosalinda Medina, Robin Lewis West; Music, John R. Graham; Editors, Joe McFadden, Corey Yaktus; a Bombshell Pictures/Epic Slap production; Color; Rated R; 108 minutes; Release date: January 8, 2010. **CAST**: Julia Voth (Trixie), Eric Cummings (Hel), America Olivo (Camero), Michael Hurst (Gage), Ron Melendez (Deputy Fuchs), William Gregory Lee (Hot Wire), Minae Noji (Kinki), Scott Hanley (Black Ice), Kevin Sorbo (Mr. Phoenix), Dennis Keiffer (MacDaddy), Lucy Lawless (Mother Superior), Renée O'Connor (Sister Batrill), Mark Lutz (Deiter Von Vondervon), Debbie Lee Carrington (Hot Pocket), Zoe Bell (Rawhide), Robert Mammana (Prison Guard John), Rich Kirby (Prison Guard Thomas), Jim Klock (Officer Spanky with a "Tude"), Danny Nero (Officer Big Gun McFluff), Christine Nguyen (Nasty Nubile Escort), Katelynne Friedman (Lily the Languid), Krystal Badia (Sister Sara), Paul Karami (The Sheik le Freak), Astrid Swan (Lady Liberty), Aisha Cain (Harem Aussie Code Blue), Sabine Varnes (Bathroom Bitch Varla), Eurlyne Epper (Bathroom Bitch Rosie), Rick Jacobson (Horndog), Brian Peck (Wrong Place – Wrong Time), Eric Gruendemann (Father Malone), Michael Belasco (Totally Awful Background Artist), Karen Austin (Narrator), Thaddeus (Himself)

Bitch Slap © Freestyle Releasing

BRUTAL BEAUTY: TALES OF THE ROSE CITY ROLLERS (Cinema Purgatorio) Producer/Director, Chip Mabry; Executive Producers, Chip Mabry, Bret Johnson, Kim Stegeman; Photography, Eli Dorsey; Music, John Askew; Editor, Ben Meader; American Toaster productions; Color; Not rated; 80 minutes; Release date: January 8, 2010. Documentary on Portland, Oregon's Rose City Rollers roller derby league. **WITH** Marollin' Monroe, Cadillac, Madame Bumpsalot, White Flight, Rhea Derange, Scratcher in the Eye, Blood Clottia, Rocket Mean, Grace Lightning

Brutal Beauty
© Cinema Purgatorio

MINE (Film Movement) Producers, Geralyn Pezanoski, Erin Eseenmacher; Director, Geralyn Pezanoski; Photography, Arlo Rosner, Jason Rhein; Editor, Jen Bradwell; a Smush Media production; Color; Not rated; 81 minutes; Release date: January 15, 2010. Documentary in which victims of Hurricane Katrina attempt to reunite with the pets they lost during the devastation. **WITH** Karen O'Toole, Gloria Richardson, Malvin Cavalier, Jessie Pullins, Tiffany Mansfield, Jeremy Mansfield, Randy Turner

Malvin Cavalier in *Mine* © Film Movement

LEONARD COHEN LIVE AT THE ISLE OF WIGHT 1970 (Pulsar/Sony Music Entertainment) Producer/Director, Murray Lerner; Executive Producer, Steve Berkowitz; Photography, Andy Carchrae, Jack Hazan, and others; Editors, Einar Westerlund, George Panos; an MFL production; Color; 16mm-to-Blu-ray; Not rated; 64 minutes; Release date: January 22, 2010. Leonard Cohen in concert. **WITH** Leonard Cohen, Bob Johnston, Joan Baez, Judy Collins, Kris Kristofferson

Leonard Cohen in *Live at the Isle of Wight 1970* © Pulsar/Sony

TO SAVE A LIFE (Goldwyn/Outreach Films) Producers, Steve Foster, Jim Britts, Nicole Franco; Executive Producer, Scott Evans; Co-Producer, Christina Lee Storm; Director, Brian Baugh; Screenplay, Jim Britts; Photography, C. Clifford Jones; Designer, Rachel Britts; Costumes, Christi Cecil-Stewart; Music, Timothy Michael Wynn; Editors, Dan O'Brien, Brian Baugh, Sarah Sanders; Casting, Elizabeth Lang; a New Song Pictures presentation in association with Accelerated Entertainment; Color; HD; Rated PG-13; 120 minutes; Release date: January 22, 2010. **CAST**: Randy Wayne (Jake Taylor), Deja Kreutzberg (Amy Briggs), Joshua Weigel (Chris Vaughn), Steven Crowder (Doug Moore), D. David Morin (Mark Rivers), Sean Michael Afable (Jonny Garcia), Bubba Lewis (Danny Rivers), Robert Bailey Jr. (Roger Dawson), Kim Hidalgo (Andrea Stevens), Arjay Smith (Matt

McQueen), Orion Mozon (Billy), Lamont Thompson (Clyde Williams), Trinity Scott (Kelsi), Janora McDuffie (Cari Vaughn), Laura Black (Pam Taylor), David Strazyk (Glen Taylor), Monique Edwards (Esther Dawson), Joseph Narducci (Frank), Lori Rom (Jan), Dee Baldus (Mrs. Jones), Nicole Franco (Church Woman), Lee Ann Kim (Reporter), Christian Pike (Young Roger), Jason Evans (Young Jake)

Randy Wayne, Sean Michael Afable in *To Save a Life* © Goldwyn

DROOL (Strand) Producers, John Portnoy, Todd Williams, Nick Thurlow; Executive Producers, Nils Larsen, Chad Martin, Peter Baxter, Darryn Welch, Chris Ouwinga; Director/Screenplay, Nancy Kissam; Photography, Kara Stephens; Designer, Maurin Scarlata; Music, Dana Boule; Editor, Jenn Belleville; an Upload films and Instinctive Film presentation in association with Elements Entertainment and Slamdance; Color; HD-to-DigiBeta; Not rated; 86 minutes; Release date: January 22, 2010. **CAST**: Laura Harring (Anora), Jill Marie Jones (Imogene Cochran), Oded Fehr (Cheb), Ashley Duggan Smith (Tabby Fleece), Christopher Newhouse (Little Pete Fleece), Rebecaa Newman (Princess), Dalton Alfortish (Denny), James DuMont (Mr. Wilder), Garrett Allain (Mr. Vargas), Kerrell Antonio (Officer), Ruthie Austin (Kathy K.), Andrew Breland (Rodney the Pool Boy), Michael Roth (Grimm Taylor), Jeremy Dean Turner (Vossler)

Jill Marie Jones, Laura Harring in *Drool* © Strand Releasing

POP STAR ON ICE (Sundance Channel) Producers/Directors/Screenplay/Photography/ Editors, David Barba, James Pellerito; Co-Producers, Becca Bender, Jennifer Pellerito; Music, Giovanni Spinelli; a Retribution Media production in association with the Sundance Channel; Stereo; Color; DV; Not rated; 85 minutes; Release date: January 22, 2010. Documentary on Olympic figure skating champion Johnny Weir. **WITH** Johnny Weir, Priscilla Hill, Paris Childers, Patti Weir, Oksana Baiul, Brian Boitano, Christine Brennan, Kurt Brownign, Sasha Cohen, Scott Hamilton, Brian Joubert, Stéphane Lambiel, Brian Orser, Victor Petrenko, Galina Zmievskaya

MISCONCEPTIONS (Regent/Here) Producers, Steve J. Brown, Ron Satlof, Ira Pearlstein; Executive Producers, Ted Perkins, Ed Arenas; Director, Ron Satlof, Ira Pearlstein; Photography, Curtis Graham; Music, Michael A. Levine; Editor, George Mandl; a Cineglobe-Noble group, Lineage Pictures and Misconceptions Prods. presentation; Color; DigiBeta; Not rated; 95 minutes; Release date: January 22, 2010. **CAST**: Samuel Ball (Tom Dexter), Sarah Carter (Lucy Dexter), A.J. Cook (Miranda Bliss), Orlando Jones (Terry Price-Owens), David Moscow (Sandy Price-Owens), David Sutcliffe (Parker Bliss Sr.), Tom Bower (Judge Transome), Colleen Ann Brah (Kathy), Tyler Cravens (Albert), Aerica D'Amaro (Debbie Sue Dawson), Mary Rachel Dudley (Ms. Mason), Grace Santos (Naomi), William Haze (Ron), Noelle McCutchen (Monica), Tim Powell (TV Evangelist), Matt McGee (Sales Guy), Frank Meli (Miranda's Attorney), David Nix (Process Server), Elliot Swift (Pastor), Nicole Burron (Young Mom), Mimi Rice (Head Nurse), Chase Ajdinovich, DeMario Henry, Brian Dean Fidalgo II, Shana Perkins (Dancers)

David Moscow, Orlando Jones, Mimi Rice in *Misconceptions* © Regent/Here

WATERCOLORS (Regent/Here) Producers, Larry Allen, Penny Styles McLean; Executive Producers, Adam W. Kassoff, Ben S. Louie, Lucia Owens; Director/Screenplay, David Oliveras; Photography, Melissa Holt; Designer, Ron Hansford; Music, Marcelo Cesena, Dorian Rimsin; Editor, Martinos Aristidou; a Silverlight Entertainment presentation; Color; DigiBeta; Not rated; 114 minutes; Release date: January 22, 2010. **CAST**: Tye Olson (Danny Wheeler), Kyle Clare (Carter Melman), Ellie Araiza (Andy), Casey Kramer (Miriam Wheeler), Jeffrey Lee Woods (Stephen Melman), William C. Mitchell (Mr. Frank), Ian Rhodes (Older Danny), Edward Finlay (Allan), David Schroeder (High School Principal), Brandon Lybrand (Henry), Greg Louganis (Coach Brown), Karen Black (Mrs. Martin), Bobby Rice (Donnert), Ten Travis, Jason Hawkins, Eddie Underwood (Swim Team Members), James Jones (Winning Swimmer), Chris Pohl, Kai Seixas, Ramsey Alderson, Roy Calhoun, Aren Goddo, Kenny Sanders, Kevin Tucker, Mychael Burns, Yamil Oliveras, Mario Merlos (Swimmers), Josue Rosas (Winning Swim Coach), James Elliot, Brian Abou (Paramedics)

Kyle Clare, Tye Olson in *Watercolors* © Regent/Here

MURDER IN FASHION (Regent/Here) formerly *Fashion Victim*; Producers, Mark Boot, Byron Werner, Erin McElveen; Executive Producers, J.R. Ganda, J. Grace; Director, Ben Waller; Screenplay, Linda Boroff; Photography, Byron Werner; Designer, Thomas S. Hammock; Costumes, Carla Biggert; Music, Seth Podowitz; Color; DigiBeta; Rated R; 90 minutes; Release date: January 22, 2010. **CAST**: Jonathan Trent (Andrew Cunanan), Robert Miano (Gianni Versace), Stacey Dash (Cara Wheeler), Cerina Vincent (TV Reporter), James C. Burns (Harry Spalding), Mike Wiseman (Agent Johnson), Joseph Sikora (Agent Richman), Jay Jablonski (Agent Melville), Callard Harris (Store Clerk), Robert Fun (Landlord), Omar Leyva (Caretaker), Landall Goolsby (David Madsen), Michael Garvey (Miami Bouncer), Shea Sica (Mary Ann Cunanan), Anne Underwood (Swedish Woman), Antonio Scalfini (Clerk #1), Joe Mahon, Brian Womack (Boys), Teaj Sanderson (Tom), Umoja Butler (VIP Bouncer), Makelaie Brown (Drug Dealer), Peter Quinana (Older Man), JD Brown (Gay Passerby), Daniel Utsinger (Phone Support Clerk), Saul Herckis (Hotel Clerk), Joey Abbene (Pawn Shop Man), Morgan Rogers (Police Officer), Nick Roberts (Reese), Happy Richardson (Spokesperson), Rod Britt (Stan), Marc Ambrose (Gay Reporter), Jack Kennedy (Tony), James Clark (Jules), Dave Florek (Danny Acton), Faquizi Brahimi (French Waiter), Buzz Belmondo (Modesto), Ray Kelsey (Model), Craig Chapman (Edward Swift), Jeff Hartley (Jeffrey Trail), Howard Ferguson-Woitzman (Lee Miglin), Abe Frederick (Laughing Cop), Tyler McGauley (James McNeil).

Jonathan Trent in *Murder in Fashion* © Regent/Here

STILL BILL (B-Side Entertainment) Producers, Damani Baker, Alex Vlack, Jon Fine; Executive Producers, Alex Vlack, Andrew Zuckerman; Directors, Damani Baker, Alex Vlack; Photography, Damani Baker, Jon Fine, Edward Marritz; Music, Bill Withers; Editors, Jon Fine, Sakae Ishikawa; a Late Night and Weekends presentation of a Slab Fork Films production; Color; HD; Not rated; 79 minutes; American release date: January 27, 2010. Documentary on musician Bill Withers. **WITH** Bill Withers, Marica Withers, Todd Withers, Clarence Avant, Benorce Blackmon, James Gadson, Terrell Harrison, Aneglique Kidjo, Jim James, Mervin Johnson, Ralph MacDonald, Raul Midon, Tavis Smiley, Sting, C.V. Thompson, Cornel West

Bill Withers in *Still Bill* © B-Side Entertainment

SAINT JOHN OF LAS VEGAS (IndieVest Pictures) Producers, Mark Burton, Matt Wall, Lawrence Mattis, Kelly McCormick; Executive Producers, Steve Buscemi, Stanley Tucci, Wren Arthur, Spike Lee, David Engel, David Alpert; Director/Screenplay, Hue Rhodes; Photography, Giles Nuttgens; Designer, Rosario Provenza; Costumes, Lisa Jensen; Music, David Torn; Editor, Annette Davey; Casting, Heidi Levitt; an IndieVest Pictures production in association with Olive Productions, presented with Circle of Confusion; Dolby; Color; Rated R; 85 minutes; Release date: January 29, 2010. **CAST**: Steve Buscemi (John), Romany Malco (Virgil), Sarah Silverman (Jill), Peter Dinklage (Mr. Townsend), Tim Blake Nelson (Ned), John Cho (Smitty), Emmanuelle Chriqui (Tasty D Lite), Aviva (Penny), Isabel Archuleta (Jenny), Josh Berry (Store Manager), Gorneth D'Oyley (Casino Dealer), Stephen Eiland (Mordicai), Jesse Garcia (Park Ranger), Jim Giesler (Barker), Jamie Haggan, Karen M. Hudson. Nicholas A. Nelson (Fair Attendees), Isaac Kappy (Geek), Shawn Prince (Ticket Taker), Ben Zeller (Truck Stop Owner), Matthew McDuffie (Lucypher), Danny Trejo (Bismarck), Jim "Gee" Giesler (Barker), Ernest Labreck (Ed McMahon Type)

Sarah Silverman, Steve Buscemi in *Saint John of Las Vegas* © IndieVest Pictures

OFF AND RUNNING (First Run Features) Producers, Nicole Opper, Sharese Bullock; Executive Producers, Macky Altston, Sandra Itkoff; Director, Nicole Opper; Screenplay, Avery Klein-Cloud, Nicole Opper; Photography, Jackob Akira Okada; Music, Daniel Bernard Roumain; Editor, Cheree Dillon; a Nicole Opper Prods. and ITvS production in association with NBPC; Color; DV; Not rated; 75 minutes; Release date: January 29, 2010. Documentary about the struggles faced by Avery, an adopted black girl raised by two Jewish lesbians. **WITH** Avery Klein-Cloud, Rafi Klein-Cloud, Travis Klein-Cloud, Tovah Klein-Cloud

Avery Klein-Cloud in *Off and Running* © First Run Features

FALLING AWAKE (IFC Films) Producer, Andrew Adelson; Executive Producers, Stephen Molaskey, Raul Alarcon, Brad Friedmutter, Dean Valentine; Director, Agustin; Screenplay, Agustin, Michael Baez, Doug Klozzner; Photography, Mark Schwartzbard; Designer, Alex Brook Lynn; Costumes, Beth Ann Kelleher; Music, Kevin A. Stuart; Editor, Michael Spence; a MegaFilms and CinemaLab presentation; Color; Not rated; 110 minutes; Release date: January 29, 2010. **CAST**: Jenna Dewan (Alessandra), J.D. Williams (D-Money), Nicholas Gonzalez (Eddie), Nestor Serrano (Lazaro), Julie Carmen (Angela), Michael Rivera (Lucho), Karin Duseva (Dancer), Eunice Anderson (Grandma), Flaco Navaja (Mafi), Andrew Cisneros (Jay), Gurdeep Singh (Pakistani Man), Maria Diaz (Business Woman), Ramon Fernandez (Papo), Alessandra Ramos (Meri), Mateo Gómez (Street Preacher), Kareem Savinon (Papo's Thug), Casper Martinez (DJ Capicu), Carolina Zaballa (Brazilian Girl), Ingrid Schau (Linda), Tiffany Romano (Nelly), Natalie Cortez (Anabela), Gerald Bunsen (Joe), Luis Jimenez (Pipo), Marta Vidal (Mafi's Mother), Xiomara Medina (Capicu's Girl), Jelani "Flash" Love (Bumpy)

Andrew Cisneros, Jenna Dewan in *Falling Awake* © IFC Films

PREACHER'S KID (Warner Premiere/Gener8xion Entertainment) Producers, Matthew Crouch, Stan Foster, Darryl Taja; Executive Producers, Marc Bienstock, Richard J. Cook; Director/Screenplay, Stan Foster; Photography, Dave Perkal; Designer, Simon Dobbin; Costumes, Frank Helmer; Music Supervisor, Julia Michels; Editor, Richard Nord; presented in association with Epidemic Pictures and Stan Foster Pictures; Dolby; Color; Rated PG-13; 101 minutes; Release date: January 29, 2010. **CAST**: Letoya Luckett (Angie), Tammy Townsend (Desiree), Durrell "Tank" Babbs (Devlin), Carlos Davis (Biscuit), Andre Butler (Markus), Nadiyah Hollis (Performer), Javen Campbell (Garrett), Clayton English (Terrence), Kelly Finley (Meghan), Ella Joyce (Sister Watkins), Rae'Ven Larrymore Kelly (Marcia), Gregory Alan Williams (Bishop King), Essence Atkins (Peaches), Clifton Powell (Ike), Dawnn Lewis (Mya), King Kedar (Marcus), Deetta West (Emma), Mari White (Keya), Gregory Alan Wililams (Bishop King), Frank Brennan (Teddy), Nikki Ali (Mom), Sharif Atkins (Wynton), Jerome Ro Brooks (Himself), Lem Collins (Jeff), Ginnie Randall (Mother Charles), Kierra "Kiki" Sheard (Litha)

Letoya Luckett in *Preacher's Kid* © Gener8xion Entertainment

FROZEN (Anchor Bay) Producers, Peter Block, Cory Neal; Executive Producers, Tim Williams, John Penotti, Michael Hogan; Co-Producers, Jason R. Miller, Amanda Essick, Mark Ward; Director/Screenplay, Adam Green; Photography, Will Bart; Designer, Bryan A. McBrien; Costumes, Barbara J. Nelson; Music, Andy Garfield; Editor, Ed Marx; Special Effects Coordinator, Dean Miller; Special Effects Makeup, Chris Hanson; Casting, Nancy Nayor Battino; a Bigger Boat/ArieScope Pictures production in association with a Bigger Boat; Dolby; Color; Rated R; 93 minutes; Release date: February 5, 2010. **CAST**: Emma Bell (Parker O'Neil), Shawn Ashmore (Joe Lynch), Kevin Zegers (Dan Walker), Ed Ackerman (Jason), Rileah Vanderbilt (Shannon), Kane Hodder (Cody), Adam Johnson (Rifkin), Chris York (Ryan), Peder Melhuse (Driver), Adam Green, Joe Lynch (Guys on Chairlift)

Emma Bell, Kevin Zegers, Shawn Ashmore in *Frozen* © Anchor Bay

THE KOREAN (Indican) Producer/Director/Screenplay, Thomas Dixon; Photography, Andreas Krol; Art Director, Marcus Miller; Costumes, Diane Collins; Music, Jace Vek; Editor, Alexander Wilson; Special Effects, Steve Tollin; a Storyteller presentation in association with Jonadab Pictures; Dolby; Color; HD; Rated PG-13; 98 minutes; Release date: February 5, 2010. **CAST**: Josiah D. Lee (Lee, The Korean), Jennifer Vos (Lissia), John Yost (Jude), Jack Erdie (Ray L.), Rik Billok (Sachton), Paul Adamo (Ali), Paula Bellin (The Contessa), James Cadenhead (Adam), Trevor Chae (Young Lee), Emilio Cornachione, Arnold Zigarelli (Diplomats), Joanne Cottage (Old Woman), Robert DiDonato (Abdula), David Early (Capt. Milcoy), Gregory Johnstone (CB's Guy #1), Andre Kazouh (Adel), Marcus Muzopappa (Chris), Shaun O'Donnell (Neighbor), Harry O'Toole (CB), Ginny Quaglia (Sandra), Jessica Ream (Stuardess), David Santiago (Shareef), Pumpa M. Shala (Maid), Rose Smith-Lotenero (Lily), Stephanie Trainer (Front Desk Attendant)

OCTOBER COUNTRY (Wishbone Films) Producers/Directors/Screenplay, Michael Palmieri, Donal Mosher; Photography, Palmieri; Music, Danny Grody, Donal Mosher, Michael Palmieri, Kenric Taylor; Dolby; Color; Not rated; 80 minutes; Release date: February 12, 2010. Documentary follows the struggles of a low-income family in upstate New York. **WITH** the Mosher Family

Donna Mosher in *October Country* © Wishbone Films

CÉLINE: THROUGH THE EYES OF THE WORLD (Sony/The Hot Ticket) Producer, Julie Snyder; Director, Stéphane Laporte; Color; Not rated; 120 minutes; Release date: February 17, 2010. Documentary follows singer Céline Dion during her Taking Chances Tour. **WITH** Céline Dion, René Angélil, René-Charles, Dion Angelil, Charice, Ito Yuna, Andrea Bocelli

Céline Dion in *Through the Eyes of the World* © Sony/Hot Ticket

HAPPY TEARS (Roadside Attractions) Producers, Joyce Pierpoline, Mitchell Lichtenstein; Executive Producers, Gregory Elias, Timothy J. DeBaets, Jonathan Gray; Director/Screenplay, Mitchell Lichtenstein; Photography, Jamie Anderson; Designer, Paul Avery; Costumes, Stacey Battat; Visual Effects Supervisor, Mark O. Forker; Casting, Kerry Barden, Paul Schnee; a Talent Beach Prods. presentation of a Pierpoline Films production; Dolby; Color; Rated R; 95 minutes; Release date: February 19, 2010. **CAST**: Demi Moore (Laura), Parker Posey (Jayne), Rip Torn (Joe), Ellen Barkin (Shelly), Christian Camargo (Jackson), Billy Magnussen (Ray), Roger Rees (Antiques Dealer), Sebastian Roche (Laurent), Susan Blommaert (Mallory), Victor Slezak (Eli Bell), Celia Weston, Tom McNutt (Neighbors), T. Ryder Smith (Shoe Salesman), Rich Barlow (Mitch Dawkins), Jacquelyn Conforti and Julianna Conforti (Young Jayne), Patti D'Arbanville (Nurse Marina), David King (Dr. Sims), Alyssa Klein (Young Laura), Kathy Nowrey, Kimberly Villanova (Prostitutes), David Adam Smith (Art Gallery Patron), Pete Patrikios (Driver), Melissa Ticen (Stewardess), Aldous Davidson (Waiter), Anderson Golsom (Young Ray), Suzanne Inman (Nurse), Marilyn Yoblick (Yard Sale Woman), Benjamin Brandreth (Ben), Mikey Iles (Mike), Max Iles (Max), Eve Gordon (TV Reporter)

Phyllis Kleine, Harold Kleine in *Phyllis and Harold* © Rainbow Releasing

Parker Posey, Demi Moore in *Happy Tears* © Roadside Attractions

BLOOD DONE SIGN MY NAME (Paladin) Producers, Mari Stuart, Mel Efros, Jeb Stuart, Robert K. Steel; Co-Producers, Richard King, David Martin; Director/Screenplay, Jeb Stuart; Based on the book by Tim Tyson; Photography, Steve Mason; Designer, Sandy Veneziano; Costumes, Mary Malin; Music, John Leftwich; Editor, Toby Yates; Casting, Craig, Lisa Mae & Mark Fincannon; a Real Folk production; Dolby; Widescreen; Color; Rated PG-13; 128 minutes; Release date: February 19, 2010. **CAST**: Nick Searcy (Robert Teel), Michael Rooker (D.A. Billy Watkins), Rick Schroder (Vernon Tyson), Lela Rochon (Roseanna Allen), Darrin Dewitt Henson (Eddie McCoy), Lee Norris (Roger Oakley), Omar Benson Miller (Herman Cozart), Nate Parker (Ben Chavis), Emily Alyn Lind (Julie Tyson), Gattlin Griffith (Tim Tyson), Rhoda Griffis (Isabel Taylor), Susan Walters (Martha Tyson), Gregory Alan Williams (Dr. Samuel Proctor), Cullen Moss (Larry Teel), Bonnie Johnson (Dorothy), Lem Collins (Rioter), Afemo Omilami (Golden Frinks), Natalie Alyn Lind (Boo Tyson), Lori Beth Edgeman (Judy Teel), Tim Parati (Lead Workman), Mike Pniewski (William Burgwyn), Michael May (Gerald Teel), Leslie Riley (Colleen Teel), Sahr Nguaujah (Boo Chavis), Michael Harding (Dr. Page Hudson), Sandra Ellis Lafferty (Grandma Jessie), Danny Vinson (Dick Jones), Milauna Jemai (Willie Mae Marrow), Frank Hoyt Taylor (Thad Stem), Markice Moore (Moses), D.A. Hänks ("Shades"), Chandler George Brown (Jeff Daniels), Lee Spencer (Charles), Martin Thompson (Judge Linwood Peoples), Ron Prather (Police Chief White), Bridget Gethins (Miss Fran), John Rutland (Oxford Police Officer Davis), A.C. Sanford (Henry "Dickie" Marrow), Andrew James (Jebbie), Michael Stanton Kennedy (Mayor Currin), Gil Johnson (Jack Miller), Marty Terry (Mrs. Alwin), David Ramsey (Judge Robert Martin), Tommy Hahn (Neil Cassidy), Jay Schmitt (Frank Panzet), David Lowe (Bailiff Sloan), Christine Horn (Sister Chavis), Kristin Jann-Fischer (Betsy Teel), Geordie White (Monk)

PHYLLIS AND HAROLD (Rainbow Releasing) Producer/Director, Cindy Kleine; Executive Producer, Andre Gregory; Photography, Claire Cario, Cindy Cleine; Music, Bruce Odland; Editor/Co-Producer, Jonathan Oppenheim; a Silver Penny Pictures production; Black and white/color; HD; Not rated; 84 minutes; Release date: February 19, 2020. Documentary in which Cindy Kleine examines her parents' 59-year marriage. **WITH** Phyllis Kleine, Harold Kleine, Eric Kleine, Annie McCarter, Cindy Kleine

DREAMKILLER (Delaware Pictures) Producer, Stephane Mermet; Executive Producer, Clyde Ware; Director, Catherine C. Pirotta; Screenplay, Catherine C. Pirotta, Clyde Ware; Photography, John O'Shaughnessy; Designer, Miguel Gomez; Music, Marcus Sjowall; Editor, Richard Hasley; Color; Rated R; 111 minutes; Release date: February 19, 2010. **CAST**: Dario Deak (Nick Nemet), John Savage (Agent Barnes), Tyrone Power Jr. (Agent Benett), John Colton (Dr. Stalberg), Penny Drake (Annette DeFour), Kelly Chambers (Rachel), Nick Rish (Det. Barrett), Diandra Newlin (Natalia Nemet), Karin Andrade (Debbie Torres), David Bertelsen (Dr. Kearney), Lauren Bicknell (Psych Nurse Wilson), Greg Blessing (Officer Reilley), Cheeks (Julian Stoli), Gary Hourani (Dr. Reyes), Rachel Haines (Det. Renee Ferguson), Pete Halvorsen (Rod), Ryan Johnsen (Officer Flynn), Jeanne Mount (Mrs. Bernstein), Donna Newlin (Nurse), Taryn O'Neill (Toni), Paul Oquist (Masterson), Mimi Renard (Nurse Spears), Todd Roosevelt (Officer Hendricks), Brent Horning (Brian Carter), Suzanne Turner (Capt. Karen MacPherson), Darian Weiss (Natalia's Boyfriend), America Young (Erin O'Dowell)

THE LAST NEW YORKER (Brink Film) Producers, Danny Vinik, Adam Forgash; Executive Producers, Richard Macary, Todd Olson; Director, Harvey Wang; Screenplay, Adam Forgash; Photography, Derek McKane; Designer, Tamar Gadish; Music, Dario Eskenazi; Editor, Jeff Flohr; a Sugarmans presentation of a Brink Films production; Color; HD; Not rated; 88 minutes; Release date: February 19, 2010. **CAST**: Dominic Chianese (Lenny Sugarman), Dick Latessa (Reuben), Kathleen Chalfant (Mimi), Josh Hamilton (Zach), Kate Buddeke (Connie), Catherine Lloyd Burns (Hostess), Joe Grifasi (Jerry), Ben Hammer (Moses Weiss), Ann Hu (Reporter), Jen Jones (Molly), Sylvia Kauders (Miriam Weiss), William Mahoney (McCormack), Keith Middleton (Bike Messenger), Dequina Moore (Waitress), Laith Nakli (Cabbie), Stuart Rudin (Eisenberg's Waiter), Martin Shakar (Sal), Joseph R. Sicari (Salvatore), Natalie Silverlieb (Talia), Irma St. Paule (Pearl), Gerry Vichi (Lou Fishman)

Dominic Chianese, Josh Hamilton in *The Last New Yorker* © Brink Film

THE GOOD GUY (Roadside Attractions) Producers, Linda Moran, René Bastian, Julio DePietro; Director/Screenplay, Julio DePietro; Photography, Seamus Tierney; Designer, Tommaso Ortino; Costumes, Erika Munro; Music, Tomandandy; Music Supervisor, Joe Rudge; Editor, Ray Hubley; a Whitest Pouring Films presentation in association with Belladonna Prods.; Color; Rated R; 90 minutes; Release date: February 19, 2010. **CAST**: Alexis Bledel (Beth Vest), Scott Porter (Tommy Fielding), Bryan Greenberg (Daniel Seaver), Anna Chlumsky (Lisa), Aaron Yoo (Steve-O), Andrew McCarthy (Cash), Kate Nauta (Cynthia), Trini Alvarado (Sylvia), Colin Egglesfield (Baker), Adam LeFevre (Billy), Luca Calvani (Paolo), Adrian Martinez (Larry), Eric Thal (Stephens), Rana Davis (Cashier), Steve Antonucci (Bar Patron), Jessalyn Wanlim (Jordan), Denise Vasi (Suki), Rob Bogue (Johnny), Christine Evagelista (Brooke), Sarah Glendening (Jen), Monica Steuer (Florist), Kathy Searle (Susan), Ursula Abbott (Jill), Clem Cheung (Angry Taxi Driver), Ted Koch (Foreman), Andrew Stewart-Jones (Shakespeare), Jeane Fournier (Christie), James Thomas Bligh (Ted the Cabbie), Michael Sirow (Smitten Man), David Villalobos (Stefan), Darrin Baker (Bobby), Jackie Stewart (Sofia), Ed Wheeler (Irv), Monika Baskiewicz (Christie's Friend), Al Roffe (Driver #2), Woody Boley (Wall Street Guy), Michael Simeoni (Donny)

Aaron Yoo, Bryan Greenberg in *The Good Guy* © Roadside Attractions

THE ART OF THE STEAL (Sundance Selects) Producer, Sheena M. Joyce; Executive Producer, Lenny Feinberg; Director/Photography, Don Argott; Music, West Dylan Thordson; Editor, Demian Fenton; a 9.14 Pictures presentation in association with MAJ Prods.; DTS; Color; Not rated; 101 minutes; Release date: February 26, 2010. Documentary about how the valuable artworks of the Barnes Foundation were wrested away from their designated home in Lower Merion, Pennsylvania. **WITH** John Anderson, Colin B. Bailey, Julian Bond, Carolyn T. Carluccio, David D'Arcy, Richard Feigen, D. Michael Fisher, Tom L. Freudenheim, Jim Gerlach, Richard H. Glanton, Nancy Herman, Walter Herman, Christopher Knight, Meryl Levitz, Bruce H. Mann, Robert Marmon, Toby Marmon, Ross Mitchell, Barry Munitz, Irvin Mahan, Marcelle Pick, David W. Rawson, Jay Raymond. Edward G. Rendell, Mark D. Schwartz, Harry Sefarbi, Richard Segal, Nick Tinari, Robert Zaller

Albert Barnes in *The Art of the Steal* © Sundance Selects

45365 (Seventh Art) Producers/Directors/Photography/Editors, Bill Ross IV, Turner Ross; Music, Jeff Larger, Charles Liddy, Sonya Phillips, Alan Reid, Bill Ross IV; Color; HD; Not rated; 91 minutes; Release date: February 26, 2010. Documentary which looks at the residents of Sidney, Ohio.

45365 © Seventh Art

TOE TO TOE (Strand) Producers, Emily Abt, Susan Leber; Executive Producer, Sarah Peter; Director/Screenplay, Emily Abt; Photography, Alan Jacobson; Desisnger, Tommaso Ortino; Costumes, Annie Yun; Music, Force Theory; Editor, Jeff Marcello; Casting, Paul Schnee, Kerry Barden; a Pureland Pictures presentation, in association with Susie Q. Prods.; Dolby; Color; Not rated; 106 minutes; Release date: February 26, 2010. **CAST**: Louisa Krause (Jesse), Sonequa Martin (Tosha), Ally Walker (Claire), Leslie Uggams (Grandma), Silvestre Rasuk (Rashid), Gaius Charles (Kevin), Dionne Audain (Brenda), Hina Abdullah (Mina), Maha Chehlaoui (Fatimah), Eric Chamblee (Kenda), Thuliso Dingwall (Miles), Samantha Eustace (Coach Kacie), Nancy Flores (Rashid's Mother), Michael Gabel (Bill), Angelica Gregory (Jill), Tiffani Holland (Chevelle), Jonnie Marie Horne (Aisha), James Kinstle (Rick), Alexandra Morten (Nicole), Jamie Nocher (Luke), Kendra North (Dr. Hanson), Kheedim Oh (Simon), Leslie Olabisi (Rico), Tuluv Price (Pam), Duane Rawlings (Rev. Roberts), Chris Riggi (Jason), Anshu Wahi (Sadia), Kevin Wallace (Salim), Betty Montgomery Williams (Shareese)

Sonequa Martin, Louisa Krause in *Toe to Toe* © Strand Releasing

PRODIGAL SONS (First Run Features) Producers, John Keitel, Kimberly Reed; Executive Producers, Robert Hawk, Gail Silva; Director, Kimberly Reed; Photography, John Keitel; Music, T. Griffin; Editors, Shannon Kennedy, Kimberly Reed; Color; DV; Not rated; 87 minutes; Release date: February 26, 2010. Filmmaker Kimberly Reed documents her return to her home town of Helena, Montana after a sex change operation, having once been the high school quarterback. **WITH** Kimberly Reed, Carol McKerrow, Marc McKerrow, Claire Jones, Lea McKerrow, Gordon McKerrow, Kathy McKerrow, Glenn McKerrow,

Jasmine Fuentes, Frank Mayo, Cyndee Moe, Tim O'Leary, Diana MacDonald, Todd McKerrow, Debbie McKerrow, Kelsie McKerrow, Oja Kodar, Sasha Welles, Nina Palinkas, Jan Jaima, Jakov Sedlar, David Cannon, Pita Rodriguez, Bridget Maley, John Moran

Carol McKerrow, Marc McKerrow, Kimberly Reed in *Prodigal Sons*
© First Run Features

EASIER WITH PRACTICE (Breaking Glass Pictures) Producer, Cookie Carosella, Kyle Patrick Alvarez; Director/Screenplay, Kyle Patrick Alvarez; Photography, David Morrison; Designer, Brooke Peters; Costumes, Tom Soluri; Music Supervisors, Marguerite Philips, Colin Wyatt; Editor, Frernando Collins; a Forty Second Productions presentation; Color; Not rated; 100 minutes; Release date: February 26, 2010. **CAST**: Brian Geraghty (Davy Mitchell), Kel O'Neill (Sean Mitchell), Marguerite Moreau (Samantha), Jeanette Brox (Sarah), Jenna Gavigan (Josie), Kathryn Aselton (Nicole), Eugene Byrd (Aaron), Danielle Lozeau (Amanda, Waitress), Emelie O'Hara (Crying Girl), Lucas CorVatta (Waiter), Allison Hensel (Bartender), Tracey Horsley (Hostess), Lauren Petzke (Blonde Woman), Jamie Haggani (Club Patron), Casey Wayne (Office Guy)

Brian Geraghty in *Easier with Practice* © Breaking Glass Pictures

FORMOSA BETRAYED (Screen Media) Producers, Will Tiao, David Cluck, Adam Kane; Director, Adam Kane; Screenplay, Charlie Stratton, Yann Samuell, Brian Askew, Nathaniel Goodman; Story, Will Tiao, Katie Swain; Photography, Irek Hartowicz; Designer, Anthony Rivero Stabley; Costumes, Karyn Wagner; Music, Jeff Danna; Editor, Howard E. Smith; Casting, Deborah Aquila, Claire Simon, Mary Tricia Wood; a Formosa Films presentation; Dolby; Color; Rated R; 103 minutes; Release date: February 26, 2010. **CAST**: James Van Der Beek (Jake Kelly), Wendy Crewson (Susan Kane), Will Tiao (Ming), John Heard (Tom Braxton), Tzi Ma (Kuo), Chelcie Ross (Daltry), Leslie Hope (Lisa Gilbert), Kenneth Tsang (General Tse), Adam Wang (Lee), Mintita Wattanakul (Maysing), Joseph Anthony Foronda

(Prof. Henry Wen), Tonray Ho (Mrs. Wen), Henry Chu (Wu), Jay Disney (Professor at Protest), Alex Duong (Wu), Peter F. Essig, Bob Kolbey (College Professors), Tim Grimm (Dean Goodman), Michelle Higgins (Cocktail Server), Jeff Albertson (FBI Staffer), Andrew J. Lee (Lee), Deborah Lynn (FBI Secretary), John Marengo (Businessman at Bar), Joseph Mazurk (Undercover FBI Agent), Stephen Oyoung (Interrogator), Peggy Roeder (Coroner), Lisa Wolf (Pallbearer), Tom Jay (Captain Chen)

James Van Der Beek in *Formosa Betrayed* © Screen Media

HARLEM ARIA (Magnolia) Producers, Deepak Nayar, Philip von Alvensleben; Executive Producers, Damon Wayans, Isabell von Alvensleben, Hale Coughlin; Director/ Screenplay, William Jennings; Photography, Keith Smith; Designer, Cecil Gentry; Costumes, Daniel Glicker; Music, Jeff Beal, Fabian Cooke; Editor, Sabine Hoffman; Casting, Denise Fitzgerald; a Kintop Pictures/Alive Entertainment/In Motion presentation of a Bent Nail production; American-German, 1999; Dolby; Moviecam color; Rated R; 100 minutes; Release date: March 5, 2010. **CAST**: Damon Wayans (Wes), Gabriel Casseus (Anton), Christian Camargo (Matthew), Malik Yoba (Luke), Paul Sorvino (Fabiano Grazzi), Kristen Wilson (Julia), Eyde Byrde (Auntie), Nicole Ari Parker (Clarisse), Fenton Lawless (Sgt. Scanlon), Isiah Whitlock Jr. (Manny), Charles Keating (Professor), Reno (Carla), James Saxenmeyer (James), Al Thompson (Bill), Lord Kayson (DaVinci)

Gabriel Casseus, Damon Wayans in *Harlem Aria* © Magnolia

STOLEN (IFC Films) formerly *Stolen Lives*; Producers, Anders Anderson, Al Corley, Josh Lucas, Devin Maurer, Bart Rosenblatt, Andy Steinman; Director, Anders Anderson; Screenplay, Glenn Taranto; Photography, Andy Steinman; Designer, Jennifer Spence; Costumes, Lisa Norcia; Music, Trevor Morris; an A2 Entertainment Corp./Code Entertainment production; Color; Widescreen; Rated R; 90 minutes; Release date: March 12, 2010. **CAST**: Josh Lucas (Matthew Wakefield), Jon Hamm (Tom Adkins Sr.), Rhona Mitra (Barbara Adkins), James Van

Der Beek (Diploma/Roggiani), Jessica Chastain (Sally Ann), Joanna Cassidy (Lea Adkins), Jimmy Bennett (John), Morena Baccarin (Rose Montgomery), Michael Cudlitz (Jonas), Andy Miller (William Daniels), Holt McCallany (Swede), Jude Ciccolella (Police Chief), Rick Gomez (Officer JJ), Marcus Thomas (Pete Dunne), Graham Phillips (Mark Wakefield), Christian Bender (Young Luke), Sam Hennings (Older Luke), Tom Kemp (Russell MacArthur), Kali Rocha (Coral), Benjamin Burdick (Carl Montgomery), Kim Hamilton (Miz Betsy), Bob Stephenson (Mike the Bartender), William C. Mitchell (Lou), Glenn Taranto (Chollie), Ryan Cutona (Bill Byrnes), Ty Panitz (Tom Adkins Jr.), Ray Proscia (Lawyer), Elizabeth Small (Edvena), Enuka Okuma (Officer Angie Riddick), Angela Schnaible (Girl), Jeanette Brox (Lisa), Kasey Campbell (Micha), Beth Grant (Older Edvena), Cheynne Wilbur (Old Minister), Pamela Dunlap (Shelly the Waitress), Rutanya Alda (Old Sally Ann), James Mathers (Joel Schubert), Paul Keith (Barber), Jonathan Eisley (Mick), Channing Chase (Lorraine), Charles C. Stevenson (Man getting a Cut), Bart McCarthy (Kevin Byrnes), Tonye Patano (Elsie Mauer), Beresford Bennett (Investigator), Al Corley (Uncle Sam), Liliana Rose (Jenette), Lindsey Rosenblatt (Ashley), Richard Amadril (Waiter), Charity Beyer (1950s Barmaid), Keith Brush (Examiner), Elizabeth Kouri (Pearl Wakefield)

Holt McCallany, Josh Lucas, James Van Der Beek in *Stolen* © IFC Films

GONE WITH THE POPE (Grindhouse Releasing) Executive Producers, Bob Murawski, Sage Stallone; Director/Screenplay, Duke Mitchell; Photography, Peter Santoro; Costumes, Al Pacillo; Editors, Roberto Florio, Bob Leighton; Color; Not rated; 83 minutes; Release date: March 12, 2010. **CAST**: Bill Boyd (Bill), John Bruno (John), Carl Cocomo (Carl), Lorenzo Dardado (The Pope/The Old Man), Paul DiAmico (Bartender), Steve DiBasio (Vatican Bishop), Nola Hand (Fat Woman), Jeanne Hibbard (Jean), Jim LoBiano (Luke), Pete Milo (Peter), Duke Mitchell (Paul), Jeffrey Mitchell (Junkie), Zep Mizner (Himself), John Murgia (John), Giorgio Tavolieri (Giorgio), Joe Virzi (Radio Announcer)

Gone with the Pope © Grindhouse Releasing

CHILDREN OF INVENTION (Variance) Producers, Mynette Louie, Trevor Sagan; Executive Producer, Dan Cogan; Director/Screenplay, Tze Chun; Photography, Chris Teague; Art Director, Ashley Wellbrook; Costumes, Jennifer Behar; Music, T. Griffin; Editor, Anna Boden; an Impact Partners and Sasquatch Films presentation of a Syncopation films production; Color; Not rated; 86 minutes; Release date: March 12, 2010. **CAST**: Cindy Cheung (Elaine Cheng), Michael Chen (Raymond Cheng), Crystal Chiu (Tina Cheng), Stephen Gevedon (Rob the Salesman), Frank Pando (Bruce), Kieran Campion (Dan), Jackson Ning (Michael), Remmi Franklin (Sheriff), Yan Xi (Felicia), Suzan Mikiel Kennedy (Mrs. Cutter), Ruth Zhang (Mrs. Chow), Yu Lu (Mr. Chow), Ronald Thomas (Toystore Manager), Lynn Mastio Rice (Betty Cardellini), Katie Kreisler (Lucy), Kathleen Kwan (Rosemary), Han Tang (Nancy), Dustin Sullivan (Dennis), Wai Ching Ho (Doris), Lee Wong (Great Grandpa), Kenneth Lee (Charles Cheng), Karlene Baptiste (Diner Signer), Amy Chang (Susan), Ai Cheng (Linda), Avery Pearson (Hotel Receptionist), Robert Kelly (Torres), Michael Pemberton (McCarthy), Janine Mahoney (Bank Teller), Jared Sprague (Blond Boy in Car), Mellini Kantayya (FTC Investigator), Laurie Williams (Public Defender), Linda Behrman (Police Woman)

THE EXPLODING GIRL (Oscilloscope) Producers, So Yong Kim, Karin Chien, Ben Howe, Bradley Rust Gray; Executive Producers, Jason Diamond, Josh Diamond, Billfield Cheng, Jay Van Hoy, Lars Knudsen; Director/Screenplay/Editor, Bradley Rust Gray; Photography, Eric Lin; Casting, Susan Shopmaker; a Soanbrad production, in association with MPS Prods.; Color; HD; Not rated; 80 minutes; Release date: March 12, 2010. **CAST**: Mark Rendall (Al), Zoe Kazan (Ivy), Maryann Urbano (Mom), Hunter Canning (Cary), Margot Ruth Tenenbaum (Cousin)

Mark Rendall, Zoe Kazan in *The Exploding Girl* © Oscilloscope

TALES FROM THE SCRIPT (First Run Features) Producer, Paul Robert Herman; Director, Peter Hanson; Screenplay, Peter Hanson, Paul Robert Herman; Music, T.J. Raider; Editor, J.D. Funari; a Grand River Films & Jade Tiger Films presentation; Color; DV; Not rated; 105 minutes; Release date: March 12, 2010. Documentary in which several professional Hollywood writers share their stories and experiences of working in the industry. **WITH** Allison Anders, Jane Anderson, Doug Atchison, John August, Shane Black, John D. Brancato, John Carpenter, Larry Cohen, Frank Darabont, Steven E. de Souza, Gerald Di Pego, Mark Fergus, Antwone Fisher, Naomi Foner, Joe Forte, Josh Friedman, Mick Garris, William Goldman, David Hayter, Peter Hyams, Michael January, Steve Koren, Jonathan Lemkin, Andrew W. Marlowe, Mark O'Keefe, Dennis Palumbo, Zak Penn, Billy Ray, Adam Rifkin, Jose Rivera, Mark Rosenthal, Ari Rubin, Bruce Joel Rubin, Richard Rush, Paul Schrader, Melville Shavelson, Ron Shelton, Ronald Shusett, Stephen Susco, Guinevere Turner, Kriss Turner, David S. Ward, James L. White, Michael Wolk, Kris Young, Justin Zackham

Melville Shavelson in *Tales from the Script* © First Run Features

SUICIDE GIRLS MUST DIE! (First Look) Producers, Keith Geller, Missy Suicide, Jeremy Kasten; Director, Sawa Suicide; Screenplay, Brian Fagan; Music, Thavius Beck; Editors, Jeremy Kasten, Seth Clark; Color; Rated R; 96 minutes; Release date: March 12, 2010. **CAST**: Amina Suicide (Amina), Bailey Suicide (Bailey), Bully Suicide (Bully), Daven Suicide (Daven), Evan Suicide (Evan), Fractal Suicide (Fractal), James Suicide (James), Joleigh Suicide (Joleigh), Mary Suicide (Mary), Quinne Suicide (Quinne), Rigel Suicide (Rigel), Roach Suicide (Roach), Roza Suicide (Roza), Sawa Suicide (Sawa), Soren Suicide (Soren), Don Bagley (Caretaker), Tony Ezzillo (Izzy), Ken Edling, Brandon Stumpf (Police Officers), Peter Patton (Diner Worker)

Suicide Girls Must Die! © First Look

THE HARIMAYA BRIDGE (Eleven Arts) Producers, Aaron Woolfolk, Ko Mori; Executive Producers, Danny Glover, John Kim, Naoshi Yoda; Director/Screenplay, Aaron Woolfolk; Photography, Masao Nakabori; Art Director, Takahisa Taguchi; Music, Kazunori Maruyama; Editor, John Coniglio; an Eleven Arts (U.S.)/Laterna (Japan) production in association with SSD; American-Japanese; Color; Not rated; 120 minutes; Release date: March 12, 2010. **CAST**: Ben Guillory (Daniel Holder), Saki Takaoka (Noriko Kubo), Misa Shimizu (Yuiko Hara), Danny Glover (Joseph Holder), Victor Grant (Mickey Holder), Sakura Thomas (Mariya), Misono (Saita Nakayama), Hajime Yamazaki (Kunji Inoue), Miho Shiraishi (Kayo Takeuchi), Honoka (Emi Osaki), Yukiko Kashiwagi (Ms. Kubo), Toshiyuki Kitami

(Mr. Kubo), Peter Coyote (Albert Tunney), A'da Alison Woolfolk (Lindsey Holder), Junkichi Orimoto (Tomoki Shide), Akira Hamada (Principal Shimura), Rico E. Anderson (Grant Holder), Michael T. Coleman (Ross), John Gallagher (Mark), Miho Ninagawa (Ms. Osaki), Kiyotaka Terauchi (Shinto Priest), David Ramadanoff (Orchestra Conductor), Marc McTizic (Young Daniel), Kailon Loud (Young Mickey), Aya Kazuki (Teacher #1), Yoshie Yamasaki (Waitress), Shuji Shiroshita (Sake Store Owner), Sayoko Uga (Flower Shop Owner), Noriko Sano (Inoue's Wife), Yuko Wada (Shide's Wife), Koji Kariya, Rikumi Nishimoto (Government Officials), Noriko Omura, Yoshiki Yamamoto, Hisao Miyauchi, Teruaki Konishi (Neighbors), Fukutaro Nishimori (Elderly Man), Minoru Yamamoto (Mr. Nakasone)

Misa Shimizu in *The Harimaya Bridge* © Eleven Arts

WHITE ON RICE (Variance) Producers, Duane Andersen, Dominic Fratto; Executive Producer, Howard Hayes; Director, Dave Boyle; Screenplay, Dave Boyle, Joel Clark; Photography, Bill Otto; Designer, Meg Boyle; Music, Mark Schulz; Editor, Duane Andersen; a Brainwave, Malatova Prods., Tiger Industry production; Color; Super 16-to-35mm; Rated PG-13; 83 minutes; Release date: March 12, 2010. **CAST**: Hiroshi Watanabe (Jimmy), Nae (Aiko), Mio Takada (Tak), Lynn Chen (Ramona), James Kyson-Lee (Tim Kim), Justin Kwong (Bob), Pepe Serna (Prof. Berk), Joy Osmanski (Mary), Cathy Shim (Betty), David Christenson (Waiter), Ron Eliot (Nathan), Kayako Takatsuna (Shiho), Jimmy Chunga (Stephens), Jennifer Klekas (Susan), Bruce Campbell (Voice of Muramoto), Kitana Baker (Lingerie Saleswoman), Joe Polhemus (Doctor), Naohiro Takita (Ramona's Dad), Rachel Andersen (Vicki), Christy Summerhays (Mrs. Polleys), Pat Donahue (Allan Snyder), Kurando Mitsutake (Samurai Executioner), Hiroshi Otaguro (Rebellious Samurai), Ren Urano (Samurai Clan Leader), Melanie Nelson (Megan), Dane allred (Policeman), Allsu Kubranova (Waiter's Girlfriend), Charlie Andersen (Boy Ghost), Tony Dang, John Fukuda, Chikako Omura, Hiroshi Ueha (Villagers), Rowan Andersen (Groucho), Bryce Bishop (Low Life Punk), Eric Bjarnson (The Corpse), Diana Eliot (Nathan's Wife), Jason McLoney (Old Man), Michael Ori (Wedding Band Leader), Asa Andersen, Ryan Ricks (Pumpkin Smashers)

Hiroshi Watanabe, Justin Kwong in *White on Rice* © Variance

SEVERE CLEAR (Sirk Prods.) Producers, Marc J. Perez, Kristian Fraga; Director/ Screenplay/Editor, Kristian Fraga; Photography, Mike Scotti; Music, Cliff Martinez; Color; DV; Not rated; 93 minutes; Release date: March 12, 2010. Docucmentary of footage shot on a camcorder by Marin 1st Lt. Mike Scotti during the first months of Operation Iraqi Freedom.

Severe Clear © Sirk Prods.

KIMJONGILIA (Kino Lober) Producers, Robert Pepin, David Novack, Young-sun Cho; Executive Producer, Mike Figgis; Co-Producers, Su Kim, the Saylors Brothers; Director, N.C. Heikin; Photography, Kyle Saylors; Editors, Peterson Almeida, Mary Lampson; Music, Michael Gordon; American-South Korean-French; Color; Not rated; 74 minutes; Release date: March 19, 2010. Documentary on Kim Jong Il's horrific reign of North Korea. **WITH** Kang Chol-hwan, Shin Dong-hyuk, Lee Shin, Byeon Ok-soon, Kim Cheol-woong

Shin Dong-hyuk in *Kimjongilia* © Kino Lorber

SHUTTERBUG (Cyprian Films) Producers, Minos Papas, Rossana Rizzo, Nando Del Castillo, Brett Mole; Director/Screenplay, Minos Papas; Photography, Rossana Rizzo; Music, Tao Zervas; Editors, Minos Papas, Max Lupowitz; Color; HD; Not rated; 91 minutes; Release date: March 19, 2010. **CAST**: Nando Del Castillo (Alex Santiago), Ariel Blue Sky (Barbara), Doug Barron (Maddox), Stanislava Stoyanova (Thalia), Brett Molé (Nick), Frank Cadillac (Harry), Anna Gutto (Miranda), Louis Chassis (Dominguez), Brian Dochney (Cocky Hipster), Tom Greenman (Todd), Amy Hoerler (Cherie), Brian Ish (Matthew), Terron Jones (Homeless Man), Aaron Lehmann (Avi), Emily Mitchell (Lady Lydia), George Morafetis (Nikolas Pythias), Joseph Muto (Dr. Sinha), Mark G. Phillips (Dwayne), Alison Rood, Lauren Fales (Hipster Girls), Mary Round (Angela), Ashley Thayer (Mary), Jonathan Tripp (Jonathan), Ivo Velon (Lupo)

Nando Del Castillo in *Shutterbug* © Cyprian Films

REPO MEN (UNIVERSAL) formerly *Reposession Mambo*; Producer, Scott Stuber; Executive Producers, Miguel Sapochnik, Jonathan Mone, Mike Drake, Valerie Dean, Andrew Z. Davis; Director, Miguel Sapochnik; Screenplay, Eric Garcia, Garrett Lerner; Based on the novel *The Reposession Mambo* by Eric Garcia; Photography, Enrique Chediak; Designer, David Sandefur; Costumes, Caroline Harris; Music, Marco Beltrami; Editor, Richard Francis-Bruce; Visual Effects Supervisor, Aaron Weintraub; Stunts/Fight Coordinator, Hiro Koda; Casting, Mindy Marin; a Stuber Pictures production, presented in association with Relativity Media; Dolby; Panavision; Technicolor; Rated R; 111 minutes; Release date; March 19, 2010. **CAST**: Jude Law (Remy), Forest Whitaker (Jake), Liev Schreiber (Frank), Alice Braga (Beth), Carice van Houten (Carol), Chandler Canterbury (Peter), Joe Pingue (Ray), Liza Lapira (Alva), Tiffany Espensen (Little Alva), Yvette Nicole Brown (Rhodesia), RZA (T-Bone), Wayne Ward (John), Tanya Clarke (Hooker), Max Turnbull (Larry the Lung), Howard Hoover, Robert Dodds (Salesemen), Raff Law (Young Remy), Tremayne Corion (Young Jake), Marty Adams (Obese Man), Daniel Kash (Chipped Tooth), Christian Lloyd (Addict), Dominc Cuzzocrea (Cabbie), Carlos Diaz (Cab Passenger), Imali Perera (Q Nurse), Tannis Burnett (Hallway Nurse), Michael Cram (Father), Heather Hodgson, Bruce Gooch (Remy's Customers), Laytrel McMullen, Ellie Ellwand, Alie Rutty (Jump Rope Girls), Kenny Robinson (Gruff Repo Man), Jim Annan, Alice Poon, Simon Northwood, Wayne Downer, John MacDonald (TSA Agents), Neil Whitely, Marium Carvell (Passenger), Daniel Lévesque (Curious Man), Michal Grajewski (Repo Trainee), Zoe Mugford (Technician), Philip Nessel (Sick Father), Roland Rothchild (Guard), Dennis Akayama, Matt Baram (Doctors), Katie Bergin (Woman in Bathroom), Jee-Yun Lee (Newswoman), Tino Monte (Newsman), John Picard (Raggedy Dude), Kevin Rushton (Artiforg Arm), Alicia Turner (Repo Woman), Ciara Jones (Subway Girl), Riley Jones (Young Debtor), Angelina Assereto (Bikini Girl)

Jude Law, Forest Whitaker in *Repo Men* © Universal Pictures

THE KILLING JAR (New Films Intl.) Producers, Jonathan Sachar, Patrick Durham, William Boyer, Mark Young; Director/Screenplay/Editor, Mark Young; Photography, Gregg Easterbrook; Designer, Chris Best; Costumes, Ginger Knussman; Music, Elia Cmiral; a New Films Intl. and Morningstar Pictures production; Color; Not rated; 90 minutes; Release date: March 19, 2010. **CAST**: Michael Madsen (Doe), Harold Perrineau (Dixon), Amber Benson (Noreen), Danny Trejo (Jimmy), Kevin Gage (Hank), Lew Temple (Lonnie), Lindsey Axelsson (Starr), Jonathan Sachar (O'Brien), Patrick Durham (Shaffer), Talan Torriero (Billy), Jake Busey (Greene), Emily Catherine Young (Young Girl)

SEE WHAT I'M SAYING: THE DEAF ENTERTAINERS DOCUMENTARY (Wordplay) Producer/Director, Hilari Scari; Photography, Jeff Gatesman; Music, Kubilay Uner; Editors, Marcus Taylor, Morgan R. Smith; Color; Not rated; 91 minutes; Release date: March 19, 2010. Documentary on four deaf entertainers: Robert DeMayo, TL Forsberg, Bob Hiltermann, C.J. Jones.

C.J. Jones in *See What I'm Saying* © Wordplay

DREAM BOY (Regent/here) Producers, James Bolton, Herb Hamsher; Executive Producers, James Garbus, Robert Kroupa; Director/Screenplay, James Bolton; Based on the novel by Jim Grimsley; Photography, Sarah Levy; Designer, James A. Gelarden; Costumes, Ann Walters; Music, Richard Buckner; Editors, Annette Davey, Chris Houghton; Casting, Natasha Cuba, Kerry Barden; a Garbus Kroupa Entertainment production, in association with Mettray Reformatory Pictures, Tetrahedron Prods.; Dolby; Color; Rated R; 89 minutes; Release date: March 26, 2010. **CAST**: Stephan Bender (Nathan), Maximillian Roeg (Roy), Randy Wayne (Burke), Owen Beckman (Randy), Diana Scarwid (Vivian), Tricia Mara (Evelyn), Rickie Lee Jones (Roy's Mom), Tom Gilroy (Preacher), Thomas Jay Ryan (Harland), Cindy Williamson (Mrs. Niece), Michele Adams (Mother of Three Kids), Brandon J. Blanchard, Sean M. Blanchard, Jaci LeJeune, Emiliy Nichols, Zach Nichols (Students), Robin Blanchard, Bridget Nichols (Cafeteria Workers)

Maximilian Roeg, Stephan Bender in *Dream Boy* © Regent/Here

LBS. (Truly Indie) Producers/Screenplay, Carmine Famiglietti, Matthew Bonifacio; Co-Producer, Sophia Atonini; Director, Matthew Bonifacio; Story, Carmine Famiglietti; Photography, William M. Miller; Designer, Sophia Antonini; Music, Carlo Giacco; Editor, Jim Rubino; a Brooklyn-Queens Experiment production in association with Slingshot, 2004; Color; Not rated; 99 minutes; Release date: March 26, 2010. **CAST**: Carmine Famiglietti (Neil Perota), Michael Aronov (Sacco Valenzia), Miriam Shor (Lara Griffin), Eric Leffler (Lee Dawkins), Sharon Angela (Theresa Perota), Susan Varon (Connie Perota), Fil Formicola (Lou Perota), Lou Martini Jr. (Anthony Lanzo), Patrick Michael Buckley (Vito), Sophia Antonini (Deidre), Gino Cafarelli (Dante), Tom Karlya (Michael), Rich Pecci (Carlos), Jennifer Michelle Brown (Flower Girl), Marilyn Matarrese (Bridesmaid)

Miriam Shor, Carmine Famiglietti in *Lbs.* © Truly Indie

DANCING ACROSS BORDERS (First Run Features) Producers, Anne Bass, Catherine Tatge; Director, Anne Bass; Photography, Bob Elfstrom, Anthony Forma, Tom Hurwitz, Anne Bass; Editors, Girish Bhargava, Mark Sutton; a 123 Prods. production; Color/Black and white; HD; DV; Not rated; 88 minutes; Release date: March 26, 2010. Documentary on ballet dancer Sokvannara "Sy" Sar.

Vannarin Sar, Sy Sar in *Dancing Across Borders* © First Run Features

WAKING SLEEPING BEAUTY (Walt Disney Studios) Producers, Peter Schneider, Don Hahn; Director/Narrator, Don Hahn; Screenplay/Interviews, Patrick Pacheco; Photography, Steve Green; Music, Chris Bacon; Editors, Ellen Keneshea, Vartan Nazarian, John Damien Ryan; a Stone Circle Pictures/Red Shoes production; Dolby; Color/black and white; DV; Rated PG; 86 minutes; Release date: March 26 2010. Documentary on the re-birth of the Walt Disney Studios' animation division from 1984 to 1994. **WITH** Ron Clements, Roy Disney, Jeffrey Katzenberg, Peter Schneider, Rob Minkoff, Michael Eisner, Lisa Keene, George Scribner, Gary Trousdale, Tim Burton, John Lasseter, Don Bluth, John Musker, Roger Allers, Dick Cook, Glen Keane, Kirk Wise, Mike Gabriel, Thomas Schumacher, Randy Cartwright, David Pruiksma

Peter Schneider, Roy Disney, Jeffrey Katzenberg in *Waking Sleeping Beauty* © Walt Disney Studios

CA$H! (Roadside Attractions) Producers, Naveen Chathappuram, Stephen Milburn Anderson; Executive Producer, Prema Thekkek; Director/Screenplay, Stephen Milburn Anderson; Photography, John R. Leonetti, Robert Primes; Designer, Gary Baugh; Costumes, Mary Law Weir; Music, Jessica Voccia; Editor, Mark Conte; an Immortal Thoughts production, in association with Golden Wings Cinema, Tomahawk Films; Dolby; Color; DV; Rated R; 108 minutes; Release date: March 26, 2010. **CAST**: Sean Bean (Pyke Kubic), Chris Hemsworth (Sam Phelan), Victoria Profeta (Leslie Phelan), Mike Starr (Melvin Goldberg), Glenn Plummer (Glen the Plumber), Michael Mantell (Mr. Dale), Antony Thekkek (Bahadurjit Tejeenerpeet Singh), Tim Kazurinsky (Chunky Chicken Salesman), Jeff Albertson (Chicago Police Officer), Tommy Bartlett (Ace Rental Car Patron), Josh Blue (Car Rental Salesman), Debbi Burns (Harlem Furniture Saleswoman), Greg Fawcett (News Anchor), Robert C. Goodwin (Bartender), Cheryl Hamada (Robbery Victim), Kevin R. Kelly (Range Rover Salesman), Charles Kierscht (Car Rental Customer), James Pusztay (Dept. of Motor Vehicles Clerk), Paul Sanchez (Cole), Janelle Snow (Liquor Store Clerk), Christian Stolte (Car Salesman Manager), Craig Sunderlin (Auto Sales Manager), James Warfield (Server)

Chris Hemsworth, Sean Bean in *Ca$h* © Roadside Attractions

JUST SAY LOVE (Regent/Here) Producer/Director, Bill Humphreys; Executive Producers, David J. Mauriello, Kirkland Tibbels; Screenplay, Bill Humphreys, David J. Mauriello; Based on the play by David J. Mauriello; Photography, Nathan Beaman; Designers, Michael Minahan, Julian Mitchell; Music, Hans Indigo Spencer; Editor, BBT Films; a Stagewright Films and Funny Boy Films presentation of a Stagewright production; Color; HD-to-DigiBeta; Not rated; 76 minutes; Release date: March 26, 2010. **CAST**: Matthew Jaeger (Guy), Robert Mammana (Doug), Bill Humphreys (Guy's Father)

Matthew Jaeger, Robert Mammana in *Just Say Love* © Regent/Here

GODSPEED (Lightyear Entertainment) Producers, Houston King, John Flanagan; Executive Producers, Joseph McKelheer, Cory Knauf, Leonard McLeod, Alejandro Salomon, Sean Guse, Oren Kaplan; Director/Editor, Robert Saitzyk; Screenplay, Cory Knauf, Robert Saitzyk; Story, Cory Knauf, Joseph McKelheer; Photography, Michael Hardwick; Costumes, Alexis Beck; Music, Jeremy Grody, Justin Melland; Casting, Danielle Lenniger, Joe Lorenzo; a Film Harvest, Highlander Films, Helios TV, Alterity Films production; Color; Widescreen; HD; Not rated; 99 minutes; Release date: March 26, 2010. **CAST**: Joseph McKelheer (Charlie Shepard), Cory Knauf (Luke Roberts), Courtney Halverson (Sarah Roberts), Ed Lauter (Mitch), Jessie Ward (Rebecca Shepard), Hallock Beals (Tim), Lynn A. Freedman (Belle), Ben Loosli (James Shepard), Ron Holmstrom (Oscar), June Eck (Lorelei), Bob Pond (Lorelei's Husband), Frank Loosli (Mr. Sykes), Wendy Young (Diner Waitress), Trygg Ramstad (Davey Iverson), Jacob Moore, Lauren Worley, Desiree Massi, Simon Johnson, Kaylene Rihtarschich (Kids in Field)

Joseph McKelheer, Cory Knauf in *Godspeed* © Lightyear Entertainment

BREAKING UPWARDS (IFC Films) Producers, Zoe Lister Jones, Daryl Wein; Executive Producer, Bill Lister; Director, Daryl Wein; Screenplay, Peter Duchan, Daryl Wein, Zoe Lister-Jones; Photography, Alex Bergman; Art Director, Ryan Schaefer; Music, Kyle Forester; a Mister Lister production; Color; Widescreen; HD; Not rated; 89 minutes; Release date: April 2, 2010. **CAST**: Zoe Lister Jones (Zoe), Daryl Wein (Daryl), Julie White (Joanie), Andrea Martin (Helanie), Peter Friedman (Alan), La Chanze (Maggie), Ebon Moss-Bacharach (Dylan), Olivia Thirlby (Erika), Pablo Schreiber (Turner), Heather Burns (Hannah), Tate Ellington (Brian), Francis Benhamou (Lindsay), David Call (David), Sam Rosen (Jack), Max Jenkins (Frosh), Michael Benjamin (Polyamorist), Charles Socarides (Nikkos), Michael Warner (Michael), Audrey Alison (Waitress)

Daryl Wein, Zoe Lister Jones in *Breaking Upwards* © IFC Films

DON McKAY (Image Entertainment) Producer, Jim Young; Executive Producers, William Earon, James Young, Thomas Haden Church; Co-Producer, David Denney; Director/Screenplay, Jake Goldberger; Photography, Phil Parmet; Designer, Aleta Shaffer; Costumes, Andrew Poleszak; Music, Steve Bramson; Music Supervisors, Gabe Hilfer, Jim Black; Editor, Andrew Dickler; Casting, Eyde Belasco; an Animus Films presentation; Dolby; Color; DV; Rated R; 87 minutes; Release date: April 2, 2010. **CAST**: Thomas Haden Church (Don McKay), Elisabeth Shue (Sonny), Melissa Leo (Marie), Pruitt Taylor Vince (Mel), James Rebhorn (Dr. Lance Pryce), Keith David (Otis Kent), M. Emmet Walsh (Samuel), Ted Arcidi (Officer Randall), Stephen Benson (Principal Edwards), Lonnie Farmer (Det. Ed Movitz), Amanda Donaghey (Clerk), Harley Yanoff (Ambulance Driver), Bates Wilder (Officer Tierney), Rachel Harker (School Secretary), Charlie Peabody, Lewis D. Wheeler (Officers), Melissa Rosal (Hostess), Meagan Hawkes (Colleen Simmons), Dossy Peabody (Cafeteria Worker), Robert Wahlberg (Alfred)

2012: TIME FOR CHANGE (Mangusta/Intention Media) Producers, Joao Amorim, Giancarlo Canavesio, Sol Tryon; Director, Joao Amorim; Photography, Felpe Reinheimer, Joao Amorim; Designer, Ryan Price; Editor, April Merl; a Manusta presentation in association with PostModern Times and Curious Pictures; Color; HD-to-Blu-Ray; Not rated; 85 minutes; Release date: April 9, 2010. An ecology documentary. **WITH** Maude Barlow, Policarp Chaj, Michael D. Coe, Michael Dorsey, Tiokasin Ghosthorse, Gilberto Gil, Gaspar P. Gonzalez, Mitch Horowitz, Barbara Marx Hubbard, Joel Kovel, Bernard Lietaer, Penny Livingston, Ellen Page, Daniel Pinchbeck, Dean Radin, Shiva Rea, Richard Register, Paul Stamets, Sting, Elizabeth Thompson, John Todd, Ryan Wartena, Ganga White

Daniel Pinchbeck, Sting in *2012: Time for Change* © Mangusta

VALLEY OF THE HEART'S DELIGHT (Indican) Executive Producers, Scott Rosenfelt, B. Billie Greif; Director, Tim Boxell; Screenplay, John Miles Murphy; Photography, Hiro Narita; Designer, Douglas Freeman; Costumes, Cathleen Edwards; Music, Richard Gibbs, Nicholas O'Toole; Editor, Jay Boekelheide; Casting, Robin Gurland; an Intercontinental Drift presentation of a Banana Peel Entertainment production; Dolby; Color; HD-to-35mm; Rated PG-13; 97 minutes; Release date: April 9, 2010. **CAST**: Gabriel Mann (Jack Pacheco), Pete Postlethwaite (Albion Munson), Emily Harrison (Helen Walsh), Diana Scarwid (Natalie Walsh), Bruce McGill (Horace Walsh), Tom Bower (Sheriff Ackle), Ron Roggé (Deputy Dully), Val Diamond (Sylvia Daumier), Ed Holmes (Gov. Brodie), David Barth (Ralph Rutz), Michael Sommers (Agent Callaway), Cully Fredericksen (Agent Tucker), Howard Swain (Bill Vente), Robert Kennedy (James Sullivan), Ralph Miller (Tom Stanton), Robert Ernst (Ernest Maloney), Rod Gnapp (Harlan Grasso), Phil Stockton (Mr. Brewster), Ralph Peduto (Vegetable Man), Regina Saisi (Farm Mother), Bob Sáenz (Talker One), Nick Scoggin (Organizer Two), David Pearl (Townsperson), John Robb (Hobo)

Gabriel Mann, Emily Harrison in *Valley of the Heart's Delight* © Indican

LETTERS TO GOD (Vivendi Entertainment) Producers, Cameron Kim Dawson, David Nixon; Executive Producer, Tom Swanson; Director, David Nixon; Co-Director/Story, Patrick Doughtie; Screenplay, Patrick Doughtie, Art D'Alessandro, Sandra Thrift, Cullen Douglas; Photography, Bob M. Scott; Designer, Mark E. Garner; Costumes, Beverly Safier; Music, Colin O'Malley; Editor, Patrick Tyler; Casting, Amy Baker Severson; a Possibility Pictures production in association with DNP Studios and Vertical Innovations; Dolby; Technicolor; Rated PG; 113 minutes; Release date: April 9, 2010. **CAST**: Robyn Lively (Maddy Doherty), Jeffrey S.S. Johnson (Brady McDaniels), Tanner Maguire (Tyler Doherty), Michael Christopher Bolten (Ben Doherty), Maree Cheatham (Olivia), Bailee

Madison (Samantha Perryfield), Ralph Waite (Cornelius Perryfield), Dennis Neal (Lester Stevens), Cristian Cunningham (Carl, Postal Supervisor), Christopher John Schmidt (Walter Finley), Lisa Curtis (Erin Miller), Tom Nowicki (Jack the Bartender), Derek Leonidoff (Pastor Andy), Lyanna Tumaneng (Linda Baker), Mandy Best (Nurse Jamie Lynn), Avery Sommers (Nurse Carol), Brendan Doughtie (Justin McDaniels), Salem Murphy (Dr. Rashaad), Carl Joseph Amari (Alex Wheaton), Andrea Conte (Miss Emily), Karley Scott Collins (Ashley Turner), Brett Rice (Bar Guy), Luke Shrader (John), Brad Benedict (Coach Dave), Wintley Phipps (Give Kids the World Emcee), Erin Bethea (Chemotherapy Nurse), Tyler Cravens (Samantha's Dad), Whitney Goin (Ex-Wife), Josué Gutierrez (Referee), Matt Swanson (Colt), Pam Landwirth (Miss Pamela), Lee Dawson (Joe Letter Carrier), Carol Saragusa (Cathy, Postal Clerk), McKay Ball (Sally), Savannah Godwin (Partygoer), Ashley Milchman, Brooke Milchman (Costume Party Guests), Sam Smith (Tow Truck Driver)

Michael Christopher Bolten, Bailee Madison, Tanner Maguire in *Letters to God* © Vivendi Entertainment

WHEN YOU'RE STRANGE (Abramorama) Producers, Peter Jankowski, John Beug, Jeff Jampol, Dick Wolf; Executive Producer, Bill Gutentag; Director/Screenplay, Tom DiCillo; Photography, Paul Ferrara; Editors, Mickey Blythe, Kevin Krasny; Narrator, Johnny Depp; a Wolf Films/Strange Pictures production in association with Rhino Entertainment; Color; DV; Rated R; 88 minutes; Release date: April 9, 2010. Documentary on The Doors.

The Doors in *When You're Strange* © Abramorama

THE BLACK WATERS OF ECHO'S POND (Parallel Media) Producers, Jason Loughridge, Raymond J. Markovich; Director, Gabriel Bologna, Screenplay, Sean Clark; Story, Gabriel Bologna, Michael Berenson; Photography, Massimo Zeri; Designer, Michael Fitzgerald; Music, Harry Manfredini; Editor, Michael Spencer; Casting, Corbin Bronson; a Project 8 Films production; Color; HD-to-35mm; Rated R; 92 minutes; Release date: April 9, 2010. **CAST**: Robert Patrick (Pete), Danielle Harris (Kathy), Sean Lawlor (Charles), James Duval (Rick), Nick Mennell (Josh), Mircea Monroe (Veronique), Arcadiy Golubovich (Anton), Electra Avellan (Renee), Elisa Avellan (Erica), Walker Howard (Trent), M.D. Walton (Robert), Declan Joyce (Danny), Nitsa Benchetrit (Florence), Adamo Palladino (Niegel), Jason Loughridge (Clint), Steve Eoff (The Butler), Melissa Barker (Inn Keeper), Julie Stensland (Maid), Tom Proctor (Thomas), Richard Tyson (Nicholas), Kurt Carley (The Pan)

Robert Patrick in *The Black Waters of Echo's Pond* © Parallel Media

LA MISSION (Screen Media) Producers, Benjamin Bratt, Peter Bratt, Alpita Patel; Executive Producers, Tom Steyer, Kat Taylor Dan Nelson; Director/Screenplay, Peter Bratt; Photography, Hiro Narita; Designer, Keith Neely; Music, Mark Killian; Editor, Stan Webb; a 5 Stick Films, TomKat films production; Color; HD; Rated R; 117 minutes; Release date: April 9, 2010. **CAST**: Benjamin Bratt (Che Rivera), Jeremy Ray Valdez (Jesse), Max Rosenak (Jordan), Patrick Shining Elk (Gary), Talisa Soto (Ana), Jesse Borrego (Rene), Kevin Michael Richardson (Dee), Ruben Gonzalez (Benny), Tina Huang (Dr. Chang), Melvina Jones (Regina), Rene Quinones (Esteban), Anthony Santana (Young Jesse), Erika Alexander (Lena), Christopher Borgzinner (Nacho), Edwin Brown (Virgil), Carlos Contreras (Gummy Bears Homey), Cesar Gomez (Gummy Bear), Jan Haley (Triage Nurse), Alex Hernandez (Smoke), Kamasu J. Livingston (Exotic Dancer), Isa Magomedov (Russian MD), Ramon Ovando (Little Man), Cathleen Riddley (Shell), Neo Veavea (Kenny)

Benjamin Bratt in *La Mission* © Screen Media

WHO DO YOU LOVE (Intl. Film Circuit) Producers, Les Alexander, Andrea Baynes, Jonathan Mitchell; Executive Producers, Gideon Amir, Dennis A. Brown; Director, Jerry Zaks; Screenplay, Peter Wortmann, Bob Conte; Photography, David Franco; Designer, Carey Meyer; Costumes, Christine Peters; Music, Jeff Beal; Editors, Scott Richter, Anthony Redman; Choreographer, Joann Jansen; an Alexander/Mitchell production; Color; Not rated; 91 minutes; Release date: April 9, 2010. **CAST**: Alessandro Nivola (Leonard Chess), David Oyelowo (Muddy Waters), Chi McBride (Willie Dixon), Jon Abrahams (Phil Chess), Megalyn Echikunwoke (Ivy Mills), Marika Dominczyk (Revetta Chess), Brett Beoubay (Bo Diddley's Manager), Rus Blackwell (Missouri Sheriff), Marcus Lyle Brown (Jess), Chris Burnett (Stage Manager), Joe Chrest (Malcolm Chisholm), Noell Coet (Frances), Joshua Davis (Terry Chess), Miko DeFoor (Little Walter), Honesty Edwards (Toe Tapper), Thomas Elliott (Radio DJ), J.D. Evermore (Jake), Leslie Garrett (Willie Dixon's Girlfriend), Lisa Goldstein (Sheva Chess), TJ Hassan (Lonnie Johnson), Brent Henry (Police Officer), Ian Leson (Alan Freed), Naima Imani Lett (Chess Receptionist), Earl Maddox (Bar Owner), Tendal Mann (Marshall Chess), Roy McCrerey (Hank Lakin), Hunter McGregor (Petey), Keb' Mo' (Jimmy Rogers), Ryan Puszewski (Young Leonard), Robert Randolph (Bo Diddley), Nick Reasons (Mover), Kermit Rolison (Mr. Fitzgerald), Benjamin Pete Rose (Young Phil), Heather Clark (Deloris, Waitress), Logan Stalarow (Ethan)

David Oyelowo, Alessandro Nivola in *Who Do You Love* © Intl. Film Circuit

AFTER.LIFE (Anchor Bay) Producers, Brad Michael Gilbert, William O. Perkins III, Celin Rattray; Executive Producers, Cooper Richey, Catherine Kellner, Edwin L. Marshall, James Swisher, Pamela Hirsch; Director, Agnieszka Wojtowicz-Vosloo; Screenplay, Agnieszka Wojtowicz-Vosloo, Paul Vosloo, Jakub Korolczuk; Photography, Anastas Michos; Designer, Ford Wheeler; Costumes, Luca Mosca; Music, Paul Haslinger; Editor, Niven Howie; Casting, Matthew Lessall; an Anchor Bay Films and Lleju Prods. presentation of a Plum Pictures production in association with Constellation Entertainment; Dolby; Widescreen; Color; Rated R; 103 minutes; Release date: April 9, 2010. **CAST**: Christina Ricci (Anna Taylor), Liam Neeson (Eliot Deacon), Justin Long (Paul Coleman), Chandler Canterbury (Jack), Celia Weston (Beatrice Taylor), Luz Alexandra Ramos (Diane), Josh Charles (Tom Peterson), Rosemary Murphy (Susan Whitehall), Malachy McCourt (Father Graham), Shuler Hensley (Vincent Miller), Alice Drummond (Mrs. Hutton), Sam Kressner (Acne Kid), Laurel Bryce (Young Anna), William O. Perkins III (Security Guard), Laurie Cole (School Principal), Doan Ly, Erin Ward (Teachers), Jack Rovello (Tall Kid), Prudence Wright Holmes, Celene Keller, Barbara Singer (Old Women), Jonny Fido (Stocky Teacher), Chris Jackson (Neal), Mark Gerrard (Waiter), Gurdeep Singh (Cashier), Steven Lee Merkel (Jeff), Jody Ebert (Police Officer), Mark Heskin (Frank Miller)

Christina Ricci, Liam Neeson in *After.Life* © Anchor Bay

HAVE YOU HEARD FROM JOHANNESBURG? (California Newsreel) Producer/Director, Connie Field; Screenplay, Ken Chowder, Connie Field, Gregory Scharpen; Photography, Tom Hurwitz; Editors, Gregory Scharpen, Jeffrey Stephens; a Clarity Films production; Color; DV; Not rated; 510 minutes; Release date: April 14, 2010. Seven documentary stories about South Africa: (1.) *Road to Resistance: 1948-1964*; (2.) *Hell of a Job*; (3.) *The New Generation: 1960-1977*; (4.) *Fair Play: 1958-1981*; (5.) *From Selma to Soweto: 1977-1986*; (6.) *The Bottom Line: 1965-1988*; (7.) *Free at Last: 1979-1990*.

Nelson Mandela, Walter Sisulu in *Have You Heard from Johannesburg?* © California Newsreel

THE PERFECT GAME (Slowhand) Producers, Mark W. Koch, Daniel de Liege, David Salzberg, Christian Turead, W. William Winokur, Michael O. Gallant; Executive Producer, Jim Van Eerden; Director, William Dear; Screenplay, W. William Winokur, based on his book; Photography, Bryan Greenberg; Designer, Denise Hudson; Costumes, Florence Kemper; Music, Bill Conti; Music Supervisor, Michael Fey; Editor, Chris Conlee; an IndustryWorks United presentation in association with Lone Runner Entertainment and HighRoad Entertainment; Color; Rated PG; 117 minutes; Release date: April 16, 2010. **CAST**: Clifton Collins Jr. (Cesar Fez), Cheech Marin (Padre Esteban), Jake T. Austin (Angel Macias), Moises Arias (Mario Ontiveros), Gabriel Morales (Ricardo Trevino), Jansen Panettiere (Enrique Suarez), David Koechner (Charlie), Emilie de Ravin (Frankie),

Bruce McGill (Tanner), Noberto Villareal (Ryan Ochoa), Louis Gossett Jr. (Cool Papa Bell), Frances Fisher (Betty), Carlos Padilla (Baltazar), Mario Quinonez Jr. (Gerado), Anthony Quinonez (Fidel), Alfred Rodriquez (Pepe), Carlos Gómez (Umberto Macias), Patricia Manterola (Maria), John Cothran (Clarence), William May (Juan), Matt Battaglia (Coach Terrence), Samantha Boscarino (Gloria), Emilio Cast (Pedro M.), Leticia Castillo (Senora Ontiveros), Alejandro Chabán (Javier), Oliver Dear (Spike), Doug DeBeech (Frank), Sonya Eddy (Rose), Christian Fortune (Biloxi Pitcher), Ramón Franco (Sr. Villarreal), Ruben Garfias (Sr. Suarez), Jerry Giles (Coach Esiason), Chalo González (Maria's Father), Seraly Morales (Oralia Masias), Marc Musso (Tommy), Julieta Ortiz (Senora Suarez), Jaeger Rydall (Sam Jenkins), Mat Smith (Jake T), Wyatt Smith (Jarrett), Andrew Thacher (Immigration Officer), Aaron Thompson (Cleon), Karen Trella (Brenda), Robert Blanche (Bridgeport Coach), Carlos Compean (Mexico City Coach)

Clifton Collins Jr., Moises Arias, Jansen Panettiere in *The Perfect Game* © Slowhand

THE CARTEL (Truly Indie) Producer/Director/Screenplay/Music, Bob Bowdon; Executive Producers, Bob Bowdon, Rob Pfaltzgraff; Photography, Jen Wekelo, Adrienne Campisano, Bob Bowdon; Editors, Morgan Beatty, David Wittlin, Sam Wolfson, Vinnie Randazzo; a Bowdon Media presentation in association with the Moving Picture Institute; Color; Not rated; 90 minutes; Release date: April 16, 2010. Documentary on the problems with the American public school system. **WITH** Joyce Powell, Clint Bolick, Robert Enlow, Gerard Robinson, Shelly Skinner, Bob Bowdon, Bill Baroni, Rick Berman, Hector Bonilla, Derrell Bradford, Mary Jane Cooper, John Corcoran, Angel Cordero, Jim Coston, Lucille Davy, Weysan Dun, Dana Egreczky, Robert Enlow, Walter Farrell, Adrian M. Fenty, Chester Finn, Armando A. Fusco, Dan Gaby, Michael Glascoe, Susan Grierson, David Harris, Lloyd Henderson, Jim Hooker, Lance Izunio, Beverly Jones, Lisa Kasabach, Matt Katz, Kris Kolluri, Ray Lesniak, Joseph Malone, Sandy McClure, Mary Jo McKinley, John McWorter, Tim Merrill, Theresa Minutillo, Joe Nathan, Heather Ngoma, Mike Pallante, Paul Peterson, Rick Pressler, Jarrett Renshaw, Greg Richmond, Gerard Robinson, Dana Rone, Paul Bambrick Santoyo, Lee Seglem, Jeff Tiltel, Paul Veggian, Anne Wallace, Scott Weiner, Steve Wollmer.

PORNOGRAPHY (Triple Fire Prods.) Producer, Sean Abley; Director/Screenplay, David Kittredge; Photography, Ivan Corona; Designer, Doug Prinzivalli; Music, Robb Williamson; Editors, Mike Justice, David Kittredge; Color; HD-to-DigiBeta; Not rated; 113 minutes; Release date: April 16, 2010. **CAST**: Matthew Montgomery (Michael Castigan), Pete Scherer (Matt Stevens), Walter Delmar (William/Jason), Jared Grey (Mark Anton), Nick Salamone (Billy), Dylan Vox (Jason Steele), Wyatt Fenner (Student/Angel), Sean Abley (Porn DP), Steve Callahan (Jerome/Urinal Guy), Jon Gale (Rex/Mover), Len Irving (Cop), Rasool Jahan (Realtor/Therapist), Mike Justice (Ghost Story Actor), Bob Koenig (Gaffer), Akie Kotabe (Jeremy/Adam), Joe Langer (Dr. T), Jeremy Owen (The Figure), David Pevsner (Professor), Amy Seeley (Mailbox Clerk), Larry Weissman (Harry), Bret Wolfe (Bishop Scott)

Walter Delmar, Matthew Montgomery in *Pornography* © Triple Fire Prods.

HEY WATCH THIS (Weinstein Co./Vivendi) Producers, Christian Charles, Lenny Beckerman; Executive Producers, Bob Weinstein, Harvey Weinstein, Paris Chong, Barry Gordon, Josh Klein, Ben Feigin; Director, Christian Charles; Photography, Shane Hurlbut; Costumes, Alexandra Loulias; Editor, Kyle Gilman; a mouseRoar and Anonymous Content production; Color; Rated R; 81 minutes; Release date: April 17, 2010. Cheech & Chong in concert. **WITH** Cheech Marin, Tommy Chong, Shelby Chong, Jimmy Root, Ricky Borrego, Carla Daws, Roman Garcia, Tray Hill, Kevin Karwoski, Robert Ketterer, Gerald Williams, Cassie Ybarra

Tommy Chong, Cheech Marin in *Hey Watch This* © Weinstein/Vivendi

KENNY CHESNEY: SUMMER IN 3D (Sony Pictures Entertainment) Producers, Joe Thomas, Kenny Chesney, Shaun Silva; Executive Producers, Clint Higham, Dale Morris, Don Maggi; Co-Executive Producers, Susan Nadler, Evelyn Shriver; Director, Joe Thomas; Photography, Robert W. Peterson; Designer, Mike Swinford; Editors, Skip Masters, Mark Pruett; 3D Supervisor, Ray Hannisian; a Hot Ticket presentation; Color; 3D; Not rated; 99 minutes; Release date: April 21, 2010. Country music performer Kenny Chesney in concert; with Kenny Chesney, Wyatt Beard, Jim Bob Grant, Tim Hensley, Nick Hoffman, Steve Marshall, Clayton Mitchell, Sean Paddock, "Drummie" Zeb Williams.

IN MY SLEEP (Morning Star Pictures) Producers, Allen Wolf, David Austin; Executive Producer, Ralph Winter; Director/Screenplay, Allen Wolf; Photography, Michael Hardwick; Designer, Brian Ollman; Costumes, Tashiba Jones-Wilson; Music, Conrad Pope; Editor, Peter Devaney Flanagan; Casting, Alyssa Weisberg; Presented in association with 8th Rig; Color; Rated PG-13; 90 minutes; Release date: April 23, 2010. **CAST**: Philip Winchester (Marcus), Tim Draxl (Justin), Lacey Chabert (Becky), Abigail Spencer (Gwen), Kelly Overton (Ann), Michael Badalucco (Derek), Beth Grant (Evelyn), Tony Hale (Ben), Kevin Kilner (Greg), Amy Aquino

(Det. Curwen), Aidan Mitchell (Young Marcus), Marcelle Larice (Carissa), Allan Wasserman (Dr. Schwarz), Alexandra Paul (Roxana), Patrick Labyorteaux (Rob), Bellamy Young (Olivia), Kirsten Vangsness (Madge), Shanna Collins (Jennifer), Kevin Michael Curran (David), Christopher Darga (Officer Etling), Robert Joseph (Officer Cooley), Larry Clarke (Officer Knachez), Joe Nunez (Mr. Mather), Vanessa Lee Evigan (Kelly), Bunny Levine (Rachel), Nancy Sexton (Tall Woman), Joy Bisco (Exotic Woman)

Tim Draxl, Kelly Overton, Philip Winchester in *In My Sleep* © Morning Star Pictures

FEED THE FISH (Strand) Producers, Nicholas Langholff, Alison Abrohams, Michael Matzdorff; Executive Producers, Tony Shalhoub, Robert Weiner, Bill Balzer, Peg Balzer; Director/Screenplay, Michael Matzdorff; Photography, Steven Parker; Designer, Merje Veski; Costumes, Karin Kopischke; Music, T.D. Lind; Editors, Ross Albert, Michael Matzdorff; Casting, Kari Peyton; Color; Not rated; 92 minutes; Release date: April 23, 2010. **CAST**: Tony Shalhoub (Sheriff Andersen), Ross Partridge (Joe Peterson), Katie Aselton (Sif Andersen), Barry Corbin (Axel Andersen), Vanessa Branch (Lorraine), Michael Chernus (J.P.), Carlos Kotkin (Jeffy), Michael Shalhoub (Dr. Koosa), Terry Slater (Aaron Aaronson), Ryan Bailey (Ringo the Paramedic), Patrick Cavanaugh (Hamish the Paramedic), Anne Shrake (Nurse Siembrzuch), Susan Shalhoub Larkin (Nurse H. Josephs)

Tony Shalhoub in *Feed the Fish* © Strand Releasing

BEST WORST MOVIE (Arca23A) Producers, Lindsay Rowles Stephenson, Michael Paul Stephenson, Brad Klopman, Jim McKeon, Mary Francis Groom, Ace Goerig; Executive Producers, Alan Hunter, Hugh Hunter; Director, Michael Paul Stephenson; Photography, Katie Graham, Carl Ingriago; Music, Bobby Tahouri; Editors, Andrew Matthews, Katie Graham; a Magic Stone prods. Presentation; Color; HD; Not rated; 91 minutes; Release date: April 23, 2010. Documentary in which one of the stars of the 1991 direct-to-video feature *Troll 2* explores its status as a cult movie based on how bad so many consider it to be. **WITH** George Hardy, Claudio Fragasso, Margo Prey, Jason Steadman, Darren Ewing.

George Hardy, Michael Paul Stephenson in *Best Worst Movie*
© Magic Stone Prods.

PAPER MAN (MPI Media Group) Producers, Richard N. Gladstein, Guymon Casady, Art Spigel, Ara Katz; Directors/Screenplay, Michele Mulroney, Kieran Mulroney; Photography, Eigil Bryld; Designer, Bill Groom; Costumes, Juliet Polcsa; Music, Mark McAdam; Editor, Sam Seig; Casting, Laray Mayfield; an Artfire Films presentation of a Film 360 and FilmColony production; Color; Rated R; 110 minutes; Release date: April 23, 2010. **CAST**: Jeff Daniels (Richard Dunn), Emma Stone (Abby), Ryan Reynolds (Captain Excellent), Lisa Kudrow (Claire Dunn), Hunter Parrish (Bryce), Kieran Culkin (Christopher), Arabella Field (Lucy), Eric Gilliland (UPS Guy), Louis Rosario (Bryce's Posse), Chris Parnell (Peter), Brian Russell (Dave), Jill Shackner (Sophomore Girl), Violet O'Neill (Makeout Girl), Michael Heinztman (Park Ranger)

Jeff Daniels, Ryan Reynolds in *Paper Man* © MPI Media Group

BEHIND THE BURLY Q (First Run Features) Producers, Leslie Zemeckis, Sheri Hellard, Jackie Levine; Executive Producer, Robert Zemeckis; Director/Screenplay, Robert Zemeckis; Photography, Sheri Hellard; Editor, Evan Finn; Color; HDCam; Not rated; 98 minutes; Release date: April 23, 2010. Documentary on Burlesque. **WITH** Alan Alda, Renny von Muchow, Dorothy von Muchow, John Perilli, Joan Arline, Nat Bodian, Lorraine Lee, Taffy O'Neill, Joni Taylor, Mike Iannucci, Rachel Schteir, Sunny Dare, White Fury, Kelly DiNardo, Janet Davis, David Kruh, Sean Rand, Steve Weinstein, Chris Costello, Mimi Reed, Beveryl Anderson Traube, Dixie Evans, Tempest Storm, Harry Lloyd, Sherry Britton, Sarah Jacobs, Blaze Starr, Kitty West, Betty Rowland, Dardy Minsky.

Blaze Starr in *Behind the Burly Q*
© First Run Features

ANTON CHEKHOV'S THE DUEL (High Line Pictures) Producers, Donald Rosenfeld, Mary Bing; Director, Dover Kosashvili; Screenplay, Mary Bing; Based on the novella by Anton Chekhov; Photography, Paul Sarossy; Designer, Ivo Hušnjak; Costumes, Sergio Ballo; Music, Angelo Milli; Casting, Joyce Nettles; a Flux Films presentation, in association with Mainframe Productions; Color; Not rated; 95 minutes; Release date: April 28, 2010. **CAST**: Andrew Scott (Laevsky), Fiona Glascott (Nadya), Tobias Menzies (Von Koren), Niall Buggy (Samoylenko), Michelle Fairley (Marya), Jeremy Swift (Deacon), Nicholas Rowe (Sheshkovsky), Debbie Chazen (Olga), Rik Makarem (Atchmianov), Simon Trinder (Postal Superintendent), Graham Turner (Atchmianov Sr.), Alister Cameron (Ustimovitch), Mislav Čavajda (Kirilin), Nina Serdarević (Katya), Juraj Kršٍevan Dovranič (Dmitri), Sreten Mokrovič (Nikodim), Tvrtko Jurič (Mustapha), Goran Vrbanič (Fyodor), Mladen Vulič (Kerbalay), Matija Jakšejović, Alan Katič (Officers), Boris Bakal (Clerk), Milan Banjanin (Shopkeeper), Mario Kozič (Boyko), Ilya Sarossy (Ilyana), Geraldine O'Rawe (Ilyana's Mother), Juliana Overmeer (Lady with the Lapdog), Maya Kosashvili (Woman with Baby), Douglas Ellis, Mary Bing, Lucy Ellis, Anton Ellis (Promenading Family), Neven Jercel (Tatar Horseman), Franka Gulin (Blind Masseuse), Dubravko Vušak (Organ Grinder), Tea Matanovič, Marijana Mikulič (Lovely Young Women), Igor Štaki Sestrić (Stevedore)

Fiona Glascott in *Anton Chekhov's The Duel* © High Line Pictures

GHOST BIRD (Small Change Prods.) Producer/Director/Editor, Scott Crocker; Photography, Damir Frkovic; Music, Zoë Keating; Color; Not rated; 85 minutes; Release date: April 28, 2010. Documentary on how some of the citizens of Brinkley, Arkansas are certain they still see a giant woodpecker that's been extinct for over half a century. **WITH** Dr. Richard Prum, Dr. Jerome Jackson, Dr. Scott Edwards, David Sibley, Chuck Volner, Nancy Tanner, Virginia Eckelberry, Sandra Kemmer, Tim Barksdale, David Luneau, Katie Jacques, Thomas Jacques, Dave Hamner, Mike Mills, Tom Nelson, Dr. John Fitzpatrick, Bobby Harrison, Tim Gallagher, Gene Sparling, Gabe Norton

David Sibley in *Ghost Bird* © Small Change Prods.

TOUCHING HOME (California Film Institute) Producers, Logan Miller, Noah Miller, Jeremy Zajonic; Directors/Screenplay, Logan Miller, Noah Miller; Executive Producers, Brian Vail, Gordon Radley; Photography, Ricardo Jacques Gale; Designer, Roy Rede; Costumes, Inanna Bantu; Music, Martin Davich; Editor, Robert Dalva; Casting, Michelle Metzner, Billy Damota; a Miller Brothers production; Dolby; Deluxe color; Rated PG-13;   108 minutes; Release date: April 29, 2010. **CAST**: Ed Harris (Charlie Winston), Brad Dourif (Clyde Winston), Robert Forster (Jim "Perk" Perkins), Logan Miller (Lane Winston), Noah Miller (Clint Winston), Ishiah Benben (Rachel), Evan Jones (Timmy "Mac" McClanahan), Lee Meriweather (Grandma Eleanor), Brandon Hanson (Brownie), James Carraway (Jimmy, Poker Player), Richard Conti (Poker Player), David Fine (Roy Rivers, Poker Player), Rod Gnapp (Ray Rod Rivers, Poker Player), Larry Kitagawa (Movie Patron), John Laughlin (Walter Houston), George Maguire (Pete, Poker Player), Shane Richardson (Carney #1)

Noah Miller, Ed Harris, Logan Miller in *Touching Home*
© California Film Institute

FURRY VENGEANCE (Summit Entertainment) Producers, Robert Simonds, Keith Goldberg; Executive Producers, Ira Shuman, Brendan Fraser, Jeff Skoll, Jonathan King; Director, Roger Kumble; Screenplay, Michael Carnes, Josh Gilbert; Photography, Peter Lyons Collister; Designer, Stephen Lineweaver; Costumes, Alexandra Welker; Music, Edward Shearmur; Music Supervisor, Patrick Houlihan; Editor, Lawrence Jordan; Visual Effects Supervisor, David Goldberg; Casting, Jennifer Euston; Stunts, Ernie Orsatti; Animal Voice Effects, Dee Bradley Baker; a Participant Media presentation in association with Imagenation Abu Dhabi of a Robert Simonds production; Dolby; Color; Rated PG; 91 minutes; Release date: April 30, 2010. **CAST**: Brendan Fraser (Dan Sanders), Brooke Shields (Tammy Sanders), Matt Prokop (Tyler Sanders), Ken Jeong (Neal Lyman), Angela Kinsey (Felder), Toby Huss (Wilson), Skyler Samuels (Amber), Samantha Bee (Principal Baker), Ricky Garcia (Frank), Eugene Cordero (Cheese), Patrice O'Neal (Gus), Jim Norton (Hank), Billy Bush (Drill Sergeant), Alice Drummond (Mrs. Martin), Gerry Bednob (Mr. Gupta), Alexander Chance (Security Guard), Wallace Shawn (Dr. Christian Burr), Dee Bradley Baker (Animal Voice Effects)

Brooke Shields, Brendan Fraser, Matt Prokop, Skyler Samuels in *Furry Vengeance* © Summit Entertainment

MERCY (IFC Films) Producers, Scott Caan, Vince Palomino, Phil Parmet; Executive Producer, Mary Vernieu; Director, Patrick Hoelck; Screenplay, Scott Caan; Photography, Phil Parmet; Designer, Pete Simmons; Costumes, Negar Ali; Music, Mader; Editor, Andrea Bottigliero; Casting, Mary Vernieu, Venus Kanani; a Gold Pony Films production; Dolby; Color; Not rated; 87 minutes; Release date: April 30, 2010. **CAST**: Scott Caan (Johnny), Wendy Glenn (Mercy), Troy Garity (Dane), John Boyd (Erik), James Caan (Gerry), Dylan McDermott (Jake), Alexie Gilmore (Chris), Whitney Able (Heather), Erika Christensen (Robin), Jamie Strange (Jessica), Holly Valance (Tess), Bre Blair (Beach Hotel Concierge), Dorian Brown (Dorian), Kelly Lynch (Herself), Brian Goodman (Security Guard), Mike Testone (Seedy Bartender), Scarlett Chorvat (Concierge), Balthazar Getty (Drunk Guy at Party), Pete Simmons (Guy with a Boat), Thom Cammer (Nigel), Troy Bellinghausen, A.J. Dunn, Wesley Scott, Justin Vaughn (Football Players)

Wendy Glenn in *Mercy* © IFC Films

THE WILD AND WONDERFUL WHITES OF WEST VIRGINIA (Tribeca Films) Producers, Julien Nitzberg; Storm Taylor; Executive Producers, Johnny Knoxville, Jeff Tremaine, Priya Swaminathan, Jeff Yapp; Director, Julien Nitzberg; Music, Deke Dickerson; Editor, Ben Daugherty; a Dickhouse production in association with Transition Productions, presented in association with American Express; Color; Not rated; 86 minutes; Release date: May 5, 2010. Documentary on the notorious White Family of West Virginia's Boone County in the Appalachian Mountains.

Jesco White in *The Wild and Wonderful Whites* © Tribeca Films

FLOORED (TraderFilm) Producers, James Allen Smith, Joseph Gibbons, Steve Prosniewski; Executive Producer, Karol Martesko-Fenster; Director, James Allen Smith; Photography, Chris Baron; Music, Stefan Scott Nelson; Editor, Andrew McAllister; Color; Not rated; 77 minutes; Release date: May 7, 2010. Documentary that looks at the trading floors of Chicago. **WITH** Jeff Ansani, Chris Felix, Kenny Ford, Jody Michael, Jon Najarian, Pete Najarian, Rob Prosniewski, Linda Raschke, Rick Santelli, John Tubbs, Mike Walsh

Rick Santelli in *Floored* © TraderFilm

HAPPINESS RUNS (Strand) Producer, Stephen Israel; Executive Producer, Tatiana Kelly; Director/Screenplay, Adam Sherman; Photography, Aaron Platt; Designer, Michael Fitzgerald; Costumes, Emily Batson; Music, Johnny Klimek, Reinhold Heil; Editor, Jonathan Alberts; Casting, Paul Palo, Linda Phillips-Palo; a Happiness Runs production; Dolby; Color; Not rated; 88 minutes; Release date: May 7, 2010. **CAST**: Hanna Hall (Becky), Mark L. Young (Victor), Jesse Plemons (Chad), Rutger Hauer (Insley), Rich Sickler (Harris), Mark Boone Junior (Victor's Father), Andie MacDowell (Victor's Mother), Joni Barth (Rachel's Mom), Steven Christopher Parker (Teo), Kirsten Berman (Jenny), Joseph Castanon (Little Mackie), Ingrid Coree (Louise), Sarah Kaite Coughlan (Rainn), AnnaLisa Erickson (Nancy), Darin Heames (Reggy), Jon Kellam (Peter), Paul McCarthy-

Boyington (Sam), Laura Peters (Rachel), Tyler Steelman (Nardo), John Walcutt (Becky's Father), Grace Bannon (Hippie Teen), Suzan Averitt (Tantric Yoga Devotee), Harmony Blossom (Body Painted Blue Butterfly Dancer), Vicoria De Mare (Scantily Clad Hippie), Jessica Elder, Wendy Louise, Bruna Rubio (Pregnant Hippies), Loni LiPuma (Ferris Wheel Girl), Nicole Smolen (Hippie Kid), Dana Berry, Kathryn Carner, Jennipher Foster, Kenyetta Lethridge, Laurie Mannette, Jared Melei, Eric Steelman, Channing Swift, Tony Swift (Commune Hippies)

Hanna Hall, Mark L. Young in *Happiness Runs* © Strand Releasing

MULTIPLE SARCASMS (Multiple Ventures Releasing) Producers, Brooks Branch, Chris Bongirne; Executive Producers, Patrice Auld, Keith Grinstein, Martha Moseley; Director, Brooks Branch; Screenplay, Brooks Branch, Linda Morris; Photography, Jacek Laskus; Designer, Sharon Lomofsky; Costumes, Kitty Boots; Music, George Fontenette; Editor, Plummy Tucker; Casting, Billy Hopkins, Suzanne Crowley, Kerry Barden, Jess Kelly; a New Films International presentation; Color; Rated R; 97 minutes; Release date: May 7, 2010. **CAST**: Timothy Hutton (Gabriel), Mira Sorvino (Cari), Dana Delany (Annie), Mario Van Peebles (Rocky), India Ennenga (Elizabeth), Laila Robins (Lauren), Stockard Channing (Pamela), Brett Berg (The MC), Eric Sheffer Stevens, Tim Bohn (Stage Gabriels), Nadia Dassouki (Saffron), Jason Denuszek (Drunk Hooligan), Ronald E. Giles (Odd Man Walking through Central Park), Jonathan C. Green (Mime), Leslie Lyles (Energy Specialist), Alex Manette (Erik), Julia K. Murney (Stage Cari), Aileen Quinn (School Secretary), Chris Sarandon (Larry), Marcus Schenkenberg (Sachi), Stephen Singer (Michael Rogers), Steve Sirkis (Chet), Franklin Ojeda Smith (Homeless Man), Emily Tremaine (Receptionist), Paris Yates (Elizabeth's Best Friend), Joan Jett (Lead Singer), Dougie Needles, Enzo Penizzotto, Thommy Price (Vulvic Nuisances)

Timothy Hutton, Mira Sorvino in *Multiple Sarcasms* © Multiple Ventures

TRASH HUMPERS (Drag City Film Distribution) Producers, Amina Dasmal, Charles-Marie Anthonioz, Robin Fox; Executive Producer, Agnès B.; Director/ Screenplay/ Photography, Harmony Korine; Editor, Leo Scott; an O'Salvation Cine and Alcove Entertainment production; American-British; Stereo; Color; Not rated; 78 minutes; Release date: May 7, 2010. **CAST**: Brian Kotzur (Buddy), Rachel Korine (Momma), Harmony Korine (Hervé), Travis Nicholson (Travis), Chris Gantry (Singer), Kevin Guthrie, Paige Spain, Dave Cloud, Chris Crofton, Charlie Ezel

Rachel Korine, Brian Kotzur, Travis Nicholson in *Trash Humpers*
© Drag City Film

THE OATH (Zeitgeist) Producer/Director, Laura Poitras; Executive Producers, Sally Jo Fifer, David Menschel; Photography, Kirsten Johnson, Laura Poitras; Music, Osvaldo Golijov; Editor, Jonathan Oppenheim; Produced by Praxis Films & The Independent Television Service (ITVS) in association with American Documentary/POV; Color; Not rated; 96 minutes; Release date: May 7, 2010. Documentary on how Abu Jandal and his brother-in-law Salim Hamdan became Osama bin Laden's driver and bodyguard, respectively; with Salim Hamdan, Abu Jandal.

Abu Jandal in *The Oath* © Zeitgeist

GRAVITY WAS EVERYWHERE BACK THEN (Nervous Films) Producer, Martina Batan; Director/Editor, Brent Green; Screenplay, Brent Green, Donna K., Michael McGinley; Photography, Brent Green, Jem Cohen, Pete Sillen, Jake Sillen, Holli Hopkins; Music, Brent Green, Jim Becker, Michael McGinley, Donna K., the Alabama Sacred Heart Singers; Stereo; HD; Color; Not rated; 75 minutes; Release date: May 7, 2010. **VOICE CAST**: Michael McGinley (Leonard), Donna K. (Mary).

Gravity Was Everywhere Back Then © Nervous Films

CASINO JACK AND THE UNITED STATES OF MONEY (Magnolia) Producers, Alex Gibney, Alison Ellwood, Zena Barakat; Executive Producers, Jeff Skoll, Diane Weyermann, Ben Goldhirsh, Mark Cuban, Todd Wagner, Bill Banowsky; Director/ Screenplay, Alex Gibney; Photography, Maryse Alberti; Music, David Robbins; Editor, Allison Ellwood; a Jigsaw Production, presented in association with Participant Media and Good; Dolby; HD; Color; Rated R; 118 minutes; Release date: May 7, 2010. Documentary on Washington lobbyist Jack Abramoff. **WITH** Jack Abramoff, Tom DeLay, Bob Ney, Ralph Reed, Michael Scanlon, Neil Volz; **CAST:** Stanley Tucci (Voice of Jack Abramoff), Paul Rudd (Voice of Michael Scanlon), and William Branner, Donn Dunlop, Kevin Henderson, Hal Kreitman, Kelly Brian Kuhn, Paolo Mugnaini (Actors)

Jack Abramoff in *Casino Jack and the United States of Money* © Magnolia

BEETLE QUEEN CONQUERS TOKYO (Argot Pictures) Producer/Director/Screenplay, Jessica Oreck; Co-Producers, Maiko Endo, Akito Kawahara; Photography, Sean Williams; Music, J.C. Morrison, Nate Shaw; Editors, Jessica Oreck, Maiko Endo, Akio Kawahara; American-Japanese; Color; Not rated; 90 minutes; Release date: May 12, 2010. Documentary explores the Japanese fascination with insects.

Beetle Queen Conquers Tokyo © Argot Pictures

PRINCESS KAIULANI (Roadside Attractions) Producers, Nigel Thomas, Ricardo S. Galindez, Roy J. Tjioe, Lauri Apelian, Marc Forby; Executive Producers, Jeffrey Kdau, Leilani Forby, Charlotte Walls, Wanda Watumull, Laurie Hayward, Sheryl Crown; Director/Screenplay, Marc Forby; Photography, Gabriel Beristain; Designer, Steven Lawrence; Costumes, Kathryn Morrison-Pahoa; Music, Stephen Warbeck; Editor, Beverley Mills; Casting, Kate Plantin; a Contentfilm International presentation of a Matador Pictures, Island Film Group and Trailblazer Films production in association with the Screen East Content Investment Fund; American-British; Dolby; Color; Rated PG; 130 minutes; Release date: May 14, 2010. **CAST**: Q'orianka Kilcher (Princess Ka'iulani), Barry Pepper (Thurston), Shaun Evans (Clive Davies), Jimmy Yull (Archie), Julian Glover (Mr. Davies), Tamzin Merchant (Alice Davies), Will Patton (Sanford Dole), Catherine Steadman (Miss Barnes), Kainoa Kilcher (Kaleo), Leo Anderson Akana (Queen Liliu'okalani), Ocean Kaowili (King Kalakaua), Cristina de la Diosa, Katharin "Ladie K" Mraz (Soldier's Girlfriends), Peter Banks (President Cleveland), Keith Barry (U.S. Marine), Christian Brassington (Duke), Brian Currie (Morgan), Kaialaka'iopono Faurot (Keiki Ka'iulani), Matt Goldstein (Photographer with Flashing Camera), Elizabeth Goram-Smith (Scullery Maid), Patti Hastie (Mrs. Morgan), Geoff Heise (Waterhouse), Love Hodel (Smith), Kamuela Kalilikane (Mamane), Kimo Kalilikane (Kaleuha), Timothy Lechner, Bill Ogilvie (New York Reporters), Jay Lembeck (Premier Gibson), Greg Sardinha (Singer), Martin Sensmeier (Kama'aina), Reupena Paopao Sheck (Kao), Jean Simon (Mrs. Collum), Laura Soller (Mrs. Anna Dole), Rosamund Stephen (Mrs. Cleveland), Ned Van Zandt (Senator Collum), Barbara Wilshere (Mrs. Davies), Kyra Glover, Damien Hanakeawe, Ronnie Inagaki, Danette Kepaa, Puanani Reis-Moniz, Lynda Sniffen (Hula Dancers)

THE LIVING WAKE (Mangusta Prods.) Producers, Ami Ankin, Chadwick Clough, Peter Kline, Mike O'Connell, Sol Tryon; Executive Producers, Charlie Corwin, Clara Markowicz, Justin Leitstein, Helen Cappuccino, Andy Cappuccino, Robert Bethge; Director, Sol Tryon; Screenplay, Mike O'Connell, Peter Kline; Photography, Scott Miller; Designer, Michael Grasley; Costumes, Negar Ali; Music, Carter Little, Mike O'Connell; Editor, Joe Klotz; Casting, Caroline Sinclair; an Original Media presentation, 2007; Dolby; Color; Not rated; 91 minutes; Release date: May 14, 2010. **CAST**: Mike O'Connell (K. Roth Binew/Passerby Man), Jesse Eisenberg (Mills Joaquin), Jim Gaffigan (Lampert Binew), Ann Dowd (Librarian), Eddie Pepitone (Reginald), Jill Larson (Alma Binew), Clay Allen (Moustache Man), Ami Ankin (Mother), Harlan Baker (Dr. Schoenberg), Bryan Brown (Frank), Rebecca Comerford (Psychic), Matthew Cowles (Mossman), Paul D'Amato (Rutger), Jay Devlin (Demon), Ben Duhl (Liquorsmith), Matt Dwyer, Patrick Keane (Christian Men), Howard Feller (Roy), Steve Flynn (Priest), Sam Goldfarb (Doctor), Kurt Haas (Clyde), Colombe Jacobsen-Derstine (Prostitute), Stephen Brian Jones (Farmer), Diane Kagan (Marla), Jun Kim (Ling), Tony Lewis (Bully #1), Michael Mandel (Landlord), Jillian Mavodones (Dawn's Sister), Peter Paton (Old Man), Stuart Rudin (Clock Maker), Ron Lee Savin (Waylon), Mark Schulte (Karl Binew), Caleb Wentworth (Young K. Roth), Simon Wentworth (Young Karl)

Mike O'Connell, Jesse Eisenberg in *The Living Wake* © Mangusta Prods.

ENTRE NOS (IndiePix) Producers, Joseph La Morte, Michael Skolnik; Executive Producers, Bob Alexander, Ryan Harrington, Stephen Bannatyne; Directors/Screenplay, Paola Mendoza, Gloria La Morte; Photography, Bradford Young; Designer, Adriana Serrano; Costumes, Vera Chow; Music, Gil Talmi; Editor, Gloria Le Morte; Casting, Ellyn Long Marshall, Marie E. Nelson; Color; Not rated; 81 minutes; Release date: May 14, 2010. **CAST**: Paola Mendoza (Mariana), Sebastian Villada Lopez (Gabriel), Laura Montana Cortez (Andrea), Sarita Chaudhury (Preet), Andres Munar (Antonio), Anthony Chisholm (Joe), Isabel Sung (Mi-sun), Eddie Martinez (Alejo), Jacqueline Duprey (Rosa), Annie Henk (Attendant), Felipe Bonilla (Manager), Denia Brache (Teresa), Clem Cheung (Mr. Kim), Victor Pagan (Man in Apartment), Farah Bala (Gloria), Sekou Jackson (Sekou), Ashley Teleki (Kimberly)

Shaun Evans, Q'orianka Kilcher in *Princess Kaiulani* © Roadside Attractions

Paola Mendoza, Sebastian Villada Lopez, Laura Montana Cortez in *Entre Nos* © IndiePix

IN/SIGNIFICANT OTHERS (North Poplar Pictures) Producer/Director/Editor, John Schwert; Screenplay, John Schwert, David Mulholland; Photography, Kenneth Wilson; Designer, Sean Macomber; Costumes, Amber Givens; Music, Anthony Short; Casting, Tonya Bludsworth; a Fourth Ward Productions, Inc. presentation; Color; Not rated; 99 minutes; Release date: May 14, 2010. **CAST**: Burgess Jenkins (Bruce Snow), Andrea Powell (Christina Ludum), Brian Lafontaine (Jack Rizzo), Mark Scarboro (Greg Rizzo), Tiffany Montgomery (Salem Snow), Brett Gentile (Cam), Scott Miles (Mike Holder), R. Keith Harris (Det. Thicke), David Sherrill (Miller), Calvin Walton (Det. Noel), Carver Johns (Mooney), Jeremy Decarlos (Ray), Aerli Austen (Susan), Gretchen McGinty (Joanne), Ashlee Payne (Leslie Rizzo), Jonathan Frappier (Conrad), Dave Blamy (Hiring Manager), Andy Boswell (Bartender), Andre DeRiso (Thirston), Roger Hair (SWAT Team Leader), Bill Hart (Lumber Yard Boss), Carrie Anne Hunt, Emily Pierce (Receptionists), Andrew R. Kaplan (Detective), Jason Allen King (Club Manager), Matt Mercer (Traveler), Byron Miller (Lou), Tim Ross (DJ), Addyson Vining (Rizzo Baby)

180º SOUTH (Magnolia) Producers, Tim Lynch, Rick Ridgeway, Emmett Malloy; Executive Producers, Rick Ridgeway, Dan Emmett, Liesl Copland, Ted Sarandos, Thom Zadra, DV DeVincentis; Director, Chris Malloy; Journals, Danny Moder; Story, Rick Ridgeway, Chris Malloy, Zachary Slobig, Steven Barilotti; Photography, Danny Moder; Animation & Artwork, Geoff McFetridge; Music, Ugly Casanova; Editor, Tim Wheeler; a Woodshed Films Inc. production; Color; 85 minutes; Not rated; 85 minutes; Release date: May 21, 2010. Documentary on surfer-climber Jeff Johnson's efforts to scale Cerro Corovado in Patagonia. **WITH** Jeff Johnson, Yvon Chouinard, Doug Tompkins, Keith Malloy, Makohe, Timmy O'Neill

180° South © Magnolia

MACGRUBER (Rogue) Producers, Lorne Michaels, John Goldwyn; Executive Producers, Ryan Kavanaugh, Tucker Tooley, Akiva Schaffer, Seth Meyers, Erin David; Director, Jorma Taccone; Screenplay, Will Forte, John Solomon, Jorma Taccone; Photography, Brandon Trost; Designer, Robb Wilson-King; Costumes, Susanna Puisto; Music, Matthew Compton; Editor, Jamie Gross; Casting, Sheila Jaffe; a Relativity Media/Michaels-Goldwyn production; Dolby; Color; Rated R; 90 minutes; Release date: May 21, 2010. **CAST**: Will Forte (MacGruber), Kristen Wiig (Vicki St. Elmo), Ryan Phillippe (Lt. Dixon Piper), Val Kilmer (Dieter Von Cunth), Powers Boothe (Col. James Faith), Maya Rudolph (Casey), Rhys Coiro (Yerik Novikov), Andy Mackenzie (Hoss Bender), Jasper Cole (Zeke Pleshette), Timothy V. Murphy (Constantine), Kevin Skousen (Senator Garver), Jimmy G. Giesler (Janitor), Chris Jericho (Frank Korver), Mark Henry (Tut Beemer), MVP (Vernon Freedom), The Great Khali (Tug Phelps), Kane (Tanker Lutz), The Big Show (Brick Hughes), Brandon Trost (Brick's Boyfriend), Robert Douglas Washington (Cashier), Chris Kittinger (Man in Tuxedo), Marielle Heller (Clocky), Derek Mears (Large Henchman), John Gibson (Dealer), Vic Browder (Control Room Guard), Russ Dillen (Commander), Michael-David Aragon (Machine Room Guard), Greg Alan Williams (Minister), Chad Brummett (Military Officer), Matt Wood (Bartender), Amare Stoudemire (Himself), Brian Petsos (Dude), Alan D'Antoni (Russian Guard), Cajardo Lindsey, Laurence Chavez, Matt Christmas (Railroad Guards), Michael Owen (Railroad Bodyguard), Edward A. Duran, Tomas Sanchez, Bobby Burns, Bill Leaman, Willie Weber (Compound Guards), Alan Tafoya (Charging Guard), Jason Trost (Smoking Guard), Milos Milicevic (KFBR392 Guy), Christina Rouner (News Anchor)

Ryan Phillippe, Will Forte in *MacGruber* © Rogue Pictures

AFTER THE CUP: SONS OF SAKHNIN UNITED (Variance) Roger Bennett, Alexander H. Brown, Michael Cohen; Executive Producer, Barry Tatleman; Director, Christopher Browne; Co-Director, Alexander H. Browne; Photography, Eitan Riklis; Music, Neill Sanford Livingston; Editor, Patrick Gambuti Jr.; Brownehouse Pictures, Deaf Dumb + Blind, Reboot Films presentation; Color; Not rated; 84 minutes; Release date: May 21, 2010. Documentary on how Bnei Sakhnin, a soccer team from a northern Israeli town won the National Cup in 2004. **WITH** Waji Abboud, Mazen Ghanayem, Eyal Lachman, Shimon Peres, Abbas Suan

After the Cup © Variance

RACING DREAMS (Hannover House) Producers, Bristol Baughan, Marshall Curry; Director, Marshall Curry; Photography, Alan Jacobsen, Wolfgang Held, Peter Gordon, Marshall Curry; Music, Joel Goodman; Editors, Matthew Hamachek, Marshall Curry, Mary Manhardt; a Good/White Buffalo Entertainment/Fire Tower Films presentation; Color; HD; Rated PG; 97 minutes; Release date: May 21, 2010. Documentary about 3 kids vying for the National Championship of the World Karting Association. **WITH** Annabeth Barnes, Josh Hobson, Brandon Warren

Racing Dreams © Hannover House

PICASSO AND BRAQUE GO TO THE MOVIES (Arthouse Films) Producers, Arne Glimcher, Robert Greenhut, Martin Scorsese; Executive Producer, Bonnie Hlinomaz; Director, Arne Glimcher; Photography, Peter Hlinomaz; Editor, Sabine Krayenhuhl; Narrator, Martin Scorsese; a Martin Scorsese, Robert Greenhut presentation; Color; HD; Not rated; 60 minutes; Release date: May 28, 2010. Documentary on the link between cubism and motion pictures. **WITH** Martin Scorsese, Bernice Rose, Julian Schnabel, Chuck Close, Lucas Samaras, Robert Whitman, Eric Fischl, Jennifer Wild.

Martin Scorsese in *Picasso and Braque Go to the Movies* © Arthouse Films

ONLY THE BRAVE (Indican) Producers, Lane Nishikawa, Karen Criswell, Eric Hayashi, Jay Koiwai; Director/Screenplay, Lane Nishikawa; Photography, Michael Wojciechowski; Designer, Alan E. Muraoka; Costumes, Larry Velasco; Music, Kimo Cornwell; Editor, Chisako Yokoyama; a Mission From Buddha Productions presentation; Dolby; Color; Rated R; 99 minutes; Release date: May 28, 2010. **CAST**: Tamlyn Tomita (Mary Takata), Lane Nishikawa (Sgt. Jimmy Takata), Greg Watanabe (Pvt. Freddy Watada), Mark Dacascos (Sgt. Steve "Zaki" Senzaki), Kipp Shiotani (Cpl. Johnny "Nomu" Nomura), Jason Scott Lee (Sgt. Glenn "Tak" Takase), Yuji Okumoto (Sgt. Yukio "Yuk" Nakajo), Ehecatl Chavez (Father Jordan), Sara Shields (Renee Jordan), Casey Koiwai (Johnny Nomura Jr.), Jordan

Nakahara (Betty Nomura), Ken Naraskai (Dr. Richard "Doc" Naganuma), Ken Choi (Pvt. Dave "Bullseye" Fukushima), Michael Sun Lee (Pvt. Al "Kauai" Nakamura), Garret T. Sato (Cpl. Richard "Hilo" Imamura), Christina Cellner (Genevieve), Ryun Yu (Pvt. Robert "Min" Minami), Larry Tazuma (Pvt. Frank Fukushima), Bob Kubota (Pvt. Ichiro "Ichi" Mizuno), Michael Hagiwara (Rev. Nobu "Rev" Inouye), Emily Liu (Nancy Loo), Sharon Omi (Charlene Naganuma), Ruika Rose (Rosie Naganuma), Jeff Fahey (Lt. William Terry), Guy Ecker (Sgt. Robert King), John Koyoma (Lt. Hank Hayashi), Brian Durkin (Pool Hall Soldier), Jennifer Aquino (Grace Nakajo), C. Traci Murase (Frances Nakajo), Takayo Fischer (Mrs. Nakajo), Pat Noriyuki Morita (Seigo Takata), Gina Hiraizumi (Eleanor Takase), Brian Connolly (Factory Manger), Brianne Takihara (Joni Loo), Thomas Morinaka, Randy Nakagawa, Aaron Takashi, Derek Kadota, Yuki Natsuzaki, Kurt Kuniyoshi (442 Squad), Thomas J. Metzger, Adam Dufrenne (German Soldiers)

Only the Brave © Indican

BOYBAND (Artigo/Ajemian Films) Producer, Andrea Ajemian; Director/Screenplay, Jon Artigo; Photography, Brian Crane; Designer, Alecia Orsini; Costumes, Jennifer Lynn Tremblay; Music, Kaz Gamble; Casting, Mary Vernieu, J.C. Cantu; Color; Not rated ; 98 minutes; Release date: June 4, 2010. **CAST**: Michael Copon (Brad), Ryan Pinkston (Greg), Robert Hoffman (Garth), Ming-Na (Judy Roberts), Kurt Fuller (Earl Roberts), Ryan Hansen (Tommy), Rachel Specter (Pamela Harris), Laura Breckenridge (Samantha Hughes), Brendan Miller (Derrick Davis), Eknock (Derf), Lorenzo Hooker III (Joda), Richard Riehle (Principal Collins), Tom Wright (Pete), Andrea Ajemian (Gloria), Jon Artigo (Mr. Anderson), Mark Ajemian (The Mumblah), Sam James (Donny), Joel Perez (Jordan), Nina Genatossio, Liz Eng, Laura Ferland (Girls), Nate Donaldson, Kevin G. Cox, Shaun Connolly (Guys), Ron Murphy (Coach Jackson), Paul C. McKinney (Trainer), Rich Manley (AJ Carson), Paul Costa (Slash), Brandon Meyer (Murph), Ryan Letourneau (Brian, Auditioner #1), Robb Russ (Peter), Roy Souza (Talent Show Emcee), Michael Cognata (Kyle), Rob Artigo (Locker Room Reporter), Celeste Oliva (News Reporter), Stephen Starr (Maurice), Joshua Taylor (Announcer), Barbara Guertin (Homeroom Teacher), Zak Finn (Barry), Dan Lindgren (Sully)

ROSENCRANTZ AND GUILDENSTERN ARE UNDEAD (Indican) Producers, Mike Landry, Carlos Velazquez, Russ Terlecki; Director/Screenplay, Jordan Galland; Photography, Chris Lavasseur; Designer, Darsi Monaco; Music, Sean Lennon; Editor, Connor Kalista; Off Hollywood Pictures in association with C Plus Pictures; Color; Not rated; 89 minutes; Release date: June 4, 2010. **CAST**: Jake Hoffman (Julian Marsh), Kris Lemche (Vince), Devon Aoki (Anna Berkley), John Ventimiglia (Theo Horace), Ralph Macchio (Bobby Bianchi), Jeremy Sisto (Det. Wimbly), Geneva Carr (Charlotte Lawrence), Waris Ahluwalia (Hugo Pepper), Azie Tesfai (Zadeska), Carmen Goodine (Lyuba), Joey Kern (Hamlet), Mike Landry (Mickey/Guildenstern), Carlos Velazquez (Carlo/Rosencrantz), Chip Zien (Dr. Marsh), Graeme Malcolm (Mr. Liden), Polina Frantsena (Julian's Fan), Lou

Carbonneau (Rookie Cop), Catilin Croby (Cookie), Tiffany Rene King (Girl with Glasses), Bijou Philipps (Lauren Lamont)

Ralph Macchio in *Rosencrantz and Guildenstern are Undead* © Indican

BURZYNSKI (Independent) Producer/Director/Screenplay/Editor, Eric Merola; Color; Not rated; 108 minutes; Release date: June 4, 2010. Documentary about Dr. Stanislaw Burzynski who has discovered the genetic mechanism to cure most human cancers. **WITH** Dr. Stanislaw Burzynski, Julian Whitaker, David Kessler, Michael Freidman, Joe Barton, Richard Jaffe, Jodi Fenton, Jessica Resselo, Kelsey Hill, Arize Onuekwusi, Ric Schiff, Dustin Kunnari

Stanislaw Burzynski in *Burzynski*

FINDING BLISS (Phase 4 Films) Producers, Jeff Rice, Daniel Toll, Rich Cowan, Dave Ornston; Executive Producers, Glen Hartford, Brandon Nutt, Leelee Sobieski; Director/Screenplay/Editor, Julie Davis; Photography, Peter N. Green; Designer, Vincent Defelice; Music, John Swihart; Editor, David Beatty; a Lightshow Entertainment, North by Northwest Entertainment, Cinamour Entertainment production; Dolby; Color; Rated R; 96 minutes; Release date: June 4, 2010. **CAST**: Leelee Sobieski (Jody Balaban), Matt Davis (Jeff Drake), Denise Richards (Bliss/Laura), Kristen Johnston (Irene Fox), Jamie Kennedy (Richard "Dick" Harder), Donnamarie Recco (Kathleen McDuffy), Mircea Monroe (Sindi), PJ Byrne (Gary), Caroline Aaron (Debra Balaban), Tim Bagley (Alan Balaban), Zach Cumer (Bobby Dalpes), Maggy Bashaw (13-year-old Actress), Christa Campbell (Kato), Mario Cassem (Morris Goldstein), Wes Deitrick (Agent), Sammi Hanratty (Little Jody), Bradley Hollibaugh (Bodyguard), Kimbre Lancaster (Angie), Marcus J. Spencer (Jake B. Bigg), Garry Marshall, Ron Jeremy, Stormy Daniels (Themselves), Kevin Partridge (Brett Miller), Saybher Perrigo (Lexi), David Perry (Sam), Jaylan Renz (Ted), Patrick Treadway (Marty), Pas'ta Weat (Dildo Delivery Guy), Bill A. Jones (AVN Announcer), Dany Taylor (Cute Guy), Julie Davis (Dyan Cannons)

Leelee Sobieski, Matt Davis in *Finding Bliss* © Phase 4 Films

CROPSEY (Cinema Purgatorio) Producers, Joshua Zeman, Barbara Brancaccio, Zachary Mortensen; Executive Producer, Jeffrey Levy-Hinte; Directors, Joshua Zeman, Barbara Brancaccio; Screenplay, Joshua Zeman; Photography, Chad Davidson; Music, Alexander Laserenko; Editors, Tom Patterson, Anita Gabrosek; an Antidote Films, Afterhouse Prods. Presentation of a Ghost Root production; Color; HD; Not rated; 84 minutes; Release date: June 4, 2010. Documentary that investigates the truth behind the arrest and incarceration of Andre Rand, a former worker at the now-abandoned Willowbrook State School for the mentally handicapped, accused of the murder and abduction of several children. **WITH** Donna Cutugno, Karen Schweiger, David Novarro, Raph Aquino

Joshua Zeman, Barbara Brancaccio in *Cropsey* © Cinema Purgatorio

WHIZ KIDS (Shadow) Producer, Michael Duca; Co-Producers, Tina DiFeliciantonio, Tom Shepard; Executive Producers, Greg Little, Elizabeth Friedman; Director, Tom Shepard; Co-Director/Photography, Tina DiFeliciantonio; Screenplay/Editor, Jane C. Wagner; Music, Laura Karpman; a Sandbar Pictures in collaboration with Duca di Carp Pictures + Naked Eye Productions Ltd. production; Color; Not rated; 82 minutes; Release date: June 4, 2010. Documentary on three 17-year-old American scientists. **WITH** Kelydra Welcker, Ana Cisneros Cisneros, Harmain Khan

Harmain Khan in *Whiz Kids* © Shadow Releasing

SPEED-DATING (Rockstone Releasing) Producers, Mekita Faiye, La Monde Byrd; Director/Screenplay, Joseph A. Elmore Jr.; Photography, David Daniel; Designer, Kody Busch; Costumes, Genelle Brooks; Music, Evan Hornsby; Editor, Terry Walters; Casting, Amber Bickham; an Eizzil Entertainment presentation; Color; Not rated; 88 minutes; Release date: June 4, 2010. **CAST**: Wesley Jonathan (Too Cool), Chico Benymon (Dog), Leonard Robinson (Beaver), Mekita Faiye (Danielle), Vanessa Simmons (Elizabeth), Holly Robinson Peete (Gayle), Mark Christopher Lawrence (Dr. Petesmith), Kelly Perine (Dee Jay), Howard "Chingy" Bailey (Kenneth), Roxanne Reese (Aunt B), Camille Mana (Ki Ki), Clint Howard (Dom), Chris Elliott (Inspector Green), Donielle Artese (Desire), Esther Baxter (Christine), Corey Browne (Pharoah Young), Tyreese Burnett (Bartender), Nick Chinlund (Finch), Aurora Ferlin (Willow), Ed Gale (Willie), Cameron Goodman (Hilary), Ron G. (Brian), Natalia Guslistaya (Geraldine), Jermaine Jackson (Grimly), Tanisha Lynn (Kelly), Crystal Maywald (Sensation), Keyla McNeely (Berlinda), Reign Morton (Lester), Michelle Phelps (Hot Girl in Pink Dress), Carlos Ramirez (Miguel), Tony Roberts (Pastor Dean), Ryan Sands (Stan), Mary Alexandra Stievfvater (Frenchita), Gavin Turek (Emily), Dion B. Vines (Butch), Giulini Wever (Samantha), Doug Williams (D), Danny Wooten (Kham), Karen Yelverton (Sage), Natasha Yi (Jasmine)

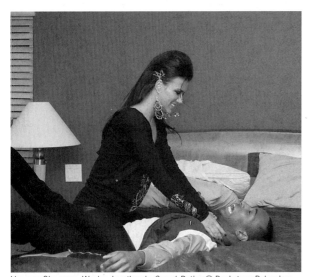

Vanessa Simmons, Wesley Jonathan in *Speed-Dating* © Rockstone Releasing

CONVENTION (IFC Films) Executive Producers, Richard Turner, Heather Winters, Joe Morley, Peter G. Chikes, Nancy M. Chikes; Producers, Jennifer Chikes, Britta Erickson, Shirley Moyers, AJ Schnack, Nathan Truesdell; Director, AJ Schnack; Photography, Steven Bognar, Daniel Junge, Laura Potiras, Julia Reichert, Wayne Robbins, AJ Schnack, Paul Taylor, Nathan Truesdell, Davis Wilson; a Bonfire Films of America and Unconventional Nonfiction production in association with Studio-on-Hudson and Just Media; Color; Not rated; 95 minutes; Release date: June 4, 2010. Documentary looking at the 2008 Democratic National Convention, as recorded by various filmmakers.

Convention © IFC Films

LIVING IN EMERGENCY: STORIES OF DOCTORS WITHOUT BORDERS (BEV Pictures) Producers, Mark Hopkins, Naisola Grimwood, Daniel Holton-Roth; Director, Mark Hopkins; Photography, Sebastian Ischer; Music, Bruno Coulais; Editors, Bob Eisenhardt, Sebastian Ischer, Doug Rossini; a Red Floor Pictures presentation; Color; Not rated; 93 minutes; Release date: June 4, 2010. Documentary on how volunteer doctors struggle to provide emergency medical care in war zones in Liberia and the Congo. **WITH** Dr. Chris Brasher, Dr. Chiara Lepora, Dr. Tom Krueger, Dr. Davinder Gill

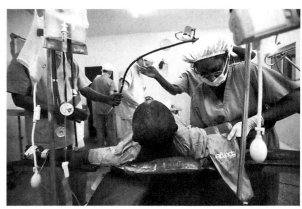

Living in Emergency © BEV Pictures

12TH AND DELAWARE (Loki Films) Executive Producer, Sheila Nevins; Directors, Heidi Ewing, Rachel Grady; Photography, Katherine Patterson; Editor, Enat Sidi; Color; Not rated; 90 minutes; Release date: June 11, 2010. Documentary on the abortion issue in Fort Pierce, Florida, where an abortion clinic is set up directly across the intersection from a pregnancy care center.

12th and Delaware © Loki Films

THE LOTTERY (Variance Films) Producers, Blake Ashman-Kipervaser, James Lawler, Madeleine Sackler; Photography, Wolfgang Held; Director/Editor, Madeleine Sackler; Music, Tunde Adebimpe, Gerard Smith; Color; Not rated; 81 minutes; Release date: June 11, 2010. Documentary in which four children compete for the Harlem Success Academy's intake lottery. **WITH** Cory Booker, Geoffrey Canada, Joel Klein, Eva Moskowitz, Susan Taylor, Dacia Toll

The Lottery © Variance Films

KINGS OF THE EVENING (Indican) Producers, Reginald T. Dorsey, Andrew P. Jones; Executive Producer, Robert Page Jones; Director/Editor, Andrew P. Jones; Screenplay, Robert Page Jones, Andrew P. Jones; Photography, Warren Yeager; Designer, William Jett; Costumes, Lynn Brannelly; Music, Kevin Toney; Casting, Phaedra Harris; a Picture Palace Films presentation; Dolby; Color; Rated PG; 100 minutes; Release date: June 11, 2010. **CAST** Tyson Beckford (Homer Hobbs), Lynn Whitfield (Gracie), Glynn Turman (Clarence Brown), Reginald T. Dorsey (Benny Potter), Linara Washington (Lucy Waters), James Russo (Ramsey), Bruce McGill (Wilfred Cheedle), Steven Williams (Mr. Gamba), Lou Myers (Counter Man), Willard E. Pugh (Henry Nicholson), Tariq Alexander (Stanley Kluntz), David Blackwell (Pawnbroker), Tish Brandt (Sadie Bloom), Jana Camp (Genya), Terrence Flack (Anthony Johnson), Clyde Jones (Reginald Crump), Tommy G. Kendrick (Manager), Justin Malloy (Franklin Cheedle), Garry Peters (Det. McCallum), Charles Quiett (Al the Bartender), LaRita Shelby (Nurse), Everett Sifuentes (Mr. Haynes), Tiffany Leigh Smith (Pretty Black Girl), Timothy Starks (Wilson), LaTeace Towns (Snazzy Lady), Keith Washington (Fletcher Henderson), Gayland Williams (Mrs. Cheedle), Tony Bottorff (Hiring Foreman), Charles Seafous, Ryan Rutledge, Tron Kendrick (Prisoners)

Lynn Whitfield in *Kings of the Evening* © Indican

THE FULL PICTURE (One Big Head Films) Producer/Director/Screenplay, Jon Bowden; Based on his play *Big Mouth*; Executive Producers, Joe Oh, Lorraine Fields, R.M. Mailloux; Photography, Clifford B. Traiman; Designer, Lucila Rafaelli; Music, Mark Degli Antoni; Editors, Peter Hathaway, Jon Bowden; Casting, Michael Ching; a Jon Bowden production; Color; HD-to-DigiBeta; Not rated; 76 minutes; Release date: June 11, 2010. **CAST** Joshua Hutchinson (Hal Foster), Bettina Devin (Gretchen Foster), Daron Jennings (Mark Foster), Lizzie Ross (Erika), Heather Mathieson (Beth Foster), Anna Fiorello (Flight Attendant), Kimberly Crandall (Ellie)

Joshua Hutchinson in *The Full Picture* © One Big Head Films

AMERICAN GRINDHOUSE (Gravitas Ventures) Producer/Director, Elijah Drenner; Executive Producer, Jeff Broadstreet; Screenplay, Elijah Drenner, Calum Waddell; Photography, Dan Greene; Music, Jason Brandt; Editors, Elijah Drenner, Dan Greene, Andrew Goldenberg; Narrator, Robert Forster; a Lux Digital Pictures production; Color/black & white; HD; Not rated; 81 minutes; Release date: June 18, 2010. Documentary on the world of exploitation movies. **WITH** Allison Anders, Judy Brown, Larry Cohen, Joe Dante, Don Edmonds, David Hess, Jack Hill, Jonathan Kaplan, Jeremy Kasten, John Landis, Herschell Gordon Lewis, William Lustig, Ted V. Mikels, Bob Minor, Kim Morgan, Eddie Muller, Fred Olen Ray, Eric Schaefer, Lewis Teague, James Gordon White, Fred Williamson.

8: THE MORMON PROPOSITION (Red Flag Releasing) Producers, Steven Greenstreet, Chris Volz, Emily Pearson; Executive Producers, Reed Cowan, Bruce Bastian; Director/Screenplay, Reed Cowan; Co-Director, Steven Greenstreet; Photography, Reed Cowan, Chris Volz; Music, Nicholas Greer; Editors, Steven Greenstreet, John Kinhart, Brian Bayerl; Narrator, Dustin Lance Black; a David v. Goliath Prod. Presentation; Color; DV; Not rated; 81 minutes; Release date: June 18, 2010. Documentary showing the great influence the Mormon Church had in insuring that Proposition 8 was passed in California, so that gay marriage was not recognized by law. **WITH** Rocky Mayor Anderson, Matt Aune, Tyler Barrick, Bruce Barton, Melissa Bird, Mac Borrowman, D. Chris Buttars, George Cole, Pali Cooper, Darren Curtis, Peter Danzig, Eric Ethington, Ryan Hollist, Ruben Israel, Derick Jones, Spencer Jones, Fred Karger, Kate Kendell, Mark Leno, Barry Lynn, David Melman, Paul Mero, Miyo, Mike Nelson, Gavin Newsom, Sarah Nicholson, Carol Lynn Pearson, Emily Pearson, Sandra Rodriguez, Gayle Ruzicka, Trevor Southey, Hal Sparks, Linda Williams Stay, George Takei, Liz Towne, Michael Waddoups, Jacob Whipple, Kathryn White, Troy Williams

8: The Mormon Proposition © Red Flag Releasing

WAH DO DEM (Wah Do Dem Prods.) Producers, Sam Fleischer, Katina Hubbard, Ben Chace, Martha Lapham, Henry Kasdon; Directors/Screenplay/Editors, Sam Fleischner, Ben Chace; Photography, Sam Fleischner; Color; DV; Not rated; 76 minutes; Release date: June 18, 2010. **CAST**: Sean Bones (Max), Norah Jones (Willow), Carl Bradshaw (Rasta Prophet), Ira Wolf-Tuton, Kevin Bewersdorf, Patrick Morrison, The Congos, Mark Gibbs.

Sean Bones, Norah Jones in *Wah Do Dem* © Wah Do Dem Prods.

THE NATURE OF EXISTENCE (Walking Shadows) Producers, Roger Nygard, Paul Tarantino; Co-Producer/Music, Billy Sullivan; Director/Screenplay, Roger Nygard; Photography/Editors, Roger Nygard, Paul Tarantino; Color; HD; Not rated; 94 minutes; Release date: June 18, 2010. Documentary in which people from around the world expound on their philosophical and religious beliefs. **WITH** Orson Scott Card, Richard Dawkins, Daniel Gilbert, Irvin Kershner, Larry Niven, King Arthur Pendragon, Sri Sri Ravi Shankar, Leonard Susskind, Julia Sweeney, Rollo Maughfling

Rollo Maughfling in *The Nature of Existence* © Walking Shadows

SOUTH OF THE BORDER (Cinema Libre Studios) Producers, Fernando Sulichin, Jose Ibanez, Rob Wilson; Executive Producers, Chris Hanley, Juan Riva, Serge Lobo; Director, Oliver Stone; Screenplay, Tariq Ali, Mark Weisbrot; Photography, Albert Maysles, Carlos Marcovich, Lucas Fuica; Music, Adam Peters; Editors, Alexis Chávez, Elisa Bonora; a Pentagram Films and New Element in association with Good Apple presentation; Color; Not rated; 78 minutes; Release date: June 25, 2010. Documentary in which filmmaker Oliver Stone interviews several South American political leaders. **WITH** Raúl Castro, Hugo Chávez, Rafael Correa, Cristina Fernández de Kirchner, Néstor Kirchner, Fernando Lugo, Evo Morales, Luiz Inácio Lula da Silva

Oliver Stone, Hugo Chávez in *South of the Border* © Cinema Libre Studios

GREAT DIRECTORS (Paladin) Producer/Director/Screenplay, Angela Ismailos; Photography, John Pirozzi; Music, Joel Douek; Editors, Christina Burchard, Sabine Hoffman; an Anisma Films presentation; Dolby; Color; Not rated; 90 minutes; Release date: July 2, 2010. Documentary in which Angela Ismalois talks with ten notable directors. **WITH** Bernardo Bertolucci, Catherine Breillat, Lilian Cavani, Stephen Frears, Todd Haynes, Angela Ismailos, Richard Linklater, Ken Loach, David Lynch, John Sayles, Agnès Varda

Angela Ismailos, Bernardo Bertolucci in *Great Directors* © Paladin

GOD OF VAMPIRES (Maxim Media/Conquest Pictures) Producers, Dharma Lin, Rob Fitz; Director/Screenplay, Rob Fitz; Photography, Silas Tyler; Designer, Kurt Bergeron; Editor, Cherry Enoki; Color; Not rated; 109 minutes; Release date: July 2, 2010. **CAST**: Dharma Lim (Frank Ng), Ben Wang (Uncle Ping), Shy Theerakulstit (Vincent), Morris Chung (Dave), Jayson Argento (Jablonski), Kurt Bergeron (Fingers), Evan Lam (Ducky), Pete O'Herne (The Fixer), John Sefel (Dominic), Lilith Astaroth, John Pungitore (Vampires)

ALL ABOUT EVIL (Peaches Christ) Producers, Darren Stein, Brian Benson, Debbie Brubaker, Joshua Grannell; Executive Producers, Robert Barber, William Barber, Anthony A. Varvaro; Director/Screenplay, Joshua Grannell; Photography, Tom Richmond; Designer, Kris Boxwell; Costumes, Frank Helmer; Music, Vinsantos; Editor, Rick LeCoompte; Casting, Jason James; a Backlash Films in

Jade Ramsey, Nikita Ramsey in *All about Evil* © Peaches Christ

association with Fog City Pictures presentation; Color; Not rated; 97 minutes; Release date: July 9, 2010. **CAST**: Natasha Lyonne (Deborah Tennis), Thomas Dekker (Steven), Cassandra Peterson (Linda), Mink Stole (Evelyn), Noah Segan (Adrian), Jack Donner (Mr. Twigs), Jade Ramsey (Veda), Nikita Ramsey (Vera), Ariel Hart (Judy), Ashley Fink (Lolita), Anthony Fitzgerald (Gene), Patrick Bristow (Peter Gorge), Julie Caitlin Brown (Tammy Tennis), Gwyneth Richards (Mrs. Moorehead), Lyndsay Kail (Claire), Santia Andrews (Janeane), Kat Turner (Veronica), Peaches Christ (Peaches), Nicholas Bearde (Det. Woods), Timmy Spence (Principal Hunter), Jennifer Taher (Nurse Helen), Mikayla Rosario (Little Debbie), Robin Calvert (Walter Tennis), Mel Shaker (Mrs. Cavanaugh), Baily Hopkins (Stephanie), Michael Brenchley (Martiny), Jamie Beardsley (Concerned Mother)

WINNEBAGO MAN (Kino) Producers, Joel Heller, James Payne, Malcolm Pullinger, Ben Steinbauer; Director, Ben Steinbauer; Screenplay, Malcolm Pullinger, Ben Steinbauer; Photography, Bradley Beesley, Berndt Mader; Music, Andrew Hoke, Taylor Holland; Editor, Malcolm Pullinger; a Bear Media presentation in association with Field Guide media, of a Do Me a Kindness production; Color; HD; Not rated; 87 minutes; Release date: July 9, 2010. Documentary in which filmmaker Ben Steinbauer tracks down Jack Debney, who was dubbed "The Angriest Man in the World" because of an outtake reel compiled from a Winnebago commercial he filmed in the 1980s. **WITH** Jack Rebney, Ben Steinbauer, Keith Gordon, Douglas Rushkoff, Alan Berliner, Nick Prueher, Joe Pickett, Charlie Sotelo, Cinco Barnes, Mike Mitchell, Alexsey Vayner

Jack Rebney in *Winnebago Man* © Kino

STANDING OVATION (Rocky Mountain Pictures) Producer, Diane Kirman; Executive Producers, James Brolin, William Lewis, Suzanne Nunez, Suzanne Burke, Wendy Martinez, A.M. Coughlin; Co-Producer, Jennifer Tini; Director/ Screenplay, Stewart Raffill; Photography, Jon Darbonne; Designer, Jim Walsh; Costumes, Krystal Tini; Music, Benedkit Brydern; Music Supervisor, Sal Dupree; Choreographers, Krystal Tini, Joanne Reagan, Anne Reagan, Debbie Apalucci; Editor, Laurie McDowell; a Kenilworth Films and West 8 Films presentation of a Brolin, Kirman, Lewis production; Dolby; Color; Rated PG; 105 minutes; Release date: July 16, 2010. **CAST**: Kayla Jackson (Brittany), Alexis Biesiada (Tatiana), Na'jee Wilson (Maya), Pilar Martin (Blaze), Kayla Raparelli (Cameron), Alanna Palombo (Alanna Wannabe), Dexter Darden (Emcee), Joei DeCarlo (Joey Batalucci), Sal Dupree (Mr. Wiggs), London Clark (Ziggy Wiggs), Erika Corvette (Angel Wiggs), Ashley Cutrona (Zita Wiggs), Devon Jordan (Twiggy Wiggs), Jeana Zettler (Zoey Wiggs), Austin Powell (Mark O'Brien), Michael Pericoloso (Mikey P.), Mykal Williams (Lead Boy), Dr. Bill Lewis (The Mayor), Mario Macaluso (Kenny Rich), Anthony Carney (Mr. Gaines), Bobby Harper (Alanna's Dad), Monique Impagliazzo (Receptionist), William McKenna (Eric), P. Brendan Mulvey (Gramps), Susie Neustadter (Mrs. Wiggs), Chrasto Parenti (Janitor), Al Sapienza (Solly DeGrand), Krystal Tini (Choreographer), Seth Rabinowitz (Boardwalk Wiseguy)

5 Ovations in *Standing Ovation* © Rocky Mountain Pictures

TO AGE OR NOT TO AGE (Sag Harbor Basement Pictures) Producers, Miriam Folcy, Joseph Zock; Executive Producer, Anthony Loera; Director/Screenplay/ Photography/ Editor, Robert Kane Pappas; Music, Spider Barbour, Paul Groueff, Mira Spektor; produced in association with RevGenetics and Solleone Health Systems; Color; DV; Not rated; 96 minutes; Release date: July 16, 2010. Documentary on scientific breakthroughs that can genetically manipulate the aging process. **WITH** Steven Austad, Nicador Austriaco, Troy Duster, Aubrey de Grey, Leonard Guarente, Cynthia Kenyon, Thomas Kirkwood, Gordon Lithgow, David Sinclair, Christoph Westphal.

Dr, Aubrey de Grey, Robert Kane Pappas in *To Age or Not to Age* © Sage Harbor Basement Pictures

THE CONTENDERS (Simmia Prods.) Producers, Raffaele Piscopiello, Paola Romagnani; Executive Producer/Editor, Ben Suenga; Director/Screenplay, Marta Mondelli; Photography, Vitaly Bokser; Art Director/Costumes, Franca Bruno; Music, Alex Trebo; a Simmia Productions and the Contenders Inc. presentation; Color; Not rated; 75 minutes; Release date: July 16, 2010. **CAST**: Anna Gutto (Nora), Adam Henry Garcia (Marc), Marta Mondelli (Veronica), Nick Stevenson (Ken), Eon Grey (Detective), Laura Caparrotti (Woman), Mélanie Cecconi (Girl)

Marta Mondelli, Adam Henry Garcia in *The Contenders* © Simmia Prods.

OPERATION: ENDGAME (Anchor Bay) formerly *Rogues Gallery*; Producers, Sean McKittrick, Michael Ohoven, Kevin Turen; Director, Fouad Mikati; Screenplay, Sam Levinson, Brian Watanabe; Photography, Arnaud Stefani; Designer, Michael Grasley; Costumes, Bonnie Stauch; Music, Ian Honeyman; Editor, Joshua Ferrazzano; an Infinity and Darko Entertainment production, presented with Infinity Media; Color; Rated R; 87 minutes; Release date: July 16, 2010. **CAST**: Joe Anderson (Fool), Odette Yustman (Temperence), Zach Galifianakis (Hermit), Ellen Barkin (Empress), Rob Corddry (Chariot), Adam Scott (Magician), Ving Rhames (Judgment), Bob Odenkirk (Emperor), Jeffrey Tambor (Devil), Maggie Q (High Priestess), Emilie de Ravin (Hierophant), Brandon T. Jackson (Tower), Beth Grant (Susan), Tim Bagley (Carl), Michael Hitchcock (Neil), Matt Baker (Bathroom Victim)

Zach Galifianakis in *Operation: Endgame* © Anchor Bay

JEAN-MICHEL BASQUIAT: THE RADIANT CHILD (Arthouse Films) Producers, Tamra Davis, David Koh, Lilly Bright, Stanley Buchtal, Alexis Manya Spraic; Executive Producer, Maja Hoffman; Director, Tamra Davis; Photography, Tamra Davis, David Koh, Harry Geller; Music, J. Ralph, Adam Horowitz, Mike Diamond; a Curiously Bright Entertainment (U.S.)/LM Media (Germany) presentation; American-German; Stereo; Color; DV; Not rated; 93 minutes; Release date: July 21, 2010. Documentary on artist Jean-Michel Basquiat. **WITH** Bruno Bischofberger, Diego Cortez, Jeffrey Deitch, Kai Eric, Fab 5 Freddy, Larry Gagosian, Fred Hoffmann, Michael Holman, Maripol, Suzanne Mallouk, Annina Nosei, Glenn O'Brien, Rene Ricard, Kenny Scharf, Julian Schnabel, Tony Shafrazi, Nicholas Taylor

Jean-Michel Basquiat in *The Radiant Child* © Arthouse Films

AUDREY THE TRAINWRECK (Independent) Producer, Adam Donaghey; Director/ Screenplay/Editor, Frank V. Ross; Photography, David Lowery; Music, John Medeski; Zero Trans Fat Prods.; Color; Not rated; 86 minutes; Release date: July 23, 2010. **CAST**: Anthony Baker (Ron Hogan), Alexi Wasser (Stacy Ryan), Danny Rhodes (Scott Kaniewski), Rebecca Spence (Kate Meyers), Jess Weixler (Tammy), Ivory Tiffin (Darci Stanton), Joe Swanberg (Jeremy Roth), Kurt Naebig (Tim Hagan), Jennifer Knox (Jenny the Bride), Sasha Gioppo (Kathy, Maid of Honor), Amy Judd (Doe-Eyes), Nick Offerman (David George), Allison Latta (Audrey), Kris Swanberg (Realtor Lady), Lonnie Phillips (Client), Nathan Adloff (Aaron), Tim Baker (Wernk-Burger), Denis Blank (Trish), Brittany Brumfield (Lisa Eichas), Zack Buell (Dan), Ainsley Elias (Darryl), Dave Moats (Jeffery), Matt Orseske (Matt), Vito Sapienza (Good News)

Anthony Baker, Jess Weixler in *Audrey the Trainwreck* © Zero Trans Fat Prods.

COUNTDOWN TO ZERO (Magnolia) Producer, Lawrence Bender; Executive Producers, Jeff Skoll, Diane Weyermann, Bruce Blair, Matt Brown; Co-Producer, Lisa Remington; Director/Screenplay, Lucy Walker; Photography, Robert Chappell, Gary Clarke, Bryan Donnell, Nick Higgins; Music, Peter Golub; Editors, Brad Fuller, Brian Johnson; Visual Effects Supervisor, Forrest Heidel; a Participant Media in association with World Security Institute and the History Channel presentation of a Lawrence Bender production; Dolby; Color; Rated PG; 91 minutes; Release date: July 23, 2010. Documentary that speculates on the world's inevitable demise because of the number of nuclear weapons in existence. **WITH** Graham Allison, James Baker III, Bruce Blair, Tony Blair, Zbigniew Brzezinski, Matthew Bunn, Richard Burt, Jimmy Carter, Mike Chinoy, Joseph Cirincione, Richard Cizik, Thomas D'Agostino, F.W. de Klerk, Pascal Fias, Alexander Glaser, Mikhail Gorbachev, Ira Helfand, Pervez Hoodhoy, R. Scott Kemp, Andrew Koch, Jeffrey Lewis, Robert McNamara, Zia Mian, Roger Molander, Rolf Mowatt-Larssen, Pervez Musharraf, Khintsagov Oleg, Ahmed Rashid, Scott Sagan, Lawrence Scott Sheets, Frank von Hippel, Valerie Plame Wilson.

Countdown to Zero © Magnolia

I WANT YOUR MONEY (Freestyle) Producer, Doug Stebleton; Executive Producers, Ray Griggs, Michael Kim Binder; Director, Ray Griggs; Screenplay, Rag Griggs, Randall Norman Desoto; Photography, Matthew Mayotte; Music, Don Harper; an RG Entertainment production; Dolby; Color; Rated PG; 92 minutes; Release date: July 28, 2010. Documentary on how the federal government has dealt with the country's financial problems; with Mike Huckabee, Stephen Moore, Michael Reagan, William Voegeli, Star Parker, Kenneth Blackwell, Edwin Meese III, Thad McCotter, Newt Gingrich, Lee Edwards, Pete Wilson, Steve Forbes, Gary Bauer, Kate Obenshain, Chris Edwards, David M. McIntosh, Lila Rose, John Stossel, Allen Icet, Rob Schaaf, John Stossel, Tom McClintock, Andrew Breitbart, George Runner, Alison Fraser; and the voices of Chris Cox (Jimmy Carter/Bill Clinton), Bill Farmer (George H.W. Bush/George W. Bush), Ray Griggs (Squirrels), Jay Lamont (Barack Obama), Jim Meskimen (Ronald Reagan), Cindy Robinson (Nancy Pelosi), Tim Russell (Ronald Reagan), Jane Edith Wilson (Sarah Palin), Mick Wingert (Arnold Schwarzenegger)

I Want Your Money © Freestyle Releasing

SMASH HIS CAMERA (Magnolia) Producers, Adam Schlesinger, Lidna Saffire; Executive Producers, Jeffrey Tarrant, William Ackman, Daniel Stern; Director, Leon Gast; Photography, Doug Don Lenzer; Music, Craig Hazen, David Wolfert; Editor, Doug Abel; a Got the Shot production; Color; HD; Rated PG-13; 90 minutes; Release date: July 30, 2010. Documentary on famed paparazzo (celebrity photographer) Ron Galella. **WITH** Ron Galella, Floyd Abrams, Joseph Basile, Dick Cavett, Chuck Close, Bonnie Fuller, Betty Burke Galella, Michael Hess, Thomas Hoving, Peter Howe, Elaine Kaufman, Robert Kennedy Jr., Neil Leifer, John Loengard, Martin London, M.C. Marden, David McGough, Robert Redford, Stuart Schlesinger, Paul Schumlback, Marvin Scott, Liz Smith, Nick Stepowyj, Kerry Sulkowicz, Jim Tooey

Marlon Brando, Ron Galella in *Smash His Camera* © Magnolia

WHAT'S THE MATTER WITH KANSAS? (Tallgrass Films) Producers, Laura Cohen, Jow Winston; Director, Joe Winston; Based on the book by Thomas Frank; Photography, T.W. Li; Music, Eric Lambert, Earhole Studios; Editors, Joe Winston, Alex MacKenzie; Stereo; Color; Not rated; 90 minutes; Release date: July 30, 2010. Documentary explores the religious right and its effect on middle-class voters. **WITH** Alyssa Barden, Brittany Barden, Dawn Barden, Matthew Barden, Nicholas Barden, Rob Barden, Tiffany Barden, Brad Bennett, Cindie Bennett, Julie Burkhart, Angel Dillard, Katy Dillard, Reagan Dillard, Rob Dillard, Thomas Etheredge, Hilda Flores, Jose Flores, Pastor Terry Fox, Thomas Frank, Mark Gietzen, Dan Glickman, Garrett Harmon, Connie Kelly, Steve LaRue, M.T. Liggett, Bob Lippoldt, Dr. Jason Lisle, Terry McLachlan, Reuben Mendoza, Velia Mendoza, Troy Newman, Randy Roberts, Lynn Schneider, Penney Schwab, Dale Swenson, Donn Teske, Kathy Teske, Tyler Teske, Zachary Teske

Brittany Barden in *What's the Matter with Kansas?* ©Tallgrass Films

DARK HOUSE (Lightning Media) Producers, Mark Sonoda, Nick Allan; Executive Producer, Charles Melander; Director/Screenplay, Darin Scott; Story, Kerry Douglas Dye, Darin Scott; Photography, Phil Lee; Designer, Susan Genito; Costumes, Glenda Maddox; Music, Vincent Gillioz; Editor, Charles Bornstein; Makeup/Creature Effects, Megan Areford; Visual Effects Supervisor, Al Magliochetti; Casting, Ivy Isenberg; a Fatal Frame Pictures presentation in association with Red Shogun Pictures; Dolby; Color; HD-to-35mm; Rated R; 85 minutes; Release date: July 30, 2010. **CAST**: Meghan Ory (Claire Thompson), Jeffrey Combs (Walston), Diane Salinger (Miss Darrode), Matt Cohen (Rudy), Bevin Prince (Ariel), Shelly Cole (Lily), Ryan Melander (Bruce), Danso Gordon (Eldon), Scott Whyte (Moreton), Ian Reed Kesler (Reed), Erin Cummings (Paula Clark), Meghan Maureen McDonough (Samantha), Mathew Melander (Rusty), Michael Albala (Harris Payne), Annalise Basso (Sally), Richard Chaves (Detective), Cruz Chung (Water Torture Victim), Tom Duilhet (Templar Knight), Gillian Foreman (Fingernail Wraith), Quinten Lopez (Andy), Michael Lovern (Plant Man), Natalie Marie (Corpse Fog), R.A. Mihailoff (The Brutal Butcher), Scotty Noyd Jr. (Spike), Mia Pollini (Brenda), Maley Pullos (Young Tammy), Amirali Raissina (Evil Clown), Courtney Robinson (Young Claire), Garrett Ryan (Mark), James Ryen (Uniformed Cop), Don Stark (Gorog), Terrell Tilford (Det. Williams), Stephen Walter (The Executioner), Kathryn Weisbeck (Woman on Rack), Time Winters (Caldecote), Ariauna Albright, Jade Brandais, Lauren Carter, Natalie Sutherland (Witches), Veronica Bennett, Ameona Leigh Almund, Andrea VanEpps (Suicide Vampires), Michael Gaglio (Torture Victim), Johnny Giacalone, Ryan Turek, Andy White, Jeromy Thorsen (Zombies), Kayla Gwyneth Morrisey (Woman's Talking Head), Felix Vicious (Hanging Body Parts)

Dark House © Lightning Media

CATS & DOGS: THE REVENGE OF KITTY GALORE (WB) Producers, Andrew Lazar, Polly Johnsen; Executive Producers, Brent O'Connor, Bruce Berman; Director, Brad Peyton; Screenplay, Ron J. Friedman, Steve Bencich; Based on characters created by John Requa, Glenn Ficarra; Photography, Steven Poster; Designer, Rusty Smith; Music, Christopher Lennertz; Editor, Julie Rogers; Special Effects Coordinator, Tony Lazarowich; Animatronic Cat and Dog Creator, Lee Romaire; Casting, Kristy Carlson; a Mad Chance/Polymorphic Pictures production, presented in association with Village Roadshow Pictures; Dolby; Technicolor; Rated PG; 82 minutes; Release date: July 30, 2010. **CAST** Chris O'Donnell (Shane), Jack McBrayer (Chuck), Fred Armisen (Friedrich), Kiernan Shipka (Little Girl), Michael Beattie (Angus MacDougall), Jeff Bennett (Duncan MacDougall), Malcolm Stewart (Capt. Fleming), Ingrid Tesch (Mom), Amitai Marmorstein (Playland Worker), Robert Hewko (Old Man), Mark Burgess (Used Car Salesman), Sage Brocklebank (Park Patron); **VOICE CAST**: James Marsden (Diggs), Nick Nolte (Butch), Christina Applegate (Catherine), Katt Williams (Seamus), Bette Midler (Kitty Galore), Neil Patrick Harris (Lou), Sean Hayes (Mr. Tinkles), Wallace Shawn (Calico), Roger Moore (Tab Lazenby), Joe Pantoliano (Peek), Michael Clarke Duncan (Sam), Paul Rodriguez (Crazy Carlito), J.K. Simmons (Gruff K-9), Elizabeth Daily (Scrumptious/Patches/Catherine's Niece), Phil LaMarr (Paws/Cat Spy Analyst), Dawn Chubai (Reporter), Keith Dallas (Coit Tower Guard), Pascale Hutton (Jackie), Grey DeLisle (Security Bulldog/Catherine's Niece/Cat Spy Analyst), Len Morganti (Rex), Betty Phillips (Cat Lady), Chris Parson (Hep Cat/Cat Spy Analyst), Bumper Robinson (Cool Cat/Dog Killa/Cat Spy Analyst/Slim), Rick D. Wasserman (Rocky), Roger L. Jackson (Inmate Fat Cat), Bonnie Cahoon (Dog PA), André Sogliuzzo (Snobby K-9), Carlos Alazraqui (Cat Gunner/Cat Spy Analyst)

THE NEW YEAR (Independent) Producers/Screenplay, Brett Haley, Elizabeth Kennedy; Director, Brett Haley; Photography, Rob C. Givens; Music, Austin Donohue; Costumes, Tara Tona; Color; Not rated; 96 minutes; Release date: July 30, 2010. **CAST**: Trieste Kelly Dunn (Sunny), Ryan Hunter (Isaac), Kevin Wheatley (Neal), Linda Lee McBride (Amy), Marc Petersen (Daniel Elliott), Lance Brannon (Glen), David McElfresh (Bobby), Justin McElfresh (Andy), Carol Kahn Parker (Laura), Victor Aminger (Partygoer)

Trieste Kelly Dunn in *The New Year* © Haley/Kennedy

THE DRY LAND (Freestyle) Producer, Heather Rae; Executive Producers, Sergio Aguero, America Ferrera; Co-Producers, Jason Michael Berman, Margo Johnston, Mark G. Mathis; Director/Screenplay, Ryan Piers Williams; Photography, Gavin Kelly; Designer, David Baca; Costumes, Jerry Carnivale; Music, Dean Parks; Music Supervisor, April Kimble; Editor, Sabine Hoffman; Casting, Jeanne McCarthy, Nicole Abellera; a Maya Entertainment presentation in association with Take Fountain Prods. and Besito Films; Dolby; Technicolor; Rated R; 92 minutes; Release date: July 30, 2010. **CAST**: Ryan O'Nan (James), America Ferrera (Sarah), Wilmer Valderrama (Raymond Gonzales), Jason Ritter (Michael), Melissa Leo (Martha), June Diane Raphael (Susie), Diego Klattenhoff (Henry), Evan Jones (Joe Davis), Benito Martinez (David Valdez), Ethan Suplee (Jack), Sasha Spielberg (Sally), Ana Claudia Talancón (Adrian), Barry Shabaka Henley (Col. Stephen Evans), Arron Shiver (Police Officer), Jeremiah Bitsui (Luis), Johnnie Hector (Police Officer), Misty Upham (Gloria), Jenny Gabrielle (Tina), Esodie Geiger (Nurse), Russell Friendberg (Dr. Stephenson), Kate Schroeder (Kathy), Therese Olson (Sasha), Candice Costello (Veronica)

America Ferrera, Ryan O'Nan in *The Dry Land* © Freestyle Releasing

LUCKY DAYS (Seminal Films) Producer, Luke Zarzecki; Executive Producers, Angelica Torn, Rip Torn, Jacqueline Guttman, Rui DaSilva, Mathius Mack Gertz; Producer Emeritus, Paul Newman; Directors, Angelica Torn, Tony Torn; Screenplay, Angelia Torn; Photography, Nils Kenaston; Music, Christopher North; Editors, Los Tres Amigos; Presented in association with Torn Page Prods.; Color; HD; Not rated; 103 minutes; Release date: August 6, 2010. **CAST**: Angelica Torn (Virginia), Federico Castelluccio (Vincent), Luke Zarzecki (Zeth), Will Patton (J.C.), Rip Torn (Bobo), Anne Jackson (Corkie), Tina Benko (Nina), Marilyn Sokol (Cherie), Gary Wolf (Felix), Tony Torn (Bobby), Gail Gerber (Bobby), Timothy Doyle (Dr. Marion), Justin Grace (Joey), Denise Lute (Frenchie), Ralphie (Thomas Wolff), Maureen Shannon (Mauve), Frank Wood (Dr. Ginger)

Rip Torn in *Lucky Days* © Seminal Films

THE WILDEST DREAM (National Geographic Entertainment) Producers, Anthony Geffen, Claudia Perkins; Executive Producer, Mike Medavoy; Director, Anthony Geffen; Screenplay, Mark Halliley; Photography, Ken Sauls, Chris Opernshaw; Art Director, Humphrey Bagham; Costumes, Jane Wrigley; Music, Joel Douek; Editor, Peter Miller; an Altitude Films production with Atlantic Prods.; Dolby; Color; Rated PG; 92 minutes; Release date: August 6, 2010. Documentary in which Conrad Anker and his team attempt to retrace George Mallory's steps in his ill-fated 1924 effort to scale Mt. Everest; with Conrad Anker, Leo Houlding; and VOICES: Liam Neeson (Narrator), Hugh Dancy (Andrew Irvine), Ralph Fiennes (George Mallory), Natasha Richardson (Ruth Mallory), Alan Rickman (Noel Odell)

Conrad Anker in *The Wildest Dream* © National Geographic Entertainment

LAST LETTERS FROM MONTE ROSA (Julesworks) Producer, Curtis Mattikow; Executive Producers, Stanley Taub, Berj Terzian; Director, Ari Taub; Screenplay/Photography, Caio Ribeiro; Designer, Joanna Wright; Costumes, Cyrus Lee; Editors, Ari Taub, Caio Ribeiro; Music, Sergei Dreznin; a WWII Film Productions in association with Julesworks Releasing, LCC presentation; Color; Not rated; 88 minutes; Release date: August 6, 2010. **CAST**: Davidé Borella (Pietro), Achim Buchner (Franz), Markus Kirschbaum (Hans), Adán Latonda (Mario), Frank Licari (Pepino), Thomas Pohn (Lt. Waldheim), Rafael Quiles (Marcello), Carmine Rapaolo (Alberto), Dieter Riesle (Otto), Fabio Sartor (Lt. Pietro), Dirk Schmidt (Wulfe), Stephan Schützler (Schultz), Wolfram Teufel (Kreuger), Frank Voß (Johann), Milton Welsh (Thomas), Daniel Asher, C.J. Barkus (US Frontline Soldiers), Gianluca Bianco, Michael Castignetti, Rick Cavallaro, Othmar Dickbauer, Zura Kiria, Massimo Lozza, Stefano Paolillo, Jamie Taub (Italian Soldiers), Hans-Dieter Brüchner (German Cook), Dave Clauss (German Motorcycle Driver), Pierluigi Corallo, Dan Costantini, Guilio Lupori, Stefano Quatrosi (Thugs), Nick Day, Francesco Mazzini (Partisans), Walter DeForest (Bald German Soldier), Emanuele Fortunati (Rossini's Chef), Dirk Kölling (German Bunker Sentinel), Alessandro Lombardo (Mountain Partisan Leader), Bob Manus (US War Correspondent), John McVay (American Grenade Thrower), Paul Meda (US Soldier with Tommy Gun), John O'Learly (US Soldier), Ruben Pla, Brett G. Smith (American Infantrymen), Lucio Polosa (Mooning Partisan), Ralf Rittmeyer (Retreating German Soldier), Sebastian Sartor (Italian Partisan Boy), Gerzon Schiefer (German Radio Operator), Michael Schürger (German Captain on Retreat)

Last Letters from Monte Rosa © Julesworks

THE PARKING LOT MOVIE (Redhouse) Producer/Director/Photography, Meghan Eckman; Music, Sam Retzer; Editors, Meghan Eckman, Christopher Hlad; Color; HD; Not rated; 74 minutes; Release date: August 6, 2010. Documentary on those who have worked as attendants at the Central Parking Lot in Charlottesville, Virginia. **WITH** Chris Farina, John Lindaman, Jeffrey Fleischer, John Bylander, Scott Meiggs, Tyler Magill, Patrick Baran, John Beers, Bridge Cox, Sam Duncan, Matt Datesmann, Daniel Finn, Corey Gross, Harper Hellems, Joe Lille, Jon Malesic, James McNew, Nate Millington, Gray Morris, Dan Moseley, AJ Pesch, Mark Schottinger, Rick Slade

Harper Hellems in *The Parking Lot Movie* © Redhouse

THE KID: CHAMACO (Maya Entertainment) Producers, Don Franken, Kirk Jarris, Miguel Necoechea Jr.; Executive Producers, Philip Bligh, Scott Chambers, Justin Kim, Bruce Randolph Tizes; Director, Miguel Necoechea; Screenplay, Miguel Mecoechea, Carl Bessai, Kirk Harris; Photography, Guillermo Granillo; Designer, Carlos Herrera; Music, Shaun Drew; Editor, Mario Sandoval; Color; Not rated; 90 minutes; Release date: August 6, 2010. **CAST**: Martin Sheen (Dr. Frank Irwin), Michael Madsen (Willie), Alex Perea (Abner Torres), Danny Perea (Silvana Torres), Kirk Harris (Jimmy Irwin), Sofia Espinosa (Paulina), Gustavo Sánchez Parra (Rigoberto Torres), Christian Vasquez (Wilo), Raúl Méndez (Manuel), Marco Antonio Barrera (Himself), Daniel Evangelista (Jose Daniel Evangelista), Gustavo Ganem (Poncho), Damayanti Quintanar (Ana), Joe Torrenueva (Luis Ortega), Michael Ellison (Mike), Don Franken (Ring Announcer)

Martin Sheen, Alex Perea in *The Kid: Chamaco* © Maya Entertainment

CIRCLE (Indican) Producers, James Allen Bradley, Joe Dain, Luke Daniels, Sharon Nixon Kelly, Brad Tiemann; Executive Producers, Ryan Weisfisch, Jonathan Zuck; Director, Michael W. Watkins; Screenplay, Brad Tiemann; Photography, Alan Jacoby; Designers, Andrew Baird, Marcel Victor Prefontaine; Costumes, Brandon Bernard; Music, Gunnard Doboze; Editors, David Crabtree, Brad Durante; Casting, Michael Hothorn; a Redwire Pictures production; Dolby; Color; Rated R; 88 minutes; Release date: August 27, 2010. **CAST**: Gail O'Grady (Dr. Green), Silas Weir Mitchell (Bennett), America Olivo (Britt), Jason Thompson (Gavin), Michael DeLuise (Bill Tanner), Peter Onorati (Chief), Erin Michelle Lokitz (Chloe), Kinsey Packard (Agent Randall), Erin Foster (Morgan), Will Stiles (Tristan), James Francis Kelly III (Det. Bryce), Rita Taggart (Professor McAdams), Ryan Doom (Luke), Tally Hunkins (Sherri), John Stamatakis, Sarah Burch, Jeremy Chada, Mario Sellitti, Sebastian Blue (Bound Patients), Mike Mohrhardt (Bathroom Student), Tony Lee Boggs (Dead Police Officer), Teddy Williams (Security Guard), Sitara Falcon (Lawnmower Man), Rae Sunshine Lee, Gregg Lee, Jayne Entwistle (Hospital Workers), Michael Thompson, Jon Greene (Police Officers)

Silas Weir Mitchell in *Circle* © Indican

FRUIT FLY (TLA Releasing) Producers, Don Young, H.P. Mendoza; Executive Producer, Stephen Gong; Director/Screenplay/Editor/Music, H.P. Mendoza; Photography, Richard Wong; Designer, Amy Y. Chan; Graphics and Animation, Mark Del Lima; a CAAM presentation of an Ersatz Film production; Widescreen; Color; HD; Not rated; 94 minutes; Release date: September 24, 2010. **CAST**: L.A. Reingen (Bethesda), Mike Curtis (Windham), Theresa Navarro (Sharon), Aaron Zaragoza (Jacob), E.S. Park (Karen), Christian Cagigal (Gaz Howard), Don Wood (Tracy), Michelle Talgarow (Geraldine), Christina Augello (Dirty Judy), Shelly Kim, M. Cat Alleyne, Nanrisa Lee (Hags), Casey Ley (Mike), Sam Roemer (Greg), Ryan Morales (Manny), James Lontayao (Kenji), Sohr Picart (Auntie Josephine), H.P.

Mendoza (Mark), Marilet Martinez (Jacob's Mother), Tim Bland (Castro Man), Bethany Del Lima, Owen Otto (Art Buyers), Tim Luym (Poleng Owner), Amara Dan (New Girl at Bar), Chi-Hui Yang (Club Bouncer)

Fruit Fly © TLA Releasing

THEY CAME TO PLAY (Area 23a) Producer, Lori Miller; Executive Producer, Ronnie Planalp; Director, Alex Rotaru; Photography, Brian O'Connell, Adrian Popescu; Editors, Harrison Engle, Drew Kilcoin; a Vault presentation of a Miller/Rotaru production; Color; HD; Not rated; 91 minutes; Release date: August 13, 2010. Documentary on the Van Cliburn International Piano Competition in Fort Worth, Texas. **WITH** Van Cliburn, Henri Delbeau, Annette Dimedio, Greg Fisher, Mark Fuller, Clark Griffith, Ken Iisaka, Slava Levin, Drew Mays, James Raphael, Esfir Ross, Anne-Marie Rouchon, Eberhard Zagrosek

Esfir Ross in They Came to Play © Area 23a

THE PEOPLE I'VE SLEPT WITH (People Pictures) Producers, Koji Steven Sakai, Quentin Lee; Executive Producers, Tien Lee, Sam Kwok, Brian Yang; Director, Quentin Lee; Screenplay, Koji Steven Sakai; Photography, Quyen Tran; Designer, Mona Nahm; Music, Steven Pranoio; Editor, Aldo Velasco; a 408 Films production; Color; HD; Not rated; 86 minutes; Release date: August 13, 2010. **CAST**: Karin Anna Cheung (Angela), Wilson Cruz (Gabriel), Archie Kao (Jefferson), Lynn Chen (Juliet), James Shigeta (Charles Yang), Chris Zylka (Mr. Hottie), Randall Park (Nice but Boring Guy), Stacie Rippy (Becky), Elizabeth Sung (Mrs. Lee), Cathy Shim (Nikki), Kelly Nienaltowski (Pregnant Woman), Tim Chiou (Fred), Dana Lee (Mr. Lee), Perry Smith (Mrs. Robinson), Sherry Weston (Dr.

Richards), Rane Jameson (Lawrence), Maya Parish (Marissa), Shu Lan Tuan (Older Angela), Traber Burns (Priest), Keo Woolford (Lenny Kai), Danny Vasquez (Ron), Rylan Williams (Preston), Justin Huen, Tim Watters, Michael Coulombe, Sarah Grant, Michael Marcel, Tristan Wand, Dexter de Sah, Evan Martinez, Denise Lee, David Binck, Wa Yang, Brian Watters (Angela's Lovers), Edward Gunawan (Gabriel's Lover)

Rane Jameson, Karin Anna Cheung in The People I've Slept With © People Pictures

NESHOBA (First Run Features) Producers/Directors/Editors, Micki Dickoff, Tony Pagano; Co-Producer, Christie Webb; Screenplay, Micki Dickoff; Photography, Tony Pagano; Music, Chris Davis; a Pro Bono and Pagano production; Color/black and white; Beta SP-to-DigiBeta; Not rated; 90 minutes; Release date: August 13, 2010. Documentary on the 1964 murder of three civil rights workers in Mississippi. **WITH** Edgar Ray "Preacher" Killen, Ben Chaney, Carolyn Goodman, Rita Bender, Jewel McDonald, Deborah Posey, Buford Posey, Dave Dennis, Florence Mars, Jerry Mitchell

Edgar Ray Killen in Neshoba © First Run Features

HIDING DIVYA (Net Effect Media) Producer, Rohi Mirza Pandya; Executive Producers, Gitesh Pandya, Deep Katdare, Vijay Vaidyanathan; Director/Screenplay, Rehana Mirza; Photography, Renato Falcao; Designer, Artai Nath; Music, Samrat Chakrabarti; Editor, Michelle Botticelli; Color; Not rated; 88 minutes; Release date: August 20, 2010. **CAST**: Pooja Kumar (Palini "Linny" Shah), Madhur Jaffrey (Divya Shah), Deep Katdare (Ravi Das), Madlaine Massey (Jia Shah), Kunal Sharma (Daniel), Stu Richel (John Cooper, "Uncle John"), Olivia Ordway Guerrieri (Young Linny), Norm Golden (Fred Mason), Ajay Naidu (Divya's Husband), Sabina Shah (Divya's Sister), Elisa De La Roche (Heena Auntie), Anupama Torgal (Kavita Auntie), Manu Narayan (Irfana Auntie's Son), Sorab Wadia (Sari Shop Owner), Nina Metha (Sari Shop Assistant), Sakina Jaffrey (Dr. Sharma), Meetu chilana (Meghana), Savera Hunsberger (Little Girl throwing Holi), Jerold E. Solomon, Andrea Smith, John Sladek (Patients), Jackie Chung, Leoni Pimentel (Police Officers), Neil Shah (Temple Caretaker), Anna Itty (Caretaker's Wife), Peter Stoeher (Priest), Sam Weerahandi (Samosa Complainer), DJ Rekha (Herself), Chris Keogh (Beefy Biker), Anju Bhambri, Sargam Bhambri, Arun Bhambri, Vishal Bhambri, Zainab Bibi, Privina Patel (Little India), Amit Patel, Chirag Patel, Vihar Patel (Hip Hop Sasians)

Pooja Kumar, Madhur Jaffrey in *Hiding Divya* © Net Effect Media

CALVIN MARSHALL (Broken Sky Films) Producers, Anne Lundgren, Michael Matondi; Executive Producer, Mark Cunningham; Director/Screenplay/Editor, Gary Lundgren; Photography, Patrick Neary; Designer, Ryan Maimberg; Costumes, Claudia Everett; Music, John Ashew; Dolby; Color; Rated R; 93 minutes; Release date: August 20, 2010. **CAST**: Alex Frost (Calvin Marshall), Jeremy Sumpter (Caselli), Michelle Lombardo (Tori Jensen), Steve Zahn (Coach Little), Jane Adams (June Marshall), Diedrich Bader (Fred Deerfield), Andrew Wilson (Ernie), Cynthia Watros (Karen), Abraham Benrubi (Coach Dewey), Catherine E. Coulson (Caramae), Douglas Rowe (Skeeter), Josh Fadem (Simon), Rosie Thomas (Sondra), Terri McMahon (Mrs. Jensen), Jimmy Garcia (Bryce), Michael Matondi (Glenn), James Peck (Mo), Renee Hewitt (Diana), Brian Amlin (B-Sauce), Bill Rowe (Tolkeim), Jackson Rowe (Johnson), Greg K. Sorenson (White Oaks Coach), Grace Thorsen (Leah)

MODERN LOVE IS AUTOMATIC (S&Z Prods.) Producers, Zach Clark, Sydney-Chanele Dawkins; Director/Screenplay/Editor, Zach Clark; Photography, Darryl Pittman; Costumes, Denise Farthing; Music, Adam Blais; Dolby; Color; HD; Not rated; 93 minutes; Release date: August 20, 2010. **CAST**: Melodie Sisk (Lorraine Schultz), Maggie Ross (Adrian), Hannah Bennett (Alaina), David Berkenblitt (Mr. Schultz), Monte Brown (Sex Shop Clerk), Carlos Bustamante (Mitch), Diana Cherkas (Emily), Ray Converse (Gary), Joel Esslinger (Fifi), Leo Goodman (Charlie), Matt Hartman (Ben), Rebecca A. Herron (Dolores), Christina Holleran (Sharon), Lydia Hyslop (Shirley), Lenny Levy (That's Soft Customer), Keller Lindler (Britney), Sandy Lisiewski (Boutique Owner), Morgaine Lowe (Yvonne), Gary Mahmoud (Dr. Mike), Marissa Molnar (Antoinette), Erik Morrison (Rick), Gil Nelson (Rodney), Tom Neubauer (Steve Luxury), Ellie Nicoll (Mistress Audrey), Cassio Portella (Edge Support Customer), Cinni Strickland (Mrs. Schultz), Ada Valaitis (Lori)

Melodie Sisk in *Modern Love is Automatic* © S&Z Prods.

NICK SABAN: GAMECHANGER (Flashlight Media Group) Producers, Grant Guffin, Trey Reynolds; Director, Trey Reynolds; Screenplay, Grant Guffin; Music, James Joseph; Editor, Michael Skilleter; Color; Not rated; 88 minutes; Release date: August 27, 2010. Documentary on Alabama football coach Nick Saban. **WITH** Nick Saban, Bill Belichick, Bobby Bowden, Paul Finebaum, Cecil Hurt, Joe Manchin III, Mal Moore, Bill Parcels, Jimmy Sexton, Gene Stallings

BAGHDAD TEXAS (Loudhouse Prod.) Producer/Music, Booka Michel; Executive Producer, Edythe Michel; Director, David H. Hickey; Screenplay, David H. Hickey, Saneye Ferrell, Al No'Mani; Photography, Robb Bindler; Designer, Derek Horton; Costumes, Stephen Chudej; Editor, Cory Van Dyke; Casting, Toni Cobb Brock; Color; HD; Not rated; 90 minutes; Release date: August 27, 2010. **CAST**: Al No'mani (Brando), Barry Tubb (Seth), Robert Prentiss (Randall), Ryan Boggus (Limon), Melinda Renna (Carmen), Shaneye Ferrell (Kathy), Brett Brock (Jimmy Glasscock), Daryl Humphries (Tommy Dickerson), Mark Keller (TV News Anchor), Kerry Awn (News Reporter at Fair), Patrick Prout (Boy with Pig), Douglas Balentine (Ron, the FBI Field Agent), Jacob Michel (Boy in Park), Billy Joe Martinez (Pedro), Rodney Garza (Jose), R. John Cameron (Tooter Manley), Booka Michel (Sheriff), Wesam Hassan (Administrator on Plane), Abraham Lara (Preacher), Wasim Hassan (Captain), Patty Griffin (Becky), Lizabeth Cardenas (Lori), Brian Crabb (Deputy)

Steve Zahn, Alex Frost in *Calvin Marshall* © Broken Sky Films

Robert Prentiss, Barry Tubb, Ryan Boggus in *Baghdad Texas* © Loudhouse Prod.

HIGHWATER (Outsider/Apostrophe) Producer, C. Rich Wilson; Director/Screenplay, Dana Brown; Photography, J. Steven Matzinger; Music, Phil Marshall, Switchfoot, Ryan Ferguson; Editors, Dana Brown, Wes Brown; Color; Not rated; 90 minutes; Release date: August 27, 2010. Documentary on the professional surfing tournaments held on the North Shore of Ohau. **WITH** David Sanderson, Kelly Slater

Highwater © Outsider

MAKE-OUT WITH VIOLENCE (Factory25) Producers/Directors, The Deagol Brothers; Executive Producers, Vicki Mead, Kyle Lehning, Zach Duensing, Greg High; Screenplay, The Deagol Brothers, Eric Lehning, Cody DeVos; Photography, David Bousquet, James King, Kevin Doyle; Art Director, Iwonka Waskowski; Costumes, Lauren Sandidge; Music, Jordan Lehning; Editors, The Deagol Brothers, Brad Bartlett; a Limerent Pictures production; Color; HD; Not rated; 105 minutes; Release date: August 27, 2010. **CAST**: Eric Lehning (Patrick), Cody DeVos (Carol), Leah High (Addy), Brett Miller (Beetle), Tia Shearer (Anne Haran), Jordan Lehning (Rody), Josh Duensing (Brian), Shellie Marie Shartzer (Wendy), Amanda Bailey (Donna Carrigan), David Carney (Motorcyclist), Jack Doyle (Mr. Darling), Kevin Doyle (The Professor), Patricia Doyle (Mrs. Carrigan), Zach Duensnig, Gail Sparks (Hunters), Steve Duensing (Mr. Hearst), Chris Edgerton (Gator), David Fuqua (Guru), Lori D. Hall (Anne's Mom), Alexandra Huff (Anne's Sister), Janet Ivey (Mrs. Hearst), Amanda Jones (Party Singer), Bob King (Preacher), Cheri Glor (Librarian), Mike Luckett (The Trespasser), Beau McCombs (Shades), Megan McNabb (Parking Lot Girl), David Mead (Mr. Carrigan), Aaron Miller (Laundromat Guy), Ryan Roshangah, Devon Miller (Freshmen Girls), Dale Rainey (Janie Carlise), Lauren Sandidge (Ann Ferguson), John Silvestro (Anne's Dad)

Make-Out with Violence © Factory25

ETIENNE! (Day O Productions) Producers, Jeremy Boering, Kurt Schemper, Joel David Moore, Giacun Caduff; Executive Producers, Jeff Mizushima, Joshua H. Miller, Tim Jackson, Reiko Kondo; Director/Screenplay/Editor, Jeff Mizushima; Photography, Tim van der Linden, Eric Kim, Jeff Mizushima; Music, Mark Bachle; a Cineasta Prods., Jacques a Bale Pictures production; FotoKem color; 16mm-to-DV; Not rated; 88 minutes; American release date: September 3, 2010. **CAST**: Richard Vallejos (Richard), Megan Harvey (Elodie), Molly Livingston (Molly), Matt Garron (Matt), David Fine (Kenly), Caveh Zahedi (Man in Coat), Courtney Halverson (Tara), Jeremiah Turner (Doug), Lisa Straussberg (Shannon), Rachel Stolte (Rachel), Debaveye Thibault (Backpacker), Marisa Pedroso (Marion), David Chien (Asian Dude in Underwear), Rinalda Caduff (One-Eyed Woman), Jerry Mosher (Dr. Mosher), Sarah Virden (Sarah), Tim Armstrong (60-Year-Old Man), Solon Bixler (Solon), Diane Alexander (Jogger), Vito Razi (Vito), David Bou (Disgruntled Gentleman), Sophia Kim (Sophia), Claudia Pedroso (Marion's Mother), Anthony Kuan (Anthony), Kenley Gaffke (Hostel Clerk)

Richard Vallajos in *Etienne!* © Day O Productions

CLEAR BLUE TUESDAY (CAVU) Producers, Elizabeth Lucas, Alexander Hammer, Daniel Wallace, Trish Whitehurst; Executive Producer, Al Parinello; Director, Elizabeth Lucas; Screenplay, Elizabeth Lucas, Becca Ayers, Julie Danao-Salkin, Vedant Gokhale, Robi Hager, Erin Hill, Cassandra Kubinski, Brother Love, Greg Naughton, Jan O'Dell, Jeremy Schonfeld, Asa Somers; Photography, Raoul Germain; Designer, Bendetta Brentan; Costumes, Mark Richard Caswell; Music, Curtis Moore; Editor, Alexander Hammer; Casting, Michael Cassara; an Al Parinello and Clear Blue Prods. presentation in association with the Harmony Entertainment Group; Color; Not rated; 106 minutes; Release date: September 3, 2010. **CAST**: Becca Ayers (Rose Burns), Julie Danao (Reena Santiago Isaacs), Vedant Gokhale (Jain Mahajan), Erin Hill (Etta Cummins), Cassandra Kubinski (Samantha Putnam), Brother Love (Syd Black), Greg Naughton (Jack King), Jan O'Dell (Caroline King), Jeremy Schonfeld (Daniel Isaacs), Asa Somers (Kyle Cassimer), Chris Anderson (Guy with Vulcan Ears), Mary Ellen Ashley (Filthy Homeless Woman), Christian Campbell (Obnoxious Co-Worker), Sarah-Jane Casey (Girlfriend Who Dies), R. Scott Denny, Jill Gorrie, Jesse Johnson, Kristoffer Lowe, Kristin McDonald, Diane Phelan, Emily Van Fleet, Rebecca Weiner (The Board), Robi Hager (Ricardo Santiago), Christopher J. Hanke (Samantha's Boyfriend), Thadd Krueger (Guy at Urinal), Michael Lanning (Friendly Guitar Player), Marsha Lawson (Secretary), Kelvin Moon Loh (Guy in Stall), Patricia Mikes (Nurse), James Naughton (Executive), Chris Orbach (Dave the Picard Fan), Al Parinello (Security Guard), Rahman (Cab Driver), Samantha Stockwell (Abby)

THE WINNING SEASON (Lionsgate) Producers, Gia Walsh, Kara Baker, Daniela Taplin Lundberg, Celine Rattray, Galt Niederhoffer; Executive Producers, Pamela Hirsch, Sam Rockwell, Joseph C. Grano, Andrea Grano, Daniel Crown, Nick Quested, Reagan Silber, Jeanne O'Brien, David Sweeney, Jamie Carmichael, Erick Kwack; Director/Screenplay, James C. Strouse; Photography, Frankie DeMarco; Designer, Stephen Beatrice; Costumes, Vicki Farrell; Editor, Joe Klotz; Casting, Kerry Barden, Paul Schnee; a Gigi Films and Plum Pictures in association with Sneaky Pete Productions presentation; Dolby; Color; HD; Rated PG-13; 100 minutes; Release date: September 3, 2010. **CAST**: Sam Rockwell (Bill), Emma Roberts (Abby), Margo Martindale (Donna), Rob Corddry (Terry), Jessica Hecht (Stacey), Shana Dowdeswell (Molly), Shareeka Epps (Lisa), Meaghan Witri (Tamra), Emily Rios (Kathy), Melanie Hinkle (Mindy), Rooney Mara (Wendy), Vanessa Gordillo (Flor), Connor Paolo (Damon), Melissa Graver (New Rome Forward), Clarke Thorell (Prairie Hill Coach), Rod Brogan (Rick), Kevin Breznahan (Joel), Brian Berrebbi (Manager), Rhonda Keyser (Uno's Waitress), Sara Chase (Outback Waitress), William Wiggins, Colby Minifie (Teens), Colleen Broomall (New Rome Center), Jennifer Regan (Concerned Mother), Devin Ratray (Security Officer), Ed Jewett, E.J. Carroll, Harry L. Seddon (Announcers), Caitlin Colford (Prairie Hill's Center), Seth Herzog (Mascot), Lynn Mancinelli, Pauline Sherrow, Angelina Aucello (Cheerleaders), Robert Keir (Arcade Boy), Caitlin Colford (Trish), Marceline Hugot (Dr. Parsons)

(back row) Sam Rockwell, Rooney Mara, Emily Rios, Meaghan Witri, Margo Martindale; (front row) Vanessa Gordillo, Shareeka Epps, Emma Roberts, Melanie Hinkle in *The Winning Season* © Lionsgate

LEGENDARY (Samuel Goldwyn Films) Producers, Steve Barnett, Mike Pavone, David Karl Calloway; Director, Mel Damski; Screenplay, John Posey; Photography, Kenneth Zunder; Designer, Claire Breaux; Music, James A. Johnson; Editor, Mitch Stanley; a WWE Studios presentation; Dolby; Color; Rated PG-13; 107 minutes; Release date: September 10, 2010. **CAST**: John Cena (Mike Chetley), Patricia Clarkson (Sharon Chetley), Devon Graye (Cal Chetley), Danny Glover (Harry "Red" Newman), Tyler Posey (Billy Barrow), Madeleine Martin (Luli Stringfellow), John Posey (Stu Tennent), Courtney J. Clark (Lori), J.D. Evermore (Terry Jay), Lara Grice (Laura Melton), Kareem J. Grimes (Theo "Gnat" Henderson), Ted Olivares (Donald Worthington), Andrew Sensenig (Larry Edwards), Raymond D. Sweet (Earl Johnson), Angelena Swords (Jill), Deneen Tyler (Judge Gardner), Christopher Alan Weaver (Joe Easley), Marc Lagattuta (Referee #1), Yvonne Misiak (Waitress), Aaron Sauer (Policeman). Vince Antoine (Claremont Coach), Robert Hermann (Northside Coach), Patrick Cox (Son of a Bitch)

Devon Graye, Patricia Clarkson in *Legendary* © Samuel Goldwyn

MODUS OPERANDI (The Zoo) Producers, Jon Krill, Laurie Foote, Mark Foote, Shalyse Dominique, Zebedee LeTendre, Barry Poltermann, Andrew Swant, Gilbert Trejo, Sean Williamson; Executive Producers, Janet Beasley, Bobby Ciraldo, Nicole Johnson; Director/Story/Editor, Frankie Latina; Screenplay, Frankie Latina, Andrew Swant; Additional Material, Mark Borchardt, Ryan Plato, Randy Russell; Photography, Mark Escribano; Costumes, Jennifer Rau; a Sasha Grey presentation in association with Reign Supreme Entertainment and Special Entertainment; Color; Not rated; 80 minutes; Release date: September 10, 2010. **CAST**: Randy Russell (Stanley Cashay), Danny Trejo (Director Holiday), Mark Borchardt (Dallas Deacon), Michael Sottile (Squire Parks), Barry Poltermann (Casey Thunderbird), Nikki Johnson (Black Licorice), Mark Metcalf (Copper Gore), Andrew Swant (Agent Xanadu), Bobby Ciraldo (Marcelio Maserati), Patrick Buckley (The Cowboy), Samwell (Adonis), Sarah Price (Agent Airheart), Robert Glenn Jones (CIA Supervisor), Ayesha Mohan (Ayesha Ayesha), Michael Sean Hayden (Surveillance Double Agent), Kelly Cunningham (Josephina), Tara Angilello (Sadi Main), Carlo Besasie (Vinnie Tortellini), Adrian Israel Deleon (The Cleaner), Shalyse Dominique (Kohe), Emily Margaret Heitzer (Mrs. Squire Parks), Jennifer Johung (Jo Jo), Xay Leplae (The One-Eyed Man), Natasha Nafrini (Aspiring Actress), Dan Ollman (The Specialist), Eamonn O'Neill (McCormick Hardcastle), Tina Poppy (Agent Poppyseed), Andrew Rosas (Horror Film Director), Leah Stuller (Venchenza Esposito), Reaiah True (Stanley's Wife), Maureen Waoh-Tobin (Black Ice), Elizabeth Bolin, Lena Song (Bikini Girls), Carey Borth (Bride Zombie), Darrell Cherney (Shirtless Kisser), Jennifer Kim (Chopsticks), Liza Scharhag (Zarana)

Randy Russell in *Modus Operandi* © The Zoo

LOVELY, STILL (Monterey Media) Producers, Lars Knudsen, Jay Van Hoy, Dana Altman; Director/Screenplay, Nicholas Fackler; Photography, Sean Kirby; Designer, Stephen Altman; Costumes, Ruth Ciemnoczolowski; Music, Nate Wolcott, Mike Mogis; Editor, Douglas Crise; Casting, Eyde Belasco; a Parts and Labor, North Sea Films production; Color; HD; Rated PG; 92 minutes; Release date: September 10, 2010. **CAST**: Martin Landau (Robert Malone), Ellen Burstyn (Mary), Adam Scott (Mike), Elizabeth Banks (Alex), Mark Booker (Harold), Leo Fitzpatrick (Pharmacist), Candice Rose (Young Mary), Har Mar Superstar (Peter), Scott Beehner (Supermarket Cashier), Susan Cannella, Laura Pearson (Women Discussing Zoo in Bar), Brett Comstock (Girl in Café), Kali Cook (Cute Girl in bar), Brendan Greene-Walsh (Cute Bartender), Chris Wiig (Grocery Store Worker), Zoey Newman (Michelle)

Ellen Burstyn, Martin Landau in *Lovely, Still* © Monterey Media

RACE TO NOWHERE (Reel Link) Producer, Vicki Abeles; Directors, Vicki Abeles, Jessica Congdon; Screenplay, Jessica Congdon, Maimone Attia; Photography, Maimone Attia, Sophie Constantinou; Music, Mark Adler; Editor, Jessica Congdon; Color; Not rated; 85 minutes; Release date: September 10, 2010. Documentary on the toll the modern educational system takes on its pupils. **WITH** Vicki Abeles, Jamey Abeles, Zach Abeles, Deborah Stipek, Ken Ginsburg, Madeline Levine, Denise Pope, Sara Bennett, Wendy Mogel

Race to Nowhere © Reel Ink

THE AFTERLIGHT (Wintersea) Producers, Alexandre Fuchs, Pegah Easton; Directors/ Screenplay/Editors, Alexei Kaleina, Craig Macneill; Photography, Zoë White; Designer, Chloe Lee; Music, Nathan Matthew David; Color; HD; Not rated; 87 minutes; Release date: September 10, 2010. **CAST**: Michael Kelly (Andrew), Jicky Schnee (Claire), Ana Asensio (Maria), Rip Torn (Carl), Morgan Taddeo (Lucy), Rhoda Pauley (Carol), Alex Cranmer (Doctor), Brian Allen, Brent Biedekaap, Ryan Boice, Samantha Geer, James Kane, Aaron Richardson (Construction Workers), Charlie Nadan, Freddie Babock, Noah Poland (Boys), Derek Mead (Boy Swinging Stick), Diane Smikle (Office Worker), Steph Van Vlack (Secretary)

Morgan Taddeo in *The Afterlight* © Wintersea

WHO IS HARRY NILSSON (AND WHY IS EVERYBODY TALKIN' ABOUT HIM?) (Kino Lorber) Producers, David Leaf, John Scheinfeld; Executive Producer, Lee Blackman; Co-Producer/Editor, Peter S. Lynch II; Director/Screenplay, John Scheinfeld; Photography, James Mathers; Music, Harry Nilsson; an LSL Prods. presentation; Color/Black and white; DV; 16mm-to-DV; Not rated; 117 minutes; Release date: September 10, 2010. Documentary on musician Harry Nilsson. **WITH** Gerry Beckley, Lee Blackman, Perr Botkin Jr., Ray Cooper, Micky Dolenz, Stanley Dorfman, Terry Gilliam, Bruce Grakal, Doug Hoefer, Dustin Hoffman, Mark Hudson, Danny Hutton, Eric Idle, Rick Jarrard, Al Kooper, Trevor Lawrence, Randy Newman, Annie Nilsson, Beau Nilsson, Diane Nilsson, Olivia Nilsson, Una Nilsson, Zach Nilsson, Yoko Ono, May Pang, Van Dyke Parks, Richard Perry, Dick Smothers, Tom Smothers, Ringo Starr, Joan Taylor, Jon Voight, Jimmy Webb, Paul Williams, Robin Williams, Brian Wilson, Fred Wolf

Harry Nilsson in *Who is Harry Nilsson?* © Kino Lorber

LOGAN (Real Bean Entertainment) Producer/Director, Kyle Lawrence; Screenplay, Kyle Lawrence, Caleb Doyle, Brian Lawrence, Matt Martin, Tyler Skrobonja; Photography, John Grove; Music, David Clevenger; Editor, Kyle Lawrence; Casting, Mike Ketcher; a Logan Films production; Color; HD; Not rated; 93 minutes; Release date: September 10, 2010. **CAST**: Leo Howard (Logan Hoffman), Booboo Stewart (Ben), Patrick Probst (Tyler Hoffman), Abigail Isom (Allison), Nicole Cummins (Carlie), Colin Ritchie (Sebastian), Emily Berry (Mrs. Hoffman), Tim Schall (Mr. Hoffman), Collins Lewis (Principal Ward), Caleb Doyle (Gavin), Evan Smith (Movie Theatre Band Student), Brady Hardin (Mr. Hardin), Charles Heuvelman (Mr. Burgesen), Joe Koestner (Mr. Spradley), Christian Probst (Gavin's Friend), Fivel Stewart (Leader of Clique Girls), Ariel Hayes (Clique Girl), Daniel Schlef (Gus), Alyssa Wolf, Mitchell List (English Students), Justin Denman (Lineman), Steve Miner (Student)

AHEAD OF TIME (Vitagraph) Producer, Zeva Oelbaum; Executive Producers, Patti Kenner, Doris Schechter, Denise Benmosche; Director/Photography, Bob Richman; Music, Ted Reichman; Editor, Sabine Krayenbuhl; a Reel Inheritance Films, PDD production; American-Israeli; Color/Black and white; HD; Not rated; 73 minutes; Release date: September 10, 2010. Documentary on journalist, author and humanitarian Ruth Gruber, as she looks back on her life at the age of 97; with Ruth Gruber, Davd Sobel, Harold Ickes, Manya Hartmayer Breuer, Ike Aronowitz, Mordechai Rossmann, Tom Segev, Eli Wallach

Ruth Gruber in *Ahead of Time* © Vitagraph

THE TRIAL (Mountain Top Releasing) Producer/Director, Gay Wheeler; Executive Producers, Robert Whitlow, Kathy Whitlow, Brad Mix, John Ayers, Reid McGraw; Screenplay, Mark Freiburger, Gary Wheeler, Robert Whitlow; Based on the novel by Robert Whitlow; Photography, Tom Priestley; Designer, John D. Kretschmer; Music, Rob Pottorf; Editor, Jonathan Olive; Casting, Beveryl Holloway; a Whitlow Films and Level Path productions; Color; Rated PG-13; 90 minutes; Release date: September 10, 2010. **CAST**: Matthew Modine (Kent "Mac" McClain), Bob Gunton (Joe Whetstone), Robert Forster (Ray Morrison), Clare Carey (Dr. Anna Wilkes), Randy Wayne (Pete Thomason), Rance Howard (Judge Danielson), Nikki Deloach (Mindy), Burgess Jenkins (Harry O'Ryan), Larry Bagby (Spencer Hightower), Brett Rice (Dr. Newbern), Bonnie Johnson (Jury Forewoman), R. Keith Harris (Lt. Monroe), David Dwyer (Alex Hightower), Danny Vinson (Rodney MacFarland), Kera O'Bryon (Angela Hightower's Voice), Gary Moore (Car Salesman), Sandra W. Van Natta (Dean Marjorie Plant), Andrew R. Kaplan (District Attorney), Wendy Foster (Spencer Hightower's Girlfriend), Chandler McIntyre (Sandy), Brian Lafontaine (Dr. Eastman), Mark Scarboro (Gene Nelson), Rebekah James (Kathy), Ted Johnson (Bank Manager), Zachary T. Robbins (Hunter Wilkes)

Bob Gunton, Matthew Modine, Rance Howard in *The Trial*
© Mountain Top Releasing

EL SUPERSTAR: THE UNLIKELY RISE OF JUAN FRANCES (Cinema Libre) Producer, Chris B. Moore, Lara Bergthold; Executive Producers, Norman Lear, George Lopez; Director, Amy French; Screenplay/Music, Amy French, Spencer John French; Photography, Stephanie Martin; Designer, Celin Diano; Costumes, Sara Walbridge; Editor, Timothy M. Snell; Stereo; Color; Not rated; 90 minutes; Release date: September 17, 2010. **CAST**: Spencer John French (Juan Francés), Lupe Ontiveros (Nena), Danny Trejo (E.J. "El Jardinero"), Elisa Bocanegra (Chuchi), Maria Esquivel (Angelica), David Franco (Narciso), Pej Vahdat (Amir), Sam Golzari (Mahmoud), Danny Mora (Bar Owner), Kerry Carney (Mrs. French), Hayden Angus Moore (Baby Juan), Jean McGowan (Red Headed Woman), Pablo Motta (Juan's Bass Player), Andres Renteria (Juan's Drummer), Oscar Schedin (Juan's Guitar Player), Domigo Siete (Themselves), Neslon Del Rosario (Hot for Narcisso), Louis Jacobs (Philip Fancydance), Antonia Vassileva (Dancer Maria), Jebbel Arce (Dancer Maria), Zibby Allen (Girlfriend Fan), Maria Forero (Girl Fan), Angel Perez (Boyfriend Fan), Carlos Alvarez (Himself), Daniel H. Fonseca, James V. Perez Hildardo Ramirez, Luis Humberto Estrella Ruiz, Feliz Valeriano, Genaro Lopez, Permin Moctezuma, Maria G. Otero, Sonia Portillo, Blanca Mayorga, Judith Huapaya (The Cinco Singers), Anthony Rincon (Boy Fan), Luis Perez (Man Fan), Sara Trujillo (Lady Fan), Steve Wilcox (Numero Uo Fan), Anthony Valadez (DJ Shyboy), Patricia Rae (Angry Radio Listener), Allan Oppenheimer (Mr. French), Jeffrey Emerson (Ryan)

Spencer John French in *El Superstar* © Cinema Libre

Elijah Wood, Malin Akerman in *The Romantics* © Paramount Famous

BIKER FOX (Fox Subliminal Films) Producers, Jeremy Lamberton, Todd Lincoln, Biker Fox; Executive Producer, Frank Palmer DeLarzelere III; Director/Screenplay, Jeremy Lamberton; Photography, Jeremy Lamberton, Biker Fox; Music Supervisor, Peymon Maskan; Editors, Jeremy Lamberton, Elvis Ripley; a Wolf Howling production in association with Sunday Town Prods. and Lookout Mountain Prods.; Color; Not rated; 88 minutes; Release date: September 10, 2010. Documentary on Tulsa-based health advocate and car parts-supplier Frank P. DeLarzelere III (Biker Fox). **WITH** Frank P. DeLarzelere III

CHOSIN (Post Factory Films) Director, Brian Iglesias; Producers/Screenplay, Brian Iglesias, Anton Sattler; Photography, Adam Ahlbrandt; Music, Will Bates; Editors, Adam Ahlbrandt, Brian Iglesias; Anton Sattler; Color; Not rated; 86 minutes; Release date: September 10, 2010. Documentary looks back on the bloody Korean War battle of the Chosin Reservoir Campaign.

Frank P. DeLarzelere III in *Biker Fox* © Fox Subliminal Films

Chosin © Post Factory Films

THE ROMANTICS (Paramount Famous) Producers, Daniela Taplin Lundberg, Gal Niederhoffer, Jennifer Todd, Suzanne Todd, Michael Benaroya, Taylor Kephart; Executive Producers, Riva Marker, Katie Holmes, Pamela Hirsch, Celina Rattray, Ron Stein; Director/Screenplay, Galt Niederhoffer, based on her novel; Photography, Sam Levy; Designer, Tim Grimes; Costumes, Danielle Kays; Editor, Jacob Craycroft; a Team Todd, Plum Pictures and Benaroya presentation in association with 10th Hole Prods.; Dolby; Color; Rated PG-13; 94 minutes; Release date: September 10, 2010. **CAST**: Katie Holmes (Laura Rosen), Josh Duhamel (Tom), Anna Paquin (Lila Hayes), Malin Akerman (Tripler), Adam Brody (Jake), Dianna Agron (Minnow), Jeremy Strong (Pete), Rebecca Lawrence (Weesie), Elijah Wood (Chip Hayes), Candice Bergen (Augusta), Rosemary Murphy (Grandmother Hayes), James I. Schaffer (William Hayes), Warren F. McKnight (Rev. Barlett)

KINGS OF PASTRY (First Run Features) Producers, Flora Lazar, Frazer Pennebaker; Executive Producer, Frazer Pennebaker, Nick Fraser; Directors, Chris Hegedus, D.A. Pennebaker; Photography, Chris Hegedus, D.A. Pennebaker, Nick Doob; Music Supervisor, Alex Toledano; Color; DV; Not rated; 84 minutes; Release date: September 15, 2010. Documentary in which France's top pastry chefs compete for the Meilleurs Ouvriers de France honor. **WITH** Sebastien Canonne, Jacquy Pfeiffer, Rachel Beaudry, Philippe Rigollot, Stephane Glacier, Regis Lazard, Frederique Lazard, Philippe Urraca

Jacquy Pfeiffer in *Kings of Pastry* © First Run Features

MUSIC MAKES A CITY (Owsley Brown Presents) Producers, Owsley Brown III, Robin Burke; Co-Producers, Cornelia Calder, Anne Flatté; Directors, Owsley Brown III, Jerome Hiler; Editors, Anne Flatté, Nathaniel Dorsky; Color; Not rated; 103 minutes; Release date: September 17, 2010. Documentary on the Louisville Orchestra.

Music Makes a City © Owsley Brown

SWEETHEARTS OF THE PRISON RODEO (Cinema Purgatorio) Producers, Bradley Beesley, Amy Dobson, James Payne; Executive Producers, Juilie Goldman, Krysanne Katsoolis, Caroline Stevens; Director, Bradley Beesley; Photography, Alan Novey; Music, Jason Quever; Editor, Louisiana Kreutz; a Fieldguide Media production in association with Super Alright, Cactus Three; Color; HD; Not rated; 89 minutes; Release date: September 17, 2010. Documentary on how the inmates of Eddie Warrior Women's Correctional Center in Taft, Oklahoma, compete in the Oklahoma State Penitentiary Rodeo; with Danny Liles, Jamie Brooks, Brandy Witte, Crystal Herrington, Monty Baker, Rhonda Buffalo, Ashley Burris

Sweethearts of the Prison Rodeo © Cinema Purgatorio

LAST DAY OF SUMMER (E1 Entertainment) Producers, Kevin Arbouet, Larry Strong, Vlad Yudin, Edwin Mejia; Director/Screenplay, Vlad Yudin, Photography, Patryk Rebisz; Designer, Joseph Polacik; Costumes, Michael Bevins; Music, Marc Aaron Jacobs, Peter Himmelman; Editor, Susan Graef; a Vladar Company production; Color; Rated R; 105 minutes; Release date: September 17, 2010. **CAST**: DJ Qualls (Joe), Nikki Reed (Stefanie), William Sadler (Mr. Crolick), Adam Scarimbolo (Joey), Jason Cruz (Timmy the Rapper), Yury Tsykun (Black Harry), Chris Bashinelli (Skateboarder), E.J. Carroll (Ken), Chris Cullen, Lisa Stansbury (Customers), Donnell Rawlings, Cory Kahaney (Cops), Lawrence Feeney (Motel Clerk), Marc Menchaca (Shipping Employee), Wass Stevens (Video Store Clerk), Robin Taylor (Jason), Igor Zhivotovsky (Yuri), Heather Dilly (Cook #1)

DJ Qualls, Nikki Reed in *Last Day of Summer* © E1 Entertainment

THE OTHER CITY (Cabin Films) Producers, Sheila C. Johnson, Jose Antonio Vargas; Executive Producers, Sheila C. Johnson, Michelle Freeman; Director, Susan Koch; Screenplay, Jose Antonio Vargas; Color; HD; Not rated; 90 minutes; Release date: September 17, 2010. Documentary on a section of Washington, D.C. that has been especially devastated by the AIDS crisis. **WITH** Jose Antonio Vargas, J'Mia Edwards, Ron Daniels, Jose Ramirez, Larry Kramer, Eleanor Holmes Norton, Frank Rich, Colbert King

Jose Ramirez in *The Other City* © Cabin Films

Paul Gordon in *The Happy Poet* © St. Chris Film

THE FREEBIE (Phase 4 Films) Producer, Adele Romanski; Executive Producers, Mark Duplass, Katie Aselton; Director/Screenplay, Katie Aselton; Photography, Benjamin Kasulke; Designers, Jessica Anisman, Marguerite Phillips; Music, Julian Wass; Editor, Nat Sanders; a Freebie presentation; Color; Rated R; 78 minutes; Release date: September 17, 2010. **CAST**: Dax Shepard (Darren), Katie Aselton (Annie), Frankie Shaw (Coffee Girl), Ross Partridge (Bartender), Sean Nelson (John), Bellamy Young (Jessica), Leonora Gershman (Lea), Ken Kennedy (Ken), Marguerite Phillips (Emily), Scott Pitts (Scott), Joshua Leonard (Dinner Party Guest), Houston Wages (Guy)

Kate Selton, Dax Shepard in *The Freebie* © Phase 4 Films

THE HAPPY POET (St. Chris Film) Producers, David Hartstein, Paul Gordon; Executive Producer, Chris Ohlson; Director/Screenplay/Editor, Paul Gordon; Photography, Lucas Millard; Designer, Caroline Karlen; Music, John Jordan; Color; HD; Not rated; 85 minutes; Release date: September 17, 2010. **CAST**: Paul Gordon (Bill), Jonny Mars (Donnie), Chris Doubek (Curtis), Liz Fisher (Agnes), Amy Myers Martin (Lily), Ricardo Lerma (Banker), Sam Wainwright Douglas (Buddy), Carlos Treviño (Derrick), Emily Ramshaw (Emily), Laura Stromberg (Laura), Liz Fisher (Agnes), Tre Spaw (Lars), Carolyn Gordon (Bill's Mom), Eleanor Cheetham (Eleanor), Robie Gay (Randy)

THE VIRGINITY HIT (Columbia) Producers, Will Ferrell, Adam McKay, Chris Henchy, Peter Principato, Paul Young; Executive Producer, Owen Burke; Co-Produer, Amy Hobby; Directors/Screenplay, Andrew Gurland, Huck Botko; Photography, Luke Geissbuhler; Editor, Geoffrey Richman; Casting, Jodi Collins; a Gary Sanchez production; Dolby; Color; DV; Rated R; 87 minutes; Release date: September 17, 2010. **CAST**: Matt Bennett (Matt), Zack Pearlman (Zack), Jacob Davich (Jacob), Justin Kline (Justin), Krysta Rodriguez (Krysta), Nicole Weaver (Nicole), Harry Zittel (Harry), Savannah Welch (Becca), Seth Barrish (Matt's Biological Dad), Tina Parker (Tina), Sunny Leone (Sunny), Daniel Weber (Daniel), John McLeaish (Inkeeper), Ramona Tyler (Mom), Bernard Hocke (Dad), David Jensen (Nicole's Dad), Keri Parker (Keri Ann), Kathleen Barnes (Kathleen), Mallory Slack (Mallory), Dacia Fernandez (Dacia), Amanda Punch (Amanda), Ashton Leigh (Ashton), Rebecca Barras (Rebecca), Carina Kaiser (Carina), Danie Coleman (Frat House Stripper), Susan LaBreque (Matt's Biological Mom), Felipe Echavarria (Men's Store Clerk), James L. Conner (Men's Store Security), M'bita Bakari (Security Guard), Bill Posley (Hipster), Tyler Humphrey (Fundraising Kid), A.J. Allegra, Cody Bruno, Jason Cenac, Brandon Moore, Patrick Noonan (Frat Guys), Lee Nguyen, Joshua Beller, Scott Sierzega (Response Films), Walter Enquist (DJ), Randall Riley (Security Guard), Lesley White (Dress Shop Owner)

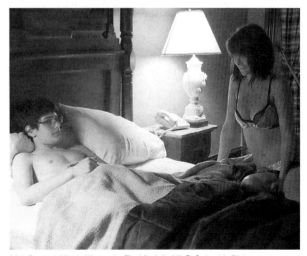

Matt Bennett, Nicole Weaver in *The Virginity Hit* © Columbia Pictures

3 BILLION AND COUNTING (Frogbite Prods.) Producer/Director/Screenplay, Dr. Rutledge; Co-Producer, Helene Udy; Photography, Aaron Krummel; Color; Not rated; 102 minutes; Release date: September 17, 2010; Documentary about the increasing number of malaria cases causing death throughout the world.

3 Billion and Counting © Frogbite Prods.

PICTURE ME (Strand) Producers, David Hochschild, Sara Ziff, Ole Schell, James Lefkowitz; Directors, Ole Schell, Sara Ziff; Photography, Ole Schell; Music, Jordan Galland, Morningwood; Editors, Sara Ziff, Ole Schell, James Lefkowitz; Animation, The Boos; a Digital Bazooka production; Color; Not rated; 80 minutes; Release date: September 24, 2010. Documentary on the world of modeling. **WITH** Sara Ziff, Missy Rayder, Cameron Russell, Sena Cech, Caitriona Balfe, Lisa Cant.

Ole Schell, Sara Ziff in *Picture Me* © Strand Releasing

100 VOICES: A JOURNEY HOME (MOD3 Prods.) Producers, Matthew Asner, Danny Gold, Michael Lam, Nathan Lam; Executive Producer, Metuka Benjamin; Directors, Matthew Asner, Danny Gold; Screenplay, Matthew Asner, Danny Gold, Michael Lam, Michael Mayhew; Photography, Anthony Melfi, Jeff Alred; Music, Charles Fox; Editor, Michael Mayhew; Color; Not rated; 91 minutes; Release date: September 22, 2010. Documentary in which Cantor Nate Lam gathers 72 other cantors from around the world to perform at the Warsaw Opera House. **WITH** Ari Brown, Nathan Lam, Alberto Misrachi, Simon Spiro, Faith Steinsnyder

100 Voices © MOD3 Prods.

THE BIG UNEASY (Independent) Producer, Karen Murphy; Director/Screenplay, Harry Shearer; Photography, Arlene Nelson; Editor, Tom Roche; Color; Not rated; 98 minutes; Release date: September 24, 2010. Documentary in which performer and New Orleans resident Harry Shearer sets out to prove that the Hurricane Katrina disaster could have been prevented.

TIBET IN SONG (Guge Prods.) Producer, Yodo Thonden: Executive Producer, Anne Corcos; Director, Ngawang Choephel; Screenplay, Ngawang Choephel, Tara Steele; Photography, Carrie Lederer, Ngawang Choephel, Tim Bartlett; Editor, Tim Bartlett; a Guge production; Color; Not rated; 86 minutes; Release date: September 24, 2010. Documentary about the threat the present political climate poses to Tibet's folk-singing tradition.

Tibet in Song © Guge Prods.

LIKE DANDELION DUST (Blue Collar Releasing) Producers, Kevin Downes, Bobby Downes, Kerry David; Executive Producers, Shelene M. Bryan, Geoff Ludlow; Director/ Editor, Jon Gunn; Screenplay, Stephen J. Rivele, Michael LaChance; Based on the novel by Karen Kingsbury; Photography, Reynaldo Villalobos; Designer, Shawn Carroll; Costumes, Stephen Chudej; Music, Nathan Larson; Casting, Amanda Koblin, Amanda Harding, Beverly Holloway; a Downes Brothers production in association with Lucky Crow Films; Dolby; Panavision; Color; DV; Rated PG-13; 100 minutes; Release date: September 24, 2010. **CAST**: Mira Sorvino (Wendy Porter), Barry Pepper (Rip Porter), Cole Hauser (Jack Campbell), Kate Levering (Molly Campbell), Maxwell Perry Cotton (Joey

Campbell), L. Scott Caldwell (Allyson Bower), Abby Brammell (Beth Norton), Kirk B.R. Woller (Bill Norton), Brett Rice (Judge), Brooke Bryan (Cammie Norton), Blake Michael Bryan (Jonah Norton), Rus Blackwell (Curtis Golding), Chad Gundersen, Timothy Twisdale (Cops), Brian F. Durkin (Bar Patron), Gregory Albrecht (Attorney), Neil Ronco (Tom Alonzo), Tim Powell (Steve Tergen)

Robert H. Jackson in *Nuremberg*
© Schulberg/Metropolis

Barry Pepper, Mira Sorvino in *Like Dandelion Dust* © Blue Collar Releasing

FRICTION (Hyrax Films) Producer/Director/Photography/Editor, Cullen Hoback; Executive Producers, Derick Campbell, Al McKinnon; Screenplay, Cullen Hoback, Jerome Schwartz; Music, Brent Knopf, Dave Lowensohn; Color; Not rated; 89 minutes; Release date: September 24, 2010. **CAST**: Amy Mathison (Amy), Jeremy Mathison (Jerry), August Thompson (August), Ernest Thompson (Terry Plant)

Amy Mathison in *Friction* © Hyrax Films

NUREMBERG (Schulberg/Metropolis) Producers, Stuart Schulberg, Pare Lorentz; Director/Screenplay, Stuart Schulberg; Music, Hans-Otto Borgmann; Resoration by Sandra Schulberg, Josh Waletzky; Narrator, Liev Schreiber; Black and white; Not rated; 78 minutes; Release date: September 29, 2010. 1948 film on the Nuremberg trials produced by the Allies at the time of trials but previously unreleased in American.

CHAIN LETTER (New Films Intl.) Producers, Deon Taylor, Michael J. Pagan; Executive Producers, Robert Smith, Todd Slater, Nesim Hason, Roxanne Avent; Director, Deon Taylor; Screenplay, Deon Taylor, Michael J. Pagan; Photography, Philip Lee; Designer, George Goodridge; Costumes, Chasia; Music, Vincent Gillioz, Marcus Blanchard; Editors, James Coblentz, Howard Smith; a New Films presentation of a Deon Taylor Enterprises and Tiger Tail Entertainment production; Color; Rated R; 97 minutes; Release date: October 1, 2010. **CAST**: Nikki Reed (Jessie Campbell), Keith David (Det. Jim Crenshaw), Brad Dourif (Mr. Smirker), Betsy Russell (Sgt. Hamill), Bai Ling (Jai Pham), Matt Cohen (Johnny Jones), Cherilyn Wilson (Rachael Conners), Noah Segan (Dante), Michael Bailey Smith (Chain Man), Clifton Powell (Coach), Brian Tee (Brian Yee), Michael J. Pagan (Michael Grant), Cody Kasch (Neil Conners), Patrick St. Esprit (Dean Jones), Deborah Geffner (Irene), Terrence Evans (Mr. Bradford), Jonathan Hernandez (Carlos), Andy Arness (Coroner), Goldie Chan (Asian Girl Texter), Eliot Benjamin (Kevin), Big Spence (Murder Suspect), Mark S. Allen (Anchor on the Scene), Madison Bauer (Jane Campbell), Roshni Shukla (Emo Girl), Christina Marie (CSI Agent), Sheila Ellis, Jeff Sutherland, Leslie Goodman (Detectives), Phil Austin (Philip Campbell), Jessica Ritchie (Britney), David Zahedian (Brad), Niki McElroy (Fine Girl), Kenyon Page (Gamer), Kate Enggren (Debra Jones), Bonnie Jean Shelton (Judy Conenrs), Ryan Calavano (Student #1), Joy Stern (Punk Hair with Trench Coat), Cory Montgomery (Yelling Gamer), Mike Stahl (Police Officer), Charles Fleisher (Frank Wiggins), Aysha Aubrey, Ashya Shamroukh (Pretty Girls), Naeem Alvi (EMT), Lyn Ross (Shirley), Matthew Mongillo (Priest), Khatira Razada (Miss Garrett), Richar Moorhouse (Uncle Bob), Pat Ridley (Man with Cell Phone), Ivan Gonzalez (Winston), Daniel Garcia (Freshman Boy), Kelly Stringfellow (Townsperson), Johann Tate (Office Burt), Derek Colston (Barber), De Mann (Scientist), Joel Shnowski (Freeman)

THE HUNGRY GHOSTS (Virgil Films) Producers, Stefan C. Schaefer, Diane Crespo, Tina Thor, Howard Axel; Executive Producers, Joe Scarpinito, Joe Laurita; Director/ Screenplay, Michael Imperioli; Photography, Dan Hersey; Co-Producer/ Designer, Victoria Imperioli; Costumes, Beth Kelleher; Music, Elijah Amitin, La Dolce Vita; Editor, Erin Greenwell; Casting, Meredith Tucker; a Cicala Filmworks, Cinema Dante, TMT Entertainment Group production; Color; Rated R; 106 minutes; Release date: October 1, 2010. **CAST**: Steve Schirripa (Frank), Aunjanue Ellis (Nadia), Nick Sandow (Gus), Sharon Angela (Sharon), Tina Benko (Abby), Paul Calderon (Carl), Joe Caniano (Joey), E.J. Carroll (Eddie), Selma Cifka (Doris), Emory Cohen (Matthew), Vincent Curatola (Nicky Z), Elzbieta Czyzewska (Mrs. Dunleavy), Sanjit De Silva (Mohammed), Suzanne Didonna (Waitress), Ken Forman (Train Conductor), John Frey (Dealer), Rachel Gittler (Park Pedestrian), Jerry Grayson (Jerry), Jim Hendricks (Ansel), Moe Hindi (Hospital Patient),

Sondra James (Lucy), Zohra Lampert (Ruth), Giselle Liberatore (Grace), Cerrone May (Passenger on Train), Ajay Naidu (Laurence), Tom Phillips (Tommy), Bess Rous (Lisette), Joseph Scarpinito (Louis), Stefan C. Schaefer (Tim), Jenna Stern (Lisa), Chris Tardio (Brian), Angelica Torn (Roberta), John Ventimiglia (James), Darlene Violette (Sandy)

Steve Schirripa, Emory Cohen in *The Hungry Ghosts* © Virgil Films

IS IT JUST ME? (TLA Releasing) Producers, JC Calciano, Michael Amato; Director/ Screenplay, JC Calciano; Photography, Joshua W. Smith; Music, Christopher Farrell; Editor, Cynthia Ludwig; a D'fi Films and Whitestone Acquisitions presentation; Color; HD; Not rated; 92 minutes; Release date: October 1, 2010. **CAST**: Nicholas Downs (Blaine), David Loren (Xander), Adam Huss (Cameron), Michelle Laurent (Michelle), Bob Rumnock (Bob), Bruce Gray (Ernie), Paul A. Becker, Michael Elepterakis, Oscar Rodriguez, Brandon Wright (GoGo Dancers), Jed Bernard (Drunk Guy), Bryce Blais (Drew), Michael Hennessy, Alisa Campbell, Jeremiah Dupre (Bartenders), Lynne Chaille (Ronnie), Gabriel Coble, Derek Soldenski (Neighbors), Michael Donahue (Antonio), Christopher King (Frontier Model), Brody Kramer (Man in Bed), Beau Nelson (Guy), Keith Roenke (Barista), Brian Schulze (Cameron's Friend), Chris Tisa (Coffee Patron)

David Loren, Nicholas Downs in *Is it Just Me?* © TLA Releasing

HATCHET II (Dark Sky Films) Producers, Cory Neal, Sarah Elbert, Derek Curl; Director/ Screenplay, Adam Green; Photography, Will Barratt; Designer, Bryan A. McBrien; Costumes, Heather Allison; Music, Andy Garfield; Editor, Ed Marx; Creature and Makeup Effects, Robert Pendergraft; Stunts, Kane Hodder; an ArieScope Pictures production; Color; Not rated; 85 minutes; Release date: October 1, 2010. **CAST**: Danielle Harris (Marybeth), Tony Todd (Rev. Zombie), Kane Hodder (Victor Crowley/Thomas Crowley), Parry Shen (Justin), Tom Holland (Bob), R.A. Mihailoff (Trent), AJ Bowen (Layton), Alexis Peters (Avery), Ed Ackerman (Cleatus), David Foy (Chad), Colton Dunn (Vernon), Rick McCallum (John), John Carl Buechler (Jack Cracker), Kathryn Fiore (Shyann Crowley), Mercedes McNab (Misty), Joleigh Fioravanti (Jenna), Joel Murray (Shapiro), Rileah Vanderbilt (Young Victor Crowley), Cody Blue Snider (Young Sampson), BJ McDonnell, Nick Principe, Joe Lynch (Hunters), Shawn Ashmore, Jason Richard Miller (Fishermen), Emma Bell (Girl on TV), Charlayne DeVillier, Sarah Agor, Laura Catalina Ortiz (Bayou Beaver Girls), Adam Green (Puking Guy), Mike Mendez, Dave Parker, Ryan Schifrin, Marcus Dunstan, Steven Barton, Lloyd Kaufman (Featured Hunters)

Danielle Harris in *Hatchet II* © Dark Sky Films

BARRY MUNDAY (Magnolia) Producers, Matthew Weaver, Eric Kopeloff, Mickey Barold, Stone Douglass; Executive Producers, Scott Prisand, Marcos Siega, Carl Levin, Rob Ortiz, Barry Habib, Jeff Davis; Director/Screenplay, Chris D'Arienzo; Based on the novel *Life is a Strange Place* by Frank Turner; Photography, Morgan Pierre Susser; Designer, Paul Oberman; Costumes, Frank Helmer; Editor, Joan Sobel; Casting, Mary Vernieu, JC Cantu; a Far Hills/Stick N' Stone and Corner Store Entertainment Productions presentation; Color; Rated R; 94 minutes; Release date: October 1, 2010. **CAST**: Patrick Wilson (Barry Munday), Judy Greer (Ginger Farley), Jean Smart (Carol Munday), Chloë Sevigny (Jennifer Farley), Malcolm McDowell (Mr. Farley), Billy Dee Williams (Lonnie Green), Cybill Shepherd (Mrs. Farley), Shea Whigham (Donald), Missi Pyle (Lida Griggs), Mae Whitman (Candice), Colin Hanks (Heavy Metal Greg), Emily Procter (Deborah), Christopher McDonald (Dr. Preston Edwards), Kyle Gass (Jerry Sherman), Chris D'Arienzo (Newton Creech), Matt Winston (Kyle Pennington), Kirk Ward, Joe Nunez (Roadies), Jenica Bergere (Janice the Midwife), Diana Terranova (Bennie), Michael Durrell (Father Walsh), Monica Allgeier (Young Woman), Razaaq Adoti (Spiro), Willam Belli (Felicia), Barret Swatek (Lucy), Becca Sweitzer (Waitress), Sam Pancake (D.J.), Bruna Rubio (Sasha), Tori White (Barry's Nurse), Michael Rivkin (Maury Knox), Michael Rivkin (Maury Knox), Marcelo Tubert (Dr. Shriver), William Stanford Davis (Greenskeeper), Trieu Tran (Moe), Julia Boyd (Makeout Girl), Jillian Schmitz (Strip Club Dancer), Geoffrey Gould (Barry Co-Worker), Rebecca Howard (Tracy), Eurydice Davis (Tammy), Cynthia Adkisson (Young

Jennifer), Marnie Alexenburg (Secretary #1), Ashley Guerrero (Beautiful Girl), Kristoffer Kjornes, James Kim (Bar Patrons), Youlanda Davis (Office Manager), Kristina Sefeldt (Ex-Girlfriend), Andrew Magarian (Candice's Dad), Barry Habib (Dr. Habib), Jeff Sanders (Bouncer), Yvonne Huff (Nurse), Jennifer M. Coll (Denise), Charlotte Roller (2-year-old Corneilia), Gary Spritz (Jersey Boy)

Judy Greer, Patrick Wilson in *Barry Munday* © Magnolia

S&MAN (HDNet Films) Producers, Jason Kliot, Lawrence Mattis, Joana Vicente; Director/Screenplay, J.T. Petty; Photography, Patrick McGraw; Editor, Andy Grieve; Color; Not rated; 84 minutes; Release date: October 1, 2010. Semi-Documentary on underground horror and fetish films. **WITH** Bill Zebub, Fred Vogel, Carol J. Clover, Debbie D, Freddie Dingo, Michelle Glick, Eric Marcisak

S&Man © HDNet Films

DOUCHEBAG (Paladin) Producers, Jonathan Schwartz, Marius Markevicius; Executive Producers, Audrey Wilf, Zygi Wilf; Director, Drake Doremus; Screenplay, Lindsay Stidham, Drake Doremus, Jonathan Schwartz, Andrew Dickler; Photography, Scott Uhlfelder, Chris Robertson; Music, Jason Torbert, Casey Immoor; Music Supervisor, Tiffany Anders; Editors, a Super Crispy Entertainment presentation in association with Sorrento Prods. of a Jonathan Schwartz production; Dolby; Color; HD; Not rated; 81 minutes; Release date: October 1, 2010. **CAST**: Andrew Dickler (Sam Nussbaum), Ben York Jones (Tom Nussbaum), Marguerite Moreau (Steph), Nicole Vicius (Mary Barger #2), Amy Ferguson (Sarah), Wendi McLendon-Covey (Mary Barger #1), David Cuddy, Michael Reilly (Party Goers), Lindsay Stidham, Charlotte Derby (Bus Stop Girls), Leslie Dawn Forsyth (Barbie), Biambu Garrett (Tea Shop Worker), Spencer Gray (The Douchebag), Sahara Hite (Stoner Chick), Joseph A. Lamantia (Tux Shop Owner), Jasmine Lowe (Tea Shop Girl), Marlo McSweeney (Roller Rink Worker), Jeanine Oda (Drive-Thru Girl), Douglas Pierson, Brian Spillane (Museum Patrons), Kyrra Richards (Tom's Girlfriend)

Ben York Jones, Andrew Dickler in *Douchebag* © Paladin

ZENITH (Cinema Purgatorio) Producers, George Lekovic, Jason Robards III; Director/ Screenplay, Vladan Nikolic; Photography, Vladimir Subotic; Art Director, Grace Yun; Costumes, Vera Chow; Music, Luigi Colarullo; Editor, Milica Zec; Color; Not rated; 93 93 minutes; Release date: October 1, 2010. **CAST**: Jason Robards III (Ed), Zohra Lampert (Ms. Minor), David Thornton (David Berger), Jay O. Sanders (Oberts), Raynor Scheine (Dale), Kenneth Anderson (Lanky Man), Ana Asensio (Lisa), Tim Biancalan (Hank Mirren), Michael Cates (Vito), Ohene Cornelius (Ralph), Moises De Pena (Seducer), Michael A. Figueroa (Gigolo), Arthur French (Mateo), Kelly Kirklyn (Nurse), Al Nazemian (Nimble), Justin Reinsilber (The Inspector), Bernie Rachelle (Schleimann), Joe Salters (Bald Man), Peter Scanavino (Jack), Gordon Joseph Weiss (Dr. Burns), Vladimir Bibic (Man #1), Didier Flamand (Rich Man), Dan Foley (Customer), Janis Grossman (Seedy Urban Creature), Derrick Jones (Urban Guy), Neal Marshad (Parishoner), Annamarie Russo, Ginamarie Russo (Madis), Doug Shapiro (Doctor #1), Marcel Simoneau (Clerk), Suzana Stankovic (Club Dancer), Brad Thomason (Man in Business Suit), Jonathan Pitts Wiley (Attendant)

Zenith © Cinema Purgatorio

CASE 39 (Paramount) Producers, Steve Golin, Kevin Misher; Director, Christian Alvart; Screenplay, Ray Wright; Photography, Hagen Bogdanksi; Designer, John Willett; Costumes, Monique Prodhomme; Music, Michl Britsch; Editor, Mark Goldbatt; Visual Effects Supervisor, Chris Watts; Casting, Randi Hiller, Sarah Halley Finn; a Misher Films/Anonymous Conente production; Dolby; Hawk Scope Widescreen; Deluxe Color; Rated R; 104 minutes; Release date: October 1, 2010. **CAST**: Renée Zellweger (Emily Jenkins), Jodelle Ferland (Lilith Sullivan), Ian McShane (Det. Barron), Bradley Cooper (Doug), Callum Keith Rennie (Edward Sullivan), Adrian Lester (Wayne), Kerry O'Malley (Margaret Sullivan), Cynthia Stevenson (Nancy), Alexander Conti (Diego), Philip Cabrita (Javier), Vanesa Tomasino (Javier's Wife), Mary Black (Custody Judge), Domenico D'Ambrosio (Plainclothes Cop), Benita Ha (Therapist), John Carroll (Judge), Michael Bean, Lesley Ewen (Co-Workers), David Patrick Green (Chief Psychiatrist), Dee Jay Jackson (Bus Driver), Taya Calicetto (Young Emily), Alisen Down (Emily's Mother), Darryl Quon (Inmate), Suzanne Bastien, Jane Braithwaite (Nurses), Fulvio Cecere (Fire Marshal), Colin Lawrence (Police Sergeant), Dagmar Midcap (News Anchor), Fran Gebhard (Coordinator), Bill Mondy (Interviewer), Andrew Airlie (Doctor), Sarah Jane Redmond (Barron's Wife), Charles Zuckermann (Demon Person), Yvonne Valdez (Mrs. Lynch), Paul Duchart (Priest), Daniel Bacon (Businessperson), Darren E. Scott (Young Cop), Dalias Blake (Detention Center Cop), Phillip Mitchell (Lead Guard)

Bradley Cooper in *Case 39* © Paramount Pictures

CASH CROP (Sierra Films) Producer, Noah Workman; Executive Producer, Scott Ramage; Photography, Adam Ross, Robert Eras, Glen Mordeci, Danny Smith; Editor, Randy Ross; Color; Not rated; 83 minutes; Release date: October 1, 2010. Documentary showing how marijuana has become California's biggest cash crop.

FREAKONOMICS (Magnolia) Introduction and Transitional Segments: Producer, Mary Rohlich; Director/Screenplay, Seth Gordon; Photography, Bradford Whitaker; Editor, Luis Lopez; Graphics and Animation, Lopez, Clay Tweel; *A Roshonda by Any Other Name*: Producers, Jeremy Chilnick, Morgan Spurlock, Joanna Chejade-Bloom; Director, Morgan Spurlock; Screenplay, Jeremy Chilnick, Morgan Spurlock; Photography, Daniel Marracino; Editor, Tova Goodman; Music, Jon Spurney; *Pure Corruption*: Producers, Peter Bull, Alex Gibney, Alexandra Johnes; Director, Alex Gibney; Screenplay, Peter Bull, Alex Gibney; Photography, Darren Lew, Junji Aoki, Ferne Pearlstein; Editor, Sloane Klevin; Music, Human; Animation, Brady E. Poulsen; *It's Not Always a Wonderful Life*: (Animated) Producers, Eugene Jarecki, Kathleen Fournier; Director/Screenplay, Eugene Jarecki; Editor, Doug Blush; Music, Peter Nashel, Pete Miser; Designer, Joe Posner; Narrator: Melvin Van Peebles; *Can You Bribe a Ninth Grader to Succeed?*: Director, Rachel Grady, Heidi Ewing; Photography, Tony Hardmon, Rob Vanalkemade; Editors, Michael Taylor, Sloane Klevin; Music, Paul Brill, Ionic Furjanic; a Chad Troutwine in association with Cold Fusion Media of a Green Film & Magnolia Pictures presentation; Dolby; Color; Rated PG-13; 86 minutes; Release date: October 1, 2010. Documentary in which various directors spotlight diverse topics: Sumo wrestling; baby names; bribing students to bring up their grades; and the drop in crime.

Freakonomics © Magnolia

IDIOTS AND ANGELS (Plympton) Producer, Biljana Labovic; Director/ Screenplay/ Animation, Bill Plympton; Art Directors, Bill Plympton, Biljana Labovic; Editor, Keivn Palmer; Color; Not rated; 78 minutes; Release date: October 6, 2010.

Idiots and Angels © Plympton

MY SOUL TO TAKE (Rogue) Producers, Wes Craven, Iya Labunka, Anthony Katagas; Executive Producers, Ryan Kavanaugh, Tucker Tooley, Andrew Rona; Director/Screenplay, Wes Craven; Photography, Petra Korner; Designer, Adam Stockhausen; Costumes, Kurt and Bart; Music, Marco Beltrami; Music Supervisor, Ed Gerrard; Editor, Peter McNulty; Casting, Avy Kaufman; a Corvus Corax production, presented in association with Relativity Media; Dolby; Super 35 Widescreen; 3D; Color; Rated R; 107 minutes; Release date: October 8, 2010. **CAST**: Max Thieriot (Bug), John Magaro (Alex), Denzel Whitaker (Jerome), Zena Grey (Penelope), Nick Lashaway (Brandon), Paulina Olszynski (Brittany), Jeremy Chu (Jay), Emily Meade (Fang), Raúl Esparza (Abel), Jessica Hecht (May), Frank Grillo (Paterson), Danai Gurira (Jeanne-Baptiste), Harris Yulin (Dr. Blake), Shareeka Epps (Chandelle), Elena Hurst (Maria), Dennis Boutsikaris (Principal Pratt), Felix Solis (Mr. Kaiser), Trevor St. John (Lake), Shannon Walsh (Melanie Pratt), Alexandra Wilson (Sarah), Eric Zuckerman (Gus), Alberto Vazquez (Officer Ramirez), Lou Sumrall (Quint), Lynnanne Zager (Betty O'Neil, Podcast Host), Michael Bell (Podcast Guest), Robert Clotworthy (Voice of News Anchor), Terri Douglas (Riverton Radio Host), Amber Efé (Other Nurse), Hannah Hodson, Nicole Brittany Patrick (Girls in Hallway), Christopher Place (The Ripper), Richard Rutkowski (News Anchor), Courtney Stow, Kaitlyn Stow (Young Leah)

Max Thieriot, John Magaro in *My Soul to Take* © Rogue Pictures

JIM (Area 23a) Producers, Vanessa Morris-Burke, Jeremy Morris-Burke; Executive Producer, Kristina Szandtner; Director/Screenplay/Photography/Editor, Jeremy Morris-Burke; Designers, Michael Byrnes, Suzanne Wang; Costumes, Rabiah Troncelliti; a Tinmouth Films and Jim and Susan Prods. presentation; Color; Not rated; 102 minutes; Release date: October 8, 2010. **CAST**: Dan Illian (Jim Kotofsky), Vanessa Morris-Burke (Susan Kotofsky), Abigail Savage (#3774), Michael Strelow (Niskaa), Atticus Cain (Nicodemus), Carolyn Morrison (Algrithmia), Michelle Ries (Lorigen Spokesperon), Amy Heidt (Eva Kismeckler), Nichole Donje (Dr. Lyndholm), Eric C. Bailey (Steve Gimbler), Maxwell Zener (Dan Muckler), Theresa Faelte-Lee (Dr. Simmons), Victor Dickerson (Earl), Gavin-Keith Umeh (Tyrone), Jack Wallace (Rick Lavelle), Jennifer Lucas (Sheila Barton), Allen Enlow (Tyce Brigs), Matthew Kinney (Dr. Latham), Charles Barron (Injured Clone), Shawn Bell (Young Man), Rob Bradford (Erik Moxley), Christy Burke (Cheryl), Anthony E. Cabral (Lorigen Security Guard), Shawn I. Chevalier, Erik A. Williams (Generator Clones), Carlos Michael Hagene (Barista), Emily Morris (Young Woman), Paul Morris (Real Estate Agent)

Dan Illian in *Jim* © Area 23a

GOING BLIND (Lovett Prods.) Producers, Hilary Klotz Steinman, Joseph Lovett; Director/ Screenplay, Joseph Lovett; Photography, Matthew Akers; Music, Doug Maxwell, Joel Goodman; Editors, Jason Jzabo, Jamie Hogan; Color; HD; Not rated; 81 minutes; Release date: October 8, 2010. Documentary in which news producer Joseph Lovett's realization that he is going blind prompted him to speak to others who are losing their sight. **WITH** Joseph Lovett, Jessica Jones, Emmet Teran, Peter D'Elia, Patricia Williams, Steve Baskis

Jessica Jones in *Going Blind* © Lovett Prods.

I SPIT ON YOUR GRAVE: UNRATED (Anchor Bay) Producers, Lisa Hansen, Paul Hertzberg; Executive Producers, Meir Zarchi, Alan Ostroff, Jeff Klein, Gary Needle; Director, Steven R. Monroe; Screenplay, Stuart Morse; Based on the screenplay *Day of the Woman* by Meir Zarchi; Photography, Neil Lisk; Designer, Dins Danielsen; Costumes, Bonnie Stauch; Music, Corey Allen Jackson; Editor, Daniel Duncan; Visual Effects Supervisor, Kevin Little; Special Makeup Effects, Jason Collins, Elvis Jones; Casting, Danny Roth; a Cinetel Films presentation; Dolby; Widescreen; Color; Not rated; 108 minutes; Release date: October 8, 2010. **CAST**: Sarah Butler (Jennifer), Daniel Franzese (Stanley), Chad Lindberg (Matthew), Tracey Walter (Earl Woodason), Rodney Eastman (Andy), Jeff Branson (Johnny), Andrew Howard (Sheriff Storch), Saxon Sharbino (Chastity), Mollie Milligan (Mrs. Storch), Amber Dawn Landrum (Gas Station Girl)

Sarah Butler, Jeff Branson, Rodney Eastman in *I Spit on Your Grave*
© Anchor Bay

AS GOOD AS DEAD (First Look) Producers, Heidi Jo Markel, Jordan Gertner, Eve Pomerance; Director, Jonathan Mossek; Screenplay, Eve Pomerance, Erez Mossek; Photography, Frank Barrera; Designer, Jade Healy, Anne Stuhler; Costumes, Rabia Troncelliti; Music, Greg Arnold; Editors, Julie Carr, Lee Percy; an Eclectic Pictures production in association with Major Motion Pictures, First Line Entertainment, Millennium Films; Color; HD; Rated R; 92 minutes; Release date: October 8, 2010. **CAST**: Andie MacDowell (Helen Kalahan), Cary Elwes (Ethan Belfrage), Frank Whaley (Aaron), Matt Dallas (Jake), Brian Cox (Rev. Kalahan), Jess Weixler (Amy), Nicole Ansari-Cox (Kate Belfrage), Clark Middleton (Seth), Mario D'Leon (Titus), Crispian Belfrage (Brian Shepherd), Emma Kantor (Sarah), Juliette Bennett (Erica), Claudine Oriol (Marsha), Elissa Middleton (Eve), J.W. Cortes, Laurence Covington (Cops), Rawson Faux (Store Customer), John Schuman (Masked Shooter), Nasry Malak (Moe), Ian Capone (Skinhead), Amy Garay (Bus Passenger), Amira Moodie (Bus Victim), Gable (Mao), John Kelsey (Bus Driver)

Matt Dallas, Cary Elwes in *As Good as Dead* © First Look

RED WHITE & BLUE (IFC) Producers, Bob Portal, Simon Rumley; Executive Producers, Adam Goldworm, Doug Abbott, Tim League, Judy Lipsey; Director/Screenplay, Simon Rumley; Photography, Milton Kam; Designer, Josh Crist; Costumes, Tessa Justman; Music, Richard Chester; Editor, Rob Hall; a Screen Projex presentation of a Rumleyvision production, in association with Fidelity Films, Fantastic Fest; Color; HD; Not rated; 104 minutes; Release date: October 8, 2010. **CAST**: Noah Taylor (Nate), Amanda Fuller (Erica), Marc Senter (Franki), Nick Ashy Holden (Alvin), Patrick Crovo (Carl), Jon Michael Davis (Ed), Sally Jackson (Ellie), Lauren Schneider (Sarah), Julian Haddad (Lil' Alan), Kevin LaVoie (Arnold), Pete O. Partida (Lee), Eryn Brooke (Lisa), Mary Mathews (Marj), Matteson Claus (Sherry), Laurie Foxx (Pamela), Michael Price (Hardware Store Manager), Jenny Gravenstein (Druggie Rock Girl), Chris Summers (Steve), Vincent Doenges (William), Ernest James (Dano), Saxon Sharbino (Paulette), Mark Hanson (Druggie Rock Guy), Robert Sliger (Oncologist), Emily Cropper (HIV Clinician), Chance Hartman (Hotel Pick-Up), Nicole Holt (Erica's Mom), François Larosa (Erica's Mom's Boyfriend), Mitchell Parrack (Doctor), Joel Reynosa (Priest), Gary Teague (Hotel Bar Customer)

Marc Senter in *Red White & Blue* © IFC Films

CHERRY (Abramorama) Producers, Matthew Fine, Sam Kitt; Executive Producer, Paul Kurta; Director/Screenplay, Jeffrey Fine; Photography, Marvin V. Rush; Designer, Jack Ryna; Costumes, Alycia Joy Rydings; Music, Bobby Johnston; Music Supervisor, Lauren Ross; Editor, Cindy Parisotto; Casting, Matthew Lessall; a Fresh Shrimp production with Kittco Pictures; Color; HD; Not rated; 99 minutes; Release date: October 8, 2010. **CAST**: Kyle Gallner (Aaron), Laura Allen (Linda), Brittany Robertson (Beth), Esai Morales (Wes), D.C. Pierson (Wild Bill), Matt Walsh (Prof. Van Aucken), Zosia Mamet (Darcy), Adrian Aguilar (Chubby), Kirk Anderson (Phil), Desmin Borges (Joey), Matthew Felkey (Fabio), Dwight Trice Jr. (Crony), John Judd (Prof. Krause), Daniel Louis Rivas (Ray Ray), Andrew Vermette (Leif), Shawn Bernal, Ryan Young (Party Guys), Don Cochran (Parent), Tyler Corbin (Student), Kiplan Dooley (Grocery Store Clerk), Emelia Tse (Dorm Girl)

Laura Allen, Kyle Gallner, Brittany Robertson in *Cherry* © Abramorama

GHETTOPHYSICS: WILL THE REAL PIMPS AND HOS PLEASE STAND UP? (Samuel Goldwyn) Producers, William H. Arntz, E. Raymond Brown, Scott Altomare; Executive Producers, Cedra Stokes, Carl Stokes; Directors/Screenplay, William H. Arntz, E. Raymond Brown; Photography, David Bridges; Designer, Elvis Strange; Costumes, Moksha McPherrin; Music, Ryan Demarre, E. Raymond Brown, Jamahl Harris, Akil the MC; Editors, William H. Arntz, Joel Plotch; Casting, Debbie Sheridan; a GhettoPhysics production/Capture Light Industries production; Dolby; Color; Rated R; 94 minutes; Release date: October 8, 2010. **CAST**: E. Raymond Brown (Narrator/University Professor), Sabrina Revelle (Shaneesh), Shang (Himself), Mike Foy (Marvin), Kristy Lewis (White TV Host), Nina Daniels (Tamara), Alex Duong (Alex), Joseph Bayard (Dakarai), Daryl Littleton (Guy on Couch with E Ray), Marcie Barkin Goodwin (Martha, School Counselor), Tomo Kawaguchi (Asian TV Host), Micaal Sajid Stevens (World Pimp Awards Announcer); with: Dedon Kamathi, Brother Ishmael Tetteh, Cynthia McKinney, Sonia Barrett, Cornel West, KRS-One, Norman Lear, Lo Da Sho, Too Short, William H. Arntz, John Perkins, Ice T, Mac Breed, Candy, Loreal, Hook da Crook, Filmore Slim, Michael Meade, Dr. Earnest Bagner, Passionique, Reginald Simmons, Hank Wesselman, Lee Mack, Byron Katie

E. Raymond Brown in *Ghettophysics* © Samuel Goldwyn

PURE COUNTRY 2: THE GIFT (Warner Bros.) Producers, Scott Duthie, Christopher Cain, Hunt Lowry; Executive Producers, Larence Mortorff, Ben Horton, Phil Adams, Bryan Elliott, Ken Crain, James Tierney; Director, Christopher Cain; Screenplay, Dean Cain, Christopher Cain; Photography, Juan Ruiz-Anchia; Designer, Kelly Anne Ross; Music, Steve Dorff; Editor, Jack Hofstra; Casting, Jo Doster; an Angry Monkey Entertainment in association with Roserock Films presentation; Dolby; Color; Rated PG; 111 minutes; Release date: October 15, 2010. **CAST**: Katrina Elam (Bobbie), Travis Fimmel (Dale), Michael McKean (Joseph), Cheech Marin (Pedro), Bronson Pinchot (Matthew), Dean Cain (Director), William Katt (Winter), George Strait (Country Music Star), Jackie Welch (Aunt Ella), Heidi Brook Myers (Molly), Kristinda Cain (Sis), David Chattam (Restaurant Manager), Ryan Cheng (Toshia 'Pudge'), Jeremy Childs (Security Guard), Kaitlyn Dorff (Young Bobbie), J.D. Parker (Roy), Paige Rasmussen (Secretary), Benjamin Reed (Stage Manager), Jeff Schafer (Bubba), Adam Skaggs (Weston), Sean Symons (Fan), Sharon Thomas (Marilyn Montgomery), Todd Truly (Keith), Chuck David Willis (Ishi), Michael Yarma (Morita)

George Strait, Katrina Elam in *Pure Country 2* © Warner Bros.

GERRYMANDERING (Green Film Co.) Producers, Jeff Reichert, Dan O'Meara, Chris Romano; Director/Screenplay, Jeff Reichert; Photography, Gary Griffin; Music, David Wingo; Editor, Sam Pollard; a Green Film Company presentation; Color; DV; Not rated; 77 minutes; Release date: October 15, 2010. Documentary on redistricting for political advantage. **WITH** Dave Aronberg, Bill Cavala, Linda Curtis, Kathay Feng, Sam Issaccharoff, Hakeem Jeffries, Arnold Schwarzenegger, George Stonefish, Chris Swain

Arnold Schwarzenegger in *Gerrymandering* © Green Film Co.

TICKED-OFF TRANNIES WITH KNIVES (Breaking Glass Pictures) Producers, Whitney Blake, Toni Miller; Director/Screenplay/Editor, Israel Luna; Photography, Israel Luna, Todd Jenkins, Lacey Brutschy; Costumes, Chase Wade; Special Effects Makeup, Joshua Fread; Casting, Israel Luna, Whitney Blake, Toni Miller; a La Luna Entertainment presentation, in association with Toucan Prods.; Color; Not rated; 95 minutes; Release date: October 15, 2010. **CAST**: Krystal Summers (Bubbles), Kelexis Davenport (Pinky LaTrimm), William Belli (Rachel), Erica Andrews (Emma), Jenna Skyy (Tipper), Tom Zembrod (Boner), Richard D. Curtin (Fergus), Kenny Ochoa (Nacho), Gerardo Davila (Chuey), Todd Jenkins (Dr. Laccio), Chase Wade (Nurse Connie), Molly Spencer (La'Trice), Melissa Timmerman (Marcy), Souk Burrows (Flash), Curt Wheeler (Squirt), Edna Jean Robinson (Prudence), Nicole Holt (Bar Patron)

Eric Andrews, Kelexis Davenport, Krystal Summers, Jenna Skyy, William Belli in *Ticked-Off Trannies with Knives* © Breaking Glass Pictures

D.L. in *King of Paper Chasin'* © Triplebeam Entertainment

THE TWO ESCOBARS (ESPN Films) Producers/Directors/Screenplay, Jeff Zimbalist, Michael Zimbalist; From an original concept by Nick Sprague; Photography, Jeff Zimbalist; Music, Michael Furjanic; Editors, Jeff Zimbalist, Gregory O'Toole; an All Rise Films production; Color; HD; Not rated; 102 minutes; Release date: October 15, 2010. Documentary on two unrelated Escobars, Pablo, drug dealer and owner of a Colombian soccer team, and Andres, the team's captain.

BITTER FEAST (Dark Sky Films) Producers, Larry Fessenden, Brent Kunkle, Peter Phok; Executive Produces, Malik B. Ali, Badie Ali, Hamza Ali, Greg Newman; Director/ Screenplay, Joe Maggio; Photography, Michael McDonough; Designer, Beck Underwood; Costumes, Elisabeth Vastola; Music, Jeff Grace; Editor, Seth E. Anderson; Visual Effects Supervisor, Neal Jonas; Casting, Antonia Dauphin, Kathleen Backel; a Glass Eye Pix production; Color; DV-to-HD; Not rated; 103 minutes; Release date: October 15, 2010. **CAST**: James Le Gros (Peter Gray), Joshua Leonard (JT Franks), Amy Seimetz (Katherine Franks), Larry Fessenden (William Coley), Megan Hilty (Peg), Mario Batali (Gordon), Owen Campbell (Johnny), Tobias Campbell (Young Peter), Paula El Sherif (Cooking Show Guest), Allie Nelson (Fan Girl at Bookstore), Sean Reid (Co-Worker), Graham Reznick (Local Newscaster), John Speredakos (Phil), Lisa Golub (Waitress), Jesse Coleman (TV Reporter)

Andreas Escobar in *The Two Escobars* © ESPN Films

KING OF PAPER CHASIN' (Triplebeam Entertainment) Producer, Jonathan Hood; Executive Producer, D.L.; Director/Editor, La Monte Edwards; Screenplay, La Monte Edwards, D.L.; Photography, Brett Albright; Art Director, Elizabeth Ralston; Costumes, Naomi Fells; Music, Kurt Oldman; Color; Rated R; 124 minutes; Release date: October 15, 2010. **CAST**: D.L. (Carter Blanche), Jason Rivera (Dell), Piarry Oriol (Thalia), Joseph Somma (Agent Richardson), Dennis Da Menace (J.B.), Omar Knight (Derek), Al Thompson, Frduah Boateng (Sage), Sean Simms (Kenneth Coda), Avia Bushyhead (Monica), Lauren Hooper (Rachel Anderson), Sean Brathwaite (JT), J. Steven Williams (Uglyman)

Joshua Leonard in *Bitter Feast* © Dark Sky Films

N-SECURE (Bluff City Films) Producers, Valerie Enloe, Bryce Southard; Executive Producer, Julius Lewis; Director, David M. Matthews; Screenplay, Julius Lewis, Christine Taylor; Photography, Andy Dean; Art Director, Rachel Boulden; Costumes, Meriwether Nichols; Music, Marc Ellis, David M. Matthews; Editor, Bryce Southard; a David M. Matthews Film presentation; Color; Rated R; 109 minutes; Release date: October 15, 2010. **CAST:** Cordell Moore (David Alan Washington), Essence Atkins (Robin Joyner), Denise Boutte (Tina Simpson), Tempestt Bledsoe (Jill), Lamman Rucker (Isaac Roberts), Toni Trucks (Denise), Rick Ravanello (Joe Hooks), Thomas Miles (Harold Lyons), Caryn Ward (Kim), Elise Neal (Leslie), Steve Conn (Dr. Myers), BernNadette Stanis (Dr. Heather), Sabrina Tiller (Nurse Nancy), Mike Higgenbottom, T.J. Cates (Police Officers), Sisagu Otsuki, Mitsuteru Hiwatari (Asian Businessmen), Judge D. Bailey (Pastor), Michael Cunningham, Donald Meyers (Investigators), Manon Matthews (Bystander), Mike McLendon (Truck Driver), Marguerite Hibbets (Medical Examiner), Trent Dee (Motel Desk Clerk), James Buchanan (Jack), Darius Willis (Ken), David Tankersley (Doctor), Danny Thomas (Sheriff)

Denise Boutte in *N-Secure* © Bluff City Films

THE SOPRANO STATE: NEW JERSEY'S CULTURE OF CORRUPTION, PART ONE (New Jersey Pictures) Producers, Steve Kalafer, Bruce Raiffe; Executive Producer, Kelli Pyffer; Director, Peter LeDonne; Screenplay, Bob Ingle, Sandy McClure; based on their book; Photography, Steven Moskovic; Editor, Molly Wiliamson; Color/Black and white; HD; Not rated; 119 minutes; Release date: October 18, 2010. Documentary looking at New Jersey's history of political corruption. **WITH** Tony Darrow, Bob Ingle, Sandy McClure, Chris Christie.

Tony Darrow in *The Soprano State* © New Jersey Pictures

MY GIRLFRIEND'S BOYFRIEND (Opus) Producers, Rick McFarland, Alyssa Milano; Director/Screenplay, Daryn Tufts; Photography, Brandon Christenson; Designer, Kenneth Hill; Costumes, Alyson Hancey; Music, Sam Cardon; Editors, Rick McFarland, Ethan Vincent; Casting, Lauren Bass; a Fiftyfilms in association with Peace by Peace Productions presentation; Color; Rated PG; 111 minutes; Release date: October 22, 2010. **CAST:** Alyssa Milano (Jesse Young), Beau Bridges (Logan Young), Christopher Gorham (Ethan Reed), Carol Kane (Barbara), Michael Landes (Troy Parker), Tom Lenk (David Young), Kelly Packard (Suzy), Emily Tyndall (Airport Worker), Heather Stephens (Sarah), Brad Johnson (Bob), Maclain Nelson (Stewart), Daryn Tufts (Waiter), Scott Christopher (Garret), Chantel Flanders (Catie), Tavya Patch (Linda Young), David Nibley (Bill), William Rubio (Stephen), Chris Clark (Piano Player), Annette Wright (Judy), Gavin Bentley (Mike), Brandy Snow (Brandy), Stephen Carey (Matthew, Boy in Window), Paul Carey (Paul), Hannah McFarland (Hayley), Adam McFarland (Alexander), Natalie Murdock (Makeup Artist), Chase Little (Conner), Lacy Rachelle (Receptionist)

Christopher Gorham, Alyssa Milano in *My Girlfriend's Boyfriend* © Opus

RISING STARS (Screen Media) Producers, Andrew van den Houten, William M. Miller; Executive Producer, Frank Olsen; Director/Screenplay/Editor, Daniel Millican; Photography, Ron Gonzalez; Designer, Emilie Ritzmann; Costumes, Michael Bevins; Music, Ryan Shore, Jason Germaine, Benjamin Reynolds; Casting, Cindi Rush; a Doberman Entertainment production; Color; Rated PG; 90 minutes; Release date: October 22, 2010. **CAST:** Kyle Riabko (Chance), Leon Thomas III (J.R.), Jessie Payo (Eigsh), Graham Patrick Martin (Garrett), Fisher Stevens (Mo Meyerson), Rebecca St. James (Kari), Barry Corbin (Farmer), Catherine Mary Stewart (Mrs. Cage), Daniel Millican (Wim), Andrew van den Houten (Rising Stars MC), Natalie Hall (Brenna), Jordan Walker Ross (Jeremiah), Connor Hill (Kid), Lauren Ashley Carter (Natalie), Morgana Shaw (Chance's Mom), Pierce Cravens (Kevin), Ron Gonzalez (Douggie), Cori Lynn Ross (Singer), Jessie Payo (Eigsh), Preston Potter (Ben) Jason Edward Cook (Petey)

Kyle Riabko in *Rising Stars* © Screen Media

PARANORMAL ACTIVITY 2 (Paramount) Producers, Jason Blum, Oren Peli; Executive Producers, Steven Schneider, Akiva Goldsman; Co-Producer, Amir Zbeda; Director, Tod Williams; Screenplay, Michael R. Perry, Christopher Landon, Tom Pabst; Story, Michael R. Perry, based on the original film *Paranormal Activity* directed and written by Oren Peli; Photography, Michael Simmonds; Designer, Jennifer Spence; Costumes, Kristin M. Burke; Editor, Gregory Plotkin; Visual Effects Supervisor, Michael Kennedy; Prosthetic Makeup Effects, Almost Human; Stunts, Rob King; Casting, Michael Hothorn; a Blumhouse/Solana Films/Room 101 production; Dolby; Deluxe color; Rated R; 91 minutes; Release date: October 22, 2010. **CAST**: Katie Featherston (Katie), Micah Sloat (Micah), Brian Boland (Daniel Rey), Molly Ephraim (Ali Rey), Sprague Grayden (Kristi Rey), David Bierend (Surveillance Camera Expert), Seth Ginsberg (Brad), Wililam Juan Prieto, Jackson Xenia Prieto (Hunter Rey), Vivis (Martine), Harper Zelinsky (Hunter Rey, Infant)

PUNCHING THE CLOWN (Viens Films) Producers, Gregori Viens, Henry Phillips; Co-Producers, David Klein, Eric Klein, Tyrone Trullinger; Director/Editor, Gregori Viens; Screenplay, Gregori Viens, Henry Phillips; Photography, Ian Campbell; Designers, Azra Bano Ali, Barclay Wright, Tim Harmston; Music, Henry Phillips; Color; Not rated; 89 minutes; Release date: October 22, 2010. **CAST**: Henry Phillips (Henry), Ellen Ratner (Ellen Pinsky), Matthew Walker (Matt), Audrey Siegel (Becca), Guilford Adams (Fabian), Evan Arnold (Don Chase), Mark Cohen (Stupid Joe), Mik Scriba (Joel), Eddie Pepitone (Eddie), Derek Waters (Dave the Intern), Robert Babish (Owen), Robert Balderson (Jack), Rick Batalla (Lucas Cascos), Eddie Berke (Bartender), Simone Carter (Fan), Travis Clark (Travis), Cissy Conner (Kitty), Conrad Angel Corral (Mitchell), Chris Fairbanks (Daniel), Judd Fish (Skinhead), Fay Gauthier (Protestor), Nikki Glaser (Olympia), Nora Gruber (Jennie), Jim Hamilton (Barfly), Warren Herr (Café Manager), Nathan Hillen (Big Cat), Michelle Anne Johnson (Jane Crown Jones), Patrick Keane (Cig Bummer/Radio Caller), Joe Kelley Jr. (Bar Patron), Wade Kelley (Captain Chaotic), Beth Kennedy (Booker), Mike MacRae (Car Heckler), Sean Masterson (Kurt), Philip McNiven (George), Matthew Morgan (Last Cigarette Guy), Mike O'Connell (Cray), Mary Linda Phillips (Dottie), Suzie Rose (Abby), Jennifer Seifert (Carrie), Steve Sheridan (Phil), C.B. Spencer (Paige), Ryan Stout (Johnny), Lisa Valenzuela (Rita), Gregori Viens (Lawyer), Bill Wiley (Sam), Paul Willson (Bill)

Henry Phillips in *Punching the Clown*
© Viens Films

KNUCKLEHEAD (Samuel Goldwyn) Producer, Mike Pavone; Executive Producers, Steve Barnett, Dave Calloway; Director, Michael Watkins; Screenplay, Bear Aderhold, Thomas F. X. Sullivan, Adam Rifkin; Photography, Kenneth Zunder; Designer, Raymond Pumilla; Costumes, Claire Breaux; Music, Jim Johnston; Editor, Peck Prior; Casting, Denis Chamian, Elizabeth Coulon, Ania Kamieniecki-O'Hare; a WWE Studios presentation; Dolby; Color; Rated PG-13; 100 minutes; Release date: October 22, 2010. **CAST**: Mark Feuerstein (Eddie Sullivan), Melora Hardin (Mary O'Conner), Paul "Big Show" Wight (Walter Krunk), Wendie Malick

(Sister Francesca), Rebecca Creskoff (Tina), Dennis Farina (Memphis Earl), Lester Speight (Redrum), Will Patton (Vic Sullivan), Bobb'e J. Thompson (Mad Milton), Saul Rubinek (Rabbi), Kurt Doss (Henry), Lurie Poston (Todd), Mike Agresta (Fight Manager), Sean Paul Braud (Hasidic Jew), Gaven Thomas Brooks (Boy on Bus), Edrick Browne (Organizer), Hunter Burke, Garrett Hines (Teens), John Chambers (Guy on Phone), Bare Knuckle Dave (Barney), Gabrielle Chapin (Line Dancer), Felder Charbonnet (Fight Registration Official), Joe Chrest (Child Services Inspector), Thomas C. Daniel (Suga Ray's Trainer), James DuMont (Announcer), Wayne Ferrara (Police Captain), Erin Frederic (Fireman), Trey Fuller (Orphan), Shima Ghamari (Lady in Yellow), Lara Grice (Hooker), Douglas M. Griffin (Sketchy Driver), Gene Kevin Hames Jr., Shane Partlow, Chris Whetsone (Cops), Jerry Katz (Sugar Ray Rosenberg), Chris Marroy (Club Goer), Kristal McManigal (Ninja #1), Elizabeth McNulty (Singer), Sam Medina (Scary Muay Thai Fighter), Caleb Michaelson (Fred), Lacey Minchew (Cutie), Darcel White Moreno (Giggles), Lance E. Nichols (Milton's Dad), Jennifer Ramirez (Nun), Jason Reppel (Fight Spectator), Arvilla Riddick (Woman on Bus), Christian P. Roche, Thea Tucker (Fairgoers), Shawn P. Roche (Mover), Aaron Sauer (Policeman), Raymond D. Sweet (Ernest, Spectator), Margo Swisher (Sexy Nurse), Alleigh Schulz (Dancer in Bar), Daniel Vincent (Bayou Bag Man), Jearl Vinot (Trainer), Jake Austin Walker (Dennis), Spicer Williams-Crosby (Biker Chick), Gregory Williams (Very Big Guy), George Wilson (Homeless Man), Jesse James Youngblood (Dangerous Mexican), Lynette Zumo (Wrestling Fan)

Paul Wight, Mark Feuerstein in *Knucklehead* © Samuel Goldwyn

BOXING GYM (Zipporah Films) Producer/Director/Editor, Frederick Wiseman; Photography, John Davey; Color; Not rated; 91 minutes; Release date: October 22, 2010. Documentary on the gymnasium run by Richard Lord in Austin, Texas where would-be boxers of all types come to train.

THE TAQWACORES (Strand) Producer/Director, Eyad Zahra; Executive Producer, Dafvid Perse; Screenplay, Michael Muhammad Knight, Eyad Zahra; Based on the novel by Michael Muhammad Knight; Photography, JP Perry; Designer, Marwan Kamel; Music, Omar Fadel, The Kominas; Editor, Josh Rosenfield; Casting, Ryan Glorioso; a Rumanni Filmworks production; Color; Not rated; 83 minutes; Release date: October 22, 2010. **CAST**: Bobby Naderi (Yusef), Noureen Dewulf (Rabeya), Dominic Rains (Jehangir), Nav Mann (Umar), Volkan Eryaman (Amazing Ayyub), Ian Tran (Fasiq), Tony Yalda (Muzzamil), Rasika Mathus (Fatima), Anne Leighton (Lynn), Denise George (Dee Dee Ali), John Charles Meyer (Hamza), Nicholas Riley (Harun), Jim Dickson (Gas Station Bully), Ara Thorose (Lead Singer of the Gilmans), Marwan Kamel (Himself)

Dominic Rains, Nav Mann in *The Taqwacores* © Strand Releasing

BEARCITY (TLA Releasing) Producers, Heidi H. Hamelin, Lewis Tice; Director, Doug Langway; Screenplay, Douglas Langway, Lawrence Ferber; Photography, Michael Hauer; Designer, Racey North; Costumes, Kathryn Moser; Music, Kerry Muzzey; Editors, Doug Langway, Gerald C. Fernando; a Sharpleft Studios production; Color; Not rated; 105 minutes; Release date: October 22, 2010. **CAST**: Joe Conti (Tyler), Gerald McCullouch (Roger), Brian Keane (Fred), Stephen Guarino (Brent), Alex Di Dio (Simon), Gregory Hunter (Michael), James Martinez (Carlos), Sebastian La Cause (Fernando), Christian Dante White (Cory), David Drake (Dr. Straube), Peter Stickles (Executive), Ashlie Atkinson (Amy), Randy Jones (Buck), Blake Evan Sherman (Melvin), Joanthan McEwan (Ted), Jack G. Bethke (Randy), Leslie L. Smith (Greg), Kevin E. Smith (Santa), Roland Rusinek (Frank), Joe Zaso (Steve), Fernando Mateo JR. (Keith), Raul Guerra (Peter), Vayu O'Donnell (Paul), Bill McKinley (Rob), Will Bethencourt (Jack), Fergus O'Brien (Jim), Paul Mauriello (Bob), Johnathan Cerio (Danny), Trai La Trash (Drag Queen), Mark Singer (Daddy), Sherry Stregack (Nurse), Scott Maxson (John), Michael Hartney (Robbie), Joe Mannetti (Hot Daddy Bear), Elli (Heavy Bear), Mike Quirk, Vinny Lomoriello (Handsome Bears), Kerry Watterson (Muscle Bear), Gary Marcus (Cub Bartender), Cole Mangano (Muscle Cub, DJ), James Rudy Flesher (Bar Patron), Michael Musto (Himself), Dean Morris (Polar Bear)

Brian Keane, Stephen Guarino in *Bearcity* © TLA Releasing

INHALE (IFC Films) Producers, Jennifer Kelly, Nathalie Marciano, Michelle Chydzik Sowa; Director, Baltasar Kormakur; Screenplay, Walter Doty, John Clafin; Story, Christian Escario; Photography, Óttar Gudnason; Designer, Monte Hallis; Costumes, Katie Saunders; Music, James Newton Howard; Editor, Elisabet Ronaldsdottir; Casting, Carla Hool; a 26 Films production; Dolby; Color; Not rated; 83 minutes; Release date: October 22, 2010. **CAST**: Dermot Mulroney (Paul Stanton), Diane Kruger (Diane Stanton), Jordi Mollà (Aguilar), Vincent Perez (Martinez), Rosanna Arquette (Dr. Rubin), Sam Shepard (James Harrison), Mia Stallard (Chloe), David Selby (Henry White), Cesar Ramos (Ines), Kristyan Ferrer (Miguel), Arlin Alcala (Centro Medico Juarez Receptionist), Juan Avila Hernandez (Camaronito), Nick Banks (Dr. Sullivan), Richard Barela (Hotel Clerk), Daniel Barela (Used Car Salesman), Maria Bethke (Clinica Castillo Receptionist), Paul Blott (Judge Jack Abrahams), Todd Thatcher Cash (Scotty), Abraham Chaidez (Luis Ruiz), Eduardo Ambriz DeColosio (Chepe), Christian Escario (General #1), Louie Franco (Biker), J.D. Garfield (Translator), Carolyn Harvey (Old Flower Vendor), Rafael Herrera (Claudia), Lisa Hill (Strip Club Waitress), Jiji Hise (Mother in Car Crash), Rick Lamlond (Prison Guard), Celestia Loeffler (EMT), Nathalie Marciano (Carol Harrison), Quinn Mason (Son in Car Crash), Kahlil Mendez (Tico), Gabriel Merendon (Diego), Nevarez Juarez (Gordo Adalberto), Kim Nieve Larricio (Marta), Elmer Pacheco (Scraggly Dude), Jesus Payan Jr. (Obese Man), Walter Perez (Arturo), Greta Quezada (Clinica Nurse Castillo), Tamara Rose (Harrison's Secretary), Manny Rubio (Juan), Kat Sawyer (UNOS Rep), Kieran Sequoia (TV Reporter), Kisha Sierra (Aguilar's Secretary), James Tarwater (Matt Peckinsky), Paco Vallejos (Priest Francisco), Sharon Van Ivan (Hospital Administrator), Joe Adams (FBI Agent)

Cesar Ramos, Dermot Mulroney in *Inhale* © IFC Films

STRANGE POWERS: STEPHIN MERRITT AND THE MAGNETIC FIELDS (Variance) Producers, Kerthy Fix, Gail O'Hara, Alan Oxman; Executive Producer, Kerthy Fix, Paul Kloss, Pamela Tanner Boll; Directors, Kerthy Fix, Gail O'Hara; Photography, Paul Kloss, Kerthy Fix; Editor, Sarah Devorkin; a Fix Films presentation; Color/black and white; Not rated; 82 minutes; Release date: October 27, 2010. Documentary on songwriter Stephin Merritt and his band, the Magnetic Fields. **WITH** Stephin Merritt, Claudia Gonson, John Woo, Sam Davol, Shirley Simms, Daniel Handler

Stephin Merritt in *Strange Powers* © Variance

KALAMITY (Screen Media) Producer, Juliana Penaranda-Loftus; Director/Screenplay, James M. Hausler; Photography, Jim Hunter; Designer, Elizabeth Jones; Costumes, Susan O'Donnell; Music, Christopher Mangum; Editor, Chris Lorusso; Casting, Lauren Bass; Presented in association with Original 4 Releasing; Dolby; Color; Rated R; 94 minutes; Release date: October 22, 2010. **CAST**: Nick Stahl (Billy Klepack), Beau Garrett (Alice), Jonathan Jackson (Stanley Keller), Alona Tal (Ashley), Robert Forster (Tom Klepack), Sammi Hanratty (Barbie Klepack), Jill Latiano (Simge), Patricia Kalember (Terry), Anya Samantha Jordanova (Woman in Street), Michael Gabel (Sam), Courtney Pauroso (College Girl), Molyneau DuBelle (Nurse), Patrick Michael Strange, Enrique Chicas (Bar Drunks), Tyler Parkinson (Matt), James M. Hausler (Dingleberry Customer), Roger Sands, Kevin L., Chelsea Connell, Leslie Connell, Olja Ivanic, Sasha Rajic (College Students), Christopher M. Clark (Christian Phillips), Larry Carter (Professor), Kate Bliss (Girl in the Blue Dress), Daniel Michael DeLuca (Confused Man at Airport), Laurel Helen Hausler (Impatient Girl), Kathleen Murphy (Susie), Ashleigh C. Hairston (Beer Pong Player), Connie Bowman (Ticket Counter Lady), Adrian Nanney (Pool Party Guy)

Nick Stahl, Jonathan Jackson in *Kalamity* © Screen Media

SAW 3D (Lionsgate) Producers, Gregg Hoffman, Oren Koules, Mark Burg; Executive Producers, Daniel Jason Heffner, Peter Block, Jason Constantine, James Wan, Leigh Whannell, Stacey Testro; Co-Producer, Troy Begnaud; Director, Kevin Greutert; Screenplay, Patrick Melton, Marcus Dunstan; Photography, Brian Gedge; Designer, Tony Ianni; Costumes, Alex Kavanagh; Music, Charlie Clouser; Editor, Andrew Coutts; Casting, Stephanie Gorin; a Twisted Pictues presentation of a Burg/Koules/Hoffman production produced in association with a Bigger Boat and Serendipity Productions; Dolby; Deluxe color; Rated R; 91 minutes; Release date: October 29, 2010. **CAST**: Tobin Bell (Jigsaw/John), Costas Mandylor (Hoffman), Betsy Russell (Jill), Cary Elwes (Dr. Gordon), Sean Patrick Flanery (Bobby), Chad Donella (Gibson), Gina Holden (Joyce), Laurence Anthony (Rogers), Dean Armstrong (Cale), Naomi Snieckus (Nina), Rebecca Marshall (Suzanne), James Van Patten (Dr. Heffner), Sebastian Pigott (Brad), Jon Cor (Ryan), Anne Greene (Dina), Chester Bennington (Evan), Dru Viergever (Dan), Gabby West (Kara), Benjamin Clost (Jake), Kevin McGarry (Charlie), Kim Schraner (Palmer), Olunike Adeliyi (Sidney), Ish Morris (Alex), Carlos Diaz (Coroner Worker), Elizabeth Rowin (Sara), Christine Simpson (Donna Evans), Jacintha Wesselingh, Claudia Difolco, Kimberley Deon (Newscasters), Rachel Wilson (Mother), Alli Chung (Business Woman), Desmond Campbell (Business Man), Billy Oliver, Liise Keeling (Police Officers), Tanedra Howard (Simone), Shauna MacDonald (Tara), Joanna Douglas (Joan), Janelle Hutchison (Addy), Greg Bryk (Mallick), Larissa Gomes (Emily), Kevin Rushton (Trevor), Jagger Gordon, Kyle Cicerella, Simone Steene (Survivor Group Members), Simon Northwood (Lead SWAT Officer), Regan Moore, Danny Lima, Bryan Thomas, Wayne Downer, Billy Oliver, Patrick Mark, Chris McGuire (SWAT Officers), Don Gough (Limo Driver)

Chester Bennington in *Saw 3D* © Lionsgate

JOLENE (Entertainment 1) Producers, Riva Yares, Zachary Matz; Director, Dan Ireland; Screenplay, Dennis Yares; Based on the story *Jolene: My Life* by E.L. Doctorow; Photography, Claudio Rocha; Designer, Bernt Amadeus Capra; Costumes, Gail McMullen; Music, Harry Gregson-Williams; Editor, Luis Colina; a Next Turn presentation of a Riva Yares production; Color; Widescreen; Rated R; 120 minutes; Release date: October 29, 2010. **CAST**: Jessica Chastain (Jolene), Dermot Mulroney (Uncle Phil), Chazz Palminteri (Sal), Rupert Friend (Coco Leger), Michael Vartan (Brad), Denise Richards (Marin), Theresa Russell (Aunt Kay), Stephanie Likes (Kendra), Jennfier Pfalzgraff (Maya), Joses Rosete (Sid), Deena Trudy (Office Assistant), John Dobradenka (Legal Aid Lawyer), Bri Acsani (Felicia), Sally Jo Bannow (Laura), Frances Fisher (Cindy), Eddie Guerra (Frank), Ron Jordan (Boris), Amy Landers (Peggy), Benjamin Mouton (Jimmy), Travis Scott Newman (Travis, the Maitre D'), Anna Kehmeier (Party Guest), Jacqueline Torres (Rosie), Cathy Rankin (Susie), Debbie Bartlett (Brad's Mother), Cheridy Clement (Rose, Waitress), Douglas L. Cook (Mental Hospital Orderly), Jared Cur (John Bone), Barbara Glover (Sales Clerk), Greg Joseph (Country Club Pianist), Mike Lawler (Justice of the Peace), Sherry Leigh (Biker Sherry), Sidney

Malone (Brad's Mother's Friend), Lene Martin (Woman in Shelter), Ciro Mennella (Attorney), Price Mitchum (Ex-Boyfriend), Zeb Newman (Mickey Holler), Josef Rainer (Brad's Father), Klor Rowland (Burly Trucker), Jedediah Shoemaker (Brad's Best Man), Mary Ann Snyder (Nanny), Shannon Whirry (Teacher)

Jessica Chastain in *Jolene* © Entertainment 1

A SMALL ACT (HBO Documentary Films) Producers, Jennifer Arnold, Patti Lee, Jeffrey Soros; Director/Screenplay, Jennifer Arnold; Story, Thomas Schlesinger; Photography, Patti Lee; Music, Joel Goodman; Editors, Carl Pfirman, Tyler Hubby; Color; Not rated; 88 minutes; Release date: October 29, 2010. Documentary on how Chris Mburu's benefactor helped him stay in school and inspired him to start his own sponsorship fund for Kenya youths. **WITH** Chris Mburu, Patrick Kimani

Patrick Kimani in *A Small Act* © HBO Documentary Films

THE KIDS GROW UP (Shadow Distribution) Producers, Doug Block, Lori Cheatle; Co-Producer, Frank Van Den Engel; Director/Photography, Doug Block; Screenplay, Doug Block, Maeve O'Boyle; Music, H. Scott Salinas; Editor, Maeve O'Boyle; Associate Producer, Gabriel Sedgwick; a Copacetic Pictures and Hard Working Movies production in association with HBO Documentary Films, ZDF in cooperation with ARTE, Channel 4, VPRO; American-Dutch-German-British; Color; Not rated; 90 minutes; Release date: October 29, 2010. Documentary on how filmmaker Doug Block, who has chronicled most of his daughter Lucy's life on film, copes with her decision to leave home to attend college. **WITH** Lucy Block, Doug Block, Marjorie Silver, Mike Block, Carol "Kitty" Block, Josh Silver, David Silver, Romain George, Ellen Block, Karen Engwall, Doug Engwall, John Golomb, Mina Block, Margaret Silver, Anne Marino, Bernard Telsey, Michael Colberg, Mariana Alexander, Jera Foster-Fell, Liz Doland, Lucy Lydon, Georgia Stockwell, Robert "Bo" Lauder, David Engwall, Beth Engwall, Sharon Schuster, Jahmil Eady, Carol Eady, Feathers

Lucy Block in *The Kids Grow Up* © Shadow Distribution

THE LAST PLAY AT SHEA (Newmarket/D&E Entertainment) Producers, Steve Cohen, Nigel Sinclair; Executive Producers, Todd Kamelhar, Greg Whiteley, Glen Zipper; Supervising Producer, Alexandra de la Vega; Director, Paul Crowder; Screenplay, Mark Monroe; Editors, Paul Crowder, Mike J. Nichols; Narrator, Alec Baldwin; a Spitfire Pictures production; Dolby; Color; Not rated; 95 minutes; Release date: October 29, 2010. Documentary on Billy Joel and Shea Stadium and the final concerted he performed there before it was razed to make way for a newer venue. **WITH** Billy Joel, Tony Bennett, Garth Brooks, Roger Daltrey, Don Henley, Keith Hernandez, Paul McCartney, Mike Piazza, Tom Seaver, Darryl Strawberry, Steve Tyler.

Billy Joel in *The Last Play at Shea* © Newmarket

WINSTON CHURCHILL: WALKING WITH DESTINY (Moriah Films) Producers, Rabbi Marvin Hier, Richard Trank; Director/Screenplay, Richard Trank; Based on material by Richard Trank and Rabbi Marvin Hier; Photography, Jeffrey Victor; Music, Lee Holdridge; Editor, Nimrod Erez; Narrator, Ben Kingsley; Color; Not rated; 100 minutes; Release date: October 29, 2010. Documentary on Britain's former prime minister, Winston Churchill. **WITH** The voices of Bryan McArdle, Doron Avraham, Richard Ben Asher

Franklin Roosevelt, Winston Churchill in *Walking with Destiny* © Moriah Films

GUY AND MADELINE ON A PARK BENCH (Variance Films) Producers, Jasmine McGlade, Mihai Dinulescu; Director/Screenplay/Lyrics, Damien Chazelle; Music, Justin Hurwitz; Editors, Damien Chazelle, W.A.W. Parker; Choreographer, Kelly Kaleta; Color; Not rated; 82 minutes; Release date: November 5, 2010. **CAST**: Jason Palmer (Guy), Desiree Garcia (Madeline), Sandha Khin (Elena), Frank Garvin (Frank), Andre Hayward (Andre), Alma Prelec (Alma), Karen Adelman (Karen), Anna Chazelle (Laura), Bernard Chazelle (Paul), Gonzalo Digenio (John), Eli Gerstenlauer (Eli), Greg Duncan (Greg), Keith Gross-Hill (Keith), Kevin Harris (Kevin), Daniel the Juggler (Juggler), Maureen McCarthy (Landlady), Vera Meyer (Glass Harmonica Player), Beverly Palmer (Guy's Mom), Sharee Palmer (Guy's Sister), Tj Palmer (Guy's Brother), Zerek Palmer (Zerek), Joe Della Penna (Pianist), Jerry Quinn (Landlord), Willie Rodriguez (Willie), Elizabeth Tingue (Sophie), Eddie Wakes (Eddie), Suzanne Bouffard, Kelly Burk, Carolyn Glicklich, Chris Rowse (Dancers at Summer Shack), Kelly Kaleta (Dancer at Party), Vanessa Pope (Girl at Party)

Jason Palmer, Desiree Garcia in *Guy and Madeline on a Park Bench* © Variance Films

NY EXPORT: OPUS JAZZ (Factory 25) Directors, Jody Lee Lipes, Henry Joost; Screenplay/Photography, Jody Lee Lipes; Designer, Ariel Schulman; Costumes, Janicza Bravo; Music, Robert Prince; Editor, Zachary Stuart-Pontier; Thirteen for WNET.org and Supermarché in association with Bar/Suozzi Productions; Color; Widescreen; Not rated; 61 minutes; Release date: November 5, 2010. Documentary of Jerome Robbins' "ballet in sneakers," *NY Export: Opus Jazz.* **WITH** Robert Fairchild, Craig Hall, Adam Hendrickson, Rebecca Krohn, Ashley Laracey, Austin Laurent, Georgina Pazcoguin, Tiler Peck, Brittany Pollack, Amar Ramasar, Rachel Rutherford, Troy Schumacher, Gretchen Smith, Andrew Veyette, Giovanni Villalobos

NY Export: Opus Jazz © Factory 25

A MARINE STORY (Red Road Studio) Producers, Dreya Weber, Ned Farr, J.D. Disalvatore; Director/Screenplay/Editor, Ned Farr; Photography, Alexandre Naufel; Music, Craig Richey; a Last Battlefield Productions presentation; Color; Not rated; 98 minutes; Release date: November 5, 2010. **CAST**: Dreya Weber (Alexandra Everett), Paris P. Pickard (Saffron), Christine Mourad (Holly), Rob Beddall (Meth Head), Anthony Michael Jones (Leo), Jason Williams (Turk), Deacon Conroy (Burner), John Lee Ames (Dale), Brad Light (Stenny), Ned Mochel (Bill), David Avallone (Deputy Bauman), Jessica M. Bair (Lesbian Kissing on Dance Floor), Andrew Blau (Disgruntled Man in Bathrobe), Gregg Daniel (Sheriff), Amanda Deibert (Meth Head Girlfriend), Colette Divine (Gayle), Chance Havens (Jonesy), Janice Ann Johnson (Clerk), Mike McAleer (Staff Sergeant Graf), Alice Rietveld (Nona), Troy Ruptash (Joe), Jeff Sugarman (Pollard), Tracy Weatherby (Marine), Lisa Wolpe (Shelly)

Paris P. Pickard, Dreya Weber in *A Marine Story* © Red Radio Studio

VIOLET TENDENCIES (Embrem Entertainment) Producers, Casper Andreas, Jesse Archer; Executive Producers, Jimmy Balletto, Gary Russell Coder, Linda Larson, Mich Lyon, Mark Stiffler; Director, Casper Andreas; Screenplay, Jesse Archer; Photography, Timothy Naylor; Designer, Lee Clayton; Costumes, Elizabeth Edwards, Moni Briones; Music, Michael Barry; Editor, Craig Cobb; Casting, Meredith Jacobson Marciano; a Fruit Fly Films production; Color; Not rated; 99 minutes; Release date: November 5, 2010. **CAST**: Mindy Cohn (Violet), Marcus Patrick (Zeus), Jesse Archer (Luke), Samuel Whitten (Riley), Casper Andreas (Markus), Kim Allen (Salome), Adrian Armas (Darian), Armand Anthony (Vern), Dennis Hearn (Bradleigh), Andrea Cirie (Donna), Sophia Lamar (Larice), Hilary Elliott (Marjorie Max), Margret R.R. Echeverria (Audrey), Shari Albert (Ashley), Michael Scott (Stephen Miser), Michelle Akeley (Darian's Receptionist), Christopher L. Graves (Mike), John-Patrick Driscoll (The Mailman), Michael Cornacchia (Donnie the Waiter), Jonathan Chang (Andre), Brandon Gill (J Flame), Ben Pamies (Gerald), J.R. Rolley (Derek), Sonja Rzepski (Jenny), Howard Feller

(Homeless Man), Fredrick Ford (Darian's Trick), Kohl Beck (Beer Can Dan), Sal Blandino, Ali Mroczkwoski, Ryan Turner (Clipboard Fundraisers), Mike Diamon, J. Fortino, Jack Mackenroth, Michael Musto (Themselves), Marc Alan Austen (Gay Party Rabbi), Jimmy Balletto (Michael), Michael "Anita" Cavnaugh (Pissed Man), Craig Cobb (Hugger), Vincent De Paul (Chance), Dan Elhedery (Sex Party Host), Max Emerson (Max), Mike Guzman (Luke's 8-inch Trick), Clover Honey (Drag Queen), Randy Jones (Buck Winston), Carlin Langley (Fag Stag), Brandon Ellyson (Violet's Friend in the Park), Steven Polito (Hedda Lettuce), Alex Quiroga (Luke's Love Trick), Max Rhyser (Long John), Ronnie Shockley III (Little Joye), Sam Smithyman (Little Matt)

Casper Andreas, Adrian Armas in *Violet Tendencies* ©Embrem Entertainment

BENEATH THE DARK (IFC Films) formerly *Wake*; Producers, Amanda Micallef, Chad Feehan, Lea-Beth Shapiro; Executive Producer, Luke Vitale; Director/Screenplay, Chad Feehan; Photography, Jason Blount; Designer, Manuel Pérez Peña; Costumes, Emily Batson; Music, Daniel Licht; Music Supervisor, Henry Self; Editor, Michael Griffin; Visual Effects Supervisor, Jamison Goei; Casting, Deanna Brigidi; a The Fort presentation; Dolby; Technicolor; Rated R; 102 minutes; Release date: November 5, 2010. **CAST**: Josh Stewart (Paul), Jamie-Lynn Sigler (Adrienne), Chris Browning (Frank), Angela "Angie" Featherstone (Sandy), Afemo Omilami (The Man), Trevor Morgan (Jason), Christopher Gessner (Max), Robert Maxhimer (Billy), Grainger Hines (Tim), Jeannetta Arnette (Shirley), Sandy Martin (Colleen), Carlease Burke (Beatrice), Melissa Bacelar (Shawnee), Chris Hayes (Cameraman), Wade Feehan (Pledge)

Josh Stewart in *Beneath the Dark* © IFC Films

TOTAL BADASS (CrashCam Films) Producers, Kera Dacy, Bob Ray; Director/Photography, Bob Ray; Editors, Andrew Segovia, Bob Ray; Color; DV; Not rated; 91 minutes; Release date: November 10, 2010. Documentary on Austin hellraiser and underground celebrity Chad Holt.

Chad Holt in *Total Badass* © CrashCam Films

HELL ON WHEELS (CrashCam Films) Producer, Werner Campbell; Director, Bob Ray; Photography, Bob Ray, Jen White; Music, … And You Will Know Us by the Trail of Dead; Editors, Conor O'Neill, Cory Ryan; Color; DV; Not rated; 90 minutes; Release date: November 10, 2010. Documentary on female roller derby. **WITH** Lonestar Rollergirls (BGGW): Nancy Haggerty, Anya Jack, Heather Burdick, April Herman, Sara Luna, Amanda Fields; Texas Rollergirls: Lane Greer, Laurie Rourke, Theresa Papas, Amy Sherman, Rachelle Moore

Hell on Wheels © CrashCam Films

HELENA FROM THE WEDDING (Film Movement) Producers, Alexa L. Fogel, Brendan Mason; Director/Screenplay, Joseph Infantolino; Photography, Stephen Kazmierski; Designer, John Bonafede; Costumes, Natasha Noorvash; Editor, Jennifer Lilly; Casting, Suzanne Smith Crowley; a Beech Hill Films production; Dolby; Color; Not rated; 89 minutes; Release date: November 12, 2010. **CAST**: Lee Tergesen (Alex), Melanie Lynskey (Alice), Paul Fitzgerald (Nick), Gillian Jacobs (Helena), Dominic Fumusa (Don), Corey Stoll (Steven), Jessica Hecht (Lynn), Dagmara Dominczyk (Eve)

Melanie Lynskey, Dagmara Dominczyk in *Helena from the Wedding*
© Film Movement

COOL IT (Roadside Attractions) Producers, Terry Botwick, Sarah Gibson, Ondi Timoner; Executive Producer, Ralph Winter; Director, Ondi Timoner; Screenplay, Terry Botwick, Sarah Gibson, Bjorn Lomborg, Ondi Timoner; Based on the book by Bjørn Lomborg; Photography, Nasar Abich; Music, N'oa Winter Lazerus, Sarah Schachner; Editors, Debra Light, Brian Singbiel, David Timoner; a 1019 Entertainment production in association with Interloper Films; Dolby; Color; Rated PG; 88 minutes; Release date: November 12, 2010. Documentary on Danish economist Bjørn Lomborg and his theories disputing the idea of global warming. **WITH** Bjørn Lomborg

Bjørn Lomborg in *Cool It* © Roadside Attractions

EXPECTING MARY (Rocky Mountain Pictures) Producer, Kim Waltrip; Executive Producer, Jim Casey; Director/Screenplay, Dan Gordon; Photography, Michael Goi; Designer, Anthony Stabley; Costumes, Donna Barish; Music, Kevin Saunders Hayes; Editor, Marc Leif; a WonderStar Productions in association with J&J Productions presentation; Color; Rated PG; 97 minutes; Release date: November 12, 2010. **CAST**: Elliott Gould (Horace Weitzel), Linda Gray (Darnella), Lainie Kazan (Lillian Littlefeather), Cloris Leachman (Annie), Della Reese (Doris Dorkus), Olesya Rulin (Mary), Cybill Shepherd (Meg), Gene Simmons (Taylor), Fred Willard (Jerry Zee), Duncan Bravo (Phil Cutbarth), Kathy Lamkin (Molly), Kinsey Packard (Barbara), Matt Kaminsky (Joe), Morgan Krantz (Ryder), Larry Bates (Sheriff), Kristen Berman (Waitress), Mandell Butler (Tony), Jordan Del Spina (Boy), Teresa Ganzel (Shar D'onnay), Robert Harvey (Doctor), Dyana Ortelli (Crystal Lite), Raymond Singh (Indian Friend)

Olesya Rulin in *Expecting Mary* © Rocky Mountain Pictures

CON ARTIST (Plug Ugly Films) Producer/Director/Photography, Michael Sladek; Executive Producers, Gill Holland, Guilherme Campellon; Editors, Jacob Bricca, Michael Sladek; Presented in association with Ovation, The Group Entertainment, Acme Pictures, Room 5 Films and New Yorker Films; Color; Not rated; 84 minutes; Release date: November 12, 2010. Documentary on "business artist" Mark Kostabi. **WITH** Mark Kostabi, Michel Gondry, Pope Benedict XVI, Bill Clinton, Jeff Koons, Dennis Miller, Robin Leach, Maury Povich, Glenn O'Brien, Gary Indiana, Wichy Hassan, Robin Byrd, Daze, Baird Jones, Nick Zedd, Donald Kuspit, Mike Cockrill

Mark Kostabi in *Con Artist* © Plug Ugly Films

WILLIAM S. BURROUGHS: A MAN WITHIN (Oscilloscope) Producers, Carmine Cervi, Ilko Davidov, Yony Leyser; Director/Screenplay, Yony Leyser; Editor, Ilkov Davidov; Narrator, Peter Weller; a BulletProof Film production; Dolby; Color/black and white; Not rated; 74 minutes; Release date: November 12, 2010. Documentary on controverisal author William S. Burroughs. **WITH** Fred Aldrich, Laurie Anderson, Bill Ayers, Amiri Baraka, Jello Biafra, Victor Bockris, George Condo, David Cronenberg, Diane DiPrima, Patricia Elliott Marvin, Robert McColl, Thurston Moore, Tom Peschio, Iggy Pop, Genesis Breyer P-Orridge, Wayne Propst, Lee Ranaldo, Dean Ripa, Patti Smith, Sonic Youth, V. Vale, Gus Van Sant, Anne Waldman, John Waters, Hal Willner.

Patti Smith, William S. Burroughs in *A Man Within* © Oscilloscope

TODAY'S SPECIAL (Reliance Media Works) Producers, Nimitt V. Mankad, Lillian LaSalle; Director, David Kaplan; Screenplay, Aasif Mandvi, Jonathan Bines; Based on the play *Sakina's Restaurant* by Aasif Mandvi; Photography, David Tumblety; Designer, Darcy C. Scanlin; Costumes, Theresa Squire; Music, Stephane Wrembel; Editor, Chris Houghton; Songs, Siddharta Khosla; an Inimitable Pictures, Sweet 180 production; Dolby; Color; Rated R; 99 minutes; Release date: November 19, 2010. **CAST**: Aasif Mandv (Samir), Naseeruddin Shah (Akbar), Jess Weixler (Carrie), Madhur Jaffrey (Farrida), Harish Patel (Hakim), Dean Winters (Chef Steve), Kevin Corrigan (Stanton), Kevin Breznahan (Freddie), Aarti Majmudar (Henna), Ranjit Chowdhry, Kumar Pallana, Ostaro (Regulars), Amir Arison (Dr. Semaan), Saila Rao (Alpana), Sean T. Krishnan (Rasool), Debargo Sanyal (Pierre), Lee Wong (Pacific East Cook), Gregory Korostishevsky (Andrei), Emily Wilk, Chloe Cmarada (Women), Ed Jewett (Spazz), Angela Lewis (Woman Looking at Menu), Jim Wisniewski (Crying Guy), Erica Peeples (Waitress), Corrine Hong Wu (Pacific East Patron), Lucy Radack (Abigail), Buzz Bovshow (Satisfied Customer), Carlos Ibarra (Busboy), Sylvia Kauders, Lisa Stansbury, Janis Grossman, Stewart Steinberg (Restaurant Patrons), Ajay Naidu (Munnamia)

Aasif Mandvi in *Today's Special* © Reliance Media Works

FAMILY AFFAIR (C-line Films) Producers, Chico Colvard, Liz Garbus; Executive Producers, Dan Cogan, Abigail Disney; Director, Chico Colvard; Music, Miram Cutler; Color; Not rated; 82 minutes; Release date: November 19, 2010. Documentary in which filmmaker Chico Colvard looks into the abuse his sisters survived by their father.

Family Affair © C-Line Films

QUEEN OF THE LOT (Rainbow) Producer, Rosemary Marks; Director/Screenplay, Henry Jaglom; Photography, Hanania Baer; Set Decorator, Sofia Jimenez; Costumes, Cynthia Obsenares; Music, Harriet Schock; Editor, Ron Vignone; Rainbow Film Company production; FotoKem Color; Rated R; 114 minutes; Release date: November 19, 2010. **CAST**: Tanna Frederick (Maggie Chase), Noah Wyle (Aaron Lambert), Christopher Rydell (Dov Lambert), Paul Sand (Ernesto), David Proval (Caesar), Zack Norman (Kaz Naiman), Kathryn Crosby (Elizabeth Lambert), Mary Crosby (Frances Lambert Sapir), Peter Bogdanovich (Pedja Sapir), Dennis Christopher (Odin Johansen), Jack Heller (Louis Lambert), Beege Barkette (August Johansen), Daisy White (Shaelynn Roth), Ron Vignone (Gio), Diane Salinger (Hildy), Kelly DeSarla (Crowley), Sabrina Jaglom (Zoe Lambert), Simon O. Jaglom (Michael Lambert), Tess Wachter (Paula Johansen), Cooper Bass (John Johansen), Robert Clements (Parole Officer), Eliza Roberts (Erika), Wendel Meldrum (Kylie), Michael Emil, Linda Carson, Lisa Pescia, Robert Hallak, Lisa Mionie, Gary Imhoff (Dependency Busters), F.X. Feeney, Tommy Lightfoot Garrett, Dianne Lawrence, Giil Whiteley, Phil Proctor (Interviewers), Charles Matthau, Len Glasser, Craig Woods, TJ Castronovo (Card Players), Nathaniel Frederick (Butler), Natasha Danilovich (Maja, Masseuse), Phil Donlon (Cop #1)

Noah Wyle, Tanna Frederick in *Queen of the Lot* © Rainbow Releasing

REGINA SPEKTOR LIVE IN LONDON (Cinema Purgatorio) Producers, Sarah Roebuck; Director, Adria Petty; Photography, Rick Woollard, Tom Harding, Mike Metcalf; a East Pleasant Pictures production; Color; Not rated; 67 minutes; Release date: November 22, 2010. Documentary on singer Regina Spektor as she performs at London's Hammersmith Apollo Theater; **WITH** Regina Spektor.

THE LEGEND OF PALE MALE (Balcony) Producers, Frederic Lilien, Janet Hess; Executive Producer, Fred Kaufman; Director, Frederic Lilien; Screenplay, Janet Hess; Music, Lenny Williams; a Birdjail Productions presentation; Color; Not rated; 85 minutes; Release date: November 24, 2010. Documentary about a wild Redtail hawk that made its home atop a 5th Avenue co-op in Manhattan.

The Legend of Pale Male © Balcony Releasing

OPEN FIVE (Paper Moon Films) Producers, Nick Case, Ryan Watt; Executive Producer, Adam Hohenberg; Director, Kentucker Audley; Screenplay, Jake Rabinbach; Photography, Joe Swanberg; an Alarum Picutres production; Color; Not rated; 72 minutes; Release date: November 26, 2010. **CAST**: Jake Rabinbach (Jake), Kentucker Audley (Kentucker), Shannon Esper (Lucy), Genevieve Angelson (Rose), Amy Seimetz (Lynn), Caroline White (Caroline).

Open Five © Paper Moon Films

WILLETS POINT (Poseidon Productions) Producers, Ivan Velez, T.J. Collins; Director/Screenplay, T.J. Collins; Photography, Ivan Velez; Music, Richard Martinez; Editor, Stewart Frankson; Presented in association with Outta Left Field and Screen Cut Films; Dolby; Color; Not rated; 75 minutes; Release date: November 26, 2010. **CAST**: Alfredo Suarez (Guillo Blanco), Lorraine Rodriguez (Doris Blanco), Natalie Garcia (Sofia Blanco), Moses Caban (Maldo), Ivan Velez (Parts Supplier), Jimmy Strano (Landlord), Kimberli Flores (Jess, Bartender), Luis Galarza (Luis Blanco), Ramfis Myrthil (Reggie), Milagros Rivera (Sandra Hernandez), Rich Drezen, Adam Lawrence (Bar Patrons).

Lorraine Rodriguez in *Willets Point* © Poseidon Productions

DEAD AWAKE (New Films) Producers, Lucas Jarach, Anthony Gudas, Jason Price; Executive Producers, Nesim Hason, Ron Gell; Director, Omar Naim; Screenplay, John Harrington, David Boivin, Justin Urich; Story, John Harrington; Photography, David A. Armstrong; Designer, Cecilia Montiel; Costumes, Carlos Brown; Music, John Hunter; Editor, Miklos Wright; Casting, Mary Vernieu, JC Cantu; a New Films Intl. presentation in association with Tax Credit Finance LLC of a Jason Price/Lucas Jarach production; Dolby; Color; Rated R; 89 minutes; Release date: December 3, 2010. **CAST**: Nick Stahl (Dylan), Rose McGowan (Charlie), Amy Smart (Natalie), Ben Marten (Steve), Kim Grimaldi (Liz), Brian Lynner (Decko), Justin Marxen (Jack), James Serpento (Det. Milano), Jack Mishler (Mr. Brennan), Shane Simmons (David), Rachel Storey (Tracy), Justin Urich (Mad Terrence), Andrea Leon (Camilla), Livia Milano (Carmella), Phyllis Mumford (Older Nurse), Noah Harvey (Boy with Bike), Gene L. Hamilton (Older Man), Steve Kennevan (Police Desk Clerk), Richard Flemming (Mr. Stark), Betty Andrews (Waitress), Paul Nycz (Tattooed Man), Rick Septer (Creepy Man), Brittany Slater (Megan).

Nick Stahl in *Dead Awake* © New Films

SAINT MISBEHAVIN': THE WAVY GRAVY MOVIE (Argot Pictures) Producers, David Becker, Michelle Esrick; Executive Producers, DA Pennebaker, John Pritzker; Director, Michelle Esrick; Screenplay, Michelle Esrick; Photography, Daniel B. Gold; Music, Emory Joseph; Editor, Karen K.H. Simn; Dolby; Color; HD; Not rated; 87 minutes; Release date: December 3, 2010. Documentary on performer-humanitarian Wavy Gravy. **WITH** Wavy Gravy (Hugh Romney), Dr. Larry Brilliant, Jackson Browne, Ram Dass, Ramblin' Jack Elliott, The Grateful Dead, Steve Ben Israel, Michael Lang, Odetta, Bonnie Raitt, Buffy Sainte-Marie

Wavy Gravy, Bob Weir, Bonnie Raitt in *Saint Misbehavin'* © Argot Pictures

BHUTTO (First Run Features) Producers, Duane Baughman, Mark Siegel, Arleen Sorkin; Executive Producer, Glenn Aveni; Directors, Duane Baughman, Johnny O'Hara; Screenplay, Johnny O'Hara; Photography, David Ethan Sanders, Jim Mulryan, Noel Donnellon, Jens Schlosser; Music, Herb Graham Jr.; Editor, Jessica Hernández; an Icon Television Music production in association with Yellow Pad Productions; American-British; Stereo; Color; HDCAM; Not rated; 111 minutes; American release date: December 3, 2010. Documentary on the powerful Bhutto family of Pakistan and how daughter Benazir swore to avenge her father after he was overthrown from power and executed. **WITH** President Asif Ali Zardari, Tariq Ali, Condoleeza Rice, Kathleen Kennedy Townsend, Pervez Musharraf, Victoria Schofield, Dr. Reza Aslan, Arianna Huffington, Husain Haqqani, Peter Galbraith, Aseefa Bhutto Zardari, Bahkatwar Bhutto Zardari, Bilawal Bhutto Zardari, Sanam "Sunny" Bhutto, Mark Siegel, Steven Coll, Ahmed Ispahani, Akbar Ahmed, Amna Piracha, Christina Lamb, Feroz Hassan Khan, John F. Burns, Fatima Bhutto, Khurram Dastgir, Rehman Malik, Wajid Shamsul Hasan, Amy Wilentz, Ibrahim Mahlik, Shuja Nawaz, Sadia Abbas

Benazir Bhutto in *Bhutto* © First Run Features

MARS (Independent) Producers, Anish Savjani, Robert Howell, Javier Bonafont, Geoff Marslett; Director/Screenplay, Geoff Marslett; Photography, Jason Eitelbach; Designers, Tracy Duncan, Geoff Marslett; Costumes, Vanessa Nirode; Animation, Swerve Pictures, Self Assembly Films; Editors, David Fabelo, Geoff Marslett; HD; Color; Not rated; 82 minutes; Release date: December 3, 2010. **CAST**: Mark Duplass (Charlie Brownville), Zoe Simpson (Casey Cook), Paul Gordon (Hank Morrison), Cynthia Watros (Allison Guthrie), Liza Weil (Jewel), James Kochalka (Jackson), Howe Gelb (Shep), Nicole Atkins (Casey's Mom), Kinky Friedman (President of the United States), Charissa Allen (ESA Environmental Analyst), Elena Araoz (ESA Operations Manager), Nicole Atkins (Casey's Mom), Javier Bonfaont (Gepetto the Tailor), Kathy Rose Center (Reporter), Sunhee Cho (ESA Flight Dynamics Engineer), Kevin Cox (ESA Spacecraft Manager), Don Hertzfeldt (Reporter 2, 'Reckless Conclusion'), Robert Howell, Berndt Mader (Secret Service Men), Jonna Juul-Hansen (The First Lady), Nicholas Koller (Pen Sniffin' Bum), Jack Lee (Reporter 1, 'Mr. BBC'), Amber Marslett (Young Casey), Geoff Marslett (Casey's Dad), Dave Mikol (Reporter 3, 'Isidis Planatitis'), Spencer Parsons (Plebe at the ESA), Brandi Perkins (Photographer), Garry Peters (Pierre the Allergic Russian), Jeremy Pollet (Andrei the Bossy Russian), Morgan Prine (Young Casey), Jean Oliver Tchouaffe (US Press Secretary), Iskra Valtcheva (ESA Software Coordinator), Melanie West (Reporter 4, 'Indonesia')

Mars © Swerve Pictures

THE ASSISTANTS (Team Effort Films) Producers, Steve Morris, Mykel Denis, Karen P. Morris; Director/Screenplay/Editor, Steve Morris; Photography, Aaron Torres; Designer, Rebekah Bell; Costumes, Julia Van Vliet; Music, Aaron Kaplan; Casting, Karen P. Morris, Jami Rudofsky; Color; Not rated; 99 minutes; Release date: December 3, 2010. **CAST**: Chris Conner (Jack Ryder), Michael Terry (Carl Dresden), Kathleen Early (Sarah Bryman), Aaron Himelstein (Ben Goodrich), Tate Hanyok (Alex Kramer), Peter Douglas (Bill Riley), Joe Mantegna (Gary Greene), Jane Seymour (Sandy Goldman), Reiko Aylesworth (Cassie Levine), Jonathan Bennett (Zack Cooper), Joe Hernandez-Kolski (Jamie Nash), Steve Morris (Sven), Kevin Koster (Myron), Stacy Keach (Harlin W. Keyes), Mykel Denis (Bartender), Josh Walsh (Thin Garbage)

The Assistants © Team Effort Films

MESKADA (Red Flag) Producers, Jay Kubassek, Ron Stein, Jen Gatien, Michael Goodin, Shawn Rice; Executive Producers, Sig de Miguel, Stephen Vincent, Josh Sternfeld; Director/Screenplay, Josh Sternfeld; Photography, Daniel Sariano; Designer, Jack Ryan; Costumes, Amy Kramer; Music, Lee Curreri, Steve Weisberg; Editor, Phyllis K. Housen; Casting, Sig de Miguel, Stephen Vincent; an Aliquot Films presentation in association with Deer Jen & Four of a Kind productions; Color; Rated R; 98 minutes; Release date: December 3, 2010. **CAST**: Nick Stahl (Noah Cordin), Rachel Nichols (Leslie Spencer), Kellan Lutz (Eddie Arlinger), Jonathan Tucker (Shane Loakin), Grace Gummer (Nat Collins), Laura Benanti (Allison Connor), James McCaffrey (Billy Burns), Michael Cerveris (Terrence Lindy), Norman Reedus (Dennis Burrows), David Aaron Baker (DA Russ Winston), Michael Sirow (Daniel Hartfield), Kerry Bishé (Emily Cordin), Rebecca Henderson (Lyla Burrows), Kathy Searle (Jane Hartfield), Charlie Tahan (Keith Burrows), Max Antisell (Zack Cordin), J.D. Rosen (Carl Everson), Johnny Hopkins (Chris Ainslie), Anne Clare Gibbons-Brown (Town Meeting Protester), Michael Goodin (Jonathan), Rachel Heller (Anchorwoman), Jason Herman (Police Officer), Kirk LaSalle (Park Ranger), Douglas Mayer (Police Officer), Jonathan Whitcup (Commissioner Jerry Collum)

Nick Stahl in *Meskada* © Red Flag

AND EVERYTHING IS GOING FINE (IFC Films) Producers, Amy Hobby, Kathleen Russo, Joshua Blum; Director, Steven Soderbergh; Music, Forrest Gray; Editor, Susan Littenberg; Color; Not rated; 89 minutes; Release date: December 10, 2010. Documentary on monologist Spalding Gray.

Spalding Gray in *And Everything is Going Fine* © IFC Films

YOU WON'T MISS ME (Factory 25) Director, Ry Russo-Young; Screenplay, Ry Russo-Young, Stella Schnabel; Photography, Kitao Sakurai, Ku-Ling Siegel; Music, Will Bates; Editors, Gil Kofman, Ry Russo-Young; Black and white/color; Not rated; 81 minutes; Release date: December 10, 2010. **CAST**: Stella Schnabel (Shelly Brown), Simon O'Connor (Simon), Zachary Tucker (David), Borden Capalino (Jesse), Carlen Altman (Carlen), Rene Ricard (Allen B. Poor), Josephine Wheelwright (Rachel), David Anzuelo (Pablo Martinez), Gil Kofman (Don), Sarah Ball (Frank), Aaron Katz (Joe), Donald Eric Cumming (Eric), Barlow Jacobs (Sparks), Alison Wonderland (Lucy), Noah Kimerling (Dr. Schwartz)

Stella Schnabel in *You Won't Miss Me* © Factory 25

I AM SECRETLY AN IMPORTANT MAN (Independent) Executive Produces, Jay Van Joy, Lars Knudsen; Producers, Alex R. Johnson, Peter Sillen; Director, Peter Sillen; Photography, Peter Sillen; Editor, David Rivello; Color; Not rated; 87 minutes; Release date: December 15, 2010. Documentary on Seattle poet Steven J. Bernstein.

Steven J. Bernstein in *I am Secretly an Important Man*

SATAN HATES YOU (Glass Eye Pix) Producers, Larry Fessenden, Lisa Wisely, James Felix McKenney, Jeremiah Kipp; Director/Screenplay/Editor, James Felix McKenney; Photography, Eric Branco; Art Directors, Laree Love, Clifford Steele; Costumes, Chase Tyler; Color; Not rated; 94 minutes; Release date: December 17, 2010. **CAST**: Christine Spencer (Wendy), Don Wood (Marc), Angus Scrimm (Dr. Michael Gabriel), Reggie Bannister (Mickey), Michael Berryman (Mr. Harker), Christina Campanella (Holly), Jennifer Boutell (Karen), Debbie Rochon (Tina), Bradford Scobie (Scadlock), Larry Fessenden (Glumac), John Levene (The Reverend Bernie Shanks), Ruth Kulerman (Mrs. Harker), Pauley Perrette (Marie Flowers), D.W. Ferranti (Forrest Daniels), Turquoise Taylor Grant (Serena), Matt Huffman (Bob), Alan Rowe Kelly (Cokey), Brenda Cooney (Margaret), Jeb Berrier (Docto), Sean Reid (Toby), Max Brooks (Reporter), Benjamin Hugh Abel Forster (Herschel), Amy Chang (Kelly), Monique Dupree (Succubus), Michael Giannott (The Brain, Party Guest), Mick Lauer (The Voice), Daniel Mazikowski (George), Carmus Revel (Vincent), Graham Reznick (Don), Michael Vincent (Alfred), Michaela McPherson ("Duchess" Party Guest), Mike Funk ("The Masked Man" Party Guest)

Michael Berryman in
Satan Hates You
© Glass Eye Pix

AND SOON THE DARKNESS (Anchor Bay) Producers, Elizabeth Friedman, Deborah Marinoff Marcus, Chris Clark, Karen J. Lauder; Executive Producers, Ron Halpern, Flora Fernandez-Marendo, Marcus Ticotin; Director, Marcos Efron; Screenplay, Jennifer Derwingson, Marcos Efron; Based on the film directed by Robert Fuest and written by Brian Clemens and Terry Natino; Photography, Gabriel Beristain; Co-Producer, Amber Heard; Designer, Marcela Bazzano; Music, tomandandy; Editor, Todd E. Miller; Casting, Joanna Colbert, Rich Mento; an Anchor Bay Films, Abandon Pictures and Studio Canal presentation in association with Sandbar Pictures and Redrum Films; American-Argentine-French; Dolby; Technicolor; Rated R; 91 minutes; Release date: December 18, 2010. **CAST**: Amber Heard (Stephanie), Odette Yustman (Ellie), Karl Urban (Michael), Gia Mantegna (Camila), Adriana Barraza (Rosamaria), César Vianco (Calvo), Michel Noher (Chucho), Luis Sabatini (Luca), Javier Luna (Bar Owner), Andrea Verdun (Waitress), Hugo Miranda (Man in Bar), María Salomé Cari (Cleaning Woman), Jorge Booth (Hernán), Matías Paz Conde (Skinny Guy), Esteban Pastrana (Barman), Nicolas Dolensky (Cute Guy), Daniel Figuereido (Pedro), Walter Peña (Mechanic), Magdalena Peralta Antivero (Model)

OY VEY! MY SON IS GAY!! (New Generation Films) Producers, Evgeny Afineevsky, Svetlana Anufrieva, Igor Zektser, Rich Cowna; Director, Evgeny Afineevsky; Screenplay, Joseph Goldman, Martin Guigui, Evgeny Afineevsky; Photography, Peter N. Green; Designer, Vincent Defelice; Music, Eddie Grimberg, Lilo Fedida; Songs, Desmond Child; Editor, Michael Southworth; Casting, Donald Paul Pemrick, Dean E. Fonk; a Saint Juste International presentation of a New Generation Films and North by Northwest Entertainment production; Dolby; Color; Rated PG-13; 90 minutes; Release date: December 25, 2010. **CAST**: Lainie Kazan (Shirley Hirsch), Saul Rubinek (Martin Hirsch), Vincent Pastore (Carmine Ferraro), John Lloyd Young (Nelson Hirsch), Jai Rodriguez (Angelo Ferraro), Bruce Villanch (Max), Shelly Burch (Teresa Ferraro), Alexandra Mamaliger (Andrea Hirsch), Carmen Electra (Sybil Williams), Rachel Handler (Celeste), Tom Fridley (Nick), Karen-Eileen Gordon (Reporter), Heiko Obermöller (Nudelman), Scott Alan (Officer Colton), Stanislav "Slava" Medvedenko (Russian Host), Jerry Sciarrio (Dr. Herman), Jerry L. Buxbaum (Skinhead Leader), Brandon O'Neill (Lonnie), Phyllis Silver (Sophie), Pete Moroz (Photographer), Jeff Scarone (Jan), Patricia Henderson (Margaret), Eddie Levi Lee (Moisha), Leslie Lowe (Alice), Dillon McNaight (Emmitt), Khalil Beznaiguia (Bartender), Michael Adams (Lance), Shane Mabrey (Officer Fernandis), Fred Swink (Big Man), Danny Bental (Rabbi), Kyle Deluca (Anthony Ferraro)

Jai Rodriguez, John Lloyd Young in *Oy Vey! My Son is Gay!!*
© New Generation Films

FOREIGN FILMS A

2010 Releases / January 1–December 31

DAYBREAKERS

(LIONSGATE) Producers, Sean Furst, Bryan Furst, Chris Brown; Executive Producers, Jason Constantine, Peter Block; Co-Producer, Todd Fellman; Directors/Screenplay, The Spierig Brothers (Peter Spierig, Michael Spierig); Photography, Ben Nott; Designer/Costumes, George Liddle; Music, Christopher Gordon; Editor, Matt Villa; Visual Effects, Postmodern Sydney, Nauka Stusio and the Spierig Brothers; Special Make-up Effects Creator, Steve Boyle; Casting, Nikki Barrett; a Screen Australia presentation of a Lionsgate and Paradise Production in association with the Pacific Film and Television Commission and Furst Films; Australian-American; Dolby; HD Widescreen; Deluxe color; Rated R; 98 minutes; American release date: January 8, 2010

Willem Dafoe, Ethan Hawke, Claudia Karvan

CAST

Edward Dalton	**Ethan Hawke**
Lionel "Elvis Cormac"	**Willem Dafoe**
Audrey Bennett	**Claudia Karvan**
Frankie Dalton	**Michael Dorman**
Christopher Caruso	**Vince Colosimo**
Alison Bromley	**Isabel Lucas**
Charles Bromley	**Sam Neill**

Harriet Minto-Day (Lisa Barrett), Jay Laga'aia (Senator Turner), Damien Garvey (Senator Westlake), Sahaj Dumpleton (Homeless Vampire), Allan Todd (Businessman), Gabriella Di Labio (Businesswoman), Ben Siemer, Peter Welman (Police Officers), Callum McLean, Jarrad Pon, Victoria Williams, Zoe White, Aolani Roy (Vampire School Kids), Tiffany Lamb (News Reader), Renai Caruso (Coffee Shop Attendant), Chris Brown, Kirsten Cameron (Subway Commuters), Carl Rush (Al Walker), Paul Sonkkila (Gen. Williams), Todd Levi (Commissioner Turnbull), Wayne Smith (Inmate 4075B), Berni Chin, Kevin Zwierzchaczewski (Lab Technicians), Joel Spreadborough (Vampire Subject), Lisa Cunningham, Amanda Buchanan (Nurses), Jane Wallace (Bromley Assistant), Mungo McKay (Colin Briggs), Emma Randall (Ellie Landon), Charlotte Wilson (Joy Watkins), Rohan Smith (Police Officer in Car), Bryan Probets (Subsider in Kitchen), John Gibson (Det. Cosgrove), Robyn Moore (Forensic Investigator Simms), Troy Mackinder (Officer Hobbs), Christopher Kirby (Jarvis Bayom), Glen Martin (Coffee Buyer), Des Coroy (Businessman), Michelle Atkinson (Mother), David Vallon (Janitor), Candice Storey, Simon Burvill-Holmes, Anne Bennetts (Onlookers), Kellie Vella (Subsider in Garage), Scot McQade (Security Desk Officer), Jack Bradford (Security Guard #1), Jason Chin (Medic), Konrad Whitten (Weathered Human), Mark Finden (Young Vampire Cadet)

Isabel Lucas

In the year 2019, when the majority of the world's population has turned to vampirism, hunting down the few humans left, Edward Dalton realizes he must come up with a blood substitute before the fresh supplies run out.

Sam Neill © Lionsgate

Michael Dorman

Katie Jarvis, Michael Fassbender

Katie Jarvis © IFC Films

Kierston Wareing

FISH TANK

(IFC FILMS) Producers, Kees Kasander, Nick Laws; Executive Producers, Paul Trijbits, Christine Langan, David M. Thompson; Director/Screenplay, Andrea Arnold; Photography, Robbie Ryan; Designer, Helen Scott; Costumes, Jane Petrie; Music Supervisor, Liz Gallacher; Editor, Nicolas Chaudeurge; Casting, Jill Trevellick; a BBC Films and the UK Film Council in association with Limelight presentation; British, 2009; Dolby; Color; Not rated; 123 minutes; American release date: January 15, 2010

CAST

Mia	**Katie Jarvis**
Connor	**Michael Fassbender**
Joanne	**Kierston Wareing**
Tyler	**Rebecca Griffiths**
Billy	**Harry Treadaway**
Keira	**Sydney Mary Nash**
Tall Dancing Girl	**Charlotte Collins**
Keeley	**Sarah Bayes**
Keeley's Dad	**Grant Wild**
Tyler's Friends	**Carrie-Ann Savill, Toyin Ogidi**

Kirsty Smith, Chelsea Chase, Brooke Hobby (Dancing Girls), Syrus (Tennents the Dog), Alan Francis, Ben Francis (Free Runners), Jack Gordon, Jason Maza (Billy's Brothers), Michael Prior (Connor's Friend), Dave Hawley, Lisa Mahoney (Snogging Couple), Sarah Counsell (Social Worker), Sunanda Biswas, Gavin Cooper, Amir Saleem, Jody Schroeder, Fase Alzakwani, Stella McGowan, Mia Copas (Breakers), Tony Geary (Van Man), Hannah-Marie Keeble (Danton Road Girl), Joanna Horton (Kelly), Charlie Baker (Podium Girl), Peter Roue (Club DJ), Geoff McCracken (Club Man), Val King (Club Woman), Kishana Thomas, Raquel Thomas, Natasha Ilic, Maxine Brogan, Kirsty Page, Georgia Crane (Audition Girls)

A teenage girl longing to find some relief from her stifling existence in a cramped housing project, finds life further complicated when she develops strong feelings for her mother's new boyfriend.

Michael Fassbender

Ian McShane, Tom Wilkinson, Ray Winstone, John Hurt, Stephen Dillane

Melvil Poupaud, Joanne Whalley

44 INCH CHEST

(IMAGE ENTERTAINMENT) Producers, Richard Brown, Steve Golin; Executive Producers, Paul Green, Dave Morrison, Ray Winstone, Ian McShane, Louis Mellis, David Scinto, Paul Brett, Glenn Brown, Tim Smith, Stuart Ford; Co-Producer, Peter Heslop; Director, Malcolm Venville; Screenplay, Louis Mellis, David Scinto; Photography, Daniel Landin; Designer, John Stevenson; Costumes, Caroline Harris; Music, Angelo Badalamenti; Additional Music, 100 Suns; Editor, Rick Russell; Casting, Gary Davy; a Prescience Media 1 LLP, Omni Films LLP and Twilight Production & Entertainment Corporation presentation in association with IM Global of an Anonymous Content/Passenger production; British-Australian; Dolby; Color; Rated R; 95 minutes; American release date: January 15, 2010

CAST

Colin Diamond	**Ray Winstone**
Meredith	**Ian McShane**
Old Man Peanut	**John Hurt**
Archie	**Tom Wilkinson**
Liz Diamond	**Joanne Whalley**
Mal	**Stephen Dillane**
Loverboy	**Melvil Poupaud**
Dave Legeno	**Brighton Billy**
Tippi Gordon	**Steven Berkoff**
Biggie Walpole	**Andy de la Tour**
Archie's Mum	**Edna Doré**
Boy on Sofa	**Ramon Christian**

When his wife announces that she is leaving him for another man, Colin and his friends plot to kidnap and terrorize his spouse's lover.

Tom Wilkinson

Ray Winstone © Image Entertainment

THE GIRL ON THE TRAIN

(STRAND) a.k.a. *La fille du RER*; Producer, Saïd Ben Saïd; Director, André Techiné; Screenplay, André Techiné, Odile Barski, Jean-Marie Besset; Based on the play *RER* by Jean-Marie Besset; Photography, Julien Hirsch; Designer, Michèle Abbé-Vannier; Costumes, Radija Zeggaï; Music, Philip Sarde; Editor, Martine Giordano; a UGC Universal presentation of an SBS Films production, in co-production with France 2 Cinema, in association with UGC1, Sofica Soficinema 5, with the participation of Canal Plus, TPS Star, Le Centre Nationale de la Cinematographie; French, 2009; Dolby; Widescreen; Color; Not rated; 105 minutes; American release date: January 22, 2010

CAST
Jeanne	**Émilie Dequenne**
Samuel Bleistein	**Michel Blanc**
Louise	**Catherine Deneuve**
Alex	**Mathieu Demy**
Judith	**Ronit Elkabetz**
Franck	**Nicolas Duvauchelle**

Jérémy Quaegebeur (Nathan), Djibril Pavadé (Tom), Alain Cauchi (Marius), Amer Alwan (Luggage Salesman), Mélaine Leconte (Waitress), Ralphaëline Goupilleau (Officer), Arnaud Valois (Gabi), Bruno Mary (Hospital Police), Jessica Borio (Secretary), Benoît Soles (Young Lawyer), Shoshana Lok (Judith's Mother), Bertraned Soulier (Father of Little Girl), David Barbas (Police)

An aimless young woman, craving attention after her relationship with her boyfriend has disintegrated, fabricates a story about being attacked on the subway because of anti-Semitism.

Michel Blanc, Mathieu Demy, Ronit Elkabetz © Strand Releasing

Émilie Dequenne, Catherine Deneuve

Martha West, Jennifer Connelly © Newmarket

Paul Bettany

CREATION

(NEWMARKET) Producer, Jeremy Thomas; Co-Producer, Nick O'Hagan; Executive Producers, Peter Watson, Christina Yao, Janice Eymann, Jamie Laurenson, David M. Thompson; Director, Jon Amiel; Screenplay, John Collee; Story, Jon Amiel, John Collee, based on the book *Annie's Box* by Randal Keynes; Photography, Jess Hall; Designer, Laurence Dorman; Costumes, Louise Stjernsward; Music, Christopher Young; Editor, Melanie Oliver; Casting, Celestia Fox; a Jeremy Thomas presentation, in association with Ocean Pictures, BBC Films, HanWay Films, of a Recorded Picture Company production; British, 2009; Dolby; Super 35 Widescreen; Color; Rated PG-13; 108 minutes; American release date: January 22, 2010

CAST
Charles Darwin	**Paul Bettany**
Emma Darwin	**Jennifer Connelly**
Rev. Innes	**Jeremy Northam**
Thomas Huxley	**Toby Jones**
Joseph Hooker	**Benedict Cumberbatch**
Annie Darwin	**Martha West**
Parslow	**Jim Carter**

Ian Kelly (Captain Fitzroy), Guy Henry (Technician), Anabolena Rodriguez (Fuegia Basket), Paul Campbell (Boat Memory), Teresa Churcher (Mrs. Davies), Harrison Sansostri (Lenny Darwin), Zak Davies (Jemmy Button), Christopher Dunkin (George Darwin), Freya Parks (Etty Darwin), Gene Goodman (Franky Darwin), Ellie Haddington (Nanny Brodie), Richard Ridings (Thatcher), Ian Mercer (Goodman), Robert Glenister (Dr. Holland), Bill Patterson (Dr. Gully), Catherine Terris (Landlady), Ken Drury (Landlord), Nigel Bowden (Zoo Keeper)

The true story of how English naturalist Charles Darwin developed his revolutionary theory on evolution.

Simon Schwarz, Georg Friedrich © Music Box Films

Florian Lukas, Benno Fürmann

NORTH FACE

(MUSIC BOX FILMS) a.k.a. *Nordwand*; Producers, Danny Krausz, Boris Schönfelder, Rudolf Santschi, Benamin Herrmann; Director, Philipp Stölzl; Screenplay, Christoph Silber, Rupert Henning, Philipp Stölzl, Johannes Naber; Based on a script by Benedkit Roeskau; Photography, Kolja Brandt; Designer, Udo Kramer; Costumes, Birgit Hutter; Music, Christian Kolonovits; Editor, Sven Budelmann; Visual Effects Supervisors, Stefan Kessner, Max Stolzenberg; Casting, Anja Dihrberg; a Dor Film-West production; German-Austrian-Swiss, 2008; Dolby; Super 35 Widescreen; Color; Not rated; 126 minutes; American release date: January 29, 2010

CAST
Toni Kurz	**Benno Fürmann**
Andreas Hinterstoisser	**Florian Lukas**
Luise Fellner	**Johanna Wokalek**
Edi Rainer	**Georg Friedrich**
Willy Angerer	**Simon Schwarz**
Henry Arau	**Ulrich Tukur**
Emil Landauer	**Erwin Steinhauer**

Branko Samarovski (Albert von Allmen), Petra Morzé (Elisabeth Landauer), Hanspeter Müller (Schlunegger), Peter Zumstein (Adolf Rubi), Martin Schick (Christian Rubi), Erni Mangold (Grandmother Kurz), Johannes Thanheiser (Grandfather Kurz), Arnd Schimkat (Hotel Keeper), Klaus Ofczarek (Director), Martin Brambach (Editor Henze), Peter Faerber (Spiess), Traute Höss (Anna Fellner)

The true story of how two Germans and two Austrians attempted to scale the north face of the Eiger mountain in 1936.

AJAMI

(KINO LORBER) Producers, Mosh Danon, Thanassis Karathanos; Co-Producer, Talia Kleinhendler; Directors/Screenplay/Editors, Scandar Copti, Yaron Shani; Photography, Boaz Yehonatan Yacov; Designer, Yoav Sinai; Costumes, Rona Doron; an Inosan Prods. (Israel)/Twenty Twenty Vision Filmproduktion, ZDF – das kleine Fernsekspirel, Arte (Germany) production; Israeli-German, 2009; Dolby; Color; Not rated; 120 minutes; American release date: February 3, 2010

CAST
Nasri	**Fouad Habash**
Ilham	**Nisrine Rihan**
Shata	**Elias Saba**
Abu-Lias	**Youssef Sahwani**
Sido	**Abu George Shibli**
Malek	**Ibrahim Frege**

Scandar Copti (Binj), Shahir Kabaha (Omar), Hilal Kabob (Anan), Ranin Karim (Hadir), Eran Naim (Dando), Sigal Harel (Dando's Sister), Tamar Yerushalmi (Dando's Mother), Moshe Yerushalmi (Dando's Father)

Tensions mount within Ajami, a religiously mixed community of Muslims and Israelis in Tel Aviv.

This film received an Oscar nomination for foreign language film (2009).

Shahir Kabaha, Eran Naim © Kino Lorber

Fouad Habash, Shahir Kabaha, Eran Naim

Jonathan Rhys Meyers, Kasia Smutniak

Richard Durden, Jonathan Rhys Meyers

John Travolta © Lionsgate

John Travolta, Melissa Mars, Jonathan Rhys Meyers

FROM PARIS WITH LOVE

(LIONSGATE) Producer, India Osborne; Executive Producer, Virginie Besson-Silla; Co-Executive Producers, Anson Downes, Linda Rae Favila; Director, Pierre Morel; Screenplay, Adi Hasak; Based on a story by Luc Besson; Photography, Michel Abramowicz; Designer, Jacques Bufnoir; Costumes, Olivier Beriot, Corinne Bruand; Music, David Buckley; Editor, Frederic Thoraval; Stunts, Philippe Guegan; Special Effects Supervisor, Philippe Hubin; Casting, Swan Pham; a Luc Besson presentation of a EuropaCorp, M6 Films, Grive Prods. and Apipoulai Prods. co-production with the participation of Canal Plus, TPS Star and M6; French; Dolby; Super 35 Widescreen; Color; Rated R; 92 minutes; American release date: February 5, 2010

CAST

Charlie Wax	**John Travolta**
James Reese	**Jonathan Rhys Meyers**
Caroline	**Kasia Smutniak**
Ambassador Bennington	**Richard Durden**
M. Wong	**Bing Yin**
Nichole	**Amber Rose Revah**
Foreign Minister	**Eric Godon**
The Thug	**François Bredon**
Rashid	**Chems Eddine Dahmani**
The Pimp	**Sami Darr**
Chinese Punk	**Julien Hagnery**
Dir Yasin	**Mostéfa Stiti**

Rebecca Dayan (Foreign Minister's Aide), Michaël Vander-Meiren (Airport Security Official), Didier Constant (Customs Official), Alexandra Boyd (Head of the Delegation), Stephen Shagov, Mike Powers (Embassy Security), Faird Elouardi (Bearded Driver), Joaquim Almeria (Trench Coat #1), Melissa Mars (Wax's Hooker), Yin Hang (Asian Hooker "German"), David Gasman (German Tourist), Frédéric Chau (Chinese Maitre D), Tam Solo (Suicidal Pakistani)

Lowly Embassy employee James Reese gets more than he bargained for when his first official assignment teams him with volatile, trigger-happy agent Charlie Wax.

RED RIDING (THE RED RIDING TRILOGY)

(IFC FILMS) Producers, Andrew Eaton, Anita Overland, Wendy Brazington; Executive Producers, Liza Marshall, Hugo Heppell, Norman Merry; Screenplay, Tony Grisoni, based on the novels by David Peace; Casting, Nina Gold; British, 2009; Not rated; Combined running time: 302 minutes; American release date: February 5, 2010

1974:
Executive Producer, Norman Merry; Director, Julian Jarrold; Photography, Rob Hardy; Designer, Cristina Casali; Costumes, Natalie Ward; Music, Adrian Johnston; Editor, Andrew Hulme; Dolby; Color; 16mm; 104 minutes.

1980:
Executive Producer, Peter Hampden; Director, James Marsh; Photography, Igor Martinovic; Designer, Tomas Burton; Costumes, Charlotte Walter; Music, Dickon Hinchliffe; Editor, Jinx Godfrey; Dolby; Widescreen; Color; 95 minutes.

1983:
Executive Producer, Alasdair MacCuish; Director, Anand Tucker; Photography, David Higgs; Designer, Alison Dominitz; Costumes, Caroline Harris; Music, Barrington Pheloung; Editor, Trevor Waite; Dolby; Widescreen; HD; Color; 103 minutes.

Andrew Garfield © IFC Films

CAST

John Piggott (1983)	**Mark Addy**
John Dawson (1974 & 1983)	**Sean Bean**
Marjorie Dawson (1974)	**Cathryn Bradshaw**
Harold Angus (1980 & 1983)	**Jim Carter**
Bill Molloy (1974, 1980 & 1983)	**Warren Clarke**
Peter Hunter (1980)	**Paddy Considine**
Dick Alderman (1974, 1980 & 1983)	**Shaun Dooley**
Barry Gannon (1974)	**Anthony Flanagan**
Elizabeth Hall (1980)	**Julia Ford**
Eddie Dunford (1974, 1980 & 1983)	**Andrew Garfield**
Paula Garland (1984)	**Rebecca Hall**
Bob Craven (1974, 1980 & 1983)	**Sean Harris**
Bill Hadley (1974 & 1983)	**John Henshaw**
Leonard Cole (1974 & 1983)	**Gerard Kearns**
Jack Whitehead (1974 & 1980)	**Eddie Marsan**
Michel Myshkin (1974 & 1983)	**Daniel Mays**
The Ripper (1980)	**Joseph Mawle**
Tommy Douglas (1974, 1980 & 1983)	**Tony Mooney**
Maurice Jobson (1974, 1980 & 1983)	**David Morrissey**
Martin Laws (1974, 1980 & 1983)	**Peter Mullan**
Helen Marshall (1980)	**Maxine Peake**
John Nolan (1980 & 1983)	**Tony Pitts**
Eddie's Mum (1974)	**Mary Jo Randle**

Saskia Reeves (Mandy Wymer: 1983), Steve Robertson (Bob Fraser: 1974 & 1983), Cara Seymour (Mary Cole: 1974 & 1983), Lesley Sharp (Joan Hunter: 1980), Robert Sheehan (BJ: 1974, 1980 & 1983), Chris Walker (Jim Prentice: 1974, 1980 & 1983)

John Henshaw, David Morrissey, Andrew Garfield

Three separate films tell the interconnecting stories of the investigation of the disappearance of several young girls in Yorkshire. These three films originally aired on Britain's Channel 4 in March of 2009.

Sean Bean

Jakob Cedergren, Lene Maria Christensen

Jakob Cedergren © Oscilloscope

TERRIBLY HAPPY

(OSCILLOSCOPE) a.k.a. *Frygtelig lykkelig*; Producers, Thomas Gammeltoft, Tina Dalhoff; Director, Henrik Ruben Genz; Screenplay, Henrik Ruben Genz, Dunja Gry Jensen; Based on a novel by Erling Jepsen; Photography, Jorgen Johansson; Designer, Niels Sejer; Music, Kare Bjerko; Editor, Kasper Leick; a Fine and Mellow production, in co-production with DR, Nordisk Film, with support from the Danish Film Institute; Danish, 2008; Dolby; Widescreen; Color; Not rated; 100 minutes; American release date: February 5, 2010

CAST

Robert Hansen	**Jakob Cedergren**
Ingerlise Buhl	**Lene Maria Christensen**
Jørgen Buhl	**Kim Bodnia**
Dr. Zerleng	**Lars Brygmann**
Købmand Moos	**Anders Hove**

Jens Jørn Spottag (Politimeste), Henrik Lykkegaard (Priest), Bodil Jørgensen (Bartender), Peter Hesse Overgaard (Helmuth), Niels Skousen (Hansi), Lars Lunøe (Nissum), Sune Geertsen (Øko Tage), Mathilde Maack (Dorthe), Ahn Le (Mrs. Købmand Moos), Taina Anneli Berg (Lone "TP"), Puk Scharbau (Voice of Hannes Stemme), Kenn Bruun (Svend "Mangler Penge"), Mads Ole Langelund Larsen (Knud "Langfinger"), Joakim Schierning (Jannik), Bent Larsen (Betjent), Thorklid Demuth (Naboen)

Following a nervous breakdown police officer Robert Hansen is assigned to a small border town where the locals have their own way of dealing with justice.

EYES WIDE OPEN

(NEW AMERICAN VISION) a.k.a. *Einayim pkuhot*; Producers, Rafael Katz, Michael Ecklet, Isabelle Attal, David C. Barrat; Director, Haim Tabakman; Screenplay, Merav Doster; Photography, Axel Schneppat; Art Director, Avi Fahima; Costumes, Yam Brusilovsky; Music, Nathaniel Mechaly; Editor, Dov Steuer; a Pimpa Film prods. (Israel)/Riva Filmprodukttion (Germany)/Totally (France) production; Israeli-German-French, 2009; Dolby; Color; Not rated; 90 minutes; American release date: February 5, 2010

CAST

Aaron Fleischman	**Zohar Strauss**
Ezri	**Ran Danker**
Rivka Fleischman	**Tinkerbell**
Rabbi Vaisben	**Tzahi Grad**
Mordechai	**Isaac Sharry**

Avi Grayinik (Israel Fischer), Eva Zrihen-Attali (Sara), Haim Znati (Ultraorthodox Weirdo), Mati Atlas (Ex-Boy Friend), Iftacvh Ofir (Head of Yeshiva Student in the Butchery), Shafrira Zakai (Fischer's Mother), Lidor Daudi (Yakov), Tal Barak (David), Bar Kalfin (Shimon), Royi Zolicha (Nataniel), Eden Alon (Iftach)

A married butcher in Jerusalem's ultra-orthodox Jewish community must make a radical decision about his life when he falls passionately in love with a young male student.

Ran Danker, Zohar Strauss © New American Vision

Zohar Strauss, Ran Danker

THE GHOST WRITER

(SUMMIT) Producers, Roman Polanski, Robert Benmussa, Alain Sarde; Co-Producers, Timothy Burrill, Carl L. Woebcken, Christoph Fisser; Executive Producer, Henning Molfenter; Director, Roman Polanski; Screenplay, Robert Harris, Roman Polanski; Based on the novel *The Ghost* by Robert Harris; Photography, Pawel Edelman; Designer, Albrecht Konrad; Costumes, Dinah Collin; Music, Alexandre Desplat; Editor, Herve de Luze; Visual Effects Designer, Frederic Moreau; Casting, Fiona Weir; an R.P. Films, France 2 Cinema (France)/ Elfte Babelsberg Film (Germany) GmbH/Runteam III Ltd. (U.K.) production; French-German-British; Dolby; Panavision; Color; Rated PG-13; 128 minutes; American release date: February 19, 2010

Eli Wallach, Ewan McGregor

CAST

The Ghost	**Ewan McGregor**
Adam Lang	**Pierce Brosnan**
Amelia Bly	**Kim Cattrall**
Ruth Lang	**Olivia Williams**
Paul Emmett	**Tom Wilkinson**
Sidney Kroll	**Timothy Hutton**
John Maddox	**James Belushi**
Richard Rycart	**Robert Pugh**
Old Man	**Eli Wallach**
Rick Riccardelli	**Jon Bernthal**
Roy	**Tim Preece**
SKY TV Newsreader	**Anna Botting**
Stewardess	**Yvonne Tomlinson**
Taxi Driver	**Milton Welsh**
Barry	**Tim Faraday**
Lucy	**Marianne Graffam**
Alice	**Kate Copeland**
Dep	**Soogi Kang**
Duc	**Lee Hong Thay**
FBI Agent	**Jaymes Butler**
Hotel Receptionist	**Morgane Polanski**
Barman	**Glenn Conroy**
CNN Newscasters	**Robert Seeliger, Anne Wittman**
Stranger	**David Rintoul**
Journalist	**Clayton Nemrow**
Woman with Bullhorn	**Julia Kratz**
Josh	**Nyasha Hatendi**
Connie	**Daphne Alexander**
War Crime Prosecutor	**Angelique Fernandez**

Alister Mazzotti, John Keogh, Hans-Peter Sussner, Stuart Austen, Andy Güting, Robert Wallhöfer (Protection Officers), Michael S. Ruscheinsky (CNN Reporter), Mo Asumang (US Secretary of State), Sylke Ferber (Island Ferry Attendant), Desirée Erasmus (Nancy Emmett), Errol Shaker (Mainland Ferry Attendant), Errol Harewood, Talin Lopez (C.I.A. Agents on the Ferry), Joel Kirby (Motel Receptionist), Regine Hetschel (Diner Waitress), Jeff Burell (Frank), Daniel Sutton (Hatherton Stewart), Eben Young (FBI Agent)

Olivia Williams, Tom Wilkinson

Controversial former Prime Minister Adam Lang hires a ghost writer to revamp his memoirs and to replace the previous "ghost" who died under mysterious circumstances.

Timothy Hutton, James Belushi, Jon Bernthal © Summit

Kim Cattrall, Olivia Williams, Pierce Brosnan

Olivia Williams, Kim Cattrall

Ewan McGregor

Kim Cattrall, Ewan McGregor

Pierce Brosnan

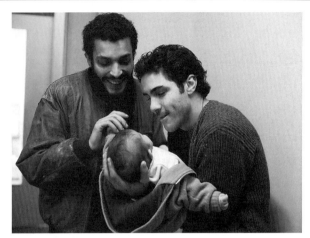

Adel Bencherif, Tahar Rahim

Reda Kateb, Tahar Rahim

Leïla Bekhti, Tahar Rahim © Sony Classics

A PROPHET

(SONY CLASSICS) a.k.a. *Un prophète*; Producers, Lauranne Bourrachot, Martine Cassinelli, Marco Cherqui; Director, Jacques Audiard; Screenplay, Thomas Bidegain, Jacques Audiard; Based on an original idea by Abdel Raouf Dafri, after an original screenplay by Abdel Raouf Dafri, Nicolas Peufaillit; Photography, Stephane Fontaine; Designer, Michel Barthelemy; Costumes, Virginie Montel; Music, Alexandre Desplat; Editor, Juliette Welfling; Casting, Richard Rousseau; a Why Not Prods., Page 114, Chic Films (France) presentation; French-Italian, 2009; Dolby; Super 35 Widescreen; Color; Rated R; 154 minutes; American release date: February 26, 2010

CAST

Malik El Djebena	**Tahar Rahim**
César Luciani	**Niels Arestrup**
Ryad	**Adel Bencherif**
Reyeb	**Hichem Yacoubi**
Jordi	**Reda Kateb**
Vcttori	**Jean-Philippe Ricci**
Prof	**Gilles Cohen**
Pilicci	**Antoine Basler**
Djamila	**Leïla Bekhti**

Pierre Leccia (Sampierro), Foued Nassah (Antaro), Jean-Emmanuel Pagni (Santi), Frédéric Graziani (Head of Detention), Slimane Dai (Lattrache), Rabah Loucif (Malik's Lawyer), Serge Onteniente (Sentecing Judge), Hervé Temime (Prosecutor), Taha Lemaizi (Hassan), Mohamed Makhtoumi (Tarik), Karim Leklou, Farid Larbi, Doula Niang (Muslims), Mamadou Minte (Latif), Guillaume Verdier (Michka), Mourad Frarema (Khalid), Zohra Benali (Mohamed's Mother), Sabar Kabbouchi , Eric Badoc, François De Courcelle (Social Workers), Nathanaël Maïni (Sampierro Guard), Charles Maestracci, Laurent Blanquet, Jean-Pierre Guinebert (Corsicans), Pascal Henault (Ceccaldi), Hakim Sid (Chemist), Mustapha Benstiti (Caillera), Alain Raymond, Didier de Backer, Patrick Mochen (Search Guards), Gilles Bellomi (Guard), Malaïc Mekeri (Belmont), Fadil Kadri (Inquiring Investigator), David Dupays (Police Commissioner), Arsène Benziane (The Bear), Kamel Ferrat (Lattrache's Chauffeur), Karim Traikia (Lattrache's Colleague), Cindy Danel (Sophie), Abdelaziz Mahtou (Mohamed Gazil), Alexandre de Seze (Head of the Court of Appeals), Kamel Saadi, Slim El Hedli, Farid Elouardi (Arabs), Veronica Ghio (Marbella's Blonde)

A petty criminal sentenced to six years in prison must quickly adapt to life behind bars as he comes between the warring prisoners.

2009 Oscar nominee for foreign language film.

Tahar Rahim, Niels Arestrup

MOTHER

(MAGNOLIA) a.k.a. *Madeo*; Producers, Seo Woo-sik, Park Tae-joon; Executive Producer, Miky Lee; Co-Executive Producers, Katharine Kim, Moon Yang-kwon; Director/Story, Bong Joon-ho; Screenplay, Park Eun-kyo, Bong Joon-ho; Photography, Hong Kyong-pyo; Designer, Ryu Seong-hie; Music, Lee Byeong-woo; Editor, Moon Sae-kyoung; a CJ Entertainment & Barunson presentation of a Barunson production; South Korean, 2009; Dolby; Widescreen; Color; Rated R; 129 minutes; American release date: March 12, 2010

Kim Hye-ja, Won Bin

CAST

Mother	**Kim Hye-ja**
Do-joon Yoon	**Won Bin**
Jin-tae	**Jin Goo**
Je-mun	**Jae-Moon Yoon**
Mi-sun	**Jun Mi-sun**
Ragman	**Lee Young-Suck**
Detective	**Song Sae-Beauk**
Ah-jung Moon	**Moon Hee-ra**
Mina	**Chun Woo-hee**
Chief	**Kim Byoung-Soon**
Mi-na	**Chun Woo-hee**
Ah-jeong's Grandma	**Kim Gin-goo**
Lawyer Kong Seok-ho	**Yum Ou-hyung**

A South Korean widow sets out to prove that her simple-minded son is innocent of the murder of a young girl.

Kim Hye-ja

Won Bin © Magnolia

Kim Hye-ja

THE GIRL WITH THE DRAGON TATTOO

(MUSIC BOX) a.k.a. *Män som hatar kvinnor* and *Millennium, Part 1: Men Who Hate Women*; Producer, Soren Staermose; Executive Producers, Anni Faurbye Fernandez, Peter Nadermann, Ole Sondberg, Mikael Wallen, Jon Mankell; Director, Niels Arden Oplev; Screenplay, Nikolaj Arcel, Rasmus Heisterberg; Based on the novel by Stieg Larsson; Photography, Eric Kress; Designer, Niels Sejer; Costumes, Cilla Rorby; Music, Jacob Groth; Editor, Anne Osterud; a Yellow Bird presentation and production, in association with SVT, ZDF, Nordisk Film; Swedish-Danish-Norwegian, 2009; Dolby; Super 35 Widescreen; Color; Not rated; 148 minutes; American release date: March 19, 2010

CAST

Mikael Blomkvist	**Michael Nyqvist**
Lisbeth Salander	**Noomi Rapace**
Erika Berger	**Lena Endre**
Martin Vanger	**Peter Haber**
Henrik Vanger	**Sven-Bertil Taube**
The Lawyer Nils Bjurman	**Peter Andersson**
Dirch Frode	**Ingvar Hirdwall**
Cecilia Vanger	**Marika Lagercrantz**
Gustav Morell	**Björn Granath**

Ewa Fröling (Harriet Vanger), Michalis Koutsogiannakis (Dragan Armanjskij), Annika Hallin (Annika Giannini), Sofia Ledarp (Malin Eriksson), Thomas Köhler ("Plague"), David Dencik (Janne Dahlman), Stefan Sauk (Hans-Erik Wennerström) Gösta Bredefeldt (Harald Vanger), Fredrik Ohlsson (Gunnar Brännlund), Jacob Ericksson (Christer Malm), Gunnel Lindblom (Isabella Vanger), Barbro Enberg (Older Lady), Reuben Sallmander (Enrico Giannini), Yasmine Garbi (Miriam Wu), Georgi Staykov (Alexander Zalachenko), Nina Norén (Agneta Salander), Emil Almén (Police Officer), Mikael Rahm (Editor), Willie Andréason (Birger Vanger), Lennart R. Svensson (Police Officer in Woods), Carl Oscar Törnros, Kalled Mustonnen, Henrik Knutsson (Huligans), Alexandra Pascalidou (TV Reporter), Theilla Bladh (Young Lisbeth), Julia Sporre (Young Harriet), Laura Lind (Jennie Giannini), Isabella Isacson (Monica Giannini), Magnus Stenius (Prison Guard Pliten), Louise Ryme (Receptionist), Pale Olofsson (Judge)

A disgraced investigative journalist teams up with a 24-year-old punkish hacker and private investigator to find out the truth behind the long-ago murder of the daughter of a powerful industrialist.

Lena Endre, Michael Nyqvist

Peter Andersson, Noomi Rapace

Noomi Rapace, Michael Nyqvist

Noomi Rapace © Music Box Films

Filippo Timi (3rd from left) © IFC Films

Filippo Timi, Giovanna Mezzogiorno

VINCERE

(IFC FILMS) Producer, Mario Gianani; Executive Producer, Olivia Sleiter; Co-Producers, Hengameh Panahi, Christian Baute; Director, Marco Bellocchio; Screenplay, Marco Bellocchio, Daniela Ceselli; Based on the book *The Secret Son of Il Duce: The Story of Albino Mussolini and His Mother Ida Dalser* by Alfredo Pieroni; Photography, Daniele Cipri; Designer, Marco Dentici; Costumes, Sergio Ballo; Music, Carlo Crivelli; Editor, Francesca Calvelli; Casting, Stefania De Santis; an Offside, 01 Distribution presentation of a Rai Cinema, Offside (Italy)/Celluloid Dreams (France) production, in collaboration with Istituto Luce; Italian-French, 2009; Dolby; Color/Black and white; Not rated; 122 minutes; American release date: March 19, 2010

CAST
Ida Dalser	**Giovanna Mezzogiorno**
Benito Mussolini	**Filippo Timi**
Riccardo Paicher	**Fausto Russo Alesi**
Rachele Mussolini	**Michela Cescon**
Pietro Fedele	**Pier Giorgio Bellocchio**
Doctor Cappelletti	**Corrado Invernizzi**
Giulio Bernardi	**Paolo Pierobon**

Bruno Cariello (The Judge), Francesca Picozza (Adelina), Simona Nobili (Mother Superior), Vanessa Scalera (Merciful Nun), Giovanna Mori (The German), Patrizia Bettini (The Singer), Silvia Ferretti (Red Shoes), Corinne Castelli (Tears), Fabrizio Costella (The Young Benito Albino)

The true story of Benito Mussolini's little-known first wife, Ida Dalser, and their offspring, as Mussolini's quest for power begins, on the eve of the First World War.

BLUEBEARD

(STRAND) a.k.a. *Barbe Bleue*; Producers, Jean-Francois Lepetit, Sylvette Frydman; Director/ Screenplay, Catherine Breillat; Photography, Vilko Filac; Designer, Olivier Jacquet; Costumes, Rose-Marie Melka; Editor, Pascale Chavance; a Flach Film, CB Films, Arte France presentation; French, 2009; Dolby; Color; HD; Not rated; 80 minutes; American release date: March 26, 2010

CAST
Barbe Bleue	**Dominique Thomas**
Marie-Catherine	**Lola Creton**
Anne	**Daphné Baïwir**
Catherine	**Marilou Lopes-Benites**
Marie-Anne	**Lola Giovannetti**
Mother Superior	**Farida Khelfa**
Mother	**Isabelle Lapouge**

Suzanne Foulquier (Bluebeard's Sister), Laure Papeyre (Ida), Adrien Ldeoux (Bluebeard's Emmissary), Jacques Triau (Bishop), Jean Bourlot (Coachman), Rose-Line Fric (Designer), Christian Urbain (Creditor), Jean-Pierre Beaussoleil (Usher), Martin Doutey (Rich Woman), Annick Orvain (Cook), Didier Brutus, David Lavallée, Jean-Philippe Lavallée (Musicians)

Badly in need of money, Marie-Catherine agrees to marry the enigmatic, wealthy Bluebeard whose previous wives seem to have disappeared without a trace.

Dominique Thomas, Lola Creton

Daphné Baïwir, Marilou Lopes-Benites © Strand Releasing

Amanda Seyfried, Julianne Moore

Amanda Seyfried, Liam Neeson

Liam Neeson, Julianne Moore, Max Thieriot, Nina Dobrev

Amanda Seyfried © Sony Classics

CHLOE

(SONY CLASSICS) Producers, Ivan Reitman, Joe Medjuck, Jeffrey Clifford; Executive Producers, Tom Pollock, Jason Reitman, Daniel Dubiecki, Olivier Courson, Ron Halpern,; Co-Producers, Jennifer Weiss, Simone Urdl; Director, Atom Egoyan; Screenplay, Erin Cressida Wilson; Based on the motion picture *Nathalie ...* , directed by Anne Fontaine, screenplay by Philippe Blasband, Anne Fontaine, Jacques Fieschi, François-Olivier Rousseau; Photography, Paul Sarossy; Designer, Philip Barker; Costumes, Debra Hanson; Music, Mychael Danna; Editor, Susan Shipton; Casting, John Buchan, Jason Knight (Canada), Joanna Colbert, Richard Mento (U.S.); a StudioCanal presentation of a Montecito Picture Company presentation; Canadian-French-American; Dolby; Deluxe color; Rated R; 96 minutes; American release date: March 26, 2010

CAST
Catherine Stewart	**Julianne Moore**
David Stewart	**Liam Neeson**
Chloe	**Amanda Seyfried**
Michael Stewart	**Max Thieriot**
Frank	**R.H. Thomson**
Anna	**Nina Dobrev**
Receptionist	**Mishu Vellani**
Bimsy	**Julie Khaner**
Alicia	**Laura DeCarteret**
Eliza	**Natalie Lisinska**
Trina	**Tiffany Knight**
Miranda	**Meghan Heffern**

Arlene Duncan (Party Guest), Kathy Maloney (Another Girl), Rosalba Martinni (Maria), Tamsen McDonough, Kathryn Kriitmaa (Waitresses), Adam Waxman (Bartender), Krysta Carter (Young Co-Ed), Severn Thompson (Nurse), Sarah Casselman (Orals Student), David Reale, Milton Barnes (Boys), Kyla Tingley (Woman behind Bar), Sean Orr, Paul Essiembre, Rod Wilson (Chloe's Clients)

Certain that her husband is having an affair, Catherine Stewart hires a prostitute to proposition him, with unexpected results.

THE ECLIPSE

(MAGNOLIA) Producer, Robert Walpole; Executive Producers, Paddy McDonald, Rebecca O'Flanagan; Co-Producers, Donal Geraghty, Cathleen Dore; Director, Conor McPherson; Screenplay, Conor McPherson, Billy Roche; Based on the story *Tales from Rain Water Pond* by Billy Roche; Photography, Ivan McCullough; Designer, Mark Geraghty; Costumes, Consolata Boyle; Music, Fionnuala Ni Chiosain; Editor, Emer Reynolds; Casting, Gail Stevens, Conagh Kearney; a Bord Scannán na hÉireann/ Irish Film Board/Radio Telefís Éireann and Broadcasting Commission of Ireland presentation of a Treasure Entertainment production; Irish, 2009; Dolby; Color; Rated R; 88 minutes; American release date: March 26, 2010

CAST
Michael Farr	**Ciarán Hinds**
Nicholas Holden	**Aidan Quinn**
Lena Morell	**Iben Hjejle**
Malachy McNeill	**Jim Norton**
Thomas Farr	**Eanna Hardwicke**
Sarah Farr	**Hannah Lynch**

Billy Roche (Jim Belton), Avian Egan (Eleanor Farr), Hilary O'Shaughnessy (TV Interviewer), Nuala Casey De Backer (Festival Organizer), Sarah Murphy (Festival Volunteer), Mia Quinn (Ghost Girl), Declan Nash (Man in Hotel Bar), Valerie Spelman (Jenny Sewell), Laurent Tavernier (Restaurant Waiter), Julie Kellegher (Hotel Waitress), Rosie O'Regan (Lantern Lady), Billy Ramsell, Mick Lynch, Donnacha Crowley, Grainne Gillis, Casper Christensen (Writers), Jean Van Sinderen-Law (Susan Holden), Ian Richard (Hand Artist), Sister Pauline, Sister Emmanuelle (Nuns)

Tormented over his wife's passing, an Irish widower agrees to serve as a driver for some of the authors gathering in his town for the literary festival and finds himself in the middle of a complicated triangle as a result.

Iben Hjejle, Ciarán Hinds © Magnolia

Aidan Quinn, Iben Hjejle

© NeoClassics

THE MISFORTUNATES

(NEOCLASSICS) a.k.a. *De helaasheid der dingen*; Producer, Dirk Impens; Co-Producers, Jeroen Beker, Frans van Gestel; Director, Felix van Groeningen; Screenplay, Christophe Drickx, Felix van Groeningen; Based on the novel *De helaasheid der dingen* by Dimitri Verhulst; Photography, Ruben Impens; Designer, Kurt Rigolle; Costumes, Ann Lauwerys; Music, Jef Neve; Editor, Nico Leunen; a Menuet (Belgium)/IDTV (Netherlands) presentation and production; Belgian-Flemish; Dolby SRD; Widescreen; Color/Black and white; HD-to-35mm; Not rated; 108 minutes; American release date: April 9, 2010

CAST
Little Gunther Strobbe	**Kenneth Vanbaeden**
Gunther Strobbe	**Valentijn Dhaenens**
Marcel "Celle" Strobbe	**Koen De Graeve**
Lowie "Petrol" Strobbe	**Wouter Hendrickx**
Pieter "Breejen" Strobbe	**Johan Heldenbergh**
Koen Strobbe	**Bert Haelvoet**
Meetje	**Gilda De Bal**
Aunt Rosie	**Natali Broods**

Pauline Grossen (Cousin Sylvie), Sofie Palmers (Gunther's Girlfriend), Guy Dermul (School Principal), Jos Geens (André), Robby Cleiren (Bailiff), Sara De Bosschere (Nele Fockedey), Wout Kelchtermans (Little Franky), Yves Degryse (Franky), Lynn Van Royen (Rostje), Ehsan Hemat (Sawasj), Sachli Gholamalizad (Mehti), Katrien Declercq (Gunther's Mother), Sten Van Gestel (Gunther's Son), Charlotte Vandermeersch (Rabbit)

13-year-old Gunther Strobbe finds himself in danger of falling into the same aimless lifestyle of his father and his three uncles who wallow in excessive drinking and fighting after moving back in with their mother.

THE WARLORDS

(MAGNET) a.k.a. *Tau ming chong*; Producers, Andre Morgan, Peter Ho-Sun Chan, Huang Jianxin; Executive Producers, Peter Lam, Kin Ngok, Andre Morgan, Han Sanping; Director, Peter Ho-Sun Chan; Collaborating Director, Raymond Yip; Screenplay, Xu Lan, Chun Tin Nam, Aubrey Lam; Photography, Arthur Wong; Designer, Yee Chung Man; Costumes, Yee Chung Man, Jessie Dai, Lee Pik-kwan; Music, Chan Kwong Wing, Peter Kam, Chatchai Pongprapaphan, Leon Ko; Action Director, Ching Siu Tung; Visual Effects Supervisor, Ng Yuen-fai; a Media Asia Films, Morgan & Chan Films (Hong Kong)/China Film Group, Warner China Film HG Corp. (China) presentation of a Morgan & Chan Films production; Hong Kong-Chinese, 2007; Dolby; Super 35 Widescreen; Color; Rated R; 113 minutes; American release date: April 2, 2010

Andy Lau, Jet Li, Takeshi Kaneshiro

CAST

General Pang Qingyun	**Jet Li**
Zhao Er-Hu	**Andy Lau**
Zhang Wen-Xiang	**Takeshi Kaneshiro**
Lian	**Jinglei Xu**
He Kui	**Zhaoqi Shi**
Zhang Shan	**Dong Dong Wang**
Jiang Da Ren	**Kuirong Wang**
Young Soldier	**Yachao Wang**
Cheng Da Ren	**Zongwan Wei**

During China's 14-year-long Taiping Rebellion, a general forms a close alliance with a pair of bandits.

© Magnet

Jinglei Xu

Jet Li

Claire van der Boom

David Roberts, Kieran Darcy-Smith

Anthony Hayes

THE SQUARE

(APPARITION) Producer, Louise Smith; Executive Producers, Nash Edgerton, Joel Edgerton, Matthew Dabner; Director, Nash Edgerton; Screenplay, Joel Edgerton, Matthew Dabner; Photography, Brad Shield; Designer, Elizabeth Mary Moore; Costumes, Sally Sharpe; Music, Francois Tetaz; Editors, Luke Doolan, Nash Edgerton; Casting, Kirsty McGregor; a Film Finance Corp. Australia presentation, in association with New South Wales Film and Television Office, of a Film Depot production, in association with Blue Tongue Films; Australian, 2008; Dolby; Super 35 Widescreen; Color; Rated R; 105 minutes; American release date: April 9, 2010

CAST

Ray Yale	**David Roberts**
Carla Smith	**Claire van der Boom**
Billy	**Joel Edgerton**
Greg Smith	**Anthony Hayes**
Martha Yale	**Lucy Bell**
Barney	**Kieran Darcy-Smith**
Leonard Long	**Brendan Donoghue**
Wendy	**Lisa Bailey**
Jake	**Peter Phelps**
Gil Hubbard	**Bill Hunter**

Paul Caesar (Sgt. Gary Miles), Mia Chippendale (Mia), Thomas Chippendale (Thomas), Amanda Crompton (Jenny), Maree D'Arcy (Greg's Mum), Luke Doolan, Greg Hatton (Greg's Mates), Tracey Furtchmann (Lauren), Paul He (Restaurant Manager), Damon Herriman (Eddie), Jacinta Hocking (News Reporter), Mia Irvin (Jake & Jenny's Baby), Eliza Logan (Rita Smith), Tony Lynch (Santa the Fireman), Hanna Mangan Lawrence (Lily), Julian Morrow (Dale), Peter Phelps (Jake), Stephen Weston (Charlie)

When Carla notices her husband has stashed away a mysterious bag of money, she plots with her lover Ray to steal the cash, a plan that goes seriously awry.

Joel Edgerton © Apparition

Guillermo Francella, Ricardo Darín

Javier Godino, Soledad Villamil, Ricardo Darín

Ricardo Darín, José Luis Gioia

Soledad Villamil, Ricardo Darín

Ricardo Darín

Soledad Villamil, Ricardo Darín

THE SECRET IN THEIR EYES

(SONY CLASSICS) a.k.a. *El Secreto de sus ojos*; Producers, Mariela Besuievsky, Juan José Campanella; Executive Producer, Gerardo Herrero, Vanessa Regone; Director/Editor, Juan José Campanella; Screenplay, Eduardo Sacheri, Juan José Campanella; Based on the novel by Eduardo Sacheri; Photography, Felix Monti; Designer, Marcelo Pont; Costumes, Cecilia Monti; Music, Jusid-Kauderer; Casting, Walter Ripell; a Tornasol (Spain)/Haddock, 100 Bares Producciones, El Secreto de Sus Ojos Aie (Argentina) production with the participation of TVE, Canal Plus; Spanish-Argentine, 2009; Dolby; HD Widescreen; Color; Rated R; 127 minutes; American release date: April 16, 2010

CAST

Benjamín Esposito	**Ricardo Darín**
Irene Menéndez Hastings	**Soledad Villamil**
Ricardo Morales	**Pablo Rago**
Isidoro Gómez	**Javier Godino**
Pablo Sandoval	**Guillermo Francella**
Inspector Báez	**José Luis Gioia**
Liliana Coloto	**Carla Quevedo**
Ordóñez	**Rudy Romano**
Juez Fortuna Lacalle	**Mario Alarcón**
Pinche Mariano	**Alejandro Abelenda**
Pinche Tino	**Sebastián Blanco**
Romano	**Mariano Argento**
Agent Cardozo	**Juan José Ortíz**
Molinari	**Kiko Cerone**
Sicora	**Fernando Pardo**

Maximilano Trento (Police Station Guard), Elvio Duvini (Juan Robles), David Di Napoli (Scribe Andretta), Sergio López Santana (Jacinto Cáceres), Pedro Kochdilian, Oscar Sánchez (Drunks), Gabriela Daniell (Alejandra Sandoval), Alicia Haydée Pennachi (Gomez's Mother), Darío Valenzuela (Foreman), Carlos Mele (Old Man in Latrine), Iván Sosa (Guardian in Questioning), Judith Buchalter (Irene's Mother), Héctor La Porta (Ministerio Bienestar, Social Civil Guard), Lilian Cuomo (Margarita), Alejandro Pérez (Thug)

Writing a novel based on a rape/murder case from twenty years ago he believes was never solved, Benjamin Esposito becomes determined to expose the guilty parties involved.

2009 Academy Award Winner for Best Foreign Language Film.

Ricardo Darín

Ricardo Darín © Sony Classics

© Producers Distribution Agency

Banksy

EXIT THROUGH THE GIFT SHOP

(PRODUCERS DISTRIBUTION AGENCY) Producer, Jaimie D'Cruz; Executive Producers, Holly Cushing, Zam Baring, James Gay-Rees; Director, Banksy; Photography, Thierry Guetta; Music, Geoff Barrow, Roni Size; Editors, Chris King, Tom Fulford; Narrator, Rhys Ifans; a Paranoid Pictures production; British-American; Color/Black and white; DV; Rated R; 86 minutes; Release date: April 16, 2010.

WITH
Banksy, Shepard Fairey, Thierry Guetta, Space Invader, André, Wendy Asher, Deborah Guetta, Jay Leno, Zeus, Christina Aguilera, Angelina Jolie, Jude Law, Brad Pitt

Documentary on guerrilla street artist Banksy.

OCEANS

(DISNEYNATURE) Producers, Jacques Perrin, Nicolas Mauvernay, Romain Le Grand; Executive Producer, Jake Eberts; DisneyNature Executive Producers, Don Hahn, Kirk Wise; Directors, Jacques Perrin, Jacques Cluzaud; Story, Jacques Perrin, Jacques Cluzaud, Stéphane Durand, François Sarano, Laurent Debas; Based on an idea by Jacques Perrin; English Language Narration Written by Michael Katims; Photography, Luc Drion, Luciano Tovoli, Philippe Ros, Laurent Charbonnier, Christophe Pottier, Eric Porjesson, Laurent Fleutoto, Thierry Thomas, Phlippe Garguli, Olivier Gueneau; Designer, Jean Rabasse; Music, Bruno Coulais; Editors, Vincent Schmitt, Catherine Mauchain; Narrator, Pierce Brosnan; a Galatée Films production, a Pathé, Notro Films, France 2 Cinéma, France 3 Cinéma co-production in association with Canal+ and TPS Star in association with Participant Media; French-Spanish-American-Swiss; Dolby; Super 35 Widescreen; Color; HD-to-35mm; Rated G; 84 minutes; American release date: April 22, 2010. Documentary which looks at the creatures of the oceans.

© Disneynature

HARRY BROWN

(SAMUEL GOLDWYN FILMS) Producers, Kris Thykier, Matthew Vaughn, Matthew Brown, Keith Bell; Executive Producers, Christos Michaels, Reno Antoniades, Tim Smith, Paul Brett, Steve Norris, Tim Haslam; Director, Daniel Barber; Screenplay, Gary Young; Photography, Martin Ruhe; Designer, Kave Quinn; Costumes, Jane Petrie; Music, Martin Phipps, Ruth Barrett; Editor, Joe Walker; Chief Makeup/Hair Designer, Jacqueline Fowler; Casting, Dan Hubbard; a MARV Partners and UK Film Council presentation in association with HanWay Films, Prescience and Framestore Features, of a MARV Partners production; British, 2009; Dolby; Super 35 Widescreen; Deluxe color; Rated R; 102 minutes; American release date: April 30, 2010

CAST
Harry Brown	**Michael Caine**
D.I. Alice Frampton	**Emily Mortimer**
D.I. Terry Hicock	**Charlie Creed Miles**
Leonard Attwell	**David Bradley**
S.I. Childs	**Iain Glen**
Stretch	**Sean Harris**
Noel Winters	**Ben Drew**
Marky	**Jack O'Connell**
Carl	**Jamie Downey**
Dean	**Lee Oakes**
Kenny	**Joseph Gilgun**
Sid Rourke	**Liam Cunningham**

Marva Alexander, Orla O'Rourke (Nurses), Liz Daniels (Kath), Marvin Stewart-Campbell (Neighbor), Lauretta Gavin (Neighbor's Wife), Rad Kaim (Doctor), Claire Hackett (Jean Winters), Ashley McGuire (Community WPC), Raza Jaffrey (Father Bracken), Martin Wilde (Boyfriend), Sian Mine (Girlfriend), Klariza Clayton (Unconscious Girl), Grace Vallorani (Linda), Sue Farr (Karaoke Singer), Forbes KB (Troy Martindale), Michelle Tate (Gang Member)

When his closest friend is senselessly killed by the marauding teens in his crumbling neighborhood, retiree Harry Brown becomes a vigilante in an effort to exact revenge and restore order.

Emily Mortimer, Michael Caine © Samuel Goldwyn Films

Jack O'Connell, Michael Caine

Sean Harris, Michael Caine

Michael Caine

BABIES

(FOCUS) a.k.a. *Bébé* (s); Producers, Alain Chabat, Amandine Billot, Christine Rouxel; Co-Executive Producer/Director/Adaptation/Photography, Thomas Balmès; Original Idea, Alain Chabat; Music, Bruno Coulais; Editor, Reynald Bertrand; French; Dolby; Color; Rated PG; 79 minutes; American release date: May 7, 2010. Documentary follows the lives of four babies from Monogolia, Namibia, San Francisco, and Tokyo, with Bayar, Hattie, Mari, Ponijao.

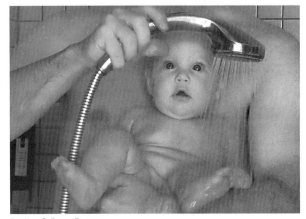

Ponijao © Focus Features

Mari

Hattie

Firat Ayverdi, Vincent Lindon

Vincent Lindon, Firat Ayverdi © Film Movement

WELCOME

(FILM MOVEMENT) Executive Producer, Christophe Rossignon; Director, Philippe Lioret; Screenplay, Philippe Lioret, Emmanuel Courcoi, Olivier Adam; Photography, Laurent Dailland; Music, Nicola Piovani; Editor, Andréa Sedlackova; Casting, Tatiana Vialle; Nord-Ouest Productions; French; Dolby; Not rated; 110 minutes; American release date: May 7, 2010

CAST
Simon Calmat	**Vincent Lindon**
Bilal	**Firat Ayverdi**
Marion Calmat	**Audrey Dana**
Mina	**Derya Ayverdi**
Bruno	**Thierry Godard**
Zoran	**Selim Akgül**
Koban	**Firat Celik**
Mirko	**Murat Subasi**

Olivier Rabourdin (Police Lieutenant), Yannick Renier (Alain), Mouafaq Rushdie (Mina's Father), Behi Djanati Ataï (Mina's Mother), Patrick Ligardes (Simon's Neighbor), Jean Pol Brissart (Judge), Blandine Pélissier (Family Court Judge)

Prevented from entering England to reunite with his girlfriend, Kurdish refugee Bilal decides to train at a local swimming pool in Calais so that he can swim across the English Channel.

Eric Cantona, Steve Evets

© IFC Films

Steve Evets (center)

LOOKING FOR ERIC

(IFC FILMS) Producer, Rebecca O'Brien; Executive Producers, Eric Cantona, Pascal Caucheteux, Vincent Maraval; Line Producer, Tim Cole; Director, Ken Loach; Screenplay, Paul Laverty; Photography, Barry Ackroyd; Designer, Fergus Clegg; Costumes, Sarah Ryan; Music, George Fenton; Editor, Jonathan Morris; Casting, Kathleen Crawford; a Sixteen Films, Canto Bros. Productions, Why Not Productions, Wild Bunch Film, Film 4, Icon Film Distribution, North West, Vision Media, France 2 Cinéma, France 2 Canal+, Ciné Cinéma, Sofica UGC 1, Diaphana Distribution, BIM Distribuzione, Les Films du Fleuve, RTBF Television Belge, La Region Wallonnee Tax Shelter of the Belgian Federal Government, Cinéart, Tornasol Films and Alta Produccion presentation; British-French-Italian-Belgian-Spanish, 2009; Dolby; Color; Not rated; 117 minutes; American release date: May 14, 2010

CAST

Eric Bishop	**Steve Evets**
Himself	**Eric Cantona**
Lily	**Stephanie Bishop**
Ryan	**Gerard Kearns**
Jess	**Stephan Gumbs**
Sam	**Lucy-Jo Hudson**
Daisy	**Cole and Dylan Williams**
Young Eric	**Matthew McNulty**
Young Lily	**Laura Ainsworth**
Eric's Father	**Maxton Beesley**
Ryan's Girlfriend	**Kelly Bowland**
Nurse	**Julie Brown**

John Henshaw (Meatballs), Justin Moorhouse (Spleen), Des Sharples (Jack), Greg Cook (Monk), Mick Ferry (Judge), Smug Roberts (Smug), Johnny Travis (Travis), Steve Marsh (Zac), Cleveland Campbell (Buz), Ryan Pope (Fenner), Omar Abdul, Adam Beresford, Ciaran Clancy, Steve Cook, Sheila Diamond, Marvin Gilbert, Ben Jackson, Wendy Kennedy, Dwyer Lynch, Jake Manning, Tom Meredith, Eddie Riley, Conor Saunders, Venn Tracey, Guy Wills (The Emperors of Rhythm)

Eric Bishop, a postman whose life is unraveling after his wife has left him, turns to his hero, footballer Eric Cantona, for advice.

Steve Evets, Eric Cantona

Barbara Mori, Hrithik Roshan

Barbara Mori © Reliance Big Pictures

KITES

(RELIANCE BIG PICTURES) Producer/Story, Rakesh Roshan; Executive Producer, Shammi Saini; Co-Producer, Sunaina Roshan; Director, Anurag Basu; Screenplay, Anurag Basu, Robin Bhatt, Akarsh Khurana; Story, Photography, Ayananka Bose; Designer, Rajat Poddar; Costumes, Suneet Varma; Music, Graeme Revell; Songs, Rajesh Roshan, Nasir Faraaz, Asif Ali Beg; Choreographers, Flexy Stu, Sandeep Soparrkar; Stunts, Spiro Razatos; a FilmKraft Prods. Production; Indian; Dolby; Widescreen; Color; Not rated; 133 minutes (also shown in 90 minute Remix version); American release date: May 21, 2010

CAST
Natasha	**Barbara Mori**
Jay Ray	**Hrithik Roshan**
Gina B. Grover	**Kangana Ranaut**
Bob Grover	**Kabir Bedi**
Tony B. Grover	**Nicholas Brown**
Robin	**Anand Tiwari**
Jamaal	**Yuri Suri**

Luce Rains, Clark Sanchez (Bounty Hunters), Steven Michael Quezada (Cop), Ivan Brutsche (Border Patrol), Dave Colon (Mexican Police), Jamie Haqqani (Police Officer), Ronald Hamilton (Railyard Worker), Madhuri Bhatia (Mrs. B. Grover), Ivan Brutsche (Border Patrol), Bob Brahamabhatt (Satpal), Shaun Webb (Officer Freeman)

A pair of Las Vegas hustlers tries to wheel and deal their way into the big time.

FATHER OF MY CHILDREN

(IFC) a.k.a. *Le père de mes enfants*; Producers, Philippe Martin, David Thion, Oliver Damian; Director/Screenplay, Mia Hansen-Løve; Photography, Pascal Auffray; Set Designer, Mathieu Menut; Costumes, Bethsabee Deryfus; Editor, Marion Monnier; Casting, Elsa Pharaon; a Les films Pelleas production, in co-production with 27 Films Poduction, Arte France Cinema; French, 2009; Color; Not rated; 110 minutes; American release date: May 21, 2010

CAST
Grégoire Canvel	**Louis-Do de Lencquesaing**
Sylvia Canvel	**Chiara Caselli**
Clémence Canvel	**Alice de Lencquesaing**
Valentine Canvel	**Alice Gautier**
Billie Canvel	**Manelle Driss**
Serge	**Eric Elmosnino**

Sandrine Dumas (Valérie), Dominique Frot (Bérénice), Antoine Mathieu (Frédéric), Elsa Pharaon (Colette), Olivia Ross (Anja), Djamshed Usmonov (Kova Asimov), Cori Shim (Ji Hong), Igor Hansen-Løve (Arthur Malkavian), Magne Brekke (Stig Janson)

Indie film producer Gregoire Canvel's high-pressure lifestyle, already taking its toll on his neglected wife and children, leads to a devastating turn of events when Gregoire finds his company facing financial ruin.

Alice Gautier, Chiara Caselli

Louis-Do de Lencquesaing, Alice de Lencquesaing © IFC Films

André Dussollier, Nicholas Marié

Dany Boon, Julie Ferrier

Dominique Pinon

MICMACS

(SONY CLASSICS) a.k.a. *Micmacs à tire-larigot*; Producers, Frederic Brillion, Gilles Legrand, Jean-Pierre Jeunet; Director, Jean-Pierre Jeunet; Screenplay, Jean-Pierre Jeunet, Guillaume Laurant; Dialogues, Guillaume Laurant; Photography, Tetsuo Nagata; Art Director, Aline Bonetto; Costumes, Madeline Fontaine; Music, Raphaël Beau; Editor, Herve Schneid; Digital Special Effects, Alain Carsoux; Special Effects, Les Versaillais; Casting, Pierre-Jacques Benichou; Stunts, Patrick Cauderlier, Jean-Claude Lagniez; an Epithète Films, Tapioca Films & Warner Bros. Entertainment France presentation; French, 2009; Dolby; Super 35 Widescreen; Color; Rated R; 104 minutes; American release date: May 28, 2010

CAST

Bazil	**Dany Boon**
Nicolas Thibault de Fenouillet	**André Dussollier**
François Marconi	**Nicolas Marié**
Slammer	**Jean-Pierre Marielle**
Mama Chow	**Yolande Moreau**
Elastic Girl	**Julie Ferrier**
Remington	**Omar Sy**
Buster	**Dominique Pinon**
Tiny Pete	**Michel Cremades**
Calculator	**Marie-Julie Baup**
Night Watchman	**Urbain Cancelier**
Gerbaud	**Patrick Paroux**
Libarski	**Jean-Pierre Becker**
Mateo	**Stéphane Butet**
Gravier	**Philippe Girard**

Doudou Masta (Head of the Rebels), Eric Naggar (Marconi's Chauffeur), Arsène Mosca (Serge, Video Store), Manon Le Moal (Lola), Félicité N'Gijol (Mrs. Cisse), Bernard Bastereaud (Her Husband), Tony Gaultier (The Horny Technician), Stéphanie Gesnel (His Partner), Noé Boon (Young Brazil)

After he is wounded by a stray bullet, former videostore clerk Bazil joins forces with an eclectic group of misfits to destroy the arms dealers responsible for his injury.

Dany Boon, Marie-Julie Baup, Omar Sy © Sony Classics

AGORA

(NEWMARKET) Producers, Fernando Bovaira, Alvaro Augustin; Executive Producers, Simon de Santiago, Jaime Ortiz de Artinano; Director, Alejandro Amenábar; Screenplay, Alejandro Amenábar, Mateo Gil; Photography, Xavi Gimenez; Designer, Guy Hendrix Dyas; Costumes, Gabriella Pescucci; Music, Dario Marianelli; Editor, Nacho Ruiz Capillas; Visual Effects, El Ranchito Visual Effects; Casting, Jina Jay; a Mod Producciones, Himenoptero and Telecino Cinema production with the participation of Canal+Espana; Spanish, 2009; Dolby; Arri Widescreen; Deluxe color; Not rated; 127 minutes; American release date: May 28, 2010

Oscar Isaac, Rachel Weisz

CAST
Hypatia	**Rachel Weisz**
Davus	**Max Minghella**
Oreste	**Oscar Isaac**
Ammonius	**Ashraf Barhom**
Synesius	**Rupert Evans**
Theon	**Michael Lonsdale**
Aspasius	**Homayoun Ershadi**
Cyril	**Sami Samir**
Olympius	**Richard Durden**
Theophiulus	**Manuel Cauchi**
Medorus	**Oshri Cohen**

Harry Borg (Prefect Evagrius), Charles Thake (Hesiquius), Yousef "Joe" Sweid (Peter), Andre Agius (Boy), Paul Barnes (Dignitary), Christopher Dingli (Student), Clint Dyer (Hierax), Wesley Ellul (Guard), Angele Galea (Chairtion), George Harris (Heladius), Jordan Kiziuk (Hypatia's Disciple), Ray Mangion (Crier via Canopica), Alan Meadows (Rabbi), Samuel Montague (Theatre Crier), Alan Paris (Bodyguard), Christopher Raikes (Hellenistic Man), Amber Rose Revah (Sidonia), Charles Sammut (Philospopher), Nikovich Sammut (Roman Officer)

The true story of 4th Century astronomer and mathematician Hypatia and her efforts to save the Alexandria library from destruction.

Rachel Weisz, Max Minghella

Rachel Weisz, Michael Lonsdale © Newmarket

Max Minghella

Sandrine Kiberlain, Vincent Lindon

Sandrine Kiberlain
© Lorber Films

MADEMOISELLE CHAMBON

(LORBER) Producers, Milena Poylo, Gilles Sacuto; Director, Stéphane Brizé; Screenplay, Stéphane Brizé, Florence Vignon; Based on the novel by Eric Holder; Photography, Antoine Héberlé; Designer, Valerie Saradijan; Costumes, Anne Dunsford; Music, Ange Ghinozzi; Editor, Anne Klotz; Casting, Brigitte Moidon; a TS Prods., F Comme Film, Arte France Cinema production, in association with Rezo Films, La Sofica Soficinema 4; French, 2009; Dolby; Panavision; Color; Not rated; 101 minutes; American release date: May 28, 2010

CAST
Jean	**Vincent Lindon**
Véronique Chambon	**Sandrine Kiberlain**
Anne Marie	**Aure Atika**
The Father	**Jean-Marc Thibault**
Jérémy	**Arthur Le Houérou**
Jean's Workmates	**Bruno Lochet, Abdallah Moundy**
Funeral Director	**Anne Houdy**
School Principal	**Michèle Goddet**
Véronique's Mother	**Geneviève Mnich**
Jean's Sisters	**Florence Hautier,**
	Jocelyne Monier
Brother-in-Law	**Jean-François Malet**

A married mason finds himself unexpectedly attracted to his son's teacher.

SPRING FEVER

(STRAND) a.k.a. *Chunfeng chenzuide yewan*; Producers, Nai An, Sylvain Busztejn; Co-Producer/Director, Lou Ye; Screenplay, Mei Feng; Photography, Zeng Jian; Designer, Peng Shaoying; Music, Peyman Yazdanian; Editors, Robin Weng, Zeng Jian, Florence Bresson; a Dream Factory HK, Rosem Films production; Hong Kong-French, 2009; Dolby; Color; DV-to-35mm; Not rated; 116 minutes; American release date: June 4, 2010

CAST
Jiang Cheng	**Qin Hao**
Luo Haitao	**Chen Sicheng**
Li Jing	**Tan Zhuo**
Wang Ping	**Wu Wei**
Lin Xue	**Jiang Jiaqi**
Boss	**Zhang Songwen**
Boss of the Restaurant	**Li Jintao**
Little Dancing Girl	**Wang Yue**

Hired by Wang Ping's wife to investigate his affair with another man, a private detective finds himself drawn into the relationship in unexpected ways.

Chen Sicheng, Wu Wei

Chen Sicheng, Qin Hao © Strand Releasing

Delphine Chaneac, Sarah Polley

Delphine Chaneac, Sarah Polley

Sarah Polley, Adrien Brody

Sarah Polley, Adrien Brody © Warner Bros.

SPLICE

(WARNER BROS.) Producer, Steve Hoban; Executive Producers, Guillermo del Toro, Don Murphy, Susan Montford, Christophe Riandee, Yves Chevalier, Sidonie Dumas; Director, Vincenzo Natali; Screenplay, Vincenzo Natali, Antoinette Terry Bryant, Douglas Taylor; Photography, Tetsuo Nagata; Designer, Todd Cherniawsky; Costumes, Alex Kavanaugh; Music, Cyrille Aufort; Editor, Michele Conroy; Visual Effects Supervisor, Robert Munroe; Visual Effects, Core Digital Pictures, BUF, Mac Guff; Special Makeup and Creature Effects, Howard Berger, Gregory Nicotero; Stunts, Plato Fountidakis, Paul Rapovski; Casting, John Buchan, Jason Knight, John Papsidera, Constance Demontoy; a Copperheart Entertainment (Canada)/ Gaumont (France) production, with the participation of Telefilm Canada, Ontario Media Development Corp.; Canadian-French; Dolby; Super 35 Widescreen; Deluxe color; Rated R; 107 minutes; American release date: June 4, 2010

CAST

Clive Nicoli	**Adrien Brody**
Elsa Kas	**Sarah Polley**
Dren	**Delphine Chaneac**
Gavin Nicoli	**Brandon McGibbon**
Joan Chorot	**Simona Maicanescu**
William Barlow	**David Hewlett**
Child Dren	**Abigail Chu**

Genetic researchers Clive Nicoli and Elsa Kas manage to create a human-animal embryo that rapidly grows into a female humanoid with amazing powers and physical abilities.

Colin Farrell, Stephen Rea

Colin Farrell © Magnolia

Colin Farrell, Alison Barry, Alicja Bachleda

Alicja Bachleda, Colin Farrell

ONDINE

(MAGNOLIA) Producers, Neil Jordan, James Flynn, Ben Browning; Executive Producers, Michael Maher, Peter Rawlinson, Ned Dowd; Line Producer, Karen Richards; Director/Screenplay, Neil Jordan; Photography, Christopher Doyle; Designer, Anna Rackard; Costumes, Eimer Ní Mhaoldomhnaigh; Music, Kjartan Sveinsson; Music Supervisors, Becky Bentham, Abbie Lister; Casting, Franke Moiselle, Nuala Moiselle, Susie Figgis; a Wayfare Entertainment presentation with the participation of Bord Scannán na Héireann/Irish Film Board of an Octagon Films/Wayfare Entertainment/Little Wave Productions production; Irish; Dolby; Color; Rated PG-13; 111 minutes; American release date: June 4, 2010

CAST
Syracuse	**Colin Farrell**
Ondine	**Alicja Bachleda**
Annie	**Alison Barry**
Alex	**Tony Curran**
Vladic	**Emil Hostina**
Maura	**Dervla Kirwan**
Priest	**Stephen Rea**
Kettle, Vladic's Henchman	**Don Wycherley**
Librarian	**Norma Sheahan**
Eion	**Conor Power**
Katie	**Olywn Hanley**

Marion O'Dwyer (Nurse, Dialysis), Mary O'Shea (Fish Co Op Worker), Gemma Reeves (Tracy, Draper's Shop), Mark Doherty (Fishery Board Man #2), Peter Gowen (Dr. Hannon), Helen Norton (Nurse), Gertrude Montgomery (Ban Garda), Reese O'Shea (Paudie), Sharon Shannon (Funeral Musician), Dashiel Jordan (Kid on Bike), Brendan McCormack (George, Fishery Board)

A fisherman finds a woman entangled in his fishing net and begins to suspect that she might be a mystical creature of the sea.

COCO CHANEL & IGOR STRAVINSKY

(SONY CLASSICS) Producers, Claudie Ossard, Chris Bolzli; Co-Producer, Veronika Zonabend; Director, Jan Kounen; Screenplay, Chris Greenhalgh; Adapted by Carlo de Boutiny, Jan Kounen from the novel *Coco & Igor* by Chris Greenhalgh; Photography, David Ungaro; Designer, Marie-Hélène Sulmoni; Costumes, Chattoune & Fab; Music, Gabriel Yared; Editor, Anny Danché; Choreographer, Dominique Brun; Casting, Gigi Akoka; a Eurowide Film Production presentation in association with Hexagon Pictures; French-Russian, 2009; Dolby; Color/Black and white; Rated R; 119 minutes; American release date: June 11, 2010

Anna Mouglalis

CAST

Igor Stravinsky	**Mads Mikkelsen**
Coco Chanel	**Anna Mouglalis**
Catherine Stravinsky	**Elena Morozova**
Misia Sert	**Natacha Lindinger**
Sergeï Diaghilev	**Grigori Manoukov**
Grand Duke Dimitri	**Rasha Bukvic**
Ernest Beaux	**Nicolas Vaude**
Arthur "Boy" Capel	**Anatole Taubman**
The Doctor	**Eric Desmarestz**
Milène Stravinsky	**Clara Guelblum**
Théodore Stravinsky	**Maxime Danielou**

Sophie Hasson (Ludmilla Stravinsky), Nikita Ponomarenko (Soulima Stravinsky), Catherine Davenier (Marie), Olivier Claverie (Joseph), Marek Kossakowski (Vaslav Nijinsky), Jérôme Pillement (Pierre Monteux), Anton Yakovlev (Anton), Irina Vavilova (Governess), Julie Farenc Deramond (Julie), Emy Lévy, Sarah Jérôme (Shop Girls), Tina Sportolaro (Secretary), Michel Ruhl (Baron), Pierre Chydivar, Agnès Vikouloff, Sacha Vikouloff (Russian Musicians), Jean-David Baschung (Doctor), Marek Tomaszewski (Pianist), David Tamaszewski (First Violin), Cyril Accorsi, Matthieu Bajolet, Caroline Baudouin, Laura Biasse, Barbara Caillieu, Marie-Laure Caradec, Damien Dreux, Sophie Gérard, Patrick Harley, Inès Hernandez, Anne Laurent, Thibaud Le Maguer, Anne Lenglet, Olivier Normand, Florent Otello, Edouard Pelleray, Judith Perron, Pascal Queneau, Enora Rivere, Julie Salgues, Jonathan Schatz, Wu Zheng (Dancers, *Le Sacre du printemps*)

Anna Mouglalis © Sony Classics

Left a penniless refugee in Paris, composer Igor Stravinsky is taken in by designer Coco Chanel with whom he begins a passionate affair.

Mads Mikkelsen, Anna Mouglalis

Mads Mikkelsen, Anna Mouglalis

Tilda Swinton, Alba Rohrwacher

Tilda Swinton, Mattia Zaccaro

Marisa Berenson, Pippo Delbono, Tilda Swinton, Alba Rohrwacher,
Mattia Zaccaro, Flavio Parenti, Maria Paiato

I AM LOVE

(MAGNOLIA) a.k.a. *Io sono l'amore*; Producers, Luca Guadagnino, Tilda Sinwton, Alessandro Usai, Francesco Melzi D'eril, Marco Morabito, Massimiliano Violante; Associate Producers, Candice Zaccagnino, Silvia Venturini Fendi, Carlo Antonelli; Line Producer, Minnie Ferrara; Director/Story, Luca Guadagnino; Screenplay, Barbara Alberti, Ivan Cotroneo, Walter Fasano, Luca Guadagnino; Photography, Yorick Le Saux; Designer, Francesca di Mottola; Costumes, Antonella Cannarozzi; Music, John Adams; Editor, Walter Fasano; Casting, Francesco Vedovati, Jorgelina Depetris; a First Sun and Mikado Film presentation; Italian; Dolby; Technicolor; Rated R; 119 minutes; American release date: June 18, 2010

CAST

Emma Recchi	**Tilda Swinton**
Edoardo Recchi Jr.	**Flavio Parenti**
Antonio Biscaglia	**Edoardo Gabbriellini**
Elisabetta Recchi	**Alba Rohrwacher**
Tancredi Recchi	**Pippo Delbono**
Eva Ugolini	**Diane Fleri**
Ida Marangon	**Maria Paiato**
Allegra Recchi	**Marisa Berenson**
Mr. Kubelkian	**Waris Ahluwalia**
Edoardo Recchi Sr.	**Gabriele Ferzetti**
Delfina	**Martina Codecasa**
Gianluca Recchi	**Mattia Zaccaro**
Dominique	**Elena Pavli**

The matriarch of a well-to-do Milanese family disrupts her life when she falls passionately in love with the young chef with whom her son plans to open a restaurant.

This film received an Oscar nomination for costume design.

Tilda Swinton © Magnolia

Agnès Jaoui, Jamel Debbouze, Jean-Pierre Bacri

Jean-Pierre Bacri, Pascale Arbillot

Pascale Arbillot

LET IT RAIN

(IFC FILMS) a.k.a. *Parlez-moi de la pluie*; Producers, Jean-Philippe Andraca, Christian Berard; Director, Agnès Jaoui; Screenplay, Agnès Jaoui, Jean-Pierre Bacri; Photography, David Quesemand; Desinger, Christian Marti; Costumes, Eve-Marie Arnault; Editor, Francois Gediger; Casting, Brigitte Moidon; a Les Films A4, StudioCanal, France 2 Cinema production; French, 2008; Dolby; Panavision; Color; Not rated; 96 minutes; American release date: June 18, 2010

CAST

Agathe Villanova	**Agnès Jaoui**
Michel Ronsard	**Jean-Pierre Bacri**
Karim	**Jamel Debbouze**
Florence	**Pascale Arbillot**
Stéphane	**Guillaume de Tonquedec**
Antoine	**Frédéric Pierrot**
Mimouna	**Mimouna Hadji**
Aurélie	**Florence Loiret-Caille**
Séverine	**Anne Werner**
Guillaume	**Laurent Jarroir**

Jean-Claude Baudracco (Ernest, Peasant #1), Didier Luc Palun (Peasant #2), Marc Betton (The Producer), Bernard Nissille (Man at Christening), Alain Bouscary (Waiter), Candide Sanchez (The Priest), Danièle Douet (Rodolphe's Mother), Sacha Rousselet, Sonam Roussel, Morgane Kerhousse (Florence as a Child), Alexandre Dobrowolski (Rodolphe), Victoria Cohen (Agathe as a Child), Myriam Arab (Young Mimouna), Isabelle Devaux (Mrs. Villanova), Antoine Garceau (Mr. Villanova), Jacques Rebouillat (Hotel Owner), Amélie Bardon (Aurélie's Friend), Sarah Barrau (Receptionist)

Author-turned-politician Agathe Villanova returns to her hometown where an interview with two incompetent journalists unfolds admist a series of trysts and love affairs.

Jean-Pierre Bacri © IFC Films

WILD GRASS

(SONY CLASSICS) a.k.a. *Les herbes folles*; Producer, Jean-Louis Livi; Executive Producer, Julie Salvador; Co-Producer, Valerio de Paolis; Director, Alain Resnais; Screenplay, Alex Réval, Laurent Herbiet; Based on the novel *L'Incident* by Christian Gailly; Photography, Eric Gautier; Designer, Jacques Saulnier; Costumes, Jackie Budin; Music, Mark Snow; Editor, Hervé de Luze; a co-production of F Comme Film – StudioCanal – France 2 Cinéma – Bim Distribuzione; French-Italian, 2009; Dolby; Panavision; Color; Rated PG; 104 minutes; American release date: June 25, 2010

CAST

Marguerite Muir	**Sabine Azéma**
Georges Palet	**André Dussollier**
Suzanne	**Anne Cosigny**
Josépha	**Emmanuelle Devos**
Bernard de Bordeaux	**Mathieu Amalric**
Lucien d'Orange	**Michel Vuillermoz**
Narrator	**Edouard Baer**
Neighbor	**Annie Cordy**
Elodie	**Sara Forestier**
Jean-Mi	**Nicolas Duvauchelle**
Marcelin Palet	**Vladimir Consigny**
Sikorsky	**Dominique Rozan**
Mickey	**Jean-Noël Brouté**

Elric Covarel-Garcia, Valéry Schatz, Stéfan Godin, Grégory Perrin (Marguerite's Acolytes), Roger-Pierre (Marcel Schwer), Paul Crauchet, Jean-Michel Ribes, Nathalie Kanoui, Adeline Ishiomin, Lisbeth Arazi Mornet (Dental Office Patients), Françoise Gillard (Shoe Saleslady), Magaly Godenaire (Watch Saleslady), Rosine Cadoret (Cinema Ticket Saleslady), Vincent Rivard (Bartender), Dorothée Blanck, Antonin Mineo, Emilie Jeauffroy (Airline Passengers), Patrick Mimoun (Jean-Baptiste Larmeur), Isabelle Des Courtils (Madame Larmeur), Candice Charles (Elodie Larmeur)

A lost wallet disrupts the lives of Georges Palet as its founder and Marguerite Muir as its owner.

André Dussollier, Mathieu Amalric

Anne Cosigny © Sony Classics

André Dussollier

Sabine Azéma

Mary Tsoni

Hristos Passalis © Kino

DOGTOOTH

(KINO) a.k.a. *Kynodontas*; Producer, Yorgos Tsourgiannis; Executive Producer, Iraklis Mavroidis; Director, Giorgos Lanthimos; Screenplay, Giorgos Lanthimos, Efthymis Filippou; Photography, Thimios Bakatakis; Art Director/Costumes, Elli Papageorgakopoulou; Editor, Yorgos Mavropsaridis; a Boo Production, co-produced by the Greek Film Center, Giorgos Lanthimos and Horsefly Productions; Greek, 2009; Color; Not rated; 94 minutes; American release date: June 25, 2010

CAST

Father	**Christos Stergioglou**
Mother	**Michelle Valley**
Older Daughter	**Aggeliki Papoulia**
Younger Daughter	**Mary Tsoni**
Son	**Hristos Passalis**
Christina	**Anna Kalaitzidou**
Dog Trainer	**Alexander Voulgaris**

A family keeps their two young daughters sheltered from the outside world, instructing them on life, language, and behavior according to their own rules.

This film received an Oscar nomination for foreign language film.

Aggeliki Papoulia, Mary Tsoni

Johan Kylén, Michael Nyqvist © Music Box

Noomi Rapace

Michael Nyqvist

Mikael Spreitz

THE GIRL WHO PLAYED WITH FIRE

(MUSIC BOX) a.k.a. *Flickan som lekte med elden*; Producer, Soren Staermose; Executive Producers, Anni Faurbye Fernandez, Peter Nadermann, Ole Sondberg, Mikael Wallen, Lone Korslund, Gunnar Carlsson; Director, Daniel Alfredson; Screenplay, Jonas Frykberg; Based on the novel by Stieg Larsson; Photography, Peter Mokrosinski; Designers, Maria Haard, Jan-Olof Agren; Costumes, Cilla Rorby; Music, Jacob Groth; Editor, Mattias Morheden; Casting, Tusse Lande; a Yellow Bird presentation and production, in association with SVT, ZDF, Nordisk Film, with the participation of Filmpool Stockholm-Malardalen, Film I Vast, Spiltan; Swedish, 2009; Dolby; Color; Rated R; 125 minutes; American release date: July 9, 2010

CAST

Lisbeth Salander	**Noomi Rapace**
Mikael Blomkvist	**Michael Nyqvist**
Erika Berger	**Lena Endre**
Malin Erikson	**Sofia Ledarp**
Nils Bjurman	**Peter Andersson**
Alexander Zalachenko	**Georgi Staykov**
Miriam Wu	**Yasmine Garbi**
Ronald Nidermann	**Mikael Spreitz**
Young Lisbeth	**Tehilla Blad**
Annika Giannini	**Annika Hallin**
Dragan Armanskij	**Michalis Koutsogiannakis**
Paolo	**Paolo Roberto**

Tanja Lorentzon (Sonja Modig), Per Oscarsson (Holger Palmgren), Alexandra Eisenstein (Journalist), Anders Ahlbom Rosendahl (Dr. Peter Teleborian), Jacob Ericksson (Christer Malm), Niklas Hjulström (Richard Ekström, Prosecutor), Magnus Knepper (Hans Faste), Ralph Carlsson (Gunnar Björk), Reuben Sallmander (Enrico), Johan Kylén (Inspector Jan Bublanski), Jörgen Berthage (Police Officer), Hans-Christian Thulin (Dag Svensson), Jennie Silfverhjelm (Mia Bergman), Pelle Bolander (Sonny Nieminen), Sunil Munshi (Dr. Sivarnandan), Daniel Gustavsson (Niklas Eriksson), Lisbeth Åkerman, Lars-Åke Gustavsson (Themselves), Thomas Lindblad (Magge Lundin), Olga Henrikson (Irina Hammujärvi), Donald Högberg (Jerker Holmberg), David Druid (Tony Scala), Ola Wahlström (Per-Åke Sandström), Dennis Önder (Refik)

When a journalist working on an explosive exposé about a sex-trafficking ring is murdered, hacker Lisbeth Salander becomes the chief suspect. Second in the series, following *The Girl with the Dragon Tattoo*.

KISSES

(OSCILLOSCOPE) Producers, Macdara Kelleher, Lance Daly, Tomas Eskilsson, Malte Forsell; Director/Screenplay, Lance Daly; Editor, J. Patrick Duffner; Photography, Lance Daly, Jake Corbett, David Grennan; Designer, Waldemar Kalinowski; Costumes, Leonie Pendergast; Music, GoBlimpsGo; Editor, J. Patrick Duffner; Casting, Mick McGinley; a Fastnet Films production; Irish, 2008; Dolby; Black and white/Color; Not rated; 72 minutes; American release date: July 16, 2010

CAST

Kylie Lawless	**Kelly O'Neill**
Dylan Dunne	**Shane Curry**
Down Under Dylan	**Stephen Rea**
Da Dunne	**Paul Roe**
Beatrice Dunne	**Neili Conroy**
Dredger Captain	**David Bendito**

Jose Jiminez (Busker), Willie Higgins (Sackman), Cathy Malone (Kylie's Ma), Elizabeth Suh (Gardiner Street Girl), Sean McDonagh (Uncle Maurice), Stephanie Kelly (Kylie's Sister), Gerry Moore (Roadie), Hilda Fay (Anita)

Living hopeless lives in a suburban housing estate outside of Dublin, a pair of pre-teens decides to run away and make their way to the city.

Kelly O'Neill, Shane Curry © Oscilloscope

Shane Curry, Kelly O'Neill

Mads Mikkelsen, Maarten Stevenson

Mads Mikkelsen, Maarten Stevenson © IFC Films

VALHALLA RISING

(IFC FILMS) Producers, Johnny Andersen, Bob Ehrhardt, Henrik Danstrup; Executive Producers, Lene Borglum, Joni Sighvatsson, Mads Peter Ole Olsen, Thorir Sigurjonsson, Yves Chevalier, Carole Sheridan, Christine Alderson; Co-Producer, Karen Smyth; Director, Nicolas Winding Refn; Screenplay, Nicolas Winding Refn, Roy Jacobsen, Matthew Read; Photography, Morten Soborg; Designer, Maurel Wear; Costumes, Gill Horn; Music, Peter-Peter, Peter Kyed; Editor, Mat Newman; Casting, Des Hamilton; a Nimbus Film presentation of a One Eye Prod. Production in association with Blind Eye Prods., La Belle Allee Prods., Scanbox Entertainment; Danish-British; Dolby; Widescreen; Technicolor; DV-to-35mm; Not rated; 92 minutes; American release date: July 16, 2010

CAST

One Eye	**Mads Mikkelsen**
Are, the Boy	**Maarten Stevenson**
Hagen	**Gordon Brown**
Gudmond	**Andrew Flanagan**
Kare	**Gary Lewis**
Hauk	**Gary McCormack**
Barde	**Alexander Morton**

Jamie Sives (Gorm), Ewan Stewart (Erik), Mathew Zajac (Malkolm), Rony Bridges (Magnus), Robert Harrison (Rodger), P. B. McBeath (Man with Pike), Callum Mitchell (Pagan Viking Guard), Stewart Porter (Kenneth), Douglas Russell (Olaf)

A mute, scarred warrior known as "One Eye" attempts to journey home only to fall in with a band of Vikings who are on route to conquer Jerusalem.

David Soul, Fred Ward

Guillaume Canet, Emir Kusturica

Vselovod Shilovsky © NeoClassics

FAREWELL

(NEOCLASSICS) a.k.a. *L'affaire farewell*; Producers, Christophe Rossignon, Bertrand Faivre, Philip Boeffard; Director/Adaptation/Dialogue, Christian Carion; Screenplay, Eric Raynaud; Based on the book *Bonjour Farewell* by Serguei Kostine; Photography, Walther Vanden Ende; Designer, Stephane Riga; Costumes, Corinne Jorry; Music, Clitn Mansell; Editor, Andrea Sedlackova; Casting, Susie Figgis, Gigi Akoka; a Nord-Ouest Films, Le Bureau, Pathe, France 2 Cinema, Blackfeet Pictures, Une Hirondelle Prods. Co-production; French, 2009; Dolby; Color; Not rated; 113 minutes; American release date: July 23, 2010

CAST

Sergei Gregoriev	**Emir Kusturica**
Pierre Froment	**Guillaume Canet**
Jessica Froment	**Alexandra Maria Lara**
Natasha	**Ingeborga Dapkunaite**
Choukov	**Oleksil Gorbunov**
Alina	**Dina Korzun**
François Mitterrand	**Philippe Magnan**
Vallier	**Niels Arestrup**
Ronald Reagan	**Fred Ward**
Hutton	**David Soul**
Feeney	**Willem Dafoe**
Igor	**Evgenie Kharlanov**
Anatoly	**Valentin Varetsky**

David Clark (Secret Service Agent), Mats Långbacka, Christian Sandström (FBI Agents), Joonas Makkonen (Finnish Border Guard), Miglen Mirtchev (KGB Agent), Lauriane Riquet (Ophélie), Timothé Riquet (Damien), Tero Saikkonen (Russian Soldier), Diane Kurger (Woman Jogging), Vselovod Shilovsky (Gorbachev)

Disillusioned by his country's Communist directives, KGB agent Sergei Gregoriev begins shipping valuable information to a French engineer stationed in Moscow.

Willem Dafoe

Alexia Fast, Ashley Judd

Goran Visnjic, Ashley Judd

Lauren Lee Smith © E1 Entertainment

HELEN

(E1 ENTERTAINMENT) Producers, Judy Tossell, Christine Haebler; Executive Producers, Kirk Shaw, Jens Meurer, Simon Fawcett, Chris Curling, Robbie Little Larry Sugar, Andrew Spaulding, Doug Mankoff; Director/Screenplay, Sandra Nettelbeck; Photography, Michael Bertl; Designer, Linda Del Rosario; Costumes, Bettina Helmi; Music, Tim Despic, James Edward Barker, David Darling; Editor, Barry Egan; Casting, Pam Dixon (U.S.), Corinne Clark, Jennifer Page (Canada); an Egoli Tossell Film (Germany)/Insight Film Studios (Canada) presentation in association with Aramid Entertainment; German-Canadian, 2009; Dolby; Super 35 Widescreen; Color; Rated R; 120 minutes; American release date: July 30, 2010

CAST

Helen Leonard	**Ashley Judd**
David	**Goran Visnjic**
Mathilda	**Lauren Lee Smith**
Dr. Sherman	**Alberta Watson**
John	**David Nykl**
Julie	**Alexia Fast**
Frank	**David Hewlett**
Susanna	**Leah Cairns**
Donna	**Ali Liebert**

Julia Keilty, Myelen Robic (Psych Nurses), Jonathan Holmes (Thief), Chleah Horsdal (Kara), Robin Nielsen (Young Man), David Quinlan (Dan), John Shaw (Prosecutor), Veena Sood (Defense Attorney), Malcolm Stewart (Wilkins), Ian Thompson (Bus Driver), Conrad Coates (Stephen), Alex Stevens (Woman)

A successful music professor finds herself losing her grip as she spirals into a deep level of clinical depression.

Lauren Lee Smith, Ashley Judd

CAIRO TIME

(IFC FILMS) Producers, Daniel Iron, David Collins; Executive Producers, Charles Pugliese, Christine Vachon; Co-Producer, Claire Welland; Director/Screenplay, Ruba Nadda; Photography, Luc Montpellier; Designer, Tamara Conboy; Costumes, Brenda Broer; Music, Niall Byrne; Music Supervisors, Stacey Horricks, David Hayman; Editor, Teresa Hannigan; Casting, John Buchan, Jason Knight; a Foundry Films presentation in association with Samson Films; Canadian-Irish, 2009; Dolby; Color; Rated PG; 88 minutes; American release date: August 6, 2010

Patricia Clarkson, Alexander Siddig

CAST

Juliette Grant	**Patricia Clarkson**
Tareq Khalifa	**Alexander Siddig**
Kathryn	**Elena Anaya**
Mark	**Tom McCamus**
Yasmeen	**Amina Annabi**
Jim	**Andrew Cullen**
Jameelah	**Mona Hala**
Hanan	**Fadia Nadda**

Mohammed Abdel Fattah (Customs Officer), Hossam Abdulla (Porter), Nabil Shazli (Manager), Ahmed Ghareeb (Propositioning Man), Mohammed

When her husband finds himself detained by his work, Juliette Grant is given a guide to show her the sights of Cairo, only to find herself falling in love with the man.

Patricia Clarkson, Alexander Siddig © IFC Films

Alexander Siddig, Patricia Clarkson

Patricia Clarkson

LEBANON

(SONY CLASSICS) Producers, Moshe Edery, Leon Edery, Einat Bikel, Uri Sabag, David Silber, Benjamina Mirnik, Ilann Girard; Executive Producer, Gil Sassover; Director/ Screenplay, Samuel Maoz; Photography, Giora Bejach; Designer, Ariel Roshko; Costumes, Hila Bargiel; Music, Nicolas Becker; Editor, Arik Lahav-Leibovici; Special Effects, Pini Klavir; Stunts, Dima Osmolovski; Casting, Hila Yuval; a United King Films presentation of a Metro Communications, Paralite Films (Israel)/Arsam Intl., Arte France (France)/Ariel Films (Germany) presentation in association with Israel Film Fund; Israeli-French-German, 2009; Dolby; Color; 16mm/HD-to-35mm; Rated R; 94 minutes; American release date: August 6, 2010

Fares Hanaya, Ashraf Barhom

CAST

Shmulik	**Yoav Donat**
Assi	**Itay Tiran**
Hertzel	**Oshri Cohen**
Yigal	**Michael Moshonov**
Gamil	**Zohar Strauss**
Syrian Captive	**Dudu Tassa**
Phalangist Members	**Ashraf Barhom**, **Fares Hanaya**
Lebanese Mother	**Reymonde Amsellem**
Lebanese Father	**Bian Antir**
Lebanese Boy	**Khaled Salama**
BMW Driver	**Iad Abu Nama**
Truck Driver	**Hussein Mahagna**
Army Doctor	**David Volach**
Cornelia	**Arye Chemer**

On the first day of the Lebanon invasion of June 1982, four Israeli soldiers enter the fray inside the cramped space of a tank.

Yoav Donat, Zohar Strauss

Reymonde Amsellem

Zohar Strauss © Sony Classics

Thure Lindhardt © Olive Films

Thure Lindhardt, David Denikc

BROTHERHOOD

(OLIVE FILMS) a.k.a. *Broderskab*; Producer, Per Holst; Executive Producer, Tomas Eskilsson; Director, Nicolo Donato; Screenplay, Rasmus Birch, Nicolo Donato; Photography, Laust Trier-Mørch; Music, Simon Brenting, Jesper Mechlenburg; Editor, Bodil Kjærhauge; an Asta Films, Film i Väst production; Danish; Dolby; Color; HD-to-35mm; Not rated; 90 minutes; American release date: August 6, 2010

CAST
Lars	**Thure Lindhardt**
Jimmy	**David Denikc**
Michael	**Nicolas Bro**
Patrick	**Morten Holst**
Ebbe	**Claus Flygare**
Mother	**Hanne Hedelund**
Father	**Lars Simonsen**

Michael Grønnemose (Laust), Anders Heinrichsen (Lasse), Jon Lange (Bo), Johannes Lassen (Kenneth), Sophie Louise Lauring (Sygeplejerske), Martin Metz (Jonas), Signe Egholm Olsen (Karina), Peter Plaugborg (Sergeant), Mads Rømer (Kim)

A closeted former serviceman joins a neo-Nazi group where he begins a passionate, secret affair with another member.

THE DISAPPEARANCE OF ALICE CREED

(ANCHOR BAY) Producer, Adrian Sturges; Executive Producers, Steve Christian, Marc Samuelson; Co-Producer, Andrew Fingret; Director/Screenplay, J. Blakeson; Photography, Philipp Blaubach; Designer, Ricky Eyres; Music, Marc Canham; Editor, Mark Eckersley; a CinemaNX and Isle of Man Film presentation of a CinemaNX production; British; Dolby; Color; Widescreen; HD; Rated R; 100 minutes; American release date: August 6, 2010

CAST
Alice Creed	**Gemma Arterton**
Danny	**Martin Compston**
Vic	**Eddie Marsan**

Vic and Danny abduct Alice Creed, demanding £2 million in ransom money from her rich father.

Gemma Arterton, Martin Compston

Martin Compston, Eddie Marsan © Anchor Bay

ANIMAL KINGDOM

(SONY CLASSICS) Producer, Liz Watts; Executive Producers, Bec Smith, Vincent Sheehan; Director/Screenplay, David Michôd; Photography, Adam Arkapaw; Designer, Jo Ford; Costumes, Cappi Ireland; Music, Antony Partos; Editor, Luke Doolan; Casting, Kirsty McGregor; a Screen Australia and Porchlight Films presentation in association with Film Victoria, Screen NSW, Fulcrum Media Finance and Showtime Australia of a Porchlight Films production; Australian; Dolby; Super 35 Widescreen; Deluxe Color; Rated R; 112 minutes; American release date: August 13, 2010

CAST

Andrew "Pope" Cody	Ben Mendelsohn
Barry "Baz" Brown	Joel Edgerton
Det. Sr. Sgt. Nathan Leckie	Guy Pearce
Darren Cody	Luke Ford
Janine "Smurf" Cody	Jacki Weaver
Craig Cody	Sullivan Stapleton
Joshua "J" Cody	James Frechcville
Ezra White	Dan Wyllie
Det. Justin Norris	Anthony Hayes
Nicky Henry	Laura Wheelwright
Catherine Brown	Mirrah Foulkes
Det. Randall Roache	Justin Rosniak
Alicia Henry	Susan Prior
Gus Emery	Clayton Jacobson
Justine Hopper	Anna Lise Phillips
Armed Robbery Detective	Anthony Ahern
Dacinta Collis	Christina Azucena
Sarah Leckie	Jacquie Brennan
Cashier	Lucia Cai
Police Radio	Michael Cody
John Harrop	Kieran Darcy-Smith
Andy Emery	Jack Heanly
Const. Peter Simmons	Josh Helman
PSG Santo	Bert Labonte
Richard Collis	Andy McPhee
Scott Leckie	Ben Ouwehand
Const. Daniel Horden	Tim Phillips

Bryce Lindemann, Paul Smits (Paramedics), Ann Michôd (Shopper), David Michôd (Reporter), Sarah Nguyen (Waitress), Tom Noble (Court Warden), Brenda Palmer (Janine's Neighbor), Dom Phelan (PSG Tom), Daniel Roche (SOG), James Saunders (PSG Gary), Michael Vice, Chris Weir (Hoods)

After his mother dies of a heroin overdose young "J" Cody is taken in by his grandmother and her dangerous brood of criminal offspring.

This film received an Oscar nomination for supporting actress (Jacki Weaver).

Andy McPhee, Sullivan Stapleton © Sony Pictures Classics

Ben Mendelsohn, Laura Wheelwright

Ben Mendelsohn, Jacki Weaver, Luke Ford

Ben Mendelsohn, Joel Edgerton

James Frecheville, Guy Pearce

Sullivan Stapleton, Jacki Weaver

Joel Edgerton, Mirrah Foulkes

Laura Wheelwright, James Frecheville

© Oscilloscope

A FILM UNFINISHED

(OSCILLOSCOPE) Producers, Itay Ken-Tor, Noemi Schory; Director/Screenplay, Yael Hersonski; Photography, Itai Ne'eman; Music, Ishai Adar; Editor, Joelle Alexis; a Belfilms production in association with MDR, SWR, Yes. Docu and Arte; German-Israeli; Color/Black and white; DV; Not rated; 89 minutes; American release date: August 18, 2010.

WITH
Interrogator	**Alexander Beyer**
Cameraman	**Rüdiger Vogler**

Documentary consisting of 60-minutes of raw footage taken by a Nazi film crew of Warsaw's Jewish ghetto in 1942, the original film intended to be used for SS propaganda.

NANNY McPHEE RETURNS

(UNIVERSAL) a.k.a. *Nanny McPhee and the Big Bang*; Producers, Lindsay Doran, Tim Bevan, Eric Fellner; Executive Producers, Debra Hayward, Liza Chasin, Emma Thompson; Co-Producer, David Brown; Director, Susanna White; Screenplay, Emma Thompson; Based on characters created by Christianna Brand; Photography, Mike Eley; Designer, Simon Elliott; Costumes, Jacqueline Durran; Music, James Newton Howard; Editor, Simon Evan-Jones; Visual Effects Supervisor, Adam McInnes; Casting, Lucy Bevan, Pippa Hall; a Universal (U.S.)/Studio Canal (France)/Relativity Media (U.S.) presentation of a Working Title (U.K.) production, in association with Three Strange Angels; British-French-American; Dolby; Super 35 Widescreen; Color; Rated PG; 109 minutes; American release date: August 20, 2010.

CAST
Nanny McPhee	**Emma Thompson**
Isabel Green	**Maggie Gyllenhaal**
Phil Green	**Rhys Ifans**
Mrs. Docherty	**Maggie Smith**
Mr. Docherty	**Sam Kelly**
Miss Topsey	**Sinead Matthews**
Missy Turvey	**Katy Brand**

Oscar Steer (Vincent Green), Asa Butterfield (Norman Green), Lil Woods (Megsie Green), Eros Vlahos (Cyril Gray), Rosie Taylor-Ritson (Celia Gray), Daniel Mays (Bleinkinsop), Ralph Fiennes (Lord Gray), Ewan McGregor (Rory Green), Bill Bailey (Farmer Macreadie), Sam Kelly (Mr. Docherty), Nonso Anozie (Sgt. Jeffreys), Ed Stoppard (Lt. Addis), Toby Sedgwick (Enemy Pilot)

During World War II, a magical nanny appears to help Isabel Green, whose husband is off fighting, and who has been left to take care of her three unruly children and her sister's spoiled offspring as well.

Lil Woods, Asa Butterfield, Oscar Steer

Maggie Smith
© Universal Studios

SOUL KITCHEN

(IFC FILMS) Producers, Klaus Maeck, Faith Akin; Co-Producers, Fabienne Vonier, Alberto Fanni, Flaminio Zadra, Paolo Colombo; Director, Faith Akin; Screenplay, Faith Akin, Adam Bousdoukos; Photography, Rainer Klausmann; Designer, Tamo Kunz; Costumes, Katrin Aschendorf; Music Supervisors, Klaus Maeck, Pia Hoffmann; Editor, Andrew Bird; Casting, Monique Akin; a Corazon Intl. production, in association with Pyramide Prods., NDR, Dorje Film; German, 2009; Dolby; Fujicolor; Not rated; 98 minutes; American release date: August 20, 2010

CAST

Zinos Kazantsakis	**Adam Bousdoukos**
Illias Kazantsakis	**Moritz Bleibtreu**
Shayn Weiss	**Birol Ünel**
Lucia Faust	**Anna Bederke**
Nadine Krüger	**Pheline Roggan**
Lutz	**Lukas Gregorowicz**
Anna Mondstein	**Dorka Gryllus**
Thomas Neumann	**Wotan Wilke Möhring**
Sokrates	**Demir Gögöl**
Nadine's Grandmother	**Monica Bleibtreu**
Mr. Jung, the Investor	**Udo Kier**

Marc Hosemann (Ziege), Cem Akin (Milli), Catrin Striebeck (Ms. Schuster from the Tax Office), Hendrik von Bültzingslöwen (Ms. Schuster's Assistant), Jan Fedder (Mr. Meyer from the Public Health Department), Julia Wachsmann (Tanja, Neumann's Fiancee), Simon Görts (Tschako), Maverick Quek (Han, the Chinese Guy), Markus Imboden (Nadine's Father), Gudrun Egner (Nadine's Mother), Arne Benzing, Piotr Gregorowicz, Hans Ludwivzak, Jan Weichsel (Bad Boy Boogiez Band), Peter Lohmeyer (Owner of *Le Papillion* Restaurant), Zarah Jane McKenzie (Waitress at *Le Papillion*), Peter Jordan (Notary Public), Wolfgang Schumacher (Doctor), Ügur Yücel (Kemal, The Bone Crusher), Philipp Baltus (Electro-DJ), Lars Rudolph (District Court Judge), Fritz Renzo Heinze (Priest), Francesco Fiannaca (Prison Officer), Bülent Celebi (Rocker guest Ali Davidson), Bernd Gajkowski, Herma Koehn (*Soul Kitchen* Guests), Joana Adu-Gyamfi (Pharmacist), Maria Ketikidou (Commissioner), Till Huster (Police Officer), Torsten Lemke (Anna's Patient), Klaus Maeck, Ernest Hausmann, Salman Kurtulan (The Bone Crusher's Patients), Emek Kavukcuŏglu (Young Real Estate Agent), Senol, Shayn' Ugurlu (Prisoner)

In Hamburg, restaurant owner Zinos Kazantsakis finds his local establishment acquiring a wider degree of popularity when he hires a professional chef, thereby causing resentment in his regular clientele.

Adam Bousdoukos, Moritz Bleibtreu

Demir Gögöl, Anna Bederke, Moritz Bleibtreu, Adam Bousdoukos, Pheline Roggan, Lukas Gregorowicz, Birol Ünel

Pheline Roggan, Adam Bousdoukos

Moritz Bleibtreu, Adam Bousdoukos © IFC Films

MAO'S LAST DANCER

Amanda Schull, Chi Cao

(GOLDWYN) Producer, Jane Scott; Executive Producer, Troy Lum; Co-Producer, Geng Ling; Director, Bruce Beresford; Screenplay, Jan Sardi; Based on the autobiography by Li Cunxin; Photography, Peter James; Designer, Herbert Pinter; Costumes, Anna Borghesi; Music, Christopher Gordon; Choreographer, Graeme Murphy; Editor, Mark Warner; Casting, Sharon Howard-Field, Nikki Barrett; a Great Scott production; Australian, 2009; Dolby; Technicolor; Rated PG; 117 minutes; American release date: August 20, 2010

CAST

Ben Stevenson	**Bruce Greenwood**
Charles Foster	**Kyle MacLachlan**
Niang	**Joan Chen**
Li Cunxin (Adult)	**Chi Cao**
Elizabeth Mackey	**Amanda Schull**
Dia	**Shuang Bao Wang**
Li Cunxin (Teenager)	**Guo Chengwu**
Li Cunxin (Child)	**Huang Wenbin**

Bruce Greenwood, Steven Heathcote, Camilla Vergotis

Aden Young (Dilworth), Madeleine Eastoe (Lori), Camilla Vergotis (Mary McKendry), Penne Hackforth-Jones (Cynthia Dodds), Jack Thompson (Judge Woodrow Seals), Chris Kirby (Mason), Suzie Steen (Betty Lou), Shu Guang Liang (Jing Tring – 8 yrs.), Ye Wang (Cunfar – 14 yrs.), Neng Neng Zhang (Gong Mei), Wan Shi Xu (Shen Yu), Shao Wei Yi (Yang Ping), Ferdinand Hoang (Consul Zhang), Hui Cong Zhan (Teacher Song), Ji Feng Sun (Headmaster), Zhi Xue Chai (Official Guan), Chang Suo Zhang (Official Chan Feng), Jie Cheng (Official Yu), Zheng Nong Yang (Cunyuan -21 yrs.), Wen Bing Zhang (Cunsang – 17 yrs.), Tian Xia (Door Soldier), Yue Hu (Long Face Boy), Jia Hui Zhang (Clumsy Sumersault Boy), Hang Yu (Boy Candidate), Bao Li (Advisor Xu), Hao Tian Xue (Shing Hua -11 yrs.), Hui Min tian (Chung Jun Town Leader), Yu Qi Zhang (Chan Lan District Chief), Hong Tao Wang (Cuncia), Ping Chen (Miss So), Peng Cao (Mr. Hung), Su Zhang (Teacher Chan), Ming Yue Ma (Lau -11 yrs.), Jian Wang (Su – 11 yrs.), Chang He (Tong -11 yrs.), Jun Ming Tian (Lujun – 12 yrs.), Xi Guo Wu (Director Wang), Gang Jiao (Teacher Gao), Jun Ping Zhu (Mistress Chiu Ho), Meng Ni Yang (Shing Hua – 15 yrs.), Zu Quan Kou (Lau – 15 yrs.), Cheng Yue Zhu (Su – 15 yrs.), Long Dai (Tong – 15 yrs.), Hong Jian Li (Lujun – 16 yrs.), Steven Heathcote (Bobby Cordner), Xiu Qing Yu (Madame Official), Jun Long Kang (Madame's Companion), Meng Wang (Bow Shooter), Feng Qi Ma (Cobbler), Ya Xuan Xu (Shing Hua – 19 yrs.), Jia Yong Sun (Lau -19 yrs.), Ke Zhu (Su - 19 yrs.), Lu Ning Chen (Tong – 19 yrs.), Hong Tao Lin (Lujun – 20 yrs.), Yang Li (Shi Dao), Fan Wang (Chinese Translator), Xiao Dong Tian (Cunfar -21 yrs.), Huai Ping Yang (Jing Tring – 15 yrs.), Monica Curran (Mrs. Tan), Lucy Egger (MC/ Orlofski), Alice Parkinson (Assistant Stage Manager), Kip Gamblin (David), Paul Stanhope (Swan Lake Conductor), Deni Hines (Anita Jones), Jon-Claire Lee (Vice Consul Lan), Min Lu, Rob Choi, Ron Lee, Cory Vi, Cheuk-Fai Chan, Sean Huling Chen (Security Guards), Qyan Tran (Consul Duty Officer), Gibson Nolte (China Desk Officer), Ted Maynard (Newsreader), Nick McKay, Nicholas Hammond (TV Reporters), Chad H. Loxsom (FBI Man), Leslie Bell (TV Presenter), Ian Meadows (WTC Backstage Manager), George Ellis (Houston Ballet Conductor), John Thwaites (Senator), Jane Harders (Senator's Wife), Leanne Atkins (Reception Guest), Dan Yang Cong (The Boy Who Asks)

The true story of how Chinese ballet star Li Cunxin defected in 1981.

Camilla Vergotis, Chi Cao © Samuel Goldwyn

Marina Foïs, Patrick Bruel , Karin Viard, Christopher Thompson © IFC Films

CHANGE OF PLANS

(IFC FILMS) a.k.a. *Le code a changé*; Producers, Christine Gozlan, Alain Terzian; Executive Producer, David Poirot; Director, Danièle Thompson; Screenplay, Danièle Thompson, Christopher Thompson; Photography, Jean-Marc Fabre; Designer, Michele Abbe; Costumes, Catherine Leterrier; Music, Nicola Piovani; Editor, Sylvie Landra; Casting, Constance Demontoy; a Thelma Films, Alter Films, StudioCanal, TF1 Films Prod., Radis Films Prod. Production, with participation of CanalPlus, CNC; French, 2009; Dolby; Widescreen; Color; Not rated; 100 minutes; American release date: August 27, 2010

CAST

Marie-Laurence "ML" Claverne	**Karin Viard**
Piotr	**Dany Boon**
Mélanie Carcassonne	**Marina Foïs**
Dr. Alain Carcassonne	**Patrick Bruel**
Sarah Mattei	**Emmanuelle Seigner**
Lucas Mattei	**Christopher Thompson**
Juliette	**Marina Hands**
Erwann	**Patrick Chesnais**

Blanca Li (Manuela), Laurent Stocker (Jean-Louis Mauzard), Pierre Arditi (Henri), Jeanne Raimbault (Doris), Isabelle Cagnat (Ms. Bollet), Marc Rioufol (Daniel Laurent), Cyrille Eldiri (Demonstrator), Michèle Brousse (Ms. Andrieux), Michel Motu (Mr. Andrieux), Guillaume Durand (Himself), Zahia Said (Nurse), Anne Agbadou-Masson (Reporter), Paul Bonfiglio (Cheesemaker), Stéphane Lauret (Lagonda Salesman), Georges Roche (Hotel Manager), David Lasserre (Dance Teacher), Jérémy Bardeau (Doctor), Julie Villers (Receptionist), Pedro Ramirez Rey, Juan Pedro Delgado, Javier Cobo Nebrera, José Maria Maldonado, Segui (Flamenco Dancers)

During the Fete de la musique, three couples are invited for dinner at the apartment of a divorce lawyer and her unemployed husband, where they discuss life and relationships.

CENTURION

(MAGNET) Producers, Christian Colson, Robert Jones; Executive Producers, Paul Smith, François Ivernel, Cameron McCracken; Director/Screenplay, Neil Marshall; Photography, Sam McCurdy; Designer, Simon Bowles; Costumes, Keith Madden; Music, Ilan Eshkeri; Editor, Chris Gill; Visual Effects Supervisor, Jacob Otterstrom; Special Prosthetic Makeup Effects, Paul Hyett; Stunts, Paul Herbert; Casting, Debbie McWilliams; a Pathé Prods. presentation in association with the U.K. Film Council in association with Warner Bros. Pictures, with the participation of Canal+ and Ciné-Cinéma of a Celador Films production; British; Dolby; Super 35 Widescreen; Color; Rated R; 97 minutes; American release date: August 27, 2010

CAST

Centurion Quintus Dias	**Michael Fassbender**
General Titus Virilus	**Dominic West**
Thax	**JJ Feild**
Septus	**Lee Ross**
Bothos	**David Morrissey**
Gorlacon	**Ulrich Thomsen**
Gorlacon's Son	**Ryan Atkinson**
Governor Agricola	**Paul Freeman**
Etain	**Olga Kurylenko**

Liam Cunningham (Brick), Noel Clarke (Marcos), Dimitri Leonidas (Leonidas), Riz Ahmed (Tarak), Imogen Poots (Arianne), Andreas Wisniewski (Commander Gratus), Dave Lengo (Vortix), Axelle Carolyn (Aeron), Dhaffer L'Abidine (Arm Wrestling Opponent), Simon Chadwick (Carlisle Messenger), Jake Marshall (Roman Officer Argos), Eoin Macken (Achivir), Dermot Keaney (Pict Hunter), Dylan Brown (Roman Guard), Rachael Stirling (Druzilla), Michael Carter (Gen. Antonius), Tom Mannion (Gen. Tesio), Peter Guinness (Gen. Cassius)

Following a bloody skirmish in which most of his men are wiped out, Quintus Dias and the survivors of Rome's Ninth Legion find themselves under attack by vengeful Pict hunters.

Michael Fassbender © Magnolia

Cécile De France, Vincent Cassel

Gérard Depardieu

Vincent Cassel, Elena Anaya © Music Box Films

Vincent Cassel, Gilles Lellouche

MESRINE: KILLER INSTINCT

(MUSIC BOX FILMS) a.k.a. *l'instinct de mort* and *Public Enemy Number One (Part 1)*; Producer, Thomas Langman; Executive Producer, Daniel Delume; Co-Producers, Maxime Remillard, Andre Rouleau; Director, Jean-Francois Richet; Screenplay, Abdel Raouf Dafri, Jean-Francois Richet; Based on the book *L'instinct de mort* by Jacques Mesrine; Photography, Eric Catelan; Designer, Emile Ghigo; Costumes, Virginie Montel; Music, Marco Beltrami; Editor, Herve Schneid; a Thomas Langman presentation of a Le Petite Reine (France)/Remstar (Canada)/Novo RPI (Italy) production in association with M6 Films; French-Canadian-Italian, 2008; Dolby; Panavision; Color; Rated R; 113 minutes; American release date: August 27, 2010

CAST

Jacques Mesrine	**Vincent Cassel**
Jeanne Schneider	**Cécile De France**
Guido	**Gérard Depardieu**
Paul	**Gilles Lellouche**
Jean-Paul Mercier	**Roy Dupuis**
Sofia	**Elena Anaya**
Sarah	**Florence Thomassin**
Jacques' Father	**Michel Duchaussoy**
Jacques' Mother	**Myriam Boyer**

Abdelhafid Metalsi (Ahmed, the Pimp), Gilbert Sicotte (The Milliardaire), Deano Clavet (Roger André), Ludivine Sagnier (Sylve Jeanjacquot), Mustapha Abourachid (Algerian Soldier), Sophiane Benrezzak, Faird Fedjer (Armed Militants), Gil Geisweiler (French Officer), Leïla Bekhti (Armed Militant's Daughter), Dorothée Brière (Suzon), Michelle Brûlé, Yves Marc Gilbert (Owners That Got Robbed), Maria Ibars Valverde (The Dark Haired Girl from the Ball), Mercè Llorens (The Blonde Girl from the Ball), Sabri Lahmer (Gégé), Manuela Gouray (Mado), Ben Badra (The Angry Customer), Frankie Pain (Lulu), Emmanuelle Carlier (The Widwife), François Hautesserre (The Accomplice from Neubourg), Jean-Claude Leguay (Tabacoff), Louis Blivet (5-year-old Sabrina), Guilhem Pellegrin (The Solicitor), Caroline Ferrus (Maggy), Arnaud Henriet (The Doorman from the Games Area), Angelo Aybar (The Games Area's Owner), Jeff Boundreault (The Immigration Officer), Benoît Théberge (The Milliardaire's Servant), Sylvain Savard (The Milliardaire's Gardener), Dominiuqe Loiseau (The Killer), Bill Anderson (The Policeman from the Arizona), Christian Bordeleau, Christine Bellier, Benoît Lavoisier (Reporters at Airport), Guy Thauvette (The Director from the USC), Jean-Loup Yale (Thibaut Mailloche), Christine Beaulieu (Lizon), Luc-Martial Dagenais (The Bank's Director), Danielle Lepine (The Lawyer), Monique Goesslin (The Warder), Laurent Imbault, Paul Stewart (Rangers)

The true story of French gangster Jacques Mesrine, covering his early years. The second half, *Mesrine: Public Enemy #1*, followed.

MESRINE: PUBLIC ENEMY #1

(MUSIC BOX FILMS) a.k.a. *l'ennemi public no 1*; Producer, Thomas Langman; Executive Producer, Daniel Delume; Co-Producers, Maxime Remillard, Andre Rouleau; Director, Jean-Francois Richet; Screenplay, Abdel Raouf Dafri, Jean-Francois Richet; Based on the book *L'instinct de mort* by Jacques Mesrine; Photography, Eric Catelan; Designer, Emile Ghigo; Costumes, Virginie Montel; Music, Marco Beltrami; Editor, Herve Schneid; a Thomas Langman presentation of a Le Petite Reine (France)/Remstar (Canada)/Novo RPI (Italy) production in association with M6 Films; French-Canadian-Italian, 2008; Dolby; Panavision; Color; Rated R; 133 minutes; American release date: September 3, 2010

CAST

Jacques Mesrine	**Vincent Cassel**
Sylvie Jeanjacquot	**Ludivine Sagnier**
François Besse	**Mathieu Amalric**
Michel Ardouin	**Samuel Le Bihan**
Charly Bauer	**Gérard Lanvin**
Superintendent Broussard	**Olivier Gourmet**
Henri Lelièvre	**Georges Wilson**
Jacques' Father	**Michel Duchaussoy**

Anne Consigny (Jacques' Lawyer), Laure Marsac (Reporter at Interview), Alain Fromager (Jacques Dallier, Reporter for *Minute*), Alain Doutey (Courthouse Chairman) Arsène Mosca (Jojo, A Policeman), Christophe Vandevelde (Inspector Gégé), Luc Thuillier (Superintendent from OCRB), Serge Biavan (Detective from the SRPJ), Pascal Elso (Superintendent from the SRPJ), Isabelle Vitari (Cashier), Michaël Vander-Meiren, David Seigneur (Policemen with Compiegne), Nicolas Abraham (Grangier), Joseph Malerba (Robert), Pscal Doucet-Bon (Compiegne, the Reporter), Emmanuel Vielly (Detective at Cemetery), Myriam Boyer (Jacques' Mother), Pascal Liger (Boxer), Gérard Jarrier (The Policeman), David Bursztein (The Sniper), Helena Soubeyrand (Friend at Arrest), Fabrice de la Villehervé (Warden), Jean-Luc Muscat, Vincent Jouan, Eric Bouhcer, Bernard Rosselli, Philippe Le Dem (Prisoners, Hospital Jail), Erik Forcinal (Prisoner, Lawyer), Fanny Sidney (16-year-old Sabrina), Alain Rimoux (The General Counsel), Olivier Barthélémy (Jailmate at Escape), Rachel Suissa (Princess Annie), Clémence Thioly (Princess Christiane), Xavier Le Tourneur (Deaville, the Corporal), Yan Brian (Supermarket CEO), Hervé Laudierè, Françoise Le Plénier (Farmers), Antoine, Floriane (Children), Jérôme Boyer, Jean-Pierre Dantan (Policemen), Clément Sasseville (Newspaper Agent, London), Martial Courcier (Aductor's Accomplice), Frédéric Constant (The Milliardaire's Son), Nicolas Woirion (Policeman, BMW Ransom), Eric Rivolier (Charlie's Wife), Benoît Marchand (Inspector Farrugia), Albert Goldberg (Saviem's Chauffeur).

The true story of gangster Jacques Mesrine, covering his final years after his return to France. Second part of the story, following *Mesrine: Killer Instinct.*

Mathieu Amalric

Olivier Gourmet

Vincent Cassel, Ludivine Sagnier

Vincent Cassel © Music Box Films

LAST TRAIN HOME

(ZEITGEIST) Producers, Mila Aung-Thwin, Daniel Cross; Director/Screenplay/ Photography, Fan Lixin; Editors, Fan Lixin, Mary Stephen; an EyeSteelFilm (Canada)/Mila Aung-Thwin (China) production; Canadian-Chinese, 2009; Color; Not rated; 85 minutes; American release date: September 3, 2010

WITH
Zhang Changhua, Chen Suqin, Zhang Qin, Zhang Yang
Documentary in which a pair of garment workers in Guangdong, South China journey for miles to visit the children they have left back home;

Zhang Qin

Zhang Qin © Zeitgeist

Ni Dahong, Sun Honglei

Xiao Shenyang, Yan Ni, Zhao Benshan © Sony Pictures Classics

A WOMAN, A GUN AND A NOODLE SHOP

(SONY CLASSICS) a.k.a. *San qiang pai an jing qi* and *A Simple Noodle Story*; Producers, Zhang Weiping, Bill Kong, Gu Hao; Executive Producer, Zhang Zhenyan; Director, Zhang Yimou; Screenplay, Xu Zhengchao, Shi Jianquan; Based on the film *Blood Simple* by Joel and Ethan Coen; Photography, Zhao Xiaoding; Designer, Han Zhong; Music, Zhao Lin; Editor, Meng Peicong; Stunts, Jiang Yanming; Chinese, 2009; a Beijing New Picture Film Co., Ltd. Film Partner (2009) International Inc. presentation; Chinese, 2009; Dolby; Color; HD Cam; Rated R; 95 minutes; American release date: September 3, 2010

CAST

Zhang	**Sun Honglei**
Li	**Xiao Shenyang**
Wang's Wife	**Yan Ni**
Wang	**Ni Dahong**
Zhao	**Cheng Ye**
Chen	**Mao Mao**
The Captain	**Zhao Benshan**
Persian	**Julien Gaudroy**

Informed of his wife's infidelity with one of his employees, Wang hires a corrupt lawman to eliminate the couple. Remake of the 1985 film *Blood Simple* which starred Frances McDormand, M. Emmet Walsh, and John Getz.

Glenn Gould

Glenn Gould © Lorber Films

GENIUS WITHIN: THE INNER LIFE OF GLENN GOULD

(LORBER) Producer, Peter Raymont; Supervising Producer, Kelly Jenkins; Directors, Michèle Hozer, Peter Raymont; Photography, Walter Corbett; Music Performed by Glenn Gould; Editor, Michèle Hozer; Produced by White Pine Pictures in association with Bravo!; Canadian, 2009; Color; Not rated; 106 minutes; American release date: September 10, 2010. Documentary on enigmatic pianist Glenn Gould.

HIDEAWAY

(STRAND) a.k.a. *Le refuge*; Producers, Claudie Ossard, Chris Bozzli; Director, François Ozon; Screenplay François Ozon, Mathieu Hippeau; Photography, Mathias Raaflaub; Set Designer, Katia Wyszkop; Costumes, Pascaline Chavanne; Music/Original Song, Louise-Ronan Choisy; Editor, Muriel Breton; Casting, Sarah Teper; a Eurowide Film Prod. Production; French, 2009; Dolby; Color; Panavision; Not rated; 88 minutes; American release date: September 10, 2010

CAST
Mousse	**Isabelle Carré**
Paul	**Louis-Ronan Choisy**
Serge	**Pierre Louis-Calixte**
Louis	**Melvil Poupaud**
The Mother	**Claire Vernet**
The Father	**Jean-Pierre Andréani**
The Woman on the Beach	**Marie Rivière**
The Doctor	**Jérome Kircher**
The Seducer	**Nicolas Moreau**
The Drug Dealer	**Emile Berling**
The Priest	**Maurice Antoni**

Dominique (Geneviève), Tania Dessources (The Nurse), Maurice Antoni (The Priest), Sylvie Haurie-Aussel (The Pharmacist), Arnaud Goudal (The Estate Agent), Kevin Sorieul (The Boy), Meie Castanho (Louise)

After her lover Louis dies of a drug overdose, a pregnant Mousse takes refuge at a beach house where she is joined by Louis' gay brother, Paul.

Isabelle Carré, Melvil Poupaud

Isabelle Carré, Louis-Ronan Choisy © Strand Releasing

BRAN NUE DAE

(FREESTYLE) Producers, Robyn Kershaw, Graeme Isaac; Executive Producers, Christopher Mapp, Matthew Street, David Whealy; Director, Rachel Perkins; Screenplay, Reg Cribb, Rachel Perkins, Jimmy Chi; Based on the stage musical by Jimmy Chi & Kuckles; Photography, Andrew Lesnie; Designer, Felicity Abbott; Costumes, Margot Wilson; Music, Cezary Skubiszewski; Choreographer, Stephen Page; Editor, Rochelle Oshlack; a Screen Australia, Omnilab Media, Mayfan Films, Robyn Kershaw Productions, Screenwest, Film Victoria, The Melbourne International Film Festival Premiere Fund, Australian Broadcasting Corporation production; Australian, 2009; Dolby; Color; Rated PG-13; 85 minutes; American release date: September 10, 2010

Ernie Dingo, Missy Higgins

CAST
Willie	**Rocky McKenzie**
Rosie	**Jessica Mauboy**
Uncle Tadpole	**Ernie Dingo**
Annie	**Missy Higgins**
Father Benedictus	**Geoffrey Rush**
Roxanne	**Deborah Mailman**
Slippery	**Tom Budge**
Roadhouse Betty	**Magda Szubanski**
Theresa	**Ningali Lawford-Wolf**
Pastor Flakkon	**Stephen Baamba Albert**
Lester	**Dan Sultan**
Tommy	**Josiah Page**
Peter	**Hunter Page**
Daryl	**Samson Page**

Geoffrey Rush

Dayle Garlett (Dorm Boy), Paully Edgar (Sam), Sylvia Clarke, Ali Torres (Women on Beach), Ferdy Mauboy (Rosie's Dad), Rowan Albert (Boy at Sun Pictures), Emma Sibosado, Sophie Kelly, Irene Shadforth (Rosie's Gang), Kelton Pell (Mean Drunk), Jimmy Edgar (Footy Coach), Tony Briggs (Scary Black Man), Peter West (Lou, Policeman), Rob Greenough (Bruce, Policeman), Brodie Taylor (Barman, Broome), Damon Lockwood (Barman, Perth), Ricardo Del Rio, Nick Britton (Priests) Patrick Duttoo Bin Amat, Michael Manolis Mavromatis, Garry Gower (Lester's Band, Knuckles), Ngaire Pigram, Tara Gower, Gina Rings, Peggy Missi, Deborah Brown, Waangenga Blanco, Sermsah Bin Saad, Trevor Jamieson, Sani Townson, Perun Bonser, David Page, Rachelle Watkins (Roebuck Hotel Dancers), Jimmy Edgar, Peter Francis, Phillip Green, Roy Wiggan (Listen to the News Dancers), Terry Nupurra, Darren Matan, Angus Malakunya, Nathan Guymangura, Jason Yirrmal, Simon Bapadjambang (The Chooky Dancers)

After being punished for an act of rebellion at his mission school in Perth, Willie runs away with the intention of returning to his home in Broome.

Jessica Mauboy

Rocky McKenzie and Company © Freestyle Releasing

Ali Larter, Wentworth Miller © Screen Gems

RESIDENT EVIL: AFTERLIFE

(SCREEN GEMS) Producers, Jeremy Bolt, Paul W.S. Anderson, Robert Kulzer, Don Carmody, Bernd Eichinger, Samuel Hadida; Executive Producers, Martin Moszkowicz, Victor Hadida; Director/Screenplay, Paul W.S. Anderson; Based on the Capcom videogame *Resident Evil*; Photography, Glen MacPherson; Designer, Arv Grewal; Costumes, Denise Cronenberg; Music, Tomandandy; Editor, Niven Howie; Special Effects Supervisor, Mark Lawton; Stunts, Rick Forsayeth; Casting, Robin D. Cook (Canada), Suzanne M. Smith (U.K.); a Constantin Film International GmbH/Davis Films/Impact Pictures production; Canadian-German-British; Dolby; Deluxe color; 3D; Rated R; 97 minutes; American release date: September 10, 2010

CAST
Alice	**Milla Jovovich**
Claire Redfield	**Ali Larter**
Bennett	**Kim Coates**
Albert Wesker	**Shawn Roberts**
Angel Ortiz	**Sergio Peris-Mencheta**
K-Mart	**Spencer Locke**
Luther West	**Boris Kodjoe**
Chris Redfield	**Wentworth Miller**

Sienna Guillory (Jill Valentine), Kacey Barnfield (Crystal), Fulvio Cecere (Wendell), Ray Olubowale (Axeman), Christopher Kano, Tatsuya Goke (Snipers), Nobuya Shimamoto, Kenta Tomeoki (Technicians), Peter Kosaka (Duty Officer), Dennis Akayama (Captain Hotaka), Shin Kawai (Umbrella Sergeant), Mika Nakashima (J Pop Girl), Takato Yamashita (Business Man), Hiromi Okuyama (Kogel Girl Undead)

In the post-apocalyptic future, Alice heads to Los Angeles, where she and several other survivors do battle with a horde of rampaging zombies. Fourth entry in the series following *Resident Evil* (2002), *Resident Evil: Apocalypse* (2004), and *Resident Evil: Extinction* (2007).

HEARTBREAKER

(IFC FILMS) a.k.a. *L'arnacoeur*; Producers, Nicolas Duval Adassovsky, Yann Zenou, Laurent Zeitoun; Director, Pascal Chaumeil; Screenplay, Laurent Zeitoun, Jérémy Doner, Yoann Gromb; Photography, Thierry Arbogast; Designer, Herve Gallet; Costumes, Laetitia Bouix, Sophie Bay-Baudens; Music, Klaus Badelt; Editor, Dorian Rigal Ansous; Casting, Tatiana Vialle; a Quad Films & Script Associes (France) presentation; French-British; Dolby; Panavision; Color; Not rated; 104 minutes; American release date: September 10, 2010

CAST
Alex	**Romain Duris**
Juliette	**Vanessa Paradis**
Mélanie	**Julie Ferrier**
Marc	**François Damiens**
Sophie	**Helena Noguerra**
Jonathan	**Andrew Lincoln**
Van Der Becq	**Jacques Frantz**
Florence	**Amandine Dewasmes**
Dutour	**Jean-Yves Lafesse**
Goran	**Jean-Marie Paris**

Tarek Boudali (Manager of Montecarlo Bay Hotel), Philippe Lacheau (The Companion), Geoffrey Bateman (Juliette's Father-in-Law), Natasha Casheman (Juliette's Mother-in-Law), Franck Massiah (Franck), Hiromi Asai (Japanese Businesswoman), Sophie Jezequel (Office Employee), Audrey Lamy (Policewoman), Dominique Gaffieri (Auctioneer), Elodie Frenck (Alex's Girlfriend), Julien Arruti (Florence's Brother), Camille Figuereos (Curling Player), Nina Melo (Young Gospel Woman), Adina Cartianu (Librarian)

Alex, who makes a living by being hired to steal away women from their boyfriends, meets his greatest challenge when he is assigned to make sure the upcoming marriage of well-to-do Juliette and Jonathan does not take place.

Romain Duris © IFC Films

Andrew Garfield,
Carey Mulligan

Domhnall Gleeson, Carey Mulligan, Keira Knightley, Andrea Riseborough
© Fox Searchlight

NEVER LET ME GO

(FOX SEARCHLIGHT) Producers, Andrew MacDonald, Allon Reich; Executive Producers, Alex Garland, Kazuo Ishiguro; Co-Producer, Richard Hewitt; Director, Mark Romanek; Screenplay, Alex Garland; Based on the novel by Kazuo Ishiguro; Photography, Adam Kimmel; Designer, Mark Digby; Costumes, Rachel Fleming, Steven Noble; Music, Rachel Portman; Music Supervisors, Randall Poster, George Drakoulias; Editor, Barney Pilling; Casting, Kate Dowd; a DNA Films and Film4 presentation; British; Dolby; Super 35 Widescreen; Color; Rated R; 104 minutes; American release date: September 15, 2010

Keira Knightley, Carey Mulligan, Andrew Garfield

CAST

Kathy	**Carey Mulligan**
Tommy	**Andrew Garfield**
Ruth	**Keira Knightley**
Young Kathy	**Isobel Meikle-Small**
Young Ruth	**Ella Purnell**
Young Tommy	**Charlie Rowe**
Miss Emily	**Charlotte Rampling**
Miss Lucy	**Sally Hawkins**
Miss Geraldine	**Kate Bowes Renna**
Madame	**Nathalie Richard**
Amanda	**Hannah Sharp**
Laurs	**Christina Carrafiell**
Arthur	**Oliver Parsons**
David	**Luke Bryant**

Fidelis Morgan (Matron), Damien Thomas (Doctor), Huggy Leaver, Charles Cork (Delivery Men), Sylvie Macdonald (Bumper Crop Girl), David Sterne (Keffers), Andrea Riseborough (Chrissie), Domhnall Gleeson (Rodney), Kate Sissons, Amy Lennox (Sitcom Girls), Anna Maria Everett (Waitress), John Gillespie, Rachel Boss (Office Workers), Lydia Wilson (Hannah), Monica Dolan (Nurse), Chidi Chickwe (George)

At Hailsham School a special class of children are specifically raised for the purpose of donating organs for those in need.

Carey Mulligan, Keira Knightley, Andrew Garfield

Roger Ashton-Griffiths, Gemma Jones

Antonio Banderas, Naomi Watts, Anna Friel

Freida Pinto, Josh Brolin

Anthony Hopkins © Sony Pictures Classics

YOU WILL MEET A TALL DARK STRANGER

(SONY CLASSICS) Producers, Letty Aronson, Stephen Tenenbaum, Jaume Roures; Co-Producers, Helen Robin, Nicky Kentish Barnes; Executive Producer, Javier Méndez; Co-Executive Producer, Jack Rollins; Director/Screenplay, Woody Allen; Photography, Vilmos Zsigmond; Designer, Jim Clay; Costumes, Beatrix Aruna Pasztor; Editor, Alisa Lepselter; Casting, Juliet Taylor, Patricia Dicerto, Gail Stevens; a Mediapro, Versátil Cinema & Gravier production in association with Antena 3 Films & Antena 3 TV, a Dippermouth production; Spanish-British; Dolby; Deluxe color; Rated R; 98 minutes; American release date: September 22, 2010

CAST

Greg	**Antonio Banderas**
Roy	**Josh Brolin**
Alfie	**Anthony Hopkins**
Helena	**Gemma Jones**
Dia	**Freida Pinto**
Charmaine	**Lucy Punch**
Sally	**Naomi Watts**
Cristal	**Pauline Collins**
Henry Strangler	**Ewen Bremner**
Alan	**Neil Jackson**
Jane	**Fenella Woolgar**
Peter Wicklow	**Jim Piddock**
Enid Wicklow	**Celia Imrie**
Jonathan	**Roger Ashton-Griffiths**
Iris	**Anna Friel**

Rupert Frazer (Jogging Partner), Kelly Harrison (Personal Trainer), Eleanor Gecks (Rollerblading Friend), Christian McKay, Philip Glenister, Jonathan Ryland, Pearce Quigley (Poker Friends), Lynda Baron (Alfie's Date), Robert Portal (Jewelry Shop Salesman), Theo James (Ray), Christopher Fulford, Johnny Harris (Ray's Friends), Alex MacQueen (Malcolm Dodds), Anupam Kher, Meera Syal (Dia's Parents), Joanna David, Geoffrey Hutchings (Alan's Parents), Natalie Walker (Alan's Sister), Shaheen Khan (Dia's Aunt), Amanda Lawrence (Medium), Zak Orth (Narrator)

Having been abandoned by her husband after 40 years, Helena seeks advice from a psychic, while her daughter Sally and her husband Roy experience their own marital problems.

BURIED

(LIONSGATE) Producers, Adrián Guerra, Peter Safran; Executive Producers, Alejandro Miranda, Rodrigo Cortés; Director/Editor, Rodrigo Cortés; Screenplay, Chris Sparling; Photography, Eduard Grau; Art Directors, María de la Cámara, Gabriel Paré; Costumes, Elisa de Andrés; Music, Victor Reyes; a Versus Entertainment production in association with The Safran Company and Dark Trick Films; Spanish-America-French; Dolby; Color; Rated R; 95 minutes; American release date: September 24, 2010

CAST
Paul Conroy **Ryan Reynolds**

VOICE CAST
Jabir	**José Luis García Pérez**
Dan Brenner	**Robert Paterson**
Alan Davenport	**Stephen Tobolowsky**
Linda Conroy	**Samantha Mathis**
Pamela Lutti	**Ivana Miño**
Maryanne Conroy/ Donna Mitchell/ Rebecca Browning	**Warner Loughlin**
Special Agent Harris	**Erik Palladino**
911 Operator	**Kali Rocha**
State Department Rep.	**Chris William Martin**
Shane Conroy	**Cade Dundish**
411 Operators	**Mary Songbird**, **Kirk Baily**
CRT Operator	**Anne Lockhart**
CRT Spokesman	**Robert Clotworthy**
Nursing Home Nurse	**Michalla Petersen**
Maryanne	**Tess Harper**
Kidnappers	**Juan Hidalgo, Abdelilah Ben Massou**
Additional Voices	**Joe Guarneri, Heath Centazzo**

Paul Conroy wakes up in a box buried six feet underground, a cell phone with a rapidly dying battery his only means of contact to the outside world.

Ryan Reynolds

Ryan Reynolds

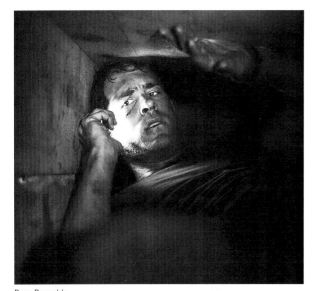

Ryan Reynolds

Ryan Reynolds © Lionsgate

Paz de la Huerta © IFC Films

Nathaniel Brown, Paz de la Huerta

ENTER THE VOID

(IFC FILMS) a.k.a. *Soudain le vide*; Producers, Brahim Chiou, Vincent Maraval, Olivier Delbosc, Marc Missonnier, Pierre Buffin, Gaspar Noé; Director/Screenplay, Gaspar Noé; Photography, Benoit Debie; Designers, Kikuo Ohta, Jean Carriere; Costumes, Tony Crosbie, Nicoletta Massone; Editors, Gaspar Noé, Marc Boucrot; Visual Effects Supervisor, Geoffrey Niquet; French-German-Italian, 2009; a Fidelite, BUF, Wild Bunch presentation; Dolby; Widescreen; Color; DV; Not rated; 154 minutes; American release date: September 24, 2010

CAST

Oscar	**Nathaniel Brown**
Linda	**Paz de la Huerta**
Alex	**Cyril Roy**
Victor	**Olly Alexander**
Mario	**Masato Tanno**
Bruno	**Ed Spear**
Little Linda	**Emily Alyn Lind**
Little Oscar	**Jesse Kuhn**

Nobu Imai (Tito), Sakiko Fukuhara (Saki), Janice Béliveau-Sicotte (Mother), Sara Stockbridge (Suzy), Stuart Miller (Victor's Father), Yemi (Carol)

Dead from a gunshot wound after a drug deal has gone bad, Oscar's ghostly spirit looks into present-day Tokyo and the sister he has left behind.

RELEASE

(TLA RELEASING) Producer/Designer/Costumes, Christian Martin; Co-Producers, Chris Broughton, Darren Flaxstone; Directors/Screenplay, Darren Flaxstone, Christian Martin; Photography, Simon Pearce; Music, Thom Petty; Editor, Darren Flaxstone; a Darren Flaxstone, Christian Martin presentation of a Bonne Idee production; British; Color; HD; Not rated; 87 minutes; American release date: October 1, 2010

CAST

Father Gillie	**Daniel Brocklebank**
Martin	**Garry Summers**
Max	**Bernie Hodges**
Rook	**Wayne Virgo**
Danny	**Simon Pearce**
Heather	**Dymphna Skehill**

While serving time in prison, a defrocked priest falls in love with a compassionate guard.

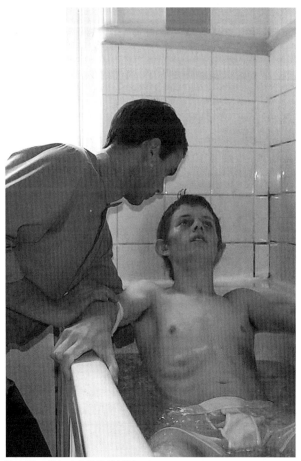

Daniel Brocklebank (left) © TLA Releasing

Kristin Scott Thomas, Sergi Lopez

Yvan Attal, Kristin Scott Thomas

Kristin Scott Thomas, Sergi Lopez

LEAVING

(IFC FILMS) a.k.a. *Partir*; Producers, Fabienne Vonier; Executive Producer, Stéphane Parthenay; Director, Catherine Corsini; Screenplay, Catherine Corsini, Gaëlle Marcé; Photography, Agnès Godard; Designer, Laurent Ott; Costumes, Anne Schotte; Editor, Simon Jacquet; Casting, Brigitte Moidon; a Pyramide Prods., Camera One, VMP, Solaire Prod. Production, in association with Cofinova 5, with the participation of Canal Plus, CineCinema; French; Dolby; Color; Not rated; 85 minutes; American release date: October 1, 2010

CAST

Suzanne	**Kristin Scott Thomas**
Ivan	**Sergi Lopez**
Samuel	**Yvan Attal**
Rémi	**Bernard Blancan**
Dubreuil	**Aladin Reibel**
David	**Alexandre Vidal**
Marion	**Daisy Broom**
Berta	**Berta Esqquirol**
Lagache	**Gérard Lartigau**

Geneviève Casile (Samuel's Mother), Philippe Laudenbach (Samuel's Father), Michèle Ernou (Mme. Auboy), Jonathan Cohen (Banker), Hélène Babu (Dorothée), Sali Cervià (The Girl at the Service Station), Asun Planas (30 Year Old), David Faure (Head of Personnel), Philippe Beglia (Antiques Dealer), Mama Prassions (Mme. Dubreuil)

Unfulfilled by her bourgeois marriage, Suzanne falls in love with the handyman set to construct her physiotherapy office, prompting her to make the bold decision to leave her husband and children.

Kristin Scott Thomas © IFC Films

TAMARA DREWE

(SONY CLASSICS) Producers, Alison Owen, Paul Trijbits, Tracey Seaward; Executive Producers, Sharon Harel, Christine Langan, Maya Amsellem; Director, Stephen Frears; Screenplay, Moira Buffini; Based on the graphic novel by Posy Simmonds; Photography, Ben Davis; Designer, Alan Macdonald; Costumes, Consolata Boyle; Music, Alexandre Desplat; Music Supervisor, Karen Elliott; Editor, Mick Audsley; Casting Leo Davis; a WestEnd Films, BBC Films and the U.K. Film Council presentation of a Ruby Films production in association with Notting Hill Films; British; Dolby; Super 35 Widescreen; Deluxe Color; Rated R; 110 minutes; American release date: October 8, 2010

CAST

Tamara Drewe	**Gemma Arterton**
Nicholas Hardiment	**Roger Allam**
Glen McCreavy	**Bill Camp**
Ben Sergeant	**Dominic Cooper**
Andy Cobb	**Luke Evans**
Beth Hardiment	**Tamsin Greig**
Jody Long	**Jessica Barden**
Casey Shaw	**Charlotte Christie**
Interviewer	**James Naughtie**
Diggory	**John Bett**
Zoe	**Josie Taylor**
Eustacia	**Bronagh Gallagher**
Tess	**Pippa Haywood**
Penny Upminster	**Susan Woolridge**
Mary	**Amanda Lawrence**
Nadia Patel	**Zahra Ahmadi**

Cheryl Campbell (Lucetta), Alex Kelly (Jody's Mum), Emily Bruni (Caitlin), Lola Frears (Poppy Hardiment), Tom Allen (Vintner), Patricia Quinn (Posh Hippy), Walter Hall (Army Geek), Joel Fry (Steve Culley), Lois Winstone (Fran Redmond), Nathan Cooper (SWIPE Band Member), Albert Clark (Boss the Dog)

Having turned herself from an ugly duckling into a stunningly lovely young lady, Tamara Drewe returns to the rural village where she grew up, causing quite a stir among the locals and attracting the attention of several men.

Bill Camp, Roger Allam, Pippa Haywood, John Bett, Tamsin Greig, Bronagh Gallagher, Lola Frears

Charlotte Christie, Jessica Barden

Luke Evans, Gemma Arterton

Gemma Arterton, Dominic Cooper © Sony Pictures Classics

NOWHERE BOY

(WEINSTEIN CO.) Producers, Douglas Rae, Robert Bernstein, Kevin Loader; Executive Producers, Jon Diamond, Christopher Moll, Tessa Ross; Co-Producers, Matt Delargy, Paul Ritchie; Co-Executive Producers, Bob Weinstein, Harvey Weinstein; Director, Sam Taylor-Wood; Screenplay, Matt Greenhalgh; Photography, Seamus McGarvey; Designer, Alice Normington; Costumes, Julian Day; Music, Alison Goldfrap, Will Gregory; Music Supervisor, Ian Neil; Editor, Lisa Gunning; Casting, Nina Gold; a Film4, U.K. Film Council presentation, in association with North West Vision and Media, LipSync Prods. and HanWay Films of an Ecosse Films production; British, 2009; Dolby; Panavision; Deluxe color; Rated R; 97 minutes; American release date: October 8, 2010

Anne-Marie Duff, Aaron Johnson

CAST

John Lennon	**Aaron Johnson**
Mimi	**Kristin Scott Thomas**
Julia	**Anne-Marie Duff**
Uncle George	**David Threlfall**
Bobby	**David Morrissey**
Paul	**Thomas Brodie Sangster**
George	**Sam Bell**
Pete	**Josh Bolt**
Marie	**Ophelia Lovibond**
Stan	**James Johnson**
Young John	**Alex Ambrose**
Marie's Friend	**Kerrie Hayes**
Schoolmistress	**Angela Walsh**
Popjoy	**Paul Ritter**
Reverend	**Richard Syms**

Angelica Jopling (Julia, aged 8), Abby Greenhalgh (Jackie, aged 6), Richard Tate (Teacher), Christopher Coghill (Cunard Yank), Ben Smith (Boy with Knife), Andrew Buchan (Fishwick), Baillie Walsh (Postman), Simon Lowe (Guitar Shop Guy), Frazer Bird (Len), James Jack Bentham (Rod), Jack McElhone (Eric), Daniel Ross (Nigel), Sam Wilmott (Colin Hanton), John Collins (Ivan), Colin Tierney (Alf), Nigel Travis (Cavern Bouncer), Lizzie Hopley (Café Waitress), Dan Armour (Percy Phillips)

Anne-Marie Duff, Kristin Scott Thomas

The story of how John Lennon's shattered family life led to his interest in becoming a musician.

Aaron Johnson © Weinstein Co.

Thomas Brodie Sangster, Aaron Johnson

Sendhil Ramamurthy, Shabana Azmi, Sally Hawkins

Sendhil Ramamurthy © UTV Motion Pictures

IT'S A WONDERFUL AFTERLIFE

(UTV) Producers, Gurinder Chada; Executive Producers, Chris Curling, Paul Mayeda Berges; Co-Producer, Michelle Fox; Director, Gurinder Chadha; Screenplay, Gurinder Chadha, Paul Mayeda Berges; Photography, Dick Pope; Designer, Nick Ellis; Costumes, Jill Taylor; Music, Craig Pruess; Songs, Bally Sagoo; Editor, Oral Norrie Ottey; Casting, Nina Gold; a Bend it Films and Indian Films presentation, in association with Studio 18; British; Dolby; Panavision; Color; Rated ; Rated PG-13; 99 minutes; American release date: October 8, 2010

CAST

Mrs. Sethi	**Shabana Azmi**
Roopi	**Goldy Notay**
DS Murthy	**Sendhil Ramamurthy**
Linda	**Sally Hawkins**
Dev	**Jimi Mistry**
Mrs. Goldstein	**Zoë Wanamaker**
D.I. Smythe	**Mark Addy**

Sanjeev Bhaskar (Curry Man), Shaheen Khan (Kebab Woman), Steve Morphew (A&E Doctor), Steve Jones (Earnest Reporter), Jamie Sives (Det. Hughes), Sacha Shilov, Teghvir Gujral, Harry Rance (Bike Kids), Ray Panthaki (Jazz), Jack Gordon (Ari), Lalita Ahmed (Old Woman at Market), Saraj Chaudhry (Young Man in Temple), Adlyn Ross (Rolling Pin Woman), Ash Varrez (Naan Man), Don Warrington (Chief Superintendent), Sanjeev Kohli, Hardeep Singh Kohli, Dar, Amer Chadha-Patel, Michael Tarat, Amit Shah (Speed Dating Men), Harvey Virdi (Overbearing Mother), Madhav Sharma (Dev's Father), Ace Bhatti (Tej), Preeya Kalidas (Karishma), Christopher Simpson (J.J. Jaan), Mo Sesay (Doctor)

A widow who has taken extreme measures to protect her overweight daughter makes it her mission to see the girl married before heading to the afterlife.

VISION

(ZEITGEIST) a.k.a. *Vision – Aus dem Leben der Hildegard von Bingen*; Producer, Markus Zimmer; Executive Producer, Hengameh Panani; Director/Screenplay, Margarethe von Trotta; Photography, Axel Block; Designer, Heike Bauersfeld; Music, Chris Heyne; Editor, Corina Dietz; a Clasart Film production presented with Concorde Classic; German, 2009; Dolby; Widescreen; Color; Not rated; 110 minutes; American release date: October 13, 2010

CAST

Hildegard von Bingen	**Barbara Sukowa**
Mönch Volmar	**Heino Ferch**
Richardis von Stade	**Hannah Herzsprung**
Abt Kuno	**Alexander Held**
Jutta	**Lena Stolze**
Richardis' Mother	**Sunnyi Melles**
Klara	**Paula Kalenberg**

Mariele Blendl (Jutta von Sponheim), Vera Lippisch (Gunhild), Annemarie Düringer (Äbtissin Tengwich), Devid Striesow (Kaiser Friedrich Barbarossa), Tristan Seith (Monk), Nicole Unger (Ursula)

The true story of how independent, free-thinking 12th Century Benedictine nun Hildegard von Bingen faced opposition from the brothers at the Disibodenberg cloister.

Barbara Sukowa, Hannah Herzsprung, Lena Stolze

Barbara Sukowa, Heino Ferch © Zeitgeist

Ari Brickman, Fernando Luján

Fernando Luján

Juan Pablo Medina, Marina de Tavira

NORA'S WILL

(MENEMSHA) a.k.a. *Cinco días sin Nora*; Producer, Laura Imperiale; Director/ Screenplay, Mariana Chenillo; Photography, Alberto Anaya Adalid; Art Director, Alejandro Garcia Castro; Music, Dario González; Editors, Oscar Figueroa Jara, Mariana Chenillo; a Cacerola Films production; Mexican, 2009; Color; Not rated; 92 minutes; American release date: October 15, 2010

CAST

José Kurtz	**Fernando Luján**
Bárbara Kurtz	**Cecilia Suárez**
Rubén Kurtz	**Ari Brickman**
Aunt Leah	**Verónica Langer**
Moisés	**Enrique Arreola**
Fabiana	**Angelina Peláez**
Nora Kurtz	**Silvia Mariscal**

Marina de Tavira (Young Nora), Juan Pablo Medina (Young José), Juan Carlos Colombo (Dr. Nurko), Martin LaSalle (Rabbi Kolatch), Max Kerlow (Rabbi Jackowitz), Fermín Martínez (Doorman), Arantza Moreno (Paola), Vanya Moreno (Laura)

After she commits suicide, Nora's ex-husband is forced to spend time with the corpse waiting for their son to arrive.

Fernando Luján © Menemsha Films

CARLOS

(IFC FILMS) Producer, Daniel Leconte; Executive Producer, Raphael Cohen; Director, Oliver Assayas, Screenplay, Oliver Assayas, Dan Franck, Daniel Leconte; Based on an original idea by Daniel Leconte; Photography, Yorick Le Saux, Denis Lenoir; Set Designer, François-Renaud Labarthe; Costumes, Jurgen Doering; Editors, Luc Barnier, Marion Monnier; Casting, Antoinette Boulat, Anja Dihrberg; French-German; Dolby; Color; Not rated; Shown at both 165 minutes and 330 minutes, plus intermission; American release date: October 15, 2010

CAST

Ilich Ramírez Sanchez, "Carlos"	**Edgar Ramírez**
Johannes Weinrich	**Alexander Scheer**
Magdalena Kopp	**Nora Von Waldst tten**
Wadie Haddad	**Ahmad Kaabour**
Hans-Joachim Klein, "Angie"	**Christoph Bach**
Anis Naccache, "Khalid"	**Rodney El-Haddad**
Gabriele Kröcher-Tiedemann, "Nada"	**Julia Hummer**
"Joseph"	**Rami Farah**
"Youssef"	**Zeid Hamdan**
Kamal Al-Issawi, "Ali"	**Talal el Jourdi**
Michel Moukharbal, "Andre"	**Fadi Abi Samra**
Wilfried Böse, "Boni"	**Aljoscha Stadelmann**
Brigitte Kuhlmann	**Katharina Schüttler**
German Militant	**Jule Böwe**
Carlos's Girlfriend	**Juana Acosta**
Amparo	**Martha Higareda**
Ambassador in the Hague	**Jean Baptiste Malartre**
Captainjean Herranz	**Olivier Cruveiller**
General Philippe Rondot	**André Marcon**
Maitre Jacques Verges	**Nicolas Briançon**
"Erik"	**Jean Baptiste Montagut**
Lana Jarrar	**Razane Jammal**
Cheikh Ahmed Zaki Yamani	**Badih Abou Chakra**
Valentin Hernandez Acosta	**Alejandro Arroyo**
Dr. Belaïd Abdessalam	**Mohammed Ourdache**
Iraqi Chargé of Affairs	**Basim Kahar**
Abdelaziz Bouteflika	**Abbes Zahmani**
Jamshid Amouzegar	**Nourredine Mirzadeh**
English Secretary	**Laura Cameron**
Chancellor Bruno Kreisky	**Udo Samel**
Otto Röesch	**Georges Kern**

The true story of Ilich Ramírez Sánchez who, between 1974 and 1994, became one of the most wanted terrorists in the world.

Badih Abou Chakra, Alejandro Arroyo, Edgar Ramirez

Edgar Ramirez

Edgar Ramirez

Edgar Ramirez © IFC Films

MONSTERS

(MAGNET) Producers, Allan Niblo, James Richardson; Executive Producers, Nigel Williams, Nick Love, Rupert Preston; Line Producer, Jim Spencer; Director/ Screenplay/Photography/Designer/ Visual Effects, Gareth Edwards; Music, Jon Hopkins; Editor, Colin Goudie; a Vertigo Films presentation; British; Dolby; Color; Not rated; 93 minutes; American release date: October 29, 2010

CAST
Andrew Kaulder   **Scoot McNairy**
Samantha Wynden   **Whitney Able**

A photojournalist agrees to escort an American tourist through a quarantined section of Mexico in hopes of reaching the safety of the U.S. border.

Scoot McNairy, Whitney Able © Magnet

Suelem © Arthouse Films

Tiao

WASTE LAND

(ARTHOUSE) Producers, Angus Aynsley, Hank Levine; Director, Lucy Walker; Co-Directors, João Jardim, Karen Harley; Photography, Dudu Miranda; Music, Moby; Editor, Pedro Kos; Brazilian-British; Color; Not rated; 98 minutes; American release date: October 29, 2010. Documentary about the 'catadores' or garbage pickers who work at Jardim Gramacho, one of the largest dumps in the world; with Vik Muniz.

This film received an Oscar nomination for documentary feature.

Vik Muniz

Rupert Grint, Bill Nighy, Emily Blunt

Rupert Everett © Freestyle Releasing

Martin Freeman

WILD TARGET

(FREESTYLE) Producers, Martin Pope, Michael Rose; Executive Producers, Steve Christian, Nigel Green, Philippe Martin, Marc Samuelson, Nigel Thomas, Charlotte Walls; Director, Jonathan Lynn; Screenplay, Lucinda Coxon; Photography, David Johnson; Art Director, Jim Glen; Costumes, Sheena Napier; Music, Michael Price; Editor, Michael Parker; a CinemaNX, Entertainment Film Distributors presentation of a Magic Light Pictures production, in association with Matador Pictures, Isle of Man Film, Cinema Four, Regent Capital; British-French; Dolby; Color; Rated PG-13; 96 minutes; American release date: October 29, 2010

CAST

Victor Maynard	**Bill Nighy**
Rose	**Emily Blunt**
Tony	**Rupert Grint**
Ferguson	**Rupert Everett**
Louisa Maynard	**Eileen Atkins**
Hector Dixon	**Martin Freeman**
Mike	**Gregor Fisher**

Graham Seed (Appraiser), Duncan Duff (Jeweller), Stephanie Lammond (Hotel Receptionist), Philip Battley (Barman), Geoff Bell (Fabian), Sia Berkeley (Hotel Receptionist), Rory Kinnear (Gerry Bailey), James O'Donnell (Barney), George Rainsford (Waiter), Alexis Rodney (Shabby Hotel Receptionist), Adrian Schiller (Forger)

Victor Maynard, a hitman tired of his violent lifestyle, balks at his latest assignment when he is ordered to kill a young woman who has stolen a precious Rembrandt from one of Victor's clients.

Eileen Atkins

Gérard Depardieu, Clovis Cornillac

Gérard Depardieu, Vahina Giocante

Jacques Gamblin (center) © IFC Films

INSPECTOR BELLAMY

(IFC FILMS) a.k.a. *Bellamy*; Producer, Patrick Godeau; Executive Producer, Françoise Galfre; Director, Claude Chabrol; Screenplay, Odile Barski, Claude Chabrol; Photography, Eduardo Serra; Designer, Françoise Benoit-Fresco; Costumes, Mic Cheminal; Music, Matthieu Chabrol; Editor, Monique Fardoulis; a co-production of Alicéleo Cinema – Alicéleo – France 2 Cinéma – DD Productions; French, 2009; Dolby; Color; Not rated; 110 minutes; American release date: October 29, 2010

CAST

Paul Bellamy	**Gérard Depardieu**
Jacques Lebas	**Clovis Cornillac**
Noël Gentil/Emile Leullet/ Denis Leprince	**Jacques Gamblin**
Françoise Bellamy	**Marie Bunel**
Nadia Sancho	**Vahina Giocante**
Mme. Leullet	**Marie Matheron**
Claire Bonheur	**Adrienne Pauly**
Alain	**Yves Verhoeven**
Bernard	**Bruno Abraham-Kremer**
Lawyer	**Rodolphe Pauly**
Gilles	**Maxence Aubenas**
TV Journalist	**Anne Maureau**
Tribunal Presdient	**Henri Cohen**
Doctors	**Thierry Calas,**
	Dominique Ratonnat
Madame Chantermerle	**Mauricette Pierre**
Taxi Driver	**Jean-Claude Dumas**
Jojo	**Matthieu Penchinat**

Police Chief Paul Bellamy finds his vacation plans interrupted by the arrival of his half-brother Jacques and a man on the lam who demands that the inspector give him protection.

Marie Bunel, Gérard Depardieu

THE GIRL WHO KICKED THE HORNET'S NEST

(MUSIC BOX FILMS) a.k.a. *Luftslottet som sprängdes*; Producer, Søren Stærmose; Executive Producers, Mikael Wallén, Ole Søndberg, Anni Faurbye Fernandez, Peter Nadermann, Lone Korslund, Gunnar Carlsson; Line Producer, Susann Billberg Rydholm; Director, Daniel Alfredson; Screenplay, Ulf Rydberg; Based on the novel by Stieg Larsson; Photography, Peter Mokrosinski; Set Designers, Maria Håård, Jan-Olf Ågren; Costumes, Cilla Rörby; Music, Jacob Groth; Editor, Håkan Karlsson; Casting, Tusse Lande; Swedish; Dolby; Color; Rated R; 148 minutes; America release date: October 29, 2010

CAST

Mikael Blomkvist	**Michael Nyqvist**
Lisbeth Salander	**Noomi Rapace**
Annika Giannini	**Annika Hallin**
Holger Palmgren	**Per Oscarsson**
Erika Berger	**Lena Endre**
Nils Bjurman	**Peter Andersson**
Christer Malm	**Jacob Ericksson**
Malin Eriksson	**Sofia Ledarp**
Inspector Jan Bublanski	**Johan Kylén**
Sonja Modig	**Tanja Lorentzon**
Monica Figuerola	**Mirja Turestedt**
Dr. Peter Teleborian	**Anders Ahlbom Rosendahl**
Hans Faste	**Magnus Krepper**
Dragan Armansky	**Michalis Koutsongiannakis**
Richard Ekström	**Niklas Hjulström**
Evert Gulberg	**Hans Alfredson**

Mikael Spreitz (Ronald Niedermann), Georgi Staykov (Alexander Zalachenko), Niklas Falk (Edklinth), Lennart Hjulström (Fredrik Clinton), Jan Holmquist (Halberg), Tanja Lorentzon (Sonja Modig), Donald Högberg (Jerker Holmberg), Aksel Morisse (Anders Jonasson), Carl-Åke Eriksson (Bertil Janeryd), Jacob Nordenson (Bertil Wadensjö), Sanna Krepper (Susanne Linder), Tomas Köhler (Plague), Johan Holmberg (Sandberg), Rolf Degerlund (Georg Nyström), Ylva Lööf (Domare), Pelle Bolander (Sonny Nieminen), Nicklas Gustavsson (Waltari), Aida Gordon (Sjuksköterska), Ismet Sabaredzovic (Miro Nikolic), Hamidja Causevic (Tomi Nikolic), Theilla Blad (Ung Lisbeth)

A wounded Lisbeth Salander enlists the help of her friend Mikael Blomkvist to help prove her innocence of the three murders for which she is being tried. Third and final installment in the series following *The Girl with the Dragon Tattoo* and *The Girl Who Played with Fire*.

Annika Hallin, Noomi Rapace

Lena Endre © Cohen Media Group

Hans Alfredson

Michael Nyqvist

Jamel Debbouze © Cohen Media Group

Jamel Debbouze (left)

Roshdy Zem

Jamel Debbouze, Sami Bouajila, Roshdy Zem

OUTSIDE THE LAW

(COHEN MEDIA GROUP) a.k.a. *Hors-la-loi*; Producer, Jean Bréhart; Director/Screenplay, Rachid Bouchareb; Photography, Christophe Beaucarne; Art Director, Yan Arlaud; Costumes, Stéphane Rollot, Edith Vesperini; Music, Armand Amar; Editor, Yannick Kergoat; from Tessalit Productions; French-Algerian-Belgian; Dolby; Color; Not rated; 138 minutes; American release date: November 3, 2010

CAST
Saïd	**Jamel Debbouze**
Messaoud	**Roshdy Zem**
Colonel Faivre	**Bernard Blancan**
Abdelkader	**Sami Bouajila**
Morvan	**Thibault de Montalembert**
The Father	**Ahmed Benaissa**
The Mother	**Chafia Boudraa**
Otami	**Samir Guesmi**
Ali	**Assad Bouab**
Picot	**Jean-Pierre Lorit**
Le Caïd	**Larbi Zekal**
Hélène	**Sabrina Seyvecou**
Sanjak	**Mourad Khon**
The Trainer	**Mohamed Djouhri**
Brahim	**Mustapha Bendou**
Hamid	**Abdelkader Secteur**

Three brothers, whose hatred of the French began when their family was evicted from their land, come together in 1954 to join the National Liberation Front in an effort to gain Algeria its freedom.

This movie received an Oscar nomination for Foreign Language Film.

RED HILL

(STRAND) Producers, Patrick Hughes, Al Clark; Executive Producers, Greg McClean, Rob Galluzzo, Craig McMahon; Director/Screenplay/Editor, Patrick Hughes; Photography, Tim Hudson; Designer, Enzo Iacono; Costumes, Nicola Dunn; Music, Dmitri Golovko, Charlie Parr; Casting, Nick Hamon; a Destination Films and Hughes House Films presentation in association with Wildheart Films, Wolf Creek Pictures, McMahon International Pictures and Screen Australia; Australian; Dolby; Color; Rated R; 95 minutes; American release date: November 5, 2010

CAST

Shane Cooper	**Ryan Kwanten**
Old Bill	**Steve Bisley**
Jimmy Conway	**Tom E. Lewis**
Alice Cooper	**Claire Van Der Boom**
Slim	**Christopher Davis**
Barlow	**Kevin Harrington**
Manning	**Richard Sutherland**
Earl	**Ken Radley**
Rex	**John Brumpton**

Cliff Ellen (Gleason), Jim Daly (Ted), Dom Phelan (Ken), Eddie Baroo (Willy), Tim Hughes (Micky Carlin), Ken Connley (Joseph Carlin), Richard E. Young (Dale), Jennifer Jarman-Walker (Martha), Elspeth Ballantyne (Old Woman), Ronald Falk (Old Man), Richard Morecroft (News Reader), Yesse Spence (News Reporter)

Relocating to the small town of Red Hill, police officer Shane Cooper finds his first day of duty turning into a nightmare when a prison break brings vengeful Jimmy Conway back to town.

Ryan Kwanten
© Strand Releasing

Ryan Kwanten, Steve Bisley

© Alamo Drafthouse

FOUR LIONS

(ALAMO DRAFTHOUSE) Producers, Mark Herbert, Derrin Schlesinger; Executive Producers, Carole Baraton, Peter Carlton, Will Clarke, Rita Dagher, Caroline Leddy, Tessa Ross, Angus Aynsley, Mark Findlay, Alex Marshall; Director, Chris Morris; Screenplay, Chris Morris, Jesse Armstrong, Sam Bain; Photography, Lol Crawley; Designer, Dick Lunn; Costumes, Charlotte Walter; Editor, Billy Sneddon; Casting, Des Hamilton; British; Dolby; Color; Rated R; 102 minutes; American release date: November 5, 2010

CAST

Omar	**Riz Ahmed**
Hassan	**Arsher Ali**
Barry	**Nigel Lindsay**
Waj	**Kayvan Novak**
Faisal	**Adeel Akhtar**
Sofia	**Preeya Kalidas**

Benedict Cumberbatch (Negotiator), Julia Davis (Alice), Craig Parkinson (Matt), Wasim Zakir (Ahmed), Mohammad Aqil (Mahmood), Karl Seth (Uncle X), William El-Gardi (Khalid), Alex MAcQueen (Malcolm Storage MP), Jonathan Maitland (Newsreader), Marcus Garvey (Marathon Policeman), Darren Boyd, Kevin Eldon (Snipers), Adil Mohammed Javed (Nabil), Toby Longworth (Heimlich Man), Danny Ashok (Phone Shop Assistant), Will Adamsdale (Alex)

A group of British jihadists decides to wage war on the world despite their total incompetence in the methods of terrorism.

MADE IN DAGENHAM

(SONY CLASSICS) Producers, Elizabeth Karlsen, Stephen Woolley; Executive Producers, Christine Langan, Tim Haslam, Norman Merry, Paul White; Line Producer, Laurie Borg; Director, Nigel Cole; Screenplay, William Ivory; Photography, John de Borman; Designer, Andrew McAlpine; Costumes, Louise St. Jernsward; Music, David Arnold; Muis Supervisor, Karen Elliott; Editor, Michael Parker; Casting, Lucy Bevan; a BBC Films presentation and UK Film Council presentation in association with HanWay Films, BMS Finance and Lip Sync Productions of a Stephen Woolley/Elizabeth Karlsen/Number 9 Films production in association with Audley Films; Dolby; Widescreen; Color; Rated R; 113 minutes; American release date: November 19, 2010

CAST

Rita O'Grady	**Sally Hawkins**
Albert Passingham	**Bob Hoskins**
Barbara Castle	**Miranda Richardson**
Connie	**Geraldine James**
Lisa Hopkins	**Rosamund Pike**
Brenda	**Andrea Riseborough**
Eddie O'Grady	**Daniel Mays**
Sandra	**Jaime Winstone**
George	**Roger Lloyd Pack**
Harold Wilson	**John Sessions**
Monty Taylor	**Kenneth Cranham**
Peter Hopkins	**Rupert Graves**
Robert Tooley	**Richard Schiff**
Eileen	**Nicola Duffett**
Monica	**Lorraine Stanley**

Matt Aubrey (Brian), Phil Cornwell (Dave), Karen Seacombe (Marge), Thomas Arnold (Martin), Sian Scott (Sharon O'Grady), Robbie Kay (Graham O'Grady), Andrew Lincoln (Mr. Clarke), Joseph Mawle (Gordon), Gina Bramhill (Hopkins' Secretary), Marcus Hutton (Grant), Joseph Kloska, Miles Jupp (Undersecretaries), Frank Baker (Frank), Philip Perry (Arthur Horovitz), Peter-Hugo Daly (Bartholomew), Simon Armstrong (Rogers), Matilda Cole (Emily), Romy Taylor (Rosie), Angus Barnett (Passing Van Driver), Birgitta Bernhard (Choir Mistress), Laurie Cannon, William Ivory, Nico Tatarowicz (Reporters), Denis Gilmore (Man on Bike), Danny Huston (Voice of American Boss), Mitchell Mullen (Kronnefeld), Matt King (Trevor Innes), Noah Taylor (Lisa Hopkins' Son), Victoria Watkins (Union Secretary), Craig Randall (Vicar), David Bond (Union Chairman), Simon Nehan (Welsh Union Man)

The true story of how the 187 women employed at the Ford Motor Company in Dagenham, England went on strike to demand pay equal to that of the male employees.

Bob Hoskins, Sally Hawkins, Geraldine James

Rosamund Pike, Rupert Graves, Richard Schiff

Miranda Richardson, Sally Hawkins, Geraldine James, Jaime Winstone, Andrea Riseborough © Sony Pictures Classics

Sally Hawkins, Nicola Duffett

Isabelle Huppert, Christopher Lambert © IFC Films

Nicolas Duvauchelle

WHITE MATERIAL

(ICF FILMS) Producer, Pascal Caucheteux; Director, Claire Denis; Screenplay, Claire Denis, Marie D'Diaye; Photography, Yves Cape; Set Designer, Saint Père Abiassi; Costumes, Judy Shrewsbury; Music, Tindersticks; Editor, Guy Lecorne; a Why Not Productions, Wild Bunch, France 3 Cinéma production; French, 2009; Dolby; Color; Not rated; 102 minutes; American release date: November 19, 2010

CAST
Maria Vial	**Isabelle Huppert**
The Boxer	**Isaach de Bankolé**
André Vial	**Christopher Lambert**
Manurel Vial	**Nicolas Duvauchelle**
The Mayor	**William Nadylam**
Lucie Vial	**Adèle Ado**

Ali Barkai (Jeep), Daniel Tchangang (José), Michel Subor (Henri Vial), David Gozlan (Hamudi)

When civil war breaks out in an unnamed African country, European farmer Maria Vial stands firm and refuses to abandon her coffee plantation.

HEARTLESS

(IFC FILMS) Producers, Richard Raymond, Pippa Cross; Executive Producers, Steve Christian, Steve Norris, Marc Samuelson, Nigel Thomas, Charlotte Walls; Director/Screenplay, Philip Ridley; Photography, Matt Gray; Designer, Ricky Eyres; Costumes, Jo Thompson; Music, David Julyan; Editors, Chris Gill, Paul Knight; Casting, Jeremy Zimmerman, Manuel Puro; a CinemaNX, Framestore, Matador Pictures production; British; Dolby; Color; Not rated; 109 minutes; American release date: November 19, 2010

CAST
Jamie Morgan	**Jim Sturgess**
Tia	**Clémence Poésy**
A.J.	**Noel Clarke**
Papa B	**Joseph Mawle**
Weapons Man	**Eddie Marsan**
Lee Morgan	**Luke Treadaway**
George Morgan	**Timothy Spall**
Marion Morgan	**Ruth Sheen**

Jack Gordon (Jeeko), Justin Salinger (Raymond Morgan), Fraser Ayres (Vinnie), David Florez, Nikita Mistry (Local Residents), Connie Hyde (Linda), Nadia Theaker (Charlie), David Sibley (Sociologist), Imogen Church (News Reporter), John MacMillan (She), Ross McCart (Young Jamie), Edward Green, James Lamb, Matt Ingram, Randell Benain (She Gang Members), Shaya Raymond, Charlie Dupré (Drunken Youths)

A shy young man who has shunned society because of a large birthmark on his face, uncovers a group of demonic East Londoners.

Joseph Mawle © IFC Films

Timothy Spall, Jim Sturgess

Peter Elliott, Africa Nile, Hugh Sacks © Freestyle Releasing

John Turturro

NC, Elle Fanning

THE NUTCRACKER IN 3D

(FREESTYLE) Producers, Andrei Konchalovsky, Paul Lowin; Executive Producer, Moritz Borman; Director, Andrei Konchalovsky; Screenplay, Andrei Konchalovsky, Chris Solimine; Additional Dialogue, Rupert Walters; Photography, Mike Southon; Designer, Kevin Phipps; Costumes, Louise St. Jernsward; Co-Producer, Jozsef Cirko; Line Producer, Laura Julian; Music Adaptation and Score, Edward Artemiev, Lyrics, Tim Rice; Editor, Henry Richardson; Senior Visual Effects Supervisor, Nicholas Brooks; Casting, Celestia Fox; a Vneshconobank presentation of a Nutcracker Holdings and HCC Media Group Ltd. Production; British-Hungarian; Dolby; 3D; Color; Rated PG; 110 minutes; American release date: November 24, 2010

CAST

Mary	**Elle Fanning**
Uncle Albert	**Nathan Lane**
The Rat Queen/Frau Eva	**Frances de la Tour**
The Rat King	**John Turturro**
Father	**Richard E. Grant**
Mother/The Snow Fairy	**Yulia Visotskaya**
Max	**Aaron Michael Drozin**
Voice of the Nutcracker	**Shirley Henderson**
The Prince	**Charlie Rowe**

Peter Elliott, Daniel Peacock (Gielgud), Alan Cox (Gielgud's Voice), Hugh Sachs (Tinker), Africa Nile (Sticks), Jonathan Coyne (Gnomad), Stuart Hopps (Butler/ The Rat Queen's Servant), Ferenc Elek (Lethal the Bat-Rat), Attila Kalmár (Screech the Bat-Rat), György Honti (The Rat Captain), Gernanda Dorogi, Kriszta Dorogi (Dr. Freud's Nieces), Verner Gresty (Little Girl's Father), Jason Harris (Lethal's Voice), Barna Ilyes (Slave), Lilla Karolyi (Little Girl), Dániel Mogács (Trolley Bus Orchestra Conductor), Richard Philipps (Dr. Freud), Péter Takátsy (Proud Rat Soldier), Andrea Tallós (Nervous Lady Rat), Béla Gados, Jácint Hergenröder, Zoltán Hetényi, László Keszég, Gyula Kormos, Ferenc Kovács, Krisztina Moskovits, Gábor Nagypál, Zsolt Sáfár Kovács (Rat Soldiers)

On Christmas Eve, Mary is taken on an adventure by the animated version of the nutcracker she has received from her uncle.

Nathan Lane

UNDERTOW

(THE FILM COLLABORATIVE) a.k.a. *Contracorriente*; Producers, Rodrigo Guerrero, Javier Fuentes-León; Executive Producers, Andrés Calderón, Cristian Conti, Michel Ruben, Émilie Georges, Ole Landsjöaasen, Christian Fürst, Annette Pisacane; Director/Screenplay, Javier Fuentes-León; Photography, Mauricio Vidal; Art Director, Diana Trujillo; Music, Selma Mutal; Editors, Roberto Benavides, Javier Fuentes-León; Casting, Rodrigo Bellott, Gustavo Vidal; Peruvian-Colombian-French-German, 2009; Dolby; Color; Not rated; 100 minutes; American release date: November 26, 2010

CAST

Miguel	**Cristian Mercado**
Santiago	**Manolo Cardona**
Mariela	**Tatiana Astengo**
Héctor	**José Chacaltana**
Pato	**Emilram Cossío**
Isaura	**Cindy Díaz**
Trinidad	**Haydée Cáceres**

Liliana Alegría Saavedra (Carlota), Germán González (Dr. Fernández), Juan Pablo Olivos (Tano), Cristian Fernández (Jacinto), Mónica Rossi (Ana), Atilia Boschetti (Sra. Rosa), María Edelmira Palomino (Doña Flor), Julio Humberto Cavero (Padre Juan), Tomás Fernández (Sabino), Alfonso Gamboa (Sergio), Jaziel Yenque Veliz (Baby)

Miguel, a fisherman who has been having an affair with another man behind his wife's back, is faced with the decision of whether or not to adhere to the wishes of his deceased male lover who asked to be buried according to the town rituals, thereby exposing their forbidden relationship.

Manolo Cardona, Cristian Mercado © The Film Collaborative

Peeter Jakobi, Per Christian Ellefsen

Peeter Jakobi, Per Christian Ellefsen © Oscilloscope

RARE EXPORTS: A CHRISTMAS TALE

(OSCILLOSCOPE) Producer, Petri Jokiranta; Co-Producers, Knut Skoglund, François-Xavier Frantz, Anna Björk; Director/Screenplay/Designer, Jalmari Helander; Based on an original idea by The Helander Brothers; Photography, Mika Orasmaa; Costumes, Saija Siekkinen; Music, Juri Seppä, Miska Seppä; Editor, Kimmo Taavila; Visual Effects, Fake Graphics; a CINET production, in association with Pomor Film, Love Streams agnès b. Productions, Davaj Film, FilmCamp, Filmpool Nord; Finnish; Dolby; Color; Rated R; 84 minutes; American release date: December 3, 2010

CAST

Riley	**Per Christian Ellefsen**
Santa Claus	**Peeter Jakobi**
Aimo	**Tommi Korpela**
Rauno Kontio	**Jorma Tommila**
Pietari Kontio	**Onni Tommila**

Jonathan Hutchings (Brian Greene), Rauno Juvonen (Piiparinen), Ilmari Järvenpää (Juuso), Risto Salmi (Sheriff), Jens Sivertsen, Sigmund Bee, Olav Pedersen, Nils M. Iselvmo (Main Elves)

In northern Finland a group of archeologists capture the "real" Santa Claus, a much more fearsome version of the one most of the world has embraced.

BARNEY'S VERSION

(SONY PICTURES CLASSICS) Producer, Robert Lantos; Executive Produer, Mark Musselman; Co-Producers, Lyse Lafontaine, Domenico Procacci, Ari Lantos; Director, Richard J. Lewis; Screenplay, Michael Konyves; Based on the novel by Mordecai Richler; Photography, Guy Dufaux; Designer, Claude Paré; Costumes, Nicoletta Massone; Music, Pasquale Catalano; Music Supervisor, Liz Gallacher; Editor, Susan Shipton; Casting, Dierdre Bowen, Nina Gold, Pam Dixon; a Serendipity Point Films in association with Fandango and Lyla Films presentation of a Robert Lantos production; Canadian; Dolby; Color; Rated R; 132 minutes; American release date: December 3, 2010

Paul Giamatti, Jake Hoffman

CAST

Barney Panofsky	Paul Giamatti
Izzy Panofsky	Dustin Hoffman
Miriam Grant Panoksfy	Rosamund Pike
The 2nd Mrs. P	Minnie Driver
Clara Chambers Charnofsky	Rachelle Lefevre
Boogie	Scott Speedman
Blair	Bruce Greenwood
Solange	Macha Grenon
Michael Panofsky	Jake Hoffman
Detective O'Hearne	Mark Addy
Charnofsky	Saul Rubinek
Kate Panofsky	Anna Hopkins
Leo	Thomas Trabacchi
Cedric	Clé Bennett
2nd Mrs. P's Father	Harvey Atkin
Rome Doctor	Massimo Wertmuller
Constable O'Malley of the North	Paul Gross
O'Malley Directors	Atom Egoyan, David Cronenberg
Jean the Matire'D at Ritz	Denys Arcand
Train Conductor	Ted Kotcheff
T/U Productions Executives	Mark Camacho, David Pryde
Bartender at Grumpy's	Paula Jean Hixson
"The Countess"	Marica Pellegrinelli
Judge at Rome Wedding	Domenico Minutoli
Uncle Irv	Howard Jerome
2nd Mrs. P's Housekeeper	Pauline Little
2nd Mrs. P's Mother	Linda Sorenson

Minnie Driver

Sam Stone, Burney Lieberman, Morty Bercovitch (Fundraising Targets), Robin Kazdan, Maury Chaykin (Wedding Guests), Larry Day (Bartender at Wedding), Sheila Hymans (Rabbi's Wife), Len Richman (Rabbi), Howard Rosenstein (Cousin Jeff), Brittany Lee Drisdelle (Girl at Café), Kyle Switzer (Production Assistant), Rebecca Croll, Ivana Shein (Receptionists), Steve Bienstock (NY Restaurant Waiter), Arthur Holden (Notary), Zack Kifell (Young Michael Panofsky), Simone Richler (Young Kate Panofsky), Arthur Grosser (Mr. Dalhousie), Pascale Bourbeau (Woman at Cemetery), Ellen David (Massage Parlor Madame), Katia Di Perna (Masseuse), Marina Eva (Leo's Girlfriend), Sandra Lavoie (Barney's One Night Stand), Harry Standjofski (Dr. Morty), Mélanie St-Pierre (O'Malley's New Co-Star), Tarah Schwartz (Reporter), Richard Lewis (Pathologist)

Barney Panofsky looks back on his mess of a life when he fell for the true love of his life while getting married to another woman.

Minnie Driver

Paul Giamatti, Dustin Hoffman

Paul Giamatti, Rosamund Pike

Paul Giamatti, Rachel Lefevre

Paul Giamatti, Scott Speedman

Rosamund Pike

Paul Giamatti © Sony Pictures Classics

APPLAUSE

(WORLD WIDE MOTION PICTURES) Producer, Mikael Christian Rieks; Director, Martin Pieter Zandvliet; Screenplay, Martin Pieter Zandvliet, Anders Frithiof August; Photography, Jesper Tøffner; Designer, Rasmus Cold; Music, Sune Martin; Editor, Per Sandholt; Casting, Gro Therp Bremer; a New Danish Screen, Nordisk Film- & TV-Fond production; Danish, 2009; Color; Rated R; 85 minutes; American release date: December 3, 2010

CAST

Thea Barfoed	**Paprika Steen**
Christian Barfoed	**Michael Falch**
Maiken	**Sara-Marie Maltha**
Tom	**Shanti Roney**
Påklæder	**Malou Reymann**
Peter	**Uffe Rørbæk Madsen**
William Barfoed	**Otto Leonard Steen Rieks**
Matthias Barfoed	**Noel Koch-Søfeldt**

Nanna Tange (Ekspedient), Michael Kastrupsen (AA Man), Annette Rønning (Bartender), Johanne Dam (Reggissør), Lars Brygmann (George), Lisbeth Holm Larsen (Receptionist), Bent Arvid Nillson (Man Kissing), Wenche Nillson (Woman Kissing)

Recovering alcoholic actress Thea Barfoed hopes to convince her ex-husband that her drinking is behind her, so she might reestablish a relationship with the two sons for whom she had relinquished custody.

Michael Falch, Paprika Steen

Otto Leonard Steen Rieks, Paprika Steen, Noel Koch-Søfeldt © World Wide Motion Pictures

Alba Rohrwacher, Pierfrancesco Favino © Film Movement

COME UNDONE

(FILM MOVEMENT) a.k.a. *Cosavogliodipiù*; Producer, Lionello Cerri; Co-Producer, Ruth Waldburger; Director, Silvio Soldini; Screenplay, Doriana Leondeff, Angelo Carbone, Silvio Soldini; Photography, Ramiro Civita; Designer, Paola Bizzarri; Costumes, Silvia Nebiolo; Music, Giovanni Venosta; Editor, Carlotta Cristiani; Casting, Jorgelina Depetris; Italian-Swiss; Vega Film; Dolby; Color; Not rated; 121 minutes; American release date: December 3, 2010

CAST

Anna	**Alba Rohrwacher**
Domenico	**Pierfrancesco Favino**
Alessio	**Giuseppe Battiston**
Miriam	**Teresa Saponangelo**
Chicca	**Monica Nappo**
Bianca	**Tatiana Lepore**

Sergio Solli (Domenico's Father-in-Law), Gisella Burinato (Aunt Ines), Gigio Alberti (Mr. Morini), Fabio Troiano (Bruno), Francesca Capelli (Agnese), Danilo Finoli (Ciro), Martina De Santis (Isa), Leonardo Nigro (Vincenzo), Adriana Del Guilmi (Anna's Mother), Raffaella Onesti (Vincent's Mother), Clelia Piscitello (Domenico's Mother-in-Law), Ninni Bruschetta (Domenico's Brother), Carla Chiarelli (Carla), Bindu de Stoppani (Enrica), Claudia Coli (Monica), Teresa Acerbis (Eliana), Paolo Riva, Michele Di Giacomo (Anna's Colleagues), Elisabetta Piccolomini (Head of Catering Service), Edwin Rojas Condor (José), Hassan Azougagh (Ahmed), Rocco Ozzimo (Barman), Stefania Casiraghi (Teacher), Adriano Passoni (Student), Federica Potenza (Domenico's Granddaughter), Sebastiano Moise (Boy on Moped), Pietro Romano (Teo), Nicoletta Maragno (Teo's Mother)

Anna's seemingly perfect married life is thrown into turmoil when she begins a passionate affair with a handsome waiter.

Geoffrey Rush

Jang Dong-gun, Kate Bosworth © Relativity Media

THE WARRIOR'S WAY

(ROGUE/RELATIVITY MEDIA) Producers, Barrie M. Osborne, Jodick Lee, Michael Peyser; Executive Producers, Tim White, Eui Hong, Matthew Jenner, David Milner, Kathy Morgan; Director/Screenplay, Sngmoo Lee; Photography, Woo-Hyung Kim; Designer, Dan Hennah; Costumes, James Acheson; Music, Javier Navarrete; Editor, Jonno Woodford-Robinson; Visual Effects Supervisor, Jason Piccioni; Casting, Liz Mullane (New Zealand), Wendy O'Brien (U.S.); a Boram Entertainment presentation of a Wellmade Star M, Sidius FNH Fuse + Media Pvt. Ltd. of a Mike's Movies/Ozworks production; New Zealand; Dolby; Color; Rated R; 100 minutes; American release date: December 3, 2010

CAST

Yang	**Jang Dong-gun**
Lynne	**Kate Bosworth**
Ron	**Geoffrey Rush**
Colonel	**Danny Huston**
Eight-Ball	**Tony Cox**
Saddest Flute	**Ti Lung**
Baby April	**Analin Rudd**
Baptiste	**Markus Hamilton**
Craig	**Rod Lousich**
Geyser	**Matt Gillanders**
Esmerelda	**Christina Asher**
Jacques	**Jed Brophy**

Carl Bland (Billy), Ian Harcourt (Lofty), Tony Wyeth (Smithy), Ryan Richards (Slug), Nic Sampson (Pug), Ashley Jones (Rug), Phil Grieve (Ivar), Eddie Campbell (Colonel's Deputy), Ebony Sushames, Aimee Renata (Mexican Daughters), Patricia Santana (Mexican Wife), Isbert Ramos (Mexican Husband), Ross Duncan (Barkeep), Makoto Murata (Sad Flue Deputy), Chontelle Melgren (Young Lynne), Cath Harkins (Lynne's Mother), Neill Rea (Lynne's Father), Elliott Officer (Lynne's Baby Brother), Ken Smith (Young Yang, 5 years), Youngmin Cho (Young Yang, 10 years), Helene Wong (Grandmother), Lee Han-garl (Greatest Swordsman), Michael Deane (Sailor), Ken McColl (Lion Tamer), David Austin (One Man Band), Brent Crozier (Cook), Matthew Burgess (Young Slug), Phoenix Brown Rigg (Young Rug), Peter Daube, John Rawls, Josh Randall, Andy Conlan, Matthew Morris, Reueben de Jong (Hell Riders), Robert Wootton, Wayne Gordon, Brenton Surgenor, Richard Coningham (Clowns), Angela McInterney, Sandra Terry, Louise Shadbolt, Anna Giordaini (Women with Bad Teeth)

After eliminiating most of his enemies, a great swordsman refuses to kill an infant and instead flees with her to a frontier town hoping to start life anew.

Jang Dong-gun

Halle Berry, Stellan Skarsgård

Chandra Wilson, Phylicia Rashad

Halle Berry © Freestyle Releasing

FRANKIE AND ALICE

(FREESTYLE) Producers, Simon Dekaric, Vincent Cirrincione, Halle Berry, Hassain Zaidi; Director, Geoffrey Sax; Screenplay, Cheryl Edwards, Marko King, Mary King, Jonathan Watters, Joe Shrapnel, Anna Waterhouse; Story, Oscar Jangier, Philip Goldberg, Cheryl Edwards; Photography, Newton Thomas Sigel; Designer, Linda Del Rosario, Richard Paris; Costumes, Ruth E. Carter; Music, Andrew Lockington; Editor, David Richardson; Casting, Juli-Ann Kay; a Cinesavvy, Inc. presentation of an Access Motion Picture, a Zaidi/Berry/Cirrincione production; Canadian; Dolby; Color; Rated R; 102 minutes; American release date: December 10, 2010

CAST

Frankie Murdoch	**Halle Berry**
Oz	**Stellan Skarsgård**
Edna	**Phylicia Rashad**
Maxine	**Chandra Wilson**
Hal	**Alex Diakun**
Nurse Susan Shaw	**Joanne Baron**
Dr. Backman	**Brian Markinson**
Dr. Strassfield	**Matt Frewer**
Pearl	**Rosalyn Coleman**
Rich Fat Cat	**Sean Tyson**
Tina	**Melanie Papalia**

Kira Clavell (Wanda), Joey Bothwell (Trish), Adrian Holmes (Cliff), James Kirk (Bobby), Kennedy Goodkey, Andrew Francis (Cops), Vanessa Morgan Mziray (Frankie, 16 years old), Michalya Eve Mckenzie (Frankie, 8 years old), Megan Charpentier (Paige, 8 years old), Katharine Isabelle (Paige), Ken Yanko (Judge Prescott), Emily Tennant (Paige, 16 years old), Scott Lyster (Pete Prescott), Ben Cole (Robert, Groom), Calvin Lee (Store Owner), Matias Hacker (Hector), Paula Puzzella (Polyester Molester), Eric Pollins (Bump and Grind Patron), Darryl Scheelar (Waiter), Rod Conway (Carl), Alexis Ioannidis (Celeste), Xantha Radley (Maria, Anorexic Girl), Colin Foo (Thin Asian Patient), Christina Schild (Annabel Prescott), Kathryn Kirkpatrick (Admission Nurse), William Phillips (Dan), Richard Cohee (Janitor), Harvey Gold, Troy Rudolph (Bar Executives), Primo Allon, Steffan Chaarria (Pool Players), Cheryl Adams (Code Green Nurse)

The true story of how Frankie Murdoch struggled with multiple personality disorder.

CASINO JACK

(ATO) Producers, Gary Howsam, Bill Marks, George Zakk; Executive Producers, Richard Rionda del Castro, Lewin Webb, Donald Zuckerman, Dana Brunetti, Patricia Eberle, Warren Nimchuk, Angelo Paletta, Domenic Serafino; Co-Producer/Screenplay, Norman Snider; Associate Producer, Rick Chad; Director, George Hickenlooper; Photography, Adam Swica; Designer, Matthew Davies; Costumes, Debra Hansen; Music, Jonathan Goldsmith; Editor, William Steinkamp; Casting, Marjorie Lecker; an ATO Pictures presentation in association with Rollercoaster Entertainment, Hannibal Pictures and Trigger Street Productions of a Rollercoaster Entertainment/MCG and Vortex Words + Pictures production in association with an Olive Branch; Canadian; Dolby; Color; Rated R; 108 minutes; American release date: December 17, 2010

CAST
Jack Abramoff	**Kevin Spacey**
Michael Scanlon	**Barry Pepper**
Pam Abramoff	**Kelly Preston**
Adam Kidan	**Jon Lovitz**
Gus Boulis	**Daniel Kash**
Bernie Sprague	**Graham Greene**
Emily Miller	**Rachelle Lefevre**
Big Tony	**Maury Chaykin**

Ruth Marshall (Susan Schmidt), Hannah Endicott-Douglas (Sarah Abramoff), John Robinson (Federal Agent Patterson), Jason Weinberg (Snake), Spencer Garrett (Tom DeLay), Yok Come Ho (Asian Factory Worker), Adam Waxman, Anna Hardwick (Lobbyists), John David Whalen (Kevin Ring), Matt Gordon (Bill Jarrell), Jeffrey R. Smith (Grover Norquist), Christian Campbell (Ralph Reed), Eric Schweig (Chief Poncho), Xenia Siamas (Flight Attendant, St. Andrews), Jeff Pustil (Bob Ney), Paolo Mancini (Scott Gleason), Cindy Dolenc (Friend), Nancy Beatty (Enid), Damir Andrei (Manny Rouvelas), Stephen Chambers (Art Dimopoulos), Oksana Kuznichenko (Blackjack Dealer), Paul Stephen (Rev. Mueller), David Fraser (Karl Rove), Pamela Matthews (Woman at Meeting), Natalie Krill (Flight Attendant, Crystal), P.J. Lazic (Chris), Mike Petersen (Senator Jarvis), Reid Morgan (Brian), Yannick Bisson (Oscar Carillo), Tina Louise Bomberry (Drinking Companion), Tony Stellisano (Roulette Operator), Mark-Cameron Fraser (Concierge), Balford Gordon (Kidan's Bodyguard), Billy Merasty (Bartender), Karl Campbell (Security Guy), Conrad Pla (Agent Hanley), Danielle Bourgon (FBI Agent), Joe Pingue (Little Tony), Ashley Wolfe (White House Aide), Linda Goranson (President Bush's Secretary), Brent Mendenhall (President Bush), Andrea Davis (Delay's Secretary), Richard Clarkin, Richard Blackburn (Partners), Judah Katz (Abbe Lowell), Brian Paul (Senator McCain), David Brandon George (Senator Burman), Duke Redbird (Senator Nighthorse), Todd Dulmage, Rob Baker (Spectators), Janet Hill (Native Woman), Kirstin Hinton (Junior Studio Executive), Kevin Louis (Prison Guard), Timothy Watters (President Clinton), John Hickenlooper (Senator Campbell), Graham Abbey (Simon Bowler), Mishael Morgan (Receptionist), Jennifer Higgin (Casino Woman), Bettina Bennett II (Natascha)

The true story of how super-lobbyist Jack Abramoff's influence over the world's wealthiest and most powerful men led to increasingly illegal activities and his eventual arrest.

Kevin Spacey, Barry Pepper

Christian Campbell, Rachelle Lefevre, Kevin Spacey, Barry Pepper

Kevin Spacey, Kelly Preston © ATO

THE ILLUSIONIST

(SONY PICTURES CLASSICS) Producers, Bob Last, Sally Chomet; Executive Producers, Philippe Carcassonne, Jake Eberts; Director/Adaptation/Music/Character Design, Sylvain Chomet; Original Screenplay, Jacques Tati; Art Director, Bjarne Hansen; Lead Compositor/Visual FX, Jean-Pierre Bouchet; Animatic, Jeann-Pierre Bouchet, James Duveen, Thomas Eide, Laurent Kircher, Pierre-Henry Lapoterie, Neil Martin, Eric Omond, Aya Suzuki, Sam Taylor, Leonard Ward; Background Layouts, Isobel Stenhouse, Bjørn-Erik Aschim; a Pathé presentation of a Django Films (UK) Cine B, France 3 Cinema co-production with the participation of Canal+, CinéCinéma, France 3 Télévisions; French-British; Dolby; Color; Rated PG; 80 minutes; American release date: December 25, 2010

VOICE CAST

The Illusionist/ French Cinema Manager	**Jean-Claude Donda**
Alice	**Eilidh Rankin**
Additional Voices	**Duncan MacNeil**
	Raymond Mearns
	James T. Muir
	Tom Urie
	Paul Bandey

An aging illusionist whose act is considered increasingly passé meets up with a teenage girl who still has the capacity for a child-like degree of wonder.

This film received an Oscar nomination for animated feature.

Alice, Showgirls © Sony Pictures Classics

Alice, The Illusionist

Billy Boy and the Britoons

Rabbit, The Illusionist

Opera Singer, The Illusionist

Guillermo Estrella, Javier Bardem, Hanaa Bouchaib

BIUTIFUL

(ROADSIDE ATTRACTIONS) Producers, Alejandro González Iñárritu, Jon Kilik, Frenando Bovaria; Executive Producer, David Linde; Co-Producers, Sandra Hermida, Ann Ruark; Associate Producers, Alfonso Cuarón, Guillermo Del Toro; Director/Story, Alejandro González Iñárritu; Screenplay, Alejandro González Iñárritu, Armando Bo, Nicolás Giacobone; Photography, Rodrigo Prieto; Designer, Brigitte Broch; Music, Gustavo Santaolalla; Editor, Stephen Mirrione; Casting, Eva Leira, Yolanda Serrano; a Menage Atroz, Mod Proucciones Production in association with Ikiru Films; Spanish-Mexican; Dolby; Color; Rated R; 148 minutes; American release date: December 29, 2010

CAST

Uxbal	**Javier Bardem**
Marambra	**Maricel Álvarez**
Tito	**Eduard Fernández**
Igé	**Diaryatou Daff**
Hai	**Taisheng Cheng**
Liwei	**Jin Luo**
Peluquería	**Manolo García**
Marquillaje	**Alessandro Bertolazzi**
Ana	**Hanaa Bouchaib**
Mateo	**Guillermo Estrella**
Ekweme	**Cheikh Ndiaye**
Samuel	**George Chibuikwem Chukwuma**
Li	**Lang Sofia Lin**

Yodian Yang (Fat Chinese Man), Tuo Lin (Barman, Bar Hai), Xueheng Chen (Chino Bodega), Xiaoyan Zhang (Jung), Ye Ailie (Father Hai), Xianlin Bao (Mother Hai), Ana Wagener (Bea), Rubén Ochandiano (Zanc), Karra Elejalde (Mendoza), Nasser Saleh (Boy), Tomás Del Estal (Man in Mourning), Ángel Luis Arjona (Dead Boy), Dolores Echepares (Funeral Lady), Adelfa Calvo (Big Woman), Manuel Solo (Doctor), Violeta Pérez (Nurse), Germán Almendros, Isaac Alcaide, Nacho Moliné (Surgeons), Carmen La Lata (Old Person), Annabel Totusaus (Secretary), Eduardo Gómez (Half-Naked Man), Ramón Elies, Juan Vicente Sánchez (Cemetery Employees), Félix Cubero (Bureaucrat), Carmen Peleteiro (Waitress), Federico Muñoz (Mayor), Leitica Albizuri (Young Girl #2), María Casado (Newscaster), Judith Hertas (News Reporter), Aroa Ortiz, Victoria M. Díaz, Sonia Cruz, Sophie Evans, Luna Jiménez Colindres, Dunia Montenegro, Rodica Ioana Unguereanu (Dancers at Strip Bar)

A single father struggling to raise two children possess the psychic abaility to convey messages from the recently deceased to their living relatives.

This film received Oscar nominations for actor (Javier Bardem) and foreign language film.

Javier Bardem, Hanaa Bouchaib

Maricel Álvarez, Javier Bardem © Roadside Attractions

Javier Bardem

ANOTHER YEAR

(SONY PICTURES CLASSICS) Producer, Georgina Lowe; Executive Producers, Gail Egan, Tessa Ross; Director/Screenplay, Mike Leigh; Photography, Dick Pope; Designer, Simon Beresford; Costumes, Jacqueline Durran; Music, Gary Yershon; Editor, Jon Gregory; Casting, Nina Gold; a Focus Features International, UK Film Council & Film4 presentation of a Thin Man Films and a Simon Channing Williams production; British; Dolby; Super 35 Widescreen; DeLuxe color; Rated PG-13; 129 minutes; American release date: December 29, 2010

CAST

Tom	**Jim Broadbent**
Gerri	**Ruth Sheen**
Mary	**Lesley Manville**
Joe	**Oliver Maltman**
Ken	**Peter Wight**
Ronnie	**David Bradley**
Carl	**Martin Savage**
Katie	**Karina Fernandez**
Tanya	**Michele Austin**
Jack	**Phil Davis**
Janet	**Imelda Staunton**
Tom's Colleague	**Stuart McQuarrie**
Mourners	**Eileen Davies, Mary Jo Randle, Ben Roberts**
Vicar	**David Hobbs**
Mr. Gupta	**Badi Uzzaman**
Mr. Gupta's Friend	**Meneka Das**
Drill Worker	**Ralph Ineson**
Allotment Lady	**Edna Doré**
Man in Bar	**Gary Powell**
Girl in Bar	**Lisa McDonald**

Throughout the course of a year, happily married Gerri and Tom are visited by various friends who reveal their discontment with their own lives.

This film received an Oscar nomination for original screenplay.

David Bradley, Lesley Manville

Jim Broadbent, Ruth Sheen

Lesley Manville, Jim Broadbent

Lesley Manville, Ruth Sheen

Ruth Sheen, Jim Broadbent

Peter Wight

Ruth Sheen, Karina Fernandez, Oliver Maltman

Oliver Maltman, Jim Broadbent, Lesley Manville, Ruth Sheen

Lesley Manville © Sony Pictures Classics

THE STRANGE CASE OF ANGELICA

(CINEMA GUILD) a.k.a. *O Estranho Caso de Angélica*; Producers, François d'Artemare, Maria João Mayer, Luis Miñarro, Renata de Almeida, Leon Cakoff; Director/Screenplay, Manoel de Oliveira; Photography, Sabine Lancelin; Sets, Christian Marti, José Pedro Penha; Costumes, Adelaide Trêpa; Editor, Valérie Loiseleux; a Filme do Tejo II, Eddie Saeta, Les Films de l'Après-Midi & Mostra Internacional de Cinema production; Portuguese; Dolby; Color; Not rated; 95 minutes; American release date: December 29, 2010

CAST

Isaac	**Ricardo Trêpa**
Angélica	**Pilar López**
Mother	**Leonor Silveira**
Engineer	**Luís Miguel Cintra**
Clementina	**Ana Maria Magalhães**
Servant	**Isabel Ruth**
Husband	**Filipe Vargas**
Justina	**Adelaide Teixeira**

Asked by a wealthy family to take the final photo of a young bride who has suddenly passed away, Isaac finds himself obsessed with the girl to the degree that she appears to come to life when he looks through his camera lens.

Pilar López

Ricardo Trêpa © Cinema Guild

Colin Farrell © Newmarket

THE WAY BACK

(NEWMARKET) Producers, Joni Levin, Peter Weir, Duncan Henderson, Nigel Sinclair; Executive Producers, Keith Clarke, John Ptak, Guy East, Simon Oakes, Tobin Armbrust, Jake Eberts, Edward Borgerding, Mohammed Khalaf, Scott Rudin, Jonathan Schwartz; Director/Screenplay, Peter Weir; Based on the book *The Long Walk: The Story of a Trek to Freedom* by Slavomir Rawicz; Photography, Russell Boyd; Designer, John Stoddart; Costumes, Wendy Stites; Music, Burkhard Dallwitz; Editor, Lee Smith; Visual Effects Supervisors, Tim Crosbie, Dennis Jones; an Exclusive Media Group, National Geographic Entertainment/ImageNation Abu Dhabi presentation of an Exclusive Films production, released in association with Wrekin Hill Entertainment and Image Entertainment; British-American-Polish; Dolby; Panavision; Color; Rated PG-13; 133 minutes; American release date: December 29, 2010

CAST

Janusz	**Jim Sturgess**
Mr. Smith	**Ed Harris**
Valka	**Colin Farrell**
Irena	**Saoirse Ronan**
Khabarov	**Mark Strong**
Tomasz	**Alexandru Potocean**
Kazik	**Sebastian Urzendowsky**
Voss	**Gustaf Skarsgård**
Zoran	**Dragos Bucur**
Andrei	**Dejan Angelov**
Bohdan	**Igor Gnezdilov**
Lazar	**Mariy Grigorov**

Yordan Bikov, Ruslan Kupenov (Garbage Eaters), Sattar Dikambayev (Mongolian Horseman), Sally Edwards (Janusz's Wife – 1939), Nikolay Mutafchiev, Valentin Ganev (Guards), Meglena Karalambova (Jansuz's Wife – 1989), Irinei Konstantinov (Jansuz – 1989), An-Zung Le (Shepherd), Stanislav Pishtalov (Commandant), Stefan Shterev (Cook), Anton Trendafilov (Steam Man), Termirkhan Tursingaliev (Young Mongolian Horseman), Hal Yamanouchi (Official)

The true story of how a small band of prisoners escaped from a Siberian gulag and crossed the Himalyans to freedom.

This film received an Oscar nomination for makeup.

FOREIGN FILMS B

2010 Releases / January 1–December 31

A YEAR AGO IN WINTER (IFC Films) a.k.a. *Im Winter ein Jahr*; Producers, Uschi Reich, Martin Moszkowicz; Executive Producers, Robert Cort, Scarlett Lacey; Director/Screenplay, Caroline Link; Photography, Bella Halben; Designer, Susann Bieling; Music, Niki Reiser; Editor, Patricia Rommel; Casting, An Dorthe Braker; a Constantin Film presentation of a production by Bavaria Filmverleih-Und Prokutions GmbH and Constantin Film Production GmbH; German, 2008; Dolby; Color; Not rated; 129 minutes; American release date: January 6, 2010. **CAST**: Karoline Herfurth (Lilli Richter), Josef Bierbichler (Max Hollander), Corinna Harfouch (Eliane Richter), Hanns Zischler (Thomas Richter), Cyril Sjöström (Alexander Richter), Mišel Maticevic (Aldo), Daniel Berini (Tom), Franz Dinda (Johannes), Karin Boyd (Renee Waters), Jacob Matschenz (Tobias Hollander), Inka Friedrich (Andrea), Hansa Czypionka (Stephan)

Karoline Herfurth in *A Year Ago in Winter* © IFC Films

IN SEARCH OF MEMORY: THE NEUROSCIENTIST ERIC KANDEL (Icarus Films) a.k.a. *Auf der Suche nach dem Gedächtnis*; Producer/Director/Screenplay, Petra Seeger; Based on the autobiography of Eric Kandel; Photography, Mario Masini, Robert Winkler; Editor, Oliver Neumann; a W-film Filmproduktion & Filmverleih production; German, 2009; Color; Not rated; 95 minutes; American release date: January 8, 2010. Documentary on Nobel Prize-winning neural scientist Eric Kandel. **WITH** Eric Kandel, Aaron Buck, Josh Dudman, Heinz Fischer, Denise Kandel, Emily Kandel, Yvonne Kandel, Juan Marcos, Mickey Stankert

Eric Kandel in *In Search of Memory* © Icarus Films

PYAAR IMPOSSIBLE! (Yash Raj) Producer/Screenplay, Uday Chopra; Director, Jugal Hansraj; Photography, Santosh Thundiyil; Photography, Ahmed Khan; Music, Salim Sulaiman; Lyrics, Anvita Dutt Guptan; Editor, Amibtah Shukla; a Yash Chopra presentation; Indian; Color; Not rated; 108 minutes; American release date: January 8, 2010. **CAST**: Uday Chopra (Abhay), Priyanka Chopra (Alisha), Dino Morea (Sidhu), Anupam Kher (Abhay's Father), Rahul Vohra (CP)

HOUSE (Janus Films) Producer/Director, Nobuhiko Obayashi; Concept, Chigumi Obayashi; Screenplay, Chiho Katsura; Photography, Yoshitaka Sakamoto; Designer, Kazuo Satsuya; Music, Asei Kobayashi, Mickie Yoshino; Japanese, 1977; Color; Not rated; 87 minutes; American release date: January 15, 2010. **CAST**: Kimiko Ikegami (Gorgeous), Eriko Tanaka (Melody), Kumiko Oba (Fantasy), Al Matsubara (Prof), Masayo Miyako (Sweet), Kung Fu (Miki Jinbo), Mieko Sato (Mac), Yoko Minamida (Gorgeous's Aunt), Saho Sasazawa (Gorgeous's Father), Haruko Yanibuchi (Ryoko), Kiyohiko Ozaki (Mr. Togo)

House © Janus Films

CHANCE PE DANCE (UTV Communications) Producer, Ronnie Screwvala; Director, Ken Ghosh; Screenplay, Ken Ghosh, Nupu Asthana; Photography, Hari vendantam; Designer, Shashikant Khamkar; Music, Sandeep Shirodkar, Adnan Sami; Dialogue, Kiran Kotrial, Manu Rishi; Lyrics, Amitabh Bhattacharya, Irfan Siddique; Editor, Shaju Chandra; a Bindass presentation; Indian; Color; Not rated; 158 minutes; American release date: January 15, 2010. **CAST**: Shahid Kapoor (Sameer Behl), Genelia (Tina Sharma), Mohnish Bahl (Rajeev Sharma), Vikas Bhalla (Gaurav), Zain Khan (Tina's Brother), Parikshat Sahni (Mr. Behl), Kurush Deboo (Sameer's Landlord), Satish Shah (School Principal)

Shahid Kapoor in *Chance Pe Dance*
© UTV Communications

ROOM AND A HALF (Seagull Films) a.k.a. *Poltory komnaty ili sentimentalnoe puteshestvie na rodinu*; Producers, Andrey Khrzhanovsky, Artem Vassiliev; Executive Producers, Lyubov Gaidukova; Director, Andrey Khrzhanovsky; Screenplay, Yuriy Arabov, Andrey Khrzahanovsky; Photography, Vladimir Brylyakov; Art Director, Marina Azizyan; Editors, Vladimir Grigorenko, Igor Malakhov; a School-studio SHAR production; Russian, 2009; Dolby; Color; Not rated; 130 minutes; American release date: January 20, 2010. **CAST**: Alisa Frieyndlih (Mother), Sergei Yursky (Father), Grigoriy Dityatkovskiy (Brodsky), Artem Smola (Young Brodsky), Evgeniy Ogandzhanyan (Brodsky in Childhood)

Alisa Frieyndlih, Sergei Yursky in *Room and a Half* © Seagull Films

THE SHAFT (Global Film Initiative) a.k.a. *Dixia de Tiankong*; Producers, Hu Giupu, Kang Jiammin, Xu Bailin, Tao Xingrui, Liu Xiuwen, Zhang Daogang, Wang Yijie, Liu Xinglun, Guo Sai; Director/Screenplay/Editor, Zhang Chi; Photography, Liu Shumin; Music, Guo Sida; Chinese; Not rated; 98 minutes; American release date: January 21, 2010. **CAST**: Luo Deyuan (Ding Baogen), Li Chen (Song Daming), Zheng Luoqian (Ding Jingshui), Huang Xuan (Ding Jingshen)

THE PARANOIDS (Oscilloscope) a.k.a. *Los paranoicos*; Producers, Sebastian Aloi, Nicolas Tacconi; Executive Producer, Sebastian Aloi; Director, Gabriel Medina; Screenplay, Nicolas Gueilburt; Photography, Lucio Bonelli; Designer, Sebastian Roses; Costumes, Paula Santos; Music, Guillermo Guareschi; Editor, Nicolas Goldbart; an Aeroplano presentation, in co-production with Mondo Cine, in association with Toct Films, Topo Films; Argentine-Spanish, 2008; Dolby; Color; Not rated; 104 minutes; American release date: January 22, 2010. **CAST**: Daniel Hendler (Luciano Gauna), Jazmín Stuart (Sofia), Walter Jackob (Manuel Sinovieck), Martín Feldman (Martin Sherman), Miguel Dedovich (Dodi), Jorge Booth (Medico), Fausto Collado (Portero), Susana Falcone (Graciela), Cecilia Gispert (Marta), Daniel Gorga (Mozo Restaurant), Maria Carolina Guzman (Mucama), Fernando Hoffman (Sagel)

Daniel Hendler, Walter Jakob, Jazmin Stuart in *The Paranoids* © Oscilloscope

FOR MY FATHER (Film Movement) a.k.a. *Sof Shavua B'Tel Aviv*; Producers, Heike Wiehle-Timm, Zvi Spielmann, Shlomo Mograbi; Director, Dror Sahavi; Screenplay, Ido Dror, Jonathan Dror; Photography, Carl-Friedrich Koschnick; Designer, Kuly Sander; Costumes, Michal Arbit; Music, Misha Segal; Editor, Fritz Busse; an Israfilm (Israel)/Relevant Film (Germany) production; Israeli-German, 2008; Dolby; Color; Not rated; 95 minutes; American release date: January 29, 2010. **CAST**: Shredi Jabarin (Tarek), Hili Yalon (Keren), Shlomo Vishinsky (Katz), Jony Arbid (Abed), Shadi Fahr-Al-Din (Salim), Rosina Kambus (Zipora), Oren Yadger (Shaul), Dina Golan (Sara), Chaim Banai (Rehavia), Michael Moshonov (Shlomi), Amir Yerushalmi (Avinoam), Khawlah Hag-Debsy (Fatma), Avital Pasternak (Adina), Adel Abou Raya (Ali), Yussuf Abu-Warda (Saleh), Uri Klausner (Dotan), Dani Israelis (Yakir)

Shredi Jabarin, Hili Yalon in *For My Father* © Film Movement

DISTRICT B13: ULTIMATUM (Magnet/EuropaCorp) a.k.a. *Banlieue 13 Ultimatum*; Producer/ Screenplay, Luc Besson, Executive Producer, Didier Hoarau; Director, Patrick Allessandrin; Photography, Jean-Francois Hensgens; Designer, Hughes Tissandier; Costumes, Thierry Delettre; Music, DA Octopuss, Track Invaders; Editor, Julien Rey; Visual Effects Supervisor, Alain Carsoux; Fight Choreographer, Cyril Raffaelli; Casting, Marc Robert, Herve Jakubowicz; a EuropaCorp, TF1 Films Prod., Ciby 2000 production, in association with Sofica EuropaCorp, with the participation of Canal Plus, CineCinema; French, 2009; Dolby; Super 35 Widescreen; Color; Rated R; 100 minutes; American release date: February 5, 2010. **CAST**: Cyril Raffaelli (Capt. Damien Tomaso), David Belle (Leïto), Philippe Torreton (President of the Republic), Daniel Duval (Walter Gassman), Elodie Young (Tao), MC Jean Gab'1 (Molko), James Deano (Karl le skin), La Fouine (Ali-K), Fabrice Feltzinger (Little Montana), Pierre-Marie Mosconi (Roland)

David Belle, Cyril Raffaelli in *District B13* © Magnet

MY NAME IS KHAN (Fox Searchlight) Producers, Hiroo Yash Johar, Gauri Khan; Director, Karan Johar; Story & Screenplay, Shibanji Bathija; Photography, Ravi K. Chandran; Designer, Sharmishta Roy; Costumes, Manish Malhotra, Shiraz Siddique; Music, Shankar Ehsaanloy; Editor, Deepa Bhatia; Casting, Shanoo Sharma, Robi Reed-Humes; a Fox Star Studios and Fox Searchlight Pictures presentation of a Dharma Productions & Red Chillies Entertainment production; Indian; Dolby; Color; Not rated; 160 minutes; American release date: February 12, 2010. **CAST**: Shah Rukh Khan (Rizwan Khan), Kajol (Mandira Khan), Christopher B. Duncan (Barack Obama), Carl Marino (Officer Vaughn), Steffany Huckaby (Kathy Baker), Jennifer Echols (Mamma Jenny), Sonya Jehan (Hasina), Shane Harper (Tim), Pallavi Sharda (Sajida Khan), Tanay Chheda (Young Rizvan), Douglas Tait (Sniper), Harmony Blossom, Kristen Marie Holly, Brittany Disston (Karma Girls), Michael William Arnold (Young Reese), Kathleen Darcy (Museum Teacher), Big Spence (Cameraman), Retson Ross, Ethynn Tanner Cerney (Locker Room Bullies), Adrian Kali Turner (Joel), Natasha Marc (Hooker), Jeremy Kilpatrick (Jimmy), Benny Nieves (Det. Garcia), Arjun Mathur (Raj), Nicolas Pajon (French Reporter), A'Ali-Salaam (Secret Service Agent), Kevin Oesetnstad (Officer John Marshall), Sheetal Menon (Radha), Arif Zakaria (Faisal Rahman), Reed Rudy (A.D.A. Jones), Tracy Weisert (School Teacher), Dominic Renda (Mark Garrick), Mike Howard (Father), Brett Glazer (Dwayne), Montgomery Paulsen (Autistic Patient), Mark S. Porro (D.A. Black), Marquis Scott (Tyler), Daniel Lee (Roger the Homeless Man), Ron Provencal (E.R. Doctor)

Shah Rukh Khan in *My Name is Khan* © Fox Searchlight

SHINJUKU INCIDENT (JCE/Emperor Motion Pictures) a.k.a. *Sansuk sigin*; Producers, Willie Chan, Solo So; Executive Producers, Jackie Chan, Albert Yeung; Director, Derek Yee; Screenplay, Derek Yee, Chun Tin-nam; Photography, Nobuyasu Kota; Designer, Oliver Wong, Chin Kar-lok; Music, Peter Kam; Editors, Cheung Ka-fai, Kwong Chi-leung; Action Choreographer, Chin Kar-lok; an Emperor Dragon Movies presentation of a Jackie Chan production; Hong Kong, 2009; Dolby; Color; Not rated; 114 minutes; American release date: February 5, 2010. **CAST**: Jackie Chan (Steelhead), Naoto Takenaka (Inspector Kitano), Daniel Wu (Jie), Xu Jing Lei (Xiuxiu/Yuko), Fan Bing Bing (Lily), Jack Kao (Gao Jie), Suet Lam (Old Ghost), Masaya Kato (Eguchi), Kenya (Nakajima), Hiroyuki Nagato (Hara Ooda), Yasuaki Kurata (Taro Watagawa), Paul Chun (Uncle De), Chin Ka Lok (Hongkie), Kenneth Low (Little Tai), Teddy Lin Chun (Tai Bao)

Jackie Chan in *Shinjuku Incident* © JCE

BAREFOOT IN TIMBUKTU (Mesch & Ugge) a.k.a. *Barfuss nach Timbuktu*; Producer, Beat Hirt; Director, Martina Egi; Photography, Frank Messmer, Bill Rosser; Editor, Christian Mueller; Swiss; Color; 16mm; HD; Not rated; 85 minutes; American release date: February 12, 2010. Documentary on Swiss-American artist-global activist-adventurer Ernst Aebi.

Ernst Aebi in *Barefoot in Timbuktu* © Mesch & Ugge

TO DIE FOR TANO (Leisure Time Features) a.k.a. *Tano da Morire*; Producers, Donatella Palermo, Loes Kamsteeg; Director, Roberta Torre; Screenplay, Roberta Torre, Gianluca Sodaro, Enzo Paglino; Photography, Daniele Cipri; Art Directors, Claudio Russo, Fabrizio Lupo; Costumes, Antonella Cannarozzi; Music/Original Songs, Nino D'Angelo; Editor, Giorgio Franchini; an ASP production in association with Dania Film, VIP National Audiovisual, Lucky Red, RAI-3, Telepiu, City of Palermo; Italian, 1997; Dolby; Color; Not rated; 76 minutes; American release date: February 12, 2010. **CAST**: Ciccio Guarino (Tano Guarrasi), Enzo Paglino (Enzo), Mimma De Rosalia (Franca Guarrasi), Maria Aliotta (Caterina), Annamaria Confalone (Modesta), Adele Aliotta (Rosa), Vincenzo di Lorenzo (Don Paliddu Billizza), Lorenzo La Rosa (Salvo lo Cicero), Giacomo D'Ignoto (Marciano), Francesca Di Cesare (Anna), Filippo Teriaca (Zio Filippo), Eleonora Teriaca (Vedova Puglisi)

Ciccio Guarino in *To Die for Tano* © Leisure Time Features

VIDEOCRACY (Lorber) Producers, Erik Gandini, Axel Arnö, Mikael Olsen; Director/Screenplay/Narrator, Erik Gandini; Executive Producer, Kristina Aberg; Co-Producers, Mikael Olsen, Axel Arno; Photography, Manuel Alberto Claro, Lukas Eisenhauer; Art Director, Martin Hultman; Music, Johan Söderberg, David Österberg, Krister Linder; Editor, Johan Söderberg; an Atmo presentation and production, in association with Zentropa, SVT, with the participation of BBC4 Storyville, Danish Broadcasting Corp., YLE FST; Swedish-Danish-British-Finnish, 2009; Dolby; Color; Not rated; 84 minutes; American release date: February 12, 2010. Documentary on the link between television and Italian politics. **WITH** Rick Canelli, Lele Mora, Marella Giovannelli, Silvio Berlusconi, Flavio Briatore, Fabrizio Corona, Simona Ventura.

Videocracy © Lorber Films

SHANGHAI RED (Indican) Producers, Oscar L. Costo, Vivian Wu; Director/Screenplay, Oscar L. Costo; Photography, Adam Kane; Designer, Jeff Knipp; Costumes, Jun Meng Feng; Music, Randy Miller; Editor, Josh Muscatine; a Shanghai Film Studios production; Chinese, 2007; Color; Not rated; 119 minutes; American release date: February 12, 2010. **CAST**: Vivian Wu (Meili Zhu), Michael Johnson (Richard Burgi), Kenny Bee (Lian Wei), Lu Yao (Bebe), Roger Yuan (Business Partner), Son Hong-lei (Lawyer), Ge You (Feng), Zhengwei Tong (Wei Ma)

LOURDES (Palisades Tartan) Producers, Martin Gaschlacht, Philippe Bober, Susanne Marian; Executive Producers, Bruno Wagner, Isabell Wiegand; Director/Screenplay, Jessica Hausner; Photography, Martin Gschlacht; Designer, Katharine Woeppermann; Costumes, Tanja Hausner; Editor, Karina Ressler; a Coop99 Filmproduktion (Austria)/Essential Filmproduktion, Thermidor Filmprodukution (Germany)/Parisienne de Production (France); Austrian-German-French, 2009; Dolby; Color; HD; Not rated; 99 minutes; American release date: February 17, 2010. **CAST**: Sylvie Testud (Christine), Léa Seydoux (Maria), Gilette Barbier (Father Hartl), Gerhard Liebmann (Pater Nigl), Bruno Todeschini (Kuno), Elina Löwensohn (Cécile), Katharina Flicker (Sonja), Lidne Prelog (Mrs. Huber), Heidi Baratta (Mrs. Spor), Jacques Pratoussy (Jean-Pierre Bely), Walter Benn (Mr. Hruby), Hubert Kramar (Mr. Oliveti), Helga Illich (Mrs. Oliveti), Bernadette Schneider (Hospitaliere), Thomas Uhlir (Max), Martin Thomas Pesl (Frank), Petra Morzé (Mother), Orsolya Tóth (Child in Wheelchair)

Sylvie Testud in *Lourdes* © Palisades Tartan

THE RED BARON (Monterey Media) a.k.a. *Der rote Baron*; Producers, Nikolai Müllerschön, Dan Maag, Roland Pellegrino, Thomas Reisser; Director/Screenplay, Nikolai Müllerschön; Photography, Klaus Merkel; Designer, Yvonne von Wallenberg; Costumes, Gudrun Schretzmeier; Music, Stefan Hansen, Dirk Reichart; Editors, Olivia Retzer, Adam P. Scott, Emmelie Mansee; German-British, 2008; Dolby; Super 35 Widescreen; Color; Rated PG-13; 106 minutes; American release date: February 19, 2010. **CAST**: Matthias Schweighöfer (Baron Manfred von Richthofen), Til Schweiger (Lt. Werner Voss), Lena Headey (Käte Otersdorf), Joseph Fiennes (Capt. Roy Brown), Maxim Mehmet (Friedrich Sternberg), Hanno Koffler (Lehmann), Volker Bruch (Lothar von Richthofen), Branislav Holicek (Wolfram von Richthofen), Jan Vlasák (Major von Richthofen), Tomás Koutník (Young Manfred von Richthoften), Tomás Ibl (Young Lothar von Richthofen), Albert Franc (Young Wolfram von Richthofen), Richard Krajco (Lanoe Hawker), Steffen Schroeder (Bodenschatz), Lukás Prikazký (Kirmaier), Ondrej Volejnik, Jirí Wohanka (German Soldiers), Iveta Jirícová (Redhead Whore), Vlastina Svátková (Blonde Whore), Axel Prahl (Gen. Ernst von Hoeppner), Gitta Schweighöfer (Kunigunde von Richthofen), Julie Engelbrecht (Isle), Luise Bähr (Sophie), Irena Máchová (Clare), Robert Nebrenský (Röuber), Ralph Misske (Menzke), Tino Mewes (Kurt Wolff), Jacob Ertemeijer (Gen. Hoeppner's Aide), Josef Vinklár (Paul von Hindeburg), Ladislav Frej (Emperor Wilhelm II), Brian Caspe (Officer Müller), Denny Ratajsky (Wounded Soldier), Pavel Myslík (Richthofen's Chauffeur), Václav Jílek (French Soldier), Adam Misik, Vladislav Rousek (Boys on Haystack), Barbora Ujfalusi (Girl on Haystack), Patrik Plesinger (Döring), Jirí Lastovka (Udel), Rostislav Novák (Löwenhardt), Zdenek Pecha (Steinhauser), Jirí Kout (Mechanic), Jan Unger (Surgeon), Igor Chmela (Wounded Soldier on Stretcher)

Matthias Schweighöfer in *The Red Baron* © Monterey Media

DEFENDOR (Sony Pictures Entertainment) Producer, Nicholas D. Tabarrok; Executive Producers, Sean Buckley, Tim Brown, Mark Stone, Tim Merkel, John Kozman; Director/Screenplay, Peter Stebbings; Photography, David Greene; Designer, Oleg Savytski; Music, John Rowley; Editor, Geoff Ashenhurst; a Darius Films production in association with Buck Films; Canadian-American-British; Panavision; Color; Rated R; 101 minutes; Release date: February 26, 2010. **CAST**: Woody Harrelson (Arthur Poppington/Defendor), Elias Koteas (Chuck Dooney), Michael Kelly (Paul Carter), Kat Dennings (Kat), Lisa Ray (Dominique Ball), Sandra Oh (Dr. Park), Charlotte Sullivan (Fay Poppington), Kristin Booth (Wendy Carter), Dakota Goyo (Jack Carter), Clark Johnson (Roger Fairbanks), Tatiana Maslany (Olga), Lyriq Bent (Wayne), Tony Nappo (Biker Cliff), James Preston Rogers (Biker Bob), Michael Cram (Blake), Graham Abbey (Constable Mike), John Paul Ruttan (Young Jack), Max Dreesen (Kid Arthur), A.C. Peterson (Radovan Kristic), Ron White (Judge Wilson), David Gardner (Grandpa Henry)

Woody Harrelson in *Defendor* © Sony Pictures Entertainment

HARLAN – IN THE SHADOW OF JEW SUESS (Zeigeist) a.k.a. *Harlan – Im Schatten von Jud Süss*; Producers, Amelie Latscha, Felix Moeller; Director/ Screenplay, Felix Moeller; Photography, Ludolph Weyer; Music, Marco Herten; Editor, Anette Fleming; a Blueprint Film, WDR, RBB, NDR production; German-French-Italian, 2008; Dolby; Black and white/Color; HD; Not rated; 99 minutes; American release date: March 3, 2010. Documentary on Third Reich filmmaker Veit Harlan; with Thomas Harlan, Maria Koerber, Caspar Harlan, Kristian Harlan, Jan Harlan, Christiane Kubrick, Jessica Jacoby, Alice Harlan, Chester Harlan, Nele Harlan, Lotte Harlan, Lena Harlan, Stefan Droessler.

Veit Harlan, Christina Soderbaum in *Harlan* © Zeitgeist

DELTA (Facets Multimedia) Producer, Viktoria Petranyi, Philippe Bober; Director, Kornél Mundruczó; Screenplay, Kornél Mundruczó, Yvette Biro; Photography, Matyas Erdely; Designer, Marton Agh; Costumes, Janos Breckl; Music, Félix Lajkó; Editor, David Jancso; a Proton Cinema, Filmpartners (Hungary)/Essential Filmproduktion (Germany) production; Hungarian-German, 2008; Dolby; Color; Not rated; 96 minutes; American release date: March 12, 2010. **CAST**: Félix Lajkó (Mihail), Orsolya Tóth (Fauna), Lili Monori (Mother), Sándor Gáspár (Mother's Lover)

Félix Lajkó , Lili Monori in *Delta* © Facets Multimedia

MY YEAR WITHOUT SEX (Strand) Producer, Bridget Ikin; Executive Producers, John Maynard, Andrew Myer, Joanna Baevski, Andrew Barlow, Paul Wiegard; Director/Screenplay, Sarah Watt; Photography, Graeme Wood; Designer, Simon McCutcheon; Editor, Denise Haratzis; a Screen Australia, Hibiscus Films production, in association with Film Victoria, South Australian Film Corp., Adelaide Film Festival, Showtime Australia; Australian, 2009; Dolby; Color; Not rated; 96 minutes; American release date: March 12, 2010. **CAST**: Sacha Horler (Natalie), Matt Day (Ross), Jonathan Segat (Louis), Maude Davey (Margaret), Katie Wall (Winona), Fred Whitlock (Greg), Sonya Suares (Rosie Singh), Portia Bradley (Ruby), Petru Gheorgiu (Con), Eddie Baroo (Tim Donnelly), Travis Cotton (Howard), Roy Davies (Old Man), Catherine Hill (Newsreader), Sean Rees-Wemyss (Blake), Lauren Mikkor (Georgia), Chloe Guymer (Chloe), Daniela Farinacci (Clinic Doctor), Rachel Maza (Intensive Care Nurse), Libby Stone (Natalie's Mother), Roger Oakley (Natalie's Father), Scott Terrill (Nurse), Rodney Afif (Hospital Doctor), Tammy McCarthy (Irene), David Vance (Radio Technician), Joe Silato (Swimming Club Santa), Anna Cattonar, Debra Waters (Pole Dancers), Klingon (Bubblehead), William McInnes (Antoinette, Radio Voice), Silas James, Benita Harrison (Petrol Station Couple), Elke Osadnik (Natalie), Carole Patullo, Leon Teague (Call Centre Workers), Barry Main, Lucienne Shenfield (Call Centre Applicant), Lara Signorino (Hairdresser), Sachin Joab (Rohit), Stella McInnes (Katie), Stella Maynard (Friend), Chelsea Bruland (Bubblehead's Rescuer), Marcelle Knapp, Christine Hua Cao (Mothers), Greg Saunders (Man in Foyer), Henry Ismailiw (Patient), Matt James (Wine Salesman)

Matt Day, Portia Bradley in *My Year without Sex* © Strand Releasing

GHOST TOWN (Lantern Films China) Producers, David Bandurski, Zhao Dayong; Director/Photography/Editor, Zhao Dayong; Music, Zhu Fangqiong; Chinese, 2008; Color; Not rated; 169 minutes; American release date: March 15, 2010. Documentary about day to day life in the mountain town of Zhizilou, China; with Yuehan, John the Elder, Pu Biqui, Li Yunai, Ah Long.

MID-AUGUST LUNCH (Zeitgeist) a.k.a. *Pranzo di Ferragosto*; Producer, Matteo Garrone; Director/Screenplay, Gianni Di Gregorio; Story, Gianni Di Gregorio, Simone Riccardini; Photography, Gian Enrico Bianchi; Designer, Susanna Cascella; Costumes, Silvia Polidori; Music, Ratchev & Carratello; Editor, Marco Spoletini; an Archimede production in collaboration with RAI Cinema; Italian, 2008; Dolby; Color; Not rated; 75 minutes; American release date: March 17, 2010. **CAST**: Gianni Di Gregorio (Gianni), Valeria De Franciscis (Gianni's Mother), Marina Cacciotti (Alfonso's Mother), Maria Cali (Aunt Maria), Grazia Cesarini Sforza (Grazia), Alfonso Santagata (Alfonso), Luigi Marchetti (Viking), Marcello Ottolenghi (Doctor), Petre Rosu (Homeless)

Gianni Di Gregorio in *Mid-August Lunch* © Zeitgeist

NEIL YOUNG TRUNK SHOW (Abramorama) Producers, Bernard Shakey, Elliott Rabinowitz, Jonathan Demme; Executive Producer, L.A. Johnson; Co-Producers, Mark Kamine, Elizabeth Hayes; Director, Jonathan Demme; Photography, Declan Quinn; Editor, Glenn Allen; a Fortissimo Films (Netherlands) presentation of a Shakey Pictures (Canada)/Clinica Estetico (U.S.) production; Dutch-Canadian-American; Dolby; Color; DV; Super 8; Not rated; 82 minutes; American release date: March 19, 2010. Documentary captures Neil Young in concert. **WITH** Neil Young, Ben Keith, Rick Rosa, Ralph Molina, Pegi Young, Anthony "Sweet Pea" Crawford, Eric Johnson, Cary Kemp.

Neil Young in *Trunk Show* © Abramorama

MANUELA AND MANUEL (Regent/Here) Producer, Frances Lausell; Executive Producer, Sonia Fritz; Director/Editor, Raul Marchand; Screenplay, Jose Ignacio Valenzuela; Photography, Sonnel Velazquez; Designer, Rafi Mercado; Costumes, Angie Olmedo; Music, Geronimo Mercado; a Caleidoscopio, Isla Films production; Puerto Rican, 2007; Color; DV; Rated PG-13; 94 minutes; American release date: March 26, 2010. **CAST**: Humberto Busto (Manuela/Manuel), Elena Iguina (Coca), Marian Pabon (Faraona), Luz Maria Rondón (Rosa), Ineabelle Colón (Margarita), Sunshine Logroño (German), Marisol Calero (Norma), Johnny Lozada (Ramon), Israel Lugo (Arturo), Adrian Garcia (Taxista), Luis Ortiz (Shadow), Sonia Fritz (Mrs. Green), Chari Lady Fox, Jamie Sunflower (Performers), Julio Ramos, Luis Freddie Vázquez (Friends), Isabel Gandia (Girl), Olga Vega (Waitress), Maine Anders (Fire Belly Dancer), Jaime Billoch (Toño), Julio J. Rodriguez, Miguel A. Quintana, Michael A. Dumas, Jose Felicicano (Dancers)

Humberto Busto in *Manuela and Manuel* © Regent/here

THE TROUBLE WITH TERKEL (Indican) Producers, Thomas Heinesen, Trine Heidegaard; Executive Producer, Kim Magnusson; Directors, Stefan Fjeldmark, Kresten Vestbjerg Andersen, Thorbjørn Christoffersen; Screenplay, Mette Heeno; Story, Anders Matthesen; Produced by Nordisk Film A/S in co-operation with A.Film and TV2/Denmark; Danish; Dolby; Color; Rated R; 88 minutes; Release date: March 26, 2010. **VOICE CAST**: Anders Mattheson (Barry Creambone), Anders Matthesen (Terkel), Randolph Kret (Leon Lozur/Stan), Heddy Burress (Sheila Buttercup), Johnny Vegas (Stewart Stardust), Eva Havata (Rita), Dan Schneider (Jason), Kristanna Loken (Joanne), Mark Fernandez (Saki), Traci Lords (Fat Doris), Chad Fifer (Silas), Chris Lackey (Gunney Sack), Danielle Fischell (Petula Baggles)

The Trouble with Terkel © Indican

THE SUN BEHIND THE CLOUDS: TIBET'S STRUGGLE FOR FREEDOM
(Balcony) Producer, Ritu Sarin; Executive Producers, Francesca von Habsburg, Lavinia Currier; Directors, Ritu Sarin, Tenzing Sonam; Screenplay, Tenzing Sonam; Photography, Graham Day, Jaimie Gramstrom, Tenzing Sonam, Stephen McCarthy, John Sergeant, Dilip Varma, Tenzin Tsetan Choklay; a White Crane Films presentation in association with Roland Films and Arch Communications; British-Austrian-French-Indian-Dutch-Chinese-American; Color; DV; Not rated; 79 minutes; American release date: March 31, 2010. Documentary on Tibet's fifty-year struggle to regain its freedom from China. **WITH** The Dalai Lama

The Dalai Lama in *The Sun Behind the Clouds* © Balcony Films

TEZA (Mypheduh Films) Producers, Haile Gerima, Karl Baumgartner; Director/Screenplay, Haile Gerima; Photography, Mario Masini; Costumes, Wassine Hailu; Music, Vijay Iyer, Jorga Mesfin; Editors, Haile Gerima, Loren Hankin; a Negod-gwad (U.S.)/Pandora Film (Germany) production; German-American; Dolby; Color; Super 16-and-HD-to-35mm; Not rated; 140 minutes; American release date: April 2, 2010. **CAST:** Aaron Arefe (Anberber), Takelech Beyene (Tadfe), Abeye Tedia, Teje Tesfahun, Nebiyu Baye, Mengistu Zelalem, Wuhib Bayu, Zenahbezu, Asrate Abrha, Araba Evelyn Johnston-Arthur, Veronika Avraham.

Aaron Arefe in *Teza* © Mypheduh Films

THE THORN IN THE HEART (Oscilloscope) a.k.a. *L'épine dans le Coeur*; Producer, Georges Bermann; Director/Screenplay, Michel Gondry; Photography, Jean-Louis Bompoint; Editor, Marie-Charlotte Moreau; a Partizan Films presentation; French, 2009; Color/Black and white; 16mm-to-HD; HD; Not rated; 86 minutes; American release date: April 2, 2010. Documentary in which filmmaker Michel Gondry pays tribute to his Aunt Suzette who had worked as a schoolteacher for 34 years. **WITH** Suzette Gondry, Jean-Yves Gondry, Sasha Allard, Remi Andre, Lucas Andreo, Laura Arjailles, Sophie Balderelli, Viviane Bastide, Henri Bec, Gabrielle Bell, Denis Bertaux, Denis Bertavy, Berthezene Denise, Francis Bertot, Gerard Bertrand, Pierre Bertrand, Lucie Blanc, Nathalie Boucknooghe, Mathis Boucknooghe, Andre Boudes, Marie-Therese Boudes, Yoni Bouisseren, Isabelle Bouisseren

Suzette Gondry, Michael Gondry in *The Thorn in the Heart* © Oscilloscope

EVERYONE ELSE (Cinema Guild) a.k.a. *Alle Anderen*; Producers, Janine Jackowski, Dirk Engelhardt, Maren Ade; Director/Screenplay, Maren Ade; Photography, Bernhard Keller; Art Directors, Silke Fischer, Volko Kamensky, Jochen Dehn; Costumes, Gitti Fuchs; Editor, Heike Parplies; a Komplizen Film production, in association with SWR, WDR, Arte; German, 2009; Dolby; Color; Not rated; 120 minutes; American release date: April 9, 2010. **CAST:** Birgit Minichmayr (Gitti), Lars Eidinger (Chris), Hans-Jochen Wagner (Hans), Nicole Marischka (Sana), Mira Partecke, Atef Vogel (Vacationers), Paula Hartmann (Rebecca), Carina N. Wiese (Chris's Sister), Laura Zedda (Baby), Claudio Melis (Man in the Car)

Birgit Minichmayr, Lars Eidinger in *Everyone Else* © Cinema Guild

BREATH MADE VISIBLE: ANNA HALPRIN (Argot Pictures) Producer/Director, Ruedi Gerber; Co-Producer, Mike King; Photography, Adam Teichman; Editors, Francoise Dumoulin, C. Peters; Music, Mario Grigorov; a ZAS Film; Swiss-American; Color; Not rated; 82 minutes; Release date: April 2, 2010. Documentary on choreographer and dance pioneer Anna Halprin. **WITH** Anna Halprin, Lawrence Halprin, Merce Cunningham, A.A. Leath, John Graham, Rana Halprin

Anna Halprin in *Breath Made Visible* © Argot Pictures

WOMEN WITHOUT MEN (IndiePix) a.k.a. *Zanan-e bedun-e mardan*; Producers, Susanne Marian, Martin Gschlacht, Philippe Bober; Executive Producers, Barbara Gladstone, Jereome de Noirmont, Oleg Kokhan; Directors, Shirin Neshat, Shoja Azari; Screenplay, Neshat Azari, Steven Henry Madoff; Based on the novella by Shahrnush Parsipur; Photography, Martin Gschlacht; Designer, Katharina Woeppermann; Costumes, Thomas Olah; Music, Ryuichi Sakamoto, Abbas Bakhtiari; Editors, George Cragg, Jay Rabinowitz, Julia Wiedwald, Patrick Lambertz, Christof Schertenleib; an Essential Filmproduktion (Germany)/Coop99 (Austria)/Parisienne de Prod. (France) production; German-Austrian-French, 2009; Dolby; Color; HD; Not rated; 100 minutes; American release date: April 9, 2010. **CAST**: Navid Akhavan (Ali), Mina Azarian (Zinat), Bijan Daneshmand (Abbas), Rahi Daneshmand (Soldier), Salma Daneshmand (Guest), Pegah Ferydoni (Faezeh), Arita Shahrzad (Farrokhlagha), Tahmoures Tehrani (Sadri), Shabnam Toloui (Munis), Orsolya Tóth (Zarin), Essa Zahir (Amir Khan)

Women without Men © IndiePix

WORLD ON A WIRE (MoMA) a.k.a. *Welt am Draht*; Producers, Peter Marthesheimer, Alexander Wesemann; Director, Rainer Wener Fassbinder; Screenplay, Rainer Werner Fassbinder, Fritz Muller-Scherz; based on the novel *Simulacron-3* by Daniel F. Galouye; Music, Gottfried Hungsberg; German, 1973 (television); Color; Not rated; 205 minutes; American release date: April 14, 2010. **CAST**: Klaus Löwitsch (Fred Stiller), Barbara Valentin (Gloria Fromm), Mascha Rabben (Eva Vollmer), Karl-Heinz Vosgerau (Herbert Siskins), Wolfgang Schenck (Franz Hahn), Günter Lamprecht (Fritz Walfang), Ulli Lommel (Rupp, Journalist), Adrian Hooven (Prof. Henry Vollmer), Ivan Desny (Guenther Lause), Joachim Hansen (Hans Edelkern), Kurt Raab (Mark Holm), Margit Carstensen (Maya Schmidt-Gentner), Ingrid Caven (Uschi, Journalist), Gottfried John (Einstein), Rudolf Lenz (Hartmann), Lieselotte Eder (Data Typist), Heinz Meier (Von Weinlaub), Peter Chatel (Hirse), Rainer Hauer (Inspector Lehner), Karl Scheydt (Inspector Stuhlfahrt), Ernst Küsters, Elhedi Ben Salem (Bodyguards), Solange Pradel (Singer), Bruce Low (Doctor), Elma Karlowa (Keeper of Cafeteria)

World on a Wire © MoMA

NOBODY'S PERFECT (Lorber) Producers, Niko von Glasow, Anne-Sophie Quancard, Frank Henschke; Executive Producer, Ewa Boroski; Director, Niko von Glasow; Screenplay, Andrew Emerson, Kiki von Glasow, Niko von Glasow; Photography, Ania Dabrowska, Andreas Kohler; Editors, Mechthild Barth, Mathias Dombrink; a Palladio Film and Westdeutscher Rundfunk production; German, 2009; Colo; 35mm/DV-to-35mm; Not rated; 84 minutes; American release date: April 16, 2010. Documentary about a nude photo shoot of 12 prenatal victims of Thalidomide. **WITH** Stefan Fricke, Sofia Plich, Bianca Vogel, Sigrid Kwella, Doris Pakendorf, Theo Zavelberg, Petra Uttenweiler, Andreas Meyer, Kim Morton, Fred Dove, Mat Fraser, Niko von Glasow, Mandel von Glasow

NoBody's Perfect © Lorber Films

NO ONE KNOWS ABOUT PERSIAN CATS (IFC Films) a.k.a. *Kasi az gorbehayeh irani khabar nadareh*; Producers, Bahman Ghobadi; Executive Producer, Roxana Saberi; Co-Producer, Mehmet Aktas; Director/Designer, Bahman Ghobadi; Screenplay, Bahman Ghobadi, Hossein M. Abkenar, Roxana Saberi; Photography, Turaj Aslani; Editor, Hayedeh Safiyari; Iranian, 2009; Dolby; Color; Widescreen; HD-to-35mm; Not rated; 101 minutes; American release date: April 16, 2010. **CAST:** Negar Shaghaghi (Negar), Ashkan Koshanejad (Ashkan), Hamed Behdad (Nader), Hichkas, Hamed Seyyed Javadi, Pouya Hosseini, Kourash Mirzaei, Arash Farazmand

Arash Farazmand in *No One Knows about Persian Cats* © IFC Films

MALICE IN WONDERLAND (Magnet) Producers, Mark Williams, Albert Martinez Martin; Director, Simon Fellows; Screenplay, Jayson Rothwell; Photography, Christopher Ross; Designer, Lisa Hall; Costumes, Alice Wolfbauer; Music, Christian Henson, Joe Henson; Casting, Alex Johnson; a Mark Williams Films/2B Pictures/Future Films production; British; Dolby; Color; Rated R; 87 minutes; American release date: April 16, 2010. **CAST**: Maggie Grace (Alice), Danny Dyer (Whitey), Matt King (Gonzo), Nathaniel Parker (Harry Hunt), Bronagh Gallagher (Hattie), Anthony Higgins (Rex), Steve Haze (Midge), Dave Lynn (Jack/Jacqui), Gary Beadle (DJ Felix Chester), Amanda Boxer (Bag Lady), Garrick Hagon (Mr. Dodgson), Paul Kaye (Caterpillar), Alan McKenna (Griffin), Fiona O'Shaughnessy (Hooker/Brothel Madam), Steve Furst (Mo), Lin Blakley (Mrs. Jones), David Frost (One Ball Barry), Tony Cook (Jimmy Three Chins)

Maggie Grace in *Malice in Wonderland* © Magnet

RAMCHAND PAKISTANI (MoMA) Producer/Treatment, Javed Jabbar; Director, Mehreen Jabbar; Screenplay, Mohammad Ahmed; Photography, Sofian Khan; Designer, Aqeel Ur Rehmann; Music, Debajyoti Mishra; Editors, Aseem Sinha, Mehreen Jabbar; a Project One production in association with JJ Media, Namak Films; Pakistani, 2008; Dolby; Color; HD; Not rated; 105 minutes; American release date: April 21, 2010. **CAST**: Shaood Alvi (Asif Hussain), Adarsh Ayaz (Moti), Atif Badar (Lalu), Karim Bux Baloch (Baloch), Nandita Das (Champa), Rashid Raooqi (Shankar), Syed Fazal Hussain (Young Ramchand), Nouman Ijaz (Abdullah), Navaid Jabbar (Older Ramchand), Salim Mairaj (Vishesh), Farooq Pareo (Suresh), Adnan Shah (Sharma), Zhalay Sharhadi (Laxmi), Maria Wasti (Kamla)

Ramchand Pakistani © Project One

THE RED BIRDS (Independent) Director/Photography, Brigitte Cornand; Music, The Birds of Martha's Vineyard; Editor, Julien Rey; a Les Films du Siamois production; French; Color; Not rated; 75 minutes; American release date: April 21, 2010. Documentary in which filmmaker Brigitte Cornand imagines 14 of her female artist friends as birds.

THE GOOD, THE BAD, THE WEIRD (IFC Films) a.k.a. *Joheunnom nabbeunnom isanghannom*; Producers, Choi Jae-won, Kim Jee-woon; Executive Producer, Miky Lee; Director, Kim Jee-woon; Screenplay, Kim Jee-woon, Kim Min-suk; Photography, Lee Mogae; Designer, Cho Hwa-sung; Costumes, Kwon Yoo-jin, Choi Eui-young; Music, Dalparan Chang Young-gyu; Editor, Nam Na-Young; a CJ Entertainment production; Korean, 2008; Dolby; Color; Not rated; 130 minutes; American release date: April 23, 2010. **CAST**: Song Kang-ho (Yoon Tae-goo, The Weird), Lee Byung-hun (Park Chang-yi, The Bad), Jung Woo-sung (Park Do-won, The Good), Jo Kyeong-hun (Doo-chae), Kim Kwang-il (Two Swords), Lee Cheong-a (Song-i), Ma Dong-seok (Bear), Oh Dal-su, Ryu Seung-su (Man-gil), Oh Seo-won (Chinese Woman), Son Byung-ho (Seo Jae-sik), Song Young-chang (Kim Pan-joo), Uhm Ji-won (Na-yeon), Yun Je-mun (Byeong-choon)

Lee Byung-Hun in *The Good, the Bad, the Weird* © IFC Films

BOOGIE WOOGIE (IFC FILMS) Producers, Danny Moynihan, Kami Naghdi, Christopher Simon, Cat Villiers; Executive Producers, Christopher Figg, Rob Whitehouse, Matthew Hobbs, Valentine Stockdale, Charles Haswell, Matias Rojas, Chris Hanley, Leonid Rozhetskin, Katrine Boorman; Director, Duncan Ward; Screenplay, Danny Moynihan, based on his novel; Photography, John Mathieson; Designer, Caroline Greville-Morris; Costumes, Claire Anderson; Music, Janusz Podrazik; Editor, Kant Pan; Art Curator, Damien Hirst; Co-Producer, Julia Stannard; Associate Producers, Steve Daly, Susan Spagna Dorfman, Jane Holzer; Casting, Gary Davy; a Constance Media, Firefly Films, Muse Prods., Autonomous/Colouframe, P&C Arcade Films, S Films, Magna Films production; British; Dolby; Color; Not rated; 94 minutes; American release date: April 23, 2010. **CAST**: Gillian Anderson (Jean Maclestone), Alan Cumming (Dewey), Heather Graham (Beth Freemantle), Danny Huston (Art Spindle), Jack Huston (Jo Richards), Christopher Lee (Alfred Rhinegold), Joanne Lumley (Alfreda Rhinegold), Simon McBurney (Robert Freign), Meredith Ostrom (Joany), Charlotte Rampling (Emille), Amanda Seyfried (Paige Prideaux), Stellan Skarsgård (Bob Maclestone), Jaime Winstone (Elaine), Gemma Atkinson (Charlotte Bailey), Alfie Allen (Photographer), Jan Uddin (Art's Partner), Rosie Fellner (Rachel Leighton), Michael Culkin (Beth's Father), Jenny Runacre (Mrs. Havermeyer), Stephen Greif (Bob's Lawyer), Sidney Cole (Cabbie), Josephine de la Baume (Frenchie), Gaetano Jouen (Himself)

John Bell, Connie Nielsen in *A Shine of Rainbows* © Freestyle Releasing

THE GOOD HEART (Magnolia) Producers, Skúli Fr. Malmquist, Thor S. Sigurjónson; Executive Producers, Sigurjón Sighvatsson, Robin O'Hara, Scott Macaulay; Director/ Screenplay, Dagur Kári; Photography, Rasmus Videbæk; Designer, Hálfdan Pedersen; Costumes, Ásta Hafiórsdóttir; Music, Slowblow; Editor, Andri Steinn Gudmundsson; Casting, Kerry Barden, Paul Schnee; a Zik Zak Filmworks production; Danish-Icelandic-American-French-German; Dolby; Color; Rated R; 95 minutes; American release date: April 30, 2010. **CAST**: Paul Dano (Lucas), Brian Cox (Jacques), Stephanie Szostak (Sarah), Damian Young (Roddie), Isild Le Besco (April), Clark Middleton (Dimitri), Edmund Lyndeck (Barber), Susan Blommaert (Nurse Nora), Naeem Uzimann (Stress Out Exerciser), Nicolas Bro (Ib Dolby), Michael J. Burg (Actor), Daniel Raymont (Markus), Bill Buell (Roger Verne), Stephen Henderson (Psychiatrist), Elissa Middleton (Mattie), André De Shields (Sooty), Ed Wheeler (Jonathan), Henry Yuk (Chin Lee), Adam S. Phillips (Patient in Therapy), Seth Sharp (Nurse Billy), Steve Axelrod (The Farmer), Aristedes Philip DuVal (Security Guard), Sonnie Brown (Nurse Woo), Halfdan Pedersen (Roger Warhol), Catherina Ren Knerr (Nurse Darlene Niles), Darren Foreman (Doctor), Michelle J. Nelson (Nurse Sheila), Alice Olivia Clarke (Nurse Mona), Guy Conan Stuart (Ben), Haraldur Jónsson (Silent Man)

THE HUMAN CENTIPEDE (FIRST SEQUENCE) (IFC Films) Producers, Tom Six, Ilona Six; Director/Screenplay, Tom Six; Photography, Goof de Koning; Music, Holeg Spies, Patrick Savage; Special Makeup Effects, Erik Hillenbrink, Rob Hillenbrink; a Six Entertainment production; Netherlands, 2009; Dolby; Color; Not rated; 90 minutes; American release date: April 30, 2010. **CAST**: Dieter Laser (Dr. Heiter), Ashley C. Williams (Lindsay), Ashlynn Yennie (Jenny), Akihiro Kitamura (Katsuro), Andreas Leupold (Det. Kranz), Peter Blankenstein (Det. Voller)

Gillian Anderson, Stellan Skarsgård, Danny Huston in *Boogie Woogie* © IFC Films

A SHINE OF RAINBOWS (Freestyle) Producers, Tina Pehme, Kim Roberts, James Flynn; Executive Producers, David Reckziegel, John Hamilton, Morgan O'Sullivan, Laura Rister; Director/Photography, Vic Sarin; Screenplay, Vic Sarin, Catherine Spear, Dennis Foon; Based on the novel by Lillian Beckwith; Designer, Tom McCullagh; Costumes, Susan Scott; Music, Keith Power; Editor, Alison Grace; Casting, John Hubbard, Ros Hubbard; a Seville Pictures presentation in association with Telefilm Canada, of a Sepia Films (Canada)/Octagon Films (Ireland) production; Canadian-Irish; 2009; Dolby; Panavision; Deluxe color; Rated PG; 101 minutes; American release date: April 23, 2010. **CAST**: Connie Nielsen (Maire O'Donnell), Aidan Quinn (Alec O'Donnell), John Bell (Tomas), Jack Gleason (Seamus), Niamh Shaw (Katie), Tara Alice Scully (Nancy), Bonnie Bollivar (Gran), Gerald Boner (Dr. Burner), Laura Doherty (Nurse), Adam Downey (Jack), Fionn O'Shea, Gary Healy (Orphan Boys), Kieran Lagan (Ned), Shane Mahon (Paddy), Joy McBrinn (Rag Lady), Ian McElhinney (Father Doyle), Greg McGuinness (Dermont), Karl O'Neill (Fergus), Frances Quinn (Mrs. Kane), Lee Satell (Rory), Sharon Simpkins (Teacher)

Dieter Laser in *The Human Centipede* © IFC Films

ROAD, MOVIE (Tribeca Film) Producers, Susan B. Landau, Ross Katz; Director/Screenplay, Dev Benegal; Photography, Michel Amathieu; Designer, Anne Seibel; Costumes, Amba Sanyal; Music, Michael Brook; Editor, Yaniv Dabach; Indian-American; Technicolor; Not rated; 95 minutes; American release date: May 5, 2010. **CAST**: Abhay Deol (Vishnu), Mohammed Faisal (The Boy), Satish Kaushik (Om), Tannishtha Chatterjee (The Woman), Veerendra Saxena (Police Chief), Amitabh Srivastava (Father), Suhia Thatte (Mother), Hardik Mehta (Masseur), Shradha Shrivastav (Sister), Roshan Taneja (OPJ)

Road, Movie © Tribeca Films

SEX & DRUGS & ROCK & ROLL (Tribeca Films) Producer, Damian Jones; Executive Producers, Kevin Phelan, Peter Hampden, Andy Serkis, Paul Viragh, Ian Neil, Ralph Kamp, Paul Brett, Steve "Harry" Harragan, Tim Smith; Director, Mat Whitecross; Screenplay, Paul Viragh; Photography, Christopher Ross, Brian Tufano; Designer, Richard Bullock; Costumes, Joanna Eatwell; Music, Chaz Jankel; Music Supervisor, Ian Neil; Casting, Toby Whale; a U.K. Film Council, Aegis Film Fund presentation; British; Dolby; Color/Black and white; DV-to-35mm; Not rated; 114 minutes; American release date: May 5, 2010. **CAST**: Andy Serkis (Ian Dury), Tom Hughes (Chaz Jankel), Ray Winstone (Bill Dury), Clifford Samuel (Charley Charles), Naomi Harris (Denise), Joseph Kennedy (Davey Payne), Arthur Darvill (Mick Gallagher), Jimmy Jagger (John Turnbull), Shakraj Soornack (Norman Watt-Roy), Mackenzie Crook (Russell Hardy), Olivia Williams (Betty Dury), Wesley Nelson (Young Ian), Ross Boatman (Pub Landlord), Bill Milner (Baxter Dury), Charlotte Beaumont (Jemima), Toby Jones (Hargreaves), Ralph Ineson (The Sulphate Strangler), Ian Neil (Photographer), Joe Siffleet (Bully Boy), Andrew Knott (Reporter), Giuseppe Circelli (Fan), Luke Evans (Clive Richards), Noel Clarke (Desmond), Alan McKenna (Policeman), Ferdy Roberts (Teacher), Georgina Edewor-Thorley (Party Girl), Poppy Miller (Carer), Michael Maloney (Graham)

Bill Milner in
Sex & Drugs & Rock & Roll
© Tribeca Films

THE TROTSKY (Tribeca Films) Producer, Kevin Tierney; Director/Screenplay, Jacob Tierney; Photography, Guy Dufaux; Designer, Anne Pritchard; Costumes, Mario Davignon; Music, Malajube; Editor, Arthur Tarnowski; a Park Ex Pictures production; Canadian; Dolby; Color; Not rated; 117 minutes; American release date: May 5, 2010. **CAST**: Jay Baruchel (Leon Bronstein), Emily Hampshire (Alexandra Leith), Geneviève Bujold (Denise Archambault), Colm Feore (Principal Berkhoff), Saul Rubinek (David Bronstein), Michael Murphy (Frank McGovern), David Julian Hirsch (Eli Bronstein), Taylor Baruchel (Taylor), Dan Beirne (Dan), Domini Blythe (Mrs. Danvers), Justin Bradley (Jimmy), Anne-Marie Cadieux (Anne Bronstein), Jesse Camacho (Skip), Darren Curtis (Taxi Driver), Angela Galuppo (Sheila), Kyle Gatehouse (Kyle), Dan Haber (Achmed), Kaniehtiio Horn (Caroline), Pat Kiely (Julien), Sarah-Jeanne Labrosse (Sarah), Ricky Mabe (Tony), Mary L. Milne (Mary), Ben Mulroney (Himself), Jessica Paré (Laura), Tommie-Amber Pirie (Sarah Bronstein), Jesse Rath (Dwight), Erika Rosenbaum (Becca), Li Li, Jesse Vinet (Private School Girls)

Ricky Mabe, Jay Baruchel, Emily Hampshire in The Trotsky © Tribeca Films

THE INFIDEL (Tribeca Films) Producers, Arvind Ethan David, Uzma Hasan, Stewart Le Marcechal, David Baddiel; Executive Producers, Omid Djalili, Cavan Ash; Director, Josh Appignanesi, Screenplay, David Baddiel; Photography, Natasha Braier; Designer, erik Rehl; Costumes, Marianne Agertoft; Music, Erran Baron Cohen; Editor, Kim Gaster; Casting, Julie Harkin; a Slingshot and Met Film production, in association with American Express; British; Dolby; Color; Not rated; 104 minutes; American release date: May 5, 2010. **CAST**: Matt Lucas (Rabbi), Archie Panjabi (Saamiya Nasir), Yigal Naor (Arshad El Masri), Omid Djalili (Mahmud Nasir), Richard Schiff (Lenny Goldberg), James Flloyd (Gary Page), Paul Kaye, Chris Wilson (Police Officers), Miranda Hart (Mrs. Keyes), Adrian Schiller (Protester), Tracy-Ann Oberman (Monty's Wife), Mina Anwar (Muna), David Schneider (Monty), Bhasker Patel (Sharif), Amit Shah (Rashid Nasir), Jason Salkey (Policeman), Stewart Scudamore (Tariq), Soraya Radford (Uzma), Michele Austin (Zadie), Shobu Kapoor (Kashmina), Syreeta Kumar (Yasmin Aktar), Rod Silvers (Rahman), Sartaj Garewal (Wasif), Jonathan Tafler (Monty's Friend), Ravin J. Ganatra (Imam), Joanna Brookes (Denise), Leah Fatania (Nabi), Christian Lees (Louis), Ricky Sekhon (Hazeem), Jonah Lees (Sammy)

Archie Punjabi, Omid Djalili, Amit Shah in The Infidel © Tribeca Films

TALENTIME (Independent) Director, Yasmin Ahmad; Photography, Low Soon-keong; Music, Pete Teo; Editors, Raja Affandy, Raja Jamaluddin; Malaysian; Color; HD-to-35mm; Not rated; 115 minutes; American release date: May 5, 2010. **CAST**: Pamela Chong (Melur), Mahesh Jugal Kishor (Mahesh), Mohd Syafie Naswip (Hafiz), Howard Hon Kahoe (Kahoe), Azean Irdawaty (Embun), Harith Iskander (Harith)

Mahesh Jugal Kishor, Pamela Chong in *Talentime* © Grand Brilliance

OSS 117: LOST IN RIO (Music Box Films) a.k.a. *OSS 117: Rio ne répond plus*; Producers, Eric Altmeyer, Nicolas Altmeyer; Director, Michel Hazanavicius; Screenplay, Michel Hazanavicius, Jean-François Halin; Based on the character created by Jean Bruce; Photography, Guillaume Schiffman; Art Director, Maamar Ech-Cheikh; Music, Ludovic Bource; Editor, Reynald Bertrand; French, 2009; Dolby; Technicolor; Not rated; 100 minutes; American release date: May 7, 2010. **CAST**: Jean Dujardin (Hubert Bonisseur de la Bath, OSS 117), Louise Monot (Dolorès Koulechov), Rüdiger Vogler (Von Zimmel), Alex Lutz (Heinrich), Reem Kherici (Carlotta), Pierre Bellemare (Lesignac), Ken Samuels (Trumendous), Serge Hazanavicius (Staman), Laurent Capelluto (Kutner), Moon Dailly (The Countess), Walter Shnorkell (Fayoelle), Philippe Herisson (Mayeux), Cirillo Luna (Hippie), Nicky Marbot (Castaing), Christelle Cornil (Mlle. Ledentu), Jean-Marie Paris, Alexandre Porfirio (Zantrax), Vincent Haquin, Alexandre Goncalves (Blue Devils), Adriana Salles (Nurse), Joseph Chanet (Chinese CIA), Patrick Vo (Chinese Pilot), Pascal Parmentier, Franck Beckmann (Germans), Jean-Claude Tran, Yin Bing (Chinese at Hotel), Chao Chen (Chinese in Taxi), Sabrine Vin (LSA Hippie)

Jean Dujardin (center) in *OSS 117: Lost in Rio* © Music Box Films

BADMAASH COMPANY (Yash Raj Films) Producer, Aditya Chopra; Executive Producer, Aashish Singh; Director/Screenplay/Story, Parmeet Sethi; Photography, Sanjay Kapoor; Designers, Sukant Panigrahy, Norman Dodge; Costumes, Ameira Punvani; Music, Pritam; Lyrics, Anvita Dutt; Choreographer, Ahmed Khan; Background Score, Julius Packiam; Color; Not rated; 144 minutes; American release date: May 7, 2010. **CAST**: Shahid Kapoor (Karan), Anushka Sharma (Bulbul), Vir Das (Chandu), Meiyang Chang (Zing), Anupam Kher (Father), Kiran Juneja, Pawan Malhotra, Jameeel Khan.

Shahid Kapoor in *Badmaash Company* © Yash Raj Films

DDR/DDR (Independent) Producer/Director/Screenplay/Editor, Amie Siegel; Photography, Christine A. Maier; German; Color; Not rated; 135 minutes; American release date: May 7, 2010. Documentary on surveillance techniques developed by the former German Democratic Republic.

DDR/DDR © Amie Siegel

CLIMATE OF CHANGE (Tribeca) Producer, Katie Bailiff; Executive Producers, Kevin Wall, Kit Williams; Director, Brian Hill; Screenplay, Simon Armitage; Photography, Roger Chapman, Tony Coldwell, Michael Timney, Wayne Vinten; Music, Nitin Swahney; Editor, Stuart Briggs; Narrator, Tilda Swinton; a Century Films production, presented in association with American Express, Participant Media and the Alliance for Climate Protection; British; Color; Not rated; 86 minutes; American release date: May 12, 2010. Documentary on the need for an unspoiled environment. **WITH** Larry Gibson, Maria Gunnoe, Judy Bonds, Solitaire Townsend, Sep Galeva, Sena Alouka

Climate of Change © Tribeca Films

HERE AND THERE (Cinema Purgatorio) a.k.a. *Tamo i ovde*, Producers, Darko Lungulov, David Nemer, George Lekovic, Vladan Nikolic; Executive Producer, Ken Del Vecchio; Director/Screenplay, Darko Lungulov; Photography, Mathis Schöningh; Costumes, Zora Mojsilovic; Music, Dejan Epjovic; Editor, Dejan Urosevic; a Penrose Film in co-production with KinoKamera; Serbian-American-German, 2009; Dolby; Color; Not rated; 85 minutes; American release date: May 14, 2010. **CAST**: David Thornton (Robert), Mirjana Karanovic (Olga), Cyndi Lauper (Rose), Branislav Trifunovic (Branko), Jelena Mrdja (Ivana), Antone Pagan (Jose Escobar), Max King (George), Fredda Lomsky (Russian Lady), Vladimir Bibic (Greek Deli Owner), Mirajan Djurdjevic (Violeta), Zeljko Erkic (Doseljenik), Lew Lew (Chinese Woman), Eliezer Meyer (Car Buyer), Goran Radakovic (Mirko), Fedja Stojanovic (Tosha Rajkovic), Vlasta Velisavljevic (Dragi, Waiter)

Mirjana Karanovic, David Thornton in *Here and There* © Cinema Purgatorio

TWO IN THE WAVE (Lorber) a.k.a. *Deux de la Vague*; Producer/Director, Emanuel Laurent; Screenplay/Narrator, Antoine De Baecque; Photography, Etienne de Grammont, Nick de Pencier; Editor, Marie-France Cuénot; a film à Trois Production; French, 2009; Black and white/Color; Not rated; 93 minutes; American release date: May 19, 2010. Documentary on filmmakers Francois Truffaut and Jean-Luc Godard's importance to the French New Wave. **WITH** Islid Le Besco

Jean-Luc Godard in *Two in the Wave* © Lorber Films

JOHN RABE (Strand) Producers, Mischa Hofmann, Jan Mojto, Benjamin Herrmann; Director/Screenplay, Florian Gallenberger; Inspired by the diaries of John Rabe; Photography, Jürgen Jürges; Designer, Tu Juhua; Music, Annette Focks; Costumes, Lisy Christl; Editor, Hansjörg Weißbrich; Casting, Cornelia von Braun; German-French-Chinese, 2009; Dolby; Cinemascope; Color; Not rated; 134 minutes; American release date: May 21, 2010. **CAST**: Ulrich Tukur (John Rabe), Daniel Brühl (Dr. Georg Rosen), Steve Buscemi (Dr. Robert Wilson), Anne Consigny (Valérie Dupres), Dagmar Manzel (Dora Rabe), Jingchu Zhang (Langshu), Teruyuki Kagawa (Prince Asaka Yasuhiko), Mathias Herrmann (Werner Fließ), Tetta Sugimoto (Nakajima Kesago), Akira Emoto (Matsui Iwane), Arata (Major Ose), Shaun Lawton (Rev. John Magee), Christian Rodska (Dr. Lewis Smythe), Gottfried John (Dr. Oskar Trautmann), Fang Yu (Hsianglin Han), Ming Li (Chang), Dong Fu Lin (Chiang Kai-Shek), Togo Igawa (Fukuda Tokuyasu), Wenkang Yuan (Gu), Qi Yi Ming (Wan), Tang Ye Fing (Chinese Singer), Christoph Hagen Dittmann (Christian Kröger), Hans Joachim Heist (Scheel), Hans-Eckart Eckhardt (Bernd Franz), Ito Yosaburo (Japanese NCO), Jia Dong Liu (Japanese Manservant), Yan Guan Ying (Lu), Zhu Yi (Dr. Hsü), Wu Yu Fang (Senior Nurse), Hsinyi Liu (Nurse), Kazuo Shimizu (Japanese Senior Officer), Takashi Nishina, Toshihiro Yashiba (Japanese Officer), Xia Rui Yan (Student), Tong Jiang (Telegraph Operator), Tomo Sora (Japanese Lieutenant), Shinichi Takashima (Japanese Soldier)

Daniel Brühl, Jingchu Zhang in *John Rabe* © Strand Releasing

PERRIER'S BOUNTY (IFC Films) Producers, Alan Moloney, Elizabeth Karlsen, Stephen Woolley; Director, Ian Fitzgibbon; Screenplay, Mark O'Rowe; Photography, Seamus Deasy; Designer, Amanda McArthur; Costumes, Keith Madden; Music, David Holmes; Editor, Tony Cranstoun; Casting, Nina Gold; a Parallel Films and Number 9 Films presentation; British-Irish; Dolby; Color; Not rated; 88 minutes; American release date: May 21, 2010. **CAST**: Cillian Murphy (Michael), Brendan Gleeson (Darren Perrier), Jim Broadbent (Jim), Jodie Whittaker (Brenda), Gabriel Byrne (Voice of the Reaper), Michael McElhatton (Ivan), Don Wycherley (Orlando), Brendan Coyle (Jerome), Conleth Hill (Russ), Domhnall Gleeson (Clifford), Patrick McCabe (Mulligan), Ned Dennehy, Glenn Speers (Clampers), Padraic Delaney (Shamie), Natalie Britton (Catherine), Liam Cunningham (The Mutt), Breffni McKenna (Dinny), Francis Magee (Hank), Wuzza Conlon (Blaise), Brendan Dempsey (Victor), Brian Doherty (Kenny), Jane Brennan (Farmhouse Battleaxe), Michael Fitzgerald (Garda), Chris Newman, Andrew Simpson (Teens)

Jim Broadbent, Cillian Murphy in *Perrier's Bounty* © IFC Films

SURVIVAL OF THE DEAD (Magnet) Producer, Paula Devonshire; Executive Producers, George A. Romero, Peter Grunwald, Art Spigel, Ara Katz, Dan Fireman, Patrice Theroux, Michael Doherty, D.J. Carson; Director/Screenplay, George A. Romero; Photography, Adam Swica; Designer, Arv Greywal; Costumes, Alex Kavanagh; Music, Robert Carli; Editor, Michael Doherty; Special Effects Make-up, Franoics Dagenais, Greg Nicotero; Visual Effects Supervisor, Colin Davies; Casting, John Buchan, Jason Knight; an Artfire Films, Romero-Grunwald Productions presentation of a Devonshire Production; Canadian-American; Dolby; Color; Rated R; 90 minutes; American release date: May 28, 2010. **CAST**: Alan Van Sprang (Sarge 'Nicotine' Crocket), Kenneth Welsh (Patrick O'Flynn), Kathleen Munroe (Janet/Jane O'Flynn), Devon Bostick (Boy), Richard Fitzpatrick (Seamus Muldoon), Athena Karkanis (Tomboy), Stefano Di Matteo (Francisco), Joris Jarsky (Chuck), Eric Woolfe (Kenny), Wayne Robson (Tawdry O'Flynn), Julian Richings (James O'Flynn), Josh Peace (D.J.), Hardee T. Lineham (Lt. Vaughn), Dru Viergever (Cheek-Biter Zombie), Mitch Risman (Drooling Zombie), John Healey (Matthew), Philippa Domville (Beth Muldoon), Miranda Millar (Zombie Girl), George Stroumboulopoulos (Talk Show Host), Pete Zedlacher (Talk Show Stooge), Michael Rhoades (Hot-Headed Good Old Boy), Brian Frank (Gut Shot Good Old Boy), Ho Chow (Fisherman), Dan Belley (Harbor Zombie), Angela Brown (Tawdry Biter), Marqus Bobesich (Dynamite Zombie), Jerry Schaefer (Fire Extinguisher Zombie), James Dunn (Hot Dog Zombie), Chad Camilleri (Flaming Zombie), Matt Birman (Lem Muldoon), Zeljko Kecojevic (Pitchfork Zombie), Kevin Rushton (Hat Zombie), Curtis Parker (Scanlon Boy), Heather Allin (Sally Muldoon), Rick Parker (Horse-Eating Zombie)

Joris Jarsky, Kathleen Munroe in *Survival of the Dead* © Magnet

DOUBLE TAKE (Kino) Producer, Emmy Oost; Director/Screenplay, Johan Grimonprez; Story, Tom McCarthy; Inspired by *25 August, 1983* by Jorge Luis Borges; Music, Christian Halten; Editors, Dieter Diependale, Tyler Huby; a Zap-o-Matik production, with Nikovantastic Film & Volya Films; Belgian-German-Dutch; Color/black and white; Not rated; 80 minutes; American release date: June 2, 2010. Semi-documentary look at director Alfred Hitchcock's late 1950's and early '60's films; with: Ron Burrage (Hitchcock Double), Mark Perry (Hitchcock Voice).

Alfred Hitchcock in *Double Take* © Kino

RAAJNEETI (Mind Blowing Films) Producer/Director, Prakash Jha; Screenplay, Anjum Rajabali, Prakash Jha; Photography, Sachin Krishn; Art Director, Jayant Deshmukh; Costumes, Priyanka Mundada; Editor, Santosh Mandal; a UTV Motion Pictures & Walkwater Media presentation; Indian; Color; Not rated; 178 minutes; American release date: June 7, 2010. **CAST**: Naseeruddin Shah (Bhaskar Sanyal), Arjun Rampal (Prithviraj Pratap), Arjun Rampal (Prithviraj Pratap), Nana Patekar (Brij Gopal), Ranbir Kapoor (Samar Pratap), Katrina Kaif (Indu Pratap), Ajay Devgan (Sooraj Kumar), Manoj Bajpai (Veerendra Pratap)

Ranbir Kapoor, Katrina Kaif in *Raajneeti* © Mind Blowing Films

GANGSTER'S PARADISE: JERUSALEMA (Anchor Bay) Producers, Tendeka Matatu, Ralph Ziman; Executive Producers, Mark Vennis, Gary Phillips, Ronnie Apteker; Director/Screenplay, Ralph Ziman; Photography, Nicolaas Hofmeyr; Designer, Flo Ballack; Costumes, Natalie Lundon; Music, Alan Lazar; Editor, David Helfand; an Anchor Bay Films, Lleju Productions and Muti Films presentation of a Tendeku Matatu production; South African, 2008; Dolby; Color; Rated R; 118 minutes; American release date: June 11, 2010. **CAST**: Rapulana Seiphemo (Lucky Kunene), Jeffrey Sekele (Nazareth), Ronnie Nyakale (Zakes Mbolelo), Shelly Meskin (Leah Friedlander), Robert Hobbs (Det. Blakkie Swart), Kenneth Nkosi (Sithole), Jafta Mamabolo (Young Kunene), Daniel Buckland (Josh Friedlander), Eugene Khumbanyiwa (Drug Dealer), Motlatsi Mahloko (Young Zakes), Kevon Kane (Van C, Drug Dealer), Louise Saint-Claire (Anna-Marie van Rensburg)

Gangster's Paradise © Anchor Bay

REEL INJUN (Lorber Films) Producers, Christina Fon, Linda Ludwick, Adam Symasnsky; Executive Producers, Catherine Bainbridge, Ernest Webb; Director, Neil Diamond; Screenplay, Catherine Bainbridge, Neil Diamond, Jeremiah Hayes; Photography, Edith Labbe; Music, Mona Laviolette, Claude Castonguay; Editor, Jeremiah Hayes; a Rezolution Pictures production in association with the National Film Board of Canada; Canadian, 2009; Color; DV; Not rated; 85 minutes; American release date: June 11, 2010. Documentary about the movies' depiction of Native Americans. **WITH** Adam Beach, R. Michael David, Clint Eastwood, Chris Eyre, Graham Greene, Charlie Hill, Jim Jarmusch, Zacharias Kunuk, Sacheen Littlefeather, Russell Means, Rod Rondeaux, Wes Studi, John Trudell.

Reel Injun © Lorber Films

HIS & HERS (Madman Entertainment) Producer, Andrew Freedman; Director/Editor, Ken Wardrop; Photography, Michael Lavelle, Kate McCullough; Music, Denis Clohessy; a Venom Film presentation; Irish, 2009; Dolby; Color; Not rated; 80 minutes; American release date: June 11, 2010. Documentary in which 70 Irish women reflect on life and relationships.

RAAVAN (Reliance Big Pictures) Producers, Mani Ratnam, Sharada Trilok; Executive Producers, Shaad Ali, B. Chintu Mohapatrea; Director/Screenplay, Mani Ratnam; Dialogue, Vijay Krishna Acharya; Photography, Santosh Sivan, V. Manikandan; Designer, Samir Chanda; Costumes, Sabyas Achi; Music, A.R. Rahman; Lyrics, Vairamuthu; Editor, Sreekar Prasad; a Madras Talkies production; Indian; Color; Widescreen; Not rated; 136 minutes; American release date: June 18, 2010. **CAST**: Abhishek Bachchan (Beera Munda), Aishwarya Rai (Ragini), Chiyaan Vikram (Dev Pratap Sharma), Govinda (Sanjeevani Kumar), Prithviraj (Dev), Nikhil Dwivedi (Lakshman)

Raavan © Reliance Big Pictures

THE AGONY AND THE ECSTASY OF PHIL SPECTOR (BBC Arena/Vixpix) Producers, Vikram Jayanti, Anthony Wall; Director, Vikram Jayanti; Photography, Maryse Alberti; Editor, Emma Matthews; Color; HD; Not rated; 102 minutes; American release date: June 30, 2010. Documentary on the ups and downs of pioneering record producer Phil Spector. **WITH** Phil Spector

Phil Spector in *The Agony and the Ecstasy of Phil Spector* © BBC Arena

I HATE LUV STORYS (UTV Communications) Producers, Hiroo Johar, Karan Johar; Director/Screenplay, Punit Malhotra; Photography, Ayankanka Bose; Designer, Amrita Mahal; Costumes, Manish Malhotra; Songs, Vishal-Shekhar; Editor, Akiv Ali; Indian; Technicolor; Not rated; 135 minutes; American release date: June 30, 2010. **CAST**: Sonam Kapoor (Simran), Imran Khan (Jay), Sammir Dattani (Raj), Samir Soni (Veer Kapoor), Aseem Tiwari (Nikhil)

Imran Khan in *I Hate Luv Storys* © UTV Communications

ONLY WHEN I DANCE (Film Movement) Producers, Giorgia Lo Savio, Nikki Parrott; Executive Producer, Jan Younghusband; Director/Photography, Beadie Finzi; Music, Stephen Hilton; Editors, Alan Levy, Felipe Lacerda; a Channel 4 presentation, in association with Arte France/NPS, of a Tigerlily Films production, in association ith Jinga Production; British-French; Color; HD; Widescreen; Not rated; 78 minutes; American release date: July 2, 2010. Documentary on two teens from a working class Brazilian neighborhood who hope to become professional ballet dancers. **WITH** Irlan Santos da Silva, Isabela Coracy Alves, Mariza Estrella, Maria Santos da Silva, Irenildo da Silva, Silvana Alves Santos, Mose Alves Santos

Irlan Santos da Silva in *Only When I Dance* © Film Movement

BEAUTIFUL ISLANDS (Eleven Arts) Producer/Director/Editor, Tomoko Kana; Executive Producer, Hirokazu Kore-eda; Photography, Minami Yukio; a Tomoko Kana production; Japanese-Italian-American, 2009; Color; HD; Rated PG; 106 minutes; American release date: July 2, 2010. Documentary on how Venice, Tuvalu and the island outpost of Shishmaref, Alaska are all in danger of being swallowed by the world's rising waters.

Beautiful Islands © Eleven Arts

[REC]2 (Magnet) Producer, Julio Fernández; Executive Producers, Julio Fernández, Carlos Fernández; Directors, Jaume Balagueró, Paco Plaza; Screenplay, Jaume Balagueró, Manu Díez, Paco Plaza,; Photography, Pablo Rosso; Designer, Gemma Fauria; Costumes, Gloria Viguer; Editor, David Gallart; Visual Effects, Alex Villagrassa; Special Makeup Effects, David Ambit; Casting, Cristina Campos; a Filmax Entertainment presentation of a Julio Fernández production for Castelao productions; Spanish, 2009; Dolby; Color; HD; Rated R; 84 minutes; American release date: July 9, 2010. **CAST**: Jonathan Mellor (Dr. Owen), Manuela Velasco (Ángela Vidal), Oscar Sánchez Zafra (Jefe), Ariel Casas (Larra), Alejandro Casaseca (Martos), Pablo Rosso (Rosso), Pep Molina (Padre Jennifer), Andrea Ros (Mire), Àlex Batllori (Ori), Pau Poch (Tito), Juli Fàbregas (Bombero), Ferran Terraza (Manu), Claudia Silva (Jennifer), Martha Carbonell (Sra. Izquierdo)

Oscar Sánchez Zafra, Claudia Silva in *[REC]2* © Magnet

AROUND A SMALL MOUNTAIN (Cinema Guild) a.k.a. *36 vues du Pic Saint-Loup*; Producers, Maurice Tinchant, Martine Marignac, Luigi Musini, Robert Cicutto, Ermanno Olmi, Sergio Castellitto, Margaret Mazzantini; Director, Jacques Rivette; Screenplay, Jacques Rivette, Pascal Bonitzer, Christine Laurent, Shirel Amitay, Sergio Castellitto; Photography, Irina Lubtchansky; Designers, Manu de Chauvigny, Giuseppe Pirotta; Costumes, Laurence Strutz; Music, Pierre Allio; Editor, Nicole Lubtchansky; a Pierre Grise Prods. Presentation of a France 2 Cinema (France)/Cinemaundici, Rai Cinema, Alien Produzioni (Italy) production; French-Italian, 2009; Dolby; Color; Not rated; 85 minutes; American release date: July 9, 2010. **CAST**: Jane Birkin (Kate), Sergio Castellitto (Vittorio), André Marcon (Alexandre), Jacques Bonnaffé (Marlo), Julie-Marie Parmentier (Clémence), Hélène de Vallombreuse (Margot), Tintin Orsoni (Wilfrid), Vimala Pons (Barbara), Mikaël Gaspar (Tom), Stéphane Laisné (Stèphane), Dominique D'Angelo (Dom), Hélène De Bissy, Pierre Baraye (Inn Patrons), Marie-Paule André (Estelle), Julie-Anne Roth (Xénie), Elodie Mamou (Elodie), Laurent Lacotte (Monsieur Gaffe), Marie Vauzelle (Madame Gaffe)

Jane Birkin, Sergio Castellitto in *Around a Small Mountain* © Cinema Guild

RED ALERT: THE WAR WITHIN (Madhu Entertainment) Producers, Rahul Aggarwal, T.P. Aggarwal; Director, Ananth Narayan Mahadevan; Screenplay, Aruna Raje; Photography, K. Rajkumar; Art Director, Sanjay Jadhav; Costumes, Shayal Sheth, Naveen Shetty; Music, Lalit Pandit; Editor, Sanjib Dutta; Indian; Color; Not rated; 120 minutes; American release date: July 9, 2010. **CAST**: Sunil Shetty (Narasimha), Sameera Reddy (Laxmi), Ayesha Dharkar (Radhakka), Seema Biswas (Saralaka), Gulshan Grover (D.I.G. Rathod), Naseeruddin Shah (Naga), Vinod Khanna (Krishna Raj), Ashish Vidyarthi (Velu), Makrand Deshpande (Raghavan), Bhagyashree (Uma)

Sunil Shetty (right) in *Red Alert* © Madhu Entertainment

ALAMAR (FilmMovement) a.k.a. *To the Sea*; Producers, Jaime Romandía, Pedro González-Rubio; Director/Screenplay/Photography/Editor, Pedro González-Rubio; Music, Fausto Palma; an MK2, Mantarraya Producciones presentation; Mexican, 2009; Color; Widescreen; HD-to-35mm; Not rated; 73 minutes; American release date: July 14, 2010. **CAST**: Jorge Machado (Jorge), Roberta Palombini (Roberta), Natan Machado Palombini (Natan), Néstor Marín (Matraca)

Jorge Machado, Natan Machado Palombini in *Alamar* © Film Movement

HENRI-GEORGES CLOUZOT'S INFERNO, (Flicker Alley) a.k.a. *L'enfer d'Henri-Georges Clouzot*; Producer, Serge Bromberg; Executive Producer, Marianne Lere; Directors, Serge Bromberg, Ruxandra Medrea; Music, Bruno Alexlu; Editor, Janice Jones; a Lobster Films presentation in co-production with France 2 Cinema; French, 2009; Color/black and white; HD and 35mm-to-HD; Not rated; 100 minutes; American release date: July 16, 2010. Documentary on filmmaker Henri-Georges Clouzot's unfinished film of the 1960's, *Inferno* starring Romy Schneider. **WITH** Bérénice Bejo, Jacques Gamblin, Catherine Allegret, Gilbert Amy, Jean-Louis Ducarme, Jacques Douy, Costa Gavras, William Lubtchansky, Lan Nguyen, Joel Stein, Bernard Stora.

Romy Schneider in *Inferno* © Flicker Alley

MUGABE AND THE WHITE AFRICAN (IFC Films) Producers, David Pearson, Eliabeth Morgan Hemlock; Executive Producers, Steve Milne, Pauline Burt; Directors, Lucy Bailey, Andrew Thompson; Photography, Andrew Thompson; Music, Johnny Pilcher; Editor, Tim Lovell; an Arturi Films production, in association with Explore Films, Film Agency for Wales and Molinare Prods.; British, 2009; Dolby; Color; HD; Not rated; 94 minutes; Release date: July 23, 2010. Documentary on how farmer Mike Campbell and his family fought to hold on to his Zimbabwe land. **WITH** Mike Campbell, Angela Campbell, Ben Freeth, Laura Freeth

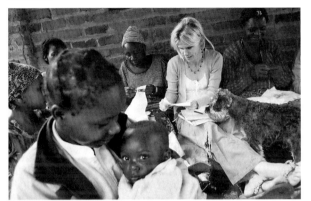

Laura Freeth in *Mugabe and the White African* © IFC Films

TIRADOR (Centerstage Prods.) a.k.a. *Slingshot*; Producers, Renato Esguerra, Antonio Del Rosario; Executive Producer, Ferdinand Lapuz; Director, Brillante Mendoza; Screenplay, Ralston Joel Jover; Photography, Brillante Mendoza, Julius Villanueva, Jeffrey Dela Cruz, Gary Tria; a Centerstage Prods. Presentation of a Rollingball production, in association with Ignatius Media; Filipino, 2007; Color; DigiBeta; Not rated; 86 minutes; American release date: July 23, 2010. Documentary looking at the Filipino slums of Quiapo. **WITH** Jiro Manio, Kristofer King, Coco Martin, Jaclyn Jose Nathan Lopez.

Tirador © Centerstage Prods.

ENEMIES OF THE PEOPLE (Intl. Film Circuit) Producer, Rob Lemkin; Executive Producer, Sandra Whipham; Directors/Screenplay/Photography, Thet Sambath, Rob Lemkin; Music, Daniel Pemberton; Editor, Stefan Ronowicz; an Old Street Films (U.K.)/Thet Sambath (Cambodia) production; British-Cambodian; Color/Black and white; HD; Not rated; 94 minutes; American release date: July 30, 2010. Documentary on the horrific genodice carried out by the Khmer Rouge from 1975 to 1979.

Suon in *Enemies of the People* © Intl. Film Circuit

WHO KILLED NANCY? (Peace Arch) Producers, Ben Timlett, Christine Anderson; Executive Producers, Ian Davies, Susan Douglas; Director, Alan G. Parker; Photography, Nick Rutter; Editor, Bill Jones; an Ipso Facto Films presentation of a Bill & Ben production in association with Double D Prods. and Moxie Makers; British, 2009; Color; DV; Not rated; 96 minutes; American release date: July 30, 2010. Documentary on the killing of Nancy Spungen by her boyfriend, Sex Pistol band member Sid Vicious. **WITH** Viviane Albertine, George Ancock, Lee Black Childers, Victor Colicchio, Steve Connolly, Esther Dior, Steve Dior, Steve English, Kenny Gordon, Peter Gravelle, Zoe Hansen< Mark Helfond, John Holmstrom, Alan Jones, Elliot Kidd, Hellin Killer, Neon Leon, Don Letts, Keith Levene, Handsome Dick Manitoba, Glen Matlock, Kris Needs, Sturgis Nikides, Alan G. Parker, Howie Pyro, George Slattery, Simone Stenfors, John Tiberi, Edward Tudor Pole, Ned Van Zandt, Kathleen Wirt; and Sophie Boyes (Nancy Spungen), Nigel Marshall (Sid Vicious), Will Cummock (Detective), Dave Twigg (Michael)

Nancy Spungen, Sid Vicious in *Who Killed Nancy?* © Peace Arch

HUGH HEFNER: PLAYBOY, ACTIVIST AND REBEL (Phase 4 Films) Producers, Victor Solnicki, Brigitte Berman, Peter Raymont; Director/Screenplay, Brigitte Berman; Photography, John Westheuser; Music, James Mark Stewart; Editors, Brigitte Berman, Richard Vandentillaart; a Metaphor Films presentation of a Victor Solnicki, Bridge Film, White Pin Pictures production, in association with Telefilm Canada, the Rogers Group of Funds, the Movie Network, Movie Central, Ontario Media Development Corp., the Canadian Television Fund, Rogers Broadcasting; Canadian; Dolby; Color/Black and white; Rated R; 124 minutes; American release date: July 30, 2010. Documentary on the founder of *Playboy* magazine, Hugh M. Hefner. **WITH** Hugh M. Hefner, Joan Baez, Tony Bennett, Pat Boone, Jim Brown, Susan Brownmiller, James Caan, Dick Cavett, Tony Curtis, Dick Gregory, Jesse Jackson, George Lucas, Bill Maher, Jenny McCarthy, Mary O'Connor, Pete Seeger, Gene Simmons, David Steinberg, Shannon Tweed, Mike Wallace, Ruth Westheimer

Hugh M. Hefner, Brigitte Berman in *Hugh Hefner* © Phase 4 Films

71: INTO THE FIRE (CJ Entertainment) a.k.a. *Into the Gunfire* and *Pohwasogeuro*; Producers, Jung Tae-won, Choi Myung-ki, Kim Jong-hyun; Director, John H. Lee; Screenplay, John H. Lee, Lee Han-hee, Kim Dong-woo; Photography, Choi Chan-min; a Taewon Entertainment production; South Korean; Dolby; Color; Not rated; 120 minutes; American release date: July 30, 2010. **CAST**: Kwon Sang-woo (Kup Kap-jo), Cha Seung-won (Park Mu-rang), T.O.P. (Oh Jung-bum), Kim Seung-Woo (Kang Suk-dae), Park Jin-hee (Hwa-Ran), Kim Sung-ryeong (Jung-bum's Mother), David McInnis (Sgt. Jones), Kim Han (Kang Suk-dae), Ki Se-Hyung, Shin Kyung-Sun (Student Soldiers)

71: Into the Fire © CJ Entertainment

THE CONCERT (Weinstein Co.) a.k.a. *Le concert*; Producer, Alain Attal; Director, Radu Mihaileanu; Screenplay, Radu Milhaileanu, Alan-Michel Blanc, Matthew Robbins; Story, Hector Cabello Reyes, Thierry Degrandi; Photography, Laurent Dailland; Designers, Cristian Niculescu, Stanislas Reydellet; Costumes, Virorica Petrovici, Maira Ramedhan Levi; Music, Armand Amar; Editor, Ludovic Troch; a Les Productions du Tresor presentation; French-Romanian-Belgian-Italian, 2009; Dolby; Widescreen; Color/black and white; Rated PG-13; 119 minutes; American release date: July 30, 2010. **CAST**: Aleksei Guskov (Andreï Filipov), Dmitri Nazarov (Sacha Grossman), Mélanie Laurent (Anne-Marie Jacquet), François Berléand (Olivier Morne Duplessis), Míou Míou (Guylène de La Rivière), Valeriy Barinov (Ivan Gavrilov), Anna Kamenkova Pavolva (Irinia Filipovna), Lionel Abelanski (Jean-Paul Carrère), Aleksandr Komissarov (Victor Vikitch), Ramzy Bedia (Owner of the 'Trou Normand')

Mélanie Laurent in *The Concert* © Weinstein Co.

THE SICILIAN GIRL (Music Box) Producers, Simonetta Amenta, Tilde Corsi, Gianni Romoli, Raphael Berdugo, Marco Amenta; Director, Marco Amenta; Screenplay, Marco Amenta, Sergio Donati, Gianni Romoli; Photography, Luca Bigazzi; Designer, Marcello Di Carlo; Costumes, Cristina Francioni; Music, Pasquale Catalano; Editor, Mirco Garrone; Casting, Pino Pellegrino, Chiara Agnello; a R&C Produzioni, Eurofilm, Roissy Films, Studio 37, Malec Production, Cite Films/France production in cooperation with RAI Cinema/Italy and Mediterranea Film/France, with the participation of Canal+ and TPS Star; Italian-French; Color; Not rated; 110 minutes; American release date: August 4, 2010. **CAST**: Veronica D'Agostino (Rita Mancuso), Gerard Jugnot (Prosecutor), Marcello Mazzarella (Don Michele Mancuso), Lucia Sardo (Rosa Mancuso), Mario Pupella (Don Salvo Rimi), Francesco Casisa (Vito), Camelo Galati (Carmelo Mancuso), Lollo Franco (Maresciallo Campisi), Miriana Faja (Young Rita), Lorenzo Rosone (Young Vito), Primo Reggiani (Lorenzo), Paolo Briguglia (Maresciallo Bruni), Roberto Bonura (Tano)

Veronica D'Agostino in *The Sicilian Girl* © Music Box Films

TERE BIN LADEN (BSK Network & Entertainment) Producers, Pooja Shetty Deora, Aarti Shetty; Executive Producer, Marjori Rodrigues; Director/Screenplay, Abhishek Sharma; Photography, Santosh Thundiyil; Art Director, Sunil Nigvekar; Costumes, Diksha Anan, Moitra; Music, Shankar Mahadevan, Ehsaan Noorani, Loy Mendonca; Editor, Suresh Pai; a Walkwater Media production; Indian; Color; Not rated; 108 minutes; American release date: August 6, 2010. **CAST**: Ali Zafar (Ali Hassan), Pradhuman Singh (Noora Chacha), Sugandha Garg (Zoya), Barry John (Ted), Rahul Singh (DJ Quershi), Nikhil Ratnaparkhi, Piyush Mishra

Ali Zafar (right) in *Tere Bin Laden* © BSK Network

MUNDO ALAS (Outsider Pictures) Producers, Luciano Campos, Marcelo Martin, Daniel Werner; Executive Producer, Nicolas Battle; Directors, Leon Gieco, Sebastian Schindel, Fernando Molnar; Screenplay, Fernanda Ribeiz, Fernando Molnar, Sebastian Schindel; Photography, Manuel Bullrich; Editor, Ernest Felder; a Magoya Films production in co-production with Incaa, Amar Assn., Dharma Group; Argentine; Dolby; Color; Not rated; 89 minutes; American release date: August 6, 2010. Documentary in which singer-songwriter León Gieco and a troupe of disabled musicians tour Argentina. **WITH** León Gieco, Alejandro David, Carina Spina, Pancho Chevez, Demian Frontera, Maxi Lemos, Rosita Bouete, Midia, Lucretia, Javier, Eduardo

Mundo Alas © Outsider Pictures

THE OXFORD MURDERS (Magnolia) Producers, Gerardo Herrero, Mariela Besuievsky, Alvaro Augustin, Kevin Loader, Frank Ribiere, Verane Frediani; Director, Alex de la Iglesia; Screenplay, Alex de la Iglesia, Jorge Guerricaechevarria; Based on the novel by Guillermo Martinez; Photography, Kiko de la Rica; Designer, Cristina Casali; Music, Roque Banos; Editor, Alejandro Lazaro; a Tornasol Films, Telecino Cinema (Spain)/Oxford Crimes (U.K.)/La Fabrique 2 (France) production; Spanish-British-French, 2008; Dolby; Widescreen; Color; Rated R; 108 minutes; American release date: August 6, 2010. **CAST**: Elijah Wood (Martin), John Hurt (Arthur Seldom), Leonor Watling (Lorna), Julie Cox (Beth), Jim Carter (Inspector Petersen), Alex Cox (Kalman), Burn Gorman (Yuri Podorov), Dominique Pinon (Frank), Anna Massey (Mrs. Eagleton), Danny Sapani (Scott), Alan David (Mr. Higgins), Tim Wallers (Defense Lawyer), James Weber Brown (Doctor), Ian East (Howard Green), Charlotte Asprey (Howard Green's Wife), Tom Frederic (Ludwig Wittgenstein), Michael Mears (Mathematician), James Howard (Newscaster), Luing Andrews (Security Guard), Sarah Crowden (Shop Assistant), Bruce Jamieson, Thomas Snowdon (Soldiers), Duane Henry, John Wark (Policemen), Bill Weston (Percussionist)

John Hurt, Elijah Wood in *The Oxford Murders* © Magnolia

ECCENTRICITIES OF A BLONDE-HAIRED GIRL (Independent) a.k.a. *Singularidades de uma Rapariga Loura*; Producers, Francois d'Artemare, Maria Joao Mayer, Louis Minarro; Director/Screenplay, Manoel de Oliveira; Based on the short story by Eca de Queiroz; Photography, Sabine Lancelin; Designers, Christian Marti, Jose Pedro Penha; Editors, Manoel de Oliveira, Catherine Krassovsky; a Filmes do Tejo II (Portugal)/Les Films de l'Apres-Midi (france)/Edie Saeta (Spain) production; Portuguese-French-Spanish; Color; HD; Not rated; 63 minutes; American release date: August 6, 2010. **CAST**: Ricardo Trêpa (Macário), Catarina Wallenstein (Luisa Vilaça), Diogo Dória (Tio Francisco), Júlia Buisel (Mãe de Luísa), Filipe Vargas (Friend)

Eccentricities of a Blonde-Haired Girl © Filmes do Tejo II

PATRIK, AGE 1.5 (Regent) Producers, Tomas Michaelsson, Lars Blomgren; Director/ Screenplay, Ella Lemhagen; Based on the play by Michael Druker; Photography, Marek Septimus Wieser; Designer, Lene Willumsen; Music, Fredrik Emilson; Editor, Thomas Lagerman; a Filmlance Intl. production; Swedish, 2008; Color; Widescreen; Rated R; 101 minutes; American release date: August 6, 2010. **CAST**: Gustaf Skarsgård (Göran Skoogh), Torkel Petersson (Sven Skoogh), Thomas Ljungman (Patrik), Annika Hallin (Eva), Amanda Davin (Isabell), Jacob Ericksson (Lennart Ljung), Anette Sevreus (Louise Ljung), Mirja Burlin (Carina Karlsson), Antti Reini (Tommy Karlsson), Marie Delleskog (Britt-Marie Svensson), Johan Kylén (Social Chief), Kristian Lima de Faria (Social Assistant), Karin de Frumerie (Receptionist), Andres Lönnbro (Urban Adler), Åsas-Lena Hjelm (Vivianne), Anna Wallander (Irja), Robin Stegmar (Police), Britta Andersson (Waitress), Richard Ulfsäter (Good-Looking Guy)

Gustaf Skarsgård, Torkel Petersson, Thomas Ljungman in *Patrik, Age 1.5* © Regent

SALT OF THIS SEA (Lorber) a.k.a. *Milh Hadha Al-Bahr*; Producers, Jacques Bidou, Marianne Dumoulin; Co-Producers, Annemarie Jacir, Pierre-Alain Meier, Joseph Rouschop, Danny Glover, Joslyn Barnes, Sawsan Asfari, Maya Sanbar, Bero Beyer, Philippe Berthet, Jaume Roures; Director/Screenplay, Annemarie Jacir; Photography, Benoit Chamaillard; Designer, Francoise Joset; Costumes, Hamada Atallah; Music, Kamran Rastegar; Editor, Michele Hubinon; a JBA Production (France)/Philistine Films (Palestine)/Thelma Film AG (Switzerland)/Tarantula (Belgium)/Louverture Films (U.S.)/Clarity World Films (U.K.)/Augustus Film (The Netherlands)/Mediapro (Spain)/Television Suisse Romande (Switzerland) production; French-Palestinian-Swiss-Belgian-American-British-Dutch-Spanish; Dolby; Color/black and white; Not rated; 109 minutes; American release date: August 13, 2010. **CAST**: Suheir Hammad (Soraya), Saleh Bakri (Emad), Riyad Ideis (Marwan), Walid Abdul Salam (Government Official), Jaber Abu Kaoud (Gas Station Attendant), Giras Abu Sabbah (Cinemateque Bouncer), Um Hussein Al Malhi (Emad's Mother), Avi Ammar (Store Attendant), Iman Aoun (Wealthy Landlord), Faras Awad (Abu Jihad), Yahya Barakat (Ziad), Ismael Dabbag (Bank Teller), Martin Daltry (Regional Manager), Hisham Daraghmeh (Fakri), Ishai Golan, Hagar Latem, Renan Latem (Agents), Shelly Goral (Irit), Franck Hammar, Avraham Shalom Levy (Policemen), Khader (Chewing Gum Boy), Reem Makhoul (Chambermaid), Juliano Mer (Hiking Leader), Ashera Ramadan (Rawan), Natalie Saadah (Back Off Girl), Jack Saadeh (Bank Manager), Sylvie Wetz (Corinne)

Suheir Hammad, Saleh Bakri in *Salt of This Sea* © Lorber Films

PEEPLI LIVE (UTV Motion Pictures) Producers, Aamir Khan, Kiran Rao; Executive Producer, B. Shrinivas Rao; Director/Screenplay, Anusha Rizvi; Photography, Shanker Raman; Designer, Suman Roy Mahapatra; Costumes, Maxima Basu; Music, Mathias Duplessy; Editor, Hemanti Sarkar; an Aamir Khan production; Indian; Color; Not rated; 105 minutes; American release date: August 13, 2010. **CAST**: Omkar Das (Natha), Raghuvir Yadav (Budhia), Shalini Vatsa (Dhaniya), Farrukh Jaffar (Amma), Malaika Shenoy (Nandita), Vishal Sharma (Deepak), Nowaz (Rakesh), Sitaram Panchal (Bhai Thakur), Nasseeruddin Shah (Salim Kidwai), Aamir Bashir (Vivek), Dan Husain (Vijay Ranjan Prasad)

Peepli Live © UTV Motion Pictures

LA SOGA (7-57 Releasing) Producers, Manny Perez, Josh Crook, Jeff Crook; Executive Producers, Patrick Pope, Jose Miguel Bonetti, Henry Mu, Celines Toribio; Director/Editor, Josh Crook; Screenplay, Manny Perez; Story, Manny Perez, Frank Molina, Michael Masucci; Photography, Zeus Morand; Designer, Jaime Whitlock; Costumes, Slobodan Strinic; Music, Evan Wilson; Music Supervisors, Rafael Evangelista, Henry Santos Jeter; Casting, Pachy Mendez; P2 Films/Lifted Prods.; Dominican; Color; Widescreen; HD; Not rated; 102 minutes; American release date: August 13, 2010. **CAST**: Manny Perez (Luisito), Denise Quiñones (Jenny), Juan Fernández (Gen. Colon), Paul Calderon (Rafa), Hemky Madera (Tavo), Alfsono Rodríguez (Franco), Joseph Lyle Taylor (Simon Burr), Margo Martindale (Flannigan), Fantino Fernandez (Young Luisito), Jaime Tirelli (Belgrado), Robinson Aybar (Efrain), Nelson Baez (The Butcher), Carmen

Brugal (Dona Irma), Coco Cabrera (Carlos Batista), Leslie Cepeda (Young Jenny), Mery Collado (Gen. Colon's Wife), Cruzmonty (Pedophile), Alexander Estrella (Margarita's Boyfriend), Guillermo Estrella (Jenny's Suitor), Elvira Grullón (Luisito's Aunt), Jean Johnny (Fellito Polanco), Antony Marte (Pres. Fernando Linares), Miguel Ángel Martínez (Luisito's Father), Pachy Méndez (Rafa's Wife), Sixta Morel (Reporter), Nuria Piera (Herself), Jose Perez (Rafa's Cousin), Diego Rafael (Young Tavo), Danilo Rodriguez (Felipe Manuel Peralta), Shino (Wellington), Sharlene Taulé (Margarita), M. Patricia Tejada (Jenny's Cousin)

Manny Perez in *La Soga* © 7057 Releasing

TALES FROM EARTHSEA (Walt Disney Studios) Producer, Toshio Suzuki; Director, Goro Miyazaki; Screenplay, Goro Miyazaki, Keiko Niwa; Based on the *Earthsea* novel series by Ursula K. Le Guin, inspired by *Shuna's Journey* by Hayao Miyazaki; Art Director, Yoji Takeshige; Directing Animator, Akihiko Yamashita; Supervising Animator, Takeshi Inamura; Color Designer, Michiyo Yasuda; Director of Digital Animation, Misunori Kataama; Music, Tamiya Tereshima; Japanese, 2006; a Studio Ghibli, Nippon Television Network, Dentsu, Hakuhodo Dump, Walt Disney Studio Home Entertainment, Mitsubishi and Toho presentation; Dolby; Color; Rated PG-13; 115 minutes; American release date: August 13, 2010. **VOICE CAST**: Willem Dafoe (Cob), Timothy Dalton (Ged/Sparrowhawk), Mariska Hargitay (Tenar), Cheech Marin (Hare), Matt Levin (Prince Arren), Blaire Restaneo (Therru), Jeff Bennett, Suzanne Blakeslee, Kat Cressida, Pat Fraley, Jessica Gee-George, Brian George, Grant George, Jess Harnell, Steve Kramer, David Lodge, Tress MacNeille, Liam O'Brien, Tara Platt, Kevin Michael Richardson, Mark Silverman, Terrence Stone, Karen Strassman, Russi Taylor (Additional Voices)

Arren in *Tales from Earthsea* © Walt Disney Studios

ALTIPLANO (First Run Features) Producers, Heino Deckert, Ma.J.De Fiction; Director/ Screenplay, Peter Brosens, Jessica Woodworth; Photography, Francisco Gózon; Art Directors, Anne Fourneri, Guillermo Isa; Editor, Nico Leunen; Belgian-German-Dutch, 2009; Dolby; Color; Not rated; 109 minutes; American release date: August 20, 2010. **CAST**: Magaly Solier (Saturnina), Jasmin Tabatabai (Grace), Olivier Gourmet (Max), Behi Djanati Ataï (Sami), Edgar Condori (Nilo/ Omar), Sonia Loaiza (Mother), Edgar Quispe (Igancio), Norma Martinez (Doctor), Rodolfo Rodriguez (Raúl), Hermelinda Luján (Rufina), Arturo Zárate (Orlando), Andreas Pietschmann (Paul), Antonio Quevedo (Soldier), Félix Cáceres (Félix), Raymundo Chillihuani (Healer), Kian Khalili (Reza)

Edgar Condori in *Altiplano* © First Run Features

MAKING PLANS FOR LENA (IFC Films) a.k.a. *Non ma fille, tu n'iras pas danser*; Producer, Pascal Caucheteux; Director, Christophe Honoré; Screenplay, Christophe Honoré, Genevieve Brisac; Photography, Laurent Brunet; Designer, Samuel Deshors; Music, Alex Beaupain; Editor, Chantal Hymans; Casting, Richard Rousseau; a Why Not Prods., France Television, Le Pacte production, with the participation of Canal Plus, France Television, Orange Cinema Series, La Region Bretagne; French, 2009; Dolby; Color; Not rated; 105 minutes; American release date: August 20, 2010. **CAST**: Chiara Mastroianni (Léna), Marina Foïs (Frédérique), Marie-Christine Barrault (Annie), Jean-Marc Barr (Nigel), Fred Ulysse (Michel), Louis Garrel (Simon), Marcial Di Fonzo Bo (Thibault), Alice Butaud (Elise), Julien Honoré (Gulven), Caroline Sihol (Florist), Donatien Suner (Anton), Lou Pasquerault (Augustine), Jean-Baptiste Fonck (José)

Louis Garrel, Chiara Mastroianni in *Making Plans for Lena* © IFC Films

THE ARMY OF CRIME (Lorber) a.k.a. *L'Armee du Crime*; Producers, Dominique Barneaud, Marc Bordure, Robert Guediguian; Director, Robert Guediguian; Screenplay, Robert Guediguian, Serge Le Peron, Gilles Taurand; Based on an original idea by Serge Le Peron; Photography, Pierre Milon; Designer, Michel Vandestien; Costumes, Christel Birot; Music, Alexandre Desplat; Editor, Bernard Sasia; Casting, Jacqueline Vicaire, Gaelle Baud; an Agat Films & Cie, StudioCala, France 3 Cinema production; French, 2009; Dolby; Color; Not rated; 138 minutes; American release date: August 20, 2010. **CAST**: Simon Abkarian (Missak Manouchian), Virginie Ledoyen (Mélinée Manouchian), Robinson Stévenin (Marcel Rayman), Grégoire Leprince-Ringuet (Thomas Elek), Lola Naymark (Monique), Yann Trégouet (Commissioner David), Ariane Ascaride (Madame Elek), Jean-Pierre Darroussin (Inspector Pujol), Ivan Franek (Feri Boczov), Adrien Jolivet (Henri Krasucki), Horatiu Malaele (Mr. Dupont), Mirza Halilovic (Petra), Olga Legrand (Olga Bancic), Esteban Carvajal-Alegria (Narek Tavkorian), Léopold Szabtaura (Simon Rayman), Paula Klein (Mr. Rayman), Boris Bergman (Mr. Rayman), George Babluani (Patriciu), Pierre Niney (Henri Keltekian), Jorgen Genuit (Raffenbach), Jean-Claude Bourbault (Joseph Darnand), Rainer Sieveret (Officer Allemand Cormeilles), Serge Avedikian (Micha Aznavourian), Pierre Banderet (Lucien Rottée), Lucas Belvaux (Joseph Epstein), Frédérique Bonnal (Concierge), Patrick Bonnel (Mr. Elek), Christine Brücher (Farmer's Wife), Alain Lenglet (Headmaster), Gérard Meylan (Cop)

Grégoire Leprince-Ringuet (center) in *The Army of Crime* © Lorber Films

WHAT IF ...? (Five & Two Pictures) a.k.a. *Notre univers impitoyable*; Producers, Caroline Benjo, Carole Scotta, Barbara Letellier, Simon Arnal; Director/Screenplay, Léa Fazer; Photography, Myriam Vinocour; Designer, Marie-Helene Sulmoni; Costumes, Isabelle Pannetier; Music, Sebastien Schuller; Editor, Francois Gedigier; a Haut & Court, M6 Films production; French, 2008; Color; Widescreen; Not rated; 86 minutes; American release date: August 20, 2010. **CAST**: Alice Taglioni (Margot Dittermann), Jocelyn Quivrin (Victor Bandini), Thierry Lhermitte (Nicolas Bervesier), Pascale Arbillot (Juliette), Scali Depeyrat (Bertrand Lavoisier), Julie Ferrier (Éléonore), Eliot Pasqualon (Antonin), Joe Sheridan (Goudal)

Thierry Lhermitte, Jocelyn Quivrin in *What If ...?* © Five & Two Pictures

THE MILK OF SORROW (Olive Films) a.k.a. *La Teta Asustada*; Producers, Antonio Chavarrias, José Maria Morales, Claudia Llosa; Director/Screenplay, Claudia Llosa; Photography, Natasha Braier; Art Directors, Susana Torres, Patricia Bueno; Music, Selma Mutal; Editor, Frank Gutierrez; a production of Wanda Visión, Oberon Cinematográfica, Vela Films; Peruvian-Italian; Dolby; Color; Not rated; 100 minutes; American release date: August 27, 2010. **CAST**: Magaly Solier (Fausta), Susi Sánchez (Aida), Efrain Solis (Noé), Marino Ballón (Tio Lucido), Bárbara Lazón (Perpetua), Delci Heredia (Carmela), Karla Heredia (Severina), Fernando Caycho (Melvin), Miller Revilla Chengay (Melvincito), Spencer Salazar (Jonathan), Summy Lapa (Chicho), María del Pilar Guerrero (Máxima), Leandro Mostorino (Jhonny), Anita Chaquiri (Abuela), Edward Llungo (Marcos), Daniel Núñez (Amadeo), Lucy Noriega (Perpetua)

Magaly Solier in *The Milk of Sorrow* © Olive Films

DANIEL & ANA (Strand) Producer, Daniel Birman Ripstein; Director/Screenplay, Michel Franco; Photography, Chuy Chávez; Photography, Enrique Chediak; Designer, Martha Papadimitriou; Music, Atto Attié; Editor, Oscar Figueroa; Almaeda Films production; Mexican; Dolby; Color; Not rated; 90 minutes; American release date: August 27, 2010. **CAST**: Darío Yazbek Bernal (Daniel), Marimar Vega (Ana), José María Torre (Rafael), Luis Miguel Lombana (Fernando), Montserrat Ontiveros (Galia)

Darío Yazbek Bernal, Marimar Vega in *Daniel & Ana* © Strand Releasing

AASHAYEIN (Reliance Big Pictures) Director/Screenplay, Nagesh Kukunoor; Photography, Sudeep Chatterjee; Art Director, Sunil Nigvekar; Costumes, Aparna Shah; Music, Salim-Suleiman; Editor, Apurva; a Percept Picture Company and T-Series presentation, in association with SIC Productions; Indian, 2009; Color; Not rated; 120 minutes; American release date: August 27, 2010. **CAST**: John Abraham (Rahul Sharma), Sonal Sehgal (Nafisa), Vikram Inamdar (Xavier), Sonali Sachdev (Doctor at Clinic), Prateeksha Lonkar (Sister Grace), Farida Jalal (Madhu), Girish Karnad (Parthasarthi), Jia Mustafa (Manju), Anaitha Nair (Padma), Sharad Wagh (Priest)

John Abraham, Sonal Sehgal in *Aashayein* © Reliance Big Pictures

SALVATION POEM (CanZion) a.k.a. *Poema de salvación*; Producers, Arturo Allen, Pablo Muñiz; Executive Producers, Matt McPherson, Marcos Witt; Director, Brian Dublín; Screenplay, Omar Quiroga, Alejandro Robino, Edurdo Marando; Based on an idea by Arturo Allen; Photography, Alexander Vatalev; Art Director, Rosana Ojeda; Editors, Guillerma García, Cecilia Palacios; VSN Producciones; Argentine, 2009; Color; Rated PG-13; 78 minutes; American release: August 27, 2010. **CAST**: Gonzalo Senestrari (Pablo), Irina Alonso (Carmen), Fernando Rosarolli (Roberto), Gian Franco (Ángel), Fernanda Ganz (Lorena), Soledad Beilis (Andrea), Mirko Sarina (Young Pablo), Lilia Pardo (Esperanza), Sapha Arias (Young Esperanza), Francisco Civic (Pastor), Fernando Armani (Music Teacher), Kevin Schiele (Literature Teacher), Sebastián Leis (Dean), César Laino (Kidnapper), Santos Lontoya (Rony), Nicolás Liern (Edgardo), Silvestre Casagrande (Marcelo), Leandro Mietta (Fernando), Diego Lublinsky (Abel Black), Felicitas Pasquale (Andrea)

CHAK JAWANA (Reliance Pictures) Producers, Balli Janjua, Rupinder Chahal; Director, Simerjit Singh; Screenplay/Costumes, Manjeet Maan, Balli Janjua; Photography, R.A. Krishna; Art Director, Manoj Kumar Kanojia; Music, Jaidev Kumar; India; Color; Not rated; 132 minutes; American release date: August 27, 2010. **CAST**: Karanjit Anmol (Dollar), Jonita Doda (Binny), Guddu (Satnam Singh), Gurkitran (Sarpanch Balkar Singh), Harisharan (Shinda), Pradeep Joshi (Talli), Gaurav Kakkar (Raja, Rajbir Singh), Shammii Malhotra (Kuldeep Kaur), Gurdas Maan (Capt. Gurjeet Singh), Sonal Minocha (Naman), Rana Ranbir (Master), Prince K.J. Singh (Boota)

Gurdas Maan, Jonita Doda in *Chak Jawana* © Reliance Pictures

WHITE WEDDING (Dada Films) Producers/Screenplay, Kenneth Nkosi, Rapulana Seiphemo, Jann Turner; Executive Producer, Ken Follett; Director, Jann Turner; Photography, Willie Nel; Art Director, Martha Sibanyoni; Music, Joel Assiazky; Editor, Tanja Hagen; a Stepping Stone Pictures production; South African, 2009; Dolby; Color; HD; Not rated; 97 minutes; American release date: September 3, 2010. **CAST**: Kenneth Nkosi (Elvis), Zandie Msutwana (Ayanda), Rapulana Seiphemo (Tumi), Jodie Whittaker (Rose), Sylvia Mngxekeza (Ayanda's Mother), Mbulelo Grootboom (Tony), Louise Saint-Claire (Mrs. Van Zyl), Grant Swanby (Slang), Marcel Van Heerden (Mr. Fanie van Zyl)

Kenneth Nkosi, Rapulana Seiphemo, Zandie Msutwana in *White Wedding* © Dada Films

WE ARE FAMILY (Dharma) Producer, Karan Johar; Executive Producer, Path Arora; Director, Sidharth Malhotra; Screenplay, Sidharth Malhotra, Karan Johar; Designer, Shashank Tere; Color; Not rated; 115 minutes; American release date: September 3, 2010. **CAST**: Kajol (Maya), Kareena Kapoor (Shreya), Arjun Rampal (Aman), Nominath Ginsberg (Ankush), Aachal Munjal (Aleya), Diya Sonecha (Anjali)

Kajol in *We are Family* © Dharma

MAX MANUS (D Films) Producers, John M. Jacobsen, Sveinung Golimo; Directors, Espen Sandberg, Joachim Roenning; Screenplay, Thomas Nordseth-Tiller; Photography, Geir Hartly Andreassen; Designer, Karli Juliusson; Costumes, Manon Rasmussen; Music, Trond Bjerknaes; Editor, Anders Refn; a John M. Jacobsen presentation; Norwegian-German-Danish, 2008; Dolby; Widescreen; Color; Not rated; 118 minutes; American release date: September 3, 2010. **CAST**: Aksel Hennie (Max Manus), Agnes Kittelsen (Ida Nikoline "Tikken" Lindebrækee), Nicolai Cleve Broch (Gregers Gram), Ken Duken (Siegfried Fehmer), Christian Rubeck (Kolbein Lauring), Knut Joner (Gunnar Sønsteby), Mads Eldøen (Edvard Tallaksen), Kyrre Haugen Sydness (Jens Christian Hauge), Viktoria Winge (Solveig Johnsrud), Pål Sverre Valheim Hagen (Roy Nilsen), Jakob Oftebro (Lars Emil Erichsen), Petter Næss (Capt. Martin Linge), Ron Donachie (Col. J.S. Wilson), Stig Henrik Hoff (Eilertsen), Oliver Stokowski (Höhler), Erik Evjen (Sigurd Jacobsen), Kjersti Holmen (Fru Jacobsen), Julia Bache-Wiig (Sykesøster Liv), Stig Hoffmeyer (Kong Haakon), Erick Aleksander Schjerven (Jon Hatland). Erik Hivju (Dr. Nordlie), Rolf Kristian Larsen (Olav), Sondre Krogtoff Larsen (Dick Henriksen)

Aksel Hennie in *Max Manus* © D Films

OUR BELOVED MONTH OF AUGUST (Independent) a.k.a. *Aquele quierdo mes de agosto*; Producers, Luis Urbano, Sandro Aguilar; Director, Miguel Gomes; Screenplay, Miguel Gomes, Mariana Ricardo, Telmo Churro; Photography, Rui Pocas; Costumes, Bruno Duarte; Editors, Telmo Churro Miguel Gomes; an O Som e a furia production; Portuguese, 2008; Dolby; Color; Not rated; 150 minutes; American release date: September 3, 2010. **CAST**: Sónia Bandeira (Tania), Fábio Oliveira (Hélder), Manuel Soares (Celestine)

Fábio Oliveira, Sónia Bandeira in *Our Beloved Month of August* © O Some e a furia production

SEQUESTRO (Paradigm) Producers, Jorge W. Atalla, Alexandre Moreira Leite; Executive Producers, Frederico Lapenda, Christian Gudegast; Director, Jorge W. Atalla; Screenplay, Jorge W. Atalla, Caio Cavechini; Photography, Arturo Querzoli; Music, Tuta Aquino, Fernando Pinheiro, Vitor Rocha; Editors, Marcelo Moraes, Marcelo Bala; a Yukon Filmworks and Midmix Entertainment presentation in association with Filmland Intl. and Paradigm Pictures; Brazilian; 2009; Dolby; Color/Black and white; HD; Not rated; 94 minutes; American release date: September 10, 2010. Documentary on Sao Paulo's Anti-Kidnapping Police Division. **WITH** Humberto Paz, Horacio Paz, Jose Ibiapina de Souza

Sequestro © Paradigm

FOOL FOR LOVE (DE MAI TINH) (Variance Films) Producers, Dustin Nguyen, Irene Trinh; Director, Truc "Charlie" Nguyen; Photography, Dominic Pereira; Music, Christopher Wong; Editors, Truc "Charlie" Nguyen, Ham Tran; an Early Risers Media Group and Wonderboy Entertainment presentation; Vietnamese; Color; Rated PG-13; 95 minutes; American release date: September 10, 2010. **CAST**: Dustin Nguyen (Dung), Truc "Charlie" Nguyen (Antoine), Kathy Uyen (Mai)

THE ANCHORAGE (General Asst.) Producers/Directors/Editors, Anders Edström, C.W. Winter; Screenplay, C.W. Winter; Photography, Anders Edström; Dolby; Swedish-American; Color; Super 16; Not rated; 86 minutes; American release date: September 17, 2010. **CAST**: Ulla Edström (Ulla), Marcus Harrling (Marcus), Elin Hamrén (Elin), Bengt Ohlsson (The Hunter)

THE GIRL (Olive Films) a.k.a. *Flickan*; Producer, David Olsson; Director, Fredrik Edfeldt; Screenplay, Karin Arrhenius; Photography, Hoyte van Hoytema; Designers, Lars Strömsten, Bernhard Winkler; Music, Dan Berridge; Editors, Therese Elfström, Malin Lindström; Sweden, 2009; Dolby; Color; Not rated; 100 minutes; American release date: September 17, 2010. **CAST**: Blanca Engstrom (The Girl), Shanti Roney (Her Father), Annika Hallin (Her Mother), Calle Lindqvist (Petter), Tova Magnusson-Norling (Anna), Leif Andrée (Gunnar), Vidar Fors (Ola), la Langhammer (Elisabeth), Emma Wigfeldt (Tina), Mats Blomgren (Ola's Father)

Blanca Engstrom in *The Girl* © Olive Films

THE TEMPTATION OF ST. TONY (Olive Films) a.k.a. *Püha Tõnu kiusamine*; Producer, Katrin Kissa; Director/ Screenplay, Veiko Õunpuu; Photography, Mart Taniel; Designer, Markku Patila; Music, Ulo Krigul; Editor, Thomas Lagerman; a Homeless Bob production in association with ATMO and Bronson Club; Estonian; Dolby; Black and white; Not rated; 110 minutes; American release date: September 17, 2010. **CAST**: Taavi Eelmaa (Tony), Ravashana Kurkova (Nadezhda), Tiina Tauraite (Tony's Wife), Sten Ljunggren (Herr Meister), Denis Lavant (Count Dionysos Korzybski), Hendrik Toompere Jr. (Actor Toivo), Katariina Lauk (Toivo's Wife), Harri Kõrvits (Director), Taavi Teplenkov (Urbo), Marika Barabanstsikova (Urbo's Wife), Rain Tolk (Kleine Willy), Liis Lepik (Tony's Child), Valeri Fjodorov (Nadezhda's Father), Evald Aavik (Priest)

Taavi Eelmaa in *The Temptation of St. Tony* © Olive Films

A MOTHER'S COURAGE: TALKING BACK TO AUTISM (First Run Features) Producer, Margrét Dagmar Ericsdóttir; Executive Producer, Kristin Olafsdottir; Director, Fridrik Thor Fridriksson; Photography, Jon Karl Helgason; Music, Sigur Rós, Björk; Editor, Thuridur Einarsdottir; Narrator, Kate Winslet; a Frontier Filmsworks in association with Klikk Productions presentation; Icelandic, 2009; Color; Not rated; 103 minutes; American release date: September 24, 2010. Documentary about Margrét Dagmar Ericsdóttir's efforts to help her autistic 11-year-old son, Keli. **WITH** Becky and Abe Meulemans, Candace Smith, Jason and Lori Collins, David G. Amaral, Jonathan Shestack, Linda Lange, Portia Iversen, Simon Baron-Cohen, David Crowe, Geraldine Dawson, Temple Grandin, Lisa Helt, Catherine Lord, Joseph E. Morrow, Soma Mukhopadhyay, Tito Mukhopadhyay, Sally Rogers, Brenda Terzich, Taylor Crowe, Thorkil Sonne, Vernon Smith

Margrét Dagmar Ericsdóttir, Keli Ericsdottir in *A Mother's Courage* © First Run Features

HOT SUMMER DAYS (Fox International) a.k.a. *Chuen sing yit luen – yit lat lat*; Producers, Fruit Chan, Paul Cheng; Directors, Tony Chan, Wing Shya; Screenplay, Tony Chan, Lucretia Ho; Photography, Sion Michel; Designer/ Costumes, Sean Kunjambu; Music, Eddie Chung, Eugene Pao; Editor, Wenders Li; Chinese-American; Dolby; Color; Rated PG; 93 minutes; American release date: October 1, 2010. **CAST**: Jacky Cheung (Wah), Nicholas Tse (Ah Wai), Rene Liu (Li Yan), Vivian Hsu (Wasabi), Jing Boran (Xiao Fang), Angela Baby (Xiao Qi), Barbie Hsu (Ding Dong), Yihong Duan (Leslie Guan), Xinbo Fu (Da Fu), Daniel Wu (Master Chef)

Jing Boran, Angela Baby in *Hot Summer Days* © Fox Intl.

IP MAN (Variance) a.k.a. *Yip Man*; Producer, Wong Bak-Ming; Director, Wilson Yip; Screenplay, Edmond Wong; Photography, O Sing-Pui; Art Director, Kenneth Mak; Music, Kenji Kawai; Editor, Cheung Ka-Fai; Martial Arts Coordinator, Hsiung Kuang; Hong Kong, 2008; Color; Rated R; 106 minutes; American release date: October 1, 2010. **CAST**: Donnie Yen (Ip Man), Simon Yam (Zhou Qing Quan), Siu-Wong fan (Jin Shan Zhao), Ka Tung Lam (Li Zhao), Yu Xing (Master Zealot Lin), You-Nam Wong (Shao Dan Yuan), Chez Zhi Hui (Master Liao), Lynn Hung (Zhang Yong Cheng), Hiroyuki Ikeuchi (Miura), Yu-Hang To (Hu Wei)

Donnie Yen in *Ip Man* © Variance

ROBERT JAY LIFTON: NAZI DOCTORS (National Center for Jewish Film) Producers/ Directors, Hannes Karnick, Wolfgang Richter; Photography/Editor, Wolfgang Richter; Music, Jan Tilman Schade; a Docfilm, Karnick & Richter production; German; Color; Not rated; 86 minutes; Release date: October 6, 2010. Documentary on the role that doctors played in the Nazi regime. **WITH** Robert Jay Lifton

Robert Jay Lifton in *Nazi Doctors* © Natl. Center for Jewish Film

RACHEL (Women Make Movies) Producer, Thierry Lenouvel; Director/ Screenplay, Simone Bitton; Photography, Jacques Bouquin; Editors, Catherine Poitevin, Jean-Michel Perez; Arte France Cinéma, Novak Productions; French-Belgian, 2009; Color; Not rated; minutes; American release date: October 8, 2010. Documentary on Rachel Corrie, who was killed trying to stop a bulldozer from plowing down some buildings.

Rachel Corrie (right) in *Rachel* © Women Make Movies

LETTERS TO FATHER JACOB (Olive Films) a.k.a. *Postia pappi Jaakobille*; Producers, Lasse Saarinen, Rimbo Salomaa; Director/Screenplay, Klaus Härö; Based on an original screenplay by Jaana Makkonen; Photography, Tuomo Hutri; Designer, Kaisa Makinen; Music, Dani Stromback; Editor, Samu Heikkila; Costumes, Sari Suominen; a Kinotaur production, with the support of YLE TV, Finnish Film Foundation, Swedish Television; Finnish-Swedish, 2009; Dolby; Widescreen; Color; Not rated; 74 minutes; American release date: October 8, 2010. **CAST**: Kaarina Hazard (Leila), Jukka Keinonen (Posteljooni), Heikki Nousiainen (Father Jacob), Kaija Pakarinen (Voice of Leilan Sisko), Esko Ronie (Vankilan Johtaja)

Kaarina Hazard, Heikki Nousiainen in *Letters to Father Jacob* © Olive Films

BOMBAY SUMMER (Katha Films) Producers, Joseph Mathew, Sanjay Bhattacharjee; Director/ Screenplay, Joseph Mathew; Photography, Amol Rathod; Art Director, Satish Chipkar; Costumes, Darshan Jalan; Editor, Pallavi Singhal; Indian, 2008; Color; Not rated; 102 minutes; American release date: October 8, 2010. **CAST:** Tannishtha Chatterjee (Geetha), Samrat Chakrabarti (Jaidev), Jatin Goswami (Madan), Gaurav Dwivedi (Zakir), Shipli Arora (Shaira), Sanjay Singh Bhadli (Paanwallah), Rakesh Harjai (Vikram), Vineet Kapoor (Chawla), Cyndy Khojol (Kili), Abhijit Lahiri (Rajesh), Shilpa Mehta (Kavita), Shwetanjali (Rai (Shenaz), Peter Demelo (Madan's Father), Ratna Hegde (Shaira's Housekeeper), Silky Jain (Anna, Receptionist), Harish Jaswani (Chawl Board President), Parandeep Singh Bawa, Ajeet Singh (Assailants)

Tannishtha Chatterjee in *Bombay Summer* © Katha Films

BUDRUS (Balcony) Producers, Roni Avni, Julia Bacha, Rula Salameh; Executive Producers, Ronit Avni, Jehane Noujaim; Director/Screenplay, Julia Bacha; Photography, Shai Pollack and others; Music, Kareem Roustom; Editors, Geeta Gandbhir, Julia Bacha; a Just Vision production with the support of the Sundance Institute Documentary Film Program; Israeli-American, 2009; Color; Not rated; 70 minutes; American release date: October 8, 2010. Documentary on how the Palestinian residents of Budrus challenged efforts by the Israeli government to run a separation barrier through their land.

Budrus © Balcony Films

URVILLE (Independent) Producers, Helge Albers, Roshanak Behesht Nedjad; Director/Screenplay/ Editor, Angela Christlieb; Photography, Yvonne Mohr; Music, Eric Hubel, Wharton Thiers; a Flying Moon production, in co-production with ZDF/Arte; German-French, 2009; Color; 81 minutes; American release date: October 15, 2010. Documentary looking at three tiny villages in France. **WITH** Denis Cremel, Michel Drappier, Nicole Gombert, Francois Grossi, Patricia Raveneau-Laurent

CARMO, HIT THE ROAD (First Run Features) Producers, Xavier Granada, Alberto Aranda, Roberto D'Avila, Murray Lipnik, Grzegorz Hajdarowicz, Elisa Alvares; Director/Screenplay, Murilo Pasta; Photography, Robbie Ryan; Art Director, Marie Lanna; Music, Zacarias M. de le Riva; Editor, Nacho Ruiz Capillas; Costumes, Iraci de Jesus; an Imagina Intl. Sales (Spain) presentation of a Contraluz Films (Spain)/Magia Filmes Producoes (Brazil)/Germi Film (Poland) production; Brazilian-Spanish-Polish, 2008; Technicolor; Not rated; 100 minutes; American release date: October 15, 2010. **CAST**: Fele Martínez (Marco Bermejo), Mariana Loureiro (Maria do Carmo), Seu Jorge (Amparo de Jesús), Márco Garcia (Diamantino dos Anjos), Paca Gabaldón (Luz Guarany), Rosi Campos (Serrana de Jesús Feliciano), Norival Rizzo (Alberto Chagas), Kiko Bertholini (Lucio Mario Espinheira), Nana Costa (Rosália Alecrim), Thaís Fersoza (Viviane Ladeira), Clarissa Kiste (Lenice Carbastaflor)

Seu Jorge, Fele Martinez in *Carmo, Hit the Road* © First Run Features

SAMSON AND DELILAH (IndiePix) Producer, Kath Shelper; Director/ Screenplay/ Photography/Music, Warwick Thornton; Designer, Daran Fulham; Editor, Roland Gallois; Australian, 2009; Dolby; Color; Not rated; 101 minutes; American release date: October 15, 2010. **CAST**: Rowan McNamara (Samson), Marissa Gibson (Delilah), Mitjili Gibson (Nana), Scott Thornton (Gonzo), Matthew Gibson (Samson's Brother), Peter Bartlett (Store Manager), Noreen Robertson (Community Lady), Kenrick "Ricco" Martin (Wheelchair Boy), Audrey Martin (Payback Auntie), Fiona Gibson (Payback Aunty), Morgaine Wallace (Checkout Lady), Tony "Brownie" Brown (Security Guard), Roland Gallois (Art Gallery Owner), Patricia Shelper (Art Store Lady), Alfreda Glynn (Art Store Customer), Rona McDonald, Jessica Sanderson (Teenagers), Tyrone Wallace, Dylan McDonald (Abductors), Trish Rigby (Waitress), Ricardo del Rio (Priest), David Page (Kenny, Green Bush Show), Pascoe Bruan (Voice of Country Radio), Steven Brown, Gregwyn Gibson (Verandah Band)

Rowan McNamara, Marissa Gibson in *Samson and Delilah* © IndiePix

THE MAN FROM NOWHERE (CJ Entertainment) a.k.a. *This Man* and *A-jeo-ssi*; Producer, Lee Tae-hun; Executive Producers, Kathrine Kim, Lee Tae-hun; Director/Screenplay, Lee Jeong-beom; Photography, Lee Tae-yoon; Designer, Yang Hong-sam; Costumes, Jang Ju-hee; Music, Shim Hyun-jung; Editor, Kim Sang bum; a United Pictures presentation of an Opus Pictures production; South Korean; Dolby; Widescreen; Color; Rated R; 119 minutes; American release date: October 15, 2010. **CAST**: Won Bin (Cha Tae-Sik), Kim Sae-ron (Jeong So-Mi), Kim Hyo-seo (Hyo-Jong), Song Yeong-cheong (Oh), Kim Hee-won (Man-seok), Kim Tae-hun (Det. Kim Chi-gon), Kim Song-oh (Jong-suk), Lee Jong-pil, Thanayong Wongtrakul, Song Yeong-chang, Baek Soo-ryeon

Won Bin in *The Man from Nowhere* © CJ Entertainment

LEGACY (Codeblack Entertainment) Producers, Arabella Page Croft, Kieran Parker, Thomas Ikimi; Executive Producers, Idris Elba, Amrit Walia; Director/Screenplay, Thomas Ikimi; Photography, Jonathan Harvey; Designer, Gordon Rogers; Costumes, Harriet Edmonds; Music, Mark Kilian; Editors, Thomas Ikimi, Richard Graham; a Black Camel Pictures/Legacy Spy production, presented in association with Kaleidoscope Prods.; Nigerian-British; Color; HD-to-35mm; Rated R; 93 minutes; American release date: October 15, 2010. **CAST**: Idris Elba (Malcolm Gray), Eamonn Walker (Darnell Gray Jr.), Monique Gabriela Curnen (Valentina Gray), Richard Brake (Scott O'Keefe), Clarke Peters (Ola Adenuga), Julian Wadham (Gregor Salenko), Gerald Kyd (Gustavo Helguerra), Mem Ferda (Andriy), Niall Greig Fulton (Vladimir), John Kazek (Dimitri), Annette Badland (Stephanie Gumpel), Lara Pulver (Diane Shaw), William Hope (Mark Star), Joe Holt (Ronny Tarbuck), Deobia Oparei (Ray Cloglamm), Juliet Howland (Anne), Christina Chong (Jane), Michael Alspaugh (Carl), Michael Callaghan (Mikhail), Finaly Harris (Darnell's Supporter), Adam Smith (Rescue Worker)

Idris Elba in *Legacy* © Codeblack Entertainment

DOWN TERRACE (Magnet) Producer, Andy Starke; Director, Ben Wheatley; Screenplay, Ben Wheatley, Robin Hill; Photography, Laurie Rose; Music, Jim Williams; Editor, Robin Hill; a Mondo Macabro Movies presentation in association with Baby Cow Films; British; Color; HD; Rated R; 89 minutes; American release date: October 15, 2010. **CAST**: Robert Hill (Bill), Robin Hill (Karl), Julia Deakin (Maggie), David Schaal (Eric), Tony Way (Garvey), Kerry Peacock (Valda), Michael Smiley (Pringle), Mark Kempner (Councillor Berman), Kitty Blue (Pringle's Kid), Gareth Tunley (Johnny), Kali Peacock (Mrs. Garvey), Luke Hartney (Spitz), Janet Hill (Mrs. Pringle), Simon Smith, Paul George, Simon Walker (Bill's Band Members)

Robert Hill, Robin Hill in *Down Terrace* © Magnet

KNOCK OUT (Aap Entertainment) Producer, Sohail Maklai; Executive Producer, Hussain Shaikh; Director, Mani Shankar; Photography, Nataraja Subramanian; Editor, Bunty Nagi; Indian; Color; Not rated; 110 minutes; American release date: October 15, 2010. **CAST**: Sanjay Dutt (Veer Vijay Singh), Irrfan Kahn (Tony Khosla), Gulshan Grover (Bapuji), Kangana Ranaut (Nidhi Srivastava), Sushant Singh (VIkram), Apoorva Lakhia (Ranvir Singh), Rukhsar (Lakshmi)

Sanjay Dutt in *Knock Out* © Aap Entertainment

Marie Bos in *Amer* © Olive Films

THE PORTUGUESE NUN (Independent) a.k.a. *A Religiosa Portuguesa*; Producers, Luis Urbano, Sandro Aguilar; Director/Screenplay, Eugène Green; Photography, Raphael O'Byrne; Designer, Ze Branco; Costumes, Margarida Morins; Editor, Valerie Loiseleux; an O Som e a furia (Portugal)/MACT Prods. (France) production; Portuguese-French; 2009; Dolby; Color; Widescreen; Not rated; 127 minutes; American release date: October 22, 2010. **CAST**: Leonor Baldaque (Julie de Hauranne), Francisco Mozos (Vasco), Diogo Dória (D. Henrique Cunha), Ana Moreira (Irma Joana), Eugène Green (Denis Verde), Adrien Michaux (Martin Dautand), Beatriz Batarda (Madalena), Carloto Cotta (D. Sebastião)

WALKAWAY (IABA Films) Producers, Shailja Gupta, Shrikant Mohta, Mahendra Soni, Varun Shah, Ruchika Lalwani, Shawn Rice; Director, Shailja Gupta; Screenplay, Shailja Gupta, Ruchika Lalwani; Photography, Trisha Solyn; Designer, Ana Monroe; Costumes, Amy Kramer; Music, Sagar Desai; Editors, Sanjay Sharma, Shailja Gupta; Color; an It's All Been Arranged production; Color; Not rated; 97 minutes; Release date: October 29, 2010. **CAST**: Manu Narayan (Darius), Samrat Chakrabarti (Shree), Manish Dayal (Vinay), Sanjiv Jhaveri (Soham), Deepti Gupta (Nidhi), Carrie Anne James (Genevieve), Pallavi Sharda (Sia), Ami Sheth (Anu)

Leonor Baldaque in *The Portuguese Nun* © O Som e furia

Sanjiv Jhaveri, Deepti Gupta in *Walkaway* © IABA Films

AMER (Olive Films) Producers, Eve Commenge, Francois Cognard; Director/Screenplay, Helene Cattet, Bruno Forzani; Photography, Manu Dacosse; Designer, Alina Santos; Costumes, Jackye Fauconnier; Editor, Bernard Beets; a Tobina Film (France)/Anonymes Films (Belgium) production, with the participation of Canal Plus; Belgian-French, 2009; Dolby; Color; Widescreen; Not rated; 88 minutes; American release date: October 29, 2010. **CAST**: Cassandra Foret (Child Ana), Charlotte Eugène-Guibbaud (Teenage Ana), Marie Bos (Adult Ana), Bianca Maria D'Amato (Ana's Mother), Harry Cleven (Taxi Driver), Jean-Michel Vovk (Ana's Father), Delphine Brual (Ana's Grandmother, Graziella), Bernard Marbaix (Ana's Dead Grandfather)

EICHMANN (Regent) Producer, Karl Richards; Director, Robert Young; Screenplay, Snoo Wilson; Photography, Michael Connor; Designer, Tibor Lazar; Costumes, Alyson Ritchie; Music, Richard Harvey; Editor, Saska Simpson; a Media 8 Entertainment presentation of a Karl Richards/E-Motion production in association with Thema Productions & Motion Investment Group' Hungarian-British, 2007; Dolby; Color; HD; Not rated; 100 minutes; American release date: October 29, 2010. Thomas Kretschmann (Adolf Eichmann), Troy Garity (Avner Less), Franka Potente (Vera Less), Stephen Fry (Minister Tormer), Delaine Yates (Miriam Frohlich), Tereza Srbova (Ingrid von Ihama), Judit Viktor (Ann Marie), Stephen Grief (Hans Lipmann), Denes Bernath (Benjamin), Bernadett Kis (Sarah), Tilly Golding (Hannah), Laszlo Berecki (David), Alexis Latham (Dubois), Scott Alexander Young (Robert Servatius), Bela Festzbaum (Dr. Kastner), Melissa Franklyn (Policewoman), Peter Ambrus (Abraham Less), Mate Endredi (Young Guard), Nikolett P. Jancsovics (Ruth), Janos Fekete (Zack), Kerstin Sekimoto (Secretary), Eszter Paloc (Interpreter), Balint Meran (German Speaking Officer), Andrew Hefler (Young Doctor), Peter Laczo (Dieter Eichmann), Krisztian Voros (Klaus Eichmann), Adam Vadas (Horst Eichmann), Viktor Noe (SS Officer), Gyula Mesterhazy (Nazi Official), Laszlo Barnak (Young Night Guard), Shy Heller (Old Night Guard), Richard Rifkin (Elderly Man), Janos Mercs (French Speaking

Officer), Attila Muller (Eichmann's Chauffeur), Istvan Goz (German Interpreter), Abdul Sattar Rehani (Husseini), Stephen Buhagiar (Locksmith), John Baddeley (Radio Voiceover)

Troy Garity, Thomas Kretschmann in *Eichmann* © Regent

AFTERSHOCK (China Lion Film Distribution) Producers, Wang Zhangjun, Gio Yanhong, Han Samping; Director, Feng Xiaogang; Screenplay, Su Xiaowei; Based on the novel by Zhang Ling; Photography, Yue Lu; Designer, Huo Tingxiao; Music, Li-guang Wang; Editor, Xiao Yang; Chinese; Color; Not rated; 130 minutes; American release date: October 29, 2010. **CAST**: Jingchu Zhang (Fang Deng/Wang Deng), Chen Daoming (Mr. Wang/Foster Dad), Chen Li (Fang Da), Fan Xu (Mom), Jin Chen (Foster Mom), Guoqiang Zhang (Fang Qiang)

Aftershock © China Lion

THE MAGICIAN (Regent) Producers, Michele Bennett, Nash Edgerton, Scott Ryan; Executive Producers, Gary Phillips, Mark Vennis; Director/Screenplay, Scott Ryan; Photography, Massimiliano Andrighetto; Editors, Nash Edgerton, Kristine Rowe, Scott Ryan; an Australian Film Finance Corporation and Film Victoria in association with Blue Tongue Films and Cherub Pictures presentation of an I Will Films Production; Australian, 2005; Dolby; Color; Not rated; 85 minutes; American release date: October 29, 2010. **CAST**: Scott Ryan (Ray Shoesmith), Ben Walker (Tony Rickards), Massimiliano Andrighetto (Massimo "Max" Totti), Kane Mason (Benny), Nathaniel Lindsay (Edna), Adam Ryan (Garage Victim)

Scott Ryan in *The Magician* © Regent

CHANGE NOTHING (Red Star Cinema) a.k.a. *Ne change rien*; Producers, Sébastien de Fonseca, Abel Ribeiro Chaves, Cédric Walter; Director/Photography, Pedro Costa; Editor, Patricia Saramago; French; Black and white; Not rated; 100 minutes; American release date: November 3, 2010. Documentary on French singer-actress Jeanne Balibar. **WITH** Jeanne Balibar, Rodolphe Burger, Hervé Loos, Arnaud Dieterlen, Joël Theux, François Loriquet, Fred Cacheux.

Jeanne Balibar in *Change Nothing* © Red Star Cinema

JEWS AND BASEBALL: AN AMERICAN LOVE STORY (7th Art) Producers, Will Hechter, Peter Miller; Director, Peter Miller; Screenplay, Ira Berkow; Photography, Antonio Rossi, Stephen McCarthy, Allen Moore; Music, Michael Roth; Narrator, Dustin Hoffman; a Clear Lake Historical Productions film; Canadian-American; Color; Not rated; 90 minutes; American release date: November 5, 2010. Documentary on Jewish Americans' association with baseball. **WITH** Martin Abramowitz, Maury Allen, Rebecca Alpert, Charles Bronfman, Melanie Greenberg, Steve Greenberg, Shawn Green, Ron Howard, Roger Kahn, Larry King, Sandy Koufax, Peter Levine, Marvin Miller, Murray Olderman, Michael Paley, Al Rosen, Mary Rotblatt, Bud Selig, Norm Sherry, Kevin Youkilis

Hank Greenberg in *Jews and Baseball* © 7th Art

SHAKE HANDS WITH THE DEVIL (Regent) Producers, Michael Donovan, Laszlo Barna; Director, Roger Spottiswoode; Screenplay, Michael Donovan; Based on the book *Shake Hands with the Devil: The Failure of Humanity* by Lt. Gen. Roméo Dallaire; Photography, Miroslaw Baszak; Designer, Louis-Martin Paradis, Lindsey Hermer-Bell; Costumes, Joyce Schure; Music, David Hirschfelder; Editor, Michel Arcand; Canadian, 2007; Dolby; Deluxe Color; Rated R; 112 minutes; American release date: November 12, 2010. **CAST**: Roy Dupuis (Lt. Gen. Roméo Dallaire), Deborah Unger (Emma), Owen Lebakeng Sejake (Gen. Henry Anyidoho), James Gallanders (Maj. Brent Beardsley), Odile Katsi Gakire (Agathe), Michel Mongeau (Luc Marchal), John Sibi-Okumu (J.R. Booh-Booh), Robert Lalonde (Gen. Maurice Baril), Tom McCamus (Phil Lancaster), Akin Omotoso (Gen. Paul Kagame), John Matchikiza (Pres. Habyarimana), Jean-Hugues Anglade (Bernard Kouchner), Strini Pillai (Bangladeshi Commander), Craig Hourqueble (Willem), Kenneth Khambula (Maj. Kamenzi), Patrice Faye (Col. Poncet), Chris Thorne (American Ambassador Rawson), Lena Slachmujilder (Odette), Philip Akin (Kofi Annan), Amanda Alden (CNN Reporter), Sarah Ashimew (Angry Woman), Raymond Awazi (Ghanian Doctor), Guy Benoni (Young Boy), David Calderisi (Boutros Boutros-Ghali), Jacqueline Donovan (Therapist), Robert Fridjhon (Frank Claeys), Daniel Janks (Troute), Stephen Backingam (British Ambassador), Odile Katesi Gakire (Agathe), Craig Hourqueie (Willem/Robert), Alexi Kamanzi (Jean-Pierre), Intore Masamba (Marcel), Remy Nasanga (Maggen), Michel Ange Nzojibwami (Col. Bagosora)

Deborah Unger, Roy Dupuis in *Shake Hands with the Devil* © Regent

DISCO AND ATOMIC WAR (Icarus Films) Producer, Kiur Aarma; Director, Jaak Kilmi; Screenplay, Jaak Kilmi, Kiur Aarma; Photography, Manfred Vainokivi, Kristjan Svirgsden, Asko Kase; Music, Ardo Ran Varres; Editor, Lauri Laasik; an Eetriüksus, Helsinki Filmi Oy co-production; Estonian-Finnish, 2009; Color; Not rated; 80 minutes; American release date: November 12, 2010. Documentary on how Western popular culture had its effect on Communist Estonia in the 1970s; with Gerada Viira (Urve), Oksar Vuks (Jaak), Toomas Pool (Toomas), Jaan-Joosep Puusaag (Joosep), Einar Kotka (Young Nikolai), Aleksandr Aug (Father of Joosep), Birgit Veemaa (Mother of Joosep), Kiur Aarma, Jaak Kilmi, Alo Kõrve, Jaan Tootsen, Liina Vahtrik, Eduard Toman (Narrators)

Disco and Atomic War © Icarus Films

ME, TOO (Olive Films) a.k.a. *Yo, también*; Producers, Manuel Gómez Cardeña, Julio Medem y Koldo Zuazua; Directors/Screenplay, Álvaro Pastor, Antonio Naharro; Photography, Alfonso Postigo; Art Director, Inés Aparicio; Costumes, Fernando García; Music, Guille Mikyway; Editor, Nino Martinez Sosa; an Alicia Produce and Promico Imagen production; Spanish, 2009; Dolby; Color; Not rated; 103 minutes; American release date: November 19, 2010. **CAST**: Lola Dueñas (Laura), Pablo Pineda (Daniel), Antonio Naharro (Santi, Daniel's Brother), Isabel García Lorca (Ma Ángeles), Pedro Álvarez Ossorio (Bernabé), Consuelo Trujillo (Consuelo), Daniel Parejo (Pedro), Lourdes Naharro (Luisa), Catalina Lladó (Pilar, Luisa's Mother), Maria Bravo (Reyes), Susan Monje (Nuria, Laura's Sister-in-Law), Joaquín Perles (Pepe), Teresa Arbolí (Rocío), Ana Peregrina (Encarni), Ana De Los Riscos (Macarena), Ramiro Alonso (Quique, Laura's Brother), Danza Móbile de Sevilla (The Dance Company)

Lola Dueñas, Pablo Pineda in *Me, Too* © Olive Films

NOTHING PERSONAL (Olive Films) Producers, Reinier Selen, Edwin van Meurs; Director/Screenplay, Uszula Antoniak; Photography, Daniel Bouquet; Costumes, Rho Roosterman-Vroegen; Music, Ethan Rose; Editor, Nathalie Alonso Casale; a Rinkel Film & TV Productions, VPRO, Fastnet Films, Family Affair Films production; Dutch-Irish, 2009; Dolby; Color; Not rated; 85 minutes; American release date: November 19, 2010. **CAST**: Stephen Rea (Martin), Lotte Verbeek (Anne), Wimie Wilhelm (Landlady)

Stephen Rea, Lotte Verbeek in *Nothing Personal* © Olive Films

KAWASAKI'S ROSE (Menemsha) a.k.a. *Kawasakiho ruze*; Producers, Rudolf Biermann, Tomás Hoffman; Director, Jan Hrebejk; Screenplay, Petr Jarchovský; Based on an idea by Petr Jarchovsky and Jan Hrebejk; Photography, Martin Sácha; Music, Ales Brezina; Editor, Vladimír Barák; Designer, Milan Býcek; Costumes, Katarina Bielikova; Casting, Mirka Hyzíková; an In Film Praha presentation; Czech, 2009; Dolby; Color; Not rated; 100 minutes; American release date: November 24, 2010. **CAST**: Lena Vlasáková (Lucie), Daniela Koláróva (Jana), Martin Huba (Pavel), Milan Mikulcík (Ludek), Antonín Kratochvil (Borek), Ladislav Chudík (Kafka), Anna Simonová (Bára), Martin Schulz (Kristian), Isao Onoda (Mr. Kawasaki), Petra Hrebícková (Radka), Ladislav Smocek (Dr. Pesek), Vladimir Kulhavy (Chief Physician)

Lenka Vlasáková, Anna Simonová in *Kawasaki's Rose* © Menemsha

BREAK KE BAAD (Reliance Big Pictures) a.k.a. *After the Break*; Producer, Kunal Kohli; Director, Danish Aslam; Screenplay, Renuka Kunzru; Photography, Andre Menezes; Designer, Minal D. Rath; Costumes, Ayesha Dasgupta; Music Score, Hitesh Sonik; Songs, Vishal Dadlani, Shekhar Ravjiani; a Kunal Kohli production; Indian; Color; Not rated; 118 minutes; American release date: November 24, 2010. **CAST**: Imran Khan (Abhay Gulati), Deepika Padukone (Aaliya Khan), Sharmila Tagore (Ayesha), Shahana Goswami (Nadia), Navin Nischol (Jeet Gulati), Lillette Dubey (Pammi), Yudhishtir Urs (Cyrus), Neelu Kohli (Kamal Gulati)

Deepika Padukone, Imran Khan in *Break ke Baad* © Reliance Big Pictures

SUMMER WARS (Gkids) Director, Mamoru Hosoda; Screenplay, Satoko Ohudera; Photography, Yukihiro Masumoto; Art Director, Youji Takeshige; Music, Akihiko Matsumoto, Tatsuro Yamashita; Animation Directors, Hiroyuki Aoyama, Shigeru Fujita, Kunihiko Hamada, Ozaki Kzautaka; Action Animation Director, Tatsuzo Nishita; Character Design, Yoshiyuki Sadamoto; Editor, Shigeru Nishiyama; Japanese, 2009; Dolby; Color; Rated PG; 114 minutes; American release date: December 3, 2010. **VOICE CAST**: Michael Sinterniklaas (Kenji), Brina Palencia (Natsuki), Pam Dougherty (Sakae), Todd Haberkorn (Sakuma), Michael Tatum (Wabisuke J.), Maxey Whitehead (Kazuma), John Swasey (Mansuke), Shelley Calene-Black (Mariko), Lydia Mackay (Naomi), Mike McFarland (Shota), Monica Rial (Yumi), Barry Yandell (Mansaku), Chuck Huber (Riichi), Cynthia Cranz (Rika), John Burgmeier (Tasuke), Christopher R. Sabat (Katsuhiko), Rob McCallum (Yorihiko), Brittney Karbowski (Yuhei), Alisan Vlkotirn (Shingo), Patrick Seitz (Kunihiko), Colleen Clinkenbeard (Noriko), Jennifer Seman (Kiyomi), Cherami Leigh (Mao), Caitlin Glass (Nana), Bill Jenkins (Kazuo), Anastasia Munoz (Yukiko), Jason Liebrecht (Ryohei), Tia Ballard (Kana)

Summer Wars © Gkids

VENGEANCE (IFC Films) a.k.a. *Fuk sau*; Producers, Michele Petin, Laurent Petin, Peter Lam, Johnnie To, Wai KA Fai, John Chong; Director, Johnnie To; Screenplay, Wai Ka Fai; Photography, Cheng Siu Keung; Art Director, Silver Cheung; Costumes, Stanley Cheung; Music, Lo Tayu; Editor, David Richardson; an ARP, Media Asia, Milkyway Image production; French-Hong Kong, 2009; Dolby; Technovision; Color; Not rated; 108 minutes; American release date: December 10, 2010. **CAST**: Johnny Hallyday (Costello), Sylvie Testud (Irene Thompson), Anthony Wong Chau-Sang (Kwai), Lam Ka Tung (Chu), Lam Suet (Fat Lok), Simon Yam (George Fung), Cheung Siu-Fai (Wolf), Felix Wong (Python), Yuk Ng Sau (Crow), Maggie Shiu (Inspector Wong), Vincent Sze (Mr. Thompson)

Lam Suet, Anthony Wong Chau-Sang, Lam Ka Tung in *Vengeance* © IFC Films

Jack Huston, Mena Suvari in *The Garden of Eden* © Roadside Attractions

BEIJING TAXI (Argot Pictures) Producers, Miao Wang, Ivana Stolkiner; Director/ Screenplay, Miao Wang; Photography, Ian Vollmer, Sean Price Williams; Editors, Sikay Tang, Miao Wang; a Three Waters production; Chinese-American; Stereo; Color; HDCAM; Not rated; 78 minutes; American release date: December 10, 2010. Documentary on the changing scene in Beijing as seen through the lives of three taxi drivers

Beijing Taxi © Argot Pictures

THE GARDEN OF EDEN (Roadside Attractions) a.k.a. *Hemingway's Garden of Eden*; Producers, Lorne Thyssen, Tim Lewiston, Bob Mahoney; Director, John Irvin; Screenplay, James Scott Linville; Based on the novel by Ernest Hemingway; Photography, Ashley Rowe; Designer, Tim Hutchinson; Costumes, Alexandra Byrne; Music, Roger Julia; Editor, Jeremy Gibbs; Casting, Dan Hubbard; a Tranquil Seas production presentation of a Devonshire Productions film in association with Berwick Street Productions PLC and Freeform Spain; British-Spanish; Dolby; Color; Rated R; 111 minutes; American release date: December 10, 2010. **CAST**: Mena Suvari (Catherine Bourne), Jack Huston (David Bourne), Caterina Murino (Marita), Carmen Maura (Madame Aurol), Richard E. Grant (Col. Boyle), Matthew Modine (David's Father), Mathias Palsvig (Young Davey), Hector Tomas (Patrice), Dritan Biba (Patron/Waiter), Luis Callejo (Monsieur Jean), Alvaro Roig (Vladimir), Yael Belicha (Girl Onlooker), Maria Miguel (Nina), Igacio Gijon Solis (Ritz Waiter), Enrique Zaldua (Waiter #2), Lola Peno (Rotund Woman), Isabella Orlowska (Constanza), Alejandro Arroyo (Man in Crowd)

THE ALIEN GIRL (Paladin) a.k.a. *Chuzhaya*; Producers, Konstantin Ernst, Igor Tolstunov; Director, Anton Bormatov; Screenplay, Vladimir Nesterenko, Sergei Sokolyuk; Based on the graphic novel by Vladimir "Adolfych" Nesterenko; Photography, Dmitri Kuvshinov, Anastasiy Michailov; Designer, Galia Sadarova, Oleg Uhov; Music, Yuri Dementev; Editor, Julia Batalova; a Konstantin Ernst and Igor Tolstunov presentation of a K3 Company, PROFIT and FIP production; Russian-American; Color; Not rated; 100 minutes; American release date: December 17, 2010. **CAST**: Natalia Romanycheva (Alien), Evgeny Tkachuk (Whiz), Kirill Poluhin (Shorty), Anatoly Otradnov (Beef), Alexander Golubkob (Milksop), Evgeny Mundun (Rasp)

THE SOUND OF INSECTS (Lorber) a.k.a. *Record of a Mummy*; Producer/ Director/ Screenplay, Peter Liechti; Based on the novel by Masahiko Shimada; Executive Producer, Franziska Reck; Photography, Matthias Kälin, Peter Liechti; Music, Norbert Mösling; Editor, Tania Stöcklin; a Liechti Filmproduktion; Swiss, 2009; Color; Not rated; 87 minutes; American release date: December 22, 2010. VOICES: Peter Mettler, Alexander Tschernek (Narrators), Doraine Green, Nikola Weisse (2nd Voices)

NÉNETTE (Kino) Director, Nicolas Philibert; Photography, Katell Dijan, Nicolas Philibert; Music, Philippe Hersant; Editor, Nicolas Philibert, Léa Masson; a Les Films d'Ici/Forum des Images production; French; Color; Not rated; 67 minutes; American release date: December 22, 2010. Documentary on Nénette, a 40-year-old orangutan, the oldest and most popular inhabitant of the Ménagerie at the Jardin des Plantes in Paris.

Nénette in *Nénette* © Kino

SECRET SUNSHINE (IFC Films) a.k.a. *Milyang*; Producer, Hanna Lee; Executive Producers, Kim In-Soo, Lee Chang-Dong; Director/Screenplay, Lee Chang-Dong; Based on the novel by Yi Chong-jun; Photography, Cho Yong-Kyu; Designer, Shin Jeom-Hui; Costumes, Cha Sun-Young, Kim Nuri; Music, Christian Basso; Editor, Kim Hyun; a CJ Entertainment, Cinema Service, Pine House Film production; South Korean, 2007; Dolby; Super 35 Widescreen; Color; Not rated; 142 minutes; American release date: December 22, 2010. **CAST**: Jeon Do-Yeon (Lee Shin-ae), Song Kang-ho (Kim Jong-chan), Seon Jung-yeop (Jun)

Jeon Do-Yeon, Song Kang-ho in *Secret Sunshine* © IFC Films

TEES MAAR KHAN (UTV) Producers, Shirish Kunder, Twinkle Khanna, Ronni Schewvala; Director, Farah Khan; Screenplay, Shirish Kunder, Ashmith Kunder; Photography, P.S. Vinod; Designer, Sabu Cryil; Music, Vishal & Shekhar, Shirish Kunder; Lyric, Anvita Dutt, Shirish Kunder, Vishal Dadlani; Editor, Shirish Kunder; a Hariom Entertainment company presentation of a Three's Company production; Indian; Color; Not rated; 135 minutes; American release date: December 22, 2010. **CAST**: Katrina Kaif (Anya), Anil Kapoor (Special Appearance), Akshay Kumar (Tabrez Mirza Kahn/Tees Maar Khan), Sanjay Dutt (Narrator), Akshaye Khanna (Atish Kapoor)

Akshay Kumar in *Tees Maar Khan* © UTV Communications

HADEWIJCH (IFC Films) Director/Screenplay, Bruno Dumont; Photography, Yves Cape; Art Director, Jean-Marc Tran; Costumes, Annie Morel Paris, Alexandra Charles; Editor, Guy Lecorne; 3B Productions; French; Color; Not rated; 105 minutes; American release date: December 24, 2010. **CAST**: Julie Sokolowski (Céline/Hadewijch), Karl Sarafidis (Nassir), Yassine Salime (Yassine), David Dewaele (David), Brigitte Mayeux-Clerget (Mother Superior), Michelle Ardenne (The Prioress), Sabrina Lechêne (The Novice), Marie Castelain (Céline's Mother), Luc-François Bouyssonie (Céline's Father)

Sabrina Lechêne, Julie Sokolowski in *Hadewijch* © IFC Films

THE RED CHAPEL (Kino Lorber) a.k.a. *Det røde kapel*; Producer, Peter Engel; Executive Producers, Mette Hoffmann Meyer, Peter Aalbæk Jenson; Director/Idea, Mads Brügger; Photography/Editor, René Johannsen; Costumes, Simon Jul; a Zentropa Rambuk presentation; Danish; Color; Not rated; 87 minutes; American release date: December 29, 2010. Documentary in which filmmaker Mads Brügger and a pair of comics journey through North Korean. **WITH** Mads Brügger, Simon Jul Jørgensen, Jacob Nossell

The Red Chapel © Kino Lorber

PROMISING NEW ACTORS

2010

KEIR GILCHRIST (*It's Kind of a Funny Story*)

JENNIFER LAWRENCE (*Winter's Bone*)

ROONEY MARA (*A Nightmare on Elm Street, The Social Network, The Winning Season, Youth in Revolt*)

ZACHARY GORDON (*Diary of a Wimpy Kid*)

ARMIE HAMMER (*The Social Network*)

CHLOË GRACE MORETZ (*Diary of a Wimpy Kid, Kick-Ass, Let Me In*)

FREIDA PINTO (*You Will Meet a Tall Dark Stranger*)

AARON JOHNSON (*The Greatest, Kick-Ass, Nowhere Boy*)

CALLAN McAULIFFE (*Flipped*)

HAILEE STEINFELD (*True Grit*)

MIA WASIKOWSKA (*Alice in Wonderland, The Kids are All Right*)

EZRA MILLER (*City Island*)

ACADEMY AWARD

Winners and Nominees 2010

BEST PICTURE

THE KING'S SPEECH

(WEINSTEIN CO.) Producers, Iain Canning, Emile Sherman, Gareth Unwin; Executive Producers, Geoffrey Rush, Tim Smith Brett, Mark Foligno, Harvey Weinstein, Bob Weinstein; Co-Producer, Peter Heslop, Simon Egan; Director, Tom Hooper; Screenplay, David Seidler; Photography, Danny Cohen; Designer, Eve Stewart; Costumes, Jenny Beavan; Music, Alexandre Desplat; Music Supervisor, Maggie Rodford; Editor, Tariq Anwar; Casting, Nina Gold; a UK Film Council presentation in association with Momentum Pictures, Aegis Film Fund, Molinare London, Filmnation Entertainment of a See Saw Films/Bedlam production; British; Dolby; Dolby; Super 35 Widescreen; Color; Rated R; 119 minutes; American release date: November 26, 2010

Geoffrey Rush, Colin Firth, Helena Bonham Carter © Weinstein Co.

CAST

King George IV (Bertie)	**Colin Firth**
Lionel Logue	**Geoffrey Rush**
Queen Elizabeth	**Helena Bonham Carter**
King Edward VIII (David)	**Guy Pearce**
Winston Churchill	**Timothy Spall**
Archbishop Cosmo Lang	**Derek Jacobi**
Myrtle Logue	**Jennifer Ehle**
King George V	**Michael Gambon**
Wallis Simpson	**Eve Best**
Princess Elizabeth	**Freya Wilson**
Princess Margaret	**Ramona Marquez**
Queen Mary	**Claire Bloom**
Stanley Baldwin	**Anthony Andrews**
Equerry	**Robert Portal**
Private Secretary	**Richard Dixon**
Robert Wood	**Andrew Havill**
Dr. Blandine Bentham	**Roger Hammond**
Laurie Logue	**Calum Gittins**
Valentine Logue	**Dominic Applewhite**
Anthony Logue	**Ben Wimsett**
Willie	**Jake Hathaway**
Lord Wigram	**Patrick Ryecart**
Lord Dawson	**Simon Chandler**
Duke of Kent	**Orlando Wells**
Duke of Gloucester	**Tim Downie**
Neville Chamberlain	**Roger Parrott**
Chauffeur for the House of Windsor	**Paul Trussell**
BBC Radio Announcer	**Adrian Scarborough**
BBC Technician	**Charles Armstrong**
Theatre Director	**David Bamber**
Nurse	**Teresa Gallagher**
Butler	**Dick Ward**
Footman	**John Albasiny**
Boy in Regent's Park	**Danny Emes**
Steward	**John Warnaby**

Colin Firth, Helena Bonham Carter

The true story of how King George VI hired speech therapist Lionel Logue to help him overcome his terrible stutter and allow him to rally the British people on the eve of World War II.

2010 Academy Award winner for Best Picture, Best Actor (Colin Firth), Best Director, and Best Original Screenplay. This film received additional Oscar nominations for supporting actor (Geoffrey Rush), supporting actress (Helena Bonham Carter), cinematography, art direction, costume design, film editing, sound mixing, and original score.

Michael Gambon

Claire Bloom

Guy Pearce

Colin Firth, Geoffrey Rush

Helena Bonham Carter, Colin Firth

Geoffrey Rush, Jennifer Ehle, Colin Firth

Geoffrey Rush, Colin Firth, Derek Jacobi

Chatter Telephone, Woody © Disney/Pixar

Aliens

Lots-o'-Huggin Bear, Buzz Lightyear, Woody

Mr. Potato Head, Bullseye, Barbie, Hamm, Ken, Woody, Jessie, Slinky Dog, Rex, Buzz Lightyear

Sparks, Twitch, Ken, Lots-o'- Huggin Bear, Chunk, Big Baby, Stretch

Barbie, Ken

Mr. Potato Head, Mrs. Potato Head, Twitch

Woody, Mr. Pricklepants, Buttercup, Trixie

Buzz Lightyear, Andy, Woody

BEST ANIMATED FEATURE
TOY STORY 3

(WALT DISNEY STUDIOS) Producer, Darla K. Anderson; Executive Producer, John Lasseter; Director, Lee Unkrich; Screenplay, Michael Arndt; Story, John Lasseter, Andrew Stanton, Lee Unkrich; Photography, Jeremy Lasky; Designer, Bob Pauley; Music, Randy Newman; Music Supervisor, Tom MacDougall; Editor, Ken Schretzmann; Story Supervisor, Jason Katz; Supervising Technical Director, Guido Quaroni; Supervising Animators, Bobby Podesta, Michael Venturini; Casting, Kevin Reher, Natalie Lyon; a Walt Disney Pictures presentation of a Pixar Animation Studios production; Dolby; 3D; Color; Rated G; 103 minutes; Release date: June 18, 2010

VOICE CAST

Woody	**Tom Hanks**
Buzz Lightyear	**Tim Allen**
Jessie	**Joan Cusack**
Lotso	**Ned Beatty**
Mr. Potato Head	**Don Rickles**
Ken	**Michael Keaton**
Rex	**Wallace Shawn**
Hamm	**John Ratzenberger**
Mrs. Potato Head	**Estelle Harris**
Andy	**John Morris**
Barbie	**Jodi Benson**
Bonnie	**Emily Hahn**
Andy's Mom	**Laurie Metcalf**
Slinky Dog	**Blake Clark**
Chatter Telephone	**Teddy Newton**
Chuckles	**Bud Luckey**
Molly	**Beatrice Miller**
Spanish Buzz	**Javier Fernandez Pena**
Mr. Pricklepants	**Timothy Dalton**
Bonnie's Mom	**Lori Alan**
Young Andy/Peatey	**Charlie Bright**
Trixie	**Kristen Schaal**
Buttercup	**Jeff Garlin**
Dolly	**Bonnie Hunt**
Twitch	**John Cygan**
Aliens	**Jeff Pidgeon**
Stretch	**Whoopi Goldberg**

Jack Angel (Chunk), R. Lee Ermey (Sarge), Jan Rabson (Sparks), Richard Kind (Bookworm), Amber Kroner (Peatrice), Brianna Maiwand (Peanelope), Jack Willis (Frog)

As Andy is about to leave for college, his toys accidentally end up at the Sunnyside Daycare Center, where things are not as rosy as they seem.
Third in the Disney/Pixar series following *Toy Story* (1995) and *Toy Story 2* (1999).

2010 Academy Award winner for Best Animated Feature and Best Original Song ("We Belong Together"). This film received additional nominations for picture, adapted screenplay, and sound editing.

BEST FEATURE DOCUMENTARY
INSIDE JOB

(SONY CLASSICS) Producers, Charles Ferguson, Audrey Marrs; Executive Producers, Jeffrey Lurie, Christina Weiss Lurie; Associate Producers, Kalyanee Mam, Anna Moot-Levin; Director, Charles Ferguson; Screenplay, Charles Ferguson, Chad Beck, Adam Bolt; Photography, Svetlana Cvetko, Kalyanee Mam; Music, Alex Heffes; Music Supervisor, Susan Jacobs; Editors, Chad Beck, Adam Bolt; Narrator, Matt Damon; a Representational Pictures production, in association with Screen Pass Pictures; Dolby; Widescreen; Color; HD; Rated PG-13; 108 minutes; Release date: October 8, 2010

WITH
William Ackman, Daniel Alpert, Jonathan Alpert, Sigridur Benediktsdottir, Willem Buiter, John Campbell, Patrick Daniel, Satyajit Das, Kristin Davis, Martin Feldstein, Jerome Fons, Barney Frank, Robert Gnaizda, Michael Greenberger, Eric Halperin, Samuel Hayes, Glenn Hubbard, Simon Johnson, Christine Lagarde, Jeffrey Lane, Andrew Lo, Lee Hsien Loong, Andri Magnson, David McCormick, Lawrence McDonald, Harvey Miller, Frederic Mishkin, Charles Morris, Frank Patrnoy, Raghuram Rajan, Kenneth Rogoff, Mouriel Roubini, Andrew Sheng, Allan Sloan, George Soros, Eliot Spitzer, Dominique Strauss-Kahn, Scott Talbott, Gillian Tett, Paul Volcker, Martin Wolf, Gylfi Zoega

Documentary on how greed and underhandedness brought about the global economic crisis.

2010 Academy Award winner for Best Documentary Feature.

Charles Morris

Robert Gnaizda

Christine Lagarde

John Campbell

Barney Frank © Sony Pictures Classics

ACADEMY AWARD FOR BEST ACTOR: Colin Firth in The King's Speech

ACADEMY AWARD FOR BEST ACTRESS: Natalie Portman in *Black Swan*

ACADEMY AWARD FOR BEST SUPPORTING ACTOR : Christian Bale in *The Fighter*

ACADEMY AWARD FOR BEST SUPPORTING ACTRESS: Melissa Leo in *The Fighter*

ACADEMY AWARD NOMINEES FOR BEST ACTOR

Javier Bardem in *Biutiful*

Jeff Bridges in *True Grit*

Jesse Eisenberg in *The Social Network*

James Franco in *127 Hours*

ACADEMY AWARD NOMINEES FOR BEST ACTRESS

Annette Bening in *The Kids are All Right*

Nicole Kidman in *Rabbit Hole*

Jennifer Lawrence in *Winter's Bone*

Michelle Williams in *Blue Valentine*

ACADEMY AWARD NOMINEES FOR BEST SUPPORTING ACTOR

John Hawkes in *Winter's Bone*

Jeremy Renner in *The Town*

Mark Ruffalo in *The Kids are All Right*

Geoffrey Rush in *The King's Speech*

ACADEMY AWARD NOMINEES FOR BEST SUPPORTING ACTRESS

Amy Adams in *The Fighter*

Helena Bonham Carter in *The King's Speech*

Hallee Steinfeld in *True Grit*

Jacki Weaver in *Animal Kingdom*

TOP BOX OFFICE

Stars and Films 2010

1

TOP
BOX OFFICE
STARS OF 2010

1. Johnny Depp
2. Angelina Jolie
3. Robert Downey, Jr.
4. Matt Damon
5. Steve Carell
6. Tom Hanks
7. Denzel Washington
8. Leonardo DiCaprio
9. George Clooney
10. Anne Hathaway

2

3

4

5

6

7

9

8

10

2010 BOX OFFICE

1. Toy Story 3 (Disney)	$414,100,000
2. Alice in Wonderland (Disney)	$334,200,000
3. Iron Man 2 (Paramount)	$311,130,000
4. Eclipse (Summit)	$300,540,000
5. Harry Potter and the Deathly Hallows Part 1 (WB)	$295,100,000
6. Inception (WB)	$292,580,000
7. Despicable Me (Universal)	$251,510,000
8. Shrek Forever After (DreamWorks)	$238,400,000
9. How to Train Your Dragon (DreamWorks)	$217,590,000
10. Tangled (Disney)	$200,300,000
11. The Karate Kid (Columbia)	$176,600,000
12. TRON Legacy (Disney)	$171,120,000
13. True Grit (Paramount)	$171,100,000
14. Clash of the Titans (WB)	$163,220,000
15. Grown Ups (Columbia)	$162,100,000
16. Little Fockers (Universal/Paramount)	$148,440,000
17. Megamind (DreamWorks)	$148,420,000
18. The King's Speech (Weinstein)	$135,460,000
19. The Last Airbender (Paramount)	$131,780,000
20. Shutter Island (Paramount)	$128,100,000
21. The Other Guys (Columbia)	$119,220,000
22. Salt (Columbia)	$118,320,000
23. Jackass 3D (Paramount)	$117,230,000
24. Valentine's Day (New Line/WB)	$110,490,000
25. Black Swan (Fox Searchlight)	$106,960,000
26. Robin Hood (Universal)	$105,270,000

5. Rupert Grint, Emma Watson in *Harry Potter and the Deathly Hallows Part 1*

26. Russell Crowe, Kevin Durand in *Robin Hood*

32. Andrew Garfield, Jesse Eisenberg in *The Social Network*

27. Chronicles of Narnia: Voyage of Dawn Treader (20th)	$104,390,000	55. Resident Evil: Afterlife (Screen Gems)	$60,130,000
28. The Expendables (Lionsgate)	$103,100,000	56. Tooth Fairy (20th Century Fox)	$60,110,000
29. Due Date (WB)	$100,540,000	57. Why Did I Get Married Too? (Lionsgate)	$60,100,000
30. Yogi Bear (WB)	$100,250,000	58. Secretariat (Disney)	$59,720,000
31. Date Night (20th Century Fox)	$98,720,000	59. Easy A (Screen Gems)	$58,410,000
32. The Social Network (Columbia)	$96,970,000	60. Takers (Screen Gems)	$57,750,000
33. The Book of Eli (WB)	$94,840,000	61. Legend of the Guardians: The Owls of Ga'Hoole (WB)	$55,680,000
34. Sex and the City 2 (New Line/WB)	$94,350,000	62. Life as We Know It (WB)	$53,380,000
35. The Fighter (Paramount)	$93,620,000	63. Letters to Juliet (Summit)	$53,100,000
36. The Town (WB)	$92,190,000	64. Wall Street: Money Never Sleeps (20th Century Fox)	$52,480,000
37. Prince of Persia: The Sands of Time (Disney)	$90,760,000	65. Predators (20th Century Fox)	$52,100,000
38. Red (Summit)	$90,370,000	66. Hot Tub Time Machine (MGM)	$50,290,000
39. Percy Jackson & the Olympians: Lightning Thief (20th)	$88,770,000	67. Kick-Ass (Lionsgate)	$48,100,000
40. Paranormal Activity 2 (Paramount)	$83,750,000	68. Killers (Lionsgate)	$47,100,000
41. Unstoppable (20th Century Fox)	$81,570,000	69. Saw 3D (Lionsgate)	$45,720,000
42. Eat Pray Love (Columbia)	$80,580,000	70. Cop Out (WB)	$44,880,000
43. Dear John (Screen Gems)	$80,100,000	71. Cats & Dogs: The Revenge of Kitty Galore (WB)	$43,590,000
44. The A-Team (20th Century Fox)	$77,230,000	72. Edge of Darkness (WB)	$43,320,000
45. Knight and Day (20th Century Fox)	$76,430,000	73. Gulliver's Travels (20th Century Fox)	$42,780,000
46. Dinner for Schmucks (Paramount/DreamWorks)	$73,100,000	74. Death at a Funeral (Screen Gems)	$42,740,000
47. The Tourist (Columbia)	$67,640,000	75. Step Up 3D (Disney)	$42,420,000
48. The Bounty Hunter (Columbia)	$67,100,000	76. The Last Exorcism (Lionsgate)	$41,100,000
49. Diary of a Wimpy Kid (20th Century Fox)	$64,100,000	77. Legion (Screen Gems)	$40,170,000
50. The Sorcerer's Apprentice (Disney)	$63,160,000	78. Burlesque (Screen Gems)	$39,450,000
51. A Nightmare on Elm Street (New Line/WB)	$63,100,000	79. The Crazies (Overture)	$39,130,000
52. The Last Song (Disney)	$62,960,000	80. For Colored Girls (Lionsgate)	$37,730,000
53. The Wolfman (Universal)	$61,980,000	81. The Back-up Plan (CBS Films)	$37,500,000
54. Get Him to the Greek (Universal)	$60,990,000	82. Vampires Suck (20th Century Fox)	$36,670,000

83. The American (Focus)	$35,610,000		92. Charlie St. Cloud (Universal)	$31,170,000
84. Green Zone (Universal)	$35,100,000		93. Morning Glory (Paramount)	$31,000,000
85. Marmaduke (20th Century Fox)	$33,650,000		94. How Do You Know (Columbia)	$30,220,000
86. Devil (Universal)	$33,610,000		95. Daybreakers (Lionsgate)	$30,110,000
87. Hereafter (WB)	$32,750,000		96. Nanny McPhee Returns (Universal)	$30,110,000
88. When in Rome (Touchstone)	$32,690,000		97. The Switch (Miramax)	$27,780,000
89. Love & Other Drugs (20th Century Fox)	$32,360,000		98. Brooklyn's Finest (Overture)	$27,170,000
90. She's Out of My League (DreamWorks)	$32,100,000		99. Machete (20th Century Fox)	$26,600,000
91. Scott Pilgrim vs. the World (Universal)	$31,530,000		100. Ramona and Beezus (20th Century Fox)	$26,170,000

42. Julia Roberts in *Eat Pray Love*

58. Diane Lane in *Secretariat*

78. Christina Aguilera in *Burlesque*

OBITUARIES
2010

James Aubrey

Barbara Billingsley

Lisa Blount

Tom Bosley

David Brown

Ian Carmichael

Maury Chaykin

Jill Clayburgh

Graham Crowden

Robert Culp

Tony Curtis

Dino DeLaurentiis

Blake Edwards

William A. Fraker

James Gammon

Harold Gould

Peter Graves

Kathryn Grayson

Corey Haim

June Havoc

COREY ALLEN (Alan Cohen), 75, Cleveland-born actor-turned-director, best remembered for sparring with James Dean in the famous knife fight in the 1955 classic *Rebel without a Cause*, died on June 27, 2010 at his home in Los Angeles. He had been suffering from Parkinson's disease. His other movies as an actor include *The Shadow on the Window, Darby's Rangers, Key Witness, Party Girl (1958), Sweet Bird of Youth*, and *The Chapman Report*. On television he won an Emmy for directing *Hill Street Blues*. He is survived by a daughter; a brother; four grandchildren; and two great-grandchildren.

JAMES AUBREY (James Aubrey Tregidgo), 62, Austria-born British actor, who played the lead role of Ralph in the 1963 version of *Lord of the Flies*, died at his home in Cranwell, Lincolnshire, England on April 6, 2010 of pancreatitis. His other movies include *Galileo, The Great Rock 'n' Roll Swindle, The Hunger, Cry Freedom*, and *Spy Game*. Survivors include his sister and a daughter.

BARBARA BILLINGSLEY (Barbara Lillian Combes), 94, Los Angeles-born actress, best remembered for playing the mom, June Cleaver, on the situation comedy *Leave it to Beaver*, died on October 16, 2010 at her home in Santa Monica, CA, of a rheumatoid disease. Her motion picture credits include *Three Wise Fools, The Arnelo Affair, Living in a Big Way, The Saxon Charm, A Kiss for Corliss, Three Guys Named Mike, Inside Straight, The Bad and the Beautiful, Invaders from Mars* (1953), *The Careless Years, Airplane!, Back to the Beach*, and *Leave it to Beaver* (1997). She is survived by her two sons; a stepson; 16 grandchildren; and 23 great-grandchildren.

LISA BLOUNT, 53, Arkansas –born actress, best remembered for playing Debra Winger's friend in the 1982 hit *An Officer and a Gentleman*, was found dead at her home in Little Rock on October 27, 2010. She had been suffering from a condition similar to multiple sclerosis. Her other movies include *September 30, 1955; Radioactive Dreams, Prince of Darkness, Out Cold, Great Balls of Fire!*, and *Box of Moonlight*. She won an Academy Award for producing the 2001 short *The Accountant*. Survivors include her mother.

TOM BOSLEY, 83, Chicago-born actor, best known for his role as patriarch Howard Cunningham on the hit sitcom *Happy Days*, died of heart failure on October 19, 2010 near his home in Palm Springs. He had been battling lung cancer. His movies include *Love with the Proper Stranger, The World of Henry Orient, Divorce American Style, The Secret War of Harry Frigg, Yours Mine and Ours* (1968), *To Find a Man, Gus, Million Dollar Mystery*, and *The Back-up Plan*. On Broadway he won a Tony Award for playing the title role in the musical *Fiorello!* He is survived by his second wife, actress Patricia Carr; a daughter from his first marriage; and three grandchildren.

ROBERT F. BOYLE, 100, Los Angeles-born art director/production designer, who received Oscar nominations for *North by Northwest, Gaily Gaily, Fiddler on the Roof*, and *The Shootist*, died on Aug. 2, 2010 in LA. His many other credits include *They Won't Believe Me, Ride the Pink Horse, Abbott and Costello Go to Mars, Operation Mad Ball, The Thrill of it All, The Russians are Coming the Russians are Coming, How to Succeed in Business without Really Trying, In Cold Blood, Mame, Winter Kills, Private Benjamin, The Best Little Whorehouse in Texas*, and *Jumpin' Jack Flash*. He was given a special Academy Award in 2008. Survivors include two daughters and three grandchildren.

DAVID BROWN, 93, New York City-born film producer, who earned Oscar nominations for *Jaws, The Verdict, A Few Good Men*, and *Chocolat*, died of kidney failure on February 1, 2010 in Manhattan. His other credits include *The Sugarland Express, The Eiger Sanction, Cocoon, Driving Miss Daisy, The Player, The Cemetery Club, Rich in Love, The Saint, Kiss the Girls, Deep Impact, Angela's Ashes*, and *Along Came a Spider*. Along with his partner Richard Zanuck he received the Irving Thalberg Award in 1991. He is survived by his wife of 51 years, *Cosmopolitan* editor Helen Gurley Brown, and his half-brother.

IAN CARMICHAEL, 89, British actor who starred for the Boulting Brothers in such comedies as *School for Scoundrels* and *I'm All Right, Jack*, died at his home in Grosmont, England on February 5, 2010. His other films include *Betrayal* (1954), *Private's Progress, Brothers in Law, Lucky Jim, Heavens Above!, Smashing Time*, and *Dark Obsession*. He is survived by his second wife; his two daughters; five grandchildren; and four great-grandchildren.

CHRISTOPHER CAZENOVE, 66, British actor died of septicemia on April 7, 2010 in London. His films include *There's a Girl in My Soup, Royal Flash, Eye of the Needle, Heat and Dust, Until September, 3 Men and a Little Lady, The Proprietor*, and *A Knight's Tale*. Survivors include his companion and his son.

CLAUDE CHABROL, 80, French filmmaker, a founder of the Nouvelle Vague movement, died on September 12, 2010 in Paris from heart failure related to a pneumothorax. His credits include *The Champagne Murders, Les Biches, The Unfaithful Wife, Le Boucher, Ten Days Wonder, Wedding in Blood, Story of Women, Madame Bovary* (1991), *Le Cérémonie, A Girl Cut in Two*, and *Inspector Bellamy*. He is survived by four children.

MAURY CHAYKIN, 61, Brooklyn-born Canadian-based character actor died on his 61st birthday, July 27, 2010 in Toronto, after battling kidney problems. His films include *The Kidnapping of the President, Soup for One, WarGames, Harry & Son, Mrs. Soffel, The Bedroom Window, Twins, Breaking In, Dances with Wolves, My Cousin Vinny, Sommersby, Whale Music, Unstrung Heroes, Devil in a Blue Dress, Cutthroat Island, The Sweet Hereafter, A Life Less Ordinary, Mousehunt, Love and Death on Long Island, Mystery Alaska, Being Julia, Where the Truth Lies*, and *Blindness*. Survivors include his wife, actress Susannah Hoffman, and their daughter.

JILL CLAYBURGH, 66, New York City-born actress, best known for her Oscar nominated role in the 1978 film *An Unmarried Woman*, died on November 5, 2010 in at her home in Lakeville, CT, after a long battle with chronic lymphocytic leukemia. Her other movies include *Portnoy's Complaint, The Thief Who Came to Dinner, The Terminal Man, Gable and Lombard, Silver Streak, Semi-Tough, Luna, Starting Over* (Oscar nomination), *It's My Turn, First Monday in October, I'm Dancing as Fast as I Can, Hanna K., Whispers in the Dark, Rich in Love, Naked in New York, Going All the Way, Running with Scissors, Love and Other Drugs*, and *Bridesmaids*. Survivors include her husband, playwright David Rabe; her daughter, actress Lily Rabe; her son; and a stepson.

GARY COLEMAN, 42, Illinois-born former child actor, who became a star on the sitcom *Diff'rent Strokes*, died in Provo, UT, on May 28, 2010 of a brain hemorrhage following a fall in his home. He was seen in such theatrical motion pictures as *On the Right Track, Jimmy the Kid, Dirty Work, Dickie Roberts: Former Child Star, An American Carol*, and *The Great Buck Howard*. He is survived by his parents.

ALAIN CORNEAU, 67, French filmmaker, best known for *Tous les Matins du Monde*, died of cancer on August, 2010 in Paris. His other credits include *France Inc., Choice of Arms, Fort Saganne*, and *Love Crime*. He is survived by his wife, filmmaker Nadine Trintignant.

JOHN CRAWFORD (Cleve Richardson), 90, Washington-born character actor died of a stroke on September 21, 2010 in Newbury Park, CA. His many films include *Cyrano de Bergerac* (1950), *Serpent of the Nile, The Key, John Paul Jones* (as George Washington), *Hell is a City, Exodus, The Longest Day, The 300 Spartans, The Victors, The Americanization of Emily, The Greatest Story Ever Told, The Poseidon Adventure, The Towering Inferno, Night Moves*, and *The Enforcer* (1976). He is survived by his longtime companion; four daughters; and two grandchildren.

GRAHAM CROWDEN, 87, Edinburgh-born actor, who appeared in such Lindsay Anderson films as *If...* and *O Lucky Man!*, died in Edinburgh on October 19, 2010. His other pictures include *One Way Pendulum, Morgan!, The File of the Golden Goose, Percy, The Ruling Class, The Abdication, The Little Prince, Jabberwocky, For Your Eyes Only, Britannia Hospital, The Missionary, The Company of Wolves, Out of Africa, A Handful of Dust, The Innocent Sleep,* and *Calendar Girls.*

ROBERT CULP, 79, Oakland-born actor, who starred in the series *I Spy* and the 1969 popular comedy *Bob & Carol & Ted & Alice*, died of a heart attack after collapsing outside his home in Los Angeles on March 24, 2010. His other films include *PT 109, The Raiders, Sunday in New York, Rhino!, Hannie Caulder, Hickey & Boggs* (which he also directed), *Goldengirl, Turk 182!,* and *The Pelican Brief.* He is survived by his daughter and two sons.

TONY CURTIS (Bernard Herschel Schwartz), 85, Bronx-born actor who starred in such top 1950s films as *The Defiant Ones* (for which he earned an Oscar nomination) and *Some Like it Hot*, died of cardiac arrest at his home in Henderson, NV, on September 29, 2010. Following his 1948 debut in *Criss Cross* (as Anthony Curtis) he was seen in such pictures as *Francis, Winchester '73, The Prince Who Was a Thief, Meet Danny Wilson, Houdini* (his first of several films opposite his first wife, Janet Leigh), *All American, Johnny Dark, The Black Shield of Falworth, The Purple Mask, Six Bridges to Cross, Trapeze, Mister Cory, Sweet Smell of Success, The Vikings, Kings Go Forth, The Perfect Furlough, Operation Petticoat, Who Was That Lady?, The Rat Race, Spartacus, Pepe, The Great Impostor, The Outsider (1961), Taras Bulba, 40 Pounds of Trouble, The List of Adrian Messenger, Captain Newman M.D., Goodbye Charlie, Sex and the Single Girl, The Great Race, Boeing Boeing, Not with My Wife You Don't!, Arrivederci, Baby!, Don't Make Waves, The Boston Strangler, Those Daring Young Men in Their Jaunty Jalopies, Suppose They Gave a War and Nobody Came?, Lepke, The Last Tycoon, Sextette, Little Miss Marker (1980), The Mirror Crack'd, Insignificance,* and *Naked in New York.* Survivors include his sixth wife and five children from his previous marriages, including actress Jamie Lee Curtis.

SUSO CECCHI D'AMICO, 96, Italian screenwriter who earned an Oscar nomination for co-scripting the 1965 farce *Casanova '70*, died in Rome on July 31, 2010. Her other credits include *The Bicycle Thief, Belissima, Senso, White Nights* (1957), *Big Deal on Madonna Street, It Started in Naples, Rocco and His Brothers, The Leopard, Shoot Loud Louder ... I Don't Understand, The Taming of the Shrew* (1967), *Lady Liberty,* and *The Innocent.* She is survived by her three children.

DOROTHY DeBORBA, 85, Los Angeles-born child actress (nicknamed "Echo") who appeared in several of the *Our Gang* shorts, died in Walnut Creek, CA, on June 2, 2010 of emphysema. From 1930 to 1933 she was one of Hal Roach's "Little Rascals" in such two-reelers as "Pups is Pups," "Helping Grandma," "Fly My Kite," "Shiver My Timbers," and "Mush and Milk." Survivors include her daughter and her son.

DINO De LAURENTIIS, 91, Naples-born motion picture producer, whose many movies include *War and Peace* (1956), *Serpico*, and *Ragtime*, died on November 10, 2010 in Beverly Hills. He received Academy Awards as the producer of the Federico Fellini films *La Strada* and *Nights of Cabiria*, and was given the Irving G. Thalberg Award in 2001. Other credits include *Bitter Rice, The Gold of Naples, Ulysses* (1954), *This Angry Age, Barabbas, Marriage Italian Style, The Bible, Barbarella, Waterloo, The Valachi Papers, Death Wish, Mandingo, Buffalo Bill and the Indians, The Shootist, Three Days of the Condor, King Kong* (1976), *Orca, The Brink's Job, King of the Gypsies, Flash Gordon, Dune, Blue Velvet, Manhunter, Breakdown, U-571,* and *Hannibal* (2001). He is survived by his second wife, five children, five grandchildren, and two great-grandchildren.

GEORGE DiCENZO, 70, New Haven-born character actor died on August 9, 2010 in Bucks County, PA. He had been in failing health since an accident the

previous year. His movies include *Across 110th Street, Close Encounters of the Third Kind, Twinkle Twinkle Killer Kane/The Ninth Configuration, Back to the Future, About Last Night...*, *18 Again*, and *A Guide to Recognizing Your Saints.* He is survived by his wife, a son, a sister, and three grandchildren.

DONAL DONNELLY, 78, British-born Ireland-raised actor died of cancer on January 4, 2010 in Chicago. He was seen in such films as *Gideon of Scotland Yard, Shake Hands with the Devil, I'm All Right Jack, The Knack ... and How to Get It, The Mind of Mr. Soames, Waterloo, The Dead, The Godfather Part III,* and *This is My Father.* Survivors include his wife and two sons.

CLIVE DONNER, 84, British director, best known for the 1965 comedy hit *What's New Pussycat*, died of Alzheimer's disease on September 7, 2010 in London. Following a career as an editor that includes such films as *Scrooge* (*A Christmas Carol;* 1951), *The Promoter* (*The Card*), and *Genevieve*, he directed such films as *The Guest* (*The Caretaker*), *Nothing but the Best, Luv, Here We Go Round the Mulberry Bush, Alfred the Great, Old Dracula* (*Vampira*), *The Nude Bomb,* and *Stealing Heaven.* There were no reported survivors.

DAVID DURSTON, 88, Pennsylvania-born filmmaker died on May 6, 2010 at his home in West Hollywood, CA, of complications from pneumonia. His films as director-writer include *The Love Statue, I Drink Your Blood,* and *Stigma.* He is survived by his companion, producer John DiBello.

BLAKE EDWARDS (William Blake Crump), 88, Tulsa-born director-writer, responsible for such classic comedies as *Breakfast at Tiffany's, Victor Victoria* (for which he received an Oscar nomination for his screenplay), and the *Pink Panther* films, died in Santa Monica, CA, on December 15, 2010 from complications of pneumonia. As an actor he did bits in such movies as *They Were Expendable, The Best Years of Our Lives,* and *Panhandle* (also producer), as a writer his credits include *All Ashore, Drive a Crooked Road, My Sister Eileen* (1955), *Operation Mad Ball, The Notorious Landlady,* and *Soldier in the Rain* (also producer), while his movies as director include *Operation Petticoat, High Time, Experiment in Terror* (also producer), *Days of Wine and Roses, The Carey Treatment,* and *Micki + Maude.* Among his pictures as director-writer are *The Pink Panther, A Shot in the Dark, The Great Race, What Did You Do in the War Daddy?, The Party, Darling Lili, Wild Rovers, The Tamarind Seed, The Return of the Pink Panther, 10, S.O.B., The Man Who Loved Women* (1983), *That's Life!, Skin Deep,* and *Switch.* In 2004 he was awarded a special Academy Award. He is survived by his second wife, actress-singer Julie Andrews; four children; one stepchild; and several grandchildren.

BEKIM FEHMIU, 74, Sarajevo-born Yugoslav actor, best known to American audiences for his leading role in the 1970 film *The Adventurers*, was found dead in his Belgrade apartment on June 15, 2010 from a self-inflicted gunshot wound. His other U.S.-released films include *I Even Met Happy Gypsies, The Deserter, Permission to Kill, Madam Kitty,* and *Black Sunday* (1977). He is survived by his wife and two sons.

EDDIE FISHER, 82, Philadelphia-born pop singer of the 1950s, known for such tunes as "I'm Yours" and "Oh, My Pa-pa," died on September 22, 2010 at his home in Berkeley, CA, of complications from hip surgery. He acted in the films *Bundle of Joy* (with then-wife Debbie Reynolds) and *Butterfield 8* (with then-wife Elizabeth Taylor). He is survived by four children, including actresses Carrie, Tricia Leigh, and Joely Fisher; his son; and six grandchildren.

WILLIAM A. FRAKER, 86, Hollywood-born cinematographer died of cancer on May 31, 2010 in Los Angeles. He earned Oscar nominations for the films *Looking for Mr. Goodbar, Heaven Can Wait* (1978), *1941* (and an additional nomination for special visual effects), *WarGames*, and *Murphy's Romance.* His other credits include *Rosemary's Baby, Bullitt, Paint Your Wagon, The Best Little Whorehouse in Texas, Protocol, The Freshman, Tombstone,* and *Town & Country.* He is survived by his wife.

Dennis Hopper

Lena Horne

Lionel Jeffries

Irvin Kershner

James MacArthur

Adele Mara

Nan Martin

Kevin McCarthy

Rue McClanahan

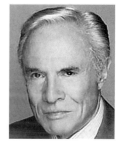

James Mitchell

Patricia Neal

Ronald Neame

Leslie Nielsen

Per Oscarsson

Fess Parker

Arthur Penn

Ingrid Pitt

Dorothy Provine

Corin Redgrave

Lynn Redgrave

JAMES GAMMON, 70, Illinois-born character actor died on July 16, 2010 at his home in Costa Mesa, CA, of cancer of the adrenal glands and the liver. He was seen in such films as *Cool Hand Luke, A Man Called Horse, Macon County Line, Urban Cowboy, Silverado, Made in Heaven, Ironweed, The Milagro Beanfield War, Major League, Coupe de Ville, I Love You to Death, Leaving Normal, The Adventures of Huck Finn, Cabin Boy, Wyatt Earp, Wild Bill, The Iron Giant* (voice), *The Cell, Cold Mountain, Silver City,* and *Appaloosa.* He is survived by his second wife, a brother, a sister, two daughters, and two grandchildren.

HAROLD GOULD (Harold Goldstein), 86, Schenectady-born character actor died of prostate cancer on September 11, 2010 in Woodland Hills, CA. His films include *The Satan Bug, Inside Daisy Clover, Harper, An American Dream, The Arrangement, Mrs. Polifax – Spy, The Sting, The Front Page* (1974), *Love and Death, Silent Movie, The Big Bus, Gus, The One and Only, Seems Like Old Times, Romero, Patch Adams, Stuart Little,* and *Freaky Friday* (2003). He is survived by his wife of 60 years, his 3 children, and five grandchildren.

PETER GRAVES (Peter Aurness), 83, Minneapolis-born actor, best known for his starring role as agent Jim Phelps on the series *Mission: Impossible,* died of a heart attack outside his home in Los Angeles on March 14, 2010. He was seen in such motion pictures as *Fort Defiance, Red Planet Mars, Stalag 17, Beneath the 12-Mile Reef, Killers from Space, The Raid, The Long Gray Line, The Naked Street, The Night of the Hunter, The Court-Martial of Billy Mitchell, Fort Yuma, It Conquered the World, Bayou (Poor White Trash), Beginning of the End, A Rage to Live, Texas Across the River, The Ballad of Josie, Airplane!,* and *Addams Family Values.* Graves is survived by his brother, actor James Arness; his wife of sixty years; and three daughters.

KATHRYN GRAYSON (Zelma Kathryn Elisabeth Hedrick), 88, North Carolina-born actress-singer, who starred in such notable MGM musicals as *Anchors Aweigh, Show Boat* (1951), and *Kiss Me Kate,* died of natural causes at her home in Los Angeles on February 17, 2010. Following her 1941 debut in *Andy Hardy's Private Secretary,* she was seen in such films as *Rio Rita* (1942), *Seven Sweethearts, Thousands Cheer, Ziegfeld Follies, Two Sisters from Boston, Till the Clouds Roll By, It Happened in Brooklyn, The Kissing Bandit, That Midnight Kiss, The Toast of New Orleans, Lovely to Look At, The Desert Song* (1953), *So This is Love,* and her last, *The Vagabond King,* in 1956. She is survived by her daughter from her second marriage, two grandchildren, and four great-grandchildren.

COREY HAIM, 38, Toronto-born actor, who as a teen starred in such 1980s movies as *Lucas* and *The Lost Boys,* died of damage to the air sacs in his lungs, pneumonia and a hardening of his heart muscle with plaque build-up within the blood vessels on March 10, 2010 in Burbank after collapsing at his mother's home near Universal City, CA. His other theatrical releases include *Firstborn, Secret Admirer, Silver Bullet, Murphy's Romance, License to Drive, Dream a Little Dream, Prayer of the Rollerboys,* and *Crank: High Voltage.* Survivors include his mother.

JUNE HAVOC (Ellen Evangeline Hovick), 97, Vancouver-born screen, stage and television actress died of natural causes at her home in Stamford, CT, on March 28, 2010. Her motion picture credits include *Four Jacks and a Jill, My Sister Eileen* (1942), *No Time for Love, Hello Frisco Hello, Hi Diddle Diddle, Brewster's Millions* (1945), *Gentleman's Agreement, When My Baby Smiles at Me, Red Hot and Blue, Mother Didn't Tell Me, Follow the Sun, Three for Jamie Dawn,* and *Can't Stop the Music.* Her life as a child performer alongside her sister Louise Hovick (Gypsy Rose Lee) was the inspiration for the musical *Gypsy.* There were no immediate survivors.

GEORGE HICKENLOOPER, 47, St. Louis-born filmmaker, who came to prominence with the 1991 documentary *Hearts of Darkness: A Filmmaker's Apocalypse,* died of natural causes on October 30, 2010 while in Denver to promote his latest movie. His other credits include *The Low Life, The Man from Elysian Fields, Factory Girl,* and *Casino Jack,* released posthumously. He is survived by his wife and son.

DENNIS HOPPER, 74, Dodge City-born actor, director, writer, best known for his iconic 1969 film *Easy Rider,* in which he starred, co-wrote (Oscar nomination), co-produced, and directed, died at his home in Venice, CA, on May 29, 2010 of complications from metastasized prostate cancer. His many other films include *Rebel without a Cause* (debut, 1955), *Giant, Gunfight at the O.K. Corral, The Story of Mankind* (as Napoleon), *From Hell to Texas, Key Witness, Night Tide, The Sons of Katie Elder, The Trip, Cool Hand Luke, Hang 'em High, True Grit, The Last Movie* (also director, co-writer, editor), *Kid Blue, The American Friend, Apocalypse Now, Out of the Blue* (also director), *Rumble Fish, The Osterman Weekend, O.C. and Stiggs, My Science Project, Blue Velvet, Hoosiers* (Oscar nomination), *River's Edge, Black Widow* (1987), *The Pick-Up Artist, Chattahoochee, Flashback, The Indian Runner, Super Mario Bros., True Romance, Chasers* (also director), *Speed, Waterworld, Carried Away, Basquiat, Edtv, Jesus' Son, Land of the Dead, 10th & Wolf, Swing Vote,* and *An American Carol.* His other directorial credits include *Colors* and *The Hot Spot.* He is survived by three daughters, and a son.

LENA HORNE, 92, Brooklyn-born singer-actress, one of the most influential and acclaimed vocalists of her time, died in New York City on May 9, 2010 of heart failure. As the first black performer signed to a contract by a major studio, she was seen in such movies as *Cabin in the Sky, Stormy Weather* (the title song became her signature tune), *Thousands Cheer, I Dood It, Broadway Rhythm, Ziegfeld Follies, Till the Clouds Roll By, Words and Music, Duchess of Idaho, Meet Me in Las Vegas, Death of a Gunfighter,* and *The Wiz.* Her awards include a lifetime Grammy and the Kennedy Center Honors. She is survived by her daughter and her granddaughter, screenwriter Jenny Lumet.

TONY IMI, 72, London-born cinematographer died in England on March 8, 2010. His films include *Inadmissible Evidence, The Slipper and the Rose, Night Crossing, Enemy Mine, Wired,* and *Shopping.* He is survived by his wife and two children.

LIONEL JEFFRIES, 83, London-born character actor-director, who came to prominence playing officious ninnies in a pair of Peter Sellers comedies of the early 1960s, *Two Way Stretch* and *The Wrong Arm of the Law,* died on February 19, 2010 in Poole, England. Among his other films as an actor are *The Quatermass Experiment (The Creeping Unknown), Bhowani Junction, Doctor at Large, All at Sea (Barnacle Bill), Dunkirk, The Nun's Story, The Trials of Oscar Wilde* (as the Marquis of Queensberry), *Fanny* (1961), *The Notorious Landlady, Call Me Bwana, The Long Ships, First Men in the Moon, Murder Ahoy!, The Spy with a Cold Nose, Arrividerci Baby! (Drop Dead Darling), Oh Dad Poor Dad Mama's Hung You in the Closet and I'm Feeling So Sad, Blast Off! (Those Fantastic Flying Fools), Chitty Chitty Bang Bang, Who Slew Auntie Roo?, Royal Flash,* and *A Chorus of Disapproval.* His directorial credits include *The Railway Children* (which he also scripted) and *Baxter.* Survivors include his wife of 48 years and three children.

MONICA JOHNSON, 54, California-born screenwriter, who collaborated with Albert Brooks on such movies as *Lost in America* and *Mother,* died of esophageal cancer on November 1, 2010. Her other credits with Brooks are *Real Life, Modern Romance, The Scout,* and *The Muse.* She also wrote *Jekyll & Hyde ... Together Again,* with her brother, Jerry Belson, and *Americathon.* She is survived by her daughter and her third husband.

ELLIOTT KASTNER, 80, Manhattan-born movie producer died of cancer on June 30, 2010 in London. His credits include *Bus Riley's Back in Town, Harper, Sweet November* (1968 and 2001 remake), *Where Eagles Dare, A Severed Head, The Long Goodbye, Jeremy, Farewell My Lovely, The Missouri Breaks, Swashbuckler, A Little Night Music, Equus, The First Deadly Sin, Garbo Talks, Angel Heart,* and *The Blob* (1988). He is survived by a son and a daughter; and three stepsons from his second marriage, one of whom is actor Cary Elwes.

BETTY LOU KEIM, 71, Massachusetts-born screen and television actress died on January 27, 2010 in Chatsworth, CA of lung cancer. Her few film roles include *These Wilder Years, Teenage Rebel, The Wayward Bus,* and *Some Came Running.*

She retired from acting after marrying actor Warren Berlinger in 1960; he survives her, along with their four children.

IRVIN KERSHNER, 87, Philadelphia-born filmmaker, who directed the *Star Wars* epic *The Empire Strikes Back* and the James Bond film *Never Say Never Again*, died from complications of cancer at his home in Los Angeles. His other movies include *Stakeout on Dope Street, Hoodlum Priest, The Luck of Ginger Coffey, A Fine Madness, The Flim-Flam Man, Loving, Up the Sandbox,* and *Eyes of Laura Mars.* Survivors include two sons.

CAMMIE KING (Eleanore Cammack King), 76, Los Angeles-born actress, who portrayed "Bonnie Blue Butler," the offspring of Clark Gable and Vivien Leigh in the classic film *Gone with the Wind*, died of cancer at her home in Fort Bragg, CA, on September 1, 2010. Her only other credit was doing the voice of "Faline" in Disney's *Bambi.* She is survived by her son, her daughter, and three grandchildren.

ART LINKLETTER (Gordon Arthur Kelly), 97, Canada-born television host-personality, known for such programs as *People are Funny* and *House Party*, died on May 26, 2010 at his home in Bel Air, CA. He was seen in the feature films *People are Funny, Champagne for Caesar, The Snow Queen,* and *Off the Menu: The Last Days of Chasen's.* He is survived by his wife of 75 years, two daughters, 7 grandchildren, and 15 great-grandchildren.

ABBEY LINCOLN (Anna Marie Wooldridge), 80, Chicago-born jazz singer-actress who starred in the films *Nothing but a Man* and *For Love of Ivy*, died in Manhattan on August 14, 2010 following a year of declining health. She was also seen in *The Girl Can't Help It* and *Mo' Better Blues.* She is survived by two brothers and a sister.

JAMES MacARTHUR, 72, Los Angeles-born actor, best known for playing Detective Danny "Danno" Williams on the long-running series *Hawaii Five-O*, died in Florida of natural causes on October 28, 2010. Following his debut in *The Young Stranger*, he was seen in such movies as *The Light in the Forest, Third Man on the Mountain, Kidnapped* (1960), *Swiss Family Robinson* (1960), *The Interns, Spencer's Mountain, Cry of Battle, Battle of the Bulge, The Love-Ins,* and *Hang 'em High.* He was the adopted son of actress Helen Hayes and playwright Charles MacArthur. He is survived by his third wife, four children, and seven grandchildren.

SIMON MacCORKINDALE, 58, British actor died of cancer on October 14, 2010 in London. His motion picture credits include *Juggernaut, Death on the Nile, The Riddle of the Sands, Cabo Blanco, The Sword and the Sorcerer,* and *Jaws 3-D.* On television he was best known for appearing on *Falcon Crest* and in the U.K. for the BBC series *Casualty.* Survivors include his second wife, actress Susan George.

JANET MacLACHLAN, 77, New York City-born actress died of a "cardiovascular incident" in Los Angeles on October 11, 2010. Her film credits include *Up Tight!,…tick…tick…tick…, Halls of Anger, Sounder, Maurie, Tightrope, The Boy Who Could Fly,* and *Heart and Souls.* Survivors include her daughter.

TOM MANKIEWICZ, 68, Los Angeles-born screenwriter-director died of cancer on July 31, 2010. His films as a writer include *Diamonds are Forever, Live and Let Die, The Man with the Golden Gun, The Cassandra Crossing, The Eagle Has Landed, Ladyhawke, Dragnet* (1987; also director), and he also directed *Delirious.* He is survived by his brother, his sister, and his stepmother.

JOE MANTELL (Joseph Mantel), 94, Brooklyn-born character actor, best known for his Oscar-nominated performance as Ernest Borgnine's pal Angie in the 1955 Academy Award winner *Marty*, died of complications of pneumonia on September 27, 2010 in Tarzana, CA. His other movies include *Storm Center, Beau James, The Sad Sack, Onionhead, The Crowded Sky, The Birds, Mister Buddwing, Chinatown, Movers & Shakers,* and *The Two Jakes.* He is survived by his wife; his son; two daughters; a grandson; and a step-grandson.

ADELE MARA (Adelaide Delgado), 87, Michigan-born actress, who appeared mainly in features for Republic Pictures, including the John Wayne films *Wake of the Red Witch* and *Sands of Iwo Jima*, died of natural causes at her home in Pacific Palisades, CA, on May 7, 2010. Her other credits include *Bells of Rosarita, Twilight on the Rio Grande, Blackmail, Robin Hood of Texas, Web of Danger, The Gallant Legion, I Jane Doe, Angel in Exile, California Passage, Back from Eternity,* and *The Big Circus.* Survived by two sons (from her marriage to producer-writer Roy Huggins, who died in 2002) and six grandchildren.

LORI MARTIN (Dawn Catherine Menzer), 62, California-born actress, who starred in the TV series adaptation of *National Velvet*, died on April 4, 2010 in Oakhurst, CA. She was seen in such films as *Machine-Gun Kelly, The FBI Story, Cape Fear* (1962), and *The Chase* (1966). After retiring from acting she went by her married name of Dawn Breitenbucher. Survivors include her son, two sisters, and a brother.

NAN MARTIN, 82, Illinois-born actress, who portrayed Ali MacGraw's disapproving mom in the 1969 comedy hit *Goodbye, Columbus*, died of complications from emphysema on March 4, 2010 in Malibu, CA. Her other films include *The Buster Keaton Story, Toys in the Attic, Bus Riley's Back in Town, The Art of Love, For Love of Ivy, Jackson County Jail, A Small Circle of Friends, Doctor Detroit, All of Me, Cast Away,* and *Shallow Hal.* Martin is survived by her husband and two sons.

KEVIN McCARTHY, 96, Seattle-born actor, who earned an Oscar nomination for playing Biff Loman in the 1951 film of *Death of a Salesman* and who starred in the 1956 sci-fi classic *Invasion of the Body Snatchers*, died of pneumonia in Hyannis, MA, on Sept. 11, 2010. His other films include *Winged Victory, Drive a Crooked Road, The Gambler from Natchez, Stranger on Horseback, An Annapolis Story, Nightmare* (1957), *The Misfits, 40 Pounds of Trouble, A Gathering of Eagles, The Prize, The Best Man* (1964), *Mirage, A Big Hand for the Little Lady, Hotel, Ace High, Kansas City Bomber, Buffalo Bill and the Indians, Invasion of the Body Snatchers* (1978 remake), *Hero at Large, Those Lips Those Eyes, My Tutor, Innerspace, The Distinguished Gentleman, Matinee, Just Cause,* and *Steal Big Steal Little.* He is survived by his second wife; three children from his first marriage; two children from his second marriage; a stepdaughter; a brother; and three grandchildren.

RUE McCLANAHAN (Eddi-Rue McClanahan), 76, Oklahoma-born actress, best known for her Emmy-winning role of Blanche Devereaux on the sitcom *The Golden Girls*, died of a brain hemorrhage on June 3, 2010. She appeared in such movies as *Five Minutes to Live* (*Door-to-Door Maniac*), *The People Next Door, The Pursuit of Happiness, They Might Be Giants, Modern Love, Dear God, Out to Sea, Starship Troopers,* and *The Fighting Temptations.* She is survived by her sixth husband, her sister, and her son from her first marriage.

VONETTA McGEE (Lawrence Vonetta McGee), 65, San Francisco-born actress died of cardiac arrest on July 9, 2010 in Berkeley, CA. She was seen in such films as *The Lost Man, The Kremlin Letter, Hammer, Melinda, Blacula, Shaft in Africa, Thomasine & Bushrod, The Eiger Sanction, Repo Man,* and *To Sleep with Anger.* She is survived by her husband, actor Carl Lumbly; her son, her mother; three brothers, and a sister.

JAMES MITCHELL, 89, Sacramento-born dancer-actor, who, following a long career in dance, became well known to fans of daytime drama for his role as Palmer Cortland on *All My Children*, died in Los Angeles of chronic obstructive pulmonary disease on January 22, 2010. He was seen in such films as *Coney Island, Border Incident, Stars in My Crown, The Toast of New Orleans, Devil's Doorway, The Band Wagon, Oklahoma!* (as the "Dream Curley"), *Deep in My Heart,* and *The Turning Point* (1977). He is survived by his partner, costume designer Albert Wolsky.

MARIO MONICELLI, 95, Italian director-writer, who received Oscar nominations for his scripts for *The Organizer* and *Casanova '70* (both of which he also directed), jumped to his death from a hospital window in Rome on November 29, 2010. He was under treatment for a tumor that appeared to be terminal. In addition to his most famous credit as a filmmaker, *Big Deal on Madonna Street*, he also made such other pictures as *Donatella*, *Boccaccio '70* (segment), *The Queens* (segment), and *Lady Liberty*. He is survived by his companion and their daughter, as well as two daughters from his second marriage.

PATRICIA NEAL (Patsy Louise Neal), 84, Kentucky-born actress, who won the Academy Award for portraying the wearied housekeeper Alma in the classic 1963 film *Hud*, died of lung cancer at her home in Edgarton, MA on August 8, 2010. Following her 1948 debut in *John Loves Mary* she was seen in such films as *The Hasty Heart*, *The Fountainhead*, *Bright Leaf*, *The Breaking Point*, *Operation Pacific*, *The Day the Earth Stood Still*, *Something for the Birds*, *A Face in the Crowd*, *Breakfast at Tiffany's*, *Psyche 59*, *In Harm's Way*, *The Subject was Roses* (Oscar nomination), *Baxter!*, *Happy Mother's Day – Love George*, *Ghost Story*, *An Unremarkable Life*, and *Cookie's Fortune*. She is survived by her sister, her brother, four children, 10 grandchildren and step-grandchildren; and a great grandchild.

RONALD NEAME, 99, British director-writer-cinematographer, known for directing such pictures as *Tunes of Glory* and *The Poseidon Adventure*, died on June 16, 2010 in Los Angeles, of complications from a fall. His credits as cinematographer include *Major Barbara*, *One of Our Aircraft is Missing* (Oscar nomination shared for special effects), and *In Which We Serve*, as photographer and co-writer on *This Happy Breed* and *Blithe Spirit*, producer on *Oliver Twist* (1948) and *The Magic Box*, and writer on *Brief Encounter* (Oscar nomination), *Great Expectations* (which he also produced; Oscar nomination for script) and *Golden Salamander* (also director). As director his other films include *The Promoter* (*The Card*), *Man with a Million* (*The Million Pound Note*), *The Man Who Never Was*, *The Horse's Mouth* (also producer), *Escape from Zahrain* (also producer), *I Could Go on Singing*, *The Chalk Garden*, *Mister Moses*, *Gambit*, *Prudence and the Pill*, *The Prime of Miss Jean Brodie*, *Scrooge*, *The Odessa File*, *Hopscotch*, *First Monday in October*, and *Foreign Body*. He is survived by his second wife; his son from his first marriage; and a grandson.

LESLIE NIELSEN, 84, Canada-born actor who made a late-career switch from mostly serious roles to comical ones died of pneumonia on November 28, 2010 in Fort Lauderdale, FL. His movies include *Ransom!* (1956), *Forbidden Planet*, *The Vagabond King*, *The Opposite Sex*, *Tammy and the Bachelor*, *The Sheepman*, *Beau Geste* (1966), *The Reluctant Astronaut*, *Rosie!*, *The Poseidon Adventure*, *Viva Knievel!*, *Airplane!*, *Prom Night* (1981), *Wrong is Right*, *Soul Man*, *Nuts*, *The Naked Gun: From the Files of Police Squad!*, *The Naked Gun 2 ½: The Smell of Fear*, *All I Want for Christmas*, *The Naked Gun 33 1/3: The Final Insult*, *Dracula: Dead and Loving It*, *Spy Hard*, *Mr. Magoo*, and *Superhero Movie*. He is survived by his fourth wife and his two daughters from his second marriage.

PER OSCARSSON, 83, Swedish actor, best known for his award-winning role in the 1968 film *Hunger*, died along with his wife in a fire at their home in Skara, Sweden, on December 30, 2010. Among his other films released in the U.S. are *My Sister My Love*, *A Dandy in Aspic*, *Doktor Glas*, *The Last Valley*, *The Night Visitor*, *Secrets*, *Montenegro*, *The Girl Who Played with Fire*, and *The Girl Who Kicked the Hornet's Nest*. He is survived by three children from his first marriage.

FESS PARKER, 85, Texas-born actor, who rose to fame playing the leading role on Disney's multi-part TV presentation of *Davy Crockett* in the mid-1950's, died on March 18, 2010 at his home in Santa Ynez, CA, of natural causes. He was seen in such motion pictures as *Untamed Frontier*, *Springfield Rifle*, *Island in the Sky*, *The Kid from Left Field*, *Them!*, *Battle Cry*, *The Great Locomotive Chase*, *Westward Ho the Wagons!*, *Old Yeller*, *The Light in the Forest*, *The Jayhawkers*, *Hell is for Heroes*, and *Smoky* (1966). During the 1960s he starred in the series *Daniel Boone*. He retired from acting in the 1970s and later opened his own winery. He is survived by his wife of 50 years and two children.

NEVA PATTERSON, 90, Iowa-born character actress died at her home in Brentwood, CA, from complications of a broken hip on December 14, 2010. Her movies include *Taxi* (1953), *Desk Set*, *An Affair to Remember*, *Too Much Too Soon*, *The Spiral Road*, *David and Lisa*, *Dear Heart*, *Skin Game*, *All the President's Men*, *The Buddy Holly Story*, *Star 80*, and *All of Me*. Survivors include her daughter.

ROBERT PAYNTER, 82, British cinematographer died on October 20, 2010 on the Isle of Wight, England. His credits include *Hannibal Brooks*, *The Nightcomers*, *An American Werewolf in London*, *Trading Places*, *The Muppets Take Manhattan*, and *Little Shop of Horrors*. Survived by a son and a daughter.

ARTHUR PENN, 88, Philadelphia-born director, best known for his groundbreaking 1967 film *Bonnie and Clyde* (for which he earned an Oscar nomination), died of congestive heart failure at his home in New York City on September 28, 2010, one day after his birthday. His other credits include *The Left-Handed Gun*, *The Miracle Worker* (Oscar nomination; he had earned a Tony for directing the piece on Broadway), *Mickey One* (and producer), *The Chase* (1966), *Alice's Restaurant* (also co-writer; Oscar nomination for directing), *Little Big Man*, *Night Moves*, *The Missouri Breaks*, *Four Friends* (and producer), *Target*, *Dead of Winter*, and *Penn & Teller Get Killed* (and producer). Survivors include his wife of 55 years, former actress Peggy Maurer; two children, and four grandchildren.

CHARLES B. PIERCE, 71, Indiana-born director-producer-set decorator died on March 5, 2010 in Tennessee. As set decorator his credits include *The Sterile Cuckoo*, *The Strawberry Statement*, and *Skyjacked*, while his films as director-producer include *The Legend of Boggy Creek*, *Bootleggers* (also writer, actor), and *The Town That Dreaded Sundown* (also actor).

INGRID PITT (possibly Ingoushka Petrov), 73, Poland-born actress, best remembered for her roles in such horror films as *The Vampire Lovers* and *Countess Dracula*, died of heart failure in London on November 23, 2010, two days after her birthday. Her other motion picture credits include *Where Eagles Dare*, *The House That Dripped Blood*, *The Wicker Man* (1973), *The Final Option*, and *Hanna's War*. She is survived by two children and a grandchild.

DOROTHY PROVINE, 75, South Dakota-born actress, who starred in such hit 1960's comedies as *It's a Mad Mad Mad Mad World* and *Good Neighbor Sam*, died of emphysema on April 25, 2010 in Silverdale, Washington. Her other films include *The Bonnie Parker Story*, *Riot in Juvenile Prison*, *The 30 Foot Bride of Candy Rock*, *The Great Race*, *That Darn Cat!* (1965), *Kiss the Girls and Make Them Die*, *Who's Minding the Mint?*, and *Never a Dull Moment* (1968). She is survived by her husband, director Robert Day; her son; and two sisters.

ROBERT B. RADNITZ, 85, Long Island-born producer specializing in "family films," who earned an Oscar nomination for the 1972 movie *Sounder*, died at his home in Malibu, CA, on June 13, 2010 of complications from a stroke. His other credits include *A Dog of Flanders* (1959), *Misty* (1961), *Island of the Blue Dolphins*, *And Now Miguel*, *My Side of the Mountain*, *The Little Ark*, *Where the Lilies Bloom*, and *Cross Creek*. He is survived by his wife.

IRVING RAVETCH, 89, Newark-born screenwriter, who earned Oscar nominations for the films *Hud* and *Norma Rae*, which he wrote with his wife, Harriet Frank Jr., died of pneumonia on September 19, 2010 in Los Angeles. Among his other films (written in collaborator with Frank) are *The Long Hot Summer*, *Home from the Hill*, *The Dark at the Top of the Stairs*, *Hombre*, *The Reivers*, *The Cowboys*, *Conrack*, *Murphy's Romance*, and *Stanley & Iris*. Survivors include Frank; a sister; and a brother.

CORIN REDGRAVE, 70, London-born actor died on April 6, 2010 in London following a short illness. He was seen in such films as *A Man for All Seasons*, *The Charge of the Light Brigade* (1968), *The Magus*, *Oh! What a Lovely War*, *When Eight Bells Toll*, *Excalibur*, *In the Name of the Father*, *Four Weddings and a Funeral*, *Persuasion*, and *Enduring Love*. Redgrave was survived by his four children, including actress Jemma Redgrave; and his sisters, actresses Vanessa and Lynn Redgrave (who would die less than a month later).

LYNN REDGRAVE, 67, London-born actress, who became a star with her Oscar-nominated performance in *Georgy Girl*, died on May 2, 2010 at her home in Kent, CT of cancer. The daughter of actors Michael Redgrave and Rachel Kempson she made her 1963 film debut in *Tom Jones* and was later seen in such pictures as *Girl with Green Eyes, Smashing Time, Last of the Mobile Hot Shots, Every Little Crook and Nanny, Everything You Always Wanted to Know about Sex*But Were Afraid to Ask, The Happy Hooker, The Big Bus, Getting it Right, Shine, Gods and Monsters* (Oscar nomination), *The Next Best Thing, How to Kill Your Neighbor's Dog, Spider, Peter Pan* (2003), *Kinsey, The Jane Austin Book Club,* and *Confessions of a Shopaholic*. Survivors include her three children, five grandchildren, and her older sister, actress Vanessa Redgrave. Her brother, actor Corin Redgrave, passed away less than a month earlier.

ERIC ROHMER, 89, French filmmaker, who came to prominence with the Oscar-nominated *My Night at Maud's*, died in Paris on January 11, 2010. His other movies include *Claire's Knee, Chloe in the Afternoon, The Marquise of O, Le Beau Mariage, Summer* (1986), *Four Adventures of Reinette and Mirabelle, A Tale of Winter,* and *A Summer's Tale*. Survivors include his brother.

LINA ROMAY (Elena Maria Romay), 91, New York City-born singer-turned-actress died on December 17, 2010 in Pasadena. The one-time vocalist for the Xavier Cugat Band, her motion picture credits include *You Were Never Lovelier, Two Girls and a Sailor, Bathing Beauty, Week-End at the Waldorf, Adventure, Love Laughs at Andy Hardy,* and *The Big Wheel*. Survivors include a son.

ZELDA RUBINSTEIN, 76, Pittsburgh-born actress, best remembered for playing the psychic in the 1982 horror hit *Poltergeist* died in Los Angeles on January 27, 2010 of natural causes. Her other films include *Under the Rainbow, Frances, Sixteen Candles, Guilty as Charged,* and *Southland Tales*. She is survived by her daughter, five grandchildren, and three great-grandchildren.

ERICH SEGAL, 72, Brooklyn-born writer, who created a sensation with his novel *Love Story*, which had been adapted from his screenplay for the 1970 film, died of a heart attack at his home in London on January 17, 2010. He had been ill with Parkinson's disease since the 1980s. In addition to earning an Oscar nomination for his *Love Story* script, he also wrote the screenplays for *Yellow Submarine, The Games, R.P.M., Jennifer on My Mind, Oliver's Story* (from his novel), *A Change of Seasons,* and *Man, Woman and Child* (from his novel). He is survived by his wife; two daughters, his mother; and two brothers.

JOHNNY SEVEN (John Anthony Fetto), 83, Brooklyn-born character actor, who portrayed Shirley MacLaine's protective brother-in-law in the Oscar-winning *The Apartment*, died in Mission Hills, CA, on January 22, 2010. His other films include *On the Waterfront, Cop Hater, The Last Mile* (1959), *Never Steal Anything Small, Guns of the Timberland, What Did You Do in the War Daddy?,* and *The Love God?* Survivors include his wife of 60 years, a son, and a grandson.

GLENN SHADIX, 58, Alabama-born character actor died on September 7, 2010 at his home in Birmingham, after being injured in a fall. His movies include *Beetle Juice, Sunset, Heathers, Meet the Applegates, Demolition Man, The Nightmare Before Christmas* (as the voice of the Mayor), *Love Affair* (1994), *Dunston Checks In, The Empty Mirror,* and *Planet of the Apes* (2001). He is survived by his sister and his mother.

JOHNNY SHEFFIELD, 79, Pasadena-born actor, best known for playing "Boy" in several Tarzan films starring Johnny Weissmuller, died on October 15, 2010 of a heart attack at his home in Chula Vista, CA, following a fall from a ladder. He made his first appearance in the role in the 1939 movie *Tarzan Finds a Son!* and his last in *Tarzan and the Huntress,* eight years later. He also starred in *Bomba, the Jungle Boy* and its sequels. Other movies include *Babes in Arms, Little Orvie, Lucky*

Cisco Kid, and *Knute Rockne All-American*. He left the business in the mid-1950s. Survivors include his wife, two sons, his daughter, a brother, and a grandson.

ALAN SILLITOE, 82, British writer, who adapted two of his "angry young man" stories into seminal films of the "New Wave" era, *Saturday Night and Sunday Morning* and *The Loneliness of the Long Distance Runner*, died in London on April 25, 2010. He is survived by his wife, his son, and his daughter.

JEAN SIMMONS, 80, London-born actress, who appeared in such notable films as *Hamlet* (for which she earned an Oscar nomination, playing Ophelia), *Elmer Gantry,* and *Spartacus*, died of lung cancer on January 22, 2010 at her home in Santa Monica, CA. Following her 1944 debut in *Give us the Moon*, she was seen in such other films as *Caesar and Cleopatra, The Way to the Stars, Great Expectations* (1946; U.S: 1947), *Black Narcissus, The Blue Lagoon* (1949), *So Long at the Fair, Trio, The Clouded Yellow, Androcles and the Lion* (her U.S. debut, in 1952), *Angel Face, Young Bess* (opposite her first husband, Stewart Granger), *The Actress, The Robe, She Couldn't Say No, The Egyptian, Desiree, Footsteps in the Fog, Guys and Dolls, Hilda Crane, This Could Be the Night, Until They Sail, The Big Country, Home Before Dark, This Earth is Mine, The Grass is Greener, All the Way Home, Life at the Top, Mister Buddwing, Divorce American Style, The Happy Ending* (Oscar nomination; directed by her second husband, Richard Brooks), and *How to Make an American Quilt*. She is survived by her two daughters and a grandson.

JOSEPH STRICK, 86, Pennsylvania-born director-writer-producer, best known for his 1967 film of James Joyce's *Ulysses* (for which he earned an Oscar nomination for his script), died in Paris on June 1, 2010 of congestive heart failure. His other pictures as director –producer include *The Savage Eye* (also writer, editor), *The Balcony, Tropic of Cancer* (also writer), and *A Portrait of the Artist as a Young Man*. His credits as producer only include *Ring of Bright Water* and *Never Cry Wolf*. He is survived by his second wife, three children from his first marriage, two children from his second marriage, a brother, a sister, and six grandchildren.

GLORIA STUART (Gloria Francis Stewart), 100, Santa Monica-born actress who starred in such early 1930s films as *The Old Dark House* and *The Invisible Man* and later made an unexpected, late career return to the screen playing the 100-year-old survivor in *Titanic*, earning an Oscar nomination (making her, at 87, the oldest performer to ever receive this honor), died at her home in Los Angeles on September 26, 2010. Her other movies include *The Kiss Before the Mirror, Roman Scandals, Gift of Gab, Maybe It's Love, Laddie, Gold Diggers of 1935, The Prisoner of Shark Island, Poor Little Rich Girl, The Girl on the Front Page, Life Begins in College, Rebecca of Sunnybrook Farm, Time Out for Murder, The Three Musketeers* (1939), *The Whistler, My Favorite Year, Wildcats, The Love Letter,* and *The Million Dollar Hotel*. She is survived by her daughter, four grandchildren, and 12 great-grandchildren.

VIRGILIO TEIXEIRA, 93, Portuguese actor died in Funchal, Madeira, Portugal on December 5, 2010. His motion picture credits include *Alexander the Great, The 7th Voyage of Sinbad, The Boy Who Stole a Million, The Happy Thieves, The Fall of the Roman Empire, Doctor Zhivago, A Man Could Get Killed,* and *Return of the Seven*.

URSULA THEISS (Ursula Schmidt), 86, Hamburg-born actress died of natural causes on June 19, 2010 in Burbank, CA. In the 1950s she was seen in the films *Monsoon, The Iron Glove, Bengal Brigade, The Americano,* and *Bandido*. She is survived by three children (two from her marriage to actor Robert Taylor, who died in 1969).

ANDRÉAS VOUTSINAS, 79, Sudan-born Greek actor, director, and acting teacher, best known for his role as Carmen Ghia in the 1968 comedy classic *The Producers*, died in Athens on June 8, 2010. His other movies include *Spirits of the Dead, Fraulein Doktor, The Twelve Chairs, A Dream of Passion, History of the World Part 1,* and *The Big Blue*. No reported survivors.

Eric Rohmer

Zelda Rubinstein

Erich Segal

Johnny Sheffield

Jean Simmons

JOHN WILLIS, 93, Tennessee-born film and theatre historian, who edited the annual volumes *Screen World* and *Theatre World*, died at his home in Manhattan on June 25, 2010 of complications from lung cancer. He had also edited the annual *Dance World* and published such books as *A Pictorial History of the American Theatre* and *A Pictorial History of the Talkies*. For more than forty years he was in charge of the Theatre World Awards which annually recognized promising new talents in the New York theatre.

NORMAN WISDOM, 95, London-born comedian-actor died on October 4, 2010 in Ballasalla on the Isle of Man following a series of strokes. Best known in the UK for his stage appearances, television series and various films, only a handful of his pictures played in the U.S.: *Trouble in Store, There Was a Crooked Man*, and *The Night They Raided Minsky's*. He was knighted in 2000. He is survived by his son and daughter.

DAVID L. WOLPER, 82, New York City-born producer, best known for such TV mini-series as *Roots* and *The Thorn Birds*, died in Beverly Hills, CA, on August 10, 2010 of congestive heart failure and complications from Parkinson's disease. His theatrical motion pictures as producer or executive producer include *The Devil's Brigade, If It's Tuesday This Must Be Belgium, The Bridge at Remagen, Willy Wonka & the Chocolate Factory, Wattstax, Imagine: John Lennon, Murder in the First*, and *L.A. Confidential*. He received an Oscar nomination for the documentary *The Race to Space* as well as the Jean Hersholt Humanitarian Award. Survivors include his third wife and three children from a previous marriage.

Joseph Strick

Gloria Stuart

Andreas Voutsinas

Norman Wisdom

David L. Wolper

Index